Real Estate Investment

Real Estate Investment

Strategies, Structures, Decisions

ANDREW BAUM
DAVID HARTZELL

Second Edition

WILEY

This edition first published 2021

Registered office

John Wiley & Sons Ltd, The Atrium, Southern Gate, Chichester, West Sussex, PO19 8SQ, United Kingdom

For details of our global editorial offices, for customer services and for information about how to apply for permission to reuse the copyright material in this book please see our website at www.wiley.com.

Library of Congress Cataloging-in-Publication Data

Names Baum, Andrew E., author. Hartzell, David, author.
Title Real estate investment strategies, structures, decisions Andrew Ellis Baum, David John Hartzell.
Description Second Edition. Hoboken Wiley, 2020. Series Wiley finance Includes index.
Identifiers LCCN 2020020370 (print) LCCN 2020020371 (ebook) ISBN 9781119526094 (hardback) ISBN 9781119526063 (adobe pdf) ISBN 9781119526155 (epub)
Subjects LCSH Real estate investment.
Classification LCC HD1382.5 .B3784 2020 (print) LCC HD1382.5 (ebook) DDC 332.6324—dc23
LC record available at httpslccn.loc.gov2020020370
LC ebook record available at httpslccn.loc.gov2020020371

SKY10059908_111423

Cover Design: Wiley
Cover Image: © piranka/Getty Images

Set in STIX Two Text 10/12 by SPi Global

Printed in Great Britain by TJ International Ltd, Padstow, Cornwall, UK

To Randee Hartzell and Karen Baum for their unfailing support

To Jamie and David Hartzell Jr and to David, Daniel and Josie Baum for helping us to understand the important things in life

Contents

Acknowledgements

We would like to thank many people without whom this book could never have been written. These are primarily our professional colleagues at Salomon Brothers, Heitman, Highwoods Properties, Prudential, Henderson, Invesco, and CBRE Investors, and our students. This means, primarily, our MBA students based at the Kenan-Flagler Business School at the University of North Carolina, the Saïd Business School at the University of Oxford, and the Judge Business School, University of Cambridge, as well as our students on the University of Reading MSc Real Estate course. In addition, our ideas have been corrected by our academic colleagues at UNC, Reading, Cambridge, and Oxford.

Some of the material in this book has appeared in a similar form in Andrew Baum's *Commercial Real Estate Investment: A Strategic Approach* (Elsevier), which was written in 2009 largely for a UK readership. In preparing much of the material both in this predecessor work and the new book, we have been very fortunate to have had the help of expert co-authors. The following have been especially helpful.

Graeme Newell of the University of Western Sydney contributed material about Australia and the box on sovereign wealth funds in Chapter 1. Nadja Savic de Jager, Shane Taylor, and Isaac Carrascal of CBRE Global Investors wrote about the continental European and Asian markets in Chapter 2. Yu Shu Ming and Ho Kim Hin of the National University of Singapore helped us with material about Asian markets, especially in Chapter 2. Ehsan Soroush and Nick Wilson contributed the box about Dubai in Chapter 2. Sabina Kalyan wrote the section on the economics of rent in Chapter 3, and Bryan MacGregor of the University of Aberdeen developed some of the forecasting material in Chapter 3. Andrew Schofield of Henderson Global Investors contributed many of the ideas in Chapter 4; Neil Crosby of the University of Reading is co-author of parts of Chapter 5; and Kieran Farrelly of CBRE Investors wrote parts of Chapters 13 and 17. Claudia Beatriz Murray of the University of Reading contributed part of Chapter 15. Tony Key contributed part of Chapter 17. Andrew Baum worked with Andrew Petersen of K&L Gates on the text *Real Estate Finance: Law, Regulation & Practice* (LexisNexis, 2008), which provided the basis for the Glossary.

In addition, we would like to thank Alex Moss, Gary McNamara, Steven Devaney, James Boyd-Philips, Daniel Baum, Jamie Hartzell, David Hartzell, Jr., Peter Struempell, Malcolm Frodsham, and Matt Richardson.

Andrew Baum would like to thank his partners at Real Estate Strategy, OPC and Property Funds Research, including Jeremy Plummer, now of CBRE Global Investors, who helped to develop many of the ideas in Chapters 15 and 16, and Nick Colley and Jane Fear, who provided many of the second edition updates.

David Hartzell would like to thank David Watkins, with SHA Capital Partners (formerly with Heitman Capital Management) in Chicago, for helping develop intuition during the many hours and years spent discussing all aspects of the real estate industry, as well as his former and current colleagues at the University of North Carolina and at the Wood Center for Real Estate Studies. Thanks also go to Brent Morris and Tim Wang at Clarion Investment for their help with data and analysis. Without the feedback, support, and good humor of thousands of MBA students at Kenan-Flagler, this book would not have been written, and life would not be nearly as much fun. Particular thanks are due to those students who helped with editing and spreadsheet development, including John Clarkson, Mike Aiken, Alexis Lefebvre, Heather Moylan, and Adam Hyder for the first edition, and Andrew Shrock, Rich Dougherty, Elliot Salman, Will McGuire, Mark Matthews, Colin Hartley, Paul Bode, and Zach Spencer for the second edition.

About the Authors

David Hartzell joined the faculty at the University of North Carolina in July 1988. During his tenure at UNC, he has taught finance and real estate courses in the undergraduate, MBA, PhD, and Executive Education Programs. He has received teaching awards at the undergraduate level at UNC, and at the MBA level at the University of Texas and at UNC.

Dave is the Steven D. Bell and Leonard W. Wood Distinguished Professor of Finance and Real Estate. He has served for most of his years at UNC as the coordinator of the Real Estate Concentration within the UNC MBA Program. In addition, he serves as the Director of the Wood Center for Real Estate Studies (www.realestate.unc.edu). He is also a Fellow of the Private Equity Research Consortium at the Kenan Institute.

He serves on the Board of Directors of Highwoods Properties, a publicly traded Real Estate Investment Trust (REIT) that invests in and develops office buildings. He serves on the Investment Committee and the Audit Committee. He is the faculty advisor and also serves on the Board of the UNC Real Estate Investment Fund, the first and only true student-managed real estate private equity fund. He was also appointed to the Investment Advisory Committee of the $100 billion North Carolina Retirement System by the NC State Treasurer in 2011.

Dave is a former vice president at Salomon Brothers Inc. in New York, where his primary focus was on institutional real estate finance and investments. Dave has worked with numerous international companies on a consulting basis, most notably Heitman Capital Management in Chicago, with whom he was affiliated from 1994 to 2010.

He received his PhD in Finance from the Business School at UNC-Chapel Hill and his MA and BS in Economics from the University of Delaware, receiving the Distinguished Alumni Award from the University of Delaware in 2000.

Andrew Baum is Professor of Practice at the Saïd Business School, University of Oxford and Professor Emeritus at the University of Reading. He was Honorary Professor of Real Estate Investment at the University of Cambridge 2009–14, and Fellow of St John's College, Cambridge 2011–14. He is Chairman of Newcore Capital Management, a real estate fund manager focused on alternatives, and advisor to several property organisations. He has held senior executive and non-executive positions with Grosvenor, The Crown Estate, CBRE Global Investors, and others. He was hired as the first director of property research for Prudential in 1987. He founded RES (a property research company) in 1990 and sold the business to Henderson Global Investors in 1997. At that time he became Chief Investment Officer (Property) at Henderson and later Director of International Property. In 2001 he founded OPC, a property research and investment company, which was sold to CBRE Investors to create CBRE Global Investment Partners, which now has over $30bn of assets under management.

He holds BSc, MPhil, and PhD degrees from the University of Reading, and is a graduate of the London Business School investment management programme, a chartered surveyor and a qualified member of the CFA Institute (ASIP). He is the author of over 50 refereed journal papers and book chapters. *PropTech 3.0: The Future of Real Estate* is the most downloaded Saïd Business School, University of Oxford report.

Baum, currently Director of the Oxford Future of Real Estate Initiative, was voted one of the top 3 most influential people in PropTech in the 2017 Lendinvest list and was winner of the UK PropTech Association Special Achievement award for 2019. He is founder and former president of the Reading Real Estate Foundation, an educational charity established to support real estate education. He was elected Academic Fellow of the Urban Land Institute in 2001, the first such election outside the USA, and Honorary Fellow of the Society of Property Researchers in 2002.

Andy and Dave are both married to their high school sweethearts, are both proud parents and (now, since the first edition) grandparents. Both played university soccer, Dave as a starter on the Division I Blue Hen soccer team at the University of Delaware, Andy for British Universities. Both play old timey mandolin less well than they would like.

Preface

It is a difficult challenge in a book like this which combines finance, law, and real estate to avoid over-complication while at the same time preventing over-simplification. This challenge is amplified many times when adopting a global perspective. In addition to periodic shocks and crashes (the latest of which, COVID-19, has shaken the foundations of real estate markets and challenged the globalization of finance), there are many different systems controlling land ownership; different approaches to investment regulation; different tax and accounting regimes; and a myriad of structures underpinning investment vehicles. To attempt to extract some global truths from this web could be regarded as over-ambitious. In deliberately adopting a global perspective, we must acknowledge the lens through which we view this world, which is designed in the UK and the USA, continental Europe and Asia, in that order.

Happily, increasing globalization allows some generalization from one US-based author and one European. We have been lucky to have worked together enough to know how and where to jump over the language barrier. The most widely accepted real estate transparency index (Jones Lang LaSalle, 2010) ranks, largely on the grounds of information availability, the UK and the USA in the top group of all global markets, with Canada, Australia, New Zealand, and Sweden. The longest, most detailed, and most heavily analysed datasets describing real estate performance in the modern era exist in the UK and the USA. The book is therefore the result of the authors' varied experience of applied property research, property fund management, international property investment, and academic research in these two leading markets and elsewhere, including the Asian, Australian, European, and developing markets.

The subject matter can be described broadly as institutional investment in real estate, and the foundation is an international and capital markets context viewed from the perspective of property investment and finance professionals. The objective of this book is to provide insights that will help global real estate investors of all types make more informed decisions.

Investors in real estate can take many different forms. At one end of the investor spectrum are individual investors hoping to increase their wealth by buying and holding investment property. By holding direct investments in buildings, they hope to earn income from rents and from selling the asset at the end of a holding period for more than they paid for it.

At the other end of the spectrum are institutional investors like sovereign wealth funds, life insurance companies, and pension funds that may hold large portfolios of individual properties, or shares in partnerships or funds, or publicly traded securities secured on real estate. They do this to add diversification to portfolios that are often dominated by securities.

At either end of the spectrum, or anywhere in between, investors should be aware of four different aspects of real estate investment, which represent the four parts of this book.

PART I: REAL ESTATE AS AN INVESTMENT: AN INTRODUCTION

First, there is a context and a history for real estate investing around the globe. How does real estate compare to other asset classes, and how has it performed over time? What basic economics and finance theories help us to understand this context?

Real estate, usually seen as an excellent but illiquid diversifier (see Chapter 1), has been a part of investor portfolios for most of the 20th and 21st centuries. Since the 1970s, real estate has become more accessible for a broader cross-section of the investing universe. Through vehicles such as Real Estate Investment Trusts (REITs), individual investors have greater access to real estate investments. In addition, the development of real estate partnerships and other ownership forms has also led to more availability for investors. Further, regulations have created an incentive for institutional investors to expand the amount of money that they invest in real estate and pension funds, life insurance companies, and high-net-worth individuals have all increased their allocations to real estate. Since the 1970s, these investors have both made and lost a great deal of wealth, depending upon when they placed their money into the real estate asset class and where that money was invested. Understanding their motivation for investing in real estate is critical to developing an investor mindset.

An important aspect of real estate markets, and investment in them, is cyclicality (see Chapter 2). In the USA since the 1970s, three complete cycles have run their course. Similar cycles have been demonstrated around the world in the UK, Europe, and Asia Pacific. Generally, prices of real estate assets reach high levels due to strong interest by investors; prices paid as the cycle takes an upswing are unrelated to the underlying supply and demand for space in the local market where tenants lease space; and when the underlying demand and supply fundamentals deteriorate in the local market, prices must adjust downward.

The US real estate market has experienced three distinct cycles since the 1960s, and each was caused by similar occurrences. Some subset of investors or lenders miscalculated the risk of owning real estate, and bought property for prices that in retrospect were too high. Once the market corrected to more accurately reflect the risk, prices fell dramatically and large amounts of individual and institutional wealth were destroyed. This happened in the USA in the 1970s, again in the 1980s and early 1990s, and most recently in the latter part of the first decade of the 21st century. Similar cyclicality was experienced at different times and for slightly different reasons around the world. To deal with the inevitable cyclicality in future real estate markets, we need to understand the economics of rent (Chapter 3) and the finance-based theories of asset pricing (Chapter 4). We have to be able to answer this question: What is a fair price for real estate?

PART II: MAKING INVESTMENT DECISIONS AT THE PROPERTY LEVEL

Few, if any, of the investors that bought property as a wealth-enhancing asset during the upside of the last cycle anticipated that the property would lose value and that they would suffer a loss in wealth due to the investment. It is more likely that they expected to earn income and to have the value of the property appreciate during their holding period. However, due to a misunderstanding of the characteristics of real estate investment, these investors were sorely disappointed in their experience.

There are numerous techniques used to evaluate real estate investments, ranging from simple back-of-the-envelope heuristics to complex and dynamic valuation models using discounted cash flow analysis and real options. One thing that has clearly changed in the real estate industry is the level of sophistication among real estate investors and the amount of time and analytical power they devote to analyzing potential real estate investments. This has partly occurred due to the increasing professionalization of the industry, and also to the large amounts of money that are being invested in the real estate asset class.

Like any investment, determining investment value and how much to pay for a real estate asset requires making some judgment regarding the future cash flows expected to be earned by the property. Generally, income from a real estate asset comes in the form of income produced by renting the property to tenants and from value appreciation during the period which the asset is held. Since these cash flows must be forecast into the future, and the future is impossible to predict, the difference between realized cash flows earned and expected cash flows can be substantial.

Risk can be defined as uncertainty of future outcomes. For those investments that exhibit greater uncertainty, the risk will be greater as well. Generally, investors in real estate have valued assets too highly because they do not fully appreciate the risk, or uncertainty, that an investment exhibits. This mis-estimation allows them to pay prices that are too high relative to the property's fair value.

The ability to model cash flows using discounted cash flow analysis is essential to understanding how to value assets (see Chapter 5). Developing expertise in generating expectations of cash flows, and adjusting valuations for the risk involved in the investment, helps to ensure that an investor does not overpay for a real estate investment. We also need to understand the impact of leases (Chapter 6) and be able to build an income statement (Chapter 7). We have to understand the common forms of debt finance, especially mortgages (Chapter 8), and model the impact of leverage and taxes (Chapter 9). In a new chapter for this second edition, we have added a case-based discussion of real estate development viability (Chapter 10).

However, while we believe that spreadsheets are wonderful (and that they should be pushed hard to explore the various option pricing and simulation techniques we do not have space to deal with properly in this book), many investors have made the mistake of letting their spreadsheet analysis make their investment decisions for them. It is important to recognize that techniques for valuation are merely tools to be used in making decisions, and are only a small part of the overall assessment process.

PART III: REAL ESTATE INVESTMENT STRUCTURES

The nature of real estate as an asset class brings with it two key problems. It is expensive to buy, leading to "lumpy" portfolios, low levels of diversification, and high levels of asset-specific risk; and it is illiquid. Various investment structures have been developed to cope with these issues, with such success that these structures now dominate the global investment strategies of most new entrants to the market.

Diversification and specific risk reduction have been the motivation for developing a private equity, or unlisted, real estate fund (Chapter 11). It is essential that we understand how carried interest structures work in joint ventures, simple co-investment funds, and private equity real estate funds (Chapter 12), and to consider how this may influence incentives and decision-making.

The same driver, plus an attempt to add liquidity, is a feature of REITs and other public equity real estate formats (Chapter 13), and liquid exposure to what should be low-risk, property-based debt income is the goal of the structured finance market described in Chapter 14.

PART IV: CREATING A GLOBAL REAL ESTATE STRATEGY

The institutional investment community has come to play a far greater role in the real estate investment universe in recent years. Pension funds and life insurance companies, as well as sovereign wealth funds and investor groups in the form of public REITs and private equity funds, have invested large amounts of wealth into the real estate asset class. Instead of purchasing one property, these investors hold portfolios of many properties, often across different property types and across different geographic markets. Real estate portfolio management requires an understanding of how the investment performance of different properties will interact when they are combined in a portfolio. One of the basic tenets of modern portfolio theory is that combining assets that perform differently over the investment horizon can lower the volatility of the portfolio relative to the volatility of the individual assets. Therefore, there is value to finding and investing in assets and sectors that are expected to perform differently in the future (Chapter 15).

One might expect this to imply the necessity of a global strategy. However, using the structures described in Part III, as global investors inevitably have and will, produces distortions that complicate the global portfolio strategy as well as the pricing approach we developed in Parts I and II. For the larger investors, these different markets are located around the world. This creates a series of very challenging problems, examined in Chapter 16.

Finally, as investors or as managers we need to understand when and where an investment strategy has been successful. Have the returns been adequate, and what drove them? This is the subject of Chapter 17, after which we draw some final conclusions – and look ahead to the future – in Chapter 18.

Real Estate Investment

PART

One

Real Estate as an Investment: An Introduction

CHAPTER 1

Real Estate – The Global Asset

1.1 THE GLOBAL PROPERTY INVESTMENT UNIVERSE

Real estate is usually identified as a discrete, or separate, component of an investment portfolio. It may be part of an allocation to 'alternatives' (financial assets that do not fall into one of the conventional investment categories of stocks, bonds, and cash); it may be part of an allocation to 'real assets' (physical assets that have an intrinsic worth and which are expected to be a hedge against inflation); or it may be part of an allocation to private markets (assets such as private equity or private debt which are not listed on a public exchange). Whichever is the case, real estate (including owner-occupied housing and farmland) constitutes a very large proportion of the world's wealth and (excluding these asset types) a significant slice of its institutional savings base.

What proportion of an investment portfolio *should* be in real estate? What proportion of the real estate portfolio should be invested in the USA, or Russia, or continental Europe?

A new investor building a global portfolio might reasonably want to know the composition by value of the 'market portfolio' – the total value of all investable assets, like stocks and bonds, added together. Given this, it is possible to imagine how your portfolio might be constituted, even if you had no views about the future performance of those assets. Assuming there were no 'friction costs', meaning the time and cost involved in accessing certain markets, which makes some less attractive than others, constructing a market portfolio would make some sense, especially given that it appears that we are less good at forecasting market returns than we think we are.

We can estimate the size of the public equity markets at any time by adding together the market capitalisation of the various global stock markets. We can do the same with publicly listed bonds. Private equity is more of a challenge, however, and real estate also creates significant difficulties. Many of the real estate assets in the world are never valued. There is a lack of transparency in many markets, and the generally low levels of information available in Asia and the emerging markets of the world mean that we do not know much about the size of the investable property markets in China, India, and Pakistan, despite their huge populations and increasingly significant gross domestic product (GDP). Even the total value of all US housing is subject to debate.

Nevertheless, we do have something to go on. While it has been estimated that real estate might comprise as much as 50% of the total value of the world's assets, this may not represent the value of the investable stock (after all, we have no intention of selling our homes in North Carolina and Oxfordshire to a sovereign wealth fund). We have no easy way of estimating the *investable* stock either, but we can have a stab at estimating the *invested* stock and adjusting that value upwards. This is the approach typically taken by analysts.

The value of the investable stock of commercial property owned by institutional investors around the world was estimated (by CBRE, 2017) to be around $27.5 trillion and by Property Funds Research (PFR) and others in 2019 at around £35 trillion. This is defined as stock that is of sufficient quality to become the focus of institutional investment. This estimate must be taken as the broadest possible guide. This value can be compared with a global equity market capitalisation of close to $69 trillion in January 2019 (World Federation of Exchanges). Assuming a typical equity exposure of say 50%, this suggests a market portfolio weight for real estate of around 20–25%. Institutional exposure (averaging around 10% globally – see Figure 1.4 later) remains below the market portfolio weight, suggesting that something appears to limit institutional investors' commitment to this asset class.

It appears that 10% is a robust estimate of current allocations to real estate. The 2018 Hodes Weill Allocations Monitor (Hodes Weill/Cornell, 2018) included research collected on a blind basis from 208 institutional investors in 29 countries. The 2018 participants held total assets under management exceeding $11.0 trillion and had portfolio investments in real estate totalling approximately $1.0 trillion or 9% of total assets. Average target allocations to real estate increased to 10.4% in 2018, up 30 basis points (bps) from 2017 and up approximately 150 bps since 2013. Despite an increase in actual allocations, institutions remained meaningfully under-invested relative to target allocations. While 92% of institutions reported that they are actively investing in real estate, institutions remained approximately 90 bps under-invested relative to target allocations.

The $35 trillion investable stock of property can be broken down to the regional level (see Table 1.1). According to similar sources, the global market is split by asset value into 28% North America and Europe, 32% Asia, and the remaining 11% in the other regions.

The USA and Japan are the two largest single-country markets in the world. The UK is the third largest global market.

TABLE 1.1 The global property investment universe ($ billion)

Asia	Australasia	Europe	Latin America	Africa/ Middle East	North America	Total
$11,490m	$730	$10,044	$1,627	$1,537	$9,992	$35,420

Sources: PFR, PGIM, IMF, and EPRA 2019.

The US institutional real estate investment market is measured by the National Council of Real Estate Investment Fiduciaries (NCREIF), whose NCREIF Property Index (NPI) consists of 8,289 investment-grade, income-producing properties with a total market value of $653 billion at the second quarter of 2019. The breakdown of the portfolio is 35% office, 25% apartments, 22% retail, 17% industrial, and 1% hotels.

In 2018 The Investment Property Forum estimated the total value of all commercial property in the UK to exceed £935 billion (a figure which includes the institutional investment universe of £509 billion). Within this £935 billion, it is estimated that 34% is retail property, 42% office property, and 14% industrial property. The remaining 10% covers a wide range of property including residential, hotels, pubs, leisure, utilities, and public service buildings. The universe used to compile the MSCI (formerly IPD) UK annual index at the end of 2018 comprised over 13,130 properties worth around £220 billion.

A truly global real estate benchmark is approaching, but for now we are limited to around 25 countries for which good data is available. For example, the MSCI Global Property Index measures the combined performance of real estate markets in 23 countries. The index is based on the MSCI (formerly IPD) indices for Australia, Austria, Belgium, Canada, Denmark, France, Germany, Ireland, Italy, Japan, Korea, Netherlands, New Zealand, Norway, Poland, Portugal, South Africa, Spain, Sweden, Switzerland, UK, USA, and the KTI Index for Finland.

As we shall see in Part II of this book, ownership of this global universe is financed through equity (some private and some public, such as that raised by public property companies) and debt (some private, such as mortgages, and some public, such as commercial mortgage-backed securities). This classification is known in the USA as the 'capital stack', and breaks down roughly as shown in Table 1.2.

The make-up of the private equity pot has recently changed as direct property ownership has been converted into fund formats, and public equity has grown as the Real Estate Investment Trust (REIT) format has been applied to more and more countries outside its US home.

PFR estimated in 2019 that 79% of the global property universe is held directly, while 13% is held in listed form and 8% is owned by private funds. Surveys suggest that there is potential for much further growth in funds. In the long run, it is reasonable to suppose that more listed and unlisted property funds will follow to convert the huge pool of government and owner-occupier-held property into an investable form. It is expected that growth in the creation of funds will continue. Prior to the crash of 2007–9, investors were taking more risk in search of maintaining attractive return levels, resulting in an increased appetite for what are called 'value-add' (higher-risk)

TABLE 1.2 The global capital stack

Private equity	Public equity	Private debt	Public debt
38%	8%	44%	10%

Source: DTZ (2015).

funds and growing interest in emerging markets on the fringes of Europe, the Middle East and North Africa, Sub-Saharan Africa, South America, and Russia. That endeavour may well recommence.

1.2 MARKET PLAYERS

The property investment market is driven by investors and fund managers, guided by advisory firms.

1.2.1 Investors

The largest global real estate investors are pension funds, insurance companies, and sovereign wealth funds (also known as government funds). Tables 1.3 and 1.4 show the world's largest sovereign wealth funds and pension funds, and what we know about their property assets. (Many insurance funds are very large but more opaque.)

TABLE 1.3 The largest sovereign wealth funds and their property assets

Domicile	Name	Estimated value of fund	Invests in real estate?	Estimated value of real estate
Norway	Norway Government Pension Fund Global	$1,053bn	Yes	$30bn
China	China Investment Corporation	$941bn	No	
Abu Dhabi	Abu Dhabi Investment Authority	$696bn	Yes	$52bn
Kuwait	Kuwait Investment Authority	$592bn	Yes	$15bn
Hong Kong	Hong Kong Monetary Authority Exchange Fund	$509bn	No	
Saudi Arabia	Saudi Arabian Monetary Authority	$506bn	No	
China	China State Administration of Foreign Exchange (SAFE)	$441bn	No	
Singapore	GIC Private Limited	$440bn	Yes	$31bn
China	National Council for Social Security Fund	$438bn	No	
Saudi Arabia	Saudi Arabia Public Investment Fund	$320bn	Yes	

Domicile	Name	Estimated value of fund	Invests in real estate?	Estimated value of real estate
Qatar	Qatar Investment Authority	$320bn	Yes	$35bn
UAE	Investment Corporation of Dubai	$240bn	Yes	$38bn
Singapore	Temasek Holdings	$238bn	Yes	$40bn
UAE	Mubadala Investment Company	$229bn	Yes	
Korea	Korea Investment Corporation	$122bn	Yes	$18bn

Source: PFR.

Insurance companies remain important, as do high net worth individuals operating through private banks and family offices. This immediately introduces us to the concept of the intermediary or capital aggregator, which is important in real estate because of the large size of the assets involved. Insurance companies, pension funds, private banks, and wealth managers are aggregators of retail (individuals') capital, and are seen as investors, largely because they have discretion or control over investment decisions. Meanwhile, aggregators of institutional capital, such as fund managers acting for pension funds, are seen not as investors but as a particular breed of advisor.

TABLE 1.4 The largest pension funds and their property assets

Domicile	Name	Total value of fund	Invests in real estate?	Estimated value of real estate
Japan	Japanese Government Pension Investment Fund	$1,552bn	Yes	$77bn
Korea	Korean National Pension Scheme	$574bn	Yes	$28bn
USA	Thrift Savings Fund	$558bn	Yes	
Netherlands	ABP Stichting Pensioenfonds	$447bn	Yes	$51bn
USA	California Public Employees Retirement System	$439bn	Yes	$34bn

(continued)

TABLE 1.4 (Continued)

Domicile	Name	Total value of fund	Invests in real estate?	Estimated value of real estate
Canada	Canada Pension Plan Investment Board	$296bn	Yes	$37bn
Singapore	Singapore Central Provident Fund	$284bn	Yes	
Netherlands	Pensioenfonds Zorg en Welzijn	$252bn	Yes	$13bn
USA	California State Teachers Retirement System	$227bn	Yes	$29bn
USA	New York State Common Retirement Fund	$221bn	Yes	$19bn
USA	New York City Board of Education Retirement System	$211bn	Yes	$14bn
USA	Malaysian Employees Provident Fund	$204bn	Yes	$6bn
USA	Florida State Board of Administration	$201bn	Yes	$22bn
USA	Florida Retirement System	$160bn	Yes	$18bn

Source: PFR.

It can be difficult to distinguish between a sovereign wealth fund, such as the Abu Dhabi Investment Authority, and a national pension fund, such as the Japanese Government Pension Investment Fund, but pension funds generally have well-defined and immediate liabilities, specifically to pay our pensions, while sovereign wealth funds may have no defined liabilities other than a broad objective to protect the nation's wealth. This is an important distinction in real estate investing, because (as we will see later in this chapter) real estate is regarded as an illiquid, long-term asset class, more suited to the investor without short-term liabilities. Hence it appears to be especially attractive to sovereign wealth funds (see Box 1.1 at the end of this chapter).

Sitting somewhere between the investor and fund manager categories are other aggregators, including real estate fund of funds managers and other advisory firms. Whether through discretionary or advisory (non-discretionary) mandates, these groups act on behalf of smaller investors to access global real estate assets and funds.

1.2.2 Fund Managers

Property investment is illiquid and difficult to diversify. An apparently obvious solution to these problems is the use of liquid traded property vehicles in place of the direct asset. A variety of legal structures exist which are capable of providing a means for investment in domestic or international real estate investment, including REITs and the new generation of unlisted property funds, both open-ended and closed-ended. In addition, work continues on the development of synthetic vehicles (derivatives) to provide solutions to these problems. These vehicles may have the primary objective of reducing tax, achieving liquidity, or aligning the interests of the investors and the managers. They exist primarily to permit co-mingling of investors, and are more fully described in Part III of this book.

As a result of the boom in funds, there has been a shift in control of the global market away from the insurance companies and pension funds which were so dominant in 1980 towards fund managers and property companies (the distinctions between which are occasionally blurred). Through the 1980s, the institutional investor dominated the industry, controlling the larger transaction business and driving best practice. In the 1990s, the effects of privatisation and outsourcing reached down to the institutions. There has consequently been a restructuring of their investment and property divisions, with the result that the power base now lies within specialist fund management operations, which may themselves be owned by what used to be insurance companies and are now financial services groups.

Table 1.5 shows the top 15 global property fund managers and the value of the assets held by those managers in Europe, the Americas, Asia, and Australasia. Significantly, there are as yet no large Asia-based managers, but Mitsubishi (Japan) and Capitaland (Singapore) would probably be on the cusp of the top 10 if they took part fully in the PFR survey.

1.2.3 Advisors

Developments in the investor and fund manager communities have created a more complex industry structure and a confusion of ownership and management. The traditional property service providers have been severely challenged by these changes. Even so, many of these businesses have been successful in creating their own fund management operations (such as LaSalle Investment Management, Savills Investment Management, and CBRE Global Investors).

Other advisors or service providers have become essential to the working of the commercial real estate investment market. These include placement agents and promoters of property funds; lawyers; tax advisors; trustees and custodians; investment brokers and agents; valuers (or appraisers in the USA); and property and asset managers, who are most easily found within the traditional service providers, but have competition in the form of specialist facilities management businesses. Recently, the emergence of WeWork and the general growth of co-working has redefined the nature of facilities management and driven hospitality and property management sectors closer together, so that property and asset management is in a state of flux.

TABLE 1.5 The PFR global manager survey, 2019 – top 20 managers by assets under management (AuM)

	Total AuM	Europe	North America	Latin America	Asia	Australasia	Middle East/ Africa
Blackstone[1]	$230,608m	$60,586m	$46,445m	–	$14,185m	–	–
Brookfield Asset Management	$193,276m	$30,169m	$146,322m	$2,606m	$7,357m	$6,557m	$265m
Nuveen/TH Real Estate	$124,566m	$33,262m	$88,175m	$143m	$988m	$1,998m	–
Hines	$119,381m	$22,384m	$91,068m	$2,840m	$2,964m	$125m	–
CBRE Global Investors[2]	$107,200m	$58,100m	$36,600m	–	$12,500m	–	–
UBS Global Asset Management	$95,413m	$37,192m	$38,748m	$262m	$17,694m	$1,517m	–
Swiss Life Asset Managers	$92,745m	$92,745m	–	–	–	–	–
MetLife Investment Management	$91,808m	$4,107m	$81,085m	$813m	–	$5,801m	$1m
AXA Investment Managers – Real Assets	$85,325m	$79,104m	$789m	–	$1,611m	$3,822m	–
JP Morgan Asset Management – Global Real Assets	$84,066m	$6,074m	$75,734m	–	$2,115m	$143m	–
AEW Global	$74,778m	$35,858m	$36,309m	–	$2,218m	$393m	–
PGIM	$72,700m	$8,800m	$52,200m	$3,200m	$8,500m	–	–
LaSalle Investment Management	$64,320m	$28,452m	$22,290m	$21m	$12,347m	$1,178m	$32m
GLP	$62,800m	$7,300m	$16,400m	$2,800m	$36,300m	–	–
DWS	$62,448m	$30,150m	$28,064m	–	$2,309m	$1,924m	–
Credit Suisse Asset Management	$61,762m	$56,265m	$2,402m	$1,270m	$1,018m	$806m	–
Invesco Real Estate	$59,353m	$11,710m	$41,340m	–	$6,303m	–	–
NYL Investors	$54,524m	–	$54,524m	–	–	–	–
Aberdeen Standard Investments	$53,718m	$51,575m	$1,146m	–	$997m	–	–
Prologis	$53,127m	$18,986m	$20,779m	$3,189m	$10,172m	–	–

Source: PFR 2019.

Note:

[1] Includes $109 billion of global assets.

[2] Data as at 31/03/2019.

1.3 PROPERTY – ITS CHARACTER AS AN ASSET CLASS

Institutional investors appear to hold less property than would be indicated by its neutral market weighting. This under-weighting can be attributed to several factors. These include the following:

1. The operational difficulties of holding property, including illiquidity, lumpiness (specific risk), and the difficulties involved in aligning the property and securities investment management processes.
2. The introduction of new alternative asset classes, some offering the income security and diversification benefits associated with real estate, including index-linked gilts, private equity, infrastructure, and private credit.
3. A lack of trust in property data, due to the nature of valuations, suspicions of smoothing in valuation-based indices, and the lack of long runs of high-frequency return histories.

The result, as we have seen, is a mismatch between the importance of the asset class in value and its weighting in institutional portfolios. Between 1980 and 2000, insurance companies reduced their property holdings from allocations as high as 10% (USA) and 20% (UK) to much lower levels. The case for property may have been overstated in the past, but suspicion regarding the asset class has reduced its appeal to institutions.

This is despite the fact that property investment has become better managed and more professionally packaged, and many of the problems associated with property investment appear to have found workable (if imperfect) solutions. By 2000, the measurement, benchmarking, forecasting, and quantitative management techniques applied to property investments had become more comparable with other asset classes. Advances in property research had provided ongoing debates with a foundation of solid evidence, and produced a clear formulation of many relevant issues. The result was an early 2000s boom in commercial and residential real estate investment across the globe, accompanied by such excellent returns that by 2005 property had become a high-performance asset class. However, the crash of 2007–9 pointed to cracks in the foundations.

By 2007, inevitably, clear overpricing had become evident in housing and in commercial property of all types in the UK, USA, and elsewhere. The ability of property investors and homeowners to take on debt secured on the value of property, coupled with the ability of lenders to securitise and sell those loans, created a wave of capital flows into the asset class and a pricing bubble. Professional responsibility took a back seat to the profit motive. Boardrooms lacked the detached yet experienced voices that advances in information and research should have made available.

London and New York had become the main centres for creative property structuring through REITs, unlisted funds, property derivatives, and mortgage-backed securities, and became the eye of the financial storm that followed. The technical advances made in information and research, and the spreading of risk made possible by the development of property investment products, did not prevent a global crisis from being incubated in the world of property investing. Worse, the global financial crisis of 2008 had its very roots in property speculation, facilitated by the packaging and re-packaging of equity, debt, and risk. It is essential, as a result of this noise, to re-examine the fundamental character of real estate as an asset class.

As with all equity-type assets, the performance of property is ultimately linked to some extent to the performance of the economy (see Chapter 3), and like all assets its performance is linked to the capital markets (see Chapter 4). The economy is the basic driver of occupier demand, and in the long term, investment returns are produced by occupiers who pay rent. However, in the shorter term – say up to 10 years – returns are much more likely to be explained by reference to changes in required returns, or yields. Required returns do not exist in a property vacuum but are instead driven by available or expected returns in other asset classes. As required returns on bonds and stocks move, so will required returns for property, followed by property prices.

Nonetheless, history shows that property is distinctly different from equities and bonds. The direct implication of property being different is its diversification potential, perhaps the strongest justification for holding it within a multi-asset portfolio. Generally, the impact of the real economy and the capital markets on the cash flow and value of real estate is distorted by several factors. It appears to be the case that these distortions contribute to the return diversity that investors crave, leading to inevitable disappointment when they reveal themselves.

1.3.1 Property Depreciates

- *Property is a real asset, and it wears out over time, suffering from physical deterioration and obsolescence, which together create depreciation.*

Commodities (say coffee, or oil) are by nature different from paper assets. Commodities will normally depreciate over time; they can have a value in use that sets a floor to minimum value; and they are generally illiquid. Finally, they may have to be valued by experts rather than priced in a secondary market. Examples include property of all types (that is, both real and personal).

Real property is, unlike equities and gilts (Treasuries in the USA), a physical asset. While, unlike personal property, it is durable (and immovable), the physical nature of buildings means that they are subject to deterioration and obsolescence, and need regular management and maintenance. Physical deterioration and functional and aesthetic obsolescence go together to create depreciation, defined as a fall in value of a piece of real property or real estate relative to an index of values of new buildings.

The problem of building depreciation or obsolescence of freehold buildings is often understated. All things equal, buildings located in areas of low land value will suffer more deterioration in performance over time than will buildings located in areas of high land value, so that poor-quality suburban offices located in out-of-town business parks with no local transport infrastructure will out-depreciate prime retail property, even in the face of attack from on-line retailing.

A failure to identify the potential impact of depreciation is very dangerous. Before the boom of 2004–7, the UK office sector failed to outperform the UK IPD universe in every year except two since 1981: depreciation was probably one of the major causes.

1.3.2 Lease Contracts Control Cash Flows

- *The cash flow delivered by a property asset is controlled or distorted by the lease contract agreed between owner and occupier.*

Unlike equities, property's income stream is governed by lease contracts, and, unlike bonds, the income from a freehold is both perpetual and may be expected to increase at lease events (rent reviews and lease ends in the UK; lease rollovers in the USA). Property's cash flow and investment characteristics flow partly from the effects of the customary occupational lease.

In a typical US lease of 3–5 years, rents will often be indexed to the consumer price index or escalated according to a fixed schedule. In continental Europe, leases of between 3 and 10 years will usually be indexed, although the degree of inflation captured by the lease rent will not always be 100%. In the UK, the initial rental income is usually fixed for the first 3–5 years, with uplifts to market rents at each rent review, sometimes upwards only. This creates a low-risk option or convertible asset. In many markets, turnover or percentage rents are adjusted to top up a base fixed amount with a percentage of the occupier's turnover, another form of option.

In Asia, commercial leases tend to be shorter, between 2 and 3 years, given the greater volatility of the emerging markets in the region. As leases are shorter, they are also not normally linked to any rental index. In Australia, larger-area office leases tend to be for 10 years with the tenant having the right of a 10-year extension, with annual rent increases. For smaller areas, the lease structure would more typically be for 3 plus 3 or 5 plus 5 years. Rent increases would normally be annual, based on CPI or fixed percentage rises, with market reviews at the beginning of the lease extension.

We deal more fully with leasing in Chapter 6. It can be seen that the precise nature of real estate as an asset in any location will vary by leasing practice and the jurisdiction which interprets those leases.

1.3.3 The Supply Side is Inelastic

- *The supply side is controlled by zoning or planning regulations, and is highly price inelastic. This means that a boom in the demand for space may be followed by a supply response, but only if permission to build can be obtained and only after a significant lag, which will be governed by the time taken to obtain a permit, prepare a site, and construct or refit a property.*

The supply side of property is regulated by local and central government. The control of supply complicates the way in which an economic event (such as a positive or negative demand shock) is translated into return. A loosening of planning policy, such as happened in many locations in the mid-1980s, created the conditions for an immediate building boom, which, in the case of the USA, was accompanied by tax breaks, further distorting supply. Nonetheless, it is difficult to vary the supply of property upwards, and even more difficult to vary it downwards. This is termed supply inelasticity.

The supply side can be both regulated and inelastic, and will sometimes produce different return characteristics for property from equities – which is otherwise the natural property analogy – in the same economic environment. More elastic supply regimes, such as those pertaining in loose planning environments in parts of Texas, or for industrial property in regeneration cities, will produce different cash flow characteristics for property investments than will highly constrained environments, such as central Paris or the West End of London. The typical industrial investment will typically deliver less-volatile rents, and will show less rental growth in times of demand expansion, than will the less elastic Paris or West End office.

1.3.4 Valuations Influence Performance

- *The returns delivered by property are likely to be heavily influenced by appraisals rather than by marginal trading prices.*

In the absence of continuously traded, deep, and securitised markets, commercial property valuations perform a vital function in the property market by acting as a surrogate for transaction prices. Property asset valuations are central to the process of performance measurement, but within both the professional and academic communities there is considerable scepticism about the ability of appraisals or valuations to fulfil this role in a reliable manner.

There is a consensus that individual valuations are prone to a degree of uncertainty. At the macro-level, it is clear that few analysts accept that appraisal-based indices reflect the true underlying performance of the property market. It is commonly held, for example, that such indices fail to capture the extent of market volatility and tend to lag underlying performance. As a consequence, issues such as the level and nature of valuation uncertainty and the causes and extent of index smoothing have generated a substantial research literature.

Some of this research indicates that valuations both lag the market and smooth the peaks and troughs of 'real' prices. Valuations – and, if valuations affect market psychology and hence prices, real estate prices – can be 'sticky'.

In many jurisdictions, the fiduciary responsibility of the valuer (appraiser) towards the client is an important influence on valuer behaviour. Claims based on accusations of professional negligence are rare but not unknown, and judicial precedent is a powerful influence on the valuation process, as is 'anchoring'. (Anchoring is a general psychological tendency by which individuals are influenced by an initial value and adjust that value to account for changes. Once the anchor – like the price you paid for your house – is set, there is a strong and continuing bias toward that value, for example in your subsequent asking price.)

It is not therefore surprising if a valuer, retained to produce a portfolio valuation on a 3-year contract, pays attention to his/her year-end 2010 valuation when undertaking the 2011 equivalent and ensures continuity by limiting the number and size of shocks a client might suffer. This can reduce changes in valuation from one period to the next.

In addition, real estate valuation is founded primarily on the use of comparable sales evidence. Similarity in property characteristics is paramount. The currency of the transaction may not be easy to control. Hence, the evidence used to value a property as at 31 December 2020 may use evidence collected over the period July to December. In a rising or falling market, this will again result in a lower variance of prices.

Hence, valuations will be based on the previous valuation plus or minus a perception of change. The perceived changes, unless based on very reliable transaction evidence, will be conservative.

The resulting issue of valuation 'smoothing' has been widely analysed. It is generally presumed to reduce the reported volatility – or risk – of real estate investment below the real level of risk suffered by investors who have to sell in a weak market or buy in a strong one.

1.3.5 Property is Not Liquid

- *Property is highly illiquid. It is expensive to trade property, there is a large risk of abortive expenditure, and the result can be a very wide bid–offer spread (a gap between what buyers will offer and sellers will accept).*

It costs much more to trade property than it costs to trade securities. There are both direct and indirect costs. Table 1.6 shows that the direct costs include taxes paid by buyers on property transactions (real property transfer taxes in the USA vary from state to state, but stamp duty in the UK is as much as 5% of the purchase price for larger commercial transactions) and fees paid by both buyers and sellers. In addition to taxes, buyers will incur survey fees, valuation fees, and legal fees, totalling (say) 1.75%. The buyers' costs, including tax, can therefore be 6.75% in the UK. Sellers will incur legal fees (say 0.5%) and brokers' fees (say 1%), so that 1.5% can be the total sellers' cost, and a round-trip purchase and sale can cost 8.25%.

These costs, which can be even higher in other jurisdictions, define one cause of the 'bid–offer spread' which inhibits liquidity. It is natural for a seller to wish to recover his total costs, so that having bought a property for £1 million he will wish to get back £1.0825 million in order not to have lost money. But in a flat or falling market buyers will not pay this price, and sellers are tempted to hang on until the selling market is stronger. Hence, liquidity will be positively related to capital growth in the market.

There are also indirect costs of transacting property. Every property is unique, which means that time and effort have to be expended on researching its physical qualities, its legal title, and its supportable market value. In addition, the process by which

TABLE 1.6 Real estate transfer costs, Europe (purchaser, % of purchase price)

Country	Due diligence costs	Agent's fee	Property transfer tax	Total cost
France	0.6%	1%	6.7–7.3%	8.6%
Germany	0.75%	1%	3.5–6.5%	6.8%
Netherlands	0.5%	1%	6%	7.5%
Poland	0.5%	1–3%	2%	4.5%
Spain	0.5%	1–3%	6%	8.5%
UK	0.8%	1%	5%	6.8%

Source: CBRE Global Investors.

properties are marketed and sold can be very risky to both sides. In many markets, including the USA and England and Wales, there is a large risk of abortive expenditure, because buyers and sellers are not committed until contracts are exchanged, and last-minute overbids by another buyer, or a price reduction (or 'chip') by the buyer, are common. The role played by professional property advisers, and the integrity of all parties who may wish to do repeat business with each other, create a sensitive balance and risk control in the transaction process. This transaction risk must also be built into a bid–offer spread (the gap between what buyers will offer and sellers will accept).

It seems obvious that an increasingly digitalised world will one day deliver instant, costless real estate transactions. Businesses will innovate ways of extracting and transferring digital data across platforms, and creating products which will encourage transaction efficiency (e.g. insurance-backed property passports). Industry groups will develop standards and protocols encouraging common standards for digital data and record-keeping, including the intelligent application of distributed ledger technology.

However, human beings will protect themselves in a *caveat emptor* world by taking their time and being thorough in the research process before committing large capital sums. Until we arrive at the instantaneous transaction, buyers and sellers will wish to pay professional advisors for risk mitigation and, on occasion, risk transfer (Baum and Saull, 2019).

Finally, the lack of a formal market-clearing mechanism for property, such as is offered by the stock market for securities, means that on occasion there may be few or no transactions, reducing the flow of comparable sales information and further increasing the perceived risk of a transaction, creating a feedback loop and self-sustaining illiquidity. This appeared to be the case, for example, in most global markets in 2007–9.

1.3.6 Large Lot Sizes Produce Specific Risk

- *Property assets are generally large in terms of capital price. This means that property portfolios cannot easily be diversified, and suffer hugely from specific risk.*

Property is heterogeneous, meaning that an investment can do well when markets do badly, and *vice versa*. Property is also 'lumpy'. Lumpiness – the large and uneven sizes of individual assets – means that direct property investment (buying buildings) requires considerably higher levels of capital investment when compared with securities, and even with significant capital investment, diversification within property portfolios may prove to be more challenging than in equity and bond portfolios. As a result, typical property portfolios contain high levels of specific risk.

This fact, coupled with the growing globalisation of property portfolios, largely explains the boom in indirect vehicles such as REITs and unlisted funds since 1990. There is also some evidence that large lot sizes have been high-beta investments (more responsive to the economy and to rises and falls in the investment market). This adds a further risk level.

Specific risk in property, whether measured as a standard deviation or as a tracking error against a benchmark (see Chapters 4 and 17), is a key problem, especially for international investors. Unlike securities, large average property capital values, an uneven distribution of these values, and the unique or heterogeneous nature of property assets creates very different real estate portfolios across investors. Property funds offer a way to limit this problem, as all three issues are minimised by investing indirectly by using diversified funds. But specific risk varies significantly between sectors, and unlisted funds (which add other risks) may be more useful in some sectors and countries than others. This is not simply a function of lot size, but also of 'diversification power' within sectors, defined as the efficiency of specific risk reduction through adding properties (Baum and Struempell, 2006; Baum, 2007).

Investors who have targeted low-risk or 'core' property as an asset class will most likely be seeking to replicate the benchmark performance with few surprises; after all, the decision to invest in property is often based on an analysis of historic risk and return characteristics produced from a market index or benchmark. The tracking error of a portfolio is therefore likely to be seen as an additional and unrewarded risk. As a result, managers may be charged with minimising tracking error – but with limited sums to invest. This is a very difficult challenge: how many properties are needed to reduce tracking error to an acceptable level?

Various studies, all of which concentrate on portfolios of properties of mixed types and geographies, have suggested that the appropriate number of properties is very large. Relevant sources include the seminal work of Markowitz (1952), Evans and Archer (1968), and Elton and Gruber (1977). A limited number of studies investigate risk reduction and portfolio size in the property market. They include Brown (1988), Brown and Matysiak (2000), Morrell (1993), and Schuck and Brown (1997). It is concluded that many assets are needed to reduce risk to the systematic level when value-weighting returns, depending on the degree of skewness of property values in the portfolio.

It is also well known that the necessary level of capital required to replicate the market will be greatly dependent on the segments of property in which one wishes to invest, as different segments of the property market exhibit vastly different lot sizes. For example, it appears obvious that a very large allocation of cash may be needed to invest in a sufficient number of shopping centres to replicate the performance of that segment with a low tracking error.

In addition, there are significant differences in the performance characteristics of properties within the different segments. Properties in some segments – for example, London offices – may experience higher variations in return than others, resulting in the probability that more properties will be needed to minimise tracking error within the segment. If London offices are also relatively expensive, the problem of assembling a market-tracking portfolio at reasonable cost is magnified.

This issue, amongst others, explains a consistent push towards the unitisation, fractionalisation, or democratisation of individual real estate assets. This push has consistently proved unsuccessful, either because market conditions have not been right, limiting either or both of the demand and supply sides, or because regulatory and tax issues have not been dealt with. In 2019, IPSX, a regulated exchange, was set up in London to trade shares in single-asset property companies. At the same time there has been a lot of noise made about the digital tokenisation of assets. Given the thoughtful approach taken by IPSX to regulation and tax transparency, this has the best chance of some success, but history has taught us to be sceptical about the likely scale of such a unitised market.

1.3.7 Leverage is Commonly Used in Real Estate Investment

- *Leverage is used in the vast majority of property transactions. This distorts the return and risk of a property investment.*

'Gearing' and 'leverage' are terms used to describe the level of a company's debt. This is typically compared with its total debt or its equity, usually expressed as a ratio or percentage. So, a company with gearing (debt to equity) of 60% has levels of debt that are 60% of its equity capital. Alternatively, gearing might be expressed as the level of a company's debt compared with its gross assets (debt plus equity). In that case, the above example would produce a gearing (debt to gross assets, or loan to value) ratio of 30%. Throughout this text we use gearing and leverage interchangeably to mean the relationship of debt to gross assets.

This concept (or these concepts) translate directly into the world of commercial real estate investment. In the right market conditions, banks have been willing to lend more against the security of property than against other assets such as equities. This is a result of property's income security and the land, bricks, and mortar salvage value of a non-performing property loan.

Banks have typically been keen to lend against the collateral security offered by real estate assets, especially when the rental income more than covers the interest payments on the loan (see Chapter 8). But the use of gearing will change the financial mathematics of the real estate investment. It reduces the amount of equity that needs to be invested; it reduces the net cash flow available to the investor by the amount of interest paid; and it reduces the net capital received by the investor on sale of the asset by the amount of the loan still outstanding. This has some complex tax and currency effects in the international context (see Chapter 16) and allows more diversification of specific risk at the asset level, because the investor can buy more properties for the same total outlay of equity. It also has two more direct implications, on return and risk.

If the prospective return or IRR on the investment without using leverage is higher than the interest rate charged, then leverage will be return-enhancing; and the greater the leverage, the greater will be the return on equity invested. In addition, the risk of the investment will be greater. The chance that the investor will lose his equity is greater the higher is the level of gearing, and the sensitivity or volatility of the prospective return will be greater. This is illustrated in Table 1.7, which shows how changing capitalisation rates (yields) on the sale of a specific property (more fully described in Baum and Crosby, 2008) produced a wider range of returns on equity (using 70% debt) than on the unleveraged investment.

TABLE 1.7 The impact of exit yields on the risk to equity (70% leverage)

Exit yield	IRR	IRR on equity
7.50%	12.00%	18.77%
8.50%	10.00%	15.10%
10.50%	6.00%	3.90%

Source: Baum and Crosby (2008).

The history of ungeared direct property returns, such as is produced by IPD in Europe and NCREIF in the USA, disguises the returns that have been available to investors' equity over most subperiods of the past 25 years. Just as homeowners can, in times of rising house prices and low interest rates, significantly enhance the return on the cash they invest by borrowing, property companies and private commercial property investors use debt finance to (hopefully) increase returns on equity – always at the cost of increasing risk.

By using rents to pay interest and (if possible) some capital repayment (amortisation), investors can enjoy a return on their equity investment in excess of the reported total return available to whole-equity investors, such as pension funds. These geared returns are rarely reported, but explain most private capital investments in global commercial property. Leverage is discussed in more detail in Chapter 9.

1.3.8 Property Appears to be an Inflation Hedge

- *Property rents appear to be related to inflation in the long run, producing a reasonable but imperfect hedge.*

For many investors, particularly pension funds which have liabilities linked to future wage levels, the need to achieve gains in money value (in nominal terms) is of less concern than the need to achieve gains in the purchasing power of assets held (in real terms).

Many investors appear to believe that there is a strong correlation between rents and inflation in the long run, and that the cash flow produced by real estate might (although subject to deterioration and obsolescence) be expected to increase in line with inflation over a long period. This is somewhat supported by theory, as the profit of an operation before rent should be positively correlated with inflation and so, therefore, should rent and profit after rent (see Chapter 3).

This belief is exemplified by the clear (73%) correlation between UK real estate and index-linked government bond yields as shown in Figure 1.1. The prices of these two

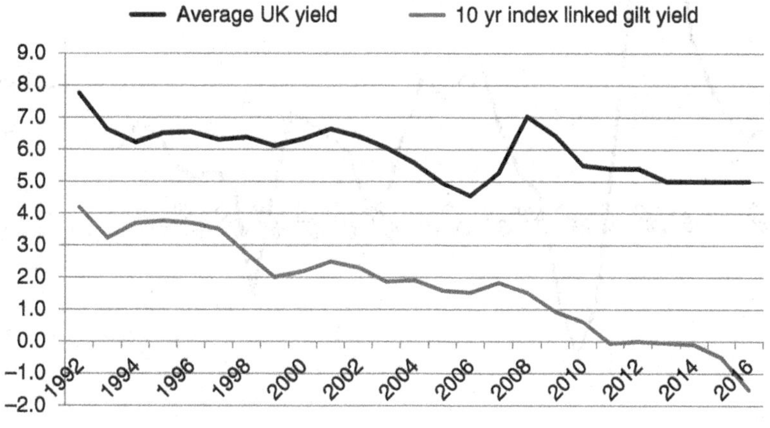

FIGURE 1.1 UK real estate and index-linked government bond yields, 1992–2017
Sources: MSCI, PFR.

asset types are strongly connected, suggesting that investors believe that the income streams and capital values are also connected. Given that the income from, and the redemption value of, index-linked government bond yields are formally indexed to inflation, investors appear to believe that property rents and prices are also linked.

The empirical evidence is, however, much less clear. Figure 1.2 shows that there has been zero correlation on an annual basis between the growth in UK commercial property rents and CPI (consumer price inflation) growth over the 35 years leading up to 2017.

It has to be said that it would be surprising if there were a contemporaneous relationship. Rents over this 35-year period were typically agreed every 5 years for 5 years in advance, and there is no formal link between the rate of inflation in any year and the rental values agreed in that year. Indeed, the parties negotiating the rent (or the valuers estimating rental values) may not have been aware of the inflation out-turn for that year until well after the negotiations were complete.

Nevertheless, and despite the complete absence of any contemporaneous correlation, it is interesting to note that annual CPI growth over this period averaged 3.23% while annual rental growth averaged 3.17%. While there is no annual correlation, there is evidence of a more complex statistical relationship.

There are many academic references to this topic, with varying conclusions, but most find a stronger long-term connection between rents and inflation than between annual returns and annual inflation.

Finally, it is common practice in many countries, including most of mainland Europe, to formally connect rents with inflation, sometimes a proportion of inflation, defined either in terms of constriction cost inflation or CPI. Where leases are for 9 or

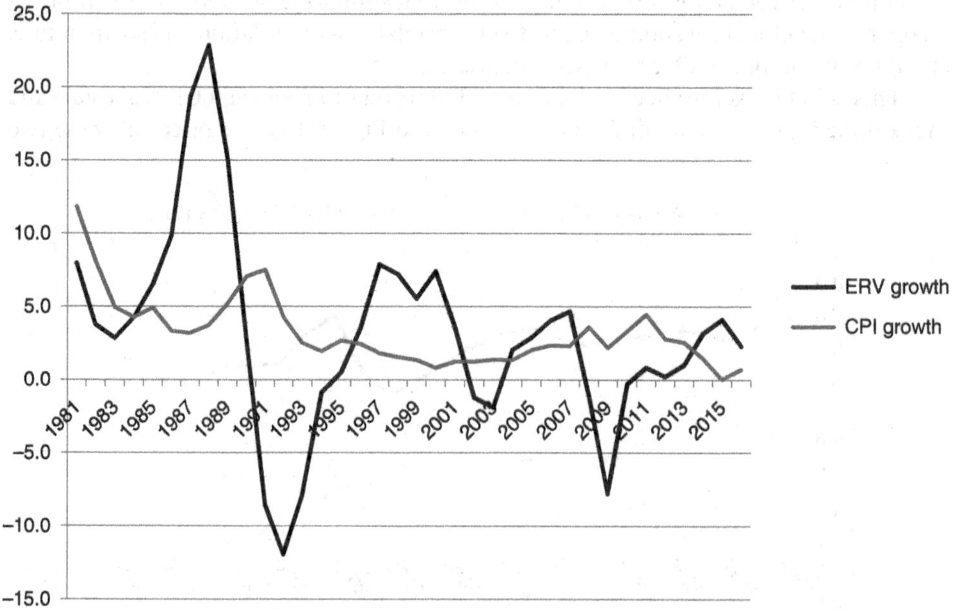

FIGURE 1.2 Are rents an inflation hedge? UK evidence, 1981–2017
Sources: MSCI, PFR.

10 years, as is typical in France and Germany, this establishes a strong link between rents and inflation, although rental values may need to be reset at the lease end if inflation has outpaced rental values affected by obsolescence.

1.3.9 Property is a Medium-Risk Asset

- *The risk of property appears low. Rent is paid before dividends, and as a real asset property will be a store of value even when it is vacant and produces no income. The volatility of annual return also appears to be lower than that of bonds. But this measure is distorted somewhat by appraisals, and the performance history of real estate suggests a medium return for a medium risk.*

Property is usually described as a medium-risk asset. In finance theory, risk and return are strongly and positively connected, so real estate returns should therefore be expected to lie between those produced by equities and those produced by bonds, and its risk profile should be similarly middling. The reported risk of property has certainly been lower than the risk of the equity market, and some data suggests a risk even lower than that of the bond market.

Rent is a superior claim on a company's assets, and paid before dividends. Property's downside risk is limited, because as a real asset property will be a store of value even when it is vacant and produces no income. In addition, leases determine the delivery of income and can produce short-term bond-like income characteristics, although returns should be more equity-like (driven by the real economy) in the longer term.

The total returns delivered by UK commercial property over the period 1971–2018 (see Table 1.8) have been less volatile even than the returns from gilts.

This data is supported by US data shown in Table 1.9, using the period 1979–2018 for US equities (S&P 500), treasuries (US 10-year Treasury 10-year index), and real estate (NCREIF NPI). This time, property has a slightly higher risk than treasuries.

Despite the UK data, any conclusion to the effect that property returns have been less volatile than the returns from gilts or treasuries is flawed. Low volatility of delivered nominal returns disguises the illiquidity of property, which introduces a risk not reflected in the volatility of notional returns based solely on valuations from period to period. In addition, valuation-based returns are themselves believed to be biased towards lower volatility than typical underlying market conditions support. There are several reasons for this, discussed above, but the effect is serial or auto-correlation between consecutive values. Where this is present, the current valuation (*Vt*) is a

TABLE 1.8 UK assets risk and return, 1971–2018

	Return	Risk
Equities	11.7%	27.5%
Gilts	9.3%	12.8%
Property	10.6%	10.5%

Sources: MSCI annual index, FTSE all-share index, FTSE 15-year gilt index.

TABLE 1.9 US assets risk and return, 1979–2018

	Return	Risk
Equities	11.6%	16.0%
Treasuries	7.0%	6.2%
Property	9.0%	7.4%

Sources: NCREIF property index, S&P 500, Barclays Capital US 10-year Treasury 10-year index.

weighted function of the present market value (*Vt**) and the immediate past valuation (*Vt* – 1), so that:

$$Vt = aVt^* + (1-a)Vt-1$$

Using this formula, a series of valuations can be 'unsmoothed' to present a representation of the imagined (unobservable) market values. Given *Vt* and *Vt* – 1, we need to assign weights (*a* and (1 – *a*)) to each. If *a* = 0.5, then the current valuation (say $10 million) is 50% of last year's valuation (say $8 million) and 50% of the present market value, which solves to $12 million. The unsmoothed series will consequently demonstrate greater volatility.

The uncertainty of the nominal dividend income produced by equities over a given holding period compares with the absolute certainty of nominal income produced by a fixed-interest security held to redemption. Commercial property falls somewhere between the two in terms of certainty of income.

Where leases are longer, such as the 10 years typical in the UK for prime or core real estate, and fixed or indexed, the principal return to the investor is an income return which is reasonably certain; and the value of the reversion at the expiry of the lease (while largely uncertain) is of reduced importance. So, the risk of commercial property, generally a medium-risk asset, depends on the lease contract, with the result that some markets compare with bonds at the least risky end of the spectrum and others with equities at the most risky end.

1.3.10 Real Estate Cycles Control Returns

- *Unlike stocks and bonds, real estate returns appear to be controlled by cycles – of 8–9 years.*

It has been suggested (e.g. by MacGregor, 1994) that repeatable patterns, or cycles, can be seen in the history of development, occupier, and investment markets. These are expressed in the form of construction activity, rents, and cap rates (initial yields), with these in turn driving capital values and returns.

The inelasticity of property supply in response to price changes is perhaps the most important variable that explains the existence of a cycle of supply, rents, capital values, and returns. Empirically, a cycle in property development is apparent, and most obvious in the London office market. Barras (1994) identified short cycles (4–5 years, the classic business cycle operating on occupier demand), long cycles (9–10 years, a tendency for severe oversupply in one cycle to feed part of the next demand cycle), long swings (20 years, associated with major phases of urban development), and long waves (50 years, technology-based). More recent data suggest cycles of 7–8 years from peak to peak of development activity.

Figure 1.3 illustrates what many would describe as a cycle in UK property returns over the period 1971–2018, with three distinct troughs.

Development activity appears to be highly pro-cyclical with GDP growth and property values (rising and falling at the same time), but exhibits sharper rises and falls. As property values rise in a strong economy, developers gain confidence and construction activity increases. Hence, current development profits have been a good explanatory variable for development activity.

There is a strong relationship between office development and changes in rents, suggesting a degree of adaptive behaviour among lenders, investors, and developers, with a tendency to follow the market, often in an exaggerated fashion. As prices rise, prices are more likely to be expected to continue to rise; development profits are a function of continued price rises; hence price rises lead to ever-increasing supply levels, which create the conditions for lower prices (this is called disaster myopia). The time lag between the inception and completion of developments creates an inevitable supply cycle.

Rents have also been strongly pro-cyclical with GDP (see Chapter 3). Barras (1994) shows how periods of growth in GDP above the long-term trend rate of growth have been coincident with periods of growth in rents above long-term trend growth. The demand side is pro-cyclical with economic growth indicators, but the inelasticity of supply means that even highly regular demand cycles can generate irregular rental

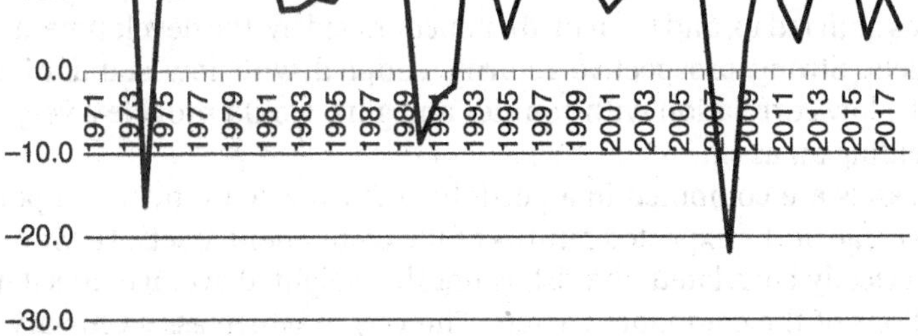

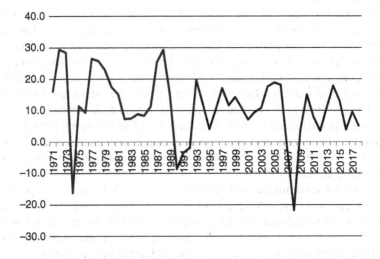

FIGURE 1.3 UK property returns, 1971–2018 (%)
Sources: MSCI 2019, Scott (1998).

cycles. Hence, rents will rise in response to economic growth and a static supply in the short term, and will continue to rise as construction activity gathers momentum; but the peak in construction activity may arrive after the peak in GDP growth, and an oversupply will result.

Some evidence of cyclicality in property yields (or cap rates – see Chapter 2) around a flat (mean-reverting) trend may be discernible over a long period. The long-run flatness of yields results in an extremely strong relationship between rental growth and capital value growth, both strongly pro-cyclical, although some extreme market movements have been strongly yield-driven (a good example being many markets in 2004–7).

Work by IPD (drawing on historic data from Scott, 1998) provides the fullest picture of long-term UK performance yet available. Data assembled from various sources covering the period 1921–2010 shows 16 'fairly distinct' peaks and troughs in the market. IPD identify six completed cycles, which ranged in length from 4 to 12 years, with an average of 8 years. The average cycle length of 8 years is interesting, as after roughly two more 8-year periods beyond 1989, the next peak of 2006–7 emerged.

1.3.11 Property Appears to be a Diversifying Asset

- *Property returns have been less well correlated with returns on equities and gilts than returns on equities and gilts have been correlated with each other. In other words, while equities and gilts have usually performed well or badly at the same time, property has outperformed or underperformed at different times, thus smoothing out the overall performance of a portfolio with assets of all three classes.*

Mathematical models based on modern portfolio theory (MPT) play an important role in the investment market, especially in the advice on investment strategy and asset allocation given by actuaries and consultants to pension funds and insurance companies (see Chapter 4).

MPT reflects the desire of investors to achieve higher returns, low individual asset risk, and (more importantly) a smooth return on the entire portfolio. Asset allocation advice has, since the acceptance of MPT, traditionally required a view on three values: the likely future return on an asset class; its risk (usually defined as volatility and measured in units of standard deviation of return over a given period); and its correlation with other asset classes. This last factor measures the extent to which upward and downward movements in the values of two variables are linked together.

MPT has both led to, and been further encouraged by, the development of asset allocation models. Strong prospective returns, coupled with low standard deviation of returns and a low correlation with equities and gilts, would provide a very strong argument for holding an asset.

When assets are combined in a portfolio, the expected return of a portfolio is the weighted average of the expected returns of the component assets. However, unless the assets are perfectly correlated, the risk is not the weighted average: it is determined by the correlations of the component assets. The way in which assets co-vary is central to portfolio risk, as low covariance produces diversification opportunities.

Correlations of 1.0 indicate perfect co-movement, correlations of 0.0 indicate independence of the returns of two assets, and correlations of −1.0 indicate that returns move in exactly opposite directions. Generally, adding assets that exhibit lower (ideally negative) correlations to a portfolio provides the greatest diversification benefits.

MSCI's UK annual index provides the longest available run of consistent annual data describing the performance of a well-diversified portfolio of real properties. The results show the following:

- Property returns have been below the return on equities but competitive with the return on gilts (see Table 1.7).
- Property volatility has been less than the volatility of equities and comparable to that of gilts (see Table 1.8).
- Property returns have been less well correlated with returns on equities and gilts than returns on equities and gilts have been correlated with each other. In other words, while equities and gilts have usually performed well or badly at the same time, property has outperformed or underperformed at different times, thus smoothing out the overall performance of a portfolio with assets of all three classes.

This is illustrated in Table 1.10. UK data suggests that property offers portfolio risk reduction to holders of bonds and equities, as property has been less highly correlated with gilts and equities than they have been with each other.

However, the reported returns on US equities, treasuries, and real estate shows a somewhat different result. There has been close to zero correlation between equities and treasuries, and also between property and treasuries, with a low positive correlation between property and equities (see Table 1.11).

The result of using UK return, risk, and correlation data (see Tables 1.8 and 1.10) in an MPT framework is a high property allocation, as shown in Table 1.12. We constructed the optimal (lowest-risk) portfolios for portfolio target returns of 10%, 10.5%, and 11%. The low return/risk portfolio not surprisingly has plenty of gilts (45%), but the optimiser selects 55% property, as this reduces the portfolio risk even below the risk of

TABLE 1.10 UK asset class correlations, 1971–2018

	Gilts	Property
Equities	0.55	0.27
Property	0.04	

Sources: IPD annual index, FTSE all-share index, FTSE 15-year gilt index.

TABLE 1.11 US asset class correlations, 1979–2018

	Treasuries	Property
Equities	0.02	0.14
Property	−0.03	

Sources: NCREIF property index, S&P 500, Barclays Capital US 10-year Treasury index.

TABLE 1.12 Optimised asset class allocations (UK)

Target return	Volatility	UK property	UK stocks	UK gilts
10.00%	8.3%	55%	0%	45%
10.50%	9.6%	80%	7%	13%
11.00%	14.4%	62%	38%	0%

TABLE 1.13 Optimised asset class allocations (USA)

Target return	Volatility	US property	US stocks	US bonds
8.00%	4.6%	39%	5%	56%
9.25%	6.2%	58%	24%	18%
10.50%	10.3%	41%	59%	0%

a portfolio of 100% gilts. The high return/risk portfolio – not surprisingly, again – has plenty (38%) of stocks, but the optimiser selects 62% property, as this again reduces the portfolio risk without excessively damaging returns. Property comprises between 55% and 80% of the optimal or efficient portfolio at all target return levels.

A similar optimisation using the more plausible US data produces similar, albeit slightly less extreme, results (Table 1.13). The recommended property allocation in the optimal portfolio varies from a minimum of 39% to a maximum of 58%.

Yet a typical allocation for institutional investors has been around 10%, around one-fifth of the optimised level (see Figure 1.4). What explains the huge difference between unconstrained theory and practice?

Valuation smoothing is a large problem colouring this data. In some years, property yields do not appear to change; and it is clear that this can be the result of a scarcity of transaction evidence and the behaviour of valuers rather than a steadily performing market.

The smoothing problem also affects the correlation numbers. Reported property correlations, such as volatility, may be artificially low. The greater the fixity of the property return series – the greater the amount of smoothing, or serial correlation – the greater will be the tendency of the correlation of that series with returns in efficient markets to be close to zero. (The correlation coefficient is determined by the covariance of two series divided by the product of their standard deviations. Low volatility depresses both the numerator and the denominator of this equation, but the impact of the covariance is likely to be greater.)

Given that three indicators are needed for assessing the appropriate weight of property in a multi-asset portfolio, two of which present two large problems, it is not surprising that property allocations in practice do not match the MPT solution. Standard deviations of returns from year to year understate true property risk; and correlations between property and the other assets may be unreliable. For this reason, various efforts have been made by academics to improve the position, which usually imply the use of statistical techniques to adjust the data (e.g. see Brown and Matysiak, 2000).

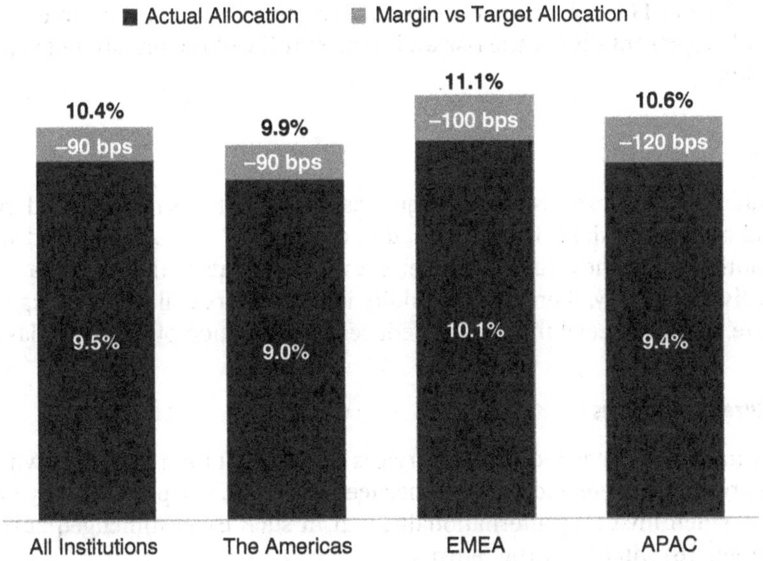

FIGURE 1.4 Actual and target real estate allocations – institutional investors
Source: Cornell Baker Program in Real Estate, Hodes Weill & Associates, 2018.

In addition, year-on-year correlations between the asset classes may be said to be of limited interest to pension funds and insurance funds with longer-term liabilities. They are more likely to be concerned with their ability to match long-term liabilities (wage inflation-linked pensions or nominally fixed endowment mortgages) without increasing the contribution rate of the employer or employee.

However, there are more limitations to this type of optimisation analysis that need to be considered, especially in a global context. These are as follows.

Specific Risk

The data used describes the returns available on the index universes of asset classes. For stocks and bonds, it is possible for investors to replicate these universes in an investment portfolio, as they are highly divisible assets and index-tracking products are available. For property, the universe used to compile the UK annual index at the end of 2018 comprised over 13,000 properties worth around £220 billion; over 7,000 properties and $640 billion comprise the US NPI universe. These universes are not investable. The investor therefore faces an additional layer of risk, which is the sampling error created by the heterogeneity and specific risk of real estate.

Leverage

The majority of property transactions involve the use of leverage (see Chapter 9). Even where the institutional investor does not use leverage on direct property acquisitions, unlisted funds will commonly be used for specialist or international investments (see

Chapters 10 and 11), and these will typically be geared. Hence, ungeared returns may not be fully representative of the risk and return profile of the investment vehicles used by investors.

Illiquidity

Real estate, unlike securities, is not a liquid asset class. This is not reflected in the volatility and correlation data. The introduction of liquidity into a property structure can significantly change the return characteristics of real estate to the point that it ceases to be attractive. Arguably, therefore, illiquidity is a necessary evil in justifying the role of real estate, but it is an evil that clearly reduces the attraction of the asset class.

Taxes, Currency, and Fees

Property investment may require the services of specialist fund managers who will typically charge *ad valorem* and performance fees. Taxes may be paid, even by tax-exempt investors, when investing internationally, and in such cases unhedged currency risk (see Chapter 16) will colour the returns.

These variables all challenge the value of a single-country, gross of tax and fees, domestic currency, unleveraged, universe of returns in deciding on an allocation to commercial property. Adding the operational challenges of investing in real estate alongside faster-moving securities, it is not surprising that allocations do not reflect the outputs of an MPT optimiser.

Alternative approaches to asset allocation do exist. The most popular alternative is the so-called 'equilibrium approach' (Litterman, 2003), which advocates a neutral position determined by the size by value of the asset class (see Chapter 4), with positions taken against that neutral weight determined by the attractiveness of market pricing. This more closely reflects the practice of professional and institutional market participants, but (as we suggested at the beginning of the chapter) still produces a higher weighting to the asset class than is observed in practice.

1.4 CONCLUSION

The cult of the equity has dominated western investment strategy in the 1980s and 1990s to the extent that equities now dominate most institutional portfolios, especially in the USA, UK, and Hong Kong. On the contrary, in Germany and some other continental European countries, bonds have always been the largest component of the mixed-asset portfolio.

The experience of property investors in the early 1990s was enough to persuade many of them that it was time to abandon the asset class. Several property companies became bankrupt; many banks developed severe shortfalls in their loan books through exposure to property loans; many householders found they owed more than they had borrowed by developing negative equity; and, worst of all, it became acutely apparent that the liquidity of property was not the same as the liquidity of equities and bonds.

Because of the liquidity and management problems associated with direct real estate ownership, the property investment market became mesmerised by the potential for securitisation or unitisation of real estate. Over the period 1990–8, real estate investment trusts in the USA and listed property trusts in Australia each saw explosive growth in markets where the legal and regulatory framework permits privately held real estate assets to be transferred into tax-efficient public vehicles. Following a boom in the creation of unlisted funds in the 1999–2006 period (see Chapter 11), the UK and Germany introduced REITs in 2007 (see Chapter 13). Property derivatives became the focus of innovation in the UK in 2005 and by 2007, swaps, structured notes, and even futures traded globally. In addition, the search for return and diversification led to globalisation, meaning a transfer of attention from domestic investors and investments to international investors and assets (see Chapter 16). But we must remember what makes real estate attractive to these investors, which is low volatility and the opportunity to diversify a securities portfolio.

Property is illiquid. This means that its required – and expected – return is higher than it would otherwise be. Innovative investment approaches incubated within the meeting rooms of US endowment funds, the Yale Investment Office being the most well-known, CPPIB (a Canadian Pension Fund), and others have emphasised the value of illiquid assets and pushed their real estate allocations to 20% plus, albeit often within a real estate private markets allocation including private credit, private equity, and infrastructure. As a result, by 2020 the dominance of benchmarks and MPT as drivers of investment allocations had weakened.

Introducing liquidity to real estate in the form of fractionalisation or securitisation may damage returns. The largest impact of improved liquidity, however, would be upon risk and diversification. Surveys have consistently shown that diversification is a powerful driver for investors to become involved with real estate as an investment. Diversification surely works only as long as the asset is truly different. Property can be a diversifier away from equities because it has bond and commodity characteristics. Taking away the illiquidity and the physical, heterogeneous, commodity nature of real estate would take away a large part of its diversification potential, and a large part of its appeal. It appears to be the case that these distortions contribute to the return diversity that investors crave, yet lead to inevitable disappointment when they reveal themselves.

Box 1.1: Sovereign Wealth Funds and Real Estate Investment

Sovereign wealth funds (SWFs) have taken on increased importance in global investment markets in recent years, operating as significant long-term investors, including real estate. According to Pensions and Investments Online (2018), sovereign wealth fund assets increased globally by 13% to a record $7.45 trillion in the year ended 31 March 2018. The largest sovereign wealth funds are shown in Table 1.14.

SWFs are government investment vehicles funded from government reserves, which are managed separately from the country's central bank. The funding sources

(continued)

(*continued*)

for these government reserves come from natural resource reserves (e.g. oil and gas), foreign exchange reserves, or pension fund reserves where there are no explicit pension liabilities.

The strategic objectives of SWFs include the management of government holdings, wealth optimisation through diversification (offsetting possible future declines in the value or stock of the country's natural resources), and supporting the development of the local economy.

SWFs have operated for over 50 years. The Kuwait Investment Authority (KIA) was established in 1953, and the 1970s increase in oil prices saw further SWFs established (e.g. the Abu Dhabi Investment Authority, ADIA), with the 1970–90 period seeing SWFs established in growing Asian economies (e.g. the Government Investment Corporation of Singapore, GIC). Since 2000, with further increases in oil prices and significant trade surpluses, a large number of new SWFs were established, over 50% of the current roster of SWFs. The Middle East and Asia now dominate the SWF universe, with several countries (including Singapore and Abu Dhabi) having more than one SWF.

TABLE 1.14 Top 10 sovereign wealth funds

Rank	Profile	Total assets	Region	Current real estate share	Total value of real estate
1	Norway Government Pension Fund Global	$1,072,840m	Europe	4%	$40,767.92m
2	China Investment Corporation	$941,417m	Asia	3%	$28,242.51m
3	Abu Dhabi Investment Authority	$696,660m	Middle East	5%	$34,833.00m
4	Kuwait Investment Authority	$592,000m	Middle East	5%	$29,600.00m
5	Hong Kong Monetary Authority I	$509,353m	Asia	3%	$15,280.59m
6	SAFE Investment Company	$439,836m	Asia	3%	$13,195.08m
7	National Council for Social Security Fund	$437,900m	Asia	5%	$21,895.00m
8	GIC Private Limited	$390,000m	Asia	7%	$27,300.00m
9	Temasek Holdings	$374,896m	Asia	16%	$59,983.36m
10	Public Investment Fund	$320,000m	Middle East	5%	$16,000.00m

Source: PFR.

Sovereign wealth funds are known to be active in real estate investment. The more established SWFs such as ADIA and GIC are experienced and sophisticated investors, with institutional maturity, performance-focused objectives, professional investment standards, and extensive risk management procedures, and we know that SWFs have increasingly adopted an active management strategy which sees them including property and private equity amongst their mandated asset classes. Strategies for property investment cover direct property, REITs, joint ventures, and co-investment with other SWFs or pension funds, unlisted property funds, equity stakes in property companies/REITs, as well as debt financing.

Through a phenomenon in international finance known as the reverse capital flow, developing countries have constantly net negative foreign investment flows to the developed countries, especially countries like China, Qatar, and UAE. The leading explanation of such capital flows is that poor institutions and a lack of protection of property rights in developing countries has led investors to seek the more stable developed countries for safe investments, including real estate and infrastructure.

CHAPTER 2

Global Property Markets and Real Estate Cycles, 1950–2020

2.1 INTRODUCTION AND BACKGROUND

Following our introduction to the market, the players, and the asset class presented in Chapter 1, this chapter describes a history of the market. In doing so, we focus on a very limited selection of the most mature countries.

In some senses, there is a global market (see Chapters 1 and 16). Nonetheless, the mature markets are limited to a minority of the world's nations, and the availability of data is highly variable in quality. This chapter reflects this inconsistency, with information provided on the USA, the UK, continental Europe, and Asia, and an example of the impact of cycles on Dubai real estate markets.

2.1.1 The Property Cycle

Inaction will be advocated in the present even though it means deep trouble in the future.

—*John Kenneth Galbraith*

In his 1955 account of the Great Crash of 1929, Galbraith said that crashes may be attributed to "men who know that things are going quite wrong [but] say that things are fundamentally sound." Nearly 80 year later he was proved right again.

Starting in 1970, the following pattern has repeated itself three times:

- Market values of existing property exceed replacement value (cost of construction), and developers expand the supply of real estate, sell buildings at completion, and earn a profit.
- Large amounts of debt and equity capital flow into the real estate industry.
- Development activity increases, creating jobs in real estate and related sectors (construction and lending).

- Additions to supply exceed tenant demand for space.
- With a glut of property, rents fall as tenant options expand (usually in conjunction with an economic downturn).
- Property values fall, ultimately dropping below replacement value.
- Given the long lead time to develop real estate, supply continues to be introduced to the market as projects that have been started are completed.
- New development stops, eliminating jobs in real estate and related industries, leading to further economic deterioration.
- Over time, the economy recovers, sometimes very slowly.
- As the economy recovers, jobs are created, increasing the demand for office space, and incomes rise, increasing the demand for retail and other space.
- Rents ultimately increase with expansion of the economy and the absorption of space by tenants.
- Because replacement value exceeds market value, developers cannot profit by adding new supply to the market and a supply shortage develops.
- As rents increase, market values ultimately rise above replacement values.
- Development slowly starts again.
- Capital flows into real estate as investors seek outsized returns based on expectations of continued value appreciation.
- Values continue to increase, further enhancing return and attracting more investors.
- Market values of existing property exceed replacement values, so developers can expand the supply of real estate, sell buildings at completion, and earn a profit.
- Large amounts of debt and equity capital flow into the real estate industry . . .
- . . . and the cycle repeats itself.

2.2 A PERFORMANCE HISTORY

2.2.1 Before 1970: Real Estate Becomes a Medium-Return Asset

Figure 2.1 shows the full UK property performance history for property, equities, and government bonds (gilts) over the period 1918–70.

As Table 2.1 shows, real estate, UK government bonds, and equities all delivered around 6–6.5% annually over the inter-war period, but equities clearly outperformed in the more inflationary period after World War II, followed by real estate, with fixed-interest gilts well behind. This establishes the expected pecking order, as the asset with the lowest expected risk (fixed-interest government bonds) delivered the lowest returns and the asset with the highest expected risk (equities) delivered the strongest returns. After 1947, real estate takes up its expected position as the medium-risk, medium-return asset class.

After World War II, the growth in availability of debt – especially mortgage finance – attracted a large number of private investors and developers to property. In the 1950s and 1960s, the reconstruction of Britain, characterized by slum clearance, comprehensive development schemes, and new towns, coupled with the ready availability of long-term mortgages at low rates of interest, enabled developers to develop and

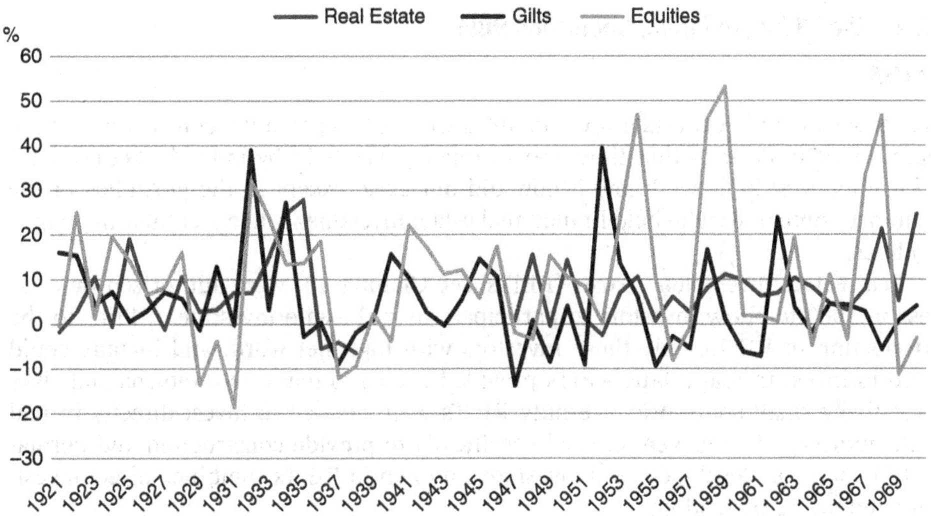

FIGURE 2.1 UK asset total returns, 1918–70 (%)
Sources: IPD, Datastream, PFR.

TABLE 2.1 UK asset mean returns, 1918–70

	Real estate	Gilts	Equities
1921–39	6.1%	6.5%	6.5%
1947–70	7.5%	1.7%	10.7%

Sources: IPD, Datastream, PFR.
Notes: Averages are geometric means; gilts are benchmark 10-year redemption yields; equities are FT all-share dividend yields; property is IPD annual universe, standing investments; property shares are FTA real estate. There is no property data 1940–46.

hold major portfolios. Rapid increases in value in the 1960s, partly fueled by growing rates of inflation and partly by the long post-war boom, went straight into the pockets of equity owners in these companies, whose borrowing costs were often fixed. At the same time, some possibly ill-judged government restrictions on development held back supply and drove up real rents.

Insurance companies had, up to the mid-1980s, been market participants as long-term mortgage lenders and as owner-occupiers or lessees of office space. Having observed the equity gains that were being made by borrowers, they began to consider exposing their own cash to the expected increasing value of property. By this route, insurance companies became equity investors in property as well as investors in property-backed, fixed-interest debt. More purchasers in the market added to pressure for higher prices.

2.2.2 The 1970s: Inflation, Boom, and Bust

The USA

The modern era of real estate investment in the USA is generally considered to have begun in 1970. Prior to that time, most property was held by individuals and institutional ownership as we know it now did not exist, except in the portfolios of life insurance companies who held limited real estate investments to offset their insurance liabilities.

Real Estate Investment Trusts (REITs, see Chapter 13) were authorized by Congress in 1960 to allow investors to participate in real estate investment. Prior to the introduction of REITs, only those investors with high net worth and income could afford to invest in real estate. REITs provided access to real estate returns and risks at relatively small share prices. Equity REITs were created to invest directly in real estate, mortgage REITs were created specifically to provide construction and permanent financing to developers and investors, and hybrid REITs combined direct investment and mortgage lending.

Growth in the REIT market was slow in the 1960s, but accelerated in the early part of the 1970s. Commercial banks were the largest providers of mortgage and construction loans at this time, but were constrained by Federal Reserve regulations as to how much of their assets they could hold in real estate loans, and also regarding the terms of the loans that they could provide. To get around these constraints, commercial banks formed mortgage REITs.

Highly leveraged mortgage REITs in the 1970s borrowed on a short-term basis using commercial paper or loans from their commercial bank sponsors, and provided financing to real estate developers and investors. Since high-quality borrowers were able to borrow from traditional lenders, mortgage REIT customers were typically lower quality and the rates they paid were higher than those charged by commercial banks. Many new REITs were formed to take advantage of the new unregulated lending market, and competitive pressures led to relaxation of underwriting standards.

REIT market capitalization increased from $0.5 billion in 1968 to $1.9 billion in 1972, and total assets controlled by REITs increased to $20 billion by the mid-1970s. The supply of office space increased by over 7% in 1971 alone, fueled by increased lending from REITs. Further growth of 5% per year in office space occurred in 1972–4, far exceeding the needs of tenants.

Favorable economic conditions for REITs reversed in 1973. The price of oil increased, as Arab oil-producing states colluded to limit the supply of crude oil to Western countries. This led to a general increase in prices around the world and in the USA, which in turn raised expectations of future inflation and interest rates. Most developers and investors had borrowed on a floating-rate basis, and as rates increased, they had difficulty staying current with increasing debt service payments. As a result, borrowers defaulted on their payments, and lenders (including REITs) foreclosed on properties. Many of the foreclosed assets exhibited high vacancy rates and low cash flow, and others were partially completed development projects. Non-performing assets held by REITs were estimated to be 75% by 1972, and investors fled the market, which drove share prices down considerably.

The REIT index reached its peak at 112.09 in January 1973, but by December 1974 it had fallen to 39.09, representing a negative 65% return over the period. Rents and values in real estate markets around the country fell precipitously with the glut of commercial space available. In addition, an increase in price inflation and interest rates led the economy into a recession in 1974 and 1975, decreasing the demand for space and further dropping rent levels and values.

The combination of a rapid increase in capital available for development and investment, highly leveraged REIT lenders competing to make loans to highly leveraged borrowers, and a slowing economy and high interest rates led to the first of our modern real estate downturns.

The downturn continued into the early 1980s, when another "perfect storm" of undisciplined capital was provided to the market and led to the beginning of the next upturn of the US real estate cycle.

The UK

The conversion of property from a vehicle for fixed-interest investment to an equity play for institutional investors was consolidated in the aftermath of the oil crisis of 1973. Loose economic policy drove a boom and, together with the rapid rise in oil prices, led to a subsequent crash in UK property markets, the equity market, and the economy as a whole. As a result of this very serious economic shock, many property companies and several banks became insolvent, many on the back of injudicious property lending, and the government was forced into the organized de-gearing of property companies in its so-called "lifeboat" operation.

Commercial property found its way into insurance company portfolios at this time, as borrowers defaulted on mortgage repayments. At the same time, property was available from distressed property companies at low prices, and the asset looked attractive as an inflation hedge, as retail prices, chased by wage increases (supported by powerful trade unions), oil prices, and loose monetary policy, leapt upwards at annual rates of 25% or more.

For a time, rents almost kept pace with inflation, taking city rents from a low of £13.50/sq. ft in 1975 to a high of £23.50/sq. ft in 1980, despite limited real growth and demand (see Table 2.2). Real rents, meanwhile, peaked in 1970.

TABLE 2.2 City office rents, nominal and real, 1960–2000

Year	Nominal rent	Inflation index	Real rent
1960	£1.38	100.00	£1.38
1965	£4.75	119.04	£3.99
1970	£12.88	148.84	£8.65
1975	£13.50	274.46	£4.92
1980	£23.50	536.87	£4.38
1985	£36.38	759.76	£4.79
1990	£50.00	1013.01	£4.94
1995	£35.00	1197.27	£2.92
2000	£50.00	1361.04	£3.67

Sources: Henderson Investors, Datastream.

2.2.3 The 1980s: New Investors Flood the Real Estate Capital Market

The USA

Several factors led to an increase in capital flows to the real estate industry in the early 1980s. Equity investment increased due to the introduction of favorable tax laws and from an expansion of pension fund and international investment. Real estate debt increased due to the relaxation of regulations for the savings and loan industry. The outcome of such a large amount of new capital flowing to the real estate industry was predictable: new development, less stringent underwriting for equity and debt investors, and a subsequent downturn.

In 1981, Congress passed the Economic Recovery and Tax Act (ERTA). After years of record high inflation and economic recession at the end of the 1970s and early 1980s, ERTA was designed to provide a stimulus to the economy in the form of tax cuts. By lowering taxes on corporations and those who provided capital for creating and investing in real assets, economic activity was expected to increase. Extremely favorable tax benefits for real estate investment were implemented, helping to spur economic growth through the creation of construction and lending jobs.

The key components of ERTA that impacted real estate investors were: (i) decreasing the useful life over which assets could be depreciated; (ii) allowing accelerated depreciation; and (iii) lowering tax rates. These factors combined to make real estate investment more attractive for investors, primarily due to tax benefits. See Box 2.1 for an example of how tax benefits increased investor returns.

Box 2.1: How Investors Took Advantage of Tax Benefits in the 1980s

Let us assume that in 1985 a limited partnership buys a 100,000 sq. ft office property located in the New Jersey suburbs of New York City for $14 million ($140/sq. ft).[1] The sponsor is a local developer, who serves as the general partner. The purchase price comprises 10% for land (not depreciable), and 90%, or $12.6 million, for the building (depreciable for tax purposes). The useful life over which an office building could be depreciated under the tax laws of 1985 was 19 years, and investors could depreciate using 175% declining balance accelerated depreciation.

In most cases, the general partner or sponsor of a limited partnership would invest no equity of its own. Instead, a percentage of the purchase price of $14 million would be charged as a fee by the sponsor at the time of purchase. If we assume that the sponsor earned a 5% fee, they would earn $700,000 at the time of the purchase and would likely also have stayed in the deal as the property manager and the leasing broker.

[1]This example was originally discussed by David Shulman in a *Barron's* article in 1991, and adapted for use here.

The partnership borrows $11.2 million of the $14 million purchase price (an 80% loan-to-value ratio), and provides $2.8 million of equity. The $2.8 million is raised from individual investors. The loan is a "bullet loan," paying interest only at a 9% rate throughout the 10-year loan term, with the entire principal coming due at the end of the loan term. Annual payments on the loan are $1.008 million ($10.08/sq. ft) and, as historically allowed by US tax laws, interest payments are fully deductible in determining taxable income for investors.

The building is 95% leased at the time of purchase, with rental rates averaging $16/sq. ft. Operating expenses in year 1 are expected to be $4.00/sq. ft. The income statement for this property in year 1 is as shown in Table 2.3.

Earning $112,000 in before-tax cash flow on an equity investment of $2.8 million provides a 4% before-tax return on equity (BTROE). Note that this is actual cash earned and distributed to the limited partners. The general partner provides this information to the limited partners at the end of the first year of ownership, also telling them that he thinks that the value of their equity increased by 10% during that time. Therefore, the total before-tax return is the sum of the ROE and the appreciation, or 14%.

The real kicker to the investment comes in the calculation of after-tax cash flow, where the impacts of depreciation and interest deductibility come into play. To calculate the depreciation deduction each year, the depreciable basis of $12.6 million is divided by the allowable useful life of the building of 19 years, and this quotient is multiplied by the accelerated depreciation factor of 175% (or 1.75). The calculation of the annual depreciation deduction is as shown in Table 2.4.

TABLE 2.3 Property income statement (1)

Gross rental revenue	$1,600,000	$16.00
– Vacancy (5%)	$80,000	$0.80
Gross effective income	$1,520,000	$15.20
– Operating expenses	$400,000	$4.00
Net operating income	$1,120,000	$11.20
– Debt service	$1,008,000	$10.08
Before-tax cash flow	$112,000	$1.12

TABLE 2.4 Depreciation calculation

Depreciable basis	$12,600,000
/ Useful life	19 years
* Depreciation factor	1.75
Depreciation	$1,160,526

(continued)

(continued)

TABLE 2.5 Property income statement after tax

Net operating income	$1,120,000
Interest	$1,008,000
Taxable income (loss)	($1,048,526)

Since depreciation and interest are deductible for tax purposes, the after-tax income statement is as shown in Table 2.5.

Tax laws in place at the time allow the limited partnership investors to report to US tax authorities that they have lost $1,048,526 in the first year of ownership. Recall that the investors pocketed $112,000 in cash flows, so that the tax losses reported are phantom losses and a result solely of favorable tax laws.

Another important aspect of the tax laws in the 1981 to 1986 period was that investors could offset active income earned from wages and salaries with phantom losses from passive real estate investments in limited partnerships. Let us assume that there was a sole investor in the office building, and that the investor earned (for the purposes of discussion) $1,048,526 in wage and salary income as an investor banker in New York. Assuming a tax rate of 40% on ordinary income, the taxpayer would have had to pay $419,410 in taxes on salary income in the absence of this real estate investment.

The tax laws in place at the time, however, allowed the investor to deduct the passive real estate loss (−$1,048,526) from active salary income to calculate taxable income, in effect reducing taxable income to $0, and saving the investor $419,410 in taxes payable that year.

If we add the savings in taxes to the before-tax cash flow, the total cash flows "earned" by the investor are as shown in Table 2.6.

The total of actual cash flow and tax savings represents the income that is available to the investor from his investment in the New Jersey office building. Dividing the total after-tax cash flow by the original equity investment provides a return on equity of 18.98%, of which almost 80% is delivered from tax savings ($419,411 / $531,411 = 78.9%). Again, if we believe that the property did appreciate by the 10% the sponsor suggested, the total return earned that year would be 28.98%, which

TABLE 2.6 Tax on salary income after real estate losses

Before-tax cash flow	$112,000
+Tax savings	$419,410
Total after-tax cash flow	$531,410

is a great return in any asset class. Most of the price increases in real estate during the 1981 to 1986 period were based on the favorable tax treatment offered by the asset class.

Investors were attracted to limited partnerships of this nature due to the enormous returns that could be earned, especially relative to alternative investment opportunities. Hungry for higher returns, investors flooded the market for real estate limited partnerships.

Sponsors of limited partnerships also earned lucrative fees (see Chapters 11 and 12), and were willing to bring them to investors at a rapid rate. For the most part, after the fees were earned, sponsors would have no further interest in the cash flows or success of the properties purchased by partnerships, giving them an incentive to create as many of them as possible. Competition to find deals by sponsors intensified, increasing market values. Development became more profitable as market values increased above replacement costs, leading to an increase in the supply of properties.

Shortly after ERTA, the Garn-Ste. Germaine (G-S) Act was passed by Congress in 1982, granting new lending powers for the savings and loan (S&L) industry. Prior to the G-S Act, S&Ls were allowed to invest only in residential mortgage loans. The passage of the Act granted S&Ls the authority to also make loans to finance the ownership of commercial property. S&Ls were willing to provide investors with high loan-to-value loans at attractive rates, expanding the supply of mortgage capital to the industry.

At the same time, pension funds increased their allocations to real estate as a result of the passage of the Employee Retirement and Income Security Act (ERISA) of 1974. The Act mandated that pension funds diversify their portfolios, which was widely interpreted as a mandate to expand investment in real estate. While slow to invest in the 1970s, pension fund participation in the asset class increased significantly in the 1980s, based on the promise of high returns, an inflation hedge, and diversification of mixed-asset portfolios.

A final source of capital came from international investors, who could borrow cheaply in their home countries and invest to earn higher yields in US real estate. The combination of new equity investors in the form of limited partnerships seeking tax benefits, pension funds, and international investors led to competition in bidding to own assets and increases in market values. Combined with expanded availability of cheap debt capital on non-restrictive terms from S&L institutions, the result was further increase in market values. A predictable increase in the supply of property followed, as developers took advantage of the positive spread between market values and replacement costs.

Meanwhile, the economy slid into a recession, and tax laws were changed in 1986 to eliminate the tax advantages that had been introduced with the ERTA in 1981. The Tax Reform Act of 1986 (TRA) ended the use of accelerated depreciation methods, and raised the useful life of commercial property to 39 years. The TRA also stopped the practice of using depreciation-based losses on passive limited partnership investments to offset income earned from active wage and salary income. The combination of these tax law changes effectively stopped the creation of limited partnership investments in their tracks.

With investors no longer able to earn large returns from depreciation-based tax losses, the market value of properties across the board fell precipitously, in some estimates by 40–50%. Investors who expected to sell assets at ever-higher prices were disappointed. The effect of the decline in property prices was most heavily felt when underlying loans matured, with lenders expecting to be paid their full principal values.

Let us assume that the value of the New Jersey office building (Box 2.1) fell by 40% to \$8.4 million over the 5-year period between the time of investment in 1985 and the loan maturity in 1990. At that time, the investors owed \$11.2 million to the bank, and were faced with several bad outcomes. The first is to attempt to sell the building. If they can net the market value of the property, they earn \$8.4 million. To pay off the loan requires \$11.2 million, so they must come up with \$2.8 million to make up the difference. Most partnerships were not willing to come out of pocket to cover losses.[2]

Instead, because most of the loans were non-recourse, many limited partnerships defaulted and turned ownership of the property back to the bank that had provided them the loan. Ill-equipped to actually own and manage properties, and facing a glut of properties on the market with values continuing to decline, savings and loan institutions and other commercial loan providers suffered huge losses, and many were forced into bankruptcy. Those that did fail were taken over by the US government, which now faced the problem of deciding what to do with the property that it owned.

The UK

By 1980, around 20% of all insurance company assets and 10% of pension fund monies were invested in commercial property, which then embarked on a protracted period of underperformance relative to the UK stock market. Pushed on by the Thatcher government's campaigns for business, privatization, and enterprise at the expense of the welfare state, equity portfolios increased in value much more quickly than property portfolios, so that more of the institutions' new money was invested in equities than in property. The result of outperformance by equities and the greater allocation of new money to that sector was a reduction in property weightings between 1980 and 1999 to averages of 5–6% for pension funds and 7–8% for insurance companies.

This period included a cycle in property values dramatic enough to rival or even exceed the boom and bust of 1972–5. The economic boom of 1986–9, when consumer expenditure growth reached levels as high as 6% a year, produced huge levels of bank liquidity. The apparent security of property for lenders enabled property companies to increase their borrowings – and financial gearing – to capture the fruits of another property boom. Residential owner-occupiers geared up and many bought second homes. According to DTZ in 1989, bank lending to property reached all-time record levels (see Table 2.7).

[2]US tax laws also require that investors pay income tax at the time of sale on all depreciation that was deducted during the ownership period, requiring a large payment from investors.

TABLE 2.7 Bank lending to property, 1981–91

Year	Nominal lending	Inflation	Real lending
1981	£5.5bn	100	£5.50bn
1983	£8.5bn	113.60	£7.48bn
1985	£12.5bn	126.49	£9.88bn
1987	£22.0bn	136.23	£16.15bn
1989	£44.6bn	154.07	£28.95bn
1991	£48.5bn	178.54	£27.16bn

Sources: DTZ, Bank of England.

2.2.4 The 1990s: The Rise of REITs

The USA

The beginning of the 1990s started with record high vacancy rates and with financial institutions owning large portfolios of real estate and bad debts. Property values continued to fall due to a weak economy and real estate market conditions. As a result, more financial institutions failed and were taken over by the US government.

The Resolution Trust Corporation (RTC) was formed to develop a strategy for liquidating government-owned properties. The challenge was significant, as there were few bidders for properties due to uncertain prospects for real estate markets. Financial institutions and the government had three options to deal with their non-performing property and loan portfolios.

1. Ignore them and hope that the market improves in the short term.
2. Manage the portfolio of assets in the hope of adding value for future sale.
3. Liquidate quickly and start over.

Many chose option 1, which ultimately led to more failures and takeovers of banks by the government. Option 2 was not optimal because banks and the government did not have the staffing or expertise available to manage properties and portfolios. Option 3 would rid the banks and the government of the problem, allow the market to discover prices for distressed assets, and hopefully lead to a subsequent upturn in property markets.

The RTC chose option 3, and decided to liquidate holdings of real estate at fire sale prices through auctions of portfolios of bad loans and properties. The first few auctions were held at large hotels that had been foreclosed upon, and the RTC placed files with information on each property and loan in the portfolio in the lobby. Analysts from potential bidders took the files and determined pricing based on the information provided.

The first auctions drew very few bidders, as prospective investors were unwilling to take the risk of investing in distressed properties. Auction winners bought portfolios for prices that were a fraction of their loan or property values. Early purchasers consisted of firms such as Goldman Sachs, J.E. Robert, Salomon Brothers, Merrill Lynch, and other institutions that saw the opportunity to buy assets cheaply, carry them for a short period, and then sell them to earn large returns. This was the birth of the private equity industry, which has evolved to become one of the primary sources of equity capital in modern real estate markets.

It took several years for the RTC to liquidate portfolios of real estate and bad loans. While there is some argument as to whether their tactics were the most efficient and fair for the real estate industry, the RTC did force transactions in an otherwise grid-locked market, which provided essential evidence of property market values. As others with capital saw the outsized returns earned by the first movers, portfolios at later auctions were sold at much higher prices.

The Commercial Mortgage-Backed Securities (CMBS) market also grew substantially as a result of RTC liquidations. Non-performing loans were pooled together by the RTC and sold at discounted prices. Buyers of the mortgage pools determined the best way to deal with each borrower. If bought at the right price, individual mortgages could be renegotiated to make it easier for a borrower to maintain, or restart, payments. Taking the suburban New Jersey office building example, let us assume that the $11.2 million loan was put into a CMBS pool and sold at a discount of 60% for $4.48 million. Further assume that the property has fallen in value to $8 million. The lender would be willing to alter the terms of the loan to the investors by reducing the loan value to $6 million, reducing payments for the borrower and, if paid in full to maturity, earning a nice return for the auction winner.

Throughout the 1990s, property markets improved in both pricing and fundamentals. A major component of the improvement was related to the growth of the REIT market beginning in 1992 with the public offering of Kimco Realty Corporation, which owned shopping centers across the USA. At the beginning of 1991, the market capitalization of the entire REIT industry was $8.7 billion, and by 2002 the total market capitalization of the industry was $161 billion. Several reasons explain this phenomenal rise, the major one of which is the introduction of the Umbrella Partnership REIT (UPREIT). Taubman Centers Inc. being the first to the market in 1992.

The UPREIT was a new structure that allowed limited partners in real estate to liquidate their holdings in exchange for partnership units that could later be transferable into shares of a publicly traded REIT. Instead of selling properties directly to the REIT and incurring a large capital gains tax liability, limited partners traded for operating partnership (OP) units in a REIT. This was deemed by tax authorities to be a like-kind exchange, and like-kind exchanges do not require payment of taxes on capital gains. OP units were fully convertible into shares of REIT common stock at some later date at the holder's discretion, and the shares could then be sold into the open market to provide liquidity. Capital gains taxes would become due at the time the shares were sold. Hence, the benefits of the UPREIT structure were deferral of taxes, and liquidity.

After 1993, most new REITs were UPREITs created as property owners converted their private holdings into public vehicles. Armed with the ability to raise capital in corporate debt and equity markets, REITs continued to grow, allowing investment in real estate equity for investors with modest incomes and net worth. This was, after all, the original reason that REIT legislation was introduced in 1960, and it had finally come to reality in the mid-1990s.

REITs in the mid-1990s were well received by investors, who saw the rise in property markets and wanted to participate in increasing incomes and values. Economic activity generally improved, interest rates generally fell, and investors were well rewarded.

In the late 1990s, however, investor psychology changed significantly, a desire for income (as provided by REITs) being replaced by a desire for growth. Fed by the promise of growth from dot.com companies, the paradigm of investment analysis changed from studying earnings in place to buying into strategies based on ideas that were expected to excel in the "new economy." Trading at infinite price-to-earnings ratios (because they did not earn any cash flow), dot.com companies sucked enormous amounts of capital from traditional "old economy" industries, which negatively impacted stock price performance.

When the dot.com bubble burst, real estate markets catering to high-tech, bio-tech, and other hot industries experienced weak fundamentals which led to an oversupply of space as these companies discontinued business operations. The 9/11 attacks hurt prospects for real estate markets in large cities, as uncertainty regarding future terrorist targets grew. Until this uncertainty settled, the prospects for real estate investment and overall economic performance were unclear.

The UK: Deep Recession, Low Inflation, and Globalization

In the downswing of the early 1990s, the pattern of 1972–5 was repeated. Interest rates rose, property rents fell, and capital values fell by even more. An economic downturn led to tenant defaults; borrowers were unable to cover interest by rent received, and their debt often exceeded the total value of the properties they owned. Properties were sold at huge discounts to their previous values. Negative equity affected new homeowners and property companies alike, in the latter case usually leading to liquidation.

Between summer 1990 and summer 1994, 15 quoted property companies, many previously glamorous and successful, became insolvent, putting such prominent schemes as Canary Wharf and Broadgate in the hands of bankers. The resulting property crash and its accompanying economic recession were both, by some measures, the most severe of the 20th century.

The 1990s was the decade during which the international property owner emerged as a long-term player in the UK property market. When (in late 1992) the UK withdrew from the European Exchange Rate Mechanism, interest rates fell, gilt yields fell, and Sterling was effectively devalued. By 1993, a London office building might have been worth only 50% of its 1989 peak, and even less in foreign currency. Bank lending had dried up (see Table 2.8), and German capital entered the UK market in 1993 at a time of distressed lenders and weak prices.

For buildings occupied on long (25-year) leases, the rent due to the owner was likely to continue unchanged for a very long time as a result of upward-only rent reviews (see Chapter 6). In some cases, market rents were not expected to regain the original rent set before the end of the lease, as nominal and real growth forecasts were both very bearish at the time. Inflation levels of around 3% were low in the context of the 1970s and 1980s, and meant that many buildings remained over-rented for years.

TABLE 2.8 Bank lending to property, 1981–99

Year	Nominal lending	Inflation	Real lending
1981	£5.5bn	100	£5.50bn
1983	£8.5bn	113.60	£7.48bn
1985	£12.5bn	126.49	£9.88bn
1987	£22.0bn	136.23	£16.15bn
1989	£44.6bn	154.07	£28.95bn
1991	£48.5bn	178.54	£27.16bn
1993	£39.8bn	188.10	£21.16bn
1995	£33.8bn	199.33	£16.96bn
1997	£35.1bn	210.60	£16.67bn
1999	£45.1bn	214.40	£20.35bn

Sources: DTZ, Bank of England.

Investors were now able to buy a fixed-income secured on property with the prospect of an equity conversion at some time – perhaps distant – in the future. Overseas purchasers (often natural fixed-income investors) could now purchase fixed-income, low-risk, bond-like real estate at very attractive prices relative to both their domestic bonds and UK gilts, whose yields fell from roughly 8.5% to 6.5% during 1993 (see Table 2.9). Sterling's devaluation meant that a larger building could now be purchased by an overseas investor for the same outlay in domestic currency terms, improving both the comfort factor of the deal and the investment gains associated with any future currency appreciation.

Steady progress was made in the 1996–2000 period, as rental growth became widely established in all sectors and lower gilt yields enabled property yields to fall.

TABLE 2.9 5-Year cost of borrowing and 10-year gilt yields, 1986–98

Year	5-Year swap	10-Year gilts	Base rate
1986	N/A	10.65	11.00
1987	9.84	9.68	8.50
1988	11.37	9.96	13.00
1989	12.37	10.26	15.00
1990	11.67	10.95	14.00
1991	10.35	9.73	10.50
1992	7.87	8.26	7.00
1993	5.88	6.10	5.50
1994	8.92	8.71	6.25
1995	7.06	7.42	6.50
1996	7.63	7.51	6.00
1997	6.86	6.29	7.25
1998	5.43	4.36	6.25

Source: Datastream.

TABLE 2.10 IPD total returns, inflation, and GDP growth, 1981–99

Year	IPD return	Inflation rate	IPD real return	GDP growth
1981	15.0	12.0	2.7	−1.3
1982	7.5	5.4	2.0	1.8
1983	7.6	5.3	2.2	3.7
1984	8.6	4.6	3.8	2.4
1985	8.3	5.7	2.5	3.8
1986	11.1	9.7	1.3	4.2
1987	25.8	3.7	21.3	4.4
1988	29.7	6.8	21.4	5.2
1989	15.4	7.7	7.1	2.1
1990	−8.4	9.3	−16.2	0.6
1991	−3.2	4.5	−7.4	−1.5
1992	−1.7	2.6	−4.2	0.1
1993	20	1.9	17.8	2.3
1994	12	2.9	8.8	4.4
1995	3.5	3.2	0.3	2.8
1996	10	2.5	7.3	2.6
1997	16.8	3.6	12.7	3.5
1998	11.8	2.8	8.8	2.2
1999	14.5	1.8	12.5	2.1

Sources: IPD, Datastream.

While double-digit returns were produced every year by the property market, market overheating was never a serious threat. Investors continued to pay more attention to equities, and in particular technology stocks, so that equities continued to outperform property. Equity portfolios began to look more dependent on smaller numbers of high-value technology stocks.

By contrast, the property market of early 2000 appeared in many ways to be well balanced, with debt, equity, and international capital all apparently comfortable with its exposure to a steadily performing and stable market. Low inflation, low interest rates, and a steadily growing economy produced returns of around 12% and 15% each year in 1998 and 1999, showing real price rises of 3–6%, and very high returns to geared equity investors (see Table 2.10).

2.2.5 2002–7: A Rising Tide Lifts All Boats

The USA

By 2002, however, US real estate had begun to look more attractive. Commercial property yields were high compared to the nil-yield and largely disastrous dot.com and telecoms stocks. In addition, banks became increasingly hungry for market share in a globally competitive finance market.

Between 2002 and 2007, the USA saw an unprecedented housing price bubble as subprime mortgages became more prevalent. Home loan underwriting standards relaxed considerably, fueled by growth in the subprime mortgage industry and securitization. With easy credit, homeowners and buyers leveraged up, in many cases borrowing more than the value of their houses. Lenders competed aggressively to originate loans, which drove mortgage rates and spreads downward. Home prices rose with cheap and easy credit.

Easy and cheap credit was also available in the commercial real estate market. In addition, equity providers had large amounts of funds to invest, allowing a great deal of liquidity to wash over all investable markets. As buyers attempted to place capital, the desire to buy and own assets led to destructive competition. In commercial real estate markets, this led to a large number of bidders for each property that was placed for sale on the market. Purchase and sale became an auction process, with finalists, chosen from among the many bidders, encouraged to bid again at even-higher prices to win the auction. In this seller's market, investors had to reformulate assumptions about cash flow expectations, and/or reduce their required rates of return on equity to be able to bid enough to own assets.

With a glut of debt and equity capital, capitalization (cap) rates (yields required by investors) dropped to unprecedented levels as low interest rates and less restrictive underwriting impacted commercial real estate pricing (see Figure 2.2). In 2002, cap rates were hovering at the 8.5–9% level, consistent with historical experience. As easy credit flowed to the sector, spurred on by increasing issuance of CMBS and Collateralized Debt Obligations (CDOs, discussed more fully in Chapter 14) backed by CMBS, investors were emboldened to pay higher and higher prices to get deals done. The precipitous drop in cap rates, in some sectors to as low as 5%, signified a bubble in commercial asset pricing that was nearly as significant as the bubble in housing markets.

Commercial mortgage lenders were forced to compete to make loans in much the same way as residential lenders were. Underwriting standards fell as originators pushed to make more loans to sell into the secondary mortgage market. Figure 2.3 shows that higher-risk interest-only (IO) loans increased as a percentage of all loans during the 2002–7 period.

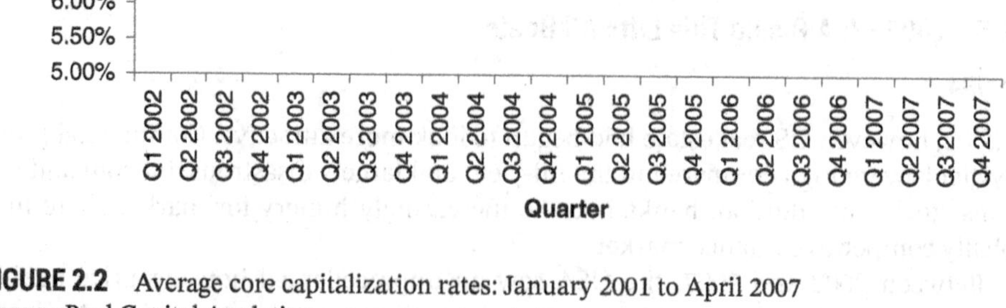

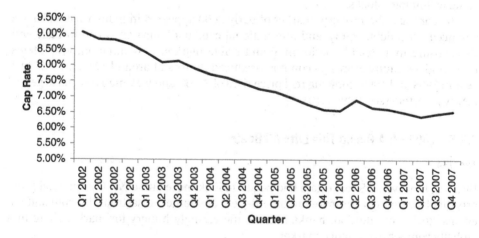

FIGURE 2.2 Average core capitalization rates: January 2001 to April 2007
Source: Real Capital Analytics.

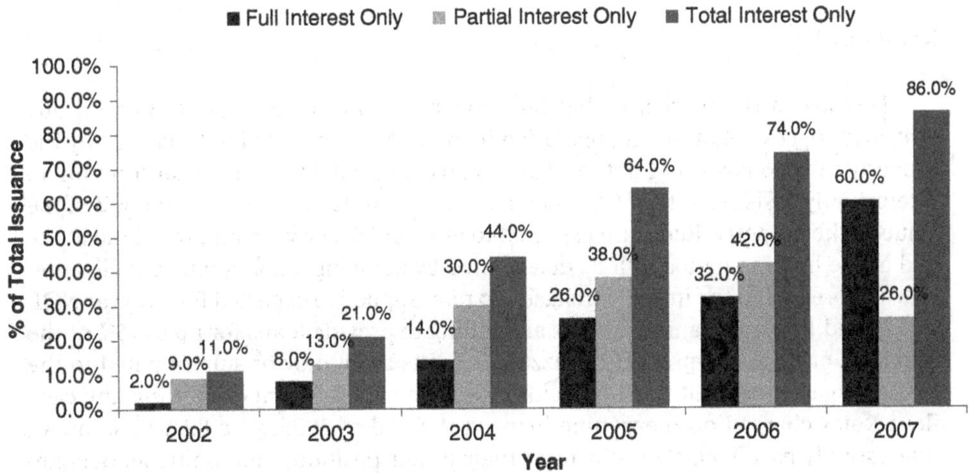

FIGURE 2.3 US mortgage loan underwriting standards decline, 2002–7
Source: Real Capital Analytics.

Interest-only loans benefit investors by allowing them to borrow more for a given level of income. However, they are more risky than amortizing loans, since principal balances are not paid down when payments are made. CMBS investors, like residential mortgage-backed securities investors, bear the ultimate risk of delinquency, default, and foreclosure, since the originators sell the loans to the secondary market (largely CMBS structures) shortly after the loan is made.

Box 2.2 provides an example of the competitive bidding process for commercial property during this period, and the impact on investors.

Box 2.2: US Real Estate Pricing in the Early 21st Century

There are two investors. The first, Mr. C, is a conservative investor. The second, Ms. R, has much higher risk tolerance. An office property became available for purchase in December 2005, and they are both planning to bid on it.[3]

A broker offered the property for sale for the owner, and (as was typical at the time) no ask price was provided. Instead, the property was offered and all willing buyers were encouraged to make a bid. The highest bidders qualified to move forward into a second round of bidding. Typically, the broker and owner would choose five finalists, who were encouraged to bid again in a final auction. In most cases, the final bids were higher than the qualifying bids.

(continued)

[3]The bones of this example are provided in "Leverage: The end of an era" by Ethan Penner (Executive Managing Director of CBRE Investors), which appeared in the November 2008 edition of the *Institutional Real Estate Letter.*

(continued)

The talk in the market is that the property is worth about $100.[4] Careful due diligence suggests that the net operating income (NOI) expected to be earned by the property in 2006 is $6.50. First mortgage loans are available for a 3-year term on an interest-only basis at a rate of 5.5%. Lenders stand willing to make loans for 80% of the value of the property. Rents are expected to grow at 5% per year, and the value at the end of the holding period will be determined by applying a going-out capitalization rate that is equal to the initial purchase cap rate, applied to expected fourth-year NOI.

In addition, mezzanine lenders are willing to provide loans for up to 15% of the purchase price of the property. Mezzanine loans are junior or subordinated to the first mortgage loan, but must be paid prior to the equity owner receiving any cash flow. Rates charged on mezzanine loans at the end of 2005 were 8.5% (also on an interest-only basis), and, in return for their junior position, mezzanine lenders are also entitled to receive 20% of the upside when the property is sold.

THE FIRST ROUND OF BIDDING

The Case of Mr. Conservative

Mr. Conservative is willing to bid on the property based on a first mortgage loan of $80 [a loan-to-value (LTV) ratio of 80%], which will require an equity investment of $20. The annual debt service on the $80 loan at 5.5% is $4.40. In year 1, the before-tax cash flow earned by Mr. C equals $2.10 (NOI of $6.50 less debt service of $4.40).

The first three years of cash flows for Mr. C are as shown in Table 2.11.

The summary statistics in Table 2.12 are useful to see how this investment performs for the lender and Mr. C.

TABLE 2.11 Before-tax cash flows to Mr. C

	Year 1	Year 2	Year 3
NOI	$6.50	$6.83	$7.17
– DS	$4.40	$4.40	$4.40
BTCF	$2.10	$2.43	$2.77

TABLE 2.12 Investment performance, Mr. C

DCR	1.48	1.55	1.63
ROE	10.5%	12.15%	13.85%

[4]To keep the example simple, we use hypothetical numbers. You are welcome to add five or six zeros, but the answers and intuition will remain the same.

DCR is the debt coverage ratio, and is calculated by dividing net operating income by debt service. This ratio is used by lenders to ensure that the income earned by the property is sufficient to pay debt service and provide a cushion. Traditionally, loan underwriters would require a debt coverage ratio of 1.3. As competition to originate loans increased, underwriting standards declined. Lenders were often willing to make loans for 1.1 or 1.2 debt coverage ratios. If a property did not earn enough to provide such a DCR, a lender might use second or third-year NOI to justify the loan. In Mr. C's case, the DCR is sufficiently high that any lender would have been willing to make him the loan.

ROE is sometimes called the "cash-on-cash" return, and represents the amount of cash flow earned by the equity investor relative to his initial equity investment. In year 1, the $2.10 in BTCF is 10.5% of the $20 equity investment.

If rents continue to grow at 5%, NOI in year 4 is expected to be $7.53. The going-out cap rate is assumed to be the same as the going-in cap rate of 6.5%, so dividing $7.53 by 6.5% gives us a selling price at the end of year 3 of $115.85. After the sale, the initial debt amount of $80 must be repaid, leaving $35.85 for Mr. C from the sale of the property in year 3.

The cash flows Mr. C expects to earn over his 3-year holding period can be summarized as shown in Table 2.13.

The IRR Mr. C expects to earn on this investment is a healthy 31.5%. This almost certainly exceeds Mr. C's cost of equity capital.

Another measure of equity investment performance is called the equity multiple, and is simply calculated as the ratio of (undiscounted) inflows divided by outflows. The multiple for Mr. C's investment is equal to 2.16 [($2.10 + $2.43 + $2.77 + $35.85) / $20]. Indicating that Mr. C more than doubles his initial outflow over the 3-year holding period.

The Case of Ms. Risky

Ms. Risky knows that she can sleep well at night if she takes out an 80% LTV loan, but she also knows about the magic of financial leverage. If she can borrow more, under certain circumstances she can magnify her return.

TABLE 2.13 Cash flows and sale proceeds, Mr. C

	Year 0	Year 1	Year 2	Year 3
Outflow	–$20.00			
BTCF		$2.10	$2.43	$2.77
Sale proceeds				$35.85
Total	–$20.00	$2.10	$2.42	$38.62

(continued)

(continued)

TABLE 2.14 Before-tax cash flows to Ms. R

	Year 1	Year 2	Year 3
NOI	$6.50	$6.83	$7.17
– DS (first)	$4.40	$4.40	$4.40
– DS (mezz)	$1.28	$1.28	$1.28
BTCF	$0.82	$1.15	$1.49

TABLE 2.15 Investment performance, Ms. R

DCR (first)	1.48	1.55	1.63
DCR (mezz)	1.14	1.20	1.26
ROE	16.4%	23.0%	29.8%

She borrows $80 under a first mortgage loan with the same terms as Mr. C, but adds a mezzanine loan as well. The mezzanine lender provides $15, which means that Ms. R only needs $5 in equity to buy the property. The rate on the mezzanine loan is 8.5%. In addition, Ms. R has to pay 20% of her upside from sale to the mezzanine lender. Her annual debt service on the mezzanine loan is $1.28 (8.5% times $15).

The cash flows she expects to earn during the first 3 years are as shown in Table 2.14.

The summary statistics in Table 2.15 are useful to see how this investment performs for the lenders and Ms. R.

The DCR for the first mortgage lender is the same as was earned for the loan to Mr. C, but the mezzanine lender's DCR is much smaller. The mezzanine lender earns a higher interest rate, and also earns 20% of the upside at the time of the sale of the property, which helps to compensate for the additional risk.

Given the lower equity investment, and the fact that the first-year return on investment (ROI) of 6.5% (equal to the going-in capitalization rate) is higher than the blended cost of debt capital (total debt service of 5.68% divided by total debt of $95) of 5.97%, the more money that can be borrowed, the higher will be the ROE. First-year ROE is 16.4% (relative to Mr. C's 10.5%), and increases in later years.

Ms. R also expects to sell the property at the end of year 5 at a 6.5% cap rate, for a price of $115.85. The distribution of cash flows to the lenders and to Ms. R is shown in Table 2.16.

Remember that part of the deal with the mezzanine lender requires Ms. R to give them 20% of the distributable cash from the sale, which equals $4.17. Subtracting this from the total distributable cash leaves $16.68 for Ms. R.

The cash flows Ms. R expects to earn can be summarized as shown in Table 2.17.

TABLE 2.16 Cash flows, lenders and Ms. R

Net sale price	$115.85
– Debt (first)	$80.00
– Debt (mezz)	$15.00
Distributable cash flow	$20.85

TABLE 2.17 Cash flows and sale proceeds, Ms. R

	Year 0	Year 1	Year 2	Year 3
Outflow	–$5.00			
BTCF		$0.80	$1.15	$1.49
Sale proceeds				$16.68
Total	–$5.00	$0.80	$1.15	$18.17

The IRR Ms. R earns on this investment is an enormous 64.56%, which is more than twice the IRR earned by Mr. C! This will clearly exceed Ms. R's hurdle rate, and she would love to be able to buy this deal at the price of $100.

Ms. R's multiple on this investment is 4.03, indicating that the inflows are more than four times her initial investment of $5. With this IRR and multiple, Ms. R is confident that others see the potential benefits of this investment as well.

Let us assume that both Mr. C and Ms. R bid $100 for the property and are both asked to join the group of finalists. Knowing that they will have to bid more than their original bid, they go back to do some more due diligence to see how much they will bid in the second round.

THE SECOND ROUND OF BIDDING

Both investors look more carefully at the property, and determine that they can bid $115. The income remains the same at $6.50, so the bid of $115 implies a capitalization rate of 5.65%. Mr. C can likely pull together a little more equity, but Ms. R has reached her maximum of $5.

The first mortgage lender is still willing to loan 80% of the value of the property, providing a loan for 80% of the $115 value, or $92.[5] For the increase, though, the lender is going to increase the rate to 5.75%. The mezzanine lender is also still

(continued)

[5]It would have been relatively easy to get an appraisal for the higher value, given the rapid growth of property values in the marketplace at this time.

(continued)

willing to lend, but knows that charging an 8.5% rate will mean the debt service for a borrower using both a first mortgage and a mezzanine loan will be greater than the NOI. Therefore, the mezzanine lender will only charge 6.5%, but in exchange for a lower rate will require 35% of the upside from sale of the property.

When the property is sold, both Mr. C and Ms. R believe that the property can be sold at the end of 3 years at a capitalization rate equal to the going-in rate of 5.65%. They both recognize that this is really aggressive, given the historical record of cap rates, but since their lenders are willing to go along with the assumption, they feel more comfortable with it.

The Case of Mr. Conservative

Given the new loan terms, Mr. C can get a first mortgage loan of $92 (still an 80% LTV ratio), so purchasing the property will require an equity investment of $23. The debt service on the $92 loan at 5.75% is $5.29. In year 1, the before-tax cash flow earned by Mr. C is equal to $1.21 (NOI of $6.50 less debt service of $5.29). The first 3 years of cash flows for Mr. C are as shown in Table 2.18.

Summary statistics are useful to see how this investment performs for the lender and Mr. C – see Table 2.19.

Naturally, since the NOI is the same as in the first round of bidding, all of these measures are lower than in the first case. DCRs are much lower than in the earlier case, meaning there is less cushion of income over debt service. The 1.23 DCR in the first year falls below the traditional required ratio of 1.3, but with the growth in income expected, year 2's DCR is nearly 1.3, and in year 3 the DCR requirement is met. Other lenders are likely willing to lend to Mr. C on the same terms, so if this bank is not willing to accept a lower DCR it will not get Mr. C's business. In the spirit

TABLE 2.18 Before-tax cash flows to Mr. C

	Year 1	Year 2	Year 3
NOI	$6.50	$6.83	$7.17
– DS	$5.29	$5.29	$5.29
BTCF	$1.21	$1.54	$1.88

TABLE 2.19 Investment performance, Mr. C

DCR	1.23	1.29	1.36
ROE	5.26%	6.70%	8.17%

TABLE 2.20 Cash flows and sale proceeds, Mr. C

	Year 0	Year 1	Year 2	Year 3
Outflow	−$23.00			
BTCF		$1.21	$1.54	$1.88
Sale proceeds				$41.27
Total	−$23.00	$1.21	$1.54	$43.15

of competition, and to make sure they earn fees from making Mr. C the loan, they agree to provide debt even at the lower DCRs.

ROEs are also lower in each of the three years from the first round of bidding. Mr. C might rationalize such low ROEs by telling himself that he will get most of his return from the sale of the asset, which the ROE does not incorporate.

As before, if rents continue to grow at 5%, NOI in year 4 is expected to be $7.53. The going-out cap rate is assumed to be the same as the going-in cap rate of 5.65%, so dividing $7.53 by 5.65% gives us a selling price at the end of year 3 of $133.27. The reader should note that there is really no reason to believe that the value at the end of the holding period will be $17.42 higher than what was expected in the first round of bidding. Rents are still expected to be $6.50, but now Mr. C (and later Ms. R) believes that, for each dollar of rent earned at the end of year 3, investors will be willing to pay a higher amount.

After the sale, the initial debt amount of $92 must be repaid, leaving Mr. C to expect an equity cash flow of $41.27 from the sale of the property in year 3.

The cash flows earned by Mr. C can be summarized as shown in Table 2.20.

The IRR Mr. C expects to earn on this investment given a price of $115 is still a strong 26.69%. Again, it is likely that Mr. C's hurdle rate is lower than this, indicating that he should invest in this deal. The multiple of inflows to outflows is 1.99.

The Case of Ms. Risky

As before, Ms. R is willing to take on the first mortgage loan at an 80% LTV, and also the mezzanine loan. In fact, given her $5 equity limit, she has to borrow from both lenders to make the deal work.

She borrows $92 under the same terms as Mr. C, but adds the mezzanine loan with the revised terms. In the second round, she borrows $18 from the mezzanine lender. She makes up the rest of the purchase price with her $5 of equity. With $110 of total debt and a $115 purchase price, the LTV ratio has increased to 96%. The new terms of the mezzanine loan require that she pay 35% of her upside from the sale.

(continued)

(continued)

TABLE 2.21 Before-tax cash flows, Ms. R

	Year 1	Year 2	Year 3
NOI	$6.50	$6.83	$7.17
– DS (first)	$5.29	$5.29	$5.29
– DS (mezz)	$1.17	$1.17	$1.17
BTCF	**$0.04**	**$0.37**	**$0.71**

TABLE 2.22 Investment performance, Ms. R

DCR (first)	1.23	1.29	1.36
DCR (mezz)	1.01	1.06	1.10
ROE	0.8%	7.4%	14.2%

The cash flows she expects to earn from operating the property during the first three years are as shown in Table 2.21.

Static measures show how the investment performs for the lender and Ms. R (Table 2.22).

The DCR for the first mortgage lender is the same as for Mr. C. The DCR for the mezzanine lender is razor thin, meaning that if there is a small reduction in NOI, Ms. R will not be able to make her debt service payments from income earned by the property. She will have to draw money from other sources, and will be in default on her loan if unable to do so. As it stands, there is a small cushion, and the DCR increases in each year thereafter, giving the lender confidence that this deal will work for him. In addition, the mezzanine lender gets a 6.5% return, plus 35% of the upside to compensate for the risk incurred.

Unlike the first-round case, the ROE to Ms. C has decreased with a higher percentage of debt. This is because the going-in cap rate (or ROI) is only 5.65%, which is lower than the weighted cost of debt of 5.87%.

After selling the property at the expected price of $133.27, Ms. R's final cash flows from the property are expected to be as shown in Table 2.23.

The new terms pay the mezzanine lender 35% of the upside, which equals $8.14. Subtracting this from the distributable cash leaves $15.13 for Ms. R.

The cash flows earned by Ms. R can be summarized as shown in Table 2.24.

The IRR Ms. R earns on this investment is a very strong 48.82%. One important point to note is that nearly all of the cash flow that Ms. R earns comes from the sale of the property. The sale of the property is assumed to occur at a cap rate of 5.65%, which is a very optimistic assumption. The larger the share of return earned for the

TABLE 2.23 Cash flows, Ms. R

Net sale price	$133.27
– Debt (first)	$92.00
– Debt (mezz)	$18.00
Distributable cash flow	$23.27

TABLE 2.24 Cash flows and sale proceeds, Ms. R

	Year 0	Year 1	Year 2	Year 3
Outflow	–$5.00			
BTCF		$0.04	$0.37	$0.71
Sale proceeds				$151.32
Total	–$5.00	$0.04	$0.37	$15.84

sale, the more speculative and risky is the project. Therefore, the 48.82% seems like a very strong return, and will please Ms. R, but it comes with a great deal of risk. The multiple on this equity investment for Ms. R is 3.25.

In this case, if both Mr. C and Ms. R bid $115, they will likely be asked to enter into a third round of bidding. They will continue to increase their bids as long as they expect to earn a return with which they feel comfortable. However, as the bids go higher, their assumptions become more aggressive and likely less realistic. In most cases, lenders will be willing to lend more and they will most likely be able to rationalize paying a higher price. This is what happened in the 2003–7 period, as deals were "priced to perfection," meaning that property economics would have to work out exactly as planned. If the economics were not as good as expected, the investors could be placed in distress.

As the new millennium progressed, the CMBS market grew as a proportion of the commercial mortgage market, to $230 billion of originations in 2007 (see Figure 2.4). This represented 52% of commercial mortgage originations that year.

From 2005 to 2007, CMBS lenders provided 50% of net new debt to the commercial mortgage market, and held about 25% of all outstanding mortgages. As will be discussed in Chapter 14, mortgage originators and CMBS issuers were able to take profits out of transactions without bearing any risk. Risk was passed on to investors in securities, who often did not have a good understanding of the true credit quality of underlying mortgages or the structures of the securities. In their quest to continue to increase profits, originators and issuers brought more and more mortgages and securities to the market, which increased the amount of mortgage debt that was available for commercial real estate.

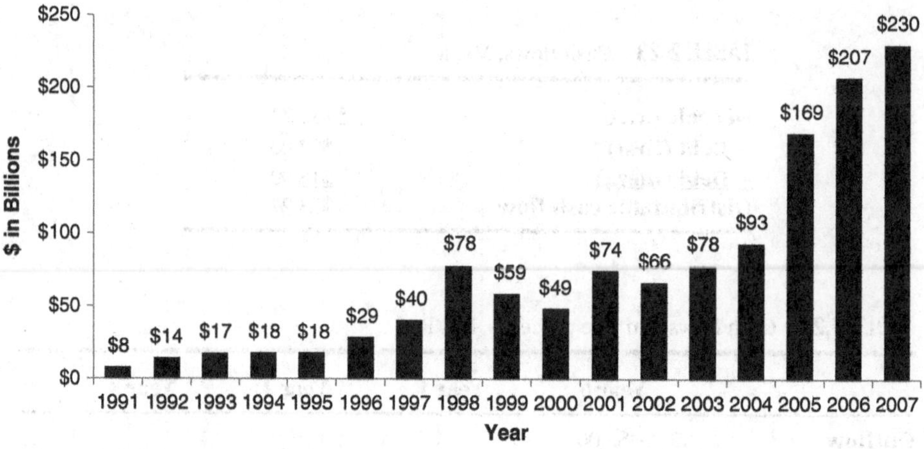

FIGURE 2.4 US CMBS issuance grows
Source: US Federal Reserve.

At the same time, CMBS lenders were crowding out traditional lenders. While commercial banks competed aggressively to originate 40% of all loans in 2005–7, insurance company issuance fell to only about 5% of new mortgages in the period.

When the commercial mortgage-backed securities market spurted in 2006 and 2007, investors were paying high prices for CMBS securities, and requiring yields that were too low for the risk involved. Figure 2.5 shows that AAA-rated CMBS securities were trading at 68 basis points (bps) over the 10-year treasury on 4 January 2007. The lowest investment-quality tranches, those rated BBB–, were yielding 140 bps over 10 years. The credit spread of 72 bps represents an extremely small premium for taking

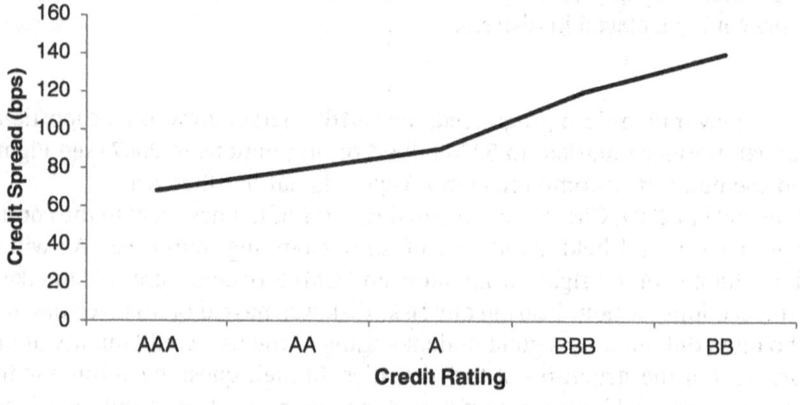

FIGURE 2.5 Spreads for CMBS reached lows in 2007
Source: JP Morgan Chase.

on much higher risk. This was due to liquid investors buying CMBS to gain a few basis points in spread over similarly rated corporate securities. Investors in CMBS felt comfortable with the risks they were taking because credit rating agencies had given the bulk of CMBS issues strong credit ratings.

As in previous cycles, tremendous flows of capital were provided to the real estate market by relatively uninformed lenders and investors. As a result, by 2007 prices were at historical highs, levels that were not supported by the underlying fundamentals of supply and demand for space. Loans were being made to satisfy demand by CMBS investors, and equity investments were being made to allocate money that had been raised by private equity funds and other investors.

The abundance of debt capital and the expected benefits of positive leverage led investors to believe that although they were paying historically high prices to own property, they would be bailed out by ever-increasing rents and values. This led them to use extremely aggressive assumptions of high future cash flow growth and low risk, which provided the basis for the high prices that they were agreeing to pay.

The UK

Following post dot.com weakness in the occupier markets, property cap rates began to fall increasingly sharply over this 5-year period. The IPD UK all-property equivalent yield fell from 7.88% in 2001 to 6.63% in 2004 and to 5.37% by the end of 2006. The total return on UK property in 2004 was 18%, a real return of 17%. In 2005, the IPD Index showed continued strong returns, with returns of 19%, equal to over 16% in real terms, and 2006 delivered another 18% return. The clear cause of the excess return performance in the years 2004–6 was a fall in cap rates (see Chapter 4).

1987, 1988, and 1993 were the only other years in IPD history since 1981 when returns have exceeded 18% nominal. Figure 2.6 shows the breakdown of returns in these years. High returns can come from three main drivers (see Chapter 4): high income returns; high rental growth; or falling cap rates. When UK property market returns were last above 18% (in 1993, when a total return of 20.2%, or 17.1% in real terms, was achieved), that return was due purely to a downward cap rate movement. Rental values in 1993 actually *fell* by 7.9%. Capital growth was driven wholly by a downward movement in equivalent yields from 10.6% in 1992 to 9.0% in 1993.

The returns delivered in 1993, 2004, 2005, and 2006 appeared to be something of an anomaly in the context of the historic pattern of returns. Since 1981, changes in yields from one year to the next have rarely exceeded ±0.5%. An annual fall in yields as significant as that seen each year from 2003 to 2006 has only been seen in one other year since the creation of the IPD UK Index. This was in 1992–3. This is shown in Figure 2.7.

2004–6 clearly shows an irregularity both in terms of the size of the yield fall and in the absolute level of yields. This in turn produced an abnormally high total return. At this point, the end of 2006, many market participants were keen to ask whether the fall in yields experienced in 2004, 2005, and 2006 was sustainable. Were we to expect further yield falls – or was this a bubble waiting to burst?

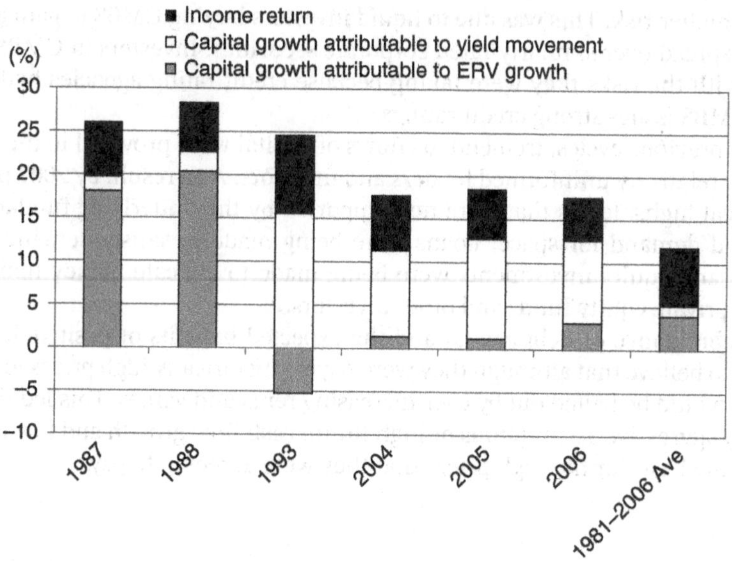

FIGURE 2.6 Analysis of IPD total returns, 1987–2006 (%)
Sources: IPD, PFR 2005.

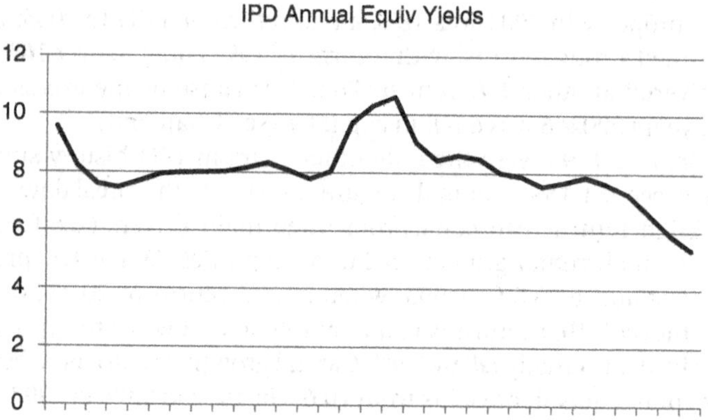

FIGURE 2.7 UK property equivalent yields (1976–2006)
Source: IPD 2007.

2.2.6 THE GLOBAL REAL ESTATE CREDIT CRISIS HITS

The USA

In 2007, defaults on residential mortgages increased as the effects of poor underwriting came home to roost. Despite the assurance of strong credit ratings provided by rating agencies, loan defaults and losses passed through to mortgage-backed security investors. Fixed-income investors exited credit markets in general as investors lost confidence in the credit quality of highly rated residential mortgage-backed securities and the CDOs that were backed by them. Further, investors reasoned that since the credit rating system was so flawed in mortgage-backed securities markets, ratings for all types of debt instruments were flawed as well. In some sense, the "toxic" nature of residential mortgage-backed securities was felt to be contagious, affecting other securities backed by similar assets in the same way. CMBS and a host of other asset-backed securities suffered from this contagion.

This distrust of the quality of ratings led to a massive exodus of capital from every fixed-income security except for those of the highest quality. As investors sold fixed-income securities due to their uncertain prospects, they bought securities that were less complex, including treasury securities and bonds of the highest credit quality. This "flight to quality" by investors depressed prices for commercial mortgage and other asset-backed securities, resulting in an increase in the yield required to compensate for the perceived higher risk. Prices of CMBS tranches fell precipitously, and yields rose to unprecedented levels (see Figure 2.8).

As the flight to quality continued, CMBS credit spreads widened to historically high levels. On 18 November 2008, the AAA spread on CMBS deals had widened to 1200 bps. The BBB– spread had widened to nearly 3500 bps. These spreads represent the cost of capital in a CMBS deal, and if security investors require such high rates, mortgages would have to be originated at incredibly high rates for an investment banker to make a profit in the CMBS market through issuing senior-subordinated securities.

The low credit spreads of early 2007 and the high credit spreads in 2008 are both extreme ends of the spectrum in the CMBS market. The low spreads of 2007 were driven by a herd of investors hungry for yield. The high spreads at the end of 2008 were driven by the same herd thundering out of the market, taking any price for what they perceived as distressed assets. In both cases, irrational investors drove pricing, and more typical spreads fall between these two extremes.

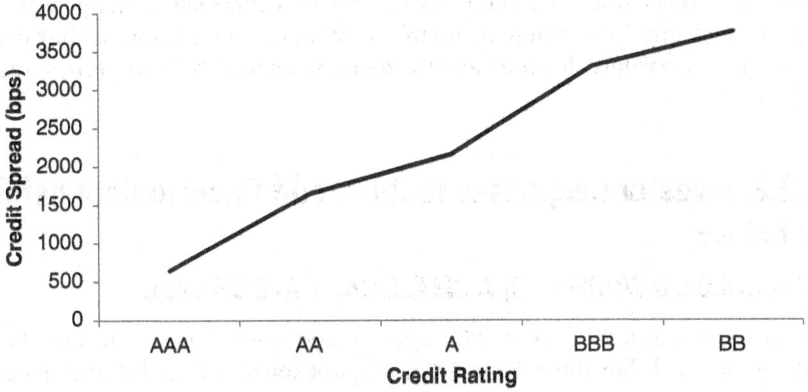

FIGURE 2.8 CMBS spreads widened to unprecedented levels in 2008
Source: JP Morgan Chase.

Since investment bankers could not make a profit issuing CMBS, none were issued. The $230 billion of loans originated in commercial markets in 2007 shrank to nearly zero in 2008. Commercial banks were also having difficulties, as they owned warehouses of mortgage assets that they had been holding in anticipation of pooling them and selling securities backed by them. As investors shunned the CMBS market, and as spreads on mortgage-backed securities increased, the investment banks could not sell the loans they held in their warehouses. The value of these assets fell, and banks began to write off large losses. As commercial banks attempted to figure out how to operate in the new credit environment, they were no longer willing to provide debt capital to the commercial real estate industry.

Together, the CMBS market and commercial banks issued 90% of new debt for commercial real estate purchases between 2005 and 2007. By 2008, they had largely ceased lending. The supply of debt fell far short of the void left by the collapse of lending from the CMBS market and from commercial banks.

Real estate is traditionally a debt-intensive industry. Banks have historically felt comfortable providing 60–80% of the value of purchased property as loans. Investor equity has historically been in the 20–40% range. As capital to lend dried up, property investors had fewer dollars available from debt to buy property. Those lenders who were still making loans required higher levels of equity and applied stricter underwriting criteria. Investors could not earn their required returns unless prices were significantly discounted. Lower prices equate to much higher capitalization rates, especially compared to cap rates that investors accepted between 2005 and 2007.

Even though buyers/investors were willing to bid with large discounts for property, owners still maintained high assessments of values for their properties. When properties were offered to the market, the ask prices were representative of those from prior to the credit crisis. With high ask prices and low bid prices from buyers who could not obtain debt at similar terms as in 2007, very few transactions occurred.

The thinking in the 2008–9 period was that prices would have to adjust to more "normal" levels. Distressed sellers would offer their properties to the market and were willing to take lower prices for their assets. This was expected to happen as owners faced maturing loans. They would be unable to refinance their loans, as they had done in the past, because values declined and the debt capacity of their properties was much lower (Box 2.3).

Box 2.3: Investor Responses to the Credit Crisis in Commercial Real Estate

WHAT COULD GO WRONG? (I) A SMALL CAP RATE CHANGE

Let us fast forward to the end of 2008, and assume that everything has worked out exactly as planned, but the sales market has weakened a little bit and instead of selling at a 5.65% cap rate, the actual rate is 6.5%. This change means that, instead of receiving $133.27 at sale, the owner only gets $115.85 ($7.53 of fourth-year NOI divided by 6.5%). The reader should recognize that a 6.5% cap rate is substantially

TABLE 2.27 Mr. C sale proceeds after a small cap rate rise

Net sale price	$115.85
– Debt	$92.00
Sale proceeds	$23.85

TABLE 2.28 Mr. C cash flows after a small cap rate rise

	Year 0	Year 1	Year 2	Year 3
Outflow	–$23.00			
BTCF		$1.21	$1.54	$1.88
Sale proceeds				$23.85
Total	–$23.00	$1.21	$1.54	$25.73

below the long-term average of cap rates, but 85 bps higher than the cap rate paid at the time of purchase.

The Impact on Mr. C

If Mr. C had bought the property for $115, he would end up selling at a price that is about equal to what he paid. His proceeds from the sale are as shown in Table 2.27.

While Mr. C's proceeds are lower than expected, he is still able to pay off his mortgage balance and have a sum of money to reinvest. Unfortunately, the sum is about equal to the $23 he originally invested, and far lower than his expectation. The cash flows he earns from the project are as shown in Table 2.28.

The actual IRR he earns from owning this project is 7.78%. This is clearly below his expectation, but at least represents a positive return on his investment. The multiple on Mr. C's equity investment is 1.24, indicating that cash inflows exceeded cash outflows.

The Impact on Ms. R

Ms. R took a more risky route, and her performance in this deal required her expectations to pan out nearly perfectly. Unfortunately, the minor cap rate rise to 6.5% affects her more than it did Mr. C. Her cash flows from selling the property at the end of year 3 are as shown in Table 2.29.

Out of this she promised the mezzanine lender 35%, so she owes them a payment of $2.05, leaving Ms. R with a final payment of $3.80, which is less than her original investment of $5. Her cash flows can be summarized as shown in Table 2.30.

(continued)

(continued)

TABLE 2.29 Ms. R sale proceeds after a small cap rate rise

Net sale price	$115.85
– Debt (first)	$92.00
– Debt (mezz)	$18.00
Sale proceeds	$5.85

TABLE 2.30 Ms. R cash flows after a small cap rate rise

	Year 0	Year 1	Year 2	Year 3
Outflow	–$5.00			
BTCF		$0.04	$0.37	$0.71
Sale proceeds				$3.90
Total	–$5.00	$0.04	$0.37	$4.51

Clearly, Ms. R loses money on this deal due to the cap rate difference between what she expected and what actually happened. Her IRR is –0.55%. Her equity multiple in this scenario is 0.99.

Post-mortem

Unfortunately, what happened to Ms. R is typical of what happened to most investors. To win a deal, they fudged assumptions to make the deal work. In this case, both she and Mr. C started the bidding with an assumption that the going-out cap rate would be 6.5%. They both changed this assumption to be far more aggressive in the second round, to rationalize paying a higher price. Their perspective on what people might be willing to pay in year 3 probably did not change that much, but they both probably figured that, if they were willing to pay a price based on a 5.65% cap rate, investors in 3 years would probably be willing to pay that much too. However, if they had not made that assumption, or another one that would increase the price they were willing to pay, they would probably not have won the deal. In the end, that probably would have been the best thing that could have happened to them.

WHAT COULD GO WRONG? (II) A LARGE CAP RATE CHANGE

In retrospect, we now know that cap rates increased to beyond 6.5% for office properties. For this example, let us assume that they have risen to 8.5%. Let us also assume that Mr. C and Ms. R have to sell the property at that rate at the end of the third year because the first mortgage loan matures. Unless they can extend the loan term, the lender will be expecting to be paid back the principal balance.

The Impact on Mr. C

In some sense, Mr. C did all the right things. He did not get sucked into a mezzanine loan, although he did pay more for the property than he probably intended to pay. At a purchase price in December 2005 of $115, he expected to earn a 26.95% IRR, but he also had to assume a very low going-out cap rate of 5.65% to earn it. What happens to Mr. C if cap rates increase to 8.5%?

An important assumption that we have to make is that the property can actually be sold. Often, in 2008, buyers were not able to obtain loans that allowed them to create a positive leverage scenario. Therefore, it is likely that Mr. C will offer the property for sale but not get any bids. Despite this, he will still owe the balance on the mortgage.

The sales price at 8.5% (which again, we assume, is the current cap rate in the marketplace) is $88.59. This price assumes that all of the other assumptions came true: rents were $6.50 in the first year, and grew by 5%. If they grew by less than 5%, this value would be even lower. Sadly for Mr. C, when he sells he must pay the $92 that he borrowed from the bank when he bought the property. His cash flows from the sale are as shown in Table 2.31.

Mr. C's investment is under water, and to sell, he must write a cheque to the bank for $3.41 out of other funds. Clearly, this was not his expectation.

The cash flows he earns from the project are as shown in Table 2.32.

TABLE 2.31 Mr. C sale proceeds after a large cap rate rise

Net sale price	$88.59
– Debt	$92.00
Sale proceeds	–$3.41

TABLE 2.32 Mr C cash flows after a large cap rate rise

	Year 0	Year 1	Year 2	Year 3
Outflow	–$23.00			
BTCF		$1.21	$1.54	$1.88
Sale proceeds				–$3.41
Total	–$23.00	$1.21	$1.54	–$1.53

(continued)

(*continued*)

In this case, the IRR is clearly negative (albeit not really meaningfully), and it is clear that this real estate investment was a bad outcome for Mr. C.

The Impact on Ms. R

Ms. R will also suffer from the sale. The net sale price she receives is the same $88.59 based on the same 8.5% cap rate, but she owes $92 on the first mortgage and $18 on the mezzanine loan. Her cash flow statement from the sale of the property is as shown in Table 2.33.

To extricate herself from the deal, and satisfy the contracts that she signed when she took out the loans, she must pay $3.41 out of pocket to the first mortgage lender, and $18 to the mezzanine lender. It is important to remember that she only invested $5 in equity to begin the deal back in December 2005. She now owes more than 4 times that amount to satisfy her debts.

As with Mr. C in this scenario, it may take a long time for Ms. R to sell the property. Despite this, she is still required to repay the balances on the two mortgages at the end of the 3-year loan term. It is likely that the lenders could extend the loan term by another year, but that is unlikely to save Ms. R from her troubles. By December 2009, real estate market conditions had not improved, and were expected to decline further.

Post-mortem

Both the banks and our investors have difficult decisions to make. Mr. C could choose to pay the shortfall or walk away from the $3.53 debt that he owes and allow the bank to foreclose on his equity interest. If he did not sign a personal guarantee (meaning the loan was non-recourse), he can walk away from the loan without any financial penalty. He will find it difficult, however, to borrow again for a long time. This may be worth the "gain" of $3.53 in debt "relief" that he gets from doing so.

Ms. R's problems are a bit more extreme. She owes far more than she invested, and most likely does not have enough funds to pay. She will most likely default on her loan and "mail in the keys," allowing the bank to foreclose. She will also be unable to borrow again for a long time, but she gets "relief" of $21.41 by exercising the implicit put option that is inherent in every mortgage instrument. As long as there is no recourse to other assets held by the borrower, the borrower can "sell" the property back to the lender at a price equal to the current balance of the loan. No one

TABLE 2.33 Ms R sale proceeds after a large cap rate rise

Net sale price	$88.59
– Debt (first)	$92.00
– Debt (mezz)	$18.00
Sale proceeds	–$21.41

borrows money expecting to do this, but in negative situations it may be the most logical and rational thing for an underwater borrower to do. At this point, someone usually suggests refinancing to solve Mr. C's and Ms. R's problems. Unfortunately, the bank will appraise the property at something close to the $88.59 value implied by an 8.5% cap rate, and then be willing to loan 80% of that amount or just a little more than $70.87. For both of our investors, they would end up owing a lot more in this scenario than if they simply walked away from the loan.

As it turns out, to avoid foreclosure and potential losses, banks and representatives of CMBS investors were willing to extend mortgage maturities or modify loan terms. Extending the mortgage maturity buys a year or two of time for the bank and the owner, in the hope that real estate and credit market conditions improve over that time. In that event, the owner can refinance or sell and come out whole. If he does not, he is in the same position facing foreclosure.

Ironically, securitization is touted as increasing the transparency and level of information in markets and also as a dampener of the amplitude of the real estate cycle. In retrospect, securitization of commercial mortgages did neither. Instead of relying on their own due diligence, investors depended solely on the ratings provided by rating agencies and, in their thirst for yield, overpaid for securities. CDOs were far too complex to be transparent and as the new few years unfolded there were untold losses for investors in CMBS and CDO issues.

The UK

Sure enough, 2006 marked the end of the bull market in UK property. The third consecutive year of returns in excess of 18% presaged the bursting of a bubble which popped in the summer of 2007.

The main driver of the boom had clearly been debt finance. Interest rates were low, and debt availability was unprecedented thanks to debt repackaging. Table 2.25 makes shocking reading for government and regulators. The coincidence of spikes in lending and a following crash is not accidental: 1989 and 2007–8 are worryingly similar, but 2007–8 is much worse.

TABLE 2.25 Bank lending to property, 1999–2008

Year	Aggregated lending
1999	£45.1bn
2000	£45.1bn
2001	£54.1bn
2002	£60.1bn
2003	£70.3bn
2004	£79.4bn
2005	£92.1bn
2006	£101.3bn
2007	£172.5bn
2008	£227.1bn

Source: De Montfort University 2008.

The UK REIT market had begun to trade at discounts to net asset value on its launch in January 2007, and moved consistently downwards from that point until, in January 2009, discounts were at an all-time high, approaching 50%. This was a sign of a correction to follow in the direct market.

From January to June 2007, the IPD monthly index had been showing positive capital growth of between 0.27% and 0.46% for each of the 6 months of the first half of the year (see Table 2.26). In the summer of 2007, the change in market sentiment was evidenced by the index producing a negative capital return in August of 0.4%. The IPD monthly index took a downward turn of over 1.5% in September. By October, market sentiment had weakened again, the UK REIT market had moved to large discounts to NAV, touching 20% in September 2007, and a year-end effect began to gather pace as valuers took 8% off values in November and December.

The market at the beginning of 2008 was damaged by the gradual realization of a global capital shortage (the credit crisis), which led to the eventual collapse of Bear Stearns in April and Lehman Brothers in September. This was expressed though a sharp increase in property yields, as shown in Figure 2.9. The yield series now clearly appeared to be mean-reverting.

TABLE 2.26 IPD UK monthly index, monthly capital returns, 2007–8

Month	Index	Capital return
Jan-07	222.82	0.27%
Feb-07	223.52	0.31%
Mar-07	224.55	0.46%
Apr-07	225.24	0.31%
May-07	225.95	0.31%
Jun-07	226.54	0.26%
Jul-07	226.03	−0.22%
Aug-07	225.13	−0.40%
Sep-07	221.58	−1.57%
Oct-07	217.44	−1.87%
Nov-07	208.80	−3.97%
Dec-07	200.09	−4.17%
Jan-08	196.04	−2.02%
Feb-08	193.12	−1.49%
Mar-08	190.62	−1.30%
Apr-08	188.80	−0.95%
May-08	186.59	−1.17%
Jun-08	182.89	−1.98%
Jul-08	179.60	−1.80%
Aug-08	176.65	−1.64%
Sep-08	171.52	−2.91%
Oct-08	164.16	−4.29%
Nov-08	154.85	−5.67%
Dec-08	145.81	−5.84%

Source: IPD.

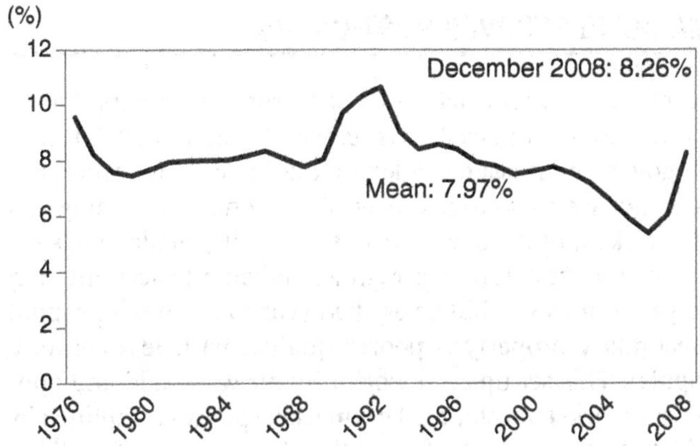

FIGURE 2.9 Property equivalent yields, 1976–2008
Source: IPD.

The unprecedented sharp yield increase, driven initially by the capital crisis, became further supported by a worsening prospect for rents, with financial services and retailing looking very weak as unemployment rose, consumer spending fell, and recession beckoned. Many big names in retailing, including Woolworths, ceased to trade from the UK high street. It became clear in early 2009 that the UK had entered recession in July 2008, and it was expected to be long and deep.

December 2008 showed the largest fall in capital values in the history of the IPD monthly index, Q4 2008 being the worst-ever quarter, and 2008 the worst year in the history of the IPD annual series dating from 1971. In 2008, values fell by 27%, wiping £46 billion from the value of the IPD universe, worth £172 billion at the beginning of the year. UK property shares were, by the end of 2008, trading at the biggest discount to NAV ever seen in recorded history: see Figure 2.10.

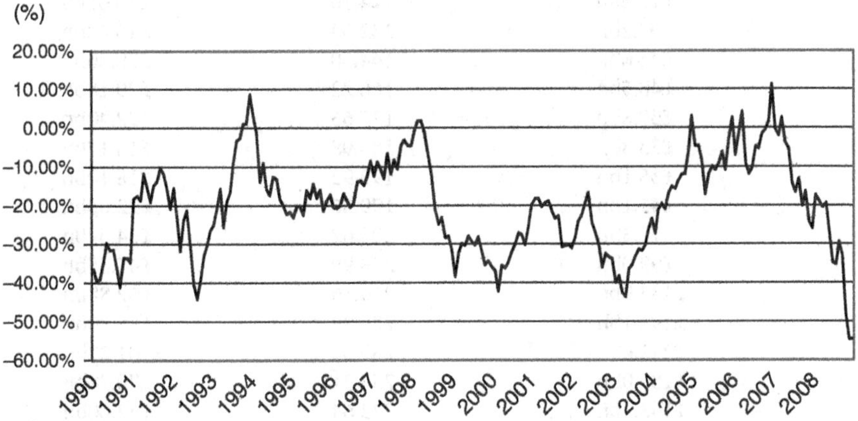

FIGURE 2.10 Estimated discount/premium to NAV, UK listed property
Source: Datastream.

2.2.7 THE MARKETS RECOVER POST-CRISIS

2008–9 were desperate years for debt-financed property owners. For cash buyers, the market looked interesting – but cash was scarce. By early 2010, UK property appeared underpriced, as government-issued index-linked bond yields were as low as 1%, and conventional long gilt yields were just over 3%. A long-term average 5% property premium over index linked, or 3% over conventional gilts, made yields of above 8% look attractive before any potential rental growth was taken into account. In retrospect, 2009 was a very good year to invest – but a very bad year to try to raise capital.

So-called secondary property – poorer quality, with less certainty of income – remained unpopular. This set up an opportunity for value-add and opportunity investment, and a two-tier market developed. This market split was amplified by the increasing unpopularity of retail property in the face of the phenomenon of on-line retailing. In the following decade, bank debt reverted to early 2000s levels (see Table 2.34).

In retrospect, UK real estate turns out to have been very cheap in 2009, thanks to ever-lower interest rates (see Figure 2.11). This phenomenon was not commonly expected, but it is very clear that lower interest rates have driven very good returns in the US and UK property markets.

Table 2.35 illustrates the strong post-crisis bounce back in the UK.

Figure 2.12 and Table 2.36 show the source of these returns – stable income returns, plus a positive yield impact and steady rent growth (just a tad less than the rate of inflation).

TABLE 2.34 Bank lending to property, 1981–2017

Year	Nominal lending	Inflation	Real lending
1981	£5.5bn	100	£5.50bn
1983	£8.5bn	113.45	£7.49bn
1985	£12.5bn	124.10	£10.07bn
1987	£22bn	132.34	£16.62bn
1989	£44.6bn	144.50	£30.86bn
1991	£48.5bn	166.22	£29.18bn
1993	£39.8bn	177.65	£22.40bn
1995	£33.8bn	185.98	£18.17bn
1997	£35.1bn	193.92	£18.10bn
1999	£45.1bn	199.55	£22.60bn
2001	£70.3bn	203.62	£34.54bn
2003	£99.0bn	208.99	£47.35bn
2005	£135.9bn	216.16	£62.88bn
2007	£193.1bn	226.33	£85.30bn
2009	£242.6bn	239.56	£101.27bn
2011	£183.0bn	258.51	£70.78bn
2013	£143.4bn	272.64	£52.60bn
2015	£133.8bn	276.73	£48.36bn
2017	£134.7bn	285.80	£47.12bn

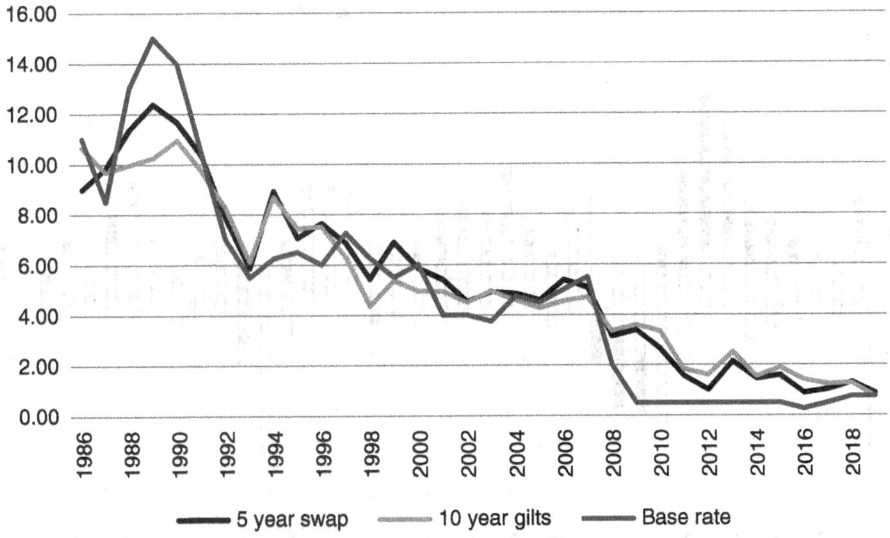

FIGURE 2.11 UK swap rates, gilt yields, and base rate, 1986–2019

TABLE 2.35 UK property returns, 1981–2019

Year	IPD return	Inflation rate	IPD real return	GDP growth
2000	10.8%	0.8%	9.9%	3.4%
2001	7.1%	1.2%	5.8%	3%
2002	9.5%	1.3%	8.1%	2.3%
2003	10.8%	1.4%	9.3%	3.3%
2004	17.6%	1.3%	16.0%	2.4%
2005	18.9%	2.1%	16.5%	3.2%
2006	18.1%	2.3%	15.4%	2.8%
2007	−3.0%	2.3%	−5.2%	2.4%
2008	−21.7%	3.6%	−24.4%	−0.3%
2009	3.7%	2.2%	1.5%	−4.2%
2010	15.1%	3.3%	11.4%	1.9%
2011	8.0%	4.5%	3.4%	1.5%
2012	3.5%	2.8%	0.7%	1.5%
2013	10.8%	2.6%	8.1%	2.1%
2014	17.8%	1.5%	16.1%	2.6%
2015	13.1%	0.0%	13.1%	2.4%
2016	3.9%	0.7%	3.2%	1.9%
2017	9.6%	2.6%	6.8%	1.9%
2018	5.1%	2.3%	2.8%	1.4%
2019	0.9%	1.8%	−0.9%	1.3%

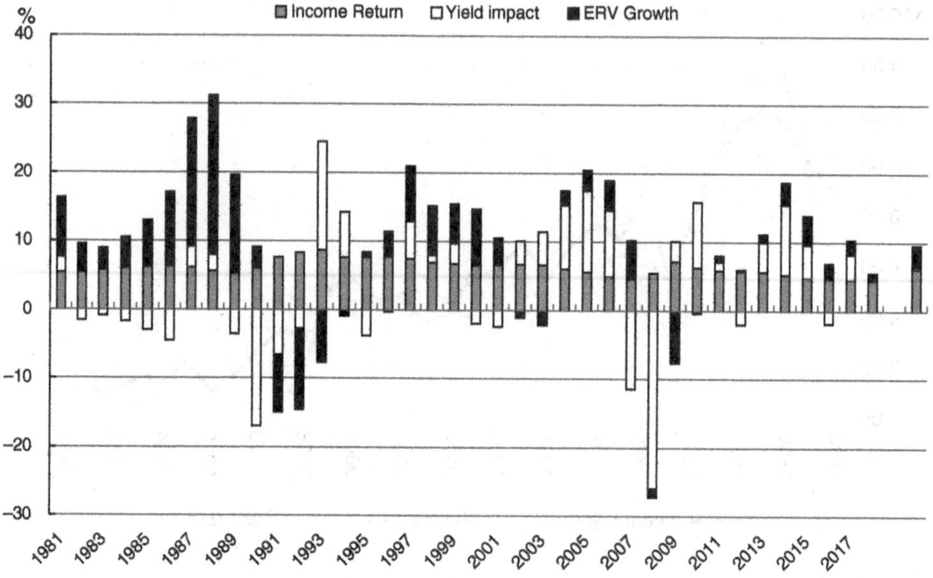

FIGURE 2.12 UK real estate return attribution, 1981–2018

TABLE 2.36 UK property return attribution, 1981–2019

Income return	Yield impact	ERV growth	Total return	Capital growth
6.18%	0.38%	3.02%	9.11%	2.77%

Figure 2.13 shows that the increase in cap rates in the post-crisis period had been wiped out by declining interest rates, which pushed cap rates to all-time lows by 2018.

2.3 THE GLOBAL MARKET

2.3.1 The European Market Develops

Figure 2.14 shows that while the USA had higher rates than the UK in the 2015–20 period, interest rates were lower in all major markets. This has helped to deliver positive returns everywhere, as shown in Table 2.37. Given low inflation rates, all four countries shown (UK, USA, Germany, and France) have delivered strong real returns.

Problems are encountered when trying to compare the performance of the real estate markets across Europe. Valuation practices vary widely and in some instances are not entirely comparable. Unlike the UK, IPD measures a tiny share of the institutional real estate stock, and coverage is particularly low for Belgium, Germany, Italy, Spain, and Sweden. In addition, the available performance history in all continental European countries is much shorter than in the UK.

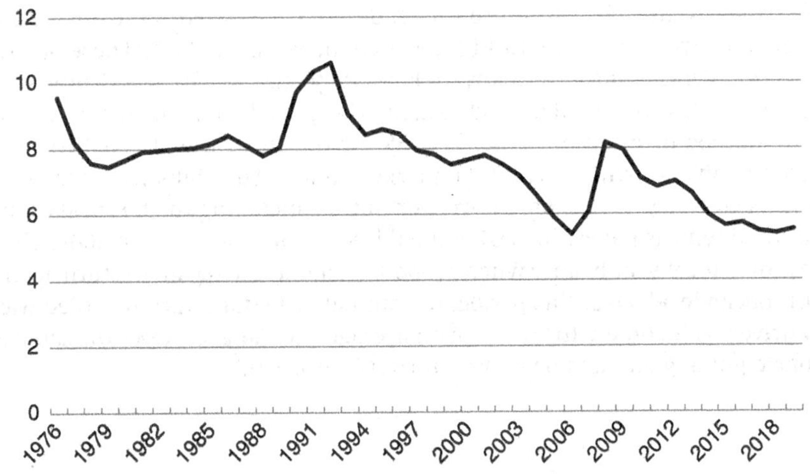

FIGURE 2.13 UK real estate cap rates, 1976–2018

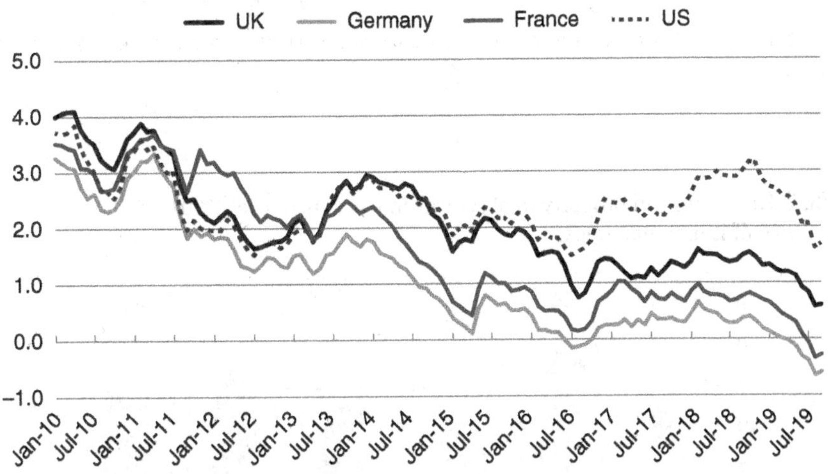

FIGURE 2.14 10-Year government bond yields, 2010–19, UK, USA, Germany, France
Source: Datastream.

TABLE 2.37 Annual average real estate returns, 2009–18

USA	UK	Germany	France
7.28%	8.93%	6.38%	6.62%

Sources: MSCI, CBREGI.

Nevertheless, the IPD Pan-European Index has measured the combined performance of property markets in 16 European countries since 2001. These are Austria, Belgium, Denmark, France, Germany, Ireland, Italy, the Netherlands, Norway, Poland, Portugal, Spain, Sweden, Switzerland, and the UK, plus the KTI index for Finland. The total IPD Europe invested universe, at €768 billion, rivals the US NCREIF Property Index (NPI) universe, which has a total market value of $653 billion (Figure 2.15).

In local currency, real estate returns for Europe including the UK peaked at 13.6% in 2006. Total returns halved in 2007 and fell into negative territory in 2008. This is the only year over the 9-year history when property generated a negative return at an aggregated European level. Over this period, the annualized total return recorded was 6.9%, mainly driven by income return, which on average was 5.4% p.a. Over the same period, Eurozone equities generated negative returns (Figure 2.16).

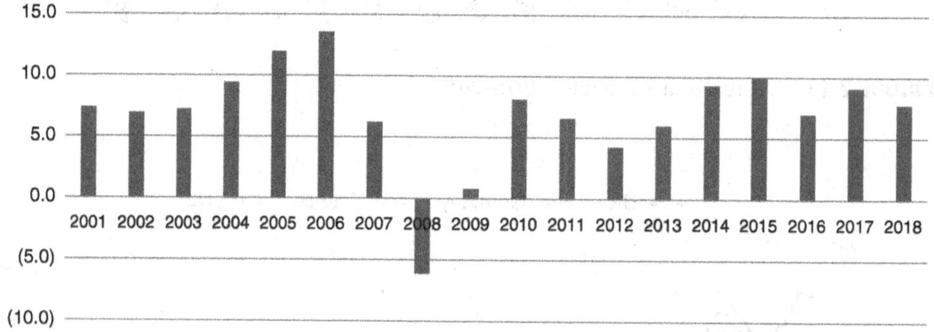

FIGURE 2.15 European property total returns in local currencies, 2001–18
Source: IPD multinational index.

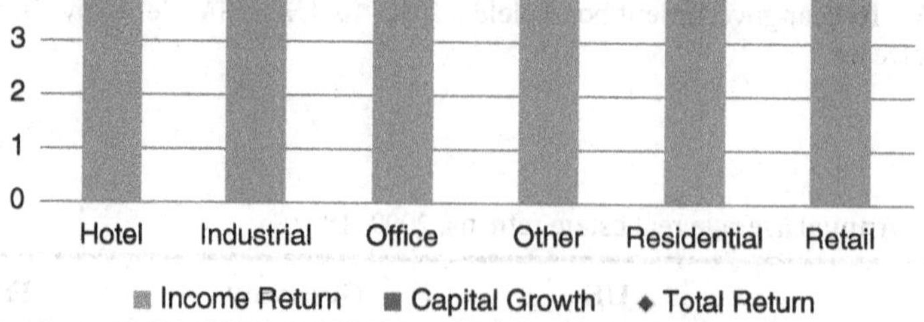

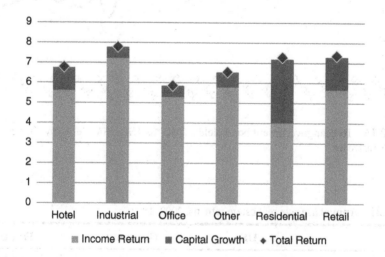

FIGURE 2.16 Europe ex-UK property average total returns by sector, 2001–18
Source: IPD multinational index.

The UK market comprises a significant portion of the IPD Pan-European Index (30% in 2018). In 2008, when the UK market generated a total return of −22%, the high weighting of the UK market turned the whole index negative.

By sector, the highest returns on the Pan-European Index over the 2001–18 period were recorded in the industrial sector, where returns were almost entirely driven by income. For the residential sector, high capital value growth partly compensated for low income yields. The office sector was the worst performer over this time period, due to falls in capital values and low income returns.

2.3.2 Asia Emerges

A consistent real estate market analysis of Asia (or Asia-Pacific) is even more difficult than a single analysis of Europe. This difficulty is compounded by the different stages of development of the Asian real estate sectors. Well-developed and mature markets in Hong Kong, Singapore, Australia, New Zealand, Japan, and Korea contrast with the developing Chinese and Indian markets and unknown territories (to most real estate investors) such as Pakistan and Indonesia. International investment interest has generally been centered on the mature markets.

While economic growth in Asia has been relatively strong for many years, the mid-1980s saw speculative currency attacks, with the US dollar falling in value against the Japanese yen, leading eventually to the Asian currency crisis in 1997. This followed the wild speculation of the Japanese "bubble economy," during which irrational exuberance and monetary easing pushed common stock and real estate prices to euphoric levels. The subsequent bursting of the bubble in 1987 caused Japan's economic and real estate slump of the 1990s and early 2000s.

The global economy picked up steadily after the dot.com boom and bust of 2000–1, primarily due to continued robust growth in China, which continued to grow as it underwent industrialization and urbanization at a pace faster than any major country. China's appetite for raw materials and capital goods transformed the country into an industrial power, which has aided the economic fortunes of the entire Asia-Pacific region, with the economies of Australia, Japan, South Korea, Thailand, and Singapore benefitting most from China's robust growth.

China's sustainable economic growth is reckoned to be around 6% p.a., while Japan's growth is much slower. This neatly exemplifies the problems encountered when attempting to generalize about Asia, and equally when building an investment strategy for the region (see Chapter 16). Japan needs a demand boost, while the Chinese government has on occasion introduced policy measures designed to cool the real estate market.

India's economic growth has exceeded that of China, but it is not a market which encourages foreign investment. In the 2020 version of the World Bank's annual *Doing Business* report, India was ranked 63rd, while China was 31st and Japan 29th. However, Asia has four of the top five – South Korea is 5th, Hong Kong 3rd, and Singapore 2nd – while New Zealand was ranked the world's easiest place to do business (World Bank, 2020).

After suffering from volatility and a credibility gap in the 1980s and early 1990s, Asian real estate as a distinct asset class produced steady, strong performance over the first two decades of the 21st century and made ground on the USA and Europe during and after the global financial crisis. Investment-grade Asian real estate has earned a permanent place in the long-term strategic plans of global investors. Initially, European and Middle Eastern private equity funds and institutions were particularly active in Asia; more recently, local core investors (such as GIC, Singapore) and investment managers have increased their influence.

The divide between the established, mature markets of Australia, New Zealand, Japan, South Korea, Singapore, and Hong Kong, on the one hand, and China, India, and the smaller emerging markets, on the other hand, is exemplified by the problems investors have in measuring market sizes. Some of MSCI's best global coverage is in Asia (New Zealand and Australia have around half their professionally managed markets indexed), but there are also real weaknesses (in China, for example, MSCI concedes that less than 4% of the market is in the index) (MSCI, 2019).

Professional investment managers are forced to use their own top-down estimates of the investment universe to determine the neutral shares for each country in a global and regional portfolio. This means that China is larger than the MSCI data would suggest. A typical Asia-Pacific portfolio might look like this: Japan 40%, China 20–25%, Australia 15–20%, Singapore, South Korea, and Hong Kong 5–10% each, and the rest of the region (Malaysia, Taiwan, New Zealand, and other emerging markets) taking up the remainder.

Steps are being taken along a road to global integration, as Asia continues to make progress as an increasingly integral and exciting part of the global property market. The absence of India, Indonesia, and Pakistan from this analysis is an obvious weakness. How long it will be before these markets and the major African, Middle Eastern, and South American countries justify essential inclusion in core global portfolios is very difficult to judge. See Box 2.4 for a Dubai example.

Box 2.4: Dubai – Losing the Plot

The Dubai residential property market became the center of global attention as a boom took hold in the mid-2000s. Investors and speculators were attaining short-term (often 6 months or less) capital gains delivering in excess of 100% IRRs via "off-plan" property purchases. Sometimes, as will be described, the returns were even more astronomical.

Were the risks these investors took commensurate with the gains? What was their rationale? How sustainable was their strategy? How did this situation develop?

1999–2001

During this period, Dubai embarked on a pioneering and visionary approach to property in the GCC (Gulf Co-operation Council) region. For the first time, pockets of strategic locations were made available for expatriate ownership via a freehold model. Under this model, expats were able to buy a small number of apartments and villas. To entice buyers, the initial property prices asked were extremely low, and buyer-conducive schemes such as rent-to-own were introduced. The initial market reaction was skeptical but soon, some regional residents began to pick up these properties as speculative investments. The risks were high, as the market was new/emerging, legislation was not in place, prices were difficult to compare, and home finance was scarce and complicated.

In spite of the risks, in retrospect it is clear that good value was to be had. Ambitious and almost surreal plans of the future Dubai were laid out, albeit difficult to believe. The vision was grand – Dubai was billed as "the new Singapore," a cross between Hong Kong and Manhattan. In the face of common criticism, "build it and they will come" became an increasingly persuasive mantra. However, the full-on marketing and PR campaign had yet to begin in earnest.

Prices of around £100/sq. ft were typical. Rental yields were around 10%, while rental rates were deemed to be competitive and expected to rise.

2002–5

Dubai became the focus of a huge international advertising campaign. The freehold property market began to pick up steam. The boom took hold as legislation supporting freehold ownership, although ambiguous, was announced, and there seemed to be a move towards market transparency.

Local Islamic (Shariah-compliant) banks, such as Amlak and Tamweel, began to participate in financing iconic projects, and such high-impact schemes as the man-made Palm Island and the Burj Dubai (the world's tallest structure on its completion, now known as Burj Khalifa) were launched. Nonetheless, skepticism still abounded as to whether Dubai could deliver on its hyper-ambitious plans. After all, the United Arab Emirates was a desert sheikhdom with only 30 years of sovereign history.

As Dubai attracted many foreign workers who came to help develop the Dubai dream, the need for housing quickly exceeded supply. Thus, savvy investors perceived this as a good opportunity to buy as rental yields were rapidly rising. The first wave of speculation began, pushing prices up and widening the new market to international investors. In addition to investment from local Emiratis, nationals from Kuwait, Saudi Arabia, and Qatar began investing heavily in Dubai. Furthermore, a few very wealthy groups from Russia, India, Pakistan, and Iran began buying property in bulk. There was a mad rush for any new residential development, and impressive schemes were being completed and delivered. People started to own, not rent, and communities began to develop. Expectations became very high, and delivered returns for investors were strong.

Prices of around £150/sq. ft became commonplace. However, rental yields were still in excess of 10–12%, and there remained room for further capital price increases. Leading government-backed developers Nakheel and the listed EMAAR became very large and began to sell land to private developers, further embedding the boom.

(*continued*)

(*continued*)

2006–7

Individual and institutional investors not initially eyeing Dubai began to catch wind of the riches being made by those who had bought and sold. Investors and agencies who had established themselves in Dubai quickly became a magnet for funds and *de facto* fund managers for friends, family, and/or clients who wanted a part of the Dubai pie. In addition to residential property, commercial property and land became hot items.

The Dubai residential market became an established investment sector, with trading in existing properties and a continuing pipeline of new projects being launched or announced. Risk premia fell, as there was greater acceptance of Dubai's position as a post-emerging property market.

Towards 2008, Dubai fever was in full stride, with a number of projects being announced every week. If all the proposed projects had been built, Dubai would have had housing for 12 million people but a population of only 1.6 million. Proposed projects such as the Trump Tower-Palm Island and the Dubai Waterfront (a waterfront community adding hundreds of miles to Dubai's coastline and proposed to be twice the size of Hong Kong) were launched. Institutional investors entered the market, debt-raising was big business (Standard Chartered, Lloyds, and other international names were now taking part), and the concentration of finance and real estate professionals and construction companies fueled a self-sustaining frenzy for all things real estate in Dubai.

Population and employment growth were being driven by the construction boom. Expectations were being fueled by the experience of the successful "flippers," many of whom were using credit cards and other forms of personal debt to raise cash for deposits before quickly selling on their rights at a profit. Often they could not afford to make the next payment. Prices of £300–400/sq. ft were well established. Rental yields fell to 7–8%.

At the peak, prices for flats and villas were being revised upwards every week. Finishing quality was an issue from the start, as developers wanted to finish the work as quickly as they could. Few buyers and fewer sellers cared about specifications and materials. Many stories were exchanged about water leakages and other defects in multi-million-dollar flats.

By this stage, speculators were paying money to reserve a place in a queue for a ticket which gave a right to put down a deposit. Those at the front of the queue flipped to those at the back for an easy profit, and some security guards managing the queues are reported to have done very well. Personal credit checks were rarely carried out on prospective buyers. A mortgage could be secured in less than 24 hours, and it was very common to have a person who earned $2,000/month owning several million-dollar plus flats and villas. Deposits might be paid with cheques drawn on Abu Dhabi banks, which took 3 days to clear in Dubai; the property would often be flipped in less than that 3 days, so no funds in Abu Dhabi were needed and infinite IRR returns were made. Many people stopped working and going to their day jobs, and a flat in Burj Dubai was reputed to have been sold by the same broker 22 times in less than 18 months.

2008–10

Upon word of Lehman's collapse, existing doubts about the plethora of new projects being announced caused prices to crash by 40–70% within 8 months. Developers defaulted on debt, borrowers defaulted on mortgages, and (because default is a criminal offence in Dubai) those who could not honor their financial commitments were put in jail. This explains the many tales of expats leaving town in a hurry, abandoning cars at the airport with the keys left in the ignition.

The majority of new projects, including Trump Tower, Dubai Waterfront, and hundreds of others, were either put on hold or cancelled. Despite its government backing, Nakheel came close to default and its bonds sold in the secondary market at huge discounts to par value.

THE ECONOMICS

Residential prices in Dubai for the period 2002–9 are shown in Table 2.38. The mean percentage index growth in 2007–8 and in 2008–9 was around 42% and −48%, respectively.

If, in 2007, I paid a 10% deposit for a $1m apartment and prices rose in line with the index, the apartment would go up in value by 42% and my equity multiply 4.2 times. If, as many did, I borrowed 50% of the deposit, my equity of $50,000 would multiply 8.4 times. I can easily flip this right at a profit.

However, if, in 2008, I paid a 10% deposit for a $1m apartment and prices fell in line with the index, the apartment would go down in value and my deposit be wiped out, leaving me with negative equity of 4.2 times my deposit. If I borrowed 50% of the deposit, my equity of $50,000 would be replaced by a personal debt of $427,000. Given that default is a criminal offence, this is a sobering thought for international investors.

TABLE 2.38 Dubai residential pricing (AED/sq. ft)

Type		2002	2003	2004	2005	2006	2007	2008	2009
Apartments	Burj Dubai	–	–	1,200	1,275	1,350	2,800	4,500	2,000
	Dubai Marina	850	836	900	1,000	1,050	1,400	1,975	1,100
	Greens	500	500	725	875	950	1,250	1,700	1,000
Villas	Lakes	550	575	700	875	1,250	1,450	2,150	1,200
	Meadows	450	500	600	800	1,150	1,500	1,775	1,100
	Ranches	450	475	620	790	1,150	1,450	2,120	1,000
	Springs	420	485	500	640	1,025	1,500	1,850	1,000

Note: The currency in the United Arab Emirates (of which Dubai is a member) is AED (Arab Emirates Dirham). It is pegged to the dollar at the fixed rate of 3.67. 1 $ = 3.67 AED.

2.4 REAL ESTATE CYCLES: CONCLUSIONS

Real estate is, and always will be, a cyclical market. Often, participants in the industry forget this and behave as if prices will always continue on an upward path. When we forget that the market is cyclical, the consequences are bad.

The current post-GFC period to 2020 provides a severe challenge to investors. Historically low interest rates have knocked on to low cap rates and higher property prices.

The long-term historical record of US capitalization rates is shown in Figure 2.17. As the figure shows, US cap rates in most periods are between 4% and 9%, averaging just over 6.6%. There are now three sustained periods where cap rates have slipped below the long-term average, including the most recent 10 years, over which time prices have been driven up by low or even negative real rates. New capital has been attracted to real estate debt and equity markets and the high yields available relative to other asset classes, which has driven asset prices up to historically high levels. In short, history repeats itself, and cycles persist. At this stage of the cycle, we always ask "Is it different this time? Are these lower cap rates a sign of an inevitable fall in prices to come – or are lower interest rates and cap rates here to stay?" The answer to this is not obvious, but if history does indeed repeat itself, another downturn will occur, followed by another recovery. The best we can do is to state the major lessons we have learned from this analysis of real estate history.

Lesson 1: Too Much Lending to Property is Dangerous

The lending of 2001–6, by the end of which period bank lending in the UK was three times the excessive 1991 level, makes previous excesses seem ascetic. By 2008, UK lending was at five times the 1991 level, and US CMBS issuance was out of control. The coincidence of geometric increases in lending and a following crash is not accidental.

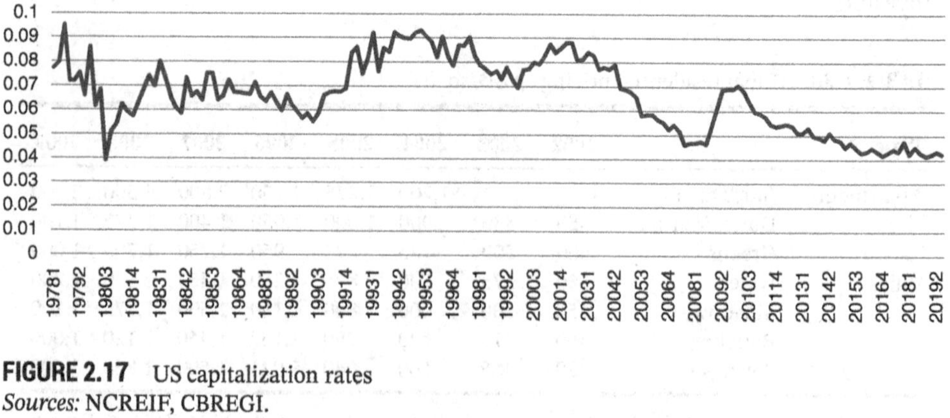

FIGURE 2.17 US capitalization rates
Sources: NCREIF, CBREGI.

Lesson 2: Yields are Mean-Reverting – Unless Real Risk-Free Rates Change

In each of 2004, 2005, and 2006, the IPD UK Index showed returns of over 18%, equal to 16% in real terms. This is well over any reasonable required return, and well in excess of average total returns on any mature real estate index, the first of which developed in the 1970s. What was driving these returns?

Over the period 1981–2006, an average property return of around 10.5% can be split into income return (around 7%) and nominal rental growth at roughly the rate of inflation (3.5%). Capitalization rate movement can add return over short periods, but its contribution over the long run has been close to zero. In the context of the historic pattern, the return breakdowns in 2004, 2005, and 2006 appear to be something of an anomaly. In each year, capital growth in excess of 12% was driven by what became known as "yield compression."

Since 1981, changes in yields from one year to the next have rarely exceeded ±0.5%. This consistency in property cap rates is well supported by theory. However, following a yield increase in 2007–10, lower real risk-free rates have driven yields consistently lower since 2010.

As we will see in Chapter 4, property cap rates can be explained as the real risk-free rate (which does not vary much over time) and a property risk premium (which should reflect consistent long-run fundamental asset qualities and not short-term fear or greed). Property cap rates *should* be mean-reverting – unless the real risk-free rate changes, as it clearly did post-2007 crash.

Lesson 3: Look at Yields on Index-Linked Securities

It is tempting to compare yields on gilts/Treasuries and yields on equities with property cap rates. The picture is confusing. But UK property yields have moved in line with index-linked bond yields since the recovery from the 1990–2 crash, since when the average premium of property cap rates over index-linked yields was around 5%. Since 2001 in particular, property cap rates tracked index-linked yields down and the two series have been strongly correlated (presumably, the capital markets see property as an inflation hedge). But by the end of 2006, the difference between equivalent yields and index-linked yields had closed from a mean of 5% to a new level of around 2.5%. This suggests that property yields were already too low, and a rise was predictable. The yield gap between real estate and indexed bonds is significant.

We develop this type of pricing analysis in Chapter 4, after examining the equally vital economics of rent in Chapter 3.

CHAPTER 3

Market Fundamentals and Rent

3.1 INTRODUCTION: THE GLOBAL PROPERTY CYCLE AND RENT

The modern era of real estate investment is generally considered to have begun in 1970. Since then, both US and UK real estate markets have experienced three distinct market cycles. As we saw in Chapter 2, all of them follow the same time line of events.

At a given point, the market value of existing property exceeds replacement value. Developers then expand the supply of real estate and debt and equity capital flows into the real estate industry. Additions to supply eventually exceed the tenant demand for space, and rents fall as tenant options expand, often in conjunction with an economic downturn. Property values fall, ultimately dropping below replacement value. New development stops, eliminating jobs in real estate and related industries, leading to further economic deterioration. As the economy recovers, new jobs create increased demand for office space, and incomes rise, increasing the demand for retail space, so that rents increase and market values ultimately rise above replacement values. Development slowly starts again. Capital flows into real estate as investors seek outsized returns based on expectations of continued value appreciation and the cycle repeats itself. This is sometimes referred to as the 'hog-cycle'.

The global real estate market is driven by common economic and financial forces, and as globalisation progresses these forces become less disparate in their effect. Nevertheless, real estate is also a spatially differentiated product, and as such different markets will exhibit uncorrelated growth and decline as local conditions dictate. Hence, Asia has largely followed a different cycle to the USA and the UK, while continental Europe has exhibited a less marked boom and bust mentality.

To understand the global property cycle and its local variations, we need to disentangle the development, occupier and investment markets. These are expressed in the form of construction activity, rents, and cap rates, with these in turn driving capital values and returns.

As we suggested in Chapter 1, development activity (which we discuss in more detail in Chapter 10) appears to be highly pro-cyclical with GDP growth (rising and falling at the same time), but exhibits sharper rises and falls. There is a strong relationship between office development and changes in rents, which have also been strongly pro-cyclical with GDP growth. Some evidence of cyclicality in property cap rates may be discernible, but the long-run flatness of yields results in an extremely strong relationship between rental growth and capital value growth, and therefore with returns. All of this points to the importance of the economics of rent in understanding the 'property cycle'.

3.2 THE ECONOMICS OF RENT

3.2.1 Rent and Operational Profits

As of 2020, annual market rents per square foot for the Gherkin, a well-known office building in the City of London, were estimated at around £60–65. Industrial space in Oxford was leasing at £10, while you could rent a house in an atmospheric area of Oxford for around £25. A coffee shop in the West End of London went for £300/sq ft. What explains these prices?

Any student of economics will immediately think of supply and demand, which is of course a correct response. But real estate is a complex economic good – unlike loaves of bread, it is heterogeneous (every piece of real estate is a monopoly of the space it occupies), immoveable and lumpy, with a limited pool of buyers or occupiers. Its supply is limited by physical geography and national and local regulations. So supply and demand, while a useful starting point in any explanation of price, is an inadequate explanation of rent.

We need to begin with the idea that, unlike bread, the human demand for most real estate (residential accommodation apart) is a derived demand, related to its ability to produce another good or service. In the case of a coffee shop, the direct demand is for coffee, while the derived demand is for the space needed to produce and sell that coffee. It follows that to understand why someone would pay £300/sq ft p.a. to rent the coffee shop, we need to understand the economics of selling coffee.

Figure 3.1 is a simplified model of the economics of any operation. The profit earned by a business can in principle be split between the property owner and the business operator.

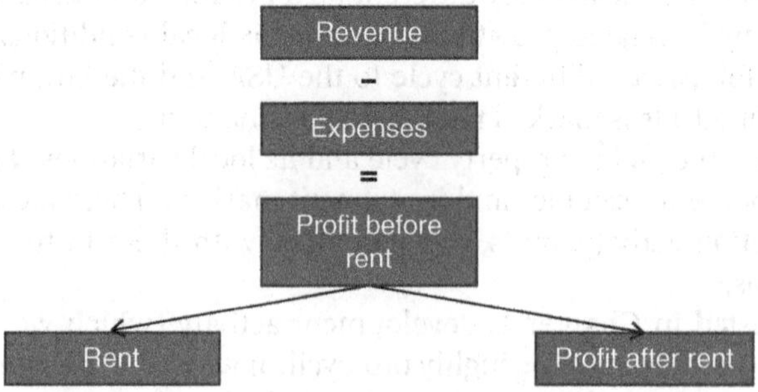

FIGURE 3.1 A real estate revenue model

First, we can identify the concept of gross profit before rent is paid as the difference between revenue and all costs except rent:

Revenue – costs (excluding rent) = gross profit including rent

Imagine a business which owns the freehold property interest of its operational premises – its profit is partly the rent it would earn if it terminated production and leased the space to someone else, and the residue is pure operational profit:

Gross profit including rent = operational profit + rent for land

The gross profit including rent is partly rent and partly operational profit, and the operational profit is a reward for any capital invested by the entrepreneur, his/her skill, and his/her labour:

Gross profit including rent = reward for entrepreneur's labour, return on capital invested, and rent for land

The profit is therefore available to be split between rent (to the landowner) and operational profit (to the operator). The proportion that goes to each will be a function of demand and supply of (i) suitable property and (ii) skilled operators.

Sometimes this distinction between rent and operational profit will be obscured. Imagine that your family has just completed the development and construction of an excellent hotel in India. Your sister is an accomplished hotel manager. She is happy to run the hotel, manage the staff, and take a salary and profit share. Your family's revenue model is driven by RevPAR (the average daily room rate multiplied by the occupancy rate) plus add-on services; its costs are employees, food, etc., and the resulting family profit is a combined reward for rent and operational profit.

If your sister is more entrepreneurial, she may suggest that she sets up a company to employ the staff and that she leases the hotel from the family for an agreed low rent plus a share of the hotel profits. As part of her costs she may pay to join a franchise to brand the hotel and receive support services. The resulting family profit is again a combined but now slightly lower and less risky reward for rent and operational profit.

If your sister is not trusted, your family might prefer to lease the hotel to Marriott International or Hilton Hotels and Resorts on a 20-year lease at an indexed rent and no profit share. The resulting family profit is simply a reward for rent, which it will wish to maximise, with all operational profit going to the hotel group, which will wish to minimise the rent. The resulting family profit is now lower and least risky.

The preferred arrangement will depend on the various parties' skills and appetite for risk. A property owner with no skill and no risk appetite will go for a lease to a well-known brand every time. It would also explain why innovative and skilful operators of space (such as Hilton and Marriott, but also co-working businesses such as WeWork and Spaces) might be able to establish valuable brands. This tension between passive low-risk rent collection and operational excellence is now being played out in the global space markets, and especially in New York and London.

3.2.2 Theories of Rent

The backdrop to this post-2007 world lies in the work of three famous economists, David Ricardo, Johann Heinrich von Thünen, and Irving Fisher. From Ricardo, we use the concept of land productivity; from von Thünen, we use the concept of location, with particular reference to transport costs; from Fisher, we use the concept of highest and best use.

Ricardo

- *Rent is that portion of the produce of the earth which is paid to the landlord for the use of the original and indestructible powers of the soil.*
- *Higher-quality land earns more rent.*
- *Rent is an unearned surplus because it derives not from skill, or effort, or capital, but from the original and indestructible powers of the soil.*

'*Rent is that portion of the produce of the earth which is paid to the landlord for the use of the original and indestructible powers of the soil*', according to Ricardo (1817). So, higher-quality land earns more rent: see Table 3.1. High-fertility soil earns more rent as long as we assume that farmers will work for a normal profit, and not be able to demand a share of the surplus revenue beyond this amount – in other words, the supply of skilled and available operators is sufficient to reduce their bargaining power to a normal or unremarkable level. Rent can then be seen as an unearned surplus because it derives not from skill, or effort, or capital, but from the original and indestructible powers of the soil. Where land is inherited, this becomes a political issue; where it is acquired for a fair price, that fair price can be very high.

If rent is that portion of the produce of the earth which is paid to the landlord for the use of the original and indestructible powers of the soil, how can we think of land for development? What are the 'original and indestructible powers of the soil' in central London? Clearly, there is no direct parallel, but we can develop an indirect analogy – the 'highest and best use' concept (see below).

TABLE 3.1 Ricardo's theory of rent

	High fertility	Medium fertility	Low fertility
Costs per acre			
Capital	£10	£10	£10
Labour	£50	£50	£50
Materials	£20	£20	£20
Normal profit	£10	£10	£10
Total	£90	£90	£90
Output per acre (tons)	20	15	10
Revenue per ton	£90	£90	£90
Revenue per acre	£180	£135	£90
Rent per acre	£90	£45	£0

von Thünen

- *The use which a piece of land is put to is a function of the cost of transport to market.*

No work on real estate is complete without a reference to the importance of location. At this point we must introduce von Thunen (1826) and his concentric ring model, which uses location – or, more precisely, transport costs – as a way of explaining land use patterns (Figure 3.2).

Table 3.2 illustrates how proximity to market, like productivity, produces an unearned surplus which falls into the lap of the landowner. Assuming fixed costs of $10 per acre, transport costs of $1 per ton per mile, variable costs of $5 per ton, and an output of two tons per acre, the rental value of the farmland closest to the town/market is much higher than the value of the land 10 miles away.

A similar idea but set in a more modern context is offered by Table 3.3. Imagine two coffee shops, one (A) located next to a station, one (B) located in a bookshop

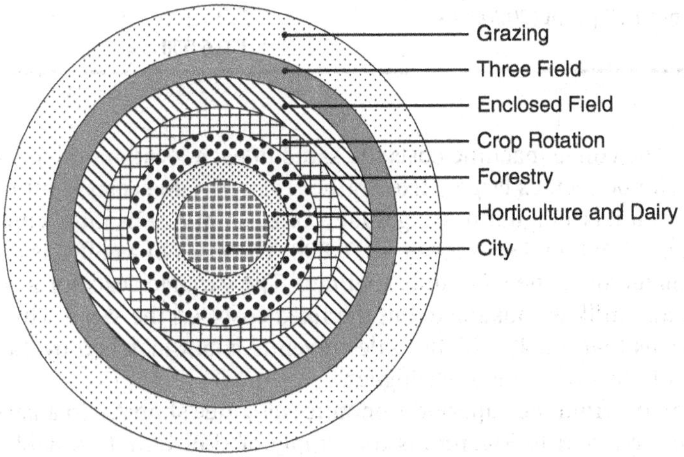

FIGURE 3.2 von Thünen's concentric rings
Source: von Thunen (1826).

TABLE 3.2 von Thünen and the value of proximity to market

Distance from market	1 mile	5 miles	10 miles
Fixed costs per ton	$10	$10	$10
Transport costs per ton per mile	$1	$5	$10
Variable costs per ton	$5	$5	$5
Total costs per ton	$16	$20	$25
Costs per acre	$32	$40	$50
Revenue per ton	$25	$25	$25
Revenue per acre	$50	$50	$50
Rent per acre	$18	$10	0

TABLE 3.3 The economics of the coffee shop

		Station (A)	Bookshop (B)
Costs			
	Equipment	£12,500	£12,500
	Energy	£20,000	£20,000
	Wages	£200,000	£200,000
Sales			
	Cups of coffee: '000 p.a.	250,000	170,000
	Price per cup	£2.50	£2.50
	Material cost per cup	£0.10	£0.10
Costs			
Fixed costs		£232,500	£232,500
Materials		£25,000	£17,000
Total costs		**£257,500**	**£249,500**
Sales revenue		**£625,000**	**£425,000**
Gross profit		*£367,500*	*£175,500*
Coffee shop 'normal' profit (20% costs)		£51,500	£49,900
Rent		**£316,000**	**£125,600**

100 m away. The coffee machine costs the same in each location; the energy costs are similar and can be seen as largely fixed rather than variable costs; staff wages are the same. Because it has a higher passing trade, coffee shop A sells more cups of coffee in a year – 250,000 – while B sells fewer – 170,000. The price of a coffee is the same, as is the cost of materials (coffee and milk) per cup. The variable costs for A are higher, as more coffee and milk is consumed, but the fixed costs are the same. This 'operational leverage' means that the 47% higher sales revenue is not matched by 3% higher total costs, and profit before rent is 109% higher.

Who benefits from the superior economics of coffee shop A? To answer this question, we need to revert to Ricardo. Is the supply of skilled and available coffee shop operators sufficient to reduce their bargaining power to a normal or unremarkable level? Or is the supply of coffee shops sufficient to reduce the bargaining power of landowners to a normal or unremarkable level? In London, New York, Sydney, or Hong Kong there are probably many more workers prepared to run a coffee shop for £50,000 (20% of running costs) than there are available suitable properties. If this is the case, almost all of the abnormal profit is economic rent, and falls to the landowner, as potential coffee shop managers and franchisees will bid up the rent until their reward hits the minimum required level of £50,000. Because A's location is closer to the market, sales are 47% higher, but the rental value of shop A is over 150% higher than the rent for B.

Proximity to market is a powerful determinant of land value and, together with the concept of agglomeration, a way of explaining urban land use patterns. Victorian cities in the UK were typically composed of a central marketplace (retail/office), surrounded by industrial and storage space which could service the retailing and be serviced by the office occupiers, in turn surrounded by housing, which was in turn surrounded by agricultural land. This setup allowed physical agglomeration of retailing, office users, and (most importantly) industrial activities, which needed physical proximity to reduce production costs and to allow the vertical integration of manufacturing activity.

By the early 21st century we could observe pressure to rearrange this hierarchy, as industrial production came to rely less on physical agglomeration (thanks largely to advances in communication technology) and transport links to the central business district (CBD) became much less important. Thanks to specialisation, manufacturing businesses now need to supply goods to national and international marketplaces via motorways/highways and airports situated outside the city core. Distribution space was also required to service these markets, but was now also increasingly required for last-mile delivery to residential areas.

Meanwhile, residential occupiers expressed a change in choice. Giving up the pleasant garden and long commute associated with suburban living, valuable knowledge workers have been pulled closer to the centre by an appreciation of the value of knowledge agglomeration and a high value placed on their own travelling time. Knowledge agglomeration economies are observable in technology, finance, media, health, and other industries (even real estate): human beings working in these fields know that they can become more valuable by exchanging knowledge at breakfast, lunch, and dinner, as well as throughout the working day. Hence areas like Brooklyn in New York and Shoreditch in London have seen the gradual conversion of warehouse space located next to the CBD into chic apartments for knowledge workers, while industrial and distribution activity has been pushed out to the suburbs.

Fisher

- *The highest and best use of a property will maximise land value or developer's profit.*
- *Generally, the use must be:*
  - *legally allowable*
    - *permitted by local zoning/planning*
    - *permitted by national regulation*
    - *permitted by covenants imposed by current or previous owners*
  - *physically possible/feasible/sustainable*
  - *financially optimal.*

In a free market for land, unencumbered by planning controls or other government interference, Irving Fisher suggested that productivity (and land values) will be maximised by property being put to its 'highest and best use'. Developers bidding for land will be able to pay more for the land if they have identified this highest and best use; existing owners will make most profit from putting land to that use.

The highest and best use in the real world must be legally allowable (permitted by local zoning/planning, permitted by national regulation, and not prohibited by covenants imposed by any current or previous owners); it must be physically possible/feasible (so that, for example, the foundations required for a high-rise building are capable of being sunk into load-bearing ground), and sustainable (so that the long-term operational costs are taken into account); and the use must be financially optimal, judged by reference to this idea of maximum productivity.

Knowledge agglomeration, plus the highest and best use concept, can be used to explain increasing density in cities and high-rise structures in the CBD (McCann and Gordon, 2005; Lizieri, 2009). The agglomeration effect decays much faster with distance in financial services than in manufacturing; ask any office worker in a large city how long is a reasonable time to travel between meetings, and we are guessing that the shorter is that time the more successful is that city. 20 minutes is a typical response in London; it is very different in Jakarta. Generally, knowledge workers will minimise travel times to and from work and between meetings in order to maximise knowledge agglomeration effects. Minimising travel time is then achieved either by large single-company campuses, such as we find in Silicon Valley; through the physical agglomeration of similar activities, such as the City of London; by identifying highly efficient public transport systems and locating next to a station; or by travelling vertically, which (subject to elevator quality) is generally quicker than lateral travel. Hence, we can expect to see centralised high-rise structures in knowledge economies, usually located at or close to public transport facilities.

3.2.3 Rent as the Price of Space

Commercial real estate can be seen as just one of many factors of production in a market economy. Human capital (labour) and physical capital (plant, machinery, information and communication technology) must be housed in space that is fit for purpose in order that occupiers (both corporates and the public sector) can generate economic output. The way in which we conceptualise the determination of rent uses the same language as the general economic theory of price: specifically, the price of productive space will be determined by the intersection of the supply and demand for space in any given period, but (as we have seen above) this idea needs to be qualified when we attempt to explain rents in the real world.

As with any other input to production, rent will be impacted by changes in productivity (both for suppliers and occupiers) and it will be subject to price 'stickiness'. Equally importantly, rent will be impacted by supply, demand, and productivity changes, but also by expectations of all three factors (and how far those expectations prove to be correct) on the part of the parties that determine price. These parties are the suppliers of space, the owners of space, and the occupiers of space.

At the most basic level, the price of occupying space is the rental value. As we will see in Chapter 6, for commercial property this will typically be expressed as a headline price per unit of space plus any incentives. Any service charge will be in addition to this.

The headline price is typically expressed in the local currency of the country, although there are important exceptions in emerging markets. The headline rent is supplemented by any incentives that the landlord might choose to give the tenant. These could take the form of rent-free periods, contributions to the fit-out, or paying the surrender fee on previously occupied space. The motive for giving incentives rather than reducing the headline rent is for the landlord to maintain evidence of higher headline rents and thereby protect the simple cap-rate valuation of the property (see Chapter 4).

In a static economy, the determinants of rent are the immediate supply and demand. A reduction in the space on the market relative to demand will result in a higher price demanded of occupiers and *vice versa*. In a market of perfect competition with no frictions, rents should in theory adjust to clear the market. However, even in this simple world, as soon as we introduce some industrial economics – the economics of corporate profitability – it soon becomes clear that even in a simple static economy prices will not necessarily adjust to clear the market.

For instance, in a world where supply was cut by an exogenous shock, but demand was static, in theory the rent would rise. However, as the use of space is merely one factor in production, the ability of the owner of space to raise the price will depend on the ability of the occupier to absorb that increased cost (either by reducing profit margins, cutting costs elsewhere in the production chain, or passing on the cost to their consumers). We explore the practical implications of this in Section 3.3.

In a dynamic, multi-period economy, the determinants of price become more complicated. For instance, if demand for space increases, the suppliers of space can respond to that need, thus mitigating the upward pressure on prices, and *vice versa*. In a perfectly competitive market, with no friction and no time lags, the rent would be maintained in perfect equilibrium by a constant response of supply to demand over the economic cycle. In this world, the only change in the rent level would come from structural changes in productivity (such as changes in the space used for each occupier, or technology-driven reductions in the cost of producing space).

3.2.4 Supply

As is the case with the provision of all production inputs, supply does not respond immediately, but with a lag. The lag will vary depending on three broad factors connected with the supply side.

First, how difficult is it to find and assemble sites and achieve planning permission in the local market? This will be impacted by physical restrictions (density of space use in the local built environment and the availability of greenfield land), as well as political attitudes towards development. The conventional wisdom is that planning authorities act to constrain supply, but planning authorities plan or zone for sufficient development to accommodate the expected growth of demand. If they did not do this, rents would rise as a proportion of GDP, which would be damaging to the economy.

Even in city centres where greenfield sites are scarce, planning authorities will over time allow an increase in the density of land use, and may allow the development of tall buildings. This has a similar effect to re-zoning greenfield sites for commercial use. Thus, in the medium term, planning authorities are unlikely to act to constrain supply, although in the short term they can certainly increase the lags involved in site assembly because of the protracted nature of achieving planning applications and the inefficiencies involved in forecasting changes in occupier demand.

The second reason for lags in the supply response is the ease of access (and thus speed) of securing development finance. As we will see in Chapter 10, real estate development is a risky business. It has therefore typically been the preserve of listed property companies, which can access capital through the equity market and are thus less subject to banks' famously cyclical willingness to take development risk onto their loan books.

The third factor is the degree of complexity of the physical construction of the building. It is clearly quicker to construct a relatively simple big-box retail or industrial warehouse on greenfield land than to construct a high-rise office block on a brownfield site or in a central business district. From conception to completion, the development process in such cases will often take 3–6 years, with the longer end of this range more common in Europe where the planning process can be particularly complex, with occasional exceptional examples taking 15–20 years (see Chapter 6).

Theoretically, the lag in the supply response time will only affect rent if the supplier has imperfectly predicted future demand. If suppliers had perfect foresight, rent levels would be unaffected by unintended over- or under-supply relative to actual demand. The rent impact is caused by the imperfect nature of predictions of supply and demand on the part of suppliers and occupiers.

The willingness of suppliers to build in anticipation of future demand will impact the behaviour of other suppliers, occupiers, government planning agencies, and commodity markets. In other words, the market for space is constantly being influenced by signals of intentions that create a multitude of potential paths for the price of productive space (rent), depending on how far market players interpret those signals. The feedback loops are endless.

The conventional 'hog-cycle' theory of high-amplitude rent cycles is thus too simplistic in a truly dynamic economy. The theory we stated at the start of this chapter was to the effect that as the demand for space increases, real estate developers will increase the supply for space. But, given the time to assemble the site, and to construct and market the building, the new space would be delivered some months after the increase in demand had initially been observed. (The time lag of construction is thus analogous to the gestation period for hogs in an agricultural economy.) By the time the space hits the market, demand may well have reduced (if it is related to a fluctuating economic cycle), resulting in oversupply. Rents will not therefore increase to the level anticipated by the developer. Developers observe this and reduce supply going forward, but this supply reduction meets the upswing in cyclical demand, leading to another cycle of supply. In other words, the 'hog-cycle' is one of perpetual imbalance between supply and demand because of the time lag between observing an increase in demand and producing the space to meet that demand.

Developers do not wait for demand to increase before switching on developments, but (if finance is available) they will try to anticipate those changes in demand. This results in three key characteristics of the supply of space.

First, there is a two-tier market. Those without capital constraints (e.g. sovereign wealth funds and listed property companies with healthy cash reserves) will be able to beat the hog-cycle by switching on supply before demand has manifested itself. Those with a constrained access to capital (such as small developers reliant on bank finance, which is of notoriously high amplitude and itself lags the demand cycle) will more likely be subject to the 'hog-cycle'.

Second, occupiers become actors in the supply of space by their ability to pre-lease space in exchange for concessionary rents and thereby to somewhat de-risk the process. This willingness to pre-lease itself becomes an important signal of future demand, and feeds back into the supply–demand decisions of other suppliers and occupiers.

A final consideration is the change in supply of different qualities of space. So far, we have focused on the provision of new space to meet increased demand. That process devalues existing space. New-built space becomes the new 'prime' or 'grade A', and sets the new top rent. Previously top-grade buildings in a particular location become 'grade B', altering their market value. Even without the provision of new space, the fact that the developer could provide space built to the newest specifications means that, as time passes, buildings that are grade A will depreciate and become grade B, C, and ultimately obsolete.

The process can be retarded by refurbishment and reconfiguration, but some incurable depreciation will remain, depending both on the complexity of the building (offices will depreciate faster than industrial sheds) and exogenous technological change (e.g. the need for cabling or new environmental standards).

Depreciation is a key factor in understanding property rents (see Chapter 1). As a result, even if the demand and supply for space was constant, the deteriorating quality of the built stock and incipient obsolescence would mean that the price of that space should fall. As price falls below replacement cost, developers will find it economically worthwhile to upgrade the space and thus secure the new top rent. In a frictionless economy, the worst-quality space would be redeveloped into the best-quality space in a constant flow, thus maintaining the average market rent at the same equilibrium level.

3.2.5 Demand

We now take a closer look at the economic determinants of demand, both cyclical and structural.

The Cyclical Demand for Space

Simply put, if rent is the price of productive space then demand for productive space is a derivative of the productive capacity of an economy. The productive capacity of the economy determines the trend rate of real economic growth. This is the level of growth at which the inputs of production (labour, space, and machinery) are used at full capacity barring frictional unemployment (of both labour and physical capital). An economy can work below capacity/trend if aggregate demand falls due to an economic shock such as a financial market crash or a fall-off in export markets. The result of the excess of supply relative to demand will be downward pressure on prices for all inputs to production, and real estate is no exception.

Similarly, an economy can work above capacity/trend if aggregate demand rises more quickly than the supply of the inputs of production. This will result in a rise in prices for all inputs. Typically, supply rises to meet demand, bringing growth back to trend. This could take the form of the inward migration of labour, or an increase in investment in plant, or – in the case of real estate – a boom in construction.

In other words, if the supply of space is constant, then an increase in the level of rent will be caused if the occupiers in that economy increase production at above-trend rates, thus generating extra demand for space. Conventionally, this can be conceptualised in terms of more firms hiring more people and therefore needing more space to house their activity. Accordingly, some argue that the true determinant of increased demand is the increase in the labour force. In that case, a sustained period of above-trend employment growth generates an increased demand for space. We see this particularly in the emerging market economies in parts of Asia, where an increase in labour participation in the market economy has coincided with the relocation of production into dense urban locations.

However, it is also possible to see an increase in the demand for space during a period of above-trend economic growth that is not associated with an increase in the rate of employment growth. For instance, a developed economy might see an increase in the growth rate as the result of a technological change that increases productivity for a sustained but short period (so that the trend growth is not structurally altered) while the economy upgrades itself to the new technology. This growth spurt would result in higher profit margins per unit of input of production. These might result in higher dividends for shareholders, or higher salaries for labour, or the willingness of the corporate occupier to demand and afford higher-quality space or more space per worker. Both of these factors would result in a rise in rents if the supply of space was constant.

The Structural Demand for Space

If the productive capacity of the economy determines the trend rate of real economic growth and thus the trend level of rental value growth, then it follows that any change in the trend rate of real economic growth will also result in a change in the trend demand for space. This can take two forms: first, a structural increase/decrease in trend economic growth; and second, a structural change in the composition of economic growth.

In the first case, the trend rate of growth will increase if the resources within that economy are increased. For instance, the labour force may increase through increased population growth, net immigration, extended working hours, extended working lives, or greater labour force participation. An example would be the increase in female labour force participation in the 1970s and 1980s in developed markets, or the transfer of Chinese workers from the non-market subsistence economy to the market economy in the 1990s and 2000s.

The resources in an economy can also be increased by investment in physical capital (plant and machinery), or by technological change in the provision of finance that results in an increase in investment capital. For example, the development of the mercantile system in the Netherlands and later Britain in the 17th century enabled the more efficient allocation of working capital to enterprises. Conversely, a decrease in trend growth rates will be caused by a reduction in resources, typically following a destructive land war or a change of government that mismanages resources. A terrible example of this is Zimbabwe in the 1990s and 2000s, and the UK Brexit issues of 2016–20 may also turn out to be a good example.

A marked change in the demand for space can also result if the composition of growth alters. This typically occurs through technological change such as the Fintech explosion of 2008–20, but could also occur when an economy joins a large free trade area (thus altering its ability to grow through exports). For instance, the European Union, the euro, and the demolition of the Berlin Wall have all changed the composition of economic – and rent – growth in Europe.

At the most crude level, a shift in economic growth from manufacturing to retail and business services will result in the obsolescence of heavy industrial sites and a shortage of retail/office space. This will have to be met by a combination of re-zoning, refurbishment, redevelopment, and urban regeneration. During this period of adjustment, which in the case of regeneration can take decades, one would expect to see market rental levels deviate substantially from trend.

Variations in Locational Demand by Use

There is another issue to consider. Occupiers' needs regarding location depend on the type of space they occupy.

Retailers are the most particular about where they are located, because the economics of retailing is essentially about relative competitive advantage between locations. Shoppers are attracted by the range and choice of goods on offer and, given a choice between two centres, they are likely to go to the location with the greatest choice of shops or goods. If the range of shops in the two places is roughly similar, then shoppers will be attracted to the one which is most accessible, has the most convenient car parking, has the most attractive, safest environment, or has more attractive facilities on offer. Accordingly, in most developed markets before the impact of online retailing was fully felt, retail rents grew in real terms because (once a retail centre has established a competitive advantage) it is hard to recreate a competing new centre or to expand the retailing offers of competing towns. Consequently, the capacity of the retailing industry nationally did not grow as fast as consumer expenditure growth in real terms, and rents grew in real terms in the long run. Figure 3.3 shows this for the major European markets, in which real rents rose at a trend rate of 3.5% over the 20 years between 1986 and 2006.

To illustrate the impact of technological change on structural demand, the rise of Amazon, Alibaba, and online retailing in general has had a major impact on retail rents. 17.5% of all retail sales were online by 2020; it was forecast that UK online retailing could take over 50% of all sales by 2030.

Given this, it is somewhat surprising that prime retail rents in the major cities continued to do well post-2006. This may be partly explained by lower online penetration

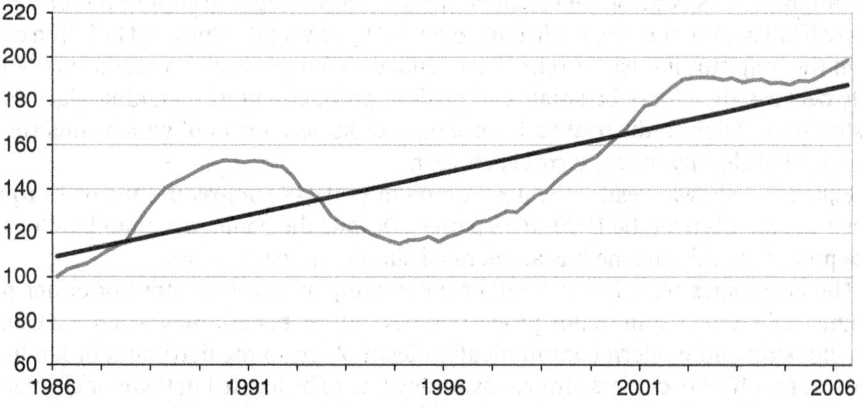

FIGURE 3.3 Real rent index, Europe retail markets 1986–2006
Source: CBRE Global Investors.

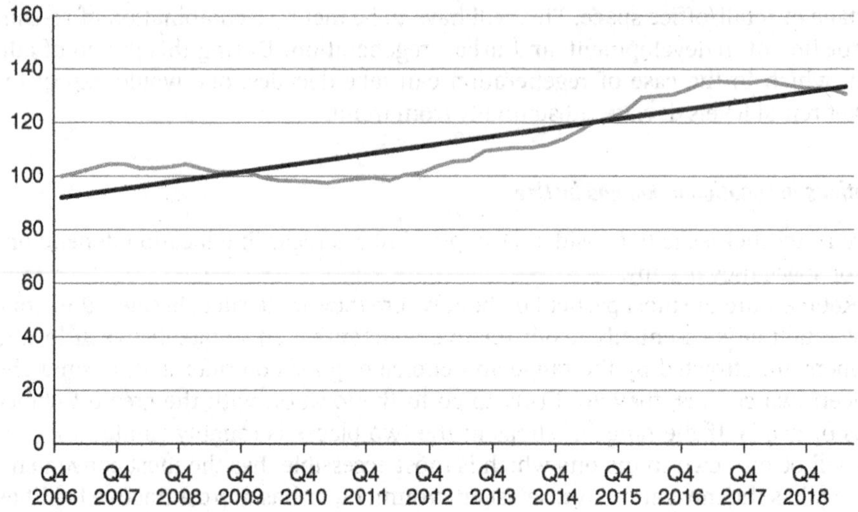

FIGURE 3.4 Real rent index, Europe retail markets 2006–18
Sources: PFR, CBRE.

in large parts of continental Europe; it may also be that prime locations act literally as shop windows for the broader online and off-line trade of the major retailers. Nevertheless, secondary retail rents have performed very poorly, and real retail rent growth in Europe 2007–18 (Figure 3.4) looks different from the 1986–2006 period, having slowed from 3.5% to 2.3%.

By contrast, light industrial businesses and warehousing occupiers have no great need to congregate together in one place, and have been relatively unfussy about where they locate, providing that road communications are satisfactory. Land is plentiful for these uses, so land values tend to be modest, placing an upper limit on the extent to which industrial rents can grow in the long run. (In the short run, rents can rise faster than building costs because there can be short-term shortages in supply, but ultimately rents will fall back to the economic rent governed by low land values and building costs.)

In the long run industrial rents have tended to fall modestly in real terms. This is partly because there may be small and gradual productivity gains taking place in the construction of light industrial and warehouse units, as a result of which construction costs may fall slightly in real terms each year.

Figure 3.5 shows negative real rent growth (−0.44%) across the major European industrial markets over the 1990–2018 period. Despite the boom in demand for logistics space post-2006, this decline has accelerated slightly in recent years.

The economics of offices are rather more complicated than those of either retail or industrial space. Of all major property types, offices benefit most from widespread car ownership and modern communication technology, to the detriment of landlords. 20 years ago, office occupiers almost invariably had to be located in town or city centres to be accessible to their customers and employees, but nowadays they have more freedom to locate on cheaper land on the edge or outside of town centres and the pattern of location is much more dispersed.

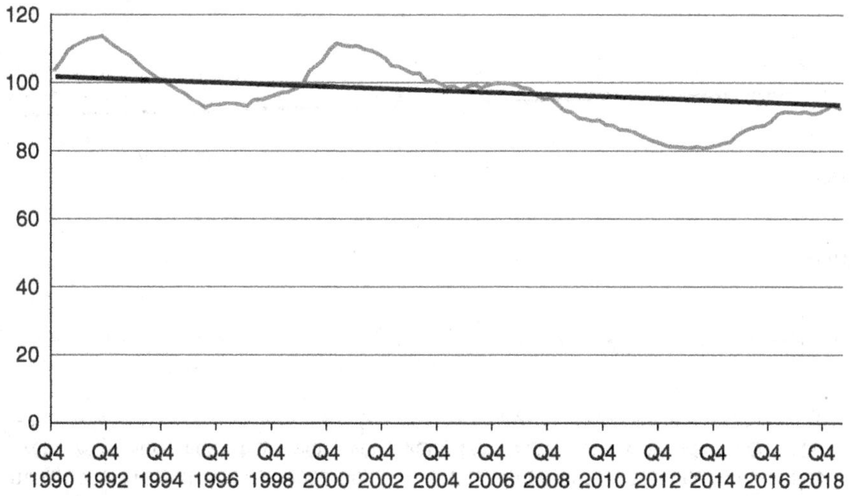

FIGURE 3.5 Real rent index, Europe industrial markets, 1990–2018
Sources: PFR, CBRE.

This freedom may, however, be curtailed by rising concerns about the environmental implications of car usage. In addition, the benefits of agglomeration seem to operate in financial and information hubs (McCann and Gordon, 2005; Lizieri, 2009), so that location has some real value for offices in places like Manhattan, Paris, Tokyo, Singapore, Hong Kong, and the City of London.

As a result of these complex forces, office rental values are gradually changing, sometimes governed by land values and sometimes governed by building costs as more plentiful, cheaper land becomes open for office occupation. Consequently, despite the service sector of the economy being by far the fastest growing in developed economies in real terms, real rental values for offices have been falling slightly in real terms over the past three decades.

Figure 3.6 shows the slightly negative trend of real rents in European office markets. This has averaged −0.3%.

3.2.6 The Relationship Between Rental Value and Rental Income

So far, we have discussed how economic factors impact the supply and demand for productive space, resulting in short-run deviations from long-run trend prices or open-market rents. However, a change in the open-market rental value of a property will not always translate directly into a change in the income receivable by the property owner. This is because changes between market rental values and income received are transmitted via the lease structure.

If we define the rental value of a property as the rent that could be charged if the unit were let in the open market on the valuation date, rental value growth between one period and another will reflect changes in the rental value of the property. By contrast, the income growth of a property between one period and another will reflect

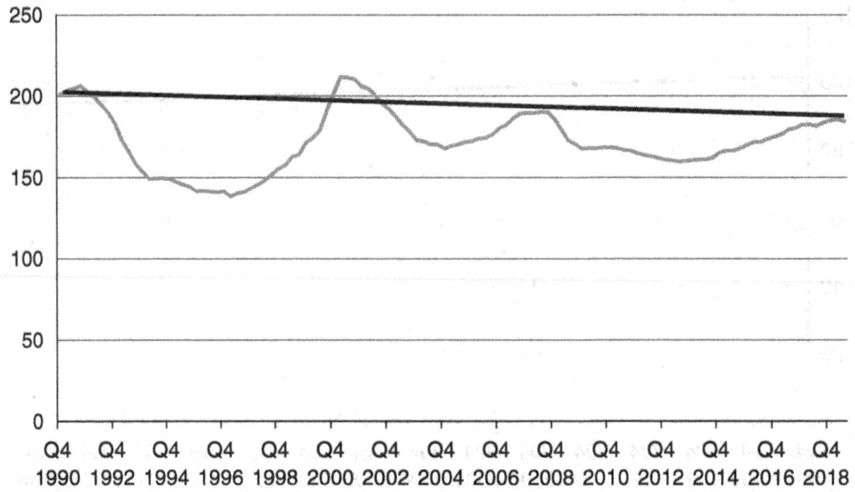

FIGURE 3.6 Real rent index, Europe office markets
Sources: PFR, CBRE.

the change in the net income receivable by the landlord. To understand how the two can vary depending on the structure of the property lease, imagine a world in which the landlord negotiates the contracted rental value of the property every single day in a perfectly competitive market for space. In this case, in order to secure the tenant, the landlord would have to adjust the contracted rent to the open-market rent in each negotiation, and estimated rental value growth would match income growth exactly.

Now imagine a situation at the other extreme, in which the landlord and tenant negotiate the contracted rent when the lease is signed, but make no provision for a further revision of that contracted rent for the duration of a very long lease (such as 42-year leases with a single review at year 21, as was common in the UK in the 1930s). In this case, unless open-market rental values are completely static for the lease duration, the rent passing will diverge from the open-market rent of the property, and income growth will not match rental value growth.

More typically, leases will fall between these two extremes. For longer leases common outside the USA and Asia, the contracted rent may be capable of being reset within the period of the lease, either with upward-only rent reviews (as in the UK or Ireland), or by means of indexation to a measure of inflation (as in much of mainland Europe). We explore the implications of this in Section 3.3.

A property where the rent passing is below the open-market rent is deemed 'reversionary' – at a lease expiry or renegotiation, the contracted rent should rise to the market level. Conversely, a property where the rent passing is higher than the open-market rent is 'over-rented', and a proportion of its income is at risk unless the market recovers before the point of the next lease break or renegotiation.

3.2.7 The Impact of Currency Movements on Rent

As we will see in Chapter 16, real estate investing becomes complicated when investors are committing capital raised in one currency to real estate investments denominated in another currency. The cost of hedging that currency risk – if it is possible – drives a wedge between the gross and net return to the investors over and above typical transaction and management fees. For investors hedging currency movements between major currency blocks, the costs are typically competed down, but for investors taking on exposure to less well-traded or long-lived currencies, the costs of hedging can prove uneconomic.

Partly for this reason, it is common practice for real estate products aimed at institutional investors in emerging market economies to have their cash flows and valuations denominated in a safe-haven currency rather than in the local currency. Practical examples of this in the European context are provided by assets in markets such as Poland which are typically priced in euros, both in terms of sale prices and rental values. This could be seen as insulating the property owner from fluctuations between the currency that is expensive to hedge (the złoty) and the currency that is either inexpensive to hedge or, ideally, the currency in which the capital was initially raised (say the euro). However, while the cash flows have been insulated at the first-order level, there is still a second-order currency risk that has not been alleviated.

Take the example of a prime Warsaw shopping centre, whose tenants are paying contracted rents denominated in Euros, but whose customers are paying for goods denominated in Złoty. Now imagine a situation in which global risk appetite sharply decreases (such as in the wake of the Lehman Brothers collapse, when the Złoty depreciated sharply against the Euro to reflect the former's emerging market risk). Even in the situation where Polish domestic demand was unaffected by the change in risk appetite and the Polish consumer spent the same Złoty amount in the shopping centre, the occupiers would find that their contracted rental payment in Euros was harder to meet.

Potentially, they could still meet the rental payment through accepting lower profit margins, but this is not sustainable in a competitive market economy. Either the increased cost has to be met by passing it on to the consumer (unlikely) or to the landlord. In other words, the fall in the złoty will result in downward pressure on market rents, despite the fact that they are denominated in euros and have supposedly been made immune to currency fluctuations. This is exactly what happened in Poland in 2009. Rents fells in Warsaw shopping centres, partly reflecting weaker domestic demand, but most obviously because the retailers' cash flows were vulnerable to the marked devaluation in the złoty.

3.2.8 Property Rents and Inflation

For many investors, particularly pension funds which have liabilities linked to future wage levels, the need to achieve gains in money value (in nominal terms) is of less concern than the need to achieve gains in the purchasing power of assets held (in real terms). The good news for real estate proponents is that both theory and data suggests a strong correlation between rents and inflation in the long run.

There are many academic references to this topic, with varying conclusions, but most find a stronger long-term connection between rents and inflation than between annual returns and annual inflation (see Chapter 1). The short-run relationship between return and inflation is weak, at best: cap rates are driven in the short term by other factors, and to expect to find a strong annual correlation between variables that are set and measured by such different processes is wildly optimistic. (We find negative correlations between inflation and capital growth in all major European markets, for example.)

Despite this, the connection between property rents and inflation can normally be expected to be strong. Theory would suggest a strong long-run correlation between rents and inflation. If we accept, following Ricardo, that rent is a surplus, then we can use an example of a single shopkeeper whose income and expenses before rent rise and fall in line with inflation, as follows:

$$\textit{Income} - \textit{expenses} = \textit{profit before rent}$$

$$\textit{Profit before rent} = \textit{rent} + \textit{profit}$$

$$\textit{Income}\,\$100 - \textit{expenses}\,\$75 = \textit{profit before rent}\,\$25$$

$$\textit{Profit before rent} = \textit{rent} + \textit{profit; if split}\ 50:50,\ \textit{rent} = \$12.50$$

If all prices double:

$$\textit{Income}\,\$200 - \textit{expenses}\,\$150 = \textit{profit before rent}\,\$50$$

$$\textit{Profit before rent} = \textit{rent} + \textit{profit; if split}\ 50:50,\ \textit{rent} = \$25$$

Using this simple theoretical example, prices double and rents double, showing a perfect correlation. To back up this theoretical relationship with empirical results prior to the impact of online retailing, we tested the relationship between net nominal rental growth and inflation in five European countries with good property data. Using IPD data for the longest available period in each country ending in 2008 and beginning in 1981 in the UK and in the early 1990s for most other markets, as summarised in Table 3.4, we found a simple average rental growth of 2.25% in the UK, Sweden,

TABLE 3.4 Nominal rent growth and inflation, European markets

	Nominal rental growth	Inflation
France	1.89%	1.98%
Germany	−0.28%	1.57%
Netherlands	2.45%	2.17%
Sweden	3.51%	1.34%
UK	3.68%	3.46%
Europe average	2.25%	2.10%

Sources: IPD, PFR.

Netherlands, Germany, and France, compared with inflation of 2.10%. Real rental growth has on average been close to zero, and the correlation between inflation and nominal rental growth across these markets has been 45%. (More up-to-date evidence suggests marginally negative real rent growth in the UK: see Chapter 4.)

3.3 FORECASTING RENTS

The link between inflation and rents is helpful in specifying models we may wish to use to forecast rents. Given the strength of this relationship, and given the way that inflation makes all values grow over time to produce meaningless correlations, it makes sense to forecast in real terms, and then to add inflation. We now examine rent forecasting, first at the national level, then at the local level.

3.3.1 Forecasting National Rents

Formal studies of the relationships between the economy and property prices were few until the collection and publication of property return data in the 1980s. Since then it has been established that the links between property and the economy are complex but strong. It is clear that there are persistent relationships which link the property market to the economy, and that these relationships can be found in rents, development activity, and cap rates. This section focuses on the links between the economy and property rents, and how these can be used to forecast the income from property investments based on forecasts of key economic variables.

The proven demand-side drivers of office rents include financial, business, and public-service sector employment. The retail drivers appear to be retail sales growth and unemployment expectations. For industrial estates and logistics, the best driver is likely to be wider GDP growth acting as a proxy for the flow of goods around the economy.

Model Types

There are, in simple terms, two ways to produce a forecasting model. The first involves establishing patterns or trends and assuming that these will continue into the future. We call this technical analysis. Examples include a linear trend (a constant increase over time) and cyclical trends. In effect, these use time as the explanatory or independent variable. All that is required to forecast the rent for a given year is the trend and the year for which the forecast is to be made. The problem with this type of model is that external factors do not change the forecast. No matter what happens, it is assumed that the pattern will persist. Thus, in property, the forecast for rents would be unchanged no matter what happens to the economy.

The second type of model is more plausible. It is one built from theory, that is, from a view of what causes changes in the dependent variable, and can be termed a causal model. Everything that follows in this chapter will concentrate on causal models.

A causal model links the variable being forecast (the dependent variable) with those which are used in the forecast (the independent variables). A good causal model has to be logical and plausible: that is, it should be based on theory. It should also be practical: the explanatory or independent variables must be forecastable, otherwise the model is an interesting historical model, but is of no value for forecasting.

Rent is the price paid by an occupier for the right to use the space for business activities. As we have seen, basic economics points to the factors which affect price, demand, and supply, and this is the basis of a plausible model. However, price, demand, and supply are all theoretical economic concepts. In order to use these concepts in practice, an empirical measure of each is required. This can be illustrated by using retail rents as an example.

Price

Price or rent has to be measured. At the national level, rent has no practical meaning unless it is measured as an index, that is, a weighted average of rents in different locations. This is similar to using the retail price index to measure price inflation.

In practice, issues such as the length of the time series, the robustness of the index construction, and the degree of sectoral and geographical disaggregation are most important in selecting an index to model. It is also possible to combine different sources, using better-quality data for the most recent period.

Demand

Rents are paid by occupiers, so plausible economics suggests that to understand rental levels it is necessary to understand what is happening to occupiers. It is not easy to measure demand directly, so a proxy variable is required. The demand by retailers for property and their ability to pay a price (the rent) depends on their profitability, which in turn depends on the demand for their goods from households. Other things being equal, increased demand should lead to higher profits and so to an ability to pay higher rents. Clearly, the ability of a retailer to pay rent will depend on factors other than the volume of sales, but this is likely to be the most important factor over time. The volume of sales can be measured either by retail sales or by consumer expenditure.

Supply

As the supply of retail space increases, other things being equal, price will fall. Supply is a relatively straightforward concept to measure, although data limitations create problems.

Poor-quality supply data is a standard problem in property research. Fortunately, this is less of a problem at the national level as supply increases relatively steadily, and the series is much less volatile than rents or the proxy variables used to represent demand and less influential in the forecast.

Supply and demand driving rent produces a plausible framework for a model based on economic theory. The next stage is to try to build the model. Building a forecasting model involves an examination of the historical data and the determination of the relationship between the dependent variable (rent) and the appropriate independent variables. In this case, this is the relationship between retail rents, consumer expenditure, and the supply of retail property. This requires the use of econometric techniques (regression analysis). The basic model as outlined above is

$$R = f(D, S)$$

In words, this means that rent is a function of demand and supply. A linear model would be

$$R = aD + bS + c$$

The historical data describing *R*, *D*, and *S* is available and is used to estimate the parameters *a*, *b*, and *c* which constitute the model, which can be used to forecast rent using forecasts of the explanatory or independent variables *D* and *S*. But a good forecasting model is not the same as a good historical model: a model is useless for forecasting if the independent variables cannot be forecasted.

Further, in using the estimated model for forecasting, it is essential to understand that it is assumed that the coefficients *a*, *b*, and *c* will remain constant in the future, in other words that the historical relationship will hold in the future. This is a basic assumption of any econometric model. In order to judge whether this is a reasonable assumption, it is possible to test statistically whether the model has been stable over time.

In practice, the regression is a best fit rather than a perfect fit. In the model, an error term *e* will be added:

$$R = aD + bS + ck + e$$

The first part of this equation is the deterministic part, in other words, the model. The second part, *e*, is the probabilistic part and defines the part of the resulting forecast which is unexplained by the model. *e* is known as the error term or the residual.

The line of best fit is calculated so that the sum of the squares of the residuals is minimised. It is important to test if the model fits the data well, that is, whether the part left unexplained (the residuals) is small. If the residuals are large, then the actual values are not very close to the values predicted by the model (the expected values), and the model is therefore of limited value.

There are further tests which a good econometric model must pass. In practice, adjustments are made to the basic model. First, inflation is removed by deflating the series. If this is not done it is possible to obtain a good 'fit' purely because there is inflation on both sides of the equation.

Second, the data is transformed into logs. (There are three reasons for this. To use regression techniques, the data has to be normally distributed and a log transformation has the effect of normalising the data; with a log transformation the coefficients can be interpreted as elasticities [sensitivities], which accords well with economic theory; and the difference in logs approximates to the rental growth rate, which makes the model easier to interpret.)

Third, as two trending variables will always have a high correlation, it is often appropriate to consider a model in differences, so that the change (rather than the level) in the independent variable leads to a change in the dependent variable.

Fourth, there may be a lagging effect. It may take some time for the change in the economy to work through to the property market. The model can be changed to include lagged values of the variables, as follows:

$$R = aR(-1) + bD + cS + dD(-1) + fS(-1) + c + e$$

Here, demand and supply are used as independent variables, both in the concurrent year and in the previous year.

Building the Model

There are two approaches to building a model. The first is to start with the broadest specification, that is, to include all the possible explanatory variables and a number of lags for each, then to eliminate those which are not significant in explaining the statistical relationships in the model. The second is to start with one explanatory variable, and to build up to a model by introducing new variables or lags.

To undertake the first, a long time series is needed, perhaps 40 years of quarterly data giving 160 observations. In property, the longest available rent series is usually less than 40 years, and is typically annual. Thus, even a broad specification of a property model has to be narrow. Fortunately, there is a school of thought in econometrics which believes that the best model is one which contains a small number of variables. This is because adding new variables always improves the statistical fit of the model but may stretch the limits of a plausible theory, and will be more difficult to build and use.

When building the model, it may become clear that one (or several) of the observations of the dependent variable does not fit the model, while the others fit well. It may be that there is a measurement problem in the dataset or that in one particular year a variable not included in the model is important. In such a case, it may be appropriate to estimate the model without the observation. This is done by introducing a dummy variable. This has the effect of removing the outlying point and so preventing it from being used in the estimation of the model. The use of a dummy variable requires a clear justification: it should not be used to improve a fundamentally poor model, but can often be used to deal with a shock of some sort or a data deficiency.

Broad specification models which include all the possible explanatory variables and lags may be better at explaining the past behaviour of a variable. This type of approach is flawed for forecasting, however, as it is difficult to estimate or forecast the value of a large number of independent variables.

An Historical Model

The following is an example of an historical model (University of Aberdeen and IPD, 1994). It uses the UK IPD rent index as the dependent variable. Other forms of model can be produced using the same data, and choosing the best is a matter of both formal statistical tests and judgement based on an understanding of the operation of the property market:

$$\begin{aligned} Rent &= 0.88 \times Rent(-1) \\ &-0.28 \times Rent(-2) \\ &+1.48 \times Consumer\ expenditure \\ &-2.36 \times Floorspace(-2) \\ &-0.09 \times Construction\ starts(-2) \\ &-0.10 \times Interest\ rate(-1) \\ &-4.88 \end{aligned}$$

Note: the model is specified in log form and real terms.

A Forecasting Model

The following is a (somewhat old, but nonetheless illustrative) model of the UK retail market. It explains or forecasts rent as the dependent variable, using consumer expenditure as the demand proxy and an extrapolated supply series based on government floorspace statistics. These are the main independent variables. The model also includes the rent level (*Rent* (−1)) in the previous year. It is clearly more parsimonious (economical) than the historical model:

$$\begin{aligned} Rent &= 0.5 \times Rent(-1) \\ &+2.7 \times Consumer\ expenditure \\ &-3.0 \times Floorspace \\ &-17.0 \end{aligned}$$

Note: the model is specified in log form and real terms.

This model passed a wide range of statistical tests, and at the time it was developed it had an excellent forecasting capability.

3.3.2 Forecasting at the Local Level

Local market forecasts are important for two related reasons. First, the sector/city is more useful as a segment for analysis than the sector/region, because the city is a more easily defined economic unit than the region. Second, regardless of the preferred portfolio categories, the management of real portfolios requires the selection of buildings to buy, sell, refurbish, or redevelop, and these require forecasts at the micro level.

The production of reliable procedures to forecast local markets is, therefore, one of the main challenges facing the property investment market. It requires a substantial amount of work, as a major investor might want views on a large number of centres.

Formal modelling at the local level is difficult. Two types of problems arise: conceptual and modelling problems, and data issues.

Conceptual and Modelling Problems

1. The definition of the appropriate local market area for which a forecast is to be produced is a problem. The local market area appropriate to one sector is unlikely to be that appropriate for another. The issue has been considered extensively in retail market modelling, but no easy solution has been credibly suggested, and the issue has received much less attention in relation to the other sectors.
2. Linked to the issue of defining local market areas is the problem that the market areas for proximate centres will overlap, as the centres are in competition.
3. In a local market where rental evidence has been based on rent reviews rather than on open-market transactions, or is smoothed or 'sticky' for some other reason, rental pressure may arise. This can be positive or negative; it refers to the difference between the provable rent and the open-market rent. When an open-market letting takes place, it is possible for the provable rent to change substantially without a change in the balance of supply and demand. There is a need, therefore, to distinguish between changes needed to reach the 'correct' rent and changes in the correct rent.
4. At the local level, many factors could potentially have an important effect on rent but cannot be formally modelled. These 'soft' variables include factors such as local business confidence, changes to planning policy on city centre car parking, and infrastructure developments.

Data Issues

1. Data for the demand variables used at the national and regional levels is generally not available at the city level. City-level retail sales, consumer expenditure data, or output data are usually unavailable. It is possible, however, to use population and employment as the basis for constructing explanatory variables. Population is linked to retail sales and employment is linked to output, and so to rents in the office and industrial sectors.
2. Whereas supply is relatively stable at the national and regional levels and so is of lesser importance in modelling, it is crucially important at the local level. A new development can dramatically change the amount of shopping space, and can have a dramatic impact on rents, so supply at the local level must be closely monitored. Reliable data describing the supply pipeline is difficult to obtain and translate into a meaningful forecast of supply, but research and information services provided at the building and tenancy level promise a solution to this problem.
3. Rent data is not available for such a wide range of centres with a sufficiently long time series and of sufficient quality to give much confidence in the result of any formal modelling.

The result of these factors is that it is probably impossible to build a meaningful econometric model from local data. One possible approach is to use the coefficients calculated at the national level to forecast the local market, as in the absence of contrary evidence it is reasonable to conclude that the same basic relationships should hold. It is, in any case, essential than a local forecast should be constrained by a framework of national forecasts. This 'top-down' approach to local forecasting can produce sensible figures. Another approach is to scrape so-called 'big data' from the ever-increasing supply of online sites, and to build local economic models from such data as mobile phone-generated activity data, Airbnb occupancy and room rates, Trip Advisor feedback, and so on. We expect to see more and more of this type of data science application.

3.4 CONCLUSION

To understand the global property cycle, we need to disentangle the development, occupier, and investment markets. The occupier markets are key, driving rents, which in turn will impact heavily on investment cash flows and returns. There may be some evidence of cyclicality in property cap rates, but there is an extremely strong relationship between rental growth and capital value growth, and therefore with returns, pointing to the importance of rent in understanding the cycle.

We began with the idea that, unlike bread, the human demand for most real estate (residential accommodation apart) is a derived demand, related to its ability to produce another good or service. It follows that to understand why someone would pay £300/sq ft p.a. to rent the coffee shop, we need to understand the economics of selling coffee, and to determine how much of the coffee shop profits will go to the landowner, in the form of rent. To understand this, we summarised the work of three famous economists, David Ricardo, Johann Heinrich von Thünen, and Irving Fisher. From Ricardo, we used the concept of land productivity; from von Thünen, we used the concept of location, with particular reference to transport costs; from Fisher, we used the concept of highest and best use.

The formation of rent in the market is determined by the intersection of the supply of, and demand for, space in any given period. But rent will be subject to institutional factors, including price 'stickiness'. Rent will be impacted not just by actual levels of supply, demand, and productivity change, but also by expectations of all three factors by the owners and occupiers of space.

A change in the open market rental value of a property will not always translate directly into a change in the income receivable by the property owner, because changes between market rental values and income received are transmitted via the lease structure. There are also several practical issues that impact on the translation of economic factors into the setting of rental values and the translation of those rental values into property income.

However, both theory and empirical evidence suggest a strong long-run correlation between rents and inflation. The link between inflation and rents is helpful in specifying models used to forecast rents. Formal rent forecasting at the national level using econometric methods can be effective and insightful; it is much harder to build a meaningful econometric model from local data.

After this discussion of the occupier market and rent, we now move on to examine the second key market – the capital market – and how cap rates can be explained. Together, cap rates and rent will enable us to understand how real estate returns are delivered, and this is the focus of Chapter 4.

CHAPTER 4

Asset Pricing, Portfolio Theory, and Real Estate

4.1 RISK, RETURN, AND PORTFOLIO THEORY

4.1.1 Introduction

In this chapter, we set out a simple process which real estate investors and fund managers can use to identify attractive markets and properties, and to decide which markets and assets should be sold. This pricing model can be applied at all levels: asset classes, countries, market sectors, and possibly for individual assets. However, it is a simplified approach used primarily in developing a strategy, and is not a substitute for the type of detailed cash flow analysis which is necessary to accurately set out the prospective returns available from a property asset taking account of the lease contract, leverage, tax, and costs. This type of cash flow analysis is dealt with fully in Part II of this book.

For the more professional and larger-scale investor and fund manager, buying and selling properties involves a series of processes. First, the ideal portfolio structure should be determined. Once this target structure is in place, the manager should identify which market sub-segments are attractively priced and should be targeted. Next, stock should be sourced from the market. Appraisals of the available properties should be undertaken. In addition, the impact of proposed purchases on portfolio risk and return should be modelled. In the acquisition process, negotiation skills should be employed, and 'due diligence' should be carried out. Due diligence describes the legal, physical, and planning enquiries and explorations prior to exchange of contracts and completion that are necessitated by the unique nature of the asset type.

Before this process can begin, how should investors decide that a market, a sector, or a property is attractively or unattractively priced?

4.1.2 Risk and Return

If investors were able to know only one thing about an investment, they would want to know the expected return. If they could have one additional piece of information, it would be the probability of failing to make that return, or downside risk. Risk is a measure of the expected return not being achieved, usually measured as the standard deviation of expected return. This approach to risk and return is sometimes called mean-variance analysis, where the mean (expected) return is the return measure and the variance is the risk measure. Sometimes, the variance is divided by the mean to produce the 'coefficient of variation'; its reciprocal (return/risk) is more intuitively appealing.

For most investment professionals, including the actuary working with a pension fund or life office, the measurement of risk rests on the concept of volatility rather than the layman's concept of the probability of a potential loss. Volatility is the fluctuation of returns around an average return. For example, one property (A) might show a 10% return each year for 5 years (see Table 4.1). Over the 5-year period, it would have shown 0% volatility as the actual return in each year was the same as the average return. If another property (B) had shown a positive return of 20% for the first 2 years, followed by a negative return of 40% in the third year and two further years of a positive return of 25%, it would have produced the same simple average return of 10% p.a. However, the volatility in returns would have been much greater. This is usually measured in units of standard deviation. This is a measure of the average distance of each observation or data item from the mean of that data.

Two other forms of risk are worth mentioning. These are competitor risk (for a fund manager, the risk of losing market share to competitors) and liability risk (for a pension or insurance fund, the risk of being unable to meet liabilities). These are both concerned with the range of expected returns in relation to something else, rather than that range in an absolute sense.

In estimating the variance or standard deviation of expected returns, historical data is often used to calculate both the expected return and the risk measure, and it is thus assumed that the past gives a good indication of the future and the range of historical returns gives a good indication of the range of possible returns for any future period. But it is important to note that the analysis should be based on expectations of return and risk: the use of historical data as a proxy is merely a convenience.

TABLE 4.1 Return and volatility

Year	Property A	Property B
1	10%	20%
2	10%	20%
3	10%	–40%
4	10%	25%
5	10%	25%
Average return	10%	10%
Standard deviation	0.00	28.06

4.1.3 Portfolio Theory

The basic concept of portfolio risk is well known: *don't put all your eggs in one basket.* Diversification is the central concept of portfolio risk and of Markowitz's Modern Portfolio Theory (MPT), developed for the equities market. As most investors hold portfolios of assets rather than one asset, the risk and return of individual assets are important only in as far as they impact the portfolio risk and return.

When assets are combined in a portfolio, the expected return of a portfolio is the weighted average of the expected returns of the component assets. However, unless the asset returns are perfectly correlated, the risk is not the weighted average: it is determined by the covariance structure of the component asset returns. The way in which asset returns co-vary is central to portfolio risk: it provides diversification opportunities.

If w_A and w_B are the weights (proportions) invested in assets A and B, E is the expected return, P is the portfolio, S^2 is the variance and ρ is the correlation coefficient:

$$w_A + w_B = 1$$

and

$$E(P) = w_A E(A) + w_B E(B)$$

$$S^2(P) = w_A^2 S^2(A) + w_B^2 S^2(B) + 2w_A w_B S(A) S(B) \rho AB$$

Consider two assets with the same expected returns. Consider first the case where their returns always move up and down together (positive correlation). The expression 'portfolio risk' reaches a maximum value. Now consider the case where, if the return on one falls, the return on the other always rises and vice versa (negative correlation). The final term has a negative value and the portfolio risk reaches a minimum value; more interestingly, the risk of the portfolio will be lower than the average risk of the two constituent assets. In such a case:

$$S^2(P) = w_A^2 S^2(A) + w_B^2 S^2(B) - 2w_A w_B S(A) S(B) \rho AB$$

MPT encourages the selection of assets which have low or negative correlation. The objective of MPT is either, for a given level of risk, to build a portfolio structure which will achieve the maximum return or, for a given return, to achieve minimum risk. The output of an optimisation analysis (see Chapter 1, and in particular Section 1.3.11) is the proportion of funds to be invested in each asset, and a measure of the expected return and the risk.

The Efficient Frontier

As stated above, the risk of a portfolio is not simply the weighted average of the risk of the component assets; it is also determined by the covariance structure of the component assets. The counter-intuitive result is that the risk of the portfolio can be lower than the average risk of the constituent assets. In addition, adding a risky (yet negatively correlated) asset to a portfolio can reduce portfolio risk.

The output of an optimisation analysis is the proportion of funds to be invested in each asset, but this will depend on the risk appetite of the investor. A high-risk portfolio will offer higher returns and a low-risk portfolio will offer lower returns. For any given return level, an optimal portfolio (one with the lowest risk for that return) can be found. There will be combinations of assets which are not optimal, meaning that by using different asset combinations it is possible to get extra return for the same risk or to have less risk for the same return. By eliminating the sub-optimal points, it is possible to construct the *efficient frontier*. Which combination of risk and return to choose along the efficient frontier depends on the investor's trade-off (or the subjective indifference function) between risk and return.

The choice of the optimum portfolio from the efficient portfolios will depend on this trade-off, which any particular investor makes between return and risk. Different investors make different trade-offs: some are less risk averse than others and so are prepared to bear additional risk for a smaller additional return.

4.1.4 Risk and Competitors

For competitor risk, the appropriate risk measure is not absolute volatility but relative volatility. If all competitors have the same portfolio, which has a high absolute risk measure, there is no competitor risk. A fund will be compared with its competitors, so if they all take risks and lose, but the fund loses less, it will be compared favourably to its peer group. However, if a fund does not take the same risk as its competitors, but constructs a lower-risk portfolio, and its competitors obtain a higher return (that is, the risk pays off), it may lose business to them. This is a particularly difficult problem, as fund managers can lose business on the basis of one year's bad results rather than the longer-term average return they are asked to deliver.

Tracking the performance of competitors is known as benchmarking. It is a variant on indexing. Rather than taking the market as a whole as an index, a specified set of competitors is used instead. The formal risk measure is the variance or standard deviation of the expected return relative to the market average or specified competitors. This is known as the *tracking error*.

Tracking error consists of two components. The first is derived from the structure of the portfolio relative to competitors (if your portfolio has a structure different from your competitors, there is a risk of underperformance) and the second is derived from the number of buildings in the portfolio and the relative value of these. This is because it is possible to have a structure for the portfolio which is identical to the market but includes a small number of properties. If only a few buildings are in the portfolio, there is a risk that poor performance for one property will have an adverse effect on the total portfolio performance. This is examined in more detail in Chapter 17.

The tracking error can be used to estimate the range of possible returns relative to the benchmark or market. The probability of outperforming can then be calculated.

4.1.5 Risk and Liabilities

A property investment portfolio might have a low tracking error against a benchmark; it may also have a low standard deviation of expected return. But if it delivers a very low income, when the investor is carrying a large debt secured on the constituent assets, there is a risk that the rental income or net operating income (NOI) will not cover the interest charge, leading to default and triggering punitive action by the lender. The risk of an investment portfolio must also be judged, therefore, by reference to liabilities.

A consideration of liabilities leads to a consideration of *duration*. Duration is calculated as the average time to the receipt of each cash flow weighted by the present value of each cash flow. It is a measure of the responsiveness of the present value of liabilities (or assets) to changes in the discount rate. To minimise this form of risk (not being able to meet liabilities), it is necessary to match the duration of liabilities to the duration of assets. Thus, if the interest rate changes, the present values of both assets and liabilities change in the same way.

This adds another dimension to risk. An immature pension fund would require high-duration assets, such as equities, which are risky in conventional terms. Real estate duration is rarely estimated (but see, for example, Van der Spek and Hoorenman, 2007) and results vary.

4.1.6 Property Portfolio Management in Practice

Until the 1980s, property portfolios tended to be seen as simple aggregations of individual buildings. There was little reference to portfolio theory in practice, and little was made of the linkages between the property market and the macro-economy or the capital markets. This has changed, and with it the emphasis has shifted from property and asset management to portfolio and fund management. At the same time, changes in the structure of the industry and pressures to outsource have created new professional service sectors, specifically fund managers and asset managers. In the industry, many different but relevant management terms are used, which we now define.

Fund management is the administration of a pool of capital, with the intention of investing the majority or all of the capital in a group of assets. Hence a property fund may have some cash, or utilise gearing.

Portfolio management is the administration of the property assets within the fund, not including the cash or gearing, but taking account of the structure of the portfolio as a whole. All or part of this function could be subcontracted by a fund manager to a property specialist. Sales and purchases might be left to the discretion of the portfolio manager (a discretionary appointment) subject to net inflows or outflows of cash imposed by the fund manager or client. More commonly, however, the property fund manager will act as the portfolio manager.

Asset management is the administration of individual property assets, not taking account of the structure of the portfolio as a whole, but with the objective of maximising the financial performance of each property asset for the client. This function is likely to be retained by a fund or portfolio manager, but might be subcontracted by a fund manager to a joint venture partner who is a specialist in the relevant property type or location. If sales and purchases require the approval of the fund manager, the appointment might be said to be advisory rather than discretionary.

Property management is the administration of the property assets, with the objective of offering satisfaction to the end user (the occupier or customer), not necessarily with the objective of maximising financial performance for the client beyond the efficient and prompt collection and payment of rent and service charges. This distinction explains the rising popularity of *facilities management*, a wholly and more comprehensive user-oriented approach to property management, sometimes called corporate real estate management. The rise of co-working and the concept of space as a service has begun to elevate the property or facilities manager to a business-critical position – which is as it should be, because (despite this being disguised by long leases under which the tenant takes responsibility for maintenance and management) the delivery of satisfactory service to a tenant should be central to the success of a property investor.

Our approach to portfolio management starts from three basic propositions. First, investment strategies are like business plans. Investment strategies should be driven by a clearly stated and understood objective, they should take account of the fund's strengths, weaknesses, opportunities, and threats (or constraints), and they should be reviewed using a form of performance appraisal.

Second, there are three ways to achieve performance objectives. These are: (i) managing portfolio structure; (ii) positive stock selection and the successful negotiation of transactions; and (iii) active management of the properties within the portfolio.

Third, the necessary technology includes three sets of models, all of which can add value. These are: (i) models used to produce forecasts or, if forecasts are mistrusted, estimates of fair value which operate at all levels for the market down to the individual building; and (ii) portfolio models, used to control risk and assist in the optimisation of portfolio planning. These are discussed in more detail in Section 4.5.

The Investment Strategy

In the objective statement, the manager needs to state what he is trying to achieve and by when. This should include a statement of required return but also of the risk to be tolerated and expected within a given timescale. Return and risk are often, but not always (see Chapter 17) stated relative to a benchmark. This process is analogous to the agreement of a mission statement.

A portfolio analysis focused on strengths, weaknesses, and constraints is a statement of where the fund is positioned and the action which is needed to be able to establish realistic objectives. Stock characteristics, market conditions, expected flows of cash, and staffing can be regarded as constraints on the fund achieving its objectives.

The strategy statement is the core of the business plan. How is the objective to be achieved, and by when?

Finally, the performance appraisal answers some highly pertinent questions. How well did we do? Did we achieve the objective? Are there any other standards of performance we should make reference to?

It needs to be recognised that more than one set of interests needs to be considered when adopting a mission and writing a business plan. The organisation may have several, sometimes conflicting, objectives. In an investment management organisation, these are all likely to relate to risk and return, a common means of measuring which are the mean and variance of annual total return. Mean-variance analysis, albeit simplistic in the context of a large and complex organisation, is useful because it is a commonly accepted theoretical foundation for investment and finance: it reflects the motivations of some actors in the business, for example some fund trustees and some research economists; and it is most easily referenced in finance and investment publications and commonly taught. However, it is not a useful way of defining the mission of most fund management organisations. Funds or managers will be concerned with other things.

The practical issues facing most investors are to do with income and capital values relative to liabilities. This concentrates the mind on solvency, which requires the advice of actuaries. Will the asset income stream be sufficient to pay the annual liabilities of the insurance or pension fund?

The practical issues facing most investment managers are to do with short-term profit and long-term enterprise value. This concentrates the outlook on revenues, costs, and market share. As in any business, managers will be concerned with competitors and business risk. This leads to the pinpointing of return relative to a competitor benchmark. This issue is dealt with in more detail in Chapter 17.

It is within this portfolio context that decisions to buy and sell buildings are made, and the precise tool used is an appraisal model.

4.2 A PROPERTY APPRAISAL MODEL

4.2.1 Introduction: The Excess Return

A key part of the due diligence process is the appraisal. Appraisal is a process used to estimate the underlying investment worth of an asset to a single purchaser. It can be contrasted with what in real estate circles is commonly called valuation, which (narrowly defined) means an estimate of the most likely selling price. This section establishes a basic framework for the estimation of the value or worth of an asset and how it can be compared to market price for the purpose of aiding buy and sell decisions.

The key objective of the portfolio construction process described above and in Chapter 15 is to create a structure for the portfolio that is most likely to achieve the investors' return and risk objectives. This would normally be by reference to market segment, such as regional location and sector type (for example, City of London offices). The identification of attractive market subsectors, cities, and districts of cities, or of market themes likely to be associated with excess returns, is the essence of the strategic appraisal process. It is normally the case that an investor will have a target rate of return for an asset and will use a discounted cash flow approach to judge whether a property is likely to achieve that target.

Individually assessed target returns fail to take account of the impact of the transaction on the portfolio, either in terms of its risk or indeed of the return impact. This needs to be the subject of a separate exercise, which is dealt with in Section 4.6 below.

The property appraisal process used in practice is reasonably common across markets (see Chapter 5). The modern investor will typically buy in or undertake research aimed at enabling a view to be formed of rent growth and movements in cap rates, often but confusingly called yields, usually derived from a view of the economy and other capital markets. Computer-based appraisal models will usually be fed with projected rents and cap rates. The investor's view of the value of the asset will typically be arrived at by using discounted cash flow, with internal rate of return (IRR) providing the typical buying rule, despite a clear view among academics that net present value (NPV) produces a superior decision. (It is not surprising that a total return or IRR measure is used in appraisals when the manager's objective is framed in terms of a total return, but the IRR rule may produce sub-optimal decisions. However, NPV can also be criticised by those familiar with option pricing techniques, and investors may be more interested in their return on equity after taxes and fees: see Chapters 9 and 17.)

The value of an investment is the present value of its expected income stream discounted at a rate which reflects its risk. However, any estimate of value depends on the views of the investor making the estimates. Price may differ from value:

(a) if the vendor has to make a forced sale for any reason;
(b) if the investor is better able to use the available information; or
(c) if the investor has different views.

For more about this, see Chapter 5.

4.2.2 The Cap Rate or Initial Yield – A Simple Price Indicator

Different property types and segments have differing qualities which are translated into the price paid for a standard unit. It is sometimes useful to describe property prices in terms of a single unit price per acre, hectare, square metre, or square foot; more often, prices are described in terms of what is commonly called *initial yield* but should be known as *cap rate*. Initial yield is an output (what an investor receives after a price is agreed and rent is received). Cap rate is an input (a divisor which when applied to rent drives price).

In theory, a *multiplier* applied to the unit of rent could more usefully be used as a unit of comparison. For example, a retail property leased for $100,000 a year and which sells for $2 million shows a multiplier of 20. This property would quite rightly be regarded as superior to one whose multiplier was 12.5.

However, the reciprocal of the multiplier (100% divided by the multiplier) is the common measure used. Hence a retail property leased for $100,000 a year which sells for $2 million shows a multiplier of 20 and a yield of 5%; an industrial property leased for $100,000 a year which sells for $1.25 million shows a lower multiplier of 12.5 and conversely a higher yield of 8%. The superior property has the lower yield, which is very confusing for many. Value is given by rent divided by cap rate.

UK *Terminology*

In the UK and other related markets, the yield is sometimes known as the initial yield, or the all-risks yield. This is defined as the net rental income divided by the current value or purchase price. There are similarities in other investment markets: these include interest-only yield, running yield, income yield, flat yield, and dividend yield.

Other yield terms in common use may serve to confuse the non-UK reader. UK idiosyncrasies in this area are explained by the unique nature of the typical UK lease for prime or high-quality property. These are long, for say 10 years, with rents fixed between rent reviews usually of 5 years duration, and with upward-only reviews to market rents. This means that changes in market rents will be expressed in differences, sometimes very big differences, between rents paid under the lease (contract rents) and market rents (sometimes called estimated rental value, or ERV).

When market rents have risen over time, market rents are likely to exceed contract rents. The asset is then 'reversionary', meaning that an income uplift can be expected at the next rent review or lease end.

When market rents have fallen over time, contract rents are likely to exceed market rents, and the excess or 'over-rented' component of the cash flow will fall away at the lease end (but not at the rent review). The upward-only rent review mechanism means that over-renting will often be a longer-lasting feature of property cash flows than a reversionary income pattern.

The *yield on reversion* is defined as the current net rental value divided by the current value or purchase price. The *equivalent yield* (also used in Australia) is the weighted average of the initial yield and the yield on reversion. It can be defined as the IRR that would be delivered assuming no change in rental value, but this has created difficulties in the case of over-rented properties. As in the case of all IRRs, the solution is found by trial and error. *Reversionary potential* is the net rental income divided by the current net rental value or vice versa.

US Terminology

For a US real estate specialist, the cap rate is used to discount a single period's cash flow, the relevant cash flow being the NOI that is expected to be earned in the first year. The formula for determining the market value of a property is still rent divided by cap rate, but more formally:

$$MV_0 = NOI_1 / cr_0$$

where MV_0 is the market value of the property at time zero, NOI_1 is a measure of expected NOI in year 1, and cr_0 is the capitalisation rate at time zero. The use of NOI rather than simply rent is explained by the fact that landlords in the USA are more likely to suffer the burden of operating expenses, while UK landlords have historically been likely to receive rents net of all costs.

The lease rent, or gross rental revenue, is adjusted to reveal the net operating income by deducting vacancy and expenses: see Chapters 5 and 7. A greater proportion of institutional US properties has been multi-tenanted than is the case in the UK, and landlords have had more responsibility for ongoing expenses, so there is more focus on NOI, while in the UK gross rental income is often assumed to be the same as net operating income.

The market yield expression may take various forms in other markets, affected by the precise definitions of the numerator (rent) and the denominator (price) and how expenses and fees are taken into account. Globally, NOI is the preferred numerator as it more precisely defines the value of this variable. Price can include or exclude purchase taxes and expenses, depending on market convention. This affects cap rates and yields, which may be calculated net or gross of such fees. From this point we assume cap rates are based on net price, or market value.

How are Cap Rates Estimated in Practice?

Cap rates are determined in asset markets where participants buy and sell properties, and are estimated by rearranging the above equation as follows:

$$cr_0 = NOI_1 / MV_0$$

Estimating the cap rate requires knowledge of net operating income and market value for properties that have recently sold. Since this information is typically known only to buyers and sellers, it is often difficult to estimate for those not involved in the transaction. We would normally try to find buildings of similar size, quality, location, and with other similar characteristics that recently transacted to attempt to estimate a cap rate to apply to the NOI for the investment opportunity. This would require estimating NOI for the comparable projects, and determining the price at which they recently sold.

Estimating the price at which a building sold can be difficult in markets such as the USA, in which most transactions are between private entities and information on transaction values are not public. Someone who is fully engaged in the real estate industry in a particular local market will typically have a good feel for the price at which properties trade. Having local information is a tremendous benefit in a local real estate market, and often represents a comparative advantage for local market participants relative to outsiders. Continued efforts to make more data public through websites and apps have so far met with limited success, as this data clearly has a commercial value.

Cap Rates are the Inverse of Price/Earnings Ratios

For readers more familiar with stock market analysis, it is useful to know that the concept of the cap rate is similar to the concept of a price/earnings, or P/E ratio. In fact, the cap rate is the reciprocal of a price/earnings, or P/E ratio. In real estate, we can substitute rent or NOI for earnings and market value for price.

The P/E ratio for a stock can be observed in the marketplace by looking at the current price of a share divided by forward earnings per share (earnings next year). The result is typically reported as a multiple of earnings per share. For example, shares of stock of utility companies may be trading at a P/E multiple of 12.5 times, implying that the current price for the average company in the industry is 12.5 times the earnings expected for next year. If an individual stock in the utility industry has expected earnings per share of $4.00, analysts will apply the 12.5 times P/E ratio to come up with an estimate of that company's stock price of $50 ($4.00 multiplied by 12.5).

Taking the reciprocal of the P/E ratio gives what is called a capitalisation rate (or cap rate) in common stock analysis. In the case of our utility stock, the cap rate is equal to

$$cr = 1/(P/E) \text{or} 1/12.5 = 0.08, \text{or} 8\%$$

With the knowledge that earnings per share (EPS) is $4.00, the estimated value of a share of the utility company's stock can be estimated either by multiplying by the P/E ratio as above, or by dividing by the cap rate as follows:

$$Price = earnings / cr = \$4.00 / 0.08 = \$50$$

What Drives the Cap Rate?

When valuing stocks, the P/E ratio will be higher for those industries or stocks that are seen by the market as having greater growth prospects. When price/earnings ratios increase, the market is willing to pay more for a given level of earnings, or operating income. That is, if the P/E ratio for utility stocks is expected to increase to 15 from 12.5, a share of stock would increase in value to $60 (15 * $4) from $50. The increase in P/E ratio may arise due to increased expectations of growth of income as a result of the business cycle, because of some competitive advantage that a firm has relative to its competitors, and for many other reasons.

Since the cap rate is the inverse of the P/E ratio, an increase in the P/E ratio indicates that the capitalisation (cap) rate has declined. A market cap rate decline to 6.6667% from 8% (equivalent to a P/E ratio rise to 15 from 12.5) implies that the value of an asset with $4 of operating income increases to $60 ($4 / 0.066667) from $50. If market conditions for an asset or an industry are expected to improve (just like an increase in P/E ratio), cap rates are expected to decline.

So, cap rates are driven by growth expectations – but what else?

One way of attacking this problem is to use Gordon's constant growth model (see Section 4.2.5 below), which suggests (assuming that cap rates do not change) that the initial yield or cap rate is a function of the total required return less the net growth in income which is expected:

$$Initial\ yield\ or\ cap\ rate = required\ return - net\ income\ growth$$

$$K = R - G$$

The required return (R) is itself a function of the risk-free rate (RFR) and a risk premium (Rp). The closest available proxy for the *risk-free rate* is the yield to redemption on government bonds. The cash flow is certain, the investment is liquid; it is cheap to manage. The *risk premium* covers factors such as uncertainty regarding the expected cash flow, both income and capital, illiquidity and management costs:

$$R = RFR + Rp$$

So:

$$K = RFR + Rp - G$$

Rental growth is the rate at which the rental value of a new building at some date in the future is expected to be higher than the current rental value of a new building. It can be separated into two components: growth in line with inflation and 'real' growth, that is growth in excess of general inflation. *Depreciation* is the rate at which the rental value of a property falls away from the rental value of an otherwise similar new property as a function of physical deterioration and of functional or aesthetic obsolescence (see Chapter 1).

Net income growth (G) is a function of the rate of real rental growth expected for new buildings in the market (G_R), plus inflation (I), net of the rate of depreciation suffered by a property as it ages (D):

$$G = G_R + I - D$$

The nominal rate of rental growth expected for new buildings in the market (G_N) is given by the rate of real rental growth expected for new buildings in the market (G_R), plus inflation (I):

$$G_N = G_R + I$$

Net income growth (G) is a function of the rate of nominal rental growth expected for new buildings in the market (G_N) net of the rate of depreciation suffered by a property as it ages (D):

$$G = G_N - D$$

Table 4.2 shows how typical cap rates for good-quality properties in the major segments may be explained by different values for these variables. In each case the risk-free rate (assume 2.5% simply for the sake of this example) plus the risk premium comprise the required total return from the investment, or hurdle rate; from this rate is deducted the expectation of net rental growth (inflationary growth plus real growth less depreciation) to produce the appropriate cap rate. If future changes in cap rates are ignored, note that the total return expected for the investment is the cap rate or initial

TABLE 4.2 Indicative sector/region cap rates (%)

Sector	RFR	+	Rp	=	I	+	G_R	−	D	+	K
Standard shops	2.5	+	3	=	2	+	0	−	0.5	+	4
Shopping centres	2.5	+	4	=	2	+	0	−	1.5	+	6
Prime offices	2.5	+	3	=	2	+	−1	−	1	+	5.5
Secondary offices	2.5	+	4	=	2	+	−1	−	2	+	7.5
Industrials	2.5	+	4	=	2	+	−1.5	−	1.5	+	7.5

yield plus net rental growth. So, for example, the required return on standard shops is (2.5% + 3%) = 5.5%; the expected return is (4% + 2% + 0% − 0.5%) = 5.5%.

In the following section, we explain how this process can be developed, using the UK market as an example.

4.2.3 The Fisher Equation

The Fisher equation (Fisher, 1930) considers the components of the interest rate, or return on an investment. It states that

$$R = l + i + RP$$

where:

- R is the interest rate or required return
- l is a reward for liquidity preference (deferred consumption)
- i is expected inflation
- RP is the risk premium

l is given by the required return on government-issued index-linked bonds (let us assume 2%). $l + i$ is the required return on government-issued conventional bonds. These returns may be regarded, respectively, as the real and nominal risk-free rates (RF_R and RF_N).

Note that $RF_N = RF_R + i$, assuming there is no inflation risk premium, so i appears to be 4.5% − 2% = 2.5%. If an inflation risk premium (an allowance for the risk that inflation turns out to be higher than expected, damaging real returns) of 0.5% is assumed, the rate of expected inflation implied by a comparison of index-linked and conventional gilt yields is 2%. This is a better analysis of prices if it is believed that investors on average prefer real risk-free assets, in which case conventional bonds have to offer higher returns (4.5% vs. 4% nominal, or 2.5% vs. 2% real).

Let us assume that RP is 3%. The Fisher equation can be rewritten as $R = RF_N + RP$. R = 4.5% + 3% = 7.5% in this case.

4.2.4 A Simple Cash Flow Model

Consider a simple nominal cash flow:

- I is the constant income, received annually in arrears
- R is the discount rate [the required return, consisting of a risk-free rate (RF_N) and a risk premium (RP)]

The value (V) is found as follows:

$$V = I/(1+R) + I/(1+R)^2 + \cdots + I/(1+R)^n$$

The discounted cash flow is a geometric progression which simplifies to

$$V = I / R$$

or

$V = I / R$ (the *correct* yield)

It is then possible to compare R with I/P (the cap rate, or current market yield) to determine if the asset is mispriced. This is a simple valuation model which ignores the possibility of income growth.

4.2.5 Gordon's Growth Model (Constant Income Growth)

Expected income growth became embedded in the behaviour of equity and property investors by the late 1950s in the USA, the UK, and other developed markets. It became necessary to extend the simple cash flow model by introducing a constant rate of growth in nominal income (G_N). Following Gordon (1962), let us assume 3% constant growth in rents, which is received annually in arrears but agreed annually in advance. Then:

$$V = I/(1+R) + I(1+G_N)/(1+R)^2 + I(1+G_N)^2/(1+R)^3 + \cdots$$

$$\cdots + I(1+G_N)^{n-1}/(1+R)^n$$

$$V = I/(R - G_N)$$

or

$(I/V) = R - G_N$ (the *correct* yield)

where P is price, it is then possible to compare $(R - G_N)$ (7.5% − 3% = 4.5%) with I/P (the current market yield).

4.2.6 A Property Valuation Model Including Depreciation

The analysis can now be extended by introducing a constant rate of depreciation (D). This produces as an approximation:

$(I/V) = R - G_N + D$ (the *correct* yield)

Let us assume a constant depreciation rate of 2%. It is then possible to compare ($R - G_N + D$ = 7.5% − 3% + 2% = 6.5%) with I/P (the current cap rate).

Alternatively, it is possible to compare the required return:

$$R = RF_N + RP$$

with the expected return:

$$(I/P) + G_N - D$$

The comparison of required return with expected return is equivalent to comparing correct yield with current yield. The correct yield is 'value' and the current yield is 'price'.

In more simple terms, let us call the initial yield *K*. Then, in equilibrium, and assuming annual growth in rent:

$$K = R - G_N + D$$

and:

$$\underset{(required\ return)}{RF_N + RP} = \underset{(expected\ return)}{K + G_N - D}$$

When markets cannot be assumed to be in equilibrium, buy and sell rules can be evolved. If $K > R - G_N + D$, buy; if $K < R - G_N + D$, sell; if $RF_N + RP > K + G_N - D$, sell; and if $RF_N + RP < K + G_N - D$, buy.

In our example, let us assume a current market cap rate of 4.5%. In this case 4.5% < 7.5% − 3% + 2% and 4.5% + 3% > 4.5% + 3% − 2% so the market is a sell.

4.3 THE MODEL COMPONENTS

The fundamental cap rate expression is therefore $K = R - G_N + D$.

Given that both the risk-free rate and growth have both real and inflation components, this can be expanded as follows:

$$K = RFR_R + i + Rp - (G_R + i - D)$$

where:

K = property cap rate
RFR_R = real risk-free rate
Rp = risk premium
G_R = expected long-term real rental growth
i = expected inflation
D = depreciation

This process requires estimates of *K*, RFR_R, *Rp*, *I*, G_R, and *D* for the market or sector. These are dealt with in turn below.

4.3.1 The Risk-Free Rate

Simplistically, the risk-free rate is the redemption yield on government bonds (UK gilts, US Treasury bonds) for the matched life of a real estate asset holding period, let us say

10 years. Assume that the redemption yield on the benchmark 10-year government bond yield at the exit date, as at 2010, is around 4%. (To be accurate, the yield curve should be taken into account, meaning that the appropriate discount rate will be different for incomes of different maturity or tenor, but this practice is unusual in real estate, perhaps because of the illiquidity of the asset class.) Government bond yields may be manipulated by government policy, as was the case in the aftermath of the global financial crisis, in which case many investors will use an average of yields over a representative period so as not to bias investment decisions due to a short-term period of historically low, or historically high, interest rates.

4.3.2 The Risk Premium

Estimating the risk premium is a topic that takes up many pages in most corporate finance and investment textbooks. Simply, however, it is clear that investors in higher-risk assets will require higher rates of return to invest in those assets. An obvious example of this occurs in the bond market. Investors will require higher risk premiums for bonds that are rated BBB relative to those rated AAA.

When valuing real estate and other financial assets, two questions arise, though, that need to be answered. The first question is 'what is risk?' and the second question is 'once we know what risk is, how should it be measured?'.

What is Risk?

The answer to 'what is risk?' in finance theory is fairly straightforward. Risk is defined as uncertainty of outcomes. The key driver of risk is the sensitivity of the cash flow to shocks created by inaccurate forecasts or unforeseeable events, and investors in assets that exhibit a greater degree of uncertainty in potential outcomes require higher rates of return.

For real estate investors, an office building that is being developed and for which no tenants have been signed to lease space is a very speculative investment with great uncertainty of future outcomes. In contrast, an existing office building that is 100% leased to a high-credit-quality tenant over a long period of time would have lower uncertainty of cash flow, and hence lower risk. Intuitively, investors would require a lower risk premium for the latter than the former. Investors in low-risk assets tend to sleep very well at nights, while high-risk asset investors do a lot of worrying – but end up richer, on average.

Risk may also differ across potential investments in other ways. For example, let us assume that an investor with a 10-year horizon identifies two identical buildings that are available for sale. The first building generates a large proportion of its cash flows over the 10-year holding period from leases in place, and a relatively small proportion of its cash flows from proceeds expected from sale at the end of the period. Since leases represent contractual cash flows to be paid by tenants, cash flows arising from them are fairly predictable. Estimating the price at which an investor can sell an asset in 10 years, however, requires speculation.

The owner of the second building earns very small amounts of cash flow from tenants during the 5-year holding period and instead expects to earn a large amount upon the sale of the asset at the end of the 5-year holding period. The owner is dependent on a relatively speculative cash flow at sale, which is based on many factors outside the owner's control. Since the second building has greater uncertainty due its reliance on sale price, an investor would require a higher risk premium to invest in it.

In some markets, where rents are fixed for periods of time, or held on longer leases with upward-only rent reviews as in the UK, it is possible to split cash flows into bond and equity components. For the equity component, the cash flow comprises the exit value and/or any expected uplift at a rent review or lease renewal, and the sensitivity of the cash flow to economic shocks will be very important indeed. For those investors interested in the real cash flow, shocks to inflation may be important.

For the bond component, assuming no default risk, the sensitivity of the nominal cash flow to economic shocks is nil. Default risk is, however, highly relevant, and will be the most important factor in the risk premium. Shocks to inflation will affect the bond income more than the equity income, because the cash flow is fixed in nominal terms and therefore has no inflation-proofing quality.

In addition, all property is subject to the extra illiquidity which affects all property much more than listed bonds and equities, and which will lead to an increase in the risk premium. The required risk premium should therefore be affected by the relative liquidity of the investment, or the extent to which it can be easily and quickly sold (see Chapter 1).

We have estimated a value for the expected long-term risk premium for the property market as 3%, the mean of an historic range. Our evidence came from (a) an analysis of ex-post delivered returns on the property market minus returns on risk-free assets (Treasury bills) and (b) adjustments based on changes in the expected attractiveness of the asset class. The delivered risk premium on real estate has shown considerable variation over the period, both within and across markets, varying between extreme values of almost ±30%, but a value of around 3% makes sense as the mean long-term delivered risk premium in the UK and USA.

The Capital Asset Pricing Model

The capital asset pricing model offers a useful means of determining a theoretically appropriate required rate of return for an asset where that asset is to be added to an already well-diversified portfolio, given that asset's non-diversifiable, systematic, or market risk. Risk in this context is derived simply from the sensitivity of the asset return to changes in market returns represented by the quantity beta (β). If the return on an asset is highly sensitive to changes in market returns, then it will increase the volatility and risk of the portfolio, and is therefore deserving of a high required return and risk premium. The attraction of the capital asset pricing model is that it can be used to place a quantified value (beta) on this sensitivity, allowing quantification of the required return. If an asset exaggerates the upturns and downturns in the portfolio, it is a risky asset and should only be purchased if the rate of return it promises is sufficiently high: that is, one that suggests that positive abnormal returns will be made.

Stocks with a beta of one have the same risk as the market in that their returns tend to move in lockstep with the market. Stocks with a beta of more than one are more volatile than the market, and are considered aggressive investments relative to the market. Stocks with a beta of less than one are less risky (or volatile) than the market and are called defensive stocks.

Beta (β) is the measure of volatility of an investment in relation to the market portfolio, which is a portfolio comprising every known asset weighted in terms of market value. Ignoring income, a β of 1.0 implies that as the market increases in value by 10%, the expected value of the new investment increases by 10%. A β of 2.0 implies that as the market increases in value by 10%, the expected value of the new investment increases by 20%. A β of 0.5 implies that as the market increases in value by 10%, the expected value of the new investment increases by 5%.

The expected return on the market portfolio [*E*(*Rm*)] should be higher than the risk-free rate (*RFR*). It comprises the risk-free rate plus an expected risk premium [*E*(*Rp*)]. The risk premium is driven by β.

$$E(Rm) = RFR + E(Rp)$$

or

$$E(Rm) = RFR + \beta * \left[E(Rm) - RFR\right]$$

If, as before, we assume a risk premium of 3%, and a risk-free rate of around 4%, the expected return (*r*) on the market (*m*) can be estimated:

$$\begin{aligned} E(Rm) &= 0.04 + 0.03 \\ &= 7.0\% \end{aligned}$$

The return on a risky investment can be similarly derived. It should comprise the risk-free rate plus a risk premium which reflects the systematic risk of the investment relative to the market. Where an investment is twice as risky as the market, the expectation is that it should earn twice the risk premium. The measure of this relative riskiness is β. Thus, the return on a risky investment *a* [*E*(*Ra*)] is given by the following:

$$E(Ra) = RFR + \beta * (Rp)$$

If, as before, we assume a risk premium of 3%, a risk-free rate of around 4%, and now an asset β of 2, the expected return on the asset can be estimated:

$$\begin{aligned} E(Ra) &= 0.04 + (2 * 0.03) \\ &= 10.0\% \end{aligned}$$

Let us assume that an historic examination of the performance of property investments in relation to the whole market has produced estimates of betas for offices, shops, and industrials (Brown and Matysiak, 2000 attempted exactly this type of analysis). The results are as follows:

$$\text{Shops}: \quad \beta = 0.7$$

$$\text{Offices}: \quad \beta = 1.3$$

$$\text{Industrials}: \quad \beta = 0.9$$

The expected or required returns are as follows:

Shops:
$$\begin{aligned} rs &= RFR + \beta * Rp \\ &= 0.04 + 0.7(0.03) \\ &= 6.1\% \end{aligned}$$

Offices:
$$\begin{aligned} ro &= RFR + \beta * Rp \\ &= 0.04 + 1.3(0.03) \\ &= 7.9\% \end{aligned}$$

Industrials:
$$\begin{aligned} ri &= RFR + \beta * Rp \\ &= 0.04 + 0.9(0.03) \\ &= 6.7\% \end{aligned}$$

The problem we encounter when applying CAPM to real estate is that it is very difficult to calculate returns on an individual property or even a portfolio of assets on a frequent basis. Unlike stocks that trade nearly continuously on international markets, a real estate property may only be traded once every 5 or 10 years. Therefore, regressions of an asset's return on the market are impossible to perform.

On the other hand, Real Estate Investment Trusts (REITs) are actively traded on open markets so calculating beta is relatively straightforward. Some would argue (as we will see in Chapter 13) that actively traded REIT shares do not accurately reflect the risk of privately held real estate, however, so developing a risk premium based on REIT betas provides inaccuracies.

4.3.3 Inflation

Long-term inflation expectations can be set at the government's target inflation rate or market consensus expectations, available from an analysis of market prices for different bond types or market surveys. For the purposes of this analysis, let us assume that the government target and/or consensus expectation is around 1.5%.

4.3.4 Real Rental Growth

Table 4.3 shows historic values of nominal and real rental growth at the segment level in the UK. Negative real rental growth of 0.7% is the average for all property.

4.3.5 Depreciation

Table 4.4 shows depreciation expectations at the UK segment level based on research undertaken over a period of years by various researchers, the latest of which is the Investment Property Forum (2011). Mean annual depreciation of 1.3% is the all-property average, combining estimated annual rental depreciation of 0.8% with estimated annual capital expenditure of 1.8%, assumed necessary to combat what would otherwise be higher rates of rental depreciation.

TABLE 4.3 UK property segment rental growth, 1981–2018

Segment	Nominal rental growth	Inflation (RPI)	Real rental growth
Standard retail	3.6%	3.8%	−0.1%
Shopping centre	4.0%	3.8%	0.2%
Retail warehouse	4.0%	3.8%	0.3%
City office	2.5%	3.8%	−1.2%
West End office	3.6%	3.8%	−0.2%
RoSE office	2.0%	3.8%	−1.7%
RoUK office	2.7%	3.8%	−1.0%
SE industrial	2.9%	3.8%	−0.9%
RoUK industrial	2.1%	3.8%	−1.6%
All property	3.0%	3.8%	−0.7%

Sources: PFR, MSCI 2019.

TABLE 4.4 Depreciation

Segment	Depreciation
Standard retail	0.6%
Shopping centre	1.0%
Retail warehouse	2.4%
City office	0.7%
West End office	1.6%
RoSE office	1.5%
RoUK office	2.3%
SE industrial	0.5%
RoUK industrial	1.3%
All property	1.3%

Source: Investment Property Forum (2011).

TABLE 4.5 'Correct' yields (1)

	RFR_N	$+Rp$	$-G_R$	$-I$	$+D$	$=K$
Mean	1.50	3.00	−0.75	1.50	1.25	5.00

4.3.6 'Correct' Yields

Using the relationship $K = RFR_N + Rp - (G_R + i - D)$, the correct yield level emerging from the reported (rounded) components is shown in Table 4.5.

Table 4.5 suggests a correct fundamental cap rate level of 5% for the UK as at the end of 2019.

4.3.7 An Analysis in Real Terms

Section 4.5 suggests that the cap rate is driven by fundamentals: gilt yields, risk premium, and growth expectations. However, there appears to be a reasonably strong long-run correlation between inflation and rental growth. If property is alternatively seen as an inflation hedge, the risk-free benchmark is the index-linked gilt and not the conventional gilt yield.

It appears that the markets believe this to be the case. Figure 4.1 shows the relationship between UK property cap rates and index-linked gilt yields. The correlation between these series is around 75%. After the 1991–3 recession, cap rates bottomed at 4.5% in the UK in 2006, and peaked at 7% in 2009. The gap (or risk premium) reached a maximum value of 6.8 in 2018, and a minimum of 2.42 in June 2007. Arguably, these extremes mark exactly the peaks and troughs of recent UK real estate markets.

The fundamental cap rate formula is $K = RFR_R + i + Rp - (G_R + i - D)$. This presumes that the risk-free benchmark for investors is the conventional (fixed-interest) gilt,

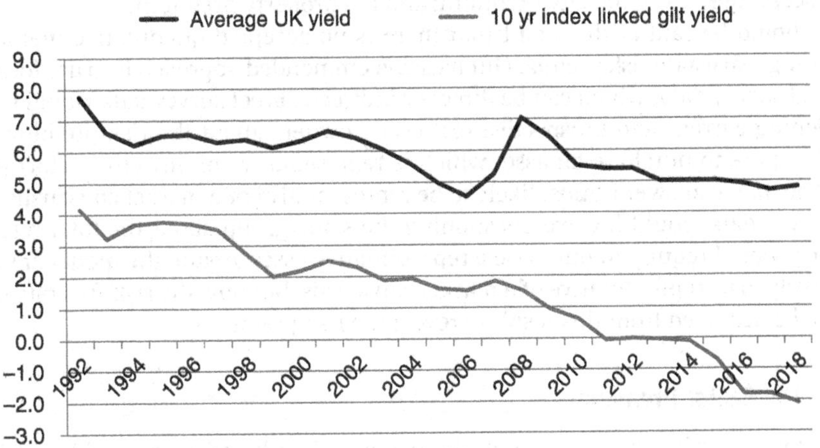

FIGURE 4.1 The UK indexed gilt–property yield gap 1992–2018
Sources: MSCI, PFR, Datastream 2010.

TABLE 4.6 'Correct' yields (2)

	RFR_R	$+Rp$	$-G_R$	$+D$	$=K$
Mean	−1.0	4.00	−0.75	1.25	5.00

Source: PFR.

which is regarded as defining the nominal risk-free rate. Instead, assuming inflation-linked rents, the index-linked gilt yield (RFR_R) is used and the equation is expressed in real terms, becoming $K = RFR_R + Rp - \left(G_R - D\right)$.

Current UK values for these variables at late 2019 are shown in Table 4.6. (Note that the risk premium is 1% higher than in the nominal analysis, as we now need to take account of the risk of rents not being correlated with inflation.)

As UK market confidence in 2019 was damaged by political uncertainty, cap rates were stubbornly sticking at higher values of around 5%.

4.4 THE REQUIRED RETURN FOR PROPERTY ASSETS

Certain research systems include the provision of a series of risk premiums for subsectors of the property market, defined by use sector and subsector, by region and by city. Where a sale or purchase is being assessed and the present value or net present value over purchase or sale price needs to be estimated, these systems establish a broad guide for estimating the risk premium which might be used in the discount rate. However, where an individual interest in property is being appraised, a further set of considerations needs to be taken into account.

This section summarises one such system which measures the issues relevant to the assessment of the individual or specific risk premium. Three main categories of premium drive the specific risk premium in this particular system. These are: the sector or subsector premium; the city premium; and the property premium.

It should be said at this point that there is no accepted quantitative method for estimating real estate risk premia. Our basic recommended approach is to use formal or informal survey data, which can be direct or indirect. Direct survey data would involve questioning current and prospective real estate owners about the risk premium they would require to purchase an asset which is representative of any city/sector/quality type. The modal answer is most likely to be representative of a market consensus. Indirect survey data would involve questioning the same group about the total return or IRR they would require to purchase a representative asset. Again, the modal answer is most likely to be representative of a market consensus, but now the risk-free rate would need to be deducted from this result to reveal the risk premium.

4.4.1 The Sector Premium

The system described herein assesses the risk premium based on a checklist of issues and using a variety of quantitative and qualitative measures. The starting point is the estimation of a premium for the whole equity-type property sector based on a presumption about the equity risk premium and the relative position of property as an asset class. Hence, the sector premium is based on the equity premium and the differential property premium.

Beyond this, the sector premiums are assessed by taking into account three factors. These are: the sensitivity of the cash flow to economic shocks, with particular reference to rental growth and depreciation; illiquidity; and other factors, including the impact on portfolio risk and the lease pattern.

4.4.2 The City Premium

The assessment of the city risk premium is based on an assessment of the riskiness of the economic structure of a city and its catchment area, together with a consideration of competing locations. The range expands from a minimum city premium for diversified and liquid cities with healthy industries to maximum premiums for illiquid cities whose economies are concentrated in weak sectors. Low liquidity values are assigned to cities and sectors where it is considered relatively difficult to raise cash from a sale at short notice.

4.4.3 The Property Premium

This section deals with the four components of the property premium, as listed below:

(a) the tenant risk class;
(b) the lease risk class;
(c) the building risk class; and
(d) the location risk class.

The relative weighting of the factors can be assessed by multiple regression analysis, whereby (given a large sample of individual property investments) the current importance of these variables in explaining cap rates or risk premiums can be assessed and their future importance hypothesised. The simple process is best illustrated by an example.

4.4.4 Example

We are considering the purchase of either of two City of London office buildings. Our estimate of the risk premium for a prime city office is 3.25% over the risk-free rate, currently 2%.

Tenant

The tenant of property A is a FTSE 350 corporate; the tenant of property B is a partnership of solicitors. Additional premium: 0.5% for building B.

TABLE 4.7 Building-specific risk premia: an example

Factor	Building A	Building B
Risk-free rate	**2.00**	**2.00**
Base premium	3.25	3.25
Tenant	0.00	0.50
Tenure	1.50	0.50
Leases	0.00	1.00
Building	0.50	0.00
Location	0.00	0.25
Premium	**5.25**	**5.50**
Discount rate	**7.25**	**7.50**

Tenure

A is leasehold, for 63 years, with low gearing (the ground rent payable to the freeholder is a small percentage of the occupational rent paid to the lessor); B is leasehold for 116 years with no gearing. Additional premia: 1.5% for building A; 0.5% for building B.

Leases

The sublease for A has 18 years to run, with no breaks and upward-only rent reviews; B has 10 years to run, with no breaks and upward-only rent reviews. Additional premium: say 1% for building B.

Building

A is an inflexible building. Extra premium: 0.5%.

Location

B has a location heavily dependent on neighbouring tenants remaining in place. Extra premium: 0.25%.

Table 4.7 summarises the cumulative effect of these individual adjustments.

See Box 4.1 for a discussion of the 'correct' asset class yields.

Box 4.1: 'Correct' Asset Class Yields

Table 4.8 shows the cap rates available on a group of UK asset classes. Each asset class has a required return, determined by the real risk-free rate (liquidity preference), expected inflation, and a risk premium. For each asset class it is possible to estimate an expected return, determined by the income return (initial yield, or cap rate), plus the expected growth in income, less depreciation.

TABLE 4.8 Asset pricing analysis (1)

	RFR_R	$+i$	$+RP$	=	K	$+G_N$	$-D$
Indexed bonds					1.5		
Govt bonds					4.0		
Equities					2.5		
Property					6.5		
Japanese bonds					2.0		
Cash					3.5		

The initial yield on a government-issued indexed bond defines the real risk-free rate (Table 4.9). The difference between the yield on fixed-interest government bonds and the yield on indexed bonds is explained by expected inflation plus a small risk premium to deal with the possibility of the inflation expectation failing to be delivered. If we take an inflation risk premium of 0.5%, deductive reasoning suggests that 2% is the expected inflation rate. The indexed bond will deliver 2% growth in income through indexation. In equilibrium, the indexed bond is set to deliver a total return of 3.5%, the required return. The fixed-interest bond will deliver a total return of 4%, outperforming the indexed bond to compensate for the inflation risk.

TABLE 4.9 Asset pricing analysis (2)

	RFR_R	$+i$	$+RP$	=	K	$+G_N$	$-D$
Indexed bonds	1.5	2.0	0.0	=	1.5	2.0	0.0
Govt bonds	1.5	2.0	0.5	=	4.0	0.0	0.0
Equities	1.5				2.5		
Property	1.5				6.5		
Japanese bonds	1.5				2.0		
Cash	1.5				3.5		

The real risk-free rate is common to all asset classes (Table 4.10). Equities and property are risky assets, riskier than bonds, and an investor will require a risk premium to compensate for this. Equities are more volatile than property, but property returns are smoothed and property is very illiquid, so a higher risk premium (4% compared to 3.5% for equities) might be justified.

In order that the market analysis is in equilibrium, income growth for equities will have to be 4.5%, assuming that depreciation is not an issue because it is dealt with by depreciation allowances in the profit and loss account, so that the yield of 2.5% is net of depreciation. If inflation of 2% is expected, real growth in earnings of 2.5% – roughly the long-term rate of UK economic growth – is needed. For property, assuming average depreciation of 1% across all sectors in line with the research

(continued)

(continued)

studies described in Chapter 1, rents need to grow at the rate of inflation (this is the historic UK average).

Equities are then set to deliver their required return of 7%, and property will deliver 7.5%.

TABLE 4.10 Asset pricing analysis (3)

	RFR_R	$+i$	$+RP$	$=$	K	$+G_N$	$-D$
Indexed bonds	1.5	2.0	0.0	=	1.5	2.0	0.0
Govt bonds	1.5	2.0	0.5	=	4.0	0.0	0.0
Equities	1.5	2.0	3.5	=	2.5	4.5	0.0
Property	1.5	2.0	4.0	=	6.5	2.0	1.0
Japanese bonds	1.5				2.0		
Cash	1.5				3.5		

What is the required return for a UK investor buying Japanese bonds? As a UK investor, say a pension fund, the investor's liabilities will be denominated in sterling. It is UK inflation that is important, and the required return is not affected by inflation prospects in Japan. There is, however, a risk above and beyond that involved in the purchase of UK government bonds. The income and capital return delivered by a Japanese bond is paid in yen, and the yen/sterling exchange rate will change over time, so that the income in sterling is uncertain and may be volatile. A risk premium of 2% is assumed. The required return is then 5.5%, and to deliver this income, growth of 3.5% is needed (Table 4.11).

TABLE 4.11 Asset pricing analysis (4)

	RFR_R	$+i$	$+RP$	$=$	K	$+G_N$	$-D$
Indexed bonds	1.5	2.0	0.0	=	1.5	2.0	0.0
Govt bonds	1.5	2.0	0.5	=	4.0	0.0	0.0
Equities	1.5	2.0	3.5	=	2.5	4.5	0.0
Property	1.5	2.0	4.0	=	6.5	2.0	1.0
Japanese bonds	1.5	2.0	2.0	No	2.0	2.0	0.0
Cash	1.5	2.0	0.0	=	3.5	0.0	0.0

However, as we shall see in Chapter 16, the market's expectation of yen appreciation is defined as the difference in interest rates – in this case represented by bond yields – in the two economies, only 2% in this case. Hence, Japanese bonds are not attractive to UK buyers. This does not mean that the market is not priced in equilibrium: simply that the likely buyer, whose natural habitat this investment represents, is not based in the UK.

Cash – say 6-month deposits – is risk free and offers neither income growth (interest rates would have to rise to deliver this) nor depreciation. As in all other asset classes except Japanese bonds, the market offers the return which is required.

4.5 FORECASTING REAL ESTATE RETURNS

A forecast of rental values (see Chapter 3) is a useful start in thinking about models for forecasting returns. But it needs to be combined with lease terms to give the expected cash flow (or, better, the expected distribution of cash flows) to calculate whether, given current price, the investment will deliver the required return. In addition, a return model will need a view of cap rates.

4.5.1 The Origin and Uses of Property Forecasts

Forecasting property rents, cap rates, prices, and returns requires an understanding of fundamental analysis. Fundamental analysis is the examination of the underlying forces that affect and connect the behaviour of the economy, asset classes, industrial sectors, and companies. The goal of fundamental analysis is to derive a forecast for the future behaviour of a market or asset from these underlying forces, either using current data or using forecasts of these variables. The rent for office space, for example, can be forecast by using current vacancy rates or by using forecasts of the future demand for and supply of space, which are in turn driven by fundamental economic variables. The usual approach is to use an econometric technique called regression analysis (see Chapter 3).

The formal forecasting of property market returns using econometric models is now relatively commonplace. To assist with investment decisions, forecasts can be produced for each sector at the national, regional, local, and individual building level. As the spatial scale becomes smaller, the task of forecasting becomes progressively more difficult. Returns could be forecast for the property market as a whole, but each sector is influenced by different factors, and it is better to consider the market as the sum of the individual sectors.

Rents can be forecast using conventional forecasting procedures, but cap rates pose more of a problem. Modelling property cap rates using regression is known to be challenging. Regression-based cap rate models typically suffer from poor explanatory power or poor diagnostics (a term used to describe an analysis of the equation), or require the forecasting of independent variables such as interest rates or equity market returns which are more difficult to forecast than the dependent variable.

Together, rent and cap rate forecasts can be used as inputs into total return forecasts. These can be used at a number of levels. The total return expected for property can be used in asset allocation for a multi-asset portfolio. Sector and region returns can be used to construct strategy for a property portfolio. Sector and region and local returns can be used to identify target areas for stock selection (buying and selling) and for active asset management.

4.5.2 Forecasting Cap Rates

Cap rates are more difficult to forecast than rents. However, based on the material presented earlier in this chapter, we can suggest that they are driven by yields on gilts, or the risk-free rate; by expectations of future net rental growth; and by the required risk premium:

$$K = RFR_R + i + Rp - (G_R + i - d)$$

The first problem is producing a good historical model. The yield series does not exhibit much volatility: property cap rates tend to move slowly upwards or downwards for a long period, and may simply be mean-reverting. In contrast, many possible explanatory variables are much more volatile. This creates modelling difficulties.

The best historical model for the all-property cap rate calculated in the RICS/IPD/Aberdeen cycles report used the following explanatory variables: the property cap rate in the previous year; the yield on long-dated gilts; net property investment; the interest rate; office and retail construction starts 1 year ago; property returns 1 year in the future; and the inflation rate.

This may produce a good historic model, but it is of little value for forecasting. Forecasts of the explanatory variables would be at least as difficult to produce as forecasts of the property cap rate. With some idea of the likely trends in these variables, it may be possible to deduce likely cap rate movements, but not to predict values with much accuracy.

Forecasting cap rates using econometric-type models is probably a waste of time, and an alternative approach using a cash flow analysis is required. There are a number of approaches that can be taken towards modelling cap rates. Cap rates may be linked to fundamentals, as above. Event-specific factors can impact on cap rates: these can include the weight of money, sentiment towards property, and recent rental growth experience, or simply cap rate movements in other assets. However, it is dangerous to use a simple lagged relationship between yields on one asset class to predict the yield on another.

Figure 4.2 illustrates the yield gap between gilts and property. Where the gap is positive, as it was before 1993, gilt yields are higher than property cap rates. After 1996, property cap rates have been higher than gilt yields. This is not a simple lead–lag relationship, but it may be meaningful if it is set in the context of the fundamental relationship:

$$K = RFR_R + i + Rp - (G_R + i - d)$$

This tells us to expect a positive relationship between gilt yields and property cap rates, but one which is complicated by the risk premium and real growth expectations. The switch to a negative yield difference post-2008 raises the question as to why this

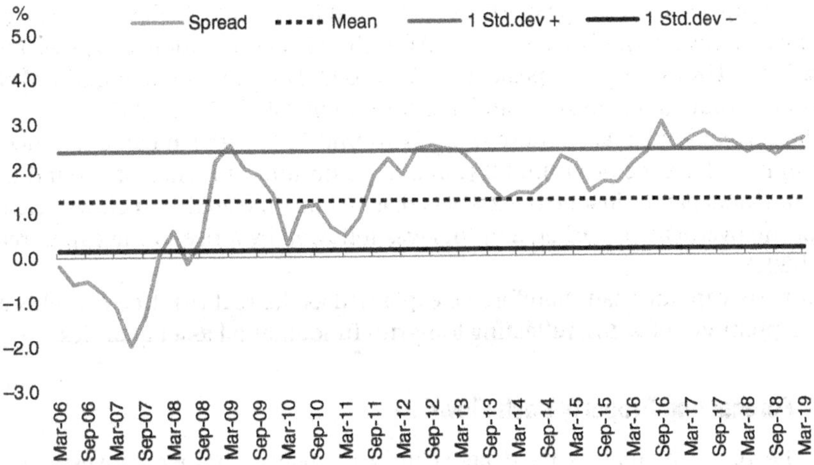

FIGURE 4.2 The UK gilt–property yield gap 2006–19
Sources: MSCI, Datastream, PFR.

may have happened. Possible explanations are that the risk premium for property has risen, anticipated growth has fallen, or there has been a combination of both – or property was looking cheap. The negative yield difference of 2005–7 suggests that the risk premium for property fell, anticipated growth increased, there had been a combination of both – or property had become overpriced.

We also know that there is a strong relationship between index-linked bond yields and property yields, and this relationship can also be used for forecasting. Figure 4.3

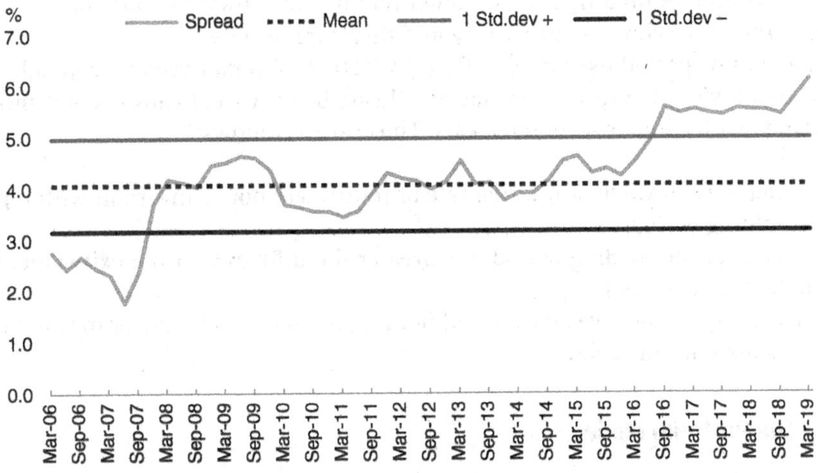

FIGURE 4.3 The UK indexed gilt–property yield gap 2006–19
Sources: MSCI, Datastream, PFR.

shows the gap between UK property cap rates and index-linked gilt yields. The correlation between these series is around 75%. After the 1991–3 recession, cap rates bottomed at 4.5% in the UK in 2006, and peaked at 7% in 2009. The gap (or risk premium) reached a maximum value of 6.8 in 2018, and a minimum of 2.42 in June 2007.

The correlation between these series is around 75%, with a mean difference of 4%, a minimum difference of around 2%, and a maximum difference of around 6%. The minimum yield gap of just below 2% was reached in June 2007, which was clearly the peak of the overheated market, and this was followed by a rise in the gap to reach 6% by mid-2018.

Property cap rates can therefore be explained as the real risk-free rate plus a property risk premium of 2–6%, reflecting long-run fundamental asset qualities.

4.5.3 Forecasting Property Cash Flows

When the rental income is fixed between rent reviews, property investments have bond components to the cash flow. The expected cash flow from the typical property investment is therefore a combination of bond and equity. Property is a hybrid, and the investment strategy must reflect this by anticipating the impact of economic and capital market forces on the value of both components of the cash flow.

The cash flow should also reflect the following factors:

1. Property income is subject to the lease, which determines the payment of rent. For example, the reversionary nature of some property investments will create an income uplift at the next review.
2. Property, more than any other mainstream investment, is a tangible asset which depreciates through physical deterioration and obsolescence.

The excess or over-rented component of the cash flow will be subject to greater risk than the portion secured by the estimated rental value (ERV); separation of the cash flow into these two component parts would therefore be wise.

The holding period used in cash flow projections should normally coincide with a lease end or review. However, this may not always be the case. In any event it should be determined with care for several reasons. These are as follows:

1. The net present value or internal rate of return will not be invariant with regard to the holding period.
2. The shorter the holding period, the greater the influence of the exit value, which will be a more risky input.
3. The manager may have an expected holding period, which may or may not equate with lease ends or reviews.

4.5.4 The Portfolio Model

The expected return on each asset should be modelled using a discounted cash flow procedure. The most attractive property will be the one for which the expected return exceeds the required return by the greatest amount. In most circumstances, this process may be optimal. However, in other circumstances it may not.

First, this ignores the impact of tax and gearing. This is dealt with in Chapter 15. Second, it ignores the impact of the purchase on the shape of the portfolio as a whole. Third, it ignores the different outlays involved. Is an excess return of 1% on a £5 million outlay superior to an excess return of 0.5% on an outlay of £10 million?

These latter two problems can be dealt with quite simply in a portfolio model. The objective of a portfolio model is to forecast cash flows and values, year by year, on all buildings held within the portfolio, in such a form as to enable the manager to model the impact of altered expectations on portfolio performance. The model allows scenarios concerning purchases, major expenditure and sales to be explored. Hence, in the above example the impact on portfolio return – and, with the necessary inputs, risk – of the two alternative purchases may be appraised. This deals quite easily with the difference in outlays, as the optimal decision will be the one which (subject to risk) has the greatest positive impact on portfolio return. The impact on the shape of the portfolio and its risk profile is also easily dealt with in the model.

4.5.5 Example

Table 4.12 shows how, assuming rising rental values and varying market cap rates, a single property moving through its 5-year review pattern and valued using a simple cap rate approach will vary in capital value. There are 3 years until the rent review, and market cap rates fall and then rise over the period. The property enjoys a sharp fall in cap rate as it passes through its rent review, reducing the risk to the investor. The property's capital value is sensitive to four variables:

(a) the income, or rent passing;
(b) the estimated rental value;
(c) the period to the rent review; and
(d) the cap rate.

In Table 4.12, the impact of the changing value and rental income on the total return delivered by the property is shown, based on the following simple return definitions.

TABLE 4.12 Portfolio modelling (1)

Data	Year 0	Year 1	Year 2	Year 3	Year 4	Year 5
Income	£1,500,000	£1,500,000	£1,500,000	£2,050,000	£2,050,000	£2,050,000
ERV*	£2,000,000	£2,000,000	£2,050,000	£2,100,000	£2,200,000	£2,220,000
Review term	3	2	1	5	4	3
Cap rate	7.50%	7.40%	7.00%	6.50%	7.25%	8.00%
Capital value	£25,366,404	£26,201,550	£28,771,696	£32,099,908	£29,733,893	£26,901,093

Note: estimated rental value, or market rent.

Income return is the net rent received over the measurement period divided by the value at the beginning of the period:

$$IR = Y_{0-1} / CV_0$$

Capital return is the change in value over the measurement period divided by the value at the beginning of the period:

$$CR = \left[CV_1 - CV_0\right] / CV_0$$

Total return is the sum of income return and capital return:

$$TR = \left[Y_{0-1} + CV_1 - CV_0\right] / CV_0$$

Table 4.13 shows the results. As the capital value rises and falls, the capital return is strongly positive, then negative. The income return is less volatile. The total return rises and falls in line with changes in capital value.

Combining this data for one property into an aggregate table describing all properties in the portfolio allows the portfolio return going forward to be modelled. Most importantly, different scenarios can be modelled, not only for out-turns of rental growth and capitalisation rate movements, but also for sales from the portfolio, additions of new buildings, and so on.

For advanced applications, financing and taxation impacts need to be dealt with, and the portfolio model can be adapted to enable regular portfolio monitoring (for example, the ranking of expected returns property by property), linkages to portfolio and facilities management systems, and client reporting.

The portfolio model can also be developed further into an arbitrage pricing system, designed to explore the sensitivity of portfolio return to various economic and capital market factors, such as changes in rates of interest, changes in expected inflation rates, changes in the value of sterling, and other relevant factors. (Portfolio performance measurement is addressed more fully in Chapter 17.)

TABLE 4.13 Portfolio modelling (2)

	Year 0	Year 1	Year 2	Year 3	Year 4	Year 5
Capital value	£25,366,404	£26,201,550	£28,771,696	£32,099,908	£29,733,893	£26,901,093
Income		£1,500,000	£1,500,000	£1,500,000	£2,050,000	£2,050,000
Income return		5.91%	5.72%	5.21%	6.89%	7.62%
Capital return		3.29%	9.81%	11.57%	−7.37%	−9.53%
Total return		9.21%	15.53%	16.78%	−0.48%	−1.91%

4.5.6 Fair Value Analysis

It has to be said that the science of forecasting real estate rents, cap rates, and returns has received criticism and lost favour post the 2007 crash. The main reason for this is the failure of forecasting systems and processes to steer investors away from the approaching rocks at that time, but there are other reasons, including the heterogeneity of real estate as an asset class and a widespread belief among investors that 'top-down' processes which require generalisations to be made about property types are less helpful than the development of themes (such as a focus on the redevelopment of poor-quality assets) plus building-by-building analysis and a consideration of the idiosyncrasies of unique assets.

One result of this change in emphasis has been a focus on longer-term modelling, so that less emphasis is placed on short-term rent growth models and cap rate movements have less impact. Value investors like to use simple metrics to assess whether assets are over- or underpriced, so a 10-year cash flow model using the long-term trend in rent growth rates (see Table 4.3) and a reversion to long-term average bond yields (producing conservative results in an era of low or negative bond yields) has value for these investors who believe it helps them to avoid overpaying for assets.

4.6 CONCLUSION: A SIMPLE WAY TO THINK ABOUT REAL ESTATE RETURNS

From Chapter 3, we can see that there should be a strong relationship between nominal rental growth and inflation. In support of this, we found a strong empirical relationship between index-linked bond yields and property yields. Figure 4.1 showed the relationship between UK property cap rates and index-linked gilt yields. The correlation between these series is around 75%, with a mean difference of 4%.

In this chapter, we developed the fundamental cap rate formula:

$$K = RFR_R + i + Rp - \left(G_R + i - D\right)$$

In equilibrium, the delivered return on real estate is the same as the required return, so:

$$K + \left(G_R + i - D\right) = RFR_R + i + Rp$$

Hence the delivered return on real estate is produced by the cap rate, or initial yield, plus net nominal rental growth. As we saw in Chapter 3, there is a strong relationship between net nominal rental growth and inflation. Real rental growth has been close to zero. We can therefore posit that the delivered return on real estate is produced by the cap rate, or initial yield, plus inflation:

$$K + i = RFR_R + i + Rp$$

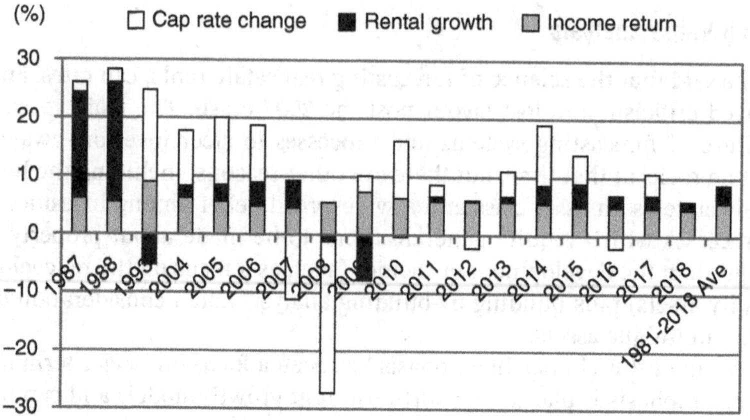

FIGURE 4.4 UK property return attribution, 1987–2018
Sources: IPD, PFR 2009.

To confirm this over a longer period, 1987–2018, Figure 4.4 shows that UK property delivered an average total return of 8.9%. Capital growth attributable to ERV growth averaged roughly 2.8%. The rate of UK inflation over the period was just over 3%, so real growth was marginally negative. Capital growth attributable to cap rate movement was just under 0.3%, and the income return was around 5.75%. In highly simplified terms, the total return of around 9% came from income of around 6% plus inflation of around 3%.

Thus it appears that, as suggested by our theoretical analysis, and confirmed by the data, we should expect the delivered long-run return on real estate to be produced by the cap rate, or initial yield, plus inflation. Cap rates have a natural value relative to indexed bonds, and overpricing should be apparent by this measure. When cap rates are low by this measure, returns may be poor, as in the period following 2006; when cap rates are high, as in 2009, there will be an additional source of return to enjoy. Cap rate adjustments are often rapid, producing shocks.

Finally, as suggested in Chapter 1, property is heterogeneous, meaning that an investment can do well when markets do badly, and *vice versa*. In Part II, we concentrate more fully on the property decision.

PART Two

Making Investment Decisions at the Property Level

CHAPTER 5

Basic Valuation and Investment Analysis

5.1 INTRODUCTION

The valuation of property, as is the case with the valuation of all privately traded assets, is an imprecise exercise. Because real estate assets trade infrequently, markets do not observe regular transactions from which to infer values. Therefore, several techniques are used in an attempt to determine the value of real property. The simplest are based on direct capital comparison, but for income-generating assets, values are found most simply by dividing rent by a cap rate (see Chapter 4), albeit most accurately by capitalising the stream of future cash flows expected to be earned by a property asset. We introduce this discounted cash flow approach in this chapter and go on to develop it in the remainder of Part II.

In his classic 1938 book *The Theory of Investment Value*, John Burr Williams (Williams, 1938) was the first to mention the idea that the value of an asset should be a function of the cash flows that are expected to be earned from an asset. Speaking of the valuation of financial assets, Williams states:

> The purchase of a stock or bond, like other transactions that give rise to the phenomenon of interest, represents the exchange of present goods for future goods – dividends, or coupons and principal, in this case the claim on future goods. To appraise the investment value, then, it is necessary to estimate the future payments. The annuity of payments, adjusted for changes in the time value of money itself, may then be discounted at the pure interest rate demanded by the investor.

The appraisal of all investments is predicated on the assumption that the current value is equal to the net present value of the future benefits (see, for example, Damodaran, 2001). This requires us to determine the most likely cash flow that the investment will produce and the discount rate which we can use to find the net present value of that cash flow. Chapter 4 introduced the concept of the required return, which is the discount rate for this purpose.

How should we apply this to real-world property valuation exercises? The answer can be found in most finance textbooks, and can be stated simply in the following equation:

$$Price_0 = \sum_{t=1}^{T} E(CF_t)/(1+r)^t$$

In this equation, price is what the investor would be willing to pay for, or the value to the investor of, the asset at the time of purchase; *T* is the total number of periods during which the investor expects to hold the asset; *E*(*CF*) is the expected cash flow expected to be earned by the asset in each of *t* periods into the future; and *r* is the discount rate that reflects a risk-free rate plus a risk premium that captures the underlying risk of the asset being valued (see Chapter 4).

From the algebra behind the equation, two things are obvious. First, for assets of the same risk (the same *r*), the higher are the expected cash flows [*E*(*CF*)] in the numerator, the higher will be the value or price that an investor would be willing to pay for the asset. Second, for assets that have the same expected cash flows [the same *E*(*CF*)], the lower the risk as measured by the discount rate (*r*) in the denominator, the higher will be the value or price that an investor would be willing to pay for the asset.

To value assets we need expected future cash flows into the future, plus an accurate measure of the risk of the asset, which we discussed in Chapter 4.

5.1.1 Cash Flow

Assume we hope to buy a property and hold it for 5 years, after which time we expect to sell it into the marketplace. Therefore, we need to forecast cash flows that we would expect to earn from the property over the 5-year holding period. When we buy a property, there may be leases in place that provide predictable cash flows in the first year, and other years within the holding period.

The certainty of cash flows from existing tenants will differ based on the property type under consideration. For example, let us assume that we are buying an industrial property that is fully leased to the US government for a 10-year period. Since there is a single tenant, and since the lease payments are guaranteed by the government to dictate a certain cash flow every year, the probability of being wrong on estimates of expected cash flows from owning this asset are very small. Therefore, uncertainty of outcomes, or risk, is low.

In contrast, an office building may have a large number of tenants that likely signed leases at different times with different terms. Typically, most, if not all, of the leases will come to the end of their term at some point during the expected holding period. If tenants vacate at the end of the lease term, new tenants will have to be found, which may take some time, and the rents that they will pay will depend on market conditions at the time the lease rolls over. Forecasting the period of vacancy, the future market rent, and when and whether or not the owner will find a qualified tenant to occupy the space represents a great deal of uncertainty. Risk in this case is higher.

Similarly, a multi-family property typically exhibits a large number of tenants, all on short-term leases that by definition roll over at the end of the lease term. Forecasting

Gross rental revenue
+ Other income
= Gross potential income
- Vacancy
= Gross effective income
- Operating expenses
= Net operating income

FIGURE 5.1 Deriving net operating income from gross rental revenue

the number of units that will be vacant, as well as rents that the owner can charge in the future, is speculative. In both the office and multi-family examples, it is critically important to be as accurate as possible in forecasting in order to ensure that a prospective purchaser does not pay too much for an asset.

Figure 5.1 shows the process by which the lease rent, or gross rental revenue, is adjusted to reveal the net operating income to be capitalised for properties in the USA.

This issue reveals a common difference in US and UK practice. Very broadly speaking, a greater proportion of US office properties is multi-tenanted than is the case in the UK, and landlords have more responsibility for ongoing expenses, so there is more focus on the impact of vacancy on net operating income (NOI). In the UK, gross rental income is often the same as NOI. Given that all of lease rents, vacancy, and operating expenses can be expected to change over time, especially if lease rents in the US have more regular changes built into them than do typically fixed 5-year rents in the UK, it is understandable that the USA has been quicker to abandon 'quick and dirty' cap rate valuation in favour of a discounted cash flow exercise.

5.1.2 Risk and the Discount Rate

Determining the denominator of the valuation equation is also critical to estimating the current value of an asset. The discount rate is often referred to as the required rate of return, the hurdle rate, or the opportunity cost of capital, as well as a number of other monikers. Throughout this section, we will use these terms interchangeably. Risk is the key driver of differential discount rates (this subject was covered fully in Chapter 4).

5.1.3 Determining Price

With estimates of cash flow and a discount rate, the price that an investor would be willing to pay for an asset can be determined using discounted cash flow (DCF) analysis, and is simply the present value of the expected cash flows discounted by the discount rate. If an investor is willing to pay more than the ask price, they can buy the property and create wealth. Of course, this conclusion relies on accurate forecasts of future cash flows. The difference between the price that the investor is willing to pay and the ask price is called the net present value (NPV).

The previous equation can be extended to show a 5-year stream of cash flows, as follows:

$$Price_0 = E(CF_1)/(1+r)^1 + E(CF_2)/(1+r)^2 + E(CF_3)/(1+r)^3 + E(CF_4)/(1+r)^4 + E(CF_5)/(1+r)^5$$

If the benefits on the right side of the equation, measured as the present value of expected future cash flows, exceed the cost on the left side of purchasing the property, the net present value will be positive.

5.1.4 Determining Return

The second application of DCF analysis is to determine what return can be earned if the property is purchased at the ask price. Here, the price on the left side of the equation is known, and we have estimates of the future cash flows. With these as inputs, the return that is earned by the property can be calculated by solving for r in the first equation. The solution is known as an internal rate of return (IRR).

Investors compare the IRR to their required rates of return, and if the IRR earned at the ask price exceeds the required rate of return, the investment will compensate the investor for the risk of the investment. If the IRR is less than the required rate of return, the investor should not commit to the investment.

5.2 ESTIMATING FUTURE CASH FLOWS

5.2.1 Introduction

This section focuses on the issues which arise when constructing a cash flow statement. The inputs can be categorised as (i) income inputs and (ii) capital inputs. The generation of some of these inputs can be challenging and complex, and a full menu of issues to consider would be very long and very detailed. This chapter sets out to introduce the basic structure only. Chapters 7 and 9 will develop this type of example further.

The data required to model real estate cash flows can be broken down into (i) current data and (ii) forecast data. Current data includes the rent currently payable; the current estimated rental value (ERV) or NOI; the lease structure and the mechanism for future rental value changes; management, rent review, purchase and sale costs; and any contractually agreed income or outflows known with some certainty. Forecast data includes expected rental value changes, redevelopment or refurbishment (capital expenditure) costs, and exit (going-out) sale price forecasts.

Our gross cash flow will be made up of income and capital. The income may increase at contractual rates, or at rent reviews. Estimation of a capital return depends on the timing of a sale; therefore, we need to estimate a likely holding period. Holding costs will be incurred during the period of ownership, and these will need to be estimated. Purchase and sale transfer costs will be payable; at each rent review or lease roll-over, a fee or commission will be payable; letting or re-letting costs may have to be faced; and management fees may be incurred. Taxes on income and capital gain will be charged. Properties have to be repaired and refurbished: even then the impact of building depreciation may have to be faced. The estimation of each of these factors will help us to reach an explicit net cash flow projection. All variables will now be briefly considered.

5.2.2 Holding Period

For purely technical reasons – that is, to avoid an infinitely long cash flow projection in a freehold analysis – a finite holding period must be utilised in the analysis model.

The over-riding concern in the choice of holding period must be the intentions of the investor. Discussions with the investor might reveal his likely or intended period of ownership. Where no intention to sell is apparent, the holding period becomes arbitrary.

While periods of 5 or 10 years are often used for convenience, it should be noted that changes in return may result from shortening or lengthening the holding period. In addition, if the holding period selected is short, then more importance is placed on the price achieved when the asset is sold, which may add risk to the proposition.

5.2.3 Lease Rent

Cash flows from investment property are generated by the lease contract (see Chapter 6). Lease terms can, in certain circumstances, dominate the property valuation, while in other cases (where there is a short lease and no rights to renew, for example) they are of lesser weight. Rarely are they peripheral to the valuation of investment property. In addition, the initial rent is affected by 'lease events' – what might happen at a break or a lease end, when tenants have the right to leave. An assessment of what might happen at the expiration of a lease is often important in assessing the most likely cash flow, and uncertainty surrounding future lease events also contributes to the risk profile of the investment, thereby influencing the discount rate. This is especially so in buildings let to single or few tenants, where assumptions surrounding the operation of breaks or renewals can lead to significant differences in appraised value.

Generally, the lease rent will be expected to change in line with a forecast of property market rents (see Chapter 3). In addition, estimates of the length of vacancy or voids will have to be made, especially in large, multi-tenanted properties.

5.2.4 Resale Price

In the cases of freeholds and long leaseholds, the selection of a holding period will trigger the assumption of a resale at the end of the period. Sale price has to be projected as the most likely selling price at that date. The most common method of market pricing is the cap rate approach, where the freehold resale price is given by:

$$MV_T = NOI_{T+1} / cr_T$$

This requires the projection of two variables: NOI (or ERV) in the year following the sale of the property and the cap rate at sale.

Estimated Rental Value at Resale

Forecasting rental growth (see Chapter 3) over the holding period is important both in the estimation of the rental flow and in the prediction of the resale price. The NOI used is for the period following the end of the holding period. If the sale is assumed in time T, the appropriate NOI estimate is for time $T + 1$.

Going-Out Capitalisation Rate

The prediction of a capitalisation rate for the subject property 5 or 10 years hence requires the estimation of two distinct trend lines. Firstly, cap rates for the type of property under consideration may be expected to change over the period. If so, the extent to which the market cap rate will change must be estimated. Second, the movement in cap rate of the subject property against an index of cap rates for such properties in a frozen state over the holding period needs to be estimated. In other words, the extent of depreciation likely to be suffered by an ageing building needs to be built into the appraisal.

A cross-section analysis may facilitate this process. Let us assume, for example, that the subject property is 10 years old, and that the appropriate capitalisation rate is 7%. Given an expectation of stable cap rates over time, the best estimate of the resale capitalisation rate after a 10-year holding period is the current cap rate on similar but 20-year-old buildings, say 8%. This leads us to the subject of depreciation.

5.2.5 Depreciation

Increases and decreases in property values (in relative terms) are a function of changes in the value of land and depreciation in the value of buildings. The building will be affected by deterioration (physical wearing out) and by obsolescence (technological or fashion changes which render the physical characteristics of the building less useful). In the office and industrial markets, there are numerous examples where changes in practice or space requirements have rendered particular types of building useless for their original purpose (floor to ceiling heights in offices, height of loading docks and equipment circulation space in factories), with the result that they have been demolished or repurposed for another use, even though they were physically sound. Capital expenditures to modernise a property and its infrastructure may minimise the impact of depreciation on value.

Deterioration can to some extent be forecast, but obsolescence caused by technological and fashion changes cannot always be foreseen within an investment time horizon. Forecasts of this kind of change over the life of a new building are particularly difficult. Nonetheless, some studies exist which examine age-related falls in rental values over time relative to new property values (e.g. Baum, 1991; IPF, 2005). These can be used as the basis for assessing the likely reduction in rental growth relative to an index of rents for new buildings. In addition to the rent impact, the exit capitalisation rate may rise as a building ages, and regular capital expenditure, refurbishment, or redevelopment may be required.

As a result of depreciation, rental values may follow a function which is a combined result of market rental growth and depreciation, at the following rate:

$$(1+g)/(1+d)$$

where:

g is the annual rate of rental growth for new buildings
d is the annual rate of depreciation.

Depreciation rates have been studied for a variety of property types, mainly office and industrial, in a variety of locations, but London has been used more than most. The results have suggested a rental value depreciation rate of less than 0.5% p.a. to more than 2% p.a.

Note that the complexity of property depreciation is illustrated by an ageing building producing a rising rental income. This may be explained by the split of investment into site and building. While the site may appreciate or depreciate in value in real terms, the building must depreciate. For illustration, assume that the current ERV (or NOI) of the subject 10-year-old building is £25/sq. ft. A rental growth estimate of 6% p.a. over the 10-year holding period is projected for the location, and rents adjust at 5-year intervals. Similar 15-year-old buildings currently let at £22/sq. ft; 20-year-old buildings currently let at £18/sq. ft. The capitalisation rate for the 10-year-old building is currently estimated at 7% and the projected resale capitalisation rate is 8% in 10 years' time when the building will be 20 years old.

The projected rental values are as follows:

Year 1–5:		= £25.00
Year 6–10:	$£22 \times (1.06)^5$	= £29.44
Year 10 (resale):	$£18 \times (1.06)^{10}$	= £32.24

The growth rate of property rents is from £25 to £32.24 over 10 years, which represents an average growth rate of 2.57% p.a. The depreciation rate is given by:

$$(1+\textit{location growth})/(1+\textit{property growth})-1=(1.06^{10}/1.0257^{1})-1=3.34\%\ \text{p.a.}$$

As the resale capitalisation rate is predicted as 8%, the resale price is therefore given by:

$$\textit{Rent}/\textit{cap rate} = £32.24/0.08\ \textit{per square foot} = £402.94\ \textit{per square foot}$$

TABLE 5.1 Depreciated cash flow

Years	Outlay	Income	Realisation
0	−£357.14		
1–5		£25	
6–10		£29.44	
10			£402.94

The current valuation is given by:

$$£25 / 0.07 = £357.14 \textit{ per square foot}$$

The gross cash flow is therefore as shown in Table 5.1.
The IRR of this investment – gross of all costs – is 8.37%.

5.2.6 Expenses

Implicit within the gross cash flow from a property investment is a series of regularly recurring expenses. These include management costs, either fees charged by an agent or professional in-house staff. In the former case they may be based on a percentage of gross rents; in the latter, they need more careful estimation, and may have to be increased over time. Repairs and maintenance will normally be covered, like insurance, by the tenant's obligations under a triple net or (in the UK) full repairing and insuring (FRI) lease. If not, they must be accounted for, as must the exceptional burden of rates (UK) or property taxes (USA) if payable by the investor.

While the property owner who provides services, for example to the common parts of a multi-tenanted office building or shopping centre, will usually expect to recover these expenses in a service (or common area maintenance) charge, the amount received may not quite match the cost of provision through a lagging effect or other causes, in which case an allowance for the service charge shortfall needs to be made.

All expenses not tied to rent must be subject to an allowance for anticipated cost inflation.

Fees

In order to strip out all costs to leave a net return estimate, acquisition fees and sale fees at the end of the holding period need to be removed from the cash flow. These will normally be percentages of purchase and sale prices. Brokerage commissions, rent review fees, legal fees, and releasing fees may all be relevant.

Taxes

Most of the analysis provided in this book assumes before-tax cash flow analysis. However, property investment appraisal for the individual investor or fund can, and should, be absolutely specific regarding the tax implications of the purchase. Thus, capital and writing down (depreciation) allowances should be taken into account where appropriate. Income or corporation tax should be removed from the income flow. Capital gains tax payable upon resale can be projected precisely by the model's insistence upon estimation of the purchase price, sale price, intervening expenditure, and holding period. Tax laws are known to change frequently, and we recommend that the analyst engage competent tax counsel to determine the impact of taxes on their investment valuation and investment feasibility analysis.

Debt Finance (Interest)

The majority of property investments are debt-financed. Private individuals, property companies, and private equity funds all use borrowed cash (debt) to purchase property. The reasons for this are several. There are usually limitations on the availability of equity capital and diversification of a portfolio can be achieved by using 50% debt finance to buy two buildings of similar cost rather than use all equity to buy one. As long as the interest rate is less than the expected return, the return will be enhanced by leverage. Debt may also hedge currency and increase the tax efficiency of a property investment for a foreign buyer (see Chapter 15).

5.3 THE DISCOUNT RATE

The principal purpose of property investment analysis in the form discussed in this chapter is the facilitation of decision-making. The basic criterion for decision-making in investment, risk considerations apart, is the expected or required rate of return. This is termed the *target rate* (sometimes the *hurdle rate*) of return.

The target rate has already appeared in Chapter 4, and should be based on the return required by the investor to compensate him for the loss of capital employed in the project which could have been employed elsewhere, that is the risk-free opportunity cost of capital (for example, the yield on Treasury bonds or redemption yield on gilts) and a risk premium. The key challenge involved in estimating the required return is the estimation of the risk premium.

In Chapter 4, we suggest that the risk premium may be built up from the following components: the property market risk premium; the sector risk premium; the location premium; and the asset premium. For an investor who is not fully diversified, which defines the vast majority, the asset premium needs to be assessed by considering the factors that create specific risk. We suggested the following: tenant risk; lease risk; location risk; and building risk.

Properties where the cash flow is more certain should have lower risk margins. For example, a heavily over-rented property (let at more than its full rental value or higher than current market rates) let on a long lease with upwards-only rent reviews to a high-quality tenant is a low-risk investment, as the level of cash flow is virtually guaranteed over a long time period. A property let on a short lease to an unstable tenant has uncertainty attached to the cash flow and should attract a higher risk premium.

One way of identifying the risk premium is to use surveys of investors, and such research is used in a number of countries. In Sweden, for example, periodic performance measurement valuations are undertaken by using DCF approaches, and these valuations are analysed to identify sector and segment target rates of return. In the UK, some *ad hoc* surveys have been undertaken; they have produced varying rates dependent on different market conditions and also vary between different sectors and segments, but risk premiums usually fall in the range between 2% and 5%. Adding debt will likely further increase an investor's risk premium.

Box 5.1 is an example of how these assumptions come together in a valuation example.

Box 5.1: A Simple Appraisal Case

An office block in a provincial UK city was built and let 17 years ago. It is currently let to a single tenant on a 25-year full repairing and insuring lease with 5-yearly upwards-only rent reviews at a current rent of £80,000 p.a. collected quarterly in advance. It now has 8 years unexpired, with the next review in 3 years. It is for sale at £1,250,000. The target rate of return is 9%.

You estimate the following information:

- The current rental value of the existing building is £100,000 p.a.
- Forecasts of rental growth rates for new buildings in the location average 4% p.a.
- The cap rate of the existing building at resale (the going-out cap rate) is estimated at 7.5%.
- The rental depreciation rate of the existing building over the next 8 years is estimated at 1% p.a., with no capital expenditure expected between now and the end of the lease.
- Other costs are rent review costs at 4% of the new rent, purchase costs at 5.75% including UK stamp duty, sale costs at 2.5%, and annual management charges at 1% of rent collected.

What would be the expected cash flow assuming a holding period of 8 years? The full cash flow quarter by quarter is set out in Table 5.2.

The total outlay including purchase costs is £1,321,875 at the beginning of quarter 1 (period 0) and immediately the first quarter's rent is received in advance for the first quarter of ownership (also period 0).

At the end of quarter 1 (period 1) the next quarter's rent is received in advance and this is repeated every quarter until the rent for the last quarter of the first 3 years is received at period 11.

After 3 years or 12 quarters, a rent review is undertaken and (assuming the rent grows by 4% p.a. in the location, less 1% p.a. for depreciation of the building) the expected net growth rate is 2.97% ((1.04/1.01) – 1). The rental value grows from £100,000 to £109,178 p.a., which is just under £27,295 per quarter. At the rent review the rent changes from £20,000 per quarter to the new amount. (Because there are no more rent reviews this rent remains static for the remainder of the 8-year unexpired term.) At quarter 12 the negotiations for the rent review generate a fee of £4,367, which can be deducted from the cash flow at that point. The new rent is collected in advance as from period 12.

TABLE 5.2 Lease cash flow (quarters)

Period	Gross income	Annual maintenance costs	Rent review, lease, purchase, sale costs	Net income	PV @ 9%	Present value
0	−£1,250,000		−£71,875	−£1,321,875	1.0000	−£1,321,875
0	£20,000	£200		£19,800	1.0000	£19,800
1	£20,000	£200		£19,800	0.9787	£19,378
2	£20,000	£200		£19,800	0.9578	£18,965
3	£20,000	£200		£19,800	0.9374	£18,561
4	£20,000	£200		£19,800	0.9174	£18,165
5	£20,000	£200		£19,800	0.8979	£17,778
6	£20,000	£200		£19,800	0.8787	£17,399
7	£20,000	£200		£19,800	0.8600	£17,028
8	£20,000	£200		£19,800	0.8417	£16,665
9	£20,000	£200		£19,800	0.8237	£16,310
10	£20,000	£200		£19,800	0.8062	£15,962
11	£20,000	£200		£19,800	0.7890	£15,622
12	£27,295	£273	£4,367	£22,654	0.7722	£17,493
13	£27,295	£273		£27,022	0.7557	£20,421
14	£27,295	£273		£27,022	0.7396	£19,986
15	£27,295	£273		£27,022	0.7239	£19,560
16	£27,295	£273		£27,022	0.7084	£19,143
17	£27,295	£273		£27,022	0.6933	£18,735
18	£27,295	£273		£27,022	0.6785	£18,335
19	£27,295	£273		£27,022	0.6641	£17,945
20	£27,295	£273		£27,022	0.6499	£17,562
21	£27,295	£273		£27,022	0.6361	£17,188
22	£27,295	£273		£27,022	0.6225	£16,822
23	£27,295	£273		£27,022	0.6093	£16,463
24	£27,295	£273		£27,022	0.5963	£16,112
25	£27,295	£273		£27,022	0.5836	£15,769
26	£27,295	£273		£27,022	0.5711	£15,433
27	£27,295	£273		£27,022	0.5589	£15,104
28	£27,295	£273		£27,022	0.5470	£14,782
29	£27,295	£273		£27,022	0.5354	£14,467
30	£27,295	£273		£27,022	0.5240	£14,158
31	£27,295	£273		£27,022	0.5128	£13,857

The cash flow is discounted at the quarterly equivalent of 9% p.a., which is 2.177%.

The sum of the last column is the net present value of the lease income less the original outlay and produces a total deficit of £770,909.

(continued)

(continued)

TABLE 5.3 Exit sale price and NPV calculation

Rental value	£126,385
/ cap rate	0.075
= estimated sale price	£1,685,134
− sale costs @ 2.5%	£41,101
= sale price net of sale costs	£1,644,033
*** PV 8 yrs @ 9%**	0.5019
= present exit value	£824,569
+ PV lease cash flow	−£770.909
= NPV	£53,660

However, at the end of the holding period the property can be sold. The sale price can be forecast as a function of the future rental value at the time of sale capitalised at the exit yield at that point. The existing rental value is £100,000 and it is growing at a net rate of 2.97% p.a. after depreciation. After 8 years it will have grown to £126,385.

The exit cap rate will be a function of the market's expectations for income and growth beyond the sale date and the return requirements of the investors at that time. It is unlikely to be the same as it is now, both because market conditions may have changed and also because upon sale, the property will be 8 years older than it is now. Even in a market where market yield levels have remained static since the purchase, the expectation for the exit yield would be different simply because the building is less attractive. Assume the older building will sell at an exit yield of 7.5% (Table 5.3).

Because a positive NPV results, this suggests that the investment will produce a higher return than the target of 9%.

Other inputs which might be considered in a DCF appraisal include the costs of debt financing on the cash flow, taxes on the net income and the sale price, and potential developments such as enhancing the existing building, changing the use, and a full redevelopment (potentially for different uses).

A fuller example incorporating many of these issues is presented in Chapters 7 and 9.

5.4 CONCLUSION

An accurate property appraisal is most likely to be achieved by capitalising the stream of future cash flows expected to be earned by a property asset. In this chapter we introduced this DCF approach. The following chapters in Part II provide a more in-depth analysis of DCF analysis as it is applied to real estate investment.

Chapter 6 provides a discussion of leasing. Since leases provide the cash flow for property, and cash flow is the key input to the DCF model, it is essential to learn the intricacies of different types of leases and how they impact the cash flow that an owner of property can expect to earn.

Chapter 7 uses leases and sale cash flows to lay the groundwork for DCF analysis for an investor that does not use debt.

Chapter 8 provides an introduction to commercial property mortgages.

Chapter 9 shows how a lender would underwrite a mortgage loan, and how the loan impacts valuation and investment performance for an equity investor.

Chapter 10 shows how property developers make decisions. We utilise similar valuation techniques as described in this chapter that are used by developers to determine the relationship between market value and the cost to construct a property.

Chapter 11 describes the unlisted real estate funds market, and Chapter 12 shows how DCF can be used to model the returns available to investors in, and managers of, joint ventures and unlisted funds when a performance fee or carried interest is agreed.

CHAPTER 6

Leasing

6.1 INTRODUCTION

In this chapter, we are generally describing US leasing practice. Cross-references are made at the end of each section to the more significant differences in UK practice and occasionally to other markets. There will be many other local variants driven by legislation or custom which we do not discuss. Local expertise is always necessary in understanding market variations in leasing practice.

Understanding real estate investment and finance requires thorough knowledge of many different types of legal documents. Among these are contracts to purchase and sell property, listing contracts, deeds, promissory notes, mortgages or deeds of trust, leases, partnership agreements, and many others. As with most legal agreements, they are negotiated and signed (or executed) before they are transacted, and after they are signed they dictate every single event that occurs thereafter. From the perspective of a real estate investor, the lease is one of the most important legal agreements. Leases are negotiated documents that dictate the rights and responsibilities of the owner of a building and the tenants who occupy space in the building, and also set out the timing and amount of payments that will be passed between tenants and the owner.

Within any large commercial building may be hidden a complex pattern of relationships created by the unique nature of property as an economic commodity. The market for property is better thought of as a market for rights in a product that may have many tiers of ownership. Consequently, a single building might represent the property rights or interests of several different parties.

For a given unit of property, there is a basic dichotomy of rights. These are the right of ownership, which may be fragmented, and the right of occupation, which (allowing for the existence of time shares and joint tenancies) is usually vested in a single legal person. In fact, the "given unit" is commonly delineated by its exclusive occupation by an organization, family, or individual.

It is especially typical in the case of commercial property (all office, shop, industrial, and institutional property, for the purposes of this book) that buildings are "owned" by non-occupiers, in contrast to residential property, where the rights of ownership and occupation are often fused within the same person. This decomposition of the ownership of commercial property produces the probability of the existence of contractual landlord/tenant relationships. The medium for these relationships is a contract or a lease, which defines the contractual relationship between the parties.

Since leases create the cash flows that are earned by the owner of a building, they are very important contracts to understand. Leases dictate every cash flow event that occurs between the landlord and the tenant from the time the lease is signed until it terminates. Lease characteristics and terms are dependent upon market conditions for space at the time the lease is negotiated and signed. In periods of low demand for space, or when large amounts of space are available, the tenant's bargaining power increases relative to the landlord's. When demand for space is strong, and there is little availability, the landlord has a favorable bargaining position.

A lease will contain provisions that specifically identify the rights and responsibilities of tenant and landlord during the lease term. These include provisions related to which party is responsible for expenses, how many parking spaces are included with the leased space, which party is responsible for tenant improvements, and other provisions specific to the agreement between the landlord and the tenant. A lease provides an estate in land, and any occupancy is deemed to be a lease if it is for a defined duration, there is an agreed rent, and there is exclusive possession of the interest.

There are many factors contained in a lease that directly affect the value and performance of interests in land and buildings. For instance, repairing liabilities, lease length, break clauses, user and assignment restrictions, and rent review patterns or escalations may all, individually or collectively, impact on the cash flow delivered by the property and its resulting capital or rental value. The differences between a UK lease governed by 5-yearly, upward-only rent reviews, a French 3-6-9 lease, and a US full-service lease with annual escalations produce very different cash flow characteristics and different valuations.

We start with some general terminology about a lease. First, the owner is also called a landlord or a lessor. A name that is used interchangeably with tenant is lessee. The formal name for a lease is a leasehold estate. A leasehold estate provides for the tenant to occupy, use, and possess the space for the duration of the lease. The owner continues to own the property. At the end of the lease term, the use and possession reverts back to the owner. If the property is sold by the owner, all existing leases in a building remain in place, and convey, or transfer, to the new owner.

6.2 LEGAL CHARACTERISTICS OF LEASES

The two major types of lease are a "Tenancy for Term of Years" and a "Tenancy from Year to Year." In both cases, use of the term "year" is misleading, as either type of lease can be written for any time period. The Tenancy for Term of Years has a fixed starting point and a fixed ending point. This type of lease can be for a day, a month, a year, or any other specified period, and at the end of that period the leased space reverts back to the owner unless some other provision allows the tenant to remain. Most leases will have a renewal period, which allows extension of the lease at the expiration of its original term. A Tenancy for Term of Years is the typical lease that is employed for most property types.

A Tenancy from Year to Year has a specific starting point, but an unspecified ending time. Typical of this type of lease is a month-to-month lease in a self-storage facility or an apartment complex. Instead of having a fixed ending date, the tenant has the right to renew the lease by continuing to use and possess the space. Either party may terminate the lease by giving notice of their intention to do so to the other party at some specified time before the end of the lease term. For example, the tenant may have to notify the landlord in writing 30 days in advance of vacating the space in a month-to-month lease. Similarly, a landlord may give 30 days' notice to a tenant indicating an intent to terminate the lease. For a Tenancy from Year to Year, there is a perpetual renewal option that is outstanding as long as the tenant continues to pay rent, or until notice to vacate is given by either party to the lease.

In the UK, the 1954 Landlord and Tenant Act provides a right for the tenant to renew the lease, although the parties may agree to "contract out" of this right. The Tenancy from Year to Year is known as a periodic tenancy. In many jurisdictions the "default" tenancy, where the parties have not explicitly specified a different arrangement, and where none is presumed under local or business custom, is the month-to-month tenancy. There are also differences between a lease and a licence (UK spelling). A licence is a personal arrangement which provides a right to use land or property, and the licensee acquires no interest. It is used to make something lawful which otherwise would be trespass, and includes tickets to concerts or athletic events.

6.3 THE LEASING PROCESS

When tenants identify space that is deemed desirable, they will typically submit a letter of intent (LOI) to the landlord with broad lease terms identified. These may include the base rent per square foot (psf) that they would like to pay, the term of the lease with start and end date, whether the rent will increase at specific intervals, how much space they would be interested in leasing, and other provisions. The LOI will often be submitted by a broker who is representing the interests of the tenant, and drawn up with the broker's assistance.

The landlord typically has a specified period within which to respond to the LOI, and will often counter with a proposal that is more beneficial to the landlord's interests. At this stage, negotiations begin and the final terms of the lease transaction are arranged. As the parties near agreement, lawyers are brought in to draft the lease. Once both parties come to terms, a lease is executed when the landlord and tenant both sign it.

In the UK, the landlord or their agent typically proposes terms. An agreement for lease creates binding heads of terms but defines necessary conditions (for example, the landlord finishing fit out or tenant improvement work) before the lease (a separate document) is activated.

6.4 IMPORTANT ECONOMIC ELEMENTS OF A LEASE

Among the many things that are negotiated, there are several issues that are critical in determining the timing of payments and the amount of cash that passes from the tenant to the landlord during the lease term. Some of the more important elements are as follows.

6.4.1 The Term of the Lease

The term of the lease dictates the period during which the tenant will occupy the space and be obligated to pay rent. The lease term could be as short as 1 month or as long as 20 years or more. In general, longer-term leases are preferred by landlords, but only if the tenant has strong credit and rents are indexed to increase or escalate at regular intervals throughout the lease term.

Terms shorter than 1 year are rare in office leasing. Terms of 3, 5, and 10 years are probably most common in the USA, but this will depend on the local market. The term of the lease will often differ according to property type. For example, apartment leases are typically for a 1-year term. Office and retail leases more often would be in the 3, 5, or 10-year range, and industrial properties will exhibit terms in the 5, 7, or 10-year range.

In the UK, 15-year terms, including a break at year 10, are common for high-quality office buildings, although the 10-year lease with a break at year 5 is increasingly familiar. So-called "secondary" properties will commonly be let for shorter terms of 3 or 5 years. Ground leases for unimproved property – bare land – can be for as long as 99, 125, or even 999 years.

The UK is unique in its use of the upward-only rent review, a palpably landlord-friendly device which gives the property owner an option to increase the rent to market levels at regular intervals but protects them from falls in market rents.

6.4.2 Base Rent and Rent Escalation Provisions[1]

The base rent will be stipulated in the initial lease document on both a square-foot basis and a total-dollar basis. The base rent will typically escalate or increase at the lease anniversary date in future years. Rent escalation tied to the Consumer Price Index (CPI) was common in the 1970s and early 1980s due to high levels of inflation. In this case, the landlord will consult official government publications that calculate the rate of inflation over the previous year, and increase the base rental rate by that amount in the following year. If the CPI increased by 3.5%, the base rent will increase by that amount, in effect indexing rents (with a 1-year lag) to inflation with annual adjustments.

Of course, it is difficult to project what consumer prices will do over a 5-year lease term. Since CPI adjustments in the future are uncertain, another more recently common escalation technique is to pre-specify the rate at which rents can increase, and adjust the base rental rate by that amount each year.

The examples we use from this point onwards will be based exclusively on US practice.

We assume that market rents at the time the least is signed are $23.00 psf, and that the lease agreement stipulates annual escalation of 3%. The rents per square foot that would be paid under this scenario are as shown in Table 6.1.

In the UK, rents are rarely index-linked, while in continental Europe this is commonplace, albeit with some restrictions on how the indexation passes through to rents, at different intervals.

---

[1]Much of the discussion in the following sections is based on office leasing, but the general techniques used can be applied to leases on all property types and sectors.

TABLE 6.1 CPI-adjusted rents

	Year 1	Year 2	Year 3	Year 4	Year 5
Rent (psf)	$23.00	$23.69	$24.40	$25.13	$25.88

6.4.3 Options

Tenant and landlord options are key elements of a lease and often consume much of the negotiation process. Common options include renewal, expansion, contraction, and termination. In each type of option, it is crucial to understand which party has the right to exercise and what the consequences entail.

Renewal Options

At the termination of the original lease, the tenant is often given the option to renew the lease for another period. For example, if the original lease term was 5 years, two 5-year renewal options may be written into the lease agreement. The renewal period could be the same as the original lease term, or it could be for a shorter or longer period. The tenant has the option to renew, and must notify the landlord of its intention to stay in the premises and extend the lease by some pre-specified time before the original lease expires (e.g. 90 days before the end of the original lease).

Renewal options typically operate to the benefit of the tenant. For example, a tenant with good credit that wishes to occupy a large amount of space in a building will have an advantageous bargaining position, especially in a weak market. The tenant may be able to negotiate a relatively low rental rate, and several renewal periods. This provides the tenant with the right to use and possess the space for potentially a long period of time.

The method for determining the lease rate at renewal is usually specified in the lease document. The rate at renewal at the end of the original lease term could be marked to current rental rates for space of similar quality. This new rate could be higher or lower than the rate the tenant is paying after 5 years on the lease that has escalated. For example, if market rents were $23.50 at the end of the fifth year, the rate the tenant pays would drop from the escalated $25.88 to the lower market rate in the first year of the renewal period. Alternatively, a lease rate for year 6 could be renegotiated between the landlord and the tenant prior to the expiration of the original lease term.

Expansion, Contraction, and Termination Options

In many cases, tenants and landlords seek to mitigate uncertainty about future space needs through other types of options. These options include expansion, contraction, and termination options. Unlike renewal options, which are almost always to the benefit of tenants, these options can be utilized to either party's advantage.

As an illustration, if a commercial tenant believes he will need additional space at some point in the future, they will often negotiate the right to expand into adjacent spaces if and when the adjacent space becomes vacant. The terms and timing of the expansion option can be predetermined if specified in the original lease document.

Alternatively, lease-expansion terms could be designed as a right of first refusal, where the tenant has the right to lease some or all of the available space at terms that are negotiated when the expansion is desired by the tenant. In this case, the expansion right is used to the benefit of the tenant.

Either party may also have the option to terminate a lease under certain conditions. For example, a landlord could negotiate a termination option for multiple reasons, but a common motive is to terminate the lease, so that the property can be redeveloped at a future date. If the landlord feels the highest and best use of the property may change during the term of the lease to a tenant, the landlord can negotiate a right to terminate the lease with a specified period of notice. Tenants may also terminate or downsize a lease if their businesses contract.

Regardless of who benefits from the aforementioned options, there is often a cost associated with each that is incurred by the exercising party. Expansion options often involve paying above-market rental rates. Contraction and termination options often involve fees and penalties tied to the cost of relocating for a landlord's termination. When a tenant wishes to vacate or decrease the amount of space they lease prior to the end of the lease term, they will be required to pay a negotiated amount that is typically based on the present value of the rent payments that the tenant otherwise would have paid if they had not terminated part or all of the lease. In addition, the landlord usually incurs costs of improving tenant space prior to the beginning of the lease term, with full expectation that the tenant will occupy the agreed-upon amount of space over the full lease term. If the tenant terminates prior to the end of the lease term, they will be required to pay a proportional amount of tenant improvements based on the time left on the lease to provide compensation to the landlord.

In the UK, the right to renewal and the ability for the landlord to terminate depend on whether the tenancy is governed by the 1954 Act: see above. Expansion and contraction rights are rare.

When a lease term expires, it is typically the tenant's responsibility to return a property to the condition it was in at the start of the lease. This is referred to as "dilapidations."

6.4.4 Measurement of Space

There are generally two ways to measure the space in a building. Usable space is the space that can be allocated to tenants. Rentable (or leasable) space is usable space plus space in the building that cannot be allocated specifically to one particular tenant, but is shared with other building occupants. The space that is not allocable to a tenant is often referred to as common area, and includes lobby space, elevators, stairways, hallways, communal bathrooms and showers, the core of the building where the elevator machinery is located, and other square footage that cannot be specifically occupied.

Typically, the landlord will use architectural plans to determine the relationship between usable and rentable space. Since the landlord expended capital to construct all of the space, they would like to earn rents on the common area as well as the space that can be allocated to individual tenants. The typical calculation is based on the ratio of total rentable space to usable space, which is often called the efficiency ratio. For example, assume that a building has 56,000 square feet of total space, but only 50,000 square feet of space that can be occupied by specific tenants. The efficiency ratio is thus 56,000 / 50,000 or 1.12.

This is important, because the amount of square feet that is leased by each tenant is multiplied by the efficiency ratio to determine the total square footage upon which they will actually have to pay rent. A simple example will help to clarify this.

Assume that local market rents are $23 per rentable square foot, and that the landlord has agreed to lease 3,000 square feet of usable space to a small real estate consulting firm. Within the lease documents, the landlord specifies that the efficiency ratio of the building is 1.12. Another way of saying this is that the "load factor" or "core factor" is 12%. Because of the load factor, the tenant will pay $23 psf based on (3,000 * 1.12) or 3,360 total square feet. Without the core factor, the tenant would have paid (3,000 * $23) or $69,000 in rents per year. Including the core factor, the tenant pays (3,360 * $23) or $77,280 in rents per year. Therefore, while the base rent is specified in the lease at $23 per rentable square foot, the actual rent paid per usable square foot is ($77,280 / 3,000), or $25.76. The higher the core factor, the higher will be the total rent payment made by the tenant.

Efficiency ratios will differ across buildings, as can annual rents paid by tenants. Let us assume that a tenant has found three different buildings in which to lease space. Building A has an efficiency ratio of 1.08, building B has an efficiency ratio of 1.12 (as above), and building C has an efficiency ratio of 1.18. The first-year cost to the tenant of leasing space in these three buildings, which all exhibit a rent of $23 psf, is $74,520, $77,280, and $81,420, respectively. Rental cost for the less efficient building (e.g. the one with the 1.18 load factor) is $6,900 higher than for the most efficient building (e.g. the one with the 1.08 load factor). Unless there is a substantial tenant advantage to having more common area, the less expensive alternative will typically be chosen.

In the UK there is a distinction between leasable and usable space. Leases do not refer to space being let, but market measurement practice is clearly understood, as a result of which rent per square foot is defined. This is based on "net internal area" for offices, which includes the footprint of the building but excludes common areas and other unusable space; gross internal area for industrials, measured from the inside of the external walls; and gross external area for some specialist buildings. For retail property, "zoning" – nothing to do with permitted land use – is commonly used to reflect the value of a shop frontage relative to its depth. Spaces closer to the street rent for higher amounts than spaces deeper into the building.

6.4.5 Expense Treatment

There are many ways that expenses are shared between landlords and tenants. The two extremes are gross (or full service) leases and fully net (or triple net) leases.

Gross Lease

The tenant pays a base rent, and the landlord is responsible for all expenses associated with operating the building. These expenses include, but are not limited to, property taxes (rates in the UK), utilities, insurance, janitorial expenses, repairs and maintenance, management, and any other expenses that are incurred. Income tax and debt service payments owed by the owner are not considered operating expenses of the property.

Under a standard gross lease, if market rents are $23 psf and first-year operating expenses (OE) are $7.50 psf, the landlord will earn gross rental revenue (GRR) of $23 psf and net operating income (NOI) of $15.50 psf during the first year. For a standard gross lease, any increases in operating expenses in later years are borne by the landlord.

For example, let us assume that lease terms provide for an escalation rate of 3% each year after the lease is signed, and that operating expenses are expected to increase by 4% p.a. In year 2, top-line rents will increase to $23.69, and operating expenses in this scenario would rise to $7.80. Therefore, the net income earned by the landlord is the difference, or $15.89. The full brunt of the increase in operating expenses is incurred by the landlord in this case. Assuming a 5-year lease term, the rental income statement per square foot for the 5-year term is shown in Table 6.2.

Total dollar amounts earned by the landlord from this lease in each year are shown in Table 6.3. These numbers assume a tenant that leases 3,000 usable square feet in a building with an efficiency ratio of 1.12, so that total leasable area is 3,360 square feet.

Note that the top-line GRR is the amount that is earned by the owner from this lease, and the NOI is the residual cash flow earned by the owner after deducting all expenses needed to operate the building. The tenant is responsible for paying $77,280 in the first year, and an escalating amount thereafter.

Many gross leases will also include an expense stop, which limits or stops the operating expenses that will be paid by the landlord. With an expense stop, the landlord's liability for payment of expenses in any year after the first year is limited to $7.50, and future operating expense increases (e.g. the $0.30 increase to $7.80 in year 2) are the sole responsibility of the tenant. For all subsequent years during the specified lease term, the tenant will pay all operating expenses in excess of $7.50 psf.

As above, the landlord will earn a net income of $15.50 in the first year. In the second year of the lease term, with the expense stop and a 3% CPI rent escalator, the net income per square foot earned by the landlord is $16.19 ($23.69 – $7.50), which is a

TABLE 6.2 Net operating income (psf)

	Year 1	Year 2	Year 3	Year 4	Year 5
GRR	$23.00	$23.69	$24.40	$25.13	$25.89
– OE	–$7.50	–$7.80	–$8.11	–$8.44	–$8.77
NOI	$15.50	$15.89	$16.29	$16.70	$17.11

TABLE 6.3 Net operating income

	Year 1	Year 2	Year 3	Year 4	Year 5
GRR	$77,280	$79,598	$81,984	$84,437	$86,957
– OE	–$25,200	–$26,208	–$27,250	–$28,325	–$29,467
NOI	$52,080	$53,390	$54,734	$56,112	$57,490

better outcome for the landlord than a standard gross lease. The income statement per square foot for a gross lease with an expense stop is as shown in Table 6.4.

In year 5, the difference in the income earned by the landlord between a standard gross lease and a gross lease with an expense stop is $1.27 psf.

Dollar amounts earned by the landlord for a lease with an expense stop are as shown in Table 6.5.

For a tenant leasing 3,360 square feet of rentable space, the difference in fifth-year NOI between a lease without an expense stop and one with an expense stop is $3,667 per year.

Note that the tenant's total expenditure for this lease structure includes the top-line rent (gross rent paid) and the amount of operating expenses in excess of the expense stop. This amount can be summarized as shown in Table 6.6.

Total expenditures are therefore higher for the tenant in the case of a lease with an expense stop, as shown in Table 6.7.

TABLE 6.4 NOI with expense stop (psf)

	Year 1	Year 2	Year 3	Year 4	Year 5
GRR	$23.00	$23.69	$24.40	$25.13	$25.88
– OE	–$7.50	–$7.50	–$7.50	–$7.50	–$7.50
NOI	$15.50	$16.19	$16.90	$17.63	$18.38

TABLE 6.5 NOI with expense stop

	Year 1	Year 2	Year 3	Year 4	Year 5
GRR	$77,280	$79,598	$81,984	$84,437	$86,957
– OE	–$25,200	–$25,200	–$25,200	–$25,200	–$25,200
NOI	$52,080	$54,398	$56,784	$59,237	$61,757

TABLE 6.6 Tenant costs (psf)

	Year 1	Year 2	Year 3	Year 4	Year 5
Gross rent paid	$23.00	$23.69	$24.40	$25.13	$25.88
+ OE overage	$0.00	$0.30	$0.61	$0.93	$1.27
Total cost	$23.00	$23.99	$25.01	$26.06	$27.15

TABLE 6.7 Tenant costs

	Year 1	Year 2	Year 3	Year 4	Year 5
Gross rent paid	$77,280	$79,598	$81,984	$84,437	$86,957
+ OE overage	$0	$1,008	$2,050	$3,125	$4,267
Total cost	$77,280	$80,606	$84,034	$87,562	$91,224

Triple Net Lease

A net lease is at the other end of the spectrum from the gross lease. In a Triple Net (or Fully Net or NNN) Lease, the tenant pays base rent to the landlord, and the tenant is responsible for paying all expenses. If the lease exhibits an escalation clause, the landlord effectively receives an indexed net cash flow that increases every year on the anniversary date of the lease.

Using the previous example, the tenant would pay first-year rent of $15.50, and then also be responsible for paying $7.50 in operating expenses in the first year. After that, any further increases in operating expenses would also be borne by the tenant. Assuming a 3% escalation rate, second-year rents paid by the tenant, and earned by the landlord, would be $15.97.

The 5-year stream of per-square-foot cash flows that are paid by the tenant in the net lease case is as shown (per square foot) in Table 6.8.

The annual rent paid by the tenant, and earned by the landlord, is shown in Table 6.9.

Assuming that operating expenses increase, as in the previous case, by 4% per year, the total amount paid by the tenant on a per-square-foot basis over the 5-year period is as shown in Table 6.10.

The total amount paid in dollars by the tenant on a per-square-foot basis over the 5-year period is as shown in Table 6.11.

It should be clear that the treatment of operating expenses can have a significant impact on the bottom-line net rents earned by the landlord, and the total amount of rent and operating expenses paid by the tenant, throughout the term of the lease. A comparison of the three lease scenarios above provides very different results. In general, the

TABLE 6.8 Net lease rents (psf)

	Year 1	Year 2	Year 3	Year 4	Year 5
Net lease rent	$15.50	$15.97	$16.45	$16.94	$17.45

TABLE 6.9 Net lease rents

	Year 1	Year 2	Year 3	Year 4	Year 5
Net lease rent	$52,080	$53,659	$55,272	$56,918	$58,632

TABLE 6.10 Total tenant expenditure (psf)

	Year 1	Year 2	Year 3	Year 4	Year 5
Net lease rent paid	$15.50	$15.97	$16.45	$16.94	$17.45
+ Operating expenses	$7.50	$7.80	$8.11	$8.43	$8.77
Total cost	$23.00	$23.77	$24.56	$25.37	$26.22

TABLE 6.11 Total tenant expenditure (psf)

	Year 1	Year 2	Year 3	Year 4	Year 5
Net lease rent paid	$52,080	$53,659	$55,272	$56,918	$58,632
+ Operating expenses	$25,200	$26,208	$27,250	$28,325	$29,467
Total cost	$77,280	$79,867	$82,522	$85,243	$88,099

landlord incurs the risk of increasing operating expenses in a standard gross lease. In a gross lease with an expense stop or a net lease, the tenant will incur the risk of increases in operating expenses.

For comparison, the NOI earned by the landlord, and the total outflow or expenditure incurred by the tenant for leases under the three different expense scenarios, is shown in Tables 6.12 and 6.13.

Summing all of the cash flows from each year, the total landlord income and tenant expenditure is summarized in Table 6.14 to show overall differences between the three types of leases.

The total income earned for the gross lease with an expense stop is $10,450 higher than the straight gross lease, showing that having the tenant pay increases in operating expenses is beneficial for the owner. Similarly, the total tenant expenditure for the gross lease with an expense stop is $10,450 higher than the straight gross lease.

TABLE 6.12 Landlord net income

	Year 1	Year 2	Year 3	Year 4	Year 5
Gross lease	$52,080	$53,390	$54,734	$56,112	$57,490
Gross lease with stop	$52,080	$54,398	$56,784	$59,237	$61,757
Net lease	$52,080	$53,659	$55,272	$56,918	$58,632

TABLE 6.13 Tenant total expenditure

	Year 1	Year 2	Year 3	Year 4	Year 5
Gross lease	$77,280	$79,598	$81,984	$84,437	$86,957
Gross lease with stop	$77,280	$80,606	$84,034	$87,562	$91,224
Net lease	$77,280	$79,867	$82,522	$85,243	$88,099

TABLE 6.14 Tenant expenditure and landlord income under different leases

	Total landlord net income	Total tenant expenditure
Gross lease	$273,806	$410,256
Gross lease with stop	$284,256	$420,706
Net lease	$276,561	$413,011

In practice, most leases fall somewhere between a fully gross lease and a fully net lease, with conditions stipulated that meet the needs of the landlord or tenant. For example, the tenant may be obligated to pay their pro rata share or property taxes and insurance, while the landlord is responsible for paying all other expenses. In other cases, the landlord may be responsible for property taxes and insurance on the building, but the tenant will be responsible for paying all other expenses. Local market conditions at the time when the lease is negotiated and signed, as well as local market conventions regarding treatment of expenses, will dictate the nature of expense sharing between landlord and tenant.

In the UK, gross leases are rare and the main alternatives are internal repairing and insuring (IRI) leases and full repairing and insuring (FRI) leases, whereby the tenant's responsibilities are defined. In addition, "service charges" are often added to rent to reimburse the landlord for the upkeep and servicing of common areas.

6.4.6 Concessions: Tenant Improvement Allowance and Rental Abatement

There are many forms of concessions, but Tenant Improvement (TI) Allowance and Rental Abatement (Free Rent) are the most common. Both concessions determine the overall out-of-pocket expenses incurred by both landlords and tenants.

Tenant Improvement Allowance or Tenant Upfit/Fitout

For a new building, the space that is conveyed in a lease transaction is known as first-generation space and is often conveyed as "shell and core" in the UK and either "cold dark shell" or "warm dark shell" in the USA. In both cases, the space runs from floor to ceiling, the floor is a concrete slab, and the ceiling is unfinished metal with bare lights hanging. For "cold dark shell," the tenant is responsible for paying to bring heating, ventilation, and air conditioning (HVAC) to the space from a central unit. "Warm dark shell" is similar in that there is a concrete slab floor and exposed ceiling, but the landlord agrees to bring the duct work for the HVAC system to somewhere inside the tenant's space. Since the landlord's cost of providing warm dark shell is higher than cold dark shell, the landlord's contribution to tenant improvement costs will often be lower for the former.

Naturally, there will be a cost for getting the space from this unfinished state to the final move-in state. Some tenants, like lawyers, banks, and other high-end service companies, will require a high standard of interior quality. The cost of converting shell space to finished space in these cases can be high. Others, like back-office tenants, will not need to spend as much. The total cost of build-out will depend on costs of construction in the local market, as well as market conditions.

A tenant will often hire a space planner or architect to design the space, and a contractor (often employed by the developer of the building) to build out the space. All designs and improvements must be approved by the owner of the building.

Tenants and landlords of first-generation space will typically share the cost of tenant improvements. The owner of a new building will include tenant improvements in the construction budget (see Chapter 10), which will pay for part of all costs for upgrading each new tenant's space. If we assume that the cost to go from cold dark shell to finished premises is $50 psf, the landlord and tenant may split the cost equally. For our 3,000 usable square foot tenant, the total cost of tenant improvements would be $150,000, with the landlord and tenant each paying $25 psf, or $75,000. This money is expended by the landlord prior to the receipt of the first rental payment. To entice tenants, the landlord may agree to fund the entire tenant improvement amount.

Second- and later-generation space is space that has already been occupied and vacated by a previous tenant. The space has been designed and finished to the old tenant's needs and specifications, with offices, conference rooms, receptions areas, copier areas, and perhaps kitchens and bathrooms already in place. The new tenant typically takes the space as is, and is responsible for any cosmetic or more involved changes that are desired. In most cases, a landlord may offer a small amount ($5–10 psf) to the new tenant for such work, which will typically only pay for new carpet and paint, as opposed to structural changes to walls and other more permanent features. Any other costs of improving the space will be paid by the tenant.

Rental Abatement (Rent-Free Periods)

Another common form of concession found in leases involves rental abatement. As with most elements found in leases, the amount of a free-rent (or rent-free) period varies substantially by market and economic conditions. In a free-rent, or rental abatement, situation, the tenant will not be required to pay rent between the date of occupation and the end of the free-rent period.

Free rent or rental abatement can be structured in a variety of ways. For example, a landlord and a tenant may agree on a $23 top-line rent for a 5-year term, but with a 1-year "free-rent" period. In this case, the tenant will not actually start paying rent to the landlord until the second year of the lease term. The 5-year lease term could be inclusive of the 1 year of free rent ("inside the term") or the term could be extended by an extra year so that there are 6 years in total to the agreement ("outside the term").

Another example of rental abatement is a 5-year lease that contains 1 month of free rent every calendar year. Alternatively, the 5 months of rent abatement could be granted at the beginning of the lease term. In either case, the 5-year lease term could be inclusive of the 5 months of free rent ("inside the term") or the term could be extended by a 5-month period ("outside the term") for a total lease term of 5 years and 5 months.

The provision of free rent to a tenant often seems unintuitive to non-real estate practitioners, who will ask why the actual rent is not simply decreased over the lease term. Instead of a $23 rent over the lease term, why not decrease the rental amount to $17? There are several reasons.

First, if a lease includes an escalation clause, second-year rents will be grown from the $23 contract rent. Second, the owner may at some point be interested in selling the property, and will inform prospective purchasers that the rental rate per square foot is the $23 psf contract rate. Similarly, if a prospective tenant were to ask what lease rates are being charged by the owner, the $23 psf contract rate will be quoted.

In many cases, free rent and tenant improvement allowances are used interchangeably, and often traded off against each other. For example, if a landlord does not have the financial resources to offer a competitive tenant improvement allowance, they will often propose a greater amount of free rent during the lease term. Alternatively, a landlord can mitigate exposure to a tenant with marginal credit by offering more free rent and less tenant improvement allowance. In that case, the tenant spends more on the build-out and the landlord incurs less upfront cost.

Rental rates and abatement will greatly depend on market conditions in existence at the time the lease is negotiated. A tenant will be able to negotiate a higher level of concessions in a relatively oversupplied market. With numerous options for space available in different buildings, the tenant will likely be able to negotiate a higher tenant improvement allowance, and a longer free-rent period. Conversely, the landlord will have more negotiating power in a relatively strong market, and will offer fewer concessions, if any at all.

In the UK, valuations or appraisals will also be based on headline rents. In Section 6.5, we explore the relationship between the headline rent, rental abatement, and effective rent in more detail. Rent-free periods are used both to provide an incentive to sign a lease and for the purpose of compensating the tenant for fitting-out (upfit) costs. Alternatively, a "premium" may be paid or received by the tenant on signing a lease. The traditional use of the term is to describe a capital sum paid at the start of a lease by a tenant to a landlord in return for a low rent or some other benefit.

The payment of this type of premium can produce advantages for both landlord and tenant. To the landlord, the receipt of an immediate cash sum rather than a flow of income is often more attractive. There may be positive implications of converting income to capital; there may also be useful accounting effects. In addition, if the tenant is paying a lower rent the landlord's income stream is likely to be more secure. The tenant, on the other side of the bargain, may prefer to use up capital in return for a reduced rental. Also, rather than holding a lease at a full market rent which might have no disposal value, the tenant will enjoy a profit rent (the difference between the rent he/she actually pays and the full market rent) which might render the leasehold interest valuable in the event that he/she wishes to dispose of it.

This situation can apply in reverse where supply exceeds demand, and in such a case the seller may be required to pay a premium to a purchaser as an inducement to take over the leasehold interest; such a premium is commonly referred to as a "reverse premium." Such a reverse premium – a cash sum – may be paid if the landlord desperately wants the tenant; anchor tenants in retail schemes provide the best examples.

Typically, in the UK market, a 5-year lease will come with 3–6 months rent free, and a 10 or 15-year lease with 6–18 months rent free. A lease signed by Nomura in the City of London in 2009 was for 20 years with between 5 and 6 years rent free, reflecting Nomura's fitting out costs but also the combined effect of a weak market and the impact of the upward-only rent review, which makes "headline rents" very important.

6.4.7 Brokerage Commissions

Another expense that is paid by the landlord is the commission that is paid to the broker who brought the tenant to the property. Commission rates will differ across markets and for different property types in each market. In general, landlords signing large leases will pay a lower percentage commission. Landlords signing smaller leases will incur a higher percentage leasing commission.

Let us assume that a tenant has negotiated a full-service gross lease which includes a $23 top-line rent paid in the first year of a 5-year lease term. At the time that the lease is signed, an annual rent escalation of 3% is included. The usable square footage is 3,000 square feet, and the load factor is 12%, creating total leasable square footage of 3,360 square feet.

Leasing commissions are based on the total amount of cash flow that is provided to the landlord over the entire lease term. For the 5-year lease, the top-line rent per square foot is multiplied by total rentable square feet within the lease to calculate the annual total lease payment. Rents paid by the tenant were as shown in Table 6.13, and total $410,256 as shown in Table 6.14. Let us assume that the brokerage commission is 6% of the total cash flow provided by the tenant over the lease term.

For the tenant described above, the calculation of brokerage commission is as shown in Table 6.15. Total commissions earned on this lease are $24,615. Commissions are typically paid in full at the beginning of the lease term. Often, half of the commission will be paid when the lease is signed, and the other half will be paid when the tenant occupies the space. In some cases, although it is rare, the commission will be spread out and paid monthly during the lease term. This favors the landlord, since the full payment is not made at the beginning of the lease term.

Several factors might impact the actual amount earned by a broker on this lease transaction. For example, the building might employ a broker-of-record or landlord's broker, as well as a tenant's broker. Both will be entitled to receipt of a commission upon execution of a lease contract. For the example above, in most cases, the landlord's broker earns 2% (one-third of the commission) of the total lease cash flow and the tenant's broker earns 4% (or two-thirds of the total commission) of the total lease cash flow.

In many markets, commissions may also be paid upon renewal of the lease at the end of the lease term. For example, if we assume that a tenant exercises the option to renew the lease for a second 5-year lease term, the original broker is often entitled to a commission at renewal. The commission rate will be lower than the original commission rate (say 1% rather than 6%), but calculated in the same way as above.

If we assume that the brokerage commission on renewals is 1%, and that rents have increased by 3% in the market over the 5-year original lease term, the top-line rent paid in the first year (e.g. year 6 of the tenant's tenure in the space) of the renewed lease term is $26.66. Subsequent rents in years 2 through 5 of the extension are $27.46, $28.28, $29.13, and $30.00, respectively. Multiplying each of these amounts by the 3,360 square

TABLE 6.15 Brokerage commission

Total lease cash flow	$410,256
× Commission rate	6%
Brokerage commission	$24,615

TABLE 6.16 Brokerage commission on renewal

Total lease cash flow	$475,541
× Commission rate	1%
Brokerage commission	$4,755

feet of leasable space gives total lease cash flows of $475,541, as shown in Table 6.16. With a commission rate of 1%, the broker would earn $4,755 at renewal.

An important notion to consider is that both tenant improvement allowance and brokerage commissions are paid before any rent income is earned by the landlord. For example, the landlord who pays 6% commission and $25 psf in tenant improvement allowance will be out-of-pocket $99,615 at the beginning of the lease term ($24,615 in commissions plus $75,000 in TI allowance), but will not receive rent payments until after the lease term commences. The delay between expenditure of cash for commissions and tenant improvements is even longer for those tenants in a free-rent situation, although it is often the case that the broker's commission will not be earned until the tenant actually begins paying rent.

In the UK, the typical commission is 10% of the first year's rent, or the headline rent if there is a rent-free period, and commission is typically paid at the time the lease is signed. The original broker will not be compensated when the lease is renewed.

6.4.8 Other Key Elements of a Lease

As with most contracts, there are numerous provisions that are important to understand. Some leases are only a few pages long, with minimal terms. Other leases can be 100 pages or more, and include terms that are relevant for the space, landlord, and tenant under consideration. As well as the lease features already discussed relating to measurement of space, rental escalation, renewal and other options, expense treatment and concessions, other key elements relate to the following:

1. The date of the lease agreement.
2. The parties to the lease, indicating clearly who the landlord and tenant are.[2]
3. The starting date, lease term, and ending date for the lease agreement.
4. A description of the leased premises.
5. The allowed use of the premises.
6. Restrictions on alterations or improvements to the property.
7. Who has responsibility for maintenance and repair of the tenant's space, the building, and the common areas.

[2]In many cases, the tenant may wish not to execute the lease with corporate credit and instead set up a bankruptcy-remote company or limited-liability company to enter into the lease agreement. In these cases, the landlord must be aware that if the terms of the lease are not met, he will not have recourse to the parent company. Often, this will be a point of negotiation that is important to the landlord in assuring that the credit quality of the lease is strong.

8. Any restrictions on the operation of the tenant's business.
9. Whether the tenant is allowed to sublet or otherwise assign part or all of the space that is leased.
10. The method of handling delinquent payments and conditions for the surrender of the premises if the tenant defaults on its lease obligations.
11. Landlord or tenant legal remedies in the event of a default.
12. The amount and type of security provided by the tenant. This can include security deposits and letters of credit. The amount, if any, typically depends on the credit of the tenant and the amount of out-of-pocket expenses incurred by the landlord.

These elements are only a subset of the topics that are relevant and important to the rights and responsibilities of the tenant and landlord. To avoid surprises, the landlord and tenant should carefully read the lease document to assure that their interests are being served.

6.4.9 Leasing Differences Across Property Types

Leases for all the major property types include most of the lease provisions discussed above. There are, however, a few differences that exist which can greatly alter the total rent paid by a tenant, and the NOI earned by a landlord.

Industrial property consists of warehouse and logistics facilities, which are mostly large boxes used for storage and the subsequent transfer of goods and products. Industrial flex space is a mixture of industrial warehouse and office space, with partitions as walls that can easily be moved as space needs change or as tenants roll over. Industrial space is usually leased for longer terms than office space, and is also more likely to be leased on a net lease basis. The tenant will be responsible for all operating expenses of the building. Tenant improvement allowances are relatively small, and often non-existent.

Retail property consists of single-tenant stand-alone buildings, small neighborhood centers, community centers, and regional shopping malls. Single-tenant buildings house drug stores, restaurants, insurance and real estate offices, video stores, and other stores that can prosper without other tenants nearby. Small neighborhood centers may include drug stores, dry cleaners, small restaurants, and sometimes a small grocery store. They exist to serve the needs of shoppers in the neighborhood for daily use items.

Community centers are larger retail properties, with a large grocery anchor, clothing stores, restaurants, and other tenants that serve a wider geographical area. The grocery anchor attracts customers to the center, and generally will pay lower rents than other tenants. Often, a shopping center developer will be required to pre-lease space to a large grocery store and a drug store prior to obtaining a construction loan. Given the importance of anchors to the developer, they are typically in a strong negotiating position, allowing them to pay low rents relative to other tenants. They are also likely to sign longer-term leases, and contract for more renewal options. Because of these factors, a retail tenant can often lock up their space for a long period of time. A community center will usually include one or more outparcels that are sold to retailers who wish to own their own property. Outparcels will often contain a national restaurant chain or a gas station.

Regional malls attract tenants from a wider geographic area, and are large open-air or enclosed facilities. Generally, a regional mall will have several large well-known "anchor tenants," attracting large numbers of shoppers to the center. Anchor tenants can typically negotiate a low lease rate, and long lease terms given their importance. A large number of smaller tenants will also lease space at a regional mall, and include a large variety of retailers. These smaller tenants are known as "shop tenants," and provide the bulk of cash flows that are earned by mall ownership.

Two features of retail leases deserve mention, as they have the potential to impact cash flows. First, tenants will generally pay all costs of common area maintenance (CAM). The landlord will be billed for the cost of maintaining and lighting the parking lot, lighting common areas, cleaning, trash removal, landscaping, and other expenses. These costs are summed, and then passed through to tenants on a *pro rata* basis, according to the number of square feet that they lease relative to the total square footage in the property. (In the UK, this is known as a service charge.)

An additional differentiating feature of retail property is the existence of percentage rents. A retail tenant will often pay a base rent that is appropriate for local market conditions and the quality of the property with respect to location, age, and other characteristics. Added to the base rent is an additional payment that is based on gross sales of the retail tenant. This additional amount is known as percentage rent. (In the UK, percentage rents are known as "turnover rents.")

The amount of percentage rent can be determined in two ways. In the first case, a tenant may be required to pay a certain percentage of gross sales above some breakpoint. For example, a small restaurant that leases 2,000 square feet of space might be required to pay 6% (the "participation percentage") of gross sales above $500,000. If gross sales exceed $500,000, the tenant must pay 6% of every dollar above that breakpoint to the landlord. For a highly successful retail shop or restaurant, the additional income earned by a landlord from percentage rent can be significant.

Calculating a "natural breakpoint" is a second technique used to determine the breakpoint above which the tenant participates in percentage rent. Let us assume that the 2,000 square foot tenant pays $18 psf for the space, so that the annual base rent is $36,000. Assume also that the participation percentage is 6%. The natural breakpoint of sales is calculated by dividing the annual base rent by the participation percentage. For this small restaurant, the natural breakpoint is ($36,000 divided by 0.06), or $600,000. As above, if gross sales are above this natural breakpoint of $600,000, the tenant must remit 6% of every dollar sold above that level as percentage rent payable to the landlord.

Other differentiating features of retail properties are exclusive use clauses, and co-tenancy clauses. Exclusive use clauses provide assurance that a tenant engaged in a specific business will be the only tenant in that business in a shopping center. This protects the tenant from competing tenants. A shop tenant (or small tenant) who agrees to sign a lease at a retail property often does so because the anchor tenant draws people to the center, and once there, customers are likely to shop at other stores that are in the same center. Co-tenancy clauses protect smaller tenants if the anchor tenant goes out of business or otherwise vacates their space. If this happens, the contracted rents paid by small tenants will decrease, in many cases significantly. For example, if the anchor vacates, the clause may say that if a new anchor is not found to occupy the space within 6 months, the tenant's rent drops to a very low rate (say $2 psf). In some cases, the rent drops to a percentage rent amount. Both ways protect the tenant.

In the UK, the charge for common area maintenance is known as service charge, and percentage rents are known as turnover rents.

6.5 LEASE ECONOMICS AND EFFECTIVE RENT

Given the many different components of a lease, it is useful to have a single measure with which to compare the economics of leasing for both the landlord and the tenant. Effective rent, a measure that takes into account differences in top-line rents, operating expenses, concessions, and other components of a lease, is designed to distil the key factors of a lease agreement down to a single number.[3]

6.5.1 Comparing Leases with Different Expense Treatment

We will begin by analyzing the three different ways that expenses are treated above, focusing first on the landlord's income statement.

The Landlord's Perspective

For each of the three scenarios, the net cash flows per square foot earned by the landlord over the lease term are as shown in Tables 6.17, 6.18, and 6.19.

TABLE 6.17 Standard gross lease NOI

Year 1	Year 2	Year 3	Year 4	Year 5
$15.50	$15.89	$16.29	$16.70	$17.11

TABLE 6.18 Gross lease with expense stop NOI

Year 1	Year 2	Year 3	Year 4	Year 5
$15.50	$16.19	$16.90	$17.63	$18.39

TABLE 6.19 Net lease NOI

Year 1	Year 2	Year 3	Year 4	Year 5
$15.50	$15.97	$16.45	$16.94	$17.45

[3]UK leasing practices with respect to effective rents are discussed in the appendix to this chapter.

TABLE 6.20 Lease present values

Scenario	Present value
Gross lease	$64.83
Gross lease / expense stop	$67.21
Net lease	$65.42

TABLE 6.21 Effective rents

Scenario	Effective rent
Gross lease	$16.24
Gross lease / expense stop	$16.83
Net lease	$16.38

From a quick look at the cash flows, it is clear that the gross lease with expense stop provides the highest net income stream to the landlord.

The effective rent measure offers a simple way of summarizing these cash flows into a single number. Calculating effective rent involves two steps. The first is to discount the stream of cash flows back to a present value using a discount rate that incorporates the risk of the tenant's payment of the contractual lease cash flow. In many cases, the tenant's bond rating is used as a discount rate. For now, let us assume that the discount rate for the tenant is 8%. Since we are comparing income streams to be paid by the same tenant, the choice of discount rate will not impact the overall results.[4]

The present value of each of the income streams at an 8% discount rate is as shown in Table 6.20. As expected, the gross lease with an expense stop provides the highest value.

The second step requires calculation of a constant annuity payment over the 5 years that could be paid out of this present value amount. Using the 8% discount rate, the annual annuity payment (or effective rent) is as shown in Table 6.21.

From this analysis, Scenario 2 is clearly preferred to the other two scenarios, with the net lease scenario the second best, and the standard gross lease providing the least benefit to the landlord.

The Tenant's Perspective

The tenant will be interested in comparing the total outflows from the three scenarios to determine which represents the smallest cash expenditure on leasing costs. The cash outflows from the three scenarios can be summarized as shown in Table 6.22.

It is clear from looking at the stream of cash flows that the gross lease provides the lowest expenditure, with the expense stop case providing the highest expenditure. We

[4]The choice of discount rate will be important if comparing lease offers from tenants with different credit quality. For lower-quality tenants, higher risk premiums and discount rates will be applied.

TABLE 6.22 Tenant cash flows

	Year 1	Year 2	Year 3	Year 4	Year 5
Gross lease					
Total cost	$23.00	$23.69	$24.40	$25.13	$25.89
Gross lease / expense stop					
Total cost	$23.00	$23.99	$25.01	$26.06	$27.15
Net lease					
Total cost	$23.00	$23.77	$24.56	$25.37	$26.22

TABLE 6.23 Tenant lease payment present values and effective rent

Scenario	Present value	Effective rent
Gross lease	$97.06	$24.31
Gross lease / expense stop	$99.35	$24.88
Net lease	$97.66	$24.46

can calculate the effective rent paid by the tenant in the same way that we calculated the effective rent earned by the landlord. These calculations are shown in Table 6.23, using the same 8% discount rate.

As might be expected, the worst scenario for the tenant (gross lease with an expense stop) is the best scenario for the landlord. The relative negotiating power of the two parties will ultimately determine how the lease and payment of expenses are structured. For example, if the tenant is a large tenant with strong credit, and is prepared to sign a long-term (e.g. 15-year) lease, the landlord may be willing to pay a higher share of expenses in order to obtain a higher-quality stream of rental income.

6.5.2 Comparing Leases with Different Concession Allowances

For any lease, there are an infinite number of possible combinations of top-line rents, expenses, and concessions in the form of free rent and tenant improvements. Comparing them can be complex and difficult. Calculating effective rent for each alternative is useful in comparing each lease alternative, as it captures all of the components of the lease agreement.

Let us start by assuming that a tenant is trying to determine which of several lease offers is best. The tenant is looking for a 5-year lease, and market rents are $23. The typical convention in the market is for a standard gross lease (without an expense stop). First-year operating expenses in all prospective buildings in the first year are $7.50 psf. As in the previous effective rent calculations, rents will escalate annually at 3% per year over the lease term. Operating expenses will increase by 4% per year. All of the lease proposals are in high-quality buildings, with similar locational quality. The typical tenant improvement allowance being offered in the marketplace at the time of lease negotiations is $25 psf.

The first landlord has offered a TI allowance of $25 psf, and 1 year of free rent "outside the term." The second landlord has offered $15 psf of TI allowance, and 1 year of free rent "inside the term." The landlord does not want to commit as much tenant improvement allowance for the shorter, inside-the-term lease period. The third landlord's proposal offers an above-market $35 in TI allowance, but no free-rent period. The fourth proposal offers $30 of TI allowance, but includes a fixed rent of $23 (e.g. no rent escalation) with no free-rent period.

Landlord's Perspective

Each lease offer provides cash flows that differ by timing and amount. For the first offer, where the concessions are offered outside the term, the cash flows paid in the form of tenant improvements at the start of the lease, and received by the landlord over the lease term, are as shown in Table 6.24.

The present value of this income stream is $36.53, and the effective rent is $7.90. Note that the equivalent annual annuity is calculated over the full 6 years of the lease term.

The second offer provides a lower TI allowance per square foot, a 1-year free-rent period, and only four additional periods of cash flows over the 5-year lease term. The cash flow stream for the landlord over the lease period is as shown in Table 6.25.

The present value of this income stream for the landlord under this proposal is $35.48, and the effective rent (equivalent annual annuity) earned is $8.89. The combination of a lower TI allowance and shorter period of earning rent payments leads to a higher effective rent calculation in the second scenario.

The third scenario does not offer any free rent, but does offer an above-market $35 psf of TI allowance. Cash flows earned by the landlord in this scenario are as shown in Table 6.26.

TABLE 6.24 Landlord cash flows – Scenario 1

Year 0	Year 1	Year 2	Year 3	Year 4	Year 5	Year 6
–$25	$0	$15.89	$16.29	$16.70	$17.11	$17.54

TABLE 6.25 Landlord cash flows – Scenario 2

Year 0	Year 1	Year 2	Year 3	Year 4	Year 5
–$15	$0	$15.89	$16.29	$16.70	$17.11

TABLE 6.26 Landlord cash flows – Scenario 3

Year 0	Year 1	Year 2	Year 3	Year 4	Year 5
–$35	$15.50	$15.89	$16.29	$16.70	$17.11

TABLE 6.27 Landlord cash flows – Scenario 4

Year 0	Year 1	Year 2	Year 3	Year 4	Year 5
–$30	$15.50	$15.20	$14.89	$14.56	$14.23

TABLE 6.28 Landlord lease options

	PV	Effective rent (psf)
Option 1	$36.53	$7.90
Option 2	$35.47	$8.88
Option 3	$28.83	$7.47
Option 4	$29.59	$7.41

The present value of this stream of income is $28.83, and the effective rent is $7.47.

In the fourth scenario, shown in Table 6.27, the landlord has offered $30 in TI allowance per square foot. In addition, the landlord has agreed to a non-escalating lease, with no free-rent period. Therefore, the top-line rent remains at $23 psf for the entire 5-year term while expenses increase. NOI earned by the landlord declines in each year.

The present value of the cash flow stream earned by the landlord is $29.59. The annuity that can be paid out of this amount for a 5-year period is $7.41.

A comparison of the four lease options is presented in Table 6.28.

From the landlord's perspective, the second option is clearly best, providing the highest effective rent payment over the lease term.

Tenant's Perspective

As the payer of lease payments, the tenant is concerned with the all-in cost of each lease option. The tenant will pay the top-line rents, and receive the TI allowance before making annual lease payments. Calculating effective rent is a useful way of comparing the different options available in the marketplace.

In this case, the tenant receives $25 in tenant improvements, enjoys 1 year of free rent, and begins making rent payments in Year 2. The present value of this stream of cash flows (over 6 years), as shown in Table 6.29, is –$67.56, and the effective rent paid by the tenant is –$14.62 psf per year.

Table 6.30 shows the case when $15 of TI is paid by the landlord, and the first year of free rent is inside the term. The present value of this stream of cash flows is –$60.77 and the effective rent paid by the tenant is –$15.22.

TABLE 6.29 Tenant cash flows – Scenario 1

Year 0	Year 1	Year 2	Year 3	Year 4	Year 5	Year 6
$25	$0	–$23.69	–$24.40	–$25.13	–$25.18	–$26.66

TABLE 6.30 Tenant cash flows – Scenario 2

Year 0	Year 1	Year 2	Year 3	Year 4	Year 5
$15	$0	–$23.69	–$24.40	–$25.13	–$25.89

With $35 of tenant improvements and no free-rent period, the present value of this stream of cash flows, as shown in Table 6.31, is –$62.07, and the effective rent paid by the tenant is –$15.54.

The present value of the stream of cash flows for a fixed rent and $30 of TI is –$61.83, and the effective rent paid by the tenant under this option is –$15.49, as shown in Table 6.32.

A comparison of the four lease options from the tenant's perspective is presented in Table 6.33.

From the tenant's perspective, the first option offers the lowest effective rent to be paid, and is clearly the best of the four options provided. The second option – which was most favorable to the landlord – is the second best option for the tenant.

As in all lease negotiations, current market conditions and relative negotiating skills will determine the final terms of the lease. Using the effective rent calculation provides an effective and simple method of comparing different lease terms for both the tenant and the landlord.

TABLE 6.31 Tenant cash flows – Scenario 3

Year 0	Year 1	Year 2	Year 3	Year 4	Year 5
$35	–$23.00	–$23.69	–$24.40	–$25.13	–$25.89

TABLE 6.32 Tenant cash flows – Scenario 4

Year 0	Year 1	Year 2	Year 3	Year 4	Year 5
$30	–$23.00	–$23.00	–$23.00	–$23.00	–$23.00

TABLE 6.33 Landlord lease options

	PV	Effective rent (psf)
Option 1	–$67.56	–$14.62
Option 2	–$60.77	–$15.22
Option 3	–$62.67	–$15.54
Option 4	–$61.83	–$15.49

6.6 CONCLUSION

In any given market conditions, leases determine the cash flows that are earned by the owner of a building. Leases dictate every cash flow event that occurs between the landlord and the tenant from the time the lease is signed until it terminates. Market conditions at the time that the lease is signed are critical in the determination of the final terms that are negotiated between a landlord and a tenant. If there is a lot of space available in the local market due to additions to supply arising from development or weak demand, the bargaining power of the landlord will be limited as the tenant will likely have numerous options available to them for renting space. If, in contrast, space is tight due to a lack of recent development activity and/or strong demand for space, the landlord will have a stronger bargaining position. As with most real estate contracts, the ultimate terms of the lease will result from a dynamic, negotiable, and interactive process.

APPENDIX: MODELING LEASE FLEXIBILITY IN THE UK

The bargaining position of the tenant may be such that they can demand inducements to sign a lease, and in a weak market a landlord will be willing to cooperate in order to lease space. In certain circumstances, as we have seen, typically to maintain investment value, landlords may wish to grant leases at rents which exceed full rental value. To induce the tenant to pay an artificially high level of rent, the landlord may offer by way of compensation an extended rent-free period, a capital sum as an inducement to sign the lease (a "reverse premium"), and/or a capital sum to assist the ingoing tenant with fitting-out costs. This may be beneficial to the tenant, who might not otherwise be able to fund the cost of fitting out new premises or who may find that it is easier to establish a business from the premises where the occupation is rent free for a period of time.

The rental level set against this background is commonly referred to in the UK as a "headline rent," meaning the rent which is contractually payable but which would not have been achieved in the open market without the payment of an extended rent-free period, capital sum, or other inducement. The range of rent-free periods and capital inducements in all sectors of the commercial leasing market is wide, and the motives for deals being struck on this artificial basis are often difficult to determine in each separate case. There is no standard practice for converting a headline rent into an "effective" rent.

There is widespread support for treating the first 3 months of any rent-free period granted to an ingoing tenant on a new lease as representing standard market practice, so that no adjustment to the rent reserved would be warranted, but there is no universal agreement as to how a rent-free period exceeding 3 months should be treated.

Where there is a rent review period in the lease, say at year 5 in a 10-year term, one school of thought amortizes this additional sum of rent on a straight-line basis until the next rent review and the annual equivalent derived is deducted from the reserved headline rent to produce the actual rent. Alternative schools of thought amortize the sum of rent over the entire term of the lease granted on a straight-line basis.

Neither of these approaches is especially rational, as the cash flow effect created by the inducement may not terminate at the first rent review, and neither may the effect persist for the entire lease term. Hence, a more appropriate approach may be to amortize the sum of the additional rent loss over the period to the next rent review at which an increase in rent is expected. This introduces the concept of probability, as we may not be able to know for sure when the cash flow effect will terminate. Simulation-based solutions as described in Baum and Crosby (2008) provide the appropriate facility for solving this problem.

Although it is possible to quantitatively model both the landlords' and tenants' positions in lease negotiations, the complexity of the relevant issues that influence the rental impact of lease terms makes a solution to pricing challenging. Examples include national legislation that may, for example, limit rent increases or offer some other form of tenant protection, and institutional factors, for example, the attitude of lenders and appraisers. The intricacy of these issues possibly explains the conservatism of many market participants towards flexi-leases and a preponderance of "standard" leases in markets. However, it also provides a potential opportunity to market participants with the ability to offer, and accurately price, flexibility in lease terms.

From the landlord's perspective, the main factors driving the required "compensation" for a non-standard lease term focus on the risk of vacancy and include, in particular, the probability of tenant vacation, the expected costs of tenant vacation, operating costs, and (less obviously) expected rental value volatility. Given data describing these variables and simulation technology, it is possible to measure the value of the options inherent in certain lease types to explore required rent adjustments for different terms (e.g. a shorter lease).

The financial implications of short leases and break clauses are reflected in rental and capital values, and it is well documented that valuers and appraisers tend to adopt conservative practices when faced with relatively novel lease structures. Research has shown that established rules-of-thumb in valuation practice are often at odds with activities in the market, and the usefulness of the direct comparison method of valuation becomes limited.

The more diversity there is in lease terms, the harder is the job of the lender and professional advisor.

Lizieri and Herd (1994) used simulation as a method of pricing break clauses. They examined approaches to the problem by practitioners and found a notable lack of consistency between valuers and in the internal logic of their assumptions. They developed a simulation approach to formally account for the probability that tenants may exercise the right to prematurely determine the lease and found evidence of inconsistency in the application of cap rate adjustments as a remedy for the impact on value of break options.

There has also been considerable interest in the potential application of option pricing techniques to property investment and development decisions (see Grenadier, 1995; Ward, 1997; Patel and Sing, 1998; Rowland, 1999). In a typical option product, the investor acquires the right to buy (call option) or sell (put option) an underlying asset before or at a pre-agreed date. In this case, since the problem is concerned with options to vacate, the price (rent) volatility of the underlying asset is a key determinant of the value of the option, with increasing volatility producing a higher value for the tenant's right to break the lease.

It is clear that both option pricing and simulation approaches can provide similar solutions to lease pricing issues. However, simulation seems more suitable in this context for a number of reasons. It can be carried out using spreadsheet-compatible analytical systems; the outputs can be integrated into conventional spreadsheet models;

and it is relatively transparent and permits the analyst to identify the key determinants of the outputs.

Example

Compare the rental value for a 15-year lease with 5-yearly upward-only rent reviews (a standard lease in the subject market) with the rental value for a 10-year lease with a 5-year break. What initial rent should be charged for the variant lease?

Assumptions

Rental value on a standard lease: £100,000 with 1 year rent free

Lease renewal probability: 20%
Lease break probability: 25%
Expected void: 3 quarters
Void volatility: 3 quarters
Empty property costs: £10,000 a year
Re-letting costs: £25,000
Expected rental growth: 1%
Rental growth volatility: 4%
Target return: 9%

Result

To equate the present values of the lease cash flows, the required year 1 rent for the variant lease increases by around 30% (see Table 6.34).

TABLE 6.34 Lease cash flows

Year	Cash flow: standard	Cash flow: variant
1	0	0
2	£100,000	£130,590
3	£100,000	£130,590
4	£100,000	£130,590
5	£100,000	£130,590
6	£108,100	£82,492
7	£108,100	£87,969
8	£108,100	£104,576
9	£108,100	£107,424
10	£108,100	£107,484
11	£115,908	£25,200
12	£115,908	£53,931
13	£115,908	£104,907
14	£115,908	£113,256
15	£115,908	£113,256
NPV	£760,940	£760,941

Explanation

The higher cash flow for the flexible lease acts as compensation for the owner, but can be lost at the first review where a break operates. At this point there is a 25% chance of a break being exercised, and the system assumes a 100% chance of any tenant using the break to bring the rent back down to the market level. After the break, there is a chance of a void and associated costs. The probability of a void falls, and the cash flow improves with every passing quarter. At the lease end in year 10, the chance of a lease renewal is very small and the cash flow recovers only as the probability of a re-letting after an expected void period rises with passing time. For more on this approach, see Baum and Crosby (2008).

CHAPTER 7

Techniques for Valuing Commercial Real Estate and Determining Feasibility: The Unleveraged Case

7.1 INTRODUCTION

In this section, we'll look at the valuation of an investment opportunity in an apartment project. We'll first value the property as an operating entity. Using the operating cash flows of the project, we'll value it as if it were all equity financed. This may seem extreme, but there are a growing number of investors, including pension funds and sovereign wealth funds, that invest in property on an unleveraged, or no-debt, basis. In general, these investors hold property for longer periods than investors that use leverage (or gearing) to finance their acquisition of property. In addition, valuing a property on an unleveraged basis allows analysts to isolate the value of a property that arises from the operation of the property itself, and separate out the impact on value of adding debt. We will show the impact that debt has on investment feasibility in Chapter 9.

Throughout the book, we'll look at valuation and feasibility on a before-tax basis, which is typical practice for real estate investors. Large sectors of the real estate investor universe consist of tax-exempt companies and institutions. Pension funds, endowments, and foundations, for example, do not pay income taxes. Real Estate Investment Trusts (REITs) are also not taxable as long as 75% of their assets are "real estate related," 75% of their total income is "real estate related" and they pass 90% of their net income through to shareholders as dividends each year.

General partnerships (GPs), limited partnerships (LPs) and limited liability corporations (LLCs) are tax-neutral vehicles that do not pay income taxes at the entity level. Instead, income earned or losses incurred are passed through the entity to individual investors or partners, and the investors pay taxes on their share of partnership income or losses. GPs, LPs, and LLCs typically include a number of investors, each having different income and tax situations. Analyzing a transaction using an arbitrary tax rate may be misleading for many of the investors, which is why we focus on before-tax analysis.

7.2 BACKGROUND ON THE INVESTMENT OPPORTUNITY

Let us assume that you lead an investment group that is interested in investing in a multi-family apartment building in the southeastern USA. The group typically holds investments for 5 years, after which time they expect to sell their properties in hopes of earning a return that is higher than what they require. The consensus among the investors is that their minimum required return is 7% for unleveraged investments. After searching the local market, you have identified a potential opportunity to buy a large garden apartment project within a mile of a large public university in the southeast. Given its proximity to campus, it is usually in high demand by students. The current owner of the property is offering it to the market for sale at a price of $48 million.

If, after performing due diligence on the property, it is determined that the $48 million asking price is reasonable, the investment group will provide equity capital to take over ownership of the property and earn future cash flows from the property over the 5-year holding period.

7.2.1 Project Details

The investment opportunity is a 258-unit apartment project, with a large swimming pool and patio area, a clubhouse, a conference and gathering facility, and a fitness center. The property sits on 20 acres of land and includes 19 buildings. It was built in 2000. Management is on-site in the clubhouse area, and the property is managed by one of the best apartment management groups in the country. Surface parking is provided at no cost to the tenants. Rents are paid on a monthly basis, and the average lease term is 1 year. Tenants include graduate students at the nearby university, young professionals who work in the area, recently hired faculty, and residents and young doctors at the nearby medical school. The project consists of 258 separate units, broken down as shown in Table 7.1.

TABLE 7.1 Apartment unit count and size

Unit type	Bedrooms	# Units	Size (sq. ft)
1 Bed 1 Bath w/ Deck	1	36	840
1 Bed 1 Bath w/ Sunroom	1	24	950
1 Bed 1 Bath w/ Den	1	30	1,054
1 Bed 1 Bath w/ Den & Sunroom	1	20	1,138
2 Bed 2 Bath	2	120	1,213
3 Bed 2.5 Bath Townhome (with attached 1-car garage)	3	28	1,545
Total / Average		258	1,148

The six types of units vary in size and configuration. One- and two-bedroom units are most popular among the prospective tenant base and comprise the largest component of the property. The larger three-bedroom units are often shared by a number of tenants or leased by families with small children. There are two floors in the three-bedroom units. All of the units have recently been renovated. The total area of rentable space is 296,184 square feet.

Recall from Chapter 5 that the price of any asset is a function of the cash flows that are expected to be earned by the asset over the period that the investor expects to hold it. A prospective investor attempts to identify every single possible cash flow event for an investment opportunity for each year during the anticipated ownership period. While it is not possible to perfectly forecast the future, the exercise of estimating future cash flows allows the analyst to identify aspects of the investment that are subject to greater uncertainty, and do further research to resolve the uncertainty if possible.

In order to determine whether the $48 million price is reasonable, and to determine the feasibility of investing in it for the investment group, discounted cash flow (DCF) techniques are employed. DCF requires estimating the cash flows that are expected to be earned by the investment opportunity in each of the years that the investor expects to own it. Naturally, with tenants already in place when the asset is acquired, there is a great deal of confidence in the accuracy of estimates for first-year rental income. In contrast, income in future years is dependent on future rental growth rates, how much will be spent to maintain and operate the building, vacancy rates, and a host of other factors, making estimates of cash flows beyond 1 year more speculative.

7.2.2 Where Do You Find Information About Income and Expenses?

If a property is offered to the market by a seller, prospective buyers can usually ask the seller or the seller's broker for information related to all aspects of the property. This is the case for the apartment investment opportunity. Audited financial statements can be requested, as well as original lease documents signed by all tenants. From these, operating cash flows can be estimated.

Prospective buyers will often be interested in making a bid on a property that is not on the market. Since information on rents paid by tenants (and earned by landlords), transaction prices, financing details, and other items are typically only known to participants in real estate transactions, obtaining information that is sufficient for a bidder to be comfortable making an offer is difficult. Generally, the real estate professionals that are most active in a local market are able to obtain the most current and most accurate information. Gathering local market information is a "barrier to entry" for outsiders, as it often takes many years of involvement in local transactions to get a good feel for rents and pricing.

For some property types, gathering information on rental rates is easier than for others. Our focus for the valuation of the apartment project is on housing. In general, it is relatively easy to determine rental rates for apartments, student housing projects, and other residential properties. For these property types, space is rented to a large number of tenants, all of whom have similar leases. For example, at the apartment facility, all tenants of similar units will pay a similar price per month. The same is true of a student housing property that is marketed to a more specific student renter base. Determining rental rates is often a simple matter of calling the leasing office and asking what types of units are available and what asking rents are for different unit sizes, or visiting an internet website.

Obtaining rental information for other types of property is more difficult. For example, determining rental rates paid for office space is not as easy as for residential properties. Calling the tenant or the owner of an office building to ask what rent is being paid by individual tenants will generally not be successful, as it is not in the interest of either party to provide that information. Further, an office building might house multiple tenants of different sizes, with each lease having different financial and other characteristics. Leases will likely differ according to rental rate paid (dependent upon when the lease was signed), lease duration, the size and credit quality of the tenant, where the tenant is located within the building, and many other factors. The area that is leased by each tenant will also vary according to tenant needs, which is another differentiating factor compared to the relatively homogeneous nature of residential property. Therefore, none of the information that would be useful in estimating earned income is available and must be estimated by the prospective investor. Similar arguments can be made for retail and industrial properties.

7.3 DEVELOPING A PRO FORMA INCOME STATEMENT

From speaking with representatives in the management office at the apartment facility, you have been able to determine the rents charged for each type of unit at the property. These monthly and annual rents are shown in Table 7.2. The total gross rental revenue (GRR) from the property is $5,145,240.

TABLE 7.2 Apartment project rent roll

Unit type	# Units	SF	Rent	Monthly CF	Annual CF	Rent PSF
1 Bed 1 Bath w/ Deck	36	840	$1,445	$52,020	$624,240	$1.72
1 Bed 1 Bath w/ Sunroom	24	950	$1,475	$35,400	$424,800	$1.55
1 Bed 1 Bath w/ Den	30	1,054	$1,545	$46,350	$556,200	$1.47
1 Bed 1 Bath w/ Den/Sunroom	20	1,138	$1,560	$31,200	$374,400	$1.37
2 Bed 2 Bath	120	1,213	$1,650	$198,000	$2,376,000	$1.36
3 Bed 2.5 Bath Townhome	28	1,545	$2,350	$65,800	$789,600	$1.52
Total / Average	258	1,148	$1,662	$428,770	$5,145,240	$1.45

Note: SF = square foot; PSF = per square foot.

In addition to the rents earned from leasing apartment units, the owner of the property will also earn non-rental income from several other sources. For example, there are 74 enclosed parking garages that are all rented, at a cost of $120/month. The total monthly non-rental income from garages is $8,880, and the annual income is $106,560. The manager also rents 50 storage units to tenants at a monthly rent of $50. The total monthly and annual income from these units is $2,500 and $30,000, respectively. Every one of the parking garages and storage units has been rented over the last 5 years, which is expected to continue into the future. Tenants also pay a non-refundable administrative fee of $150 when they apply to lease a unit. On average, 42% of all units turn or rollover in any year, for a total of 108 units. The total annual income earned by the owner from these fees is $16,200 (108 * $150). There are several other sources of non-rental income earned by the owner, including trash or rubbish collection, clubhouse and pool rentals, and pest control. The total amount earned per unit is estimated as $40/month.

A summary of the total other income on an annual basis is shown in Table 7.3.

TABLE 7.3 Other income earned by the property

Source	# Units	Cost	Monthly CF	Annual CF
Parking (tuck-under garages)	74	$120	$8,880	$106,560
Storage units	50	$50	$2,500	$30,000
Administrative fee	258	$40	$10,320	$123,840
Miscellaneous	108	$150	NA	$16,200
Total				$276,600

The total non-rental, or other, income is $276,600.

7.3.1 Calculating Total Revenues

Now that we have estimated all of the potential sources of income, let's add them up to determine the amount of revenue that we might expect to earn in the first year of owning this property. Since total rental revenue is $5,145,240 and non-rental revenue is $276,600, the total revenue from all expected sources is $5,421,840. Like an investment in a private company, this represents the top-line revenue of an income statement.

7.3.2 Estimating Vacancy Loss

At any point in time, 13 (or 5%) of the units will be vacant and not earning rent. Vacancy may be related to weakness in the demand for units relative to more attractive locations, or may arise due to the fact that tenants leave at the end of their lease term and it typically takes several weeks to perform the necessary tasks required to lease the unit to the next tenant. The latter type of vacancy is referred to as frictional vacancy.

This vacancy rate of 5% is only expected to affect rental income, as there is a long waiting list for the parking and storage units at all times. Therefore, 5% of the $5,145,240 gross rental revenue equals $257,262. This reduces revenues to the owner of the property. Total rental revenue less the $257,272 income lost from vacant units equals a gross effective income of $4,887,978.

7.3.3 Estimating Operating Expenses

To generate property revenue, the owner of the property must provide certain services and incur expenses. These expenses include paying for:

- Utilities (water, sewer, and electric) for each of the units plus for any common areas.
- Internet and cable television access for each unit.
- Landscaping and general grounds maintenance.
- Property taxes, based on the assessed value of the property, paid to local jurisdictions in exchange for services such as garbage removal, police and fire service, local schools, and other government services.
- Management of the property, including payroll for staff, license to operate, office supplies, etc.
- General maintenance of the property to ensure that it remains in top rentable condition, and that service calls for routine issues like stopped-up drains or toilets, electrical problems, etc. are dealt with in a prompt and professional manner.
- Marketing the units to prospective tenants.
- Other non-routine expenses that may arise.

For a property that is marketed broadly to prospective investors, such as this one, the buyer should be able to obtain audited financial statements with detailed summaries of expenses incurred over the past several years. Past operating expenses for the apartment project totaled 40% of the gross effective income that is generated, or $4,887,978 * 40% = $1,995,191.

For a typical rental housing property, we might also assume that there is a 2-week period between renters during which rent is not earned. During this period, the owner of the property paints all units, repairs or replaces carpets if necessary, and generally spruces up the buildings for the next tenants. For each unit, we'll assume that the cost of cleaning the carpet for a recently vacated unit is $100, and the cost of repainting a unit is $300 for a total turnover cost of $400 per unit that is vacated. Above we discussed that 42%, or 108, of the units turn or rollover each year, so the total expenses incurred to do this are $43,200.

Since carpet typically has only a 5-year useful life, it's a good idea to reserve 20% of the cost of new carpet each year. The cost of new carpet is $1,000 per unit, so for each of the 258 units, the owner reserves $200 per year for a total expense of $51,600 ($200 * 258 units).

The sum of operating expenses, turnover expenses of carpet cleaning and repainting, and the carpet reserve represents the total expenses that are expected to be paid in the first year of ownership, and equals $2,049,991 ($1,955,191 + $43,200 + $51,600).

7.3.4 Calculating Net Operating Income

The income statement demonstrating the property cash flows can be summarized as shown in Table 7.4.

TABLE 7.4 Formula for calculating NOI

Gross rental revenue (GRR)
– Vacancy (VAC)
Gross effective income (GEI)
+ Other income (OI)
Total revenue (TR)
– Total expenses (TE)
Net operating income (NOI)

Determining the first year's expected cash flow is a matter of organizing the project information presented above into the income statement as shown in Table 7.5.

TABLE 7.5 Calculation of first-year NOI

	Year 1
Gross rental revenue (GRR)	$5,145,240
– Vacancy (VAC)	$257,262
Gross effective income (GEI)	$4,887,978
+ Other income (OI)	$276,600
Total revenue (TR)	$5,164,578
– Total expenses (TE)	$2,049,991
Net operating income (NOI)	$3,114,587

For readers who have been exposed to financial accounting, net operating income (NOI) is roughly the equivalent of earnings before interest, taxes, depreciation, and amortization (EBITDA). NOI represents the operating cash flow expected to be earned by a productive asset (in this case, the apartment project) without respect to who owns it, how it is financed, or the owner's income tax consequences.

7.4 VALUATION USING NET OPERATING INCOME: SINGLE-YEAR CASH FLOW

The appraisal profession often uses NOI to determine a "quick and dirty" initial estimate of the value of a property. The concept is the same as valuing a perpetuity, where an estimate of next year's operating cash flow (e.g. next year's NOI) is divided (or capitalized) by a discount rate. The discount rate that is used is called a capitalization (or cap) rate.

7.4.1 An Aside on Capitalization Rates

Elsewhere in this book, detailed theories are presented that provide an academic perspective on the underlying components of capitalization rates. Here, we'll focus more on how they are used in practice, and what causes them to change.

Cap rates are generally used to discount a single period's cash flow. For our purposes, the relevant cash flow is the NOI that is expected to be earned in the first year. The formula for determining the market value of a property is:

$$MV_0 = NOI_1 / cr_0$$

where MV_0 is the market value of the property at time zero (e.g. today), which is what we are trying to estimate. NOI_1 is a measure of expected NOI in year 1, and cr_0 is the capitalization rate at time zero.

Estimating the Market Cap Rate

Cap rates are determined in asset markets where participants buy and sell properties, and are estimated by rearranging the above equation as follows:

$$cr_0 = NOI_1 / MV_0$$

Estimating the cap rate for our apartment project requires knowledge of NOI and market value for properties that have recently sold. Since this information is typically known only to buyers and sellers, it is often difficult to estimate for those not involved in the transaction.

In developing an estimate of a cap rate for the apartment project, we would try to find buildings of similar size, quality, location, and with other similar characteristics (e.g. in the same "industry") that recently transacted to attempt to estimate a cap rate to apply to the NOI that was calculated for the investment opportunity.

This would require estimating NOI for the comparable projects and determining the price at which they recently sold. Estimating NOI would be fairly straightforward, and we would proceed in much the same way as we did when we calculated first-year NOI for the investment opportunity. We would need to know how many bedrooms (or units) there are in the building, estimate a vacancy rate, operating and other expenses, and then estimate NOI with this information.

Estimating the actual price at which a building sold is more difficult, since most transactions are between private entities and information on transactions values is not public information. Someone who is fully engaged in the real estate industry in a particular local market will typically have a good feel for the price at which properties trade. Local market participants often have a comparative advantage over outsiders due to their knowledge of the local market.

Cap Rates are the Inverse of Price/Earnings Ratios

For readers more familiar with stock market analysis, it is useful to know that the concept of the cap rate is similar to the concept of a price/earnings, or P/E ratio. In fact, the cap rate is the reciprocal of a P/E ratio. In real estate, we substitute NOI for earnings and market value for price.

The P/E ratio for a stock can be observed in the marketplace by looking at the current price of a share divided by forward earnings per share (e.g. earnings next year). The result is typically reported as a multiple of earnings per share (EPS). For example, shares of stock of utility companies may be trading at a P/E multiple of 12.5 times, implying that the current price for the average company in the industry is 12.5 times the earnings expected for next year. If an individual stock in the utility industry has expected earnings per share of $4.00, analysts will apply the 12.5 times P/E ratio to come up with an estimate of that company's stock price of $50 (or $4.00 times 12.5).

Taking the reciprocal of the P/E ratio gives what is called a capitalization rate (or cap rate) in common stock analysis. While rarely used, it is a well-known concept. In the case of our utility stock, the cap rate is equal to:

$$cr = 1/(P/E) \text{ or } 1/12.5 = 0.08, \text{ or } 8\%$$

With the knowledge that EPS is $4.00, the estimated value of a share of the utility company's stock can be estimated either by multiplying by the P/E ratio as above, or by dividing by the cap rate as follows:

$$Earnings / cr = Price = \$4.00/0.08 = \$50$$

When valuing stocks, the P/E ratio will be higher for those industries or stocks that are seen by the market as having greater growth prospects. When P/E ratios increase, the market is willing to pay more for a given level of earnings, or operating income. That is, if the P/E ratio for utility stocks is expected to increase to 15 from 12.5, a share of stock would increase in value to $60 (15 * $4) from $50. The increase in P/E ratio may arise due to increased expectations of growth of income as a result of the business cycle, some competitive advantage that a firm has relative to its competitors, and for many other reasons.

Since the cap rate is the inverse of the P/E ratio, an increase in the P/E ratio indicates that the cap rate has declined. A market cap rate decline to 6.6667% from 8% (equivalent to a P/E ratio rise to 15 from 12.5) implies that the value of an asset with $4 of operating income increases to $60 (e.g. $4 / 0.066667) from $50. If market conditions for an asset or an industry are expected to improve (just like an increase in P/E ratio), cap rates are expected to decline.

Using Cap Rates to Value the Apartment Project

A cap rate, calculated in a similar way as for the utility stock, is what is most commonly used as a first estimate for real estate valuation. To develop an estimate of a cap rate for the apartment project, we would try to find buildings of similar size, quality, location, and with other similar characteristics (i.e. in the same "industry") that recently transacted.

Table 7.6 provides NOI, market value, and cap rate information for several recent transactions of multi-family investments.

TABLE 7.6 Recent transactions

Property name	# Units	NOI	Sale price	Cap rate
Legacy Crossroads	344	$3,173,400	$46,300,000	6.85%
Flats 55Twelve	268	$1,856,570	$30,500,000	6.09%
Century Trinity Estates	270	$2,223,450	$35,300,000	6.30%
Lenox at Patterson Place	292	$1,787,040	$26,900,000	6.64%

It is important to know details about each of the properties used as comparables (or comps) for calculation of the cap rate for the local apartment market. All of the comparable properties are about the same standard of quality and management as the investment opportunity, but differ by age and location. Three of the four are considered to be in inferior locations given their distance from employment centers and amenities. Legacy Crossroads was built in 2009, and comprises 344 units, so is larger than our prospective apartment investment. Unlike our investment opportunity, it has not been renovated. Flats 55Twelve has 268 units, and was recently renovated to a similar finish as our apartment investment. It is the closest in proximity, so its location is of similar quality to our acquisition target. There are 270 units in Century Trinity Estates, and it was built in 2001. Most of the unit interiors have been renovated. Finally, Lenox at Patterson Place consist of 292 units and was built in 1999.

The range of cap rates for recent transactions is 6.09–6.85%, indicating some variability in pricing in the local market. The two most similar properties are Flats 55Twelve and Century Trinity Estates, which exhibit lower cap rates than the other two properties. The average of the four cap rates is 6.475%, but for the two most comparable properties the average is 6.2%, which is a reasonable estimate of the cap rate for apartment properties in the local market. The cap rate at the time of purchase is known as the "going-in" cap rate.

Recalling that next year's expected NOI for the property is $3,114,587, and dividing by the 6.2% cap rate, the estimated value of the project is $50,235,274:

$$MV_0 = NOI_1 / cr_0 = \$3{,}114{,}587 / 0.062 = \$50{,}235{,}274$$

It should be clear that using this rather imprecise method provides a rough estimate of value. In this case, we would say that the estimated market value of this property should be around $50.235 million. If this is a reasonable representation of the market value, a below-market price acquisition at the asking price of $48 million would be favorable.

Calculating the Implied Cap Rate for the Apartment Investment Opportunity

Another way to evaluate the reasonableness of the asking price for the investment is to rearrange the equation and solve for the capitalization rate that is implied by the estimate of next year's NOI and the asking price. This can be done as follows:

$$NOI_1 / MV_0 = cr_0 = \$3{,}114{,}587 / \$48{,}000{,}000 = 0.064887, \text{or } 6.4887\%$$

The value of $48 million can also be obtained by rearranging the equation, and dividing NOI by the calculated cap rate of 6.4887%, or $3,114,587 / 0.064887 = $48 million.

In this case, we would say that our first estimate of value and the asking price are fairly similar, with a market cap rate of about 6.2% (determined based on our analysis of recent transactions) and an asking cap rate of 6.499% (determined by using our estimate of first-year NOI and the asking price). Our estimate of market value using first-year NOI and the estimate of a market cap rate is $50.235 million, and the asking price for the apartment project is $48 million. Since the estimate of market value is higher than the asking price, we would likely elect to analyze the property in more detail to get a better feel for its feasibility as an investment for the group.

7.5 INVESTMENT ANALYSIS USING OPERATING INCOME: MULTIPLE-YEAR CASH FLOWS

The analysis using an estimate of expected cash flow in the first year of property ownership is useful, but limited in determining investment value and feasibility. In most applications, estimates of all cash flow events expected during the period of ownership will be more useful in estimating the value of a property. The starting point is the first-year NOI that was estimated above, but a number of assumptions must be made to develop a pro forma (or expected) income statement over the 5 years that the investment group expects to own the property.

7.5.1 Operating Cash Flows from Leasing

Let us start with a discussion of how income earned may change over the 5-year holding period. First, we would expect and hope that rents would grow from year to year. Rents could be assumed to grow at the inflation rate or at a faster rate if the property is in a good location and enjoys strong demand in a supply-constrained market. In contrast, rents may grow at a slower rate if market conditions in the local area are expected to deteriorate, if the property's functionality is expected to decline with age, or if new supply of competing space is expected to be added to the market.

We can estimate a growth rate for the apartment project by looking at the historical record of rents charged by the owners in previous years. From a discussion with the management team, the average asking rent has grown at a rate of between 2% and 4%, so a growth rate estimate of 3% seems reasonable. This 3% growth rate will also be applied to all of the other income sources earned by the property.

With audited financial statements from previous years, growth rates in operating expenses can be estimated as well. If property financial statements are not available, operating expense growth rates will have to be estimated based on the age of the property, the quality of the building, and a guess at how the components of operating expenses will increase. Let's assume that operating expenses will grow at a rate that is similar to the inflation rate, and that the general price level will increase at a 2.5% rate for each of the next 5 years.

The vacancy rate has been estimated at 5%, which is the long-term vacancy rate for Class A apartments in the local market. It is extremely unlikely that vacancy will be 5% in every year of the 5-year holding period, but in most applications of discounted cash flow analysis, a constant vacancy rate is assumed. We will follow this convention, but the reader should appreciate the importance of testing feasibility results for different possible future scenarios.

This is called sensitivity analysis, and it will be discussed later in Section 7.7.

Generating a 5-year pro forma income statement is relatively straightforward. For application to the apartment project, we need only grow annual rents by 3% and operating expenses by 2.5%. It goes without saying that the actual rental growth rate is unlikely to be exactly 3% and the operating expense growth rate is unlikely to be 2.5%, but these provide a starting point for analysis.

Using the first-year NOI as a base year, and growing rents by 3% and expenses by 2.5%, provides the 5-year operating statement shown in Table 7.7.

TABLE 7.7 Multi-year income statement

	Year 1	Year 2	Year 3	Year 4	Year 5
GRR	$5,145,240	$5,299,597	$5,458,585	$5,622,343	$5,791,013
− VAC	$257,262	$264,980	$272,929	$281,117	$289,551
GEI	$4,887,978	$5,034,617	$5,185,656	$5,341,226	$5,501,462
+ OI	$276,600	$284,898	$293,445	$302,248	$311,316
TR	$5,164,578	$5,319,515	$5,479,101	$5,643,474	$5,812,778
− TE	$2,049,991	$2,101,241	$2,153,772	$2,207,616	$2,262,807
NOI	$3,114,587	$3,218,274	$3,325,329	$3,435,858	$3,549,971

Notice that NOI increases every year because revenue from leasing bedrooms and parking spaces increases at a faster rate than operating expenses.

7.5.2 Cash Flows from Disposition

At the end of the expected 5-year holding period, the investment group plans to sell the apartment project. Therefore, the value of the asset in 5 years' time must be estimated. Clearly, attempting to determine a sales price for the asset in 5 years is fraught with speculation.

Estimating the future sales price requires assumptions about the state of the market at the time of sale, which are very difficult to forecast at the beginning of the holding period. In contrast, real estate market conditions for the project might improve while it is owned by the investment group. If this is the case, cap rates will decrease over the holding period. If so, buyers will be willing to pay a higher price for each dollar of income (e.g. the P/E ratio will increase) or conversely the "going-out" cap rate at sale will be lower than the "going-in" cap rate at the time the asset was purchased. If markets are expected to weaken, a higher "going-out" capitalization rate will be assumed.

Traditionally, analysts assume that cap rates increase by 0.5% (or 50 basis points) from the time of purchase until the time of sale. For the apartment project, this means that cap rates would increase from the "going-in" cap rate of 6.489% (at the $48 million asking price) to a "going-out" cap rate of 6.989%. Hence, we are assuming a slight increase in cap rates over the period that the investment group holds the asset.

Recall that when we valued the property at the time of purchase, we assumed that NOI in year 1 was a perpetuity. Dividing expected first-year NOI of $3,114,587 by the cap rate today (time 0) or 6.489% gave us the value of $48 million.

To get the expected sale price in 5 years, we need to apply similar logic. That is, we need an estimate of NOI for the sixth year (see Table 7.8), and to divide it by the cap rate that we expect for year 5. The estimate for NOI requires another year of income projection, using the assumed growth rate for revenues of 3% and for operating expenses of 2.5%.

TABLE 7.8 Expected NOI in year 6

	Year 6
GRR	$5,964,743
– VAC	$298,237
GEI	$5,666,506
+ OI	$320,655
TR	$5,987,161
– TE	$2,319,377
NOI	$3,667,785

With this NOI estimate for the end of the sixth year, and our assumption that the prevailing cap rate in August 2014 is 6.989%, we can estimate a "going-out" valuation, or sale price, of $3,667,785 / 0.06989, or $52,479,396.

This represents a 9.34% increase in the value of the property during the time period that the investment group expects to own the asset. This corresponds to a 1.8% compounded annual growth rate (CAGR) in the asset's price.

Typically, selling expenses will be incurred when an asset is sold. These expenses will include a brokerage commission (paid by the seller), seller's attorney expenses, costs of transferring deeds, and other expenses related to the sale of the property. Assume for our purposes that these costs total 3% of the gross selling price (GSP). Therefore, the total selling expenses are 3% of $52,481,470, or $1,574,444. The net selling proceeds expected to be earned by the investment group is the GSP less the selling expenses, which equals $50,907,026.

7.6 APPLYING DISCOUNTED CASH FLOW TO ANALYZE INVESTMENT FEASIBILITY

In the introduction, it was mentioned that there are two ways in which discounted cash flow analysis can be applied. With an asking price from the seller, the investment feasibility of the project can be ascertained. The second application is to determine the maximum amount that an investor should be willing to pay and still earn their required rate of return. We'll look at these in turn.

With 5 years of projected operating cash flows, and an estimate of the net proceeds we expect to earn from selling the project, we can analyze the feasibility of the apartment investment opportunity for the investment group. We'll use the 7% return that is required by the investment group to determine its feasibility.

7.6.1 Determining Feasibility

Expected cash flows from operations and disposition for this investment have been estimated as shown in Table 7.9.

TABLE 7.9 Expected cash flows

	Year 0	Year 1	Year 2	Year 3	Year 4	Year 5
Outflow	−$48,000,000					
CF – Opns		$3,114,587	$3,218,274	$3,325,329	$3,435,858	$3,549,971
CF – Dispn		–	–	–	–	$50,907,026
Total	−$48,000,000	$3,114,587	$3,218,274	$3,325,329	$3,435,858	$54,456,997

The internal rate of return (IRR) for the stream of cash flows represented by an unleveraged investment in the apartment property is 7.934%. Since this earned rate of return exceeds the required rate of return of 7%, this represents a good investment for the investment group at the asking price of $48 million.

Some investors will also calculate the net present value (NPV) of prospective projects. Doing so generates a NPV of $1,884,538. Since the NPV is greater than zero, the investment signal from the NPV is similar to the signal from the IRR. At $48 million, investing in the apartment project represents an investment that meets and exceeds the required rate of return for the investment group.

7.6.2 Equity Multiple

Technically, the equity multiple is not a discounted cash flow technique or measure, but it has become a standard for analyzing investment feasibility. The equity multiple is the ratio of the total cash inflows relative to the cash outflows. It is not a discounted cash flow measure because the cash flows used in the calculation are simply added, rather than using a discount rate or calculating an internal rate of return. In the apartment example, the equity multiple is:

$$Equity\ multiple(EM) = Sum\ of\ all\ inflows\ /\ sum\ of\ all\ outflows$$
$$= \begin{pmatrix} \$3,114,587 + \$3,218,274 + \$3,325,329 + \$3,435,858 \\ + \$3,549,971 + \$50,907,026 \end{pmatrix} / \$48,000,000$$
$$= 1.4073$$

The equity multiple is also sometimes referred to as the return on invested capital (ROIC), and measures the total number of dollars that are earned relative to the total number of dollars that are invested. In this case, for every dollar invested at acquisition, \$1.41 is returned as cash flows from operations and from disposition at the end of the holding period. In general, the higher this number is, the better the investment looks in terms of feasibility.

7.6.3 Partitioning the Internal Rate of Return

Remember from earlier that we said that we have good confidence in our estimate of NOI in the first year since lease contracts for next year are likely in place and market conditions likely won't change much in 1 year. Our confidence about our forecasts declines as projections get further into the future. Most speculative is our estimate of what price we expect to sell the property for at the end of our holding period of 5 years. This is because our NOI estimates in year 6 are very speculative, as is our estimate of what the cap rate will be at the end of year 5. Therefore, it is useful to determine what proportion of our return is provided by operational cash flows (NOI), and what proportion is expected to be provided by sale proceeds.

To do so, we need to take the present value of the NOI cash flows at the IRR that was calculated, which is 7.934% in this example. Then, we need to take the present value of the net sale proceeds expected at the end of year 5, again discounted by the IRR. Adding these two components together should give us the price that was paid for the asset. In this way, we partition the IRR into the component produced by the NOI and the component produced by the sale of the asset.

In this case, the present value of the 5-year NOI stream is \$13,247,784 and the present value of the net sale price is \$34,752,216. The sum is \$48,000,000. Of the initial sale price, 27.6% can be attributed to the less speculative operating cash flows, and 72.4% from disposition. While this seems like a high proportion attributed to sale, the typical range is 60–75%.

TABLE 7.10 Partitioning the internal rate of return

	Amount	Percentage	IRR
PV cash from operations	\$13,247,784	27.6%	2.2%
PV cash from disposition	\$34,752,216	72.4%	5.7%
PV total cash flows	\$48,000,000	100.0%	7.93%

As a general rule of thumb, the higher the proportion that is generated from the sale, the more risky the project is to the investor. Above 80%, the investor should probably rethink its required rate of return, as risk will be higher.

7.6.4 Calculating the Maximum Price to Pay

The spread of earned over required return implies that the investment group, all else equal, could pay a higher price than the asking price and still achieve their desired return. Theoretically, the investment criterion is that the group should invest as long as IRR is greater than RRR, and that the group could increase their bid until IRR is equal to RRR. The maximum price that could be paid for the asset is simply calculated as the present value of all expected cash flows at the required rate of return of 7%.

In this case, the group could bid up to a price of $49.884 million and still earn an IRR of 7%, equivalent to its RRR. Of course, there are many other factors that would enter into the analysis, including adding debt and taxes, but these fairly straightforward calculations provide the first evidence as to whether this would represent a good investment and add wealth for the investment group.

7.7 SENSITIVITY ANALYSIS

Our analysis has been fairly static so far, in that we have made assumptions and calculated investment performance (IRR, NPV, EM) based on those assumptions. Key assumptions made are that rental rates will grow by 3% per year, operating expenses will grow by 2.5% per year, vacancy rates will be a constant 5%, and our going-out cap rate to determine our expected year 5 sale price is 50 basis points (bps), or 0.5% higher than our going-in cap rate. Naturally, any or all of these assumptions are unlikely to actually happen.

Sensitivity analysis allows us to check our results using varying assumptions, and also to show how sensitive our results are to them. For example, we can answer a lot of "What if?" questions. That is, what if rents grow more quickly, or less quickly than 3%? What if cap rates go up 100 bps, or go down 50 bps from our going-in cap rate?

Given the assumptions above, our expected IRR is 7.934%. Let us start by seeing the impact of changes in our rent growth assumption on this result.

Table 7.11 shows the results of our sensitivity analysis. Obviously, changing assumptions to be more positive increases IRR, and less favorable assumptions result in decreases to IRR. For example, assuming 4% rent growth instead of the base case 3% increases IRR to 8.14% from 7.93%. Increasing expense growth rates to 3.5% from 2.5% leads to a decrease in IRR to 7.85%. Changes in vacancy also have an impact on IRR, with higher vacancies leading to less income, and hence to lower returns.

As is typically the case, changes in going-out cap rate assumptions have large impacts on IRR. If, instead of assuming that cap rates go up by 50 bps, they increase by 100 bps, IRR drops from 7.93% to 6.73%. Similarly, if we assume that cap rates don't change at all over the holding period, the IRR rises to 9.26%.

If we call our original set of assumptions the base case, the worst case would be the assumptions with the most pessimistic view of the future (e.g. 2% rent growth, 3.5% expenses growth, 7% vacancy, and a 1% [100 bps] increase in cap rates), which completely changes the nature of this investment. The IRR calculated in this scenario is 6.21%, which falls below our investment hurdle of 7%. Clearly, this is a worst-case scenario, but there is likely a probability that these assumptions could be correct.

In contrast, if the investment turns out better than we expected and the best case occurs, the IRR earned by our investment group could be 9.75%, which is far above our hurdle rate.

The point of sensitivity analysis is to show a range of outcomes that can occur under different assumption scenarios. For those variables that alter the outcome the most, more research should be done to attempt to make the best forecast.

TABLE 7.11 Results of sensitivity analysis

	Assumption	IRR impact
	4%	8.14%
Rent growth	3%	7.93%
	2%	7.73%
	3.50%	7.85%
Expense growth	2.50%	7.93%
	1.50%	8.01%
	7%	7.71%
Vacancy	5%	7.93%
	3%	8.16%
	100 bps	6.73%
Cap rate increase	50 bps	7.93%
	0 bps	9.26%
Best case		9.75%
Base case		7.93%
Worst case		6.21%

7.8 CONCLUSION

This section has focused on valuation of a project at the entity, or total project, level. One key thing to remember is that we used NOI and net selling proceeds as our cash flow estimates. These two sets of expected cash flows are intended to represent all future cash flow events that will impact the cash flows earned by the owner of the project. In the case of the unleveraged investor investing in the entity represented by the apartment facility, this analysis is independent of who owns the project, how the project is financed, and the tax situation of the investors. The cash flows represent the overall productivity of the building as a whole.

Investors attempt to forecast every cash flow event that is likely to occur during the holding period. Using these estimates of cash flow, investment feasibility is determined by analyzing whether the IRR that is implied by the forecasts of cash flows exceeds the investor's required rate of return. For the investment group, the internal rate of return of 7.93% exceeded the required rate of return of 7%, indicating that if the cash flow estimates are correct, the investment will earn a higher return than required. In addition, the NPV of the estimated future cash flows at the 7% required rate of return is $1,884,538, which is greater than zero. In both cases, the results are favorable for investment.

The maximum amount that an investor can pay for an asset can also be determined by discounting the expected stream of cash flows by the required rate of return. Doing so provides a value of $49.884 million, indicating that the investment group can bid up to this level and still be confident that they will earn their 7% required rate of return.

CHAPTER 8

Mortgages: An Introduction

8.1 INTRODUCTION

Most real estate investments are financed with a combination of debt and equity. Debt is typically provided by an institutional lender, such as a bank, insurance company, or pension fund, or through the secondary mortgage market. The lender provides funds to the borrower for the purchase of property, and then receives cash flows in the form of debt service payments from the owner of the property over the loan term. The lender holds the loan as an asset on its balance sheet, and earns a return that compensates for the risk of the loan and the credit risk of the borrower. For the borrower, the loan represents a liability that must be paid back from the cash flow earned by the property. The interest rate on the loan is the cost of funds to the borrower.

This chapter builds on the apartment example that was provided in Chapter 7. Sections 8.2–8.5 provide a background on legal issues in the mortgage market and the lending industry. Section 8.6 provides an introduction to mortgage mathematics. This material is designed to provide an understanding of amortization schedules and calculating lender yields. Additional information includes the calculation of effective borrowing costs and penalties that commercial lenders usually charge when a borrower wishes to prepay the balance of the loan prior to the contractual loan maturity or term.

Chapter 9 introduces the reader to commercial mortgage underwriting. Based on an analysis of the borrower's credit history and the quality of the collateral, the underwriter determines whether to approve or disapprove a loan. Typically, for property, the quality and magnitude of cash flows expected to be earned by the property determine whether a loan will be approved and the amount that the lender will be willing to lend. In Chapter 9, we'll also look at the impact of debt on valuation and investment feasibility for the equity investor.

Introducing debt to an equity investment also increases the level of risk and the uncertainty of outcomes for the equity investor. Residual cash flows to the equity investor will be more volatile with debt, and the volatility increases with the amount of debt. Understanding the risks of debt is a critical component of investment analysis and should be understood by all investors.

8.2 WHAT IS A MORTGAGE?

A mortgage is legally defined as "an instrument creating a security interest in land and usually providing for foreclosure in case of a default on the debt." The lender is called a mortgagee, and the borrower is called a mortgagor. In effect, the mortgagor borrows from the mortgagee an amount that is sufficient, when combined with an equity investment from the mortgagor, to purchase a property. In exchange for the loan, the mortgagor promises to make regular payments according to the terms of the loan. Typically, the mortgagor pledges his/her property as collateral for the loan. If the mortgagor should fail to make a contractual payment as agreed in the loan documents, the mortgagee can foreclose the mortgagor's interest in the property by selling it and (hopefully) collecting an amount from the sale that is sufficient to recover the full outstanding balance on the loan.

Each mortgage typically includes two contracts: a promissory note and a mortgage instrument.

8.2.1 Promissory Note

The promissory note is a contract between the mortgagee and mortgagor that contains the terms of the loan, and represents a written promise to pay a specific number of payments of a specific amount at regular intervals for a specific period of time. The terms include the interest rate that the lender charges, the amortization period, the term or maturity of the loan, and any other provisions that affect payments. Typical commercial mortgage promissory notes require monthly payments of principal and interest. The monthly principal amortizes, or pays down, the original balance over the life of the loan. These terms are defined and examples are provided in this chapter.

8.2.2 Mortgage Instrument

The mortgage instrument creates a security interest in the property for the mortgagee. It creates the legal right of the mortgagee to foreclose on the property that serves as collateral for the loan. If the borrower defaults by not making payments according to the original schedule and terms of the promissory note, the mortgagee can take control of the property and sell it. Proceeds from the sale of the property are used to recover the amount of the loan that is outstanding at the time of default. Funds recovered over and above the amount of debt are distributed to others who have a claim on the property or the borrower.

Mortgages can be "recourse" or "non-recourse" loans. Recourse loans require the borrower to pledge additional collateral beyond the property to the lender to serve as protection should the borrower default. Non-recourse loans limit the lender's right to sell assets only to the property that is mortgaged. In this sense, the lender has no recourse to other assets that might be owned by the borrower.

Under the terms of a recourse mortgage, the mortgaged property will be sold by the lender if default occurs, and if the proceeds from sale are insufficient to cover the balance that is outstanding on the loan, the lender has recourse to other assets owned by the borrower. Additional collateral may include equity interests in other properties that the borrower owns, personal property (owner-occupied housing, automobiles, etc.) that the borrower owns, or other assets such as stocks or bonds. In all cases, the pledged assets serve as additional collateral for the mortgage loan, and the assets pledged with recourse are designed to fully repay the lender should the value of the mortgaged property be below the loan amount at the time of sale.

Another provision used by lenders to enhance their position is to require a personal guarantee from the borrower, or from someone who is in the borrowing partnership. A borrower who signs a personal guarantee and subsequently defaults is required to repay the loan balance that is outstanding at the time of default, plus any payments that are in arrears.

Credit enhancement, in the form of recourse or a personal guarantee, makes a lender more willing to lend funds for purchase of investment property, and may allow the borrower to negotiate a lower interest rate or other favorable terms. When credit is difficult to obtain, credit enhancement from the borrower is standard.

In practice, lenders will allow a grace period if payments are missed, depending upon the relationship between the lender and the borrower and the circumstances of the default. Lender practice will differ, with some lenders initiating foreclosure proceedings after a short period of time (3 months) when payments are not made by the borrower, and others allowing longer periods.

8.3 THE RISKS AND RETURNS OF MORTGAGE INVESTMENT

The mortgage lender originates and owns a mortgage as an asset on their balance sheet. As an asset, it is expected to earn a return over the holding period that it is owned. This return comes in the form of the interest rate that is charged to the borrower. The interest rate is used to calculate the debt service that is paid by the borrower, for whom the mortgage is a contractual obligation or liability.

The best-case scenario for the lender is for the borrower to make payments exactly as specified by the promissory note, and to earn the expected interest rate, or yield, on the mortgage. However, there are many types of risk that may arise in a mortgage investment.

a. *Investment risk.* First and foremost, the property must provide a strong return for the investor/borrower. Pro forma income statements must demonstrate that the investment is expected to provide sufficient return to compensate the equity investor for the risk incurred. A strong internal rate of return (IRR) and net present value (NPV) ensure that the investor can increase wealth from the investment.

b. *Default risk.* Careful underwriting, or assessment, of risk prior to originating a mortgage loan reduces the likelihood that the borrower will default. Even if the loan is carefully underwritten, however, changes in market conditions, borrower circumstances, tenant performance, or other circumstances could create a scenario where a borrower may wish to stop making debt service payments. One way to mitigate default risk is to require credit enhancement, as discussed above.

c. *Interest rate risk*. This risk arises for fixed-rate mortgages. Like any fixed-income investment that promises a fixed payment, if interest rates rise, the value of the investment declines. For the lender, this causes a reduction in the value of portfolio assets. Of course, the opposite is true as well – if interest rates decline, the value of a fixed-income asset increases.
d. *Prepayment risk*. Borrowers may have the option to prepay or call their mortgage prior to the maturity of the loan. If so, the lender will have to reinvest the proceeds of the prepayment into the current mortgage market. If rates have fallen since the loan was originated, the lender will be forced to invest in mortgages with lower contract interest rates, and earn a lower yield over the term of the original mortgage. This reduces the spread of asset return over liability cost, and reduces profit margins.

8.4 THE FINANCIAL COMPONENTS OF A MORTGAGE

Every mortgage consists of three different financial contracts: a bond, a call option, and a put option.

8.4.1 The Bond Component

The bond is fairly self-explanatory. The borrower pledges to make regular payments in order to repay the principal amount that was initially borrowed, and provide a return to the lender in the form of the interest rate charged. Like any fixed-income investment, the payment is a contractual obligation of the borrower.

Corporate bonds make regular payments of interest, followed at maturity by the total repayment of the principal amount that was borrowed. Commercial and other mortgages differ from corporate bonds in that each regular payment typically includes an interest component and a principal component. Because each payment includes a principal component, the balance is paid down slowly through the term of the loan. The lender is said to be "long a bond," because they own an asset in the form of the loan, and are the recipient of the contractual payments. The borrower is said to be "short a bond," since they owe a liability and make debt service payments.

The lender earns a yield that is equal to the IRR generated by the loan cash flows over the loan term. The outflow for the lender is the initial loan amount, and the inflows are the monthly payments of principal and interest.

8.4.2 The Call Option Component

A call option is the right, not the obligation, to buy an asset at some time in the future. Many mortgages allow the borrower an ability to repay the loan in full at any point in time, which is a form of call option. For example, a borrower may wish to refinance the original loan if interest rates fall during the loan term. At the time of refinancing, the borrower obtains a new loan for an amount equal to the balance outstanding on the old loan. With the proceeds from the new lender, the old loan is paid back in full, and the borrower has a new lending agreement with the new lender. Because the new loan offers a lower interest rate than the original loan, the borrower typically reduces monthly payment requirements, and increases before- and after-tax cash flow.[1]

Since the borrower has the option to buy back the loan at any time by paying it back in full, they are "long a call option." The borrower will exercise this call option when the present value of the monthly savings from lower debt service payments exceeds the transaction costs involved in executing the refinancing transaction. The call option is said to be "in the money" when the present value of savings in debt service payments from refinancing exceeds transaction costs.

The original lender is "short a call option," because the borrower can exercise the option at any time, and the lender must "sell" the mortgage back to the borrower at par, which is the balance outstanding at the time of refinancing.

Note that the original lender faces a great deal of interest rate risk by originating fixed-rate mortgages that allow prepayment, given the existence of this call option. The borrower will exercise the call option under two circumstances: (1) when interest rates decline, or (2) when the cash flow and value of a property increase to allow greater debt capacity. The lender receives full repayment of principal, and reinvests into the mortgage market at a lower rate than paid under the original mortgage.

Residential mortgagors can typically exercise the call option without cost, and the lender faces the full effect of interest rate risk. Commercial mortgagors, in contrast, must usually pay a fee, known as a prepayment penalty, to unwind the old mortgage to take advantage of lower interest rates from refinancing. This fee can take many forms, but is designed to fully price the borrower's call option, and reduce or eliminate the benefit to the borrower of lower interest rates and dissuade prepayment. Different methods of calculating prepayment penalties are discussed later in this chapter.

8.4.3 The Put Option Component

A put option gives the holder the right, not the obligation, to sell an asset at some future time. In a mortgage agreement, the mortgagor is long a put option, and the mortgagee is short the option, meaning that the mortgagor has control over when the option is to be exercised. So, when will the put option be exercised?

Imagine a scenario where a non-recourse mortgagor borrows $15 million on a $20 million property. Over time, newer competing developments with better amenities are built nearby, and overall real estate market conditions worsen. After 2 years of paying on a 5-year mortgage agreement, the property has declined in value to $12.5 million, and the loan balance outstanding is still close to $15 million. In the parlance of the 21st century, this loan is "under water," in that the value of the property is less than the loan amount, in this case, by $2.5 million. The investor's initial equity is completely wiped out, and if the property were sold, the investor would have to come out of pocket to cover the difference between the loan amount and the proceeds from sale.

[1] Some borrowers in the 2000–7 period were able to refinance for larger amounts than their existing mortgages. Interest rates declined, and property income and values increased, leading to an increase in debt capacity. In many cases, borrowers could take cash out of their property investments by borrowing larger amounts, paying back their old mortgages, and pocketing the difference. This practice led to a significant increase in leverage in the property industry, ultimately causing problems that led to the credit crisis in 2008. This is discussed in Chapter 13.

Let us also assume that current income thrown off by the property is insufficient to cover debt service payments, and the owner of the property is forced to use income from other sources to keep mortgage payments current. Instead of continuing to do this, the borrower may choose to default on the mortgage and allow the property to go through the foreclosure process. Since the loan is non-recourse, the borrower has not pledged any assets except for the property. By defaulting and allowing the lender to take over the asset in the foreclosure process, the borrower has exercised a put option by "selling" the asset to the lender for the balance of the loan outstanding. The borrower is not responsible for the $2.5 million loss incurred by the lender.

The put option is "in the money" when the value of the asset falls below the balance outstanding on the mortgage loan, or when the cash flow earned by the property is less than the debt service payment requirement. In either case, the incentive for the borrower is to default, turn ownership back over to the lender, and be foreclosed upon.

Of course, there are ramifications to the borrower from doing this. Needless to say, it will be more difficult for this borrower to obtain commercial mortgage financing in the future given the default and foreclosure. In addition, the borrower walks away from any equity that was invested when the property was purchased.

Lenders can and do use contractual methods to minimize the probability of borrower put option execution. Loans that allow lender recourse to other assets owned by the borrower will greatly limit borrower willingness to default. Similarly, there is no benefit of defaulting if the borrower has signed personal guarantees for the loan amount, since the $2.5 million shortfall on the loan at foreclosure would have to be paid back from other owner sources.

8.5 THE MORTGAGE MENU

A borrower in the real estate markets has many options when considering a loan. The primary distinctions between loans are with respect to the type of rate that is applied to the mortgage amount, and the amortization schedule that is applied.

8.5.1 Fixed or Floating-Rate Loans

Commercial mortgage loans can carry either a fixed or a floating rate. A fixed rate is just that – the interest rate is fixed for the entire term of the mortgage. In most cases, a fixed-rate loan will require a fixed or constant monthly payment until maturity. A borrower obtains some certainty for budgeting purposes, and interest rate risk is shifted to the lender. If interest rates rise, the value of their fixed-rate mortgage asset will fall. Conversely, the borrower enjoys a mortgage that pays interest at a lower rate than is currently available in the market.

In order to lessen their exposure to interest rate risk, lenders will offer floating-rate loans. A floating, or adjustable, rate loan provides for changes in interest rates and payments over the term of a mortgage loan. A common example is to allow the interest rate to move with movements in a market index, such as 1-year Treasury bonds, the prime rate, or the London Inter-Bank Offer Rate (LIBOR). At regular intervals, the lender changes the rate on the loan to a rate that is based on one of the indexes.

For example, a LIBOR-based loan might adjust once every year on the anniversary date of the origination of the mortgage. At the anniversary date, the lender consults a financial website to determine the current LIBOR rate. The lender typically adds a premium as specified in the original promissory note, and the sum of LIBOR plus the premium is the rate that will be charged for the following year. Note that the debt service payment on the loan will also change with the interest rate. If rates go up, debt service payments also increase, meaning that the investor's before- and after-tax cash flows decline. If the interest rate increase was unexpected, the actual return earned on the investment will be lower than what was forecast when the property was originally purchased.

Of course, interest rates could also fall between rate and payment adjustments, meaning that payments would fall as well. This benefits the borrower, and leads to higher cash flows for the equity investor.

The lender is better off with an adjustable rate loan, since the interest rate adjusts to a market rate at each anniversary date. In this way, interest rate risk is partially shifted to the borrower. The shorter the period between interest rate and payment adjustments, the more interest rate risk is shifted to the borrower.

Often, a lender will offer a slightly lower rate on a floating-rate loan to attempt to entice a borrower to take this type of loan.

8.5.2 Fully or Partially Amortizing Loans

Another choice for the borrower is between a fully amortizing and a partially amortizing loan. As the name implies, a fully amortizing loan pays off the balance in regular payments over the period of the loan. For example, a 30-year loan pays off the balance in regular payments over the 30-year period. As payments are made, the lender's exposure declines as the principal balance is paid back. If property values are constant, the owner's equity stake in the property will increase. Fully amortizing loans for commercial property were common prior to the 1990s, but their usage has declined since then. Currently, most loans are originated as partially amortizing loans.

A partially amortizing loan calculates payments as if to amortize a loan over a long period of time, say 30 years. However, the maturity of the loan will be relatively short, say 5, 7, or 10 years. Since the monthly debt service payments are calculated based on a 30-year payment period, the principal balance of the loan will not be fully paid off at the time the loan matures. A loan with a maturity of 5 years and an amortization period of 30 years is termed a "5/30" loan.

The amount outstanding at the end of the maturity is paid back out of proceeds from the sale of the asset, or from a refinancing transaction. The balance outstanding is usually a sizeable proportion of the initial loan balance, especially with shorter maturities. Examples of both fully and partially amortizing loans are presented in Chapter 9.

A third type of loan that became popular in the early decades of the 21st century is an interest-only mortgage. Instead of paying back principal over time as in the case of a fully or partially amortizing loan, the borrower of an interest-only loan pays back only interest (as the name implies) with each payment. Since the principal balance does not decrease with regular payments, lender exposure does not decrease over the life of the loan.

Recently, lenders have been offering loans that allow for the borrower to make payments based on an interest-only basis for the early parts of a loan term. For example, terms of the loan might be 5/30, with 2 years of interest-only payments. In this case, the borrower will pay interest only (IO) for 2 years, and after 2 years, the loan reverts to a 5-year maturity with payments based on a 30-year amortization period. The practice of allowing an IO period allows borrowers to increase loan amounts and decrease the amount of equity that they must invest.

8.6 AN INTRODUCTION TO MORTGAGE MATH

Let us assume that the investment group (the borrower) contracts to purchase the apartment facility introduced in Chapter 7 for $48 million, and has applied to a lender for a 75% loan-to-value ratio loan at an interest rate of 5.5%. Therefore, the group is seeking a $36 million loan, and will invest $36 million as their equity stake. As with most commercial mortgages, the borrower will make monthly payments of principal and interest over the term of the mortgage. For now, we will assume that the mortgage maturity or term is 25 years. The borrower is expected to make 300 monthly payments, ultimately paying down the entire principal balance over that period.

8.6.1 Calculating the Monthly Payment

A mortgage payment is an annuity that is paid over the term of the loan. By definition, an annuity is a constant payment, made at regular intervals, over a certain number of periods. The investment group has applied for a $36 million loan. Determining the monthly payment that they'll have to make on this loan during the loan term requires solving for the monthly annuity payment that must be paid to fully pay back the $36 million over the 300-month loan term at a 5.5% rate. In order to solve this, it's useful to know that the $36 million loan amount is a present value, 5.5% is the annual interest rate, 300 months is the term, and the unknown is the monthly annuity (or debt service) payment. To determine the monthly interest rate requires dividing 5.5% by 12, which gives 0.4583%.

Using the @PMT function in Excel, and inputting $36,000,000 as the present value, (5.5%/12 =) 0.4583% as the rate, and 300 months as the number of periods gives a monthly payment of $221,071.50. This is the monthly payment that must be made by the borrower to fulfill the terms of his promissory note for this mortgage.[2]

[2] Using a financial calculator, making sure that it's in monthly mode (12 P/YR), the keystrokes to calculate this payment are:

36000000	PV
5.5	I/YR
300	N

Solve for PMT, and the answer is $221,071.50.

8.6.2 The Mortgage Loan Constant

A calculation that is often made for mortgages is called the mortgage loan constant (MLC). Conceptually, the MLC is the monthly payment that would have to be made to repay a $1 loan given the interest rate and the term of the loan. For this reason, the MLC is also known as the installment to amortize one dollar (ITAO). To determine the monthly payment for a more typical larger loan, the ITAO would be multiplied by the initial loan balance (e.g. in our case, $36,000,000). Using Excel as above, the only difference is that $1 would be used as the present value input instead of $36,000,000.[3] The result of the calculation is a monthly payment of $0.006140875.

While it may not appear to be the case, the MLC is a useful concept when attempting to determine the impact of leverage on return, and we'll return to it later in this section. For now, note that if the MLC is multiplied by the $36 million loan amount, the product is $221,071.50, which is the same monthly payment that is calculated above. Another way to interpret the MLC is as the monthly cost of borrowing a dollar. Using the same inputs, the monthly cost is 0.61408749%. The annual MLC is calculated by simply multiplying the monthly MLC by 12, which equals 0.0736905, or 7.36905%. As a check, 7.36905% times $36,000,000 is $2,652,852, which divided by 12 is the monthly payment of $221,071.50.

The annual MLC (7.36905% in this case) is always higher than the loan rate (5.5%) for an amortizing mortgage. The MLC incorporates both the interest and principal components of the mortgage payment, whereas the loan rate simply reflects the interest component of the payment. This might be clearer in the context of separating the interest and principal payments, and developing an amortization schedule.

8.6.3 The Amortization Schedule

As mentioned above, each of the monthly $221,071.50 payments contains a principal and interest component. Since mortgage interest on residential and commercial property is tax deductible in the USA, it is essential to be able to determine how much of each payment is of interest, and how much is of principal. The calculation is relatively straightforward.[4]

In any given month, the interest payment is simply the monthly interest rate times the balance outstanding on the mortgage. For example, the monthly payment, which is fixed throughout the loan term, is $221,051.50. The interest component of the payment in the first month is (0.055/12 * $36,000,000 =) $165,000. Since each payment contains only two components, principal and interest, the principal component is the remainder of the total payment, or ($221,071.50 – $165,000 =) $56,071.50. The reader should note that the bulk of the payment in the first month is payment of interest.

To determine the amount of interest to be paid in the second month, the balance outstanding from the beginning of the loan term is reduced by the $56,071.50 that was

[3] The keystrokes for the calculator are as repeated above, but instead of a $36,000,000 loan, we would input $1 as the PV. The PMT that is calculated is 0.006140875, or 0.6140875%.

[4] The reader should note that there will be minor differences in the calculations in this section depending on whether a calculator or Excel is used, due to minor rounding errors. Unless specified, the numbers presented in the book are calculated using Excel.

paid in principal in the first month. Therefore, the balance outstanding after 1 month of payments is $35,943,928.50 ($36,000,000 – $56,071.50). The interest payment to be made in the second month is (0.055/12 * $35,943,928.50), or $164,743.00. Subtracting this interest amount from the total payment of $221,071.50 leaves $56,328.49 to be paid as principal, which decreases the balance outstanding again.

Note that the interest component in the second month has declined since it is calculated as the fixed interest rate times the balance outstanding at the beginning of the month, and the balance declines as principal is paid with each debt service payment. Conversely, since the principal component is calculated by subtracting the declining interest component from the fixed monthly payment, the principal amount increases each month. This process is repeated for each month throughout the 300-month amortization period.

The first 24 months of the amortization schedule are presented in Table 8.1, as is the balance outstanding on the mortgage at the end of every year and the last year's monthly payments of principal and interest. The reader should attempt to replicate this table using the calculation support facility of their choice.

TABLE 8.1 Amortization schedule for $36 million loan at 5.5% interest rate and 25-year maturity

Month	Beg. balance	Payment	Interest	Principal	End balance
0					
1	$36,000,000.00	$221,071.50	$165,000.00	$56,071.50	$35,943,928.50
2	$35,943,928.50	$221,071.50	$164,743.01	$56,328.49	$35,887,600.01
3	$35,887,600.01	$221,071.50	$164,484.83	$56,586.66	$35,831,013.35
4	$35,831,013.35	$221,071.50	$164,225.48	$56,846.02	$35,774,167.33
5	$35,774,167.33	$221,071.50	$163,964.93	$57,106.56	$35,717,060.76
6	$35,717,060.76	$221,071.50	$163,703.20	$57,368.30	$35,659,692.46
7	$35,659,692.46	$221,071.50	$163,440.26	$57,631.24	$35,602,061.22
8	$35,602,061.22	$221,071.50	$163,176.11	$57,895.38	$35,544,165.84
9	$35,544,165.84	$221,071.50	$162,910.76	$58,160.74	$35,486,005.10
10	$35,486,005.10	$221,071.50	$162,644.19	$58,427.31	$35,427,577.79
11	$35,427,577.79	$221,071.50	$162,376.40	$58,695.10	$35,368,882.70
12	$35,368,882.70	$221,071.50	$162,107.38	$58,964.12	$35,309,918.58
13	$35,309,918.58	$221,071.50	$161,837.13	$59,234.37	$35,250,684.21
14	$35,250,684.21	$221,071.50	$161,565.64	$59,505.86	$35,191,178.35
15	$35,191,178.35	$221,071.50	$161,292.90	$59,778.60	$35,131,399.75
16	$35,131,399.75	$221,071.50	$161,018.92	$60,052.58	$35,071,347.17
17	$35,071,347.17	$221,071.50	$160,743.67	$60,327.82	$35,011,019.34
18	$35,011,019.34	$221,071.50	$160,467.17	$60,604.33	$34,950,415.02
19	$34,950,415.02	$221,071.50	$160,189.40	$60,882.10	$34,889,532.92
20	$34,889,532.92	$221,071.50	$159,910.36	$61,161.14	$34,828,371.79
21	$34,828,371.79	$221,071.50	$159,630.04	$61,441.46	$34,766,930.33
22	$34,766,930.33	$221,071.50	$159,348.43	$61,723.07	$34,705,207.26
23	$34,705,207.26	$221,071.50	$159,065.53	$62,005.96	$34,643,201.30
24	$34,643,201.30	$221,071.50	$158,781.34	$62,290.16	$34,580,911.14
36	$33,876,585.76	$221,071.50	$155,267.68	$65,803.81	$33,810,781.95

(Continued)

TABLE 8.1 (CONTINUED)

Month	Beg. balance	Payment	Interest	Principal	End balance
48	$33,066,727.09	$221,071.50	$151,555.83	$69,515.66	$32,997,211.42
60	$32,211,186.01	$221,071.50	$147,634.60	$73,436.89	$32,137,749.12
72	$31,307,385.70	$221,071.50	$143,492.18	$77,579.31	$31,229,806.39
84	$30,352,603.95	$221,071.50	$139,116.10	$81,955.40	$30,270,648.55
96	$29,343,965.00	$221,071.50	$134,493.17	$86,578.32	$29,257,386.67
108	$28,278,430.88	$221,071.50	$129,609.47	$91,462.02	$28,186,968.86
120	$27,152,792.26	$221,071.50	$124,450.30	$96,621.20	$27,056,171.06
132	$25,963,658.78	$221,071.50	$119,000.10	$102,071.39	$25,861,587.39
144	$24,707,448.83	$221,071.50	$113,242.47	$107,829.02	$24,599,619.80
156	$23,380,378.75	$221,071.50	$107,160.07	$113,911.43	$23,266,467.33
168	$21,978,451.50	$221,071.50	$100,734.57	$120,336.93	$21,858,114.57
180	$20,497,444.52	$221,071.50	$93,946.62	$127,124.88	$20,370,319.65
192	$18,932,897.12	$221,071.50	$86,775.78	$134,295.72	$18,798,601.40
204	$17,280,096.94	$221,071.50	$79,200.44	$141,871.05	$17,138,225.88
216	$15,534,065.84	$221,071.50	$71,197.80	$149,873.70	$15,384,192.14
228	$13,689,544.86	$221,071.50	$62,743.75	$158,327.75	$13,531,217.11
240	$11,740,978.40	$221,071.50	$53,812.82	$167,258.68	$11,573,719.72
252	$9,682,497.47	$221,071.50	$44,378.11	$176,693.38	$9,505,804.09
264	$7,507,902.04	$221,071.50	$34,411.22	$186,660.28	$7,321,241.76
276	$5,210,642.33	$221,071.50	$23,882.11	$197,189.39	$5,013,452.94
288	$2,783,799.12	$221,071.50	$12,759.08	$208,312.42	$2,575,486.70
300	$220,062.88	$221,071.50	$1,008.62	$220,062.88	0.00

Several points are worth mentioning. The first relates to the principal balance and how it changes over time. As is always the case for a fully amortizing mortgage, the balance outstanding declines over time, and at the end of the term the principal is completely paid down to a balance of zero. In addition, the principal component of the payment increases in each successive month, so that principal repayment speeds up as the loan ages. If the monthly principal components were added up, the total amount of principal paid over the 300-month loan term would total the initial balance of $36 million. The last payment of $221,071.50 is comprised of a $1,008.62 interest component, and a $220,062.88 principal component.

The balance outstanding at any point in time during the 25-year term can be calculated by determining the present value of all the remaining monthly payments at the monthly interest rate for the remaining term. For example, assume the borrower wants to determine the balance outstanding as of the end of the fifth year. At that time, 60 payments of $221,071.50 would have been made, and 240 payments remain to be paid. For this application, we know that the PMT is $221,071.50, the remaining term (N) is 240, and the interest rate is 5.5% (or 0.4583% monthly). Solving for PV using a calculator or Excel, the present value of this 240-month annuity stream at a monthly rate of 5.5%/12 is $32,137,749.12, which represents the loan balance outstanding after 5 years of monthly payments.

Note that the accumulation of principal that would be paid in the first 60 monthly payments is only $3,862,250.88 (equal to the original balance of $36,000,000 less the balance at the end of 5 years of $32,137,749.12), which represents only 10.73% of the original balance. A total of $13,264,290 has been paid (60 monthly payments made of $221,071.50), but only $3,862,250.88 ($36,000,000 – $32,137,749.12) of principal has been repaid. The difference of $9,861,250.88 is the amount of interest that is paid with the first 60 payments.

Similarly, after 10 years (or 40% of the loan term), 24.84% of the original balance has been paid. After 15 years (60% of the full term of the mortgage), only 43.4% of the principal borrowed has been paid back through regular amortization. Almost 20.09% of the original loan balance ($7,321,241.76) is paid in the last 3 years of the 25-year loan term.

Figure 8.1 demonstrates how the principal balance declines over the term of the loan.

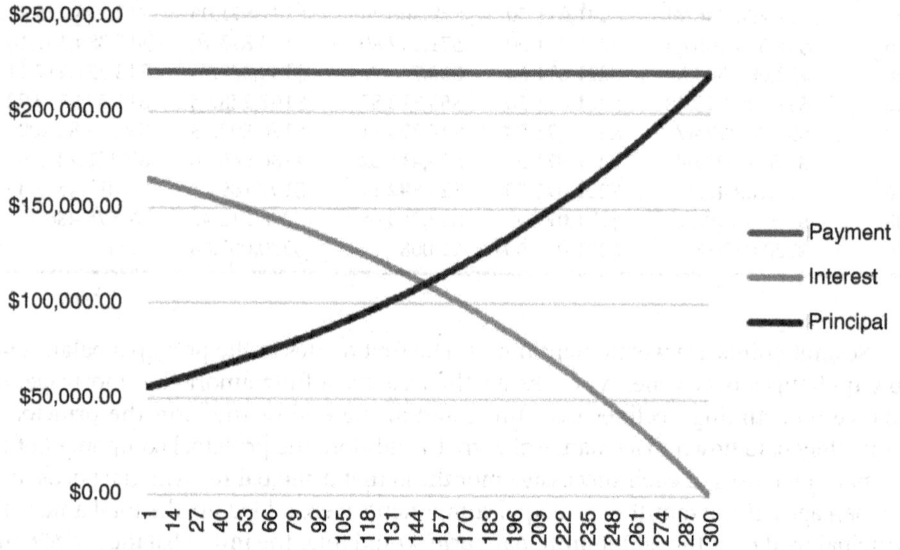

FIGURE 8.1 Graph of monthly payment, principal component, and interest component over loan maturity

The proportion of each payment that is interest declines over time, as it is calculated based on the declining balance of the loan (e.g. the monthly interest rate of 5.5%/12 multiplied by the balance outstanding at the beginning of each month). Clearly, this means that the principal component of each payment increases over time. In fact, the first payment is mostly interest, with a small relative principal payment, and the last payment is comprised mostly of principal.

8.6.4 Converting from the Contract Rate to the Compounded Rate

The astute reader will recognize that the annual contract rate on the loan is 5.5%, but since the payments are made monthly, the actual rate earned by the lender will be slightly higher than 5.5%. Because the payments are received by the lender (paid by the borrower) monthly, the 5.5% annual rate must be converted into an annual rate with monthly compounding, which means that the following calculation must be made:

$$\left(1+\left(0.055/12\right)^{12}\right)-1=5.64\%$$

Despite the fact that the rate quoted is an annual rate of 5.5%, because payments are made in monthly installments, the actual annualized rate (on a monthly compounding basis) is 5.64%.[5]

8.6.5 Determining the Cost of Borrowing

In many cases, a lender will charge fees at the inception of the loan term. These fees, in the form of loan origination fees or discount points, reduce the actual disbursement made to the borrower. A loan origination fee is charged to cover the administrative costs of underwriting the loan, and for overhead related to inputting the details of the loan and borrower into the lender's computer system. These fees may also cover any legal fees that are not allocable to the borrower at closing, the cost of recording the loan, and other expenditures incurred by the bank in the process of originating and closing the loan. Each discount point is equal to 1% of the initial loan balance, and points are charged to enhance the lender's yield. In some cases, the borrower can reduce or "buy down" the contract interest rate that is charged on the loan by paying one or more points at the beginning of the loan term.

For example, if a lender charges a 1% loan origination fee (LOF), the actual amount disbursed, and available for the property purchase, is $36,000,000 less $360,000 or $35,640,000. Payments made to the lender are still based on the original $36 million amount. Since payments are based on $36 million of loan amount, and the lender actually only disburses $35.64 million, the yield earned by the lender (and paid by the borrower) is higher than the contract rate.

Borrowing Cost without Up-front Fees

As a basis for comparison, let us assume that no up-front fees are paid by the borrower. Effective borrowing cost (EBC, or equivalently effective lender yield (ELY)) is simply an internal

[5] The astute reader will appreciate the relationship to the monthly interest rate and the monthly mortgage constant by looking at the amortization schedule. From the earlier discussion in this section, the monthly interest rate is 0.4583333% while the monthly mortgage loan constant is 0.6140875%. The difference between these two numbers, or 0.1557542%, is the principal component of the first mortgage payment. Multiplying this by the initial mortgage balance of $36,000,000 million gives the principal component of the first monthly mortgage payment, or $56,071.50.

rate of return (or yield) calculation. From the lender's perspective, for example, if there are no fees associated with the mortgage, the cash outflow is the original amount lent, or $36,000,000. The inflows are the stream of $221,071.50 cash flows that the borrower pays each month for 300 months. The reader should verify that if held to maturity, the loan will provide an annual yield (compounded monthly) of 5.64%. These cash flows are shown in Table 8.2.

TABLE 8.2 Calculation of effective borrowing costs: no up-front fees

	Paid to maturity	Prepaid in 5 years	Prepaid in 1 year
Month	Cash flows	Cash flows	Cash flows
0	–$36,000,000.00	–$36,000,000.00	–$36,000,000.00
1	$221,071.50	$221,071.50	$221,071.50
2	$221,071.50	$221,071.50	$221,071.50
3	$221,071.50	$221,071.50	$221,071.50
4	$221,071.50	$221,071.50	$221,071.50
5	$221,071.50	$221,071.50	$221,071.50
6	$221,071.50	$221,071.50	$221,071.50
7	$221,071.50	$221,071.50	$221,071.50
8	$221,071.50	$221,071.50	$221,071.50
9	$221,071.50	$221,071.50	$221,071.50
10	$221,071.50	$221,071.50	$221,071.50
11	$221,071.50	$221,071.50	$221,071.50
12	$221,071.50	$221,071.50	$35,530,990.07
58	$221,071.50	$221,071.50	
59	$221,071.50	$221,071.50	
60	$221,071.50	$32,358,820.62	
358	$221,071.50		
359	$221,071.50		
360	$221,071.50		
IRR	5.6408%	5.6408%	5.6408%

Since the balance outstanding at any point in time is the present value of these future cash flows at the lending rate, the yield will equal the rate of 5.64% whether it is held to maturity, or paid off prior to maturity. For example, the relevant cash flows are also shown in Table 8.2 for a loan that is paid off in Year 5. At payoff, the balance outstanding plus the last payment of $221,071.50 is paid. The yield of 5.64% is the same as if payments were made until the end of the 300-month term. The same yield is earned if the loan is prepaid at the end of the first year, as shown in the third column of Table 8.2.

Borrowing Costs when the Lender Charges Fees

When discount points and loan origination fees are charged by the lender, yields paid by borrowers and earned by lenders will be higher than for loans where fees are not paid up-front.

To determine the cost of borrowing, assume that our borrower had to pay one discount point (1% of the original balance), and a 1% loan origination fee, and that the loan maturity is 25 years, with monthly payments. Because of the loan origination fee and the points charged, the total amount disbursed by the lender will be net of the 2% up-front fees. These fees total 2% of the original balance, or $720,000. The amount of cash outflow provided by the lender is ($36,000,000 – $720,000 =) $35,280,000. The investor must provide $16 million of equity, plus $720,000 of up-front fees, a total of $16.72 million. Since the lender's outflow is smaller, and the inflows remain the same at $221,071.50, the IRR on these flows is higher than the contract rate of 5.5%, or the compounded rate of 5.64%.

In fact, in this case, the ELY (and hence, EBC) is 5.86%. The cash flows underlying this calculation are shown in the first column of Table 8.3. Because the payments are based on an original balance of $36,000,000 and the lender disburses only $35,280,000, the lender's yield increases by 22 basis points relative to the "no-point" case. If a lender can charge higher points and fees, the yield will increase further.

TABLE 8.3 Calculation of effective borrowing costs with points and origination fees

	Paid to maturity	Prepaid in 5 years	Prepaid in 1 year
Month	**Cash flows**	**Cash flows**	**Cash flows**
0	–$35,280,000.00	–$35,280,000.00	–$35,280,000.00
1	$221,071.50	$221,071.50	$221,071.50
2	$221,071.50	$221,071.50	$221,071.50
3	$221,071.50	$221,071.50	$221,071.50
4	$221,071.50	$221,071.50	$221,071.50
5	$221,071.50	$221,071.50	$221,071.50
6	$221,071.50	$221,071.50	$221,071.50
7	$221,071.50	$221,071.50	$221,071.50
8	$221,071.50	$221,071.50	$221,071.50
9	$221,071.50	$221,071.50	$221,071.50
10	$221,071.50	$221,071.50	$221,071.50
11	$221,071.50	$221,071.50	$221,071.50
12	$221,071.50	$21071.4972	$35,530,990.07
58	$221,071.50	$221,071.50	
59	$221,071.50	$221,071.50	
60	$221,071.50	$32,358,820.62	
358	$221,071.50		
359	$221,071.50		
360	$221,071.50		
IRR	5.8606%	6.1541%	7.8718%

Borrowing Costs when the Loan is Prepaid Prior to Maturity

When up-front fees are charged, the lender's yield (borrower's borrowing cost) is increased above the contract rate. For now, assume the 2% in fees is charged by the lender, and that all payments are calculated as in the example above. Further assume that the borrower prepays the loan in 5 years, as opposed to the 25-year case where the lender earned 5.86%. In the 25-year case, it took 300 payments for the full principal amount of $36,000,000 to be earned back by the lender. In the case of a 5-year prepayment, the principal is earned back through regular monthly payments over the first 5 years, and then in a lump sum payment at the end of the 60th payment in Year 5. Clearly, due to the impact of the time value of money, the lender's yield is higher in the case of prepayment. The question is, how much higher?

The cash flows for the 5-year prepayment case are shown in the second column of Table 8.3.

Again, the only difference from what is shown in the first column is that the entire balance outstanding at the end of the fifth year is paid back at that time. From the amortization schedule shown in Table 8.1, the amount to be paid back at the end of the fifth year is $32,137,749.12. If this loan was not prepaid at this time, the remaining principal would have come in small monthly amounts throughout the remainder of the loan term. Since it is prepaid, these principal payments are accelerated to the fifth year. When these cash flows are inserted into the IRR calculations, we obtain an ELY (or EBC) of 6.15%.

The reader should notice that when up-front fees are charged by the lender, the earlier the loan is prepaid, the earlier the principal is earned and the higher is the yield that is earned by the lender (or paid by the borrower). For example, if the loan were to be prepaid after only 1 year, the yield jumps to 7.87%, as shown in the third column of Table 8.3.

8.7 CALCULATING PREPAYMENT PENALTIES

Unlike their residential counterparts, commercial mortgage borrowers in the USA are typically restricted from prepaying mortgage balances prior to loan maturity. If the borrower wishes to terminate a mortgage contract prior to maturity, a fee must usually be paid for the privilege. Typically, a borrower will prepay (or call) their loan when interest rates fall. This is exactly the worst time for the lender to receive a prepayment, as the funds must be reinvested at the currently available lower rate. To ensure that the lender is not negatively impacted by such a prepayment, several conventions exist in the marketplace to exact a penalty on the borrower should they wish to prepay.

To make the discussion realistic, let's assume that the loan term or maturity on the apartment project has a 10-year term, but that payments are calculated based on a 25-year amortization schedule (a 10/25 loan). Therefore, the monthly payment is the same as before, and equal to $221,071.50. At the end of the 10-year term, a "balloon payment" equal to the balance outstanding after 10 years of $27,056,171.06 (see Table 8.1) is due to the lender.

8.7.1 Lockout Periods

The greatest form of protection from prepayment for the lender is the imposition of a lockout period. During the lockout period, the borrower is prohibited from prepaying any principal, in essence locking out the borrower from prepayment. While this protects the lender, borrowers do not like the inflexibility of such a contract. For example, there may be times when a borrower wishes to sell the property prior to the end of the lockout period. This might happen when the property has significantly increased in value. Under a lockout provision, the borrower is unable to sell, severely decreasing the borrower's flexibility in taking profits on an investment project. Similarly, if a property's income level increases substantially so that a loan's credit quality is enhanced, or if interest rates fall, the borrower may be able to get better loan terms. A borrower that has a loan with a lockout period would be unable to take advantage of these favorable conditions for borrowing.

Because of the restrictions inherent with lockout clauses, they are not typical. In some cases, however, a loan may be locked out for the first 2 or 3 years of its loan term, so that the lender can be assured that the loan will be outstanding for some minimum period of time.

Because of the inflexibility of lockout periods, a number of other conventions have been developed both to allow prepayments and to provide some compensation to the lender if the prepayment has a negative economic impact. These provisions generally fall into three categories: step-down prepayment penalties, yield maintenance penalties, and defeasance.

8.7.2 Step-down Prepayment Penalties

If a borrower wishes to prepay a loan that exhibits a step-down prepayment penalty, a fee must be paid to the lender when the prepayment is made. An example of a step-down penalty would have the borrower pay back 105% of the outstanding balance of the loan at the time of prepayment, but only during the first 5 years of the loan term. After 5 years of the loan term, the prepayment penalty "steps down" by 1% per year, until the penalty reduces to 0% in Year 10. At that time, all prepayments are made at par, which is equal to the outstanding balance at the time of prepayment (e.g. 100% of the balance is paid, with no additional penalty). The penalty schedule is as shown in Table 8.4.

In the case of the apartment project, if the borrower wanted to prepay at the end of Year 5, the lender would determine the penalty by multiplying 1.05 times the balance outstanding at that time. Therefore, although the balance outstanding from Table 8.1 is $32,137,749.12, the borrower would have to pay $33,744,636.58 (or 1.05 * $32,137,749.12) to sever the contract with the lender. The penalty for prepayment is 5% of the loan balance at the end of Year 5, and equal to the difference between the total amount paid and the balance outstanding, or $1,606,887.46.

Step-down prepayment penalties are uncommon, and have largely been replaced by methods that more accurately reflect the loss that a lender would incur at prepayment. The two most common methods used today are yield maintenance penalties, and defeasance.

TABLE 8.4 Step-down prepayment penalty schedule

Year	Percentage
1	105%
2	105%
3	105%
4	105%
5	105%
6	104%
7	103%
8	102%
9	101%
10	100%

8.7.3 Yield Maintenance Penalties and Yield Calculations

Unlike the arbitrary prepayment penalties in the step-down case, yield maintenance penalties are designed to allow the borrower to prepay, but also to provide compensation to the lender for the loss that would be incurred due to the repayment. Typically, with a yield maintenance clause, if a borrower wishes to prepay, they must pay a lump-sum penalty at the time of prepayment. The penalty is designed to allow the lender to earn the same yield-to-maturity (5.64% compounded monthly) that was expected in the original contract. Maintaining this yield makes the lender whole with respect to their expectations when they originated the mortgage, hence they are called "make-whole penalties."

Let us use the 10/25 mortgage loan from the previous section to demonstrate, and let us also assume that there are no points or fees paid at the beginning of the loan term. As in the previous section, the borrower wishes to prepay at the end of Year 5. If the loan had not been prepaid, the lender would have received 60 more monthly payments of $221,071.50 over the remaining 5 years until loan maturity, as well as the balance outstanding at maturity in Year 10 of $27,056,171.06. Monthly cash flows that would have been earned by the lender over the loan term if the loan had not been prepaid are as shown in Table 8.5.

TABLE 8.5 Lender's expected cash flows (1)

Month	1	2	3	...	120
Payment	$221,071.50	$221,071.50	$221,071.50		$221,071.50
Balance					$27,056,171.06
Total	$221,071.50	$221,071.50	$221,071.50	...	$27,277,242.56

Instead of paying the loan back over the 10-year term, however, assume that mortgage rates drop to 5.0% at the end of Year 5 after 60 payments have been made, and that the borrower chooses to refinance to take advantage of the lower rate. The owner of the property obtains a new loan from a different lender, and uses the proceeds to pay back the principal balance on the original loan to the original lender.

Since the balance outstanding at time of prepayment in month 60 is $32,137,749.12, the original lender has to reinvest this amount at the current 5.0% mortgage interest rate. For now, we assume that the original lender reinvests in a mortgage loan that has a 5-year maturity, and payments are made based on a 20-year amortization period.

Monthly debt service payments on the new 5/20 loan made to a new borrower at the new lower 5.0% interest rate are $212,094.92. After 60 months of payments through the end of the new loan term, the balance outstanding on the reinvested loan is $26,820,514.56.

Monthly cash flows earned by the lender by investing the proceeds of the prepayment of principal at the new lower interest rate are as shown in Table 8.6.

TABLE 8.6 Reinvested lender's income flows

Month	61	62	63	...	120
Payment	$212,094.92	$212,094.92	$212,094.92	...	$212,094.92
Balance					$26,820,514.56
Total	$212,094.92	$212,094.92	$212,094.92	...	$27,032,609.48

The important thing to note is that both the monthly payment and the balance outstanding at the end of the new 5-year loan term are lower than they would have been, had the original loan not been prepaid.

The stream of income earned by the lender over the full 5-year term of the original loan is as shown in Table 8.7.

TABLE 8.7 Lender's cash flows (2)

Month	Cash flows	
0	–$36,000,000.00	–$36,000,000.00
1–59	$221,071.50	$221,071.50
60	$221,071.50 + $32,137,749.12 – $32,127,749.12	$221,071.50
61–119	$12,094.92	$212,094.92
120	$212,094.92 + $26,820,514.56	$27,032,609.48

An explanation of this stream of cash flows now follows. At the time the original loan was made, the lender provided $36 million to the borrower. For the first 59 months, the contracted payments of $221,071.50 were paid by the borrower to the lender. In month 60, the last $221,071.50 debt service payment is made, then the borrower pays back the balance outstanding at that time of $32,137,749.12. At the same time that the principal is paid, the lender immediately makes a new loan of $32,137,749.12 to a new borrower at the new 5.0% interest rate. Based on the amortization period of 240 months, the payment made by the new borrower is $212,094.92. That loan is outstanding for 60 more payments, and then the balance outstanding of $26,820,514.56 on the loan to the new borrower is paid, along with the final monthly debt service payment at the maturity of the loan.

The IRR on this stream of cash flows is only 5.43%, which is below the 5.64% that the lender originally expected to earn over the 5-year loan term.

The yield maintenance prepayment penalty is a fee charged to the borrower at the time of refinancing that is designed to compensate the lender for the loss in yield (5.64% – 5.43%, or 21 basis points) that occurs due to the reinvestment of proceeds at the new lower interest rate and to allow the lender to earn their expected yield of 5.64% over the original 10-year term. This requires an additional payment to be made, along with the original outstanding balance at the end of 10 years, of $27,056,171.06, as contracted at the beginning of the original term.

To determine the amount of penalty, the amount of the monthly shortfall has to be calculated. The old payments for the 60 remaining months were supposed to be $221,071.50. The new payments earned on the 5.0% loan are $212,094.92. The shortfall between the old payment and the new payment is $8,976.58.

In addition to the shortfall in monthly payments, there is also a difference in the amount of principal that would have been paid to the lender at the end of the 10-year maturity in the original loan ($27,056,171.06) and the amount of principal that will be repaid on the new loan made at 5% ($26,820,514.56). The difference in these two amounts is $235,656.50.

The stream of cash flow shortfalls over the final 60 months of the original loan term is shown in Table 8.8.

TABLE 8.8 Cash flow shortfalls after prepayment

Month	Shortfall	
61–119	$8,976.58	$8,976.58
120	$8,976.58 + $235,656.51	$244,633.09

Taking the present value of these cash flows at 5.0%, the yield maintenance prepayment penalty is $659,300.00. The logic is that this is the amount that the lender would need to invest at 5.0% to earn the cash flow shortfall that is incurred because the borrower chose to refinance and prepay the original mortgage. In other words, investing $659,300.00 at a 5.0% rate over a 60-month period would allow the lender to generate a cash flow stream that pays $8,976.58 for 59 months, and $244,633.09 in month 60.

Adding the outstanding balance at time of prepayment of the original loan in the 60th month to the prepayment penalty, the borrower would have to pay $32,797,049.12 ($32,137,749.12 + $659,300.00) to sever the contract with the original lender.

When the stream of cash flows generated from investing the prepayment penalty amount is added to the stream of cash flows earned on the new 5.0% mortgage, the lender can exactly replicate the cash flows that would have been earned if the loan had not been repaid. As shown in Table 8.9, the IRR on the combined stream of cash flows is 5.64%, exactly the same as the lender originally expected to earn when the original loan was made.

TABLE 8.9 Cash flows over loan maturity with yield maintenance prepayment penalty

Month	0	1–59	60	61–119	120
Old loan	–$36,000,000.00	$221,071.50	$221,071.50		
Old loan balance			$32,137,749.12		
New loan			–$32,137,749.12	$212,094.92	$212,094.92
New loan balance					$26,820,514.56
Prepayment penalty			$659,300.00		
PP reinvestment			–$659,300.00	$8,976.58	$8,976.58
PP balance					$235,656.51
Total	–$36,000,000.00	$221,071.50	$221,071.50	$221,071.50	$27,277,242.56

This type of prepayment penalty is known as a yield maintenance penalty, because the yield or IRR earned over the entire 120-month initial loan term is 5.64%, exactly what would have been earned if the mortgage had not been prepaid. Another term used to describe this is a "make-whole" prepayment penalty.

8.7.4 Treasury Flat Prepayment Penalty

The logic of the Treasury flat prepayment penalty is similar to the yield maintenance penalty, but with one important difference. In the above section, we assumed that the amount prepaid in Year 5 was invested at the current mortgage rate of 5%. For Treasury flat penalties, the amount prepaid is assumed to be invested in a Treasury security with the same maturity as the term remaining on the loan. In this case, the index rate would be the 5-year Treasury note as of the date the loan is to be repaid, which we assume is the end of the fifth year of the loan term. Let us assume that on the date of prepayment, the 5-year Treasury yield is 1.84%.

Following the logic of the previous section, the lender's expected cash flows over the 10-year term of the loan were presented in Table 8.5. When the loan is prepaid, the balance of $32,137,749.12 is reinvested in Treasury securities to earn 1.84%, which generates income as shown in Table 8.10.

TABLE 8.10 Reinvested lender's income flows

Month	**61**	**62**	**63**	**. . .**	**120**
Payment	$160,155.50	$160,155.50	$160,155.50	. . .	$160,155.50
Balance					$25,175,050.96
Total	$160,155.50	$160,155.50	$160,155.50	. . .	$25,335,206.47

The reader should note that the income earned by the original lender is only $160,155.50 over the remaining term of the mortgage, and the outstanding balance of this new loan is $25,175,050.96. The shortfall in income relative to the original loan is $60,915.99 ($221,071.50 – $160,155.50) and the difference in the outstanding balance at the end of the term is $1,991,120.10 ($27,056,171.06 – $25,175,050.96). The income stream generated by the original loan and the reinvested prepayment amount are shown in Table 8.11.

TABLE 8.11 Lender's cash flows (2)

Month	**Cash flows**	
0	–$36,000,000.00	–$36,000,000.00
1–59	$221,071.50	$221,071.50
60	$221,071.50 + $32,137,749.12 – $32,127,749.12	$221,071.50
61–119	$160,155.50	$212,094.92
120	$160,155.50 + $25,175,050.96	$25,335,206.47

The IRR for this stream of cash flows earned by the lender is 4.08%, which is 1.56% (or 156 basis points) less than the expected return of the lender.

The penalty is designed to provide the same yield as that expected by the lender (5.64%), and is calculated by taking the present value of the shortfalls in income over the last 60 months of the original loan term. These shortfalls are shown in Table 8.12.

TABLE 8.12 Cash flow shortfalls after prepayment

Month	**Shortfall**	
61–119	$60,915.99	$60,915.99
120	$60,915.99 + $1,881,120.10	$1,994,036.09

As in the previous section, we need to calculate the present value of the 60-month payment stream of $60,915.99 for 60 months at 1.84%, which is $3,489,317.63. The present value of the difference in balance of $1,994,036.09 at the end of the loan term is $1,715,900.23. The sum of these represents the total prepayment penalty that would be due to the lender at the time of prepayment, or $5,205,217.86.

Clearly, since we are assuming that the prepaid mortgage balance is reinvested at 1.84%, there is a large difference in payments relative to the "make-whole" prepayment penalty example provided in the previous section. Further, since we discount these larger payments at a lower rate (1.84% relative to 5%), the present value of these payments is larger. This makes the total prepayment penalty much higher.

The cash flow earned by the lender over the loan term is shown in detail in Table 8.13.

TABLE 8.13 Cash flows over loan maturity with yield maintenance prepayment penalty

Month	0	1–59	60	61–119	120
Old loan	–$36,000,000.00	$221,071.50	$221,071.50		
Old loan balance			$32,137,749.12		
New loan			–$32,137,749.12	$160,155.50	$160,155.50
New loan balance					$25,175,050.96
Prepayment penalty			$5,205,217.86		
PP reinvestment			–$5,205,217.86	$60,915.99	$60,915.99
PP balance					$1,881,120.10
Total	–$36,000,000.00	$221,071.50	$221,071.50	$221,071.50	$27,277,242.56

The logic is that when the borrower chooses to prepay, they must also pay a $5,205,217.86 prepayment penalty in addition to the balance outstanding of $32,137,749.12. The total payment made at that time to sever the mortgage contract is $37,342,966.98. This amount is reinvested at the 1.84% Treasury rate to generate the same income stream that would have been earned had the loan not been prepaid. Hence, the lender earns a 5.64% IRR over the full 10-year period, which is the same as in the make-whole prepayment penalty example. The difference is that the penalty paid by the borrower is much higher ($5,205.217.86 compared to $659,300.00).

Generally, a Treasury flat prepayment penalty should dissuade a borrower from prepaying in Year 5 given the high penalty incurred. However, there are situations when a borrower might choose to prepay despite the high penalty. For example, if we assume that the property value has increased to $60 million over the first 5 years of the loan term, the borrower might be able to borrow using a 75% loan-to-value ratio, which would allow a $45,000,000 loan amount. For now, let us also assume that net operating income has increased sufficiently to still generate a debt service coverage ratio of 1.25 times, as required by the lender.

In this case, a new loan would provide the borrower with $45,000,000 of loan proceeds, and the borrower pays the $37,137,749.12 Treasury flat prepayment penalty.

Everything else being equal, the difference of $7,862,250.88 would be paid to the borrower. This is an example of a "cash-out refinancing," so named because the borrower (investor) can take cash out of the investment from the refinancing transaction.

8.7.5 Defeasance

Defeasance is similar to yield maintenance prepayment penalties, but it is far more punitive to the borrower, and beneficial to the lender. The stream of debt service payments that had been promised to the lender stops when the borrower chooses to prepay. As discussed above, yield maintenance required the borrower to pay a lump sum that made up the difference between the original payment stream and what the lender could earn if the principal prepaid were invested back into commercial mortgages at current rates. Defeasance requires the borrower to purchase US Treasury obligations that replicate the entire original stream of debt service cash flows over the remaining term of the mortgage.

With defeasance, the timing of cash flows earned by the lender stays exactly the same as it would have been had the mortgage not been prepaid. Further, the credit quality of the stream of cash flows is enhanced, in effect substituting the credit of the US government for the credit of the borrower, which is beneficial to the lender. The burden of purchasing the Treasury obligations falls to the borrower, and the stream of income provided must exactly match the promised debt service payments under the original mortgage. Purchase of Treasury obligations will entail transaction costs, and a staging of maturities of zero-coupon or coupon bonds throughout the remaining term of the mortgage.

Because few real estate investors have expertise in structuring Treasury investments to match a cash flow stream, several companies have been set up to defease a mortgage for a fee. These companies will determine the amount of penalty that must be paid, execute transactions in the Treasury market to replicate the original debt service cash flow stream, manage and monitor the Treasury securities after purchase to ensure that the original lender receives the payments, and generally oversee the process.

8.8 CONCLUSION

This chapter is designed to help the reader gain a better understanding of conventions in the mortgage market. The calculations presented are typical of most mortgage loans made in the mortgage market. It is critical for a borrower to have an understanding of how these calculations are made, and what they mean. Calculation of effective borrowing cost is particularly useful for comparing loan offerings from different lenders. The loan that has the lowest effective borrowing cost should be the one that is most beneficial to the borrower.

CHAPTER 9

Commercial Mortgage Underwriting and Leveraged Feasibility Analysis

9.1 INTRODUCTION

This chapter has two following sections. The first (Section 9.2) introduces the reader to commercial mortgage underwriting. Based on an analysis of the borrower's credit history and the quality of the collateral, the mortgage underwriter determines whether to approve or disapprove a loan request, and if the loan is approved, how much of a loan should be offered to the prospective borrower. Typically, for commercial property, the quality and magnitude of expected cash flows determine whether a loan will be approved, and how much that loan will be.

The second (Section 9.3) focuses on determining investment feasibility for a leveraged investment. Continuing with our example from Chapters 7 and 8, we look at the investment feasibility of the apartment project, adding debt and taxes. Using before-tax discounted cash flow analysis, we can assess whether the investment meets the investment objectives of the investment group.

9.2 MORTGAGE UNDERWRITING AND THE UNDERWRITING PROCESS

In most cases, the purchaser of a property for investment purposes will finance a large proportion of the cost using mortgage debt. The borrower will apply to a lender for a loan that is based on the price that the investor is willing to pay for the property, and the mortgage application is underwritten by the lender. The mortgage underwriter's goal is to determine whether a borrower will be able to make payments based on the terms of the promissory note, and to estimate the likelihood of borrower default in making these payments. If default is likely, the lender will not commit funds to the borrower.

We use the loan characteristics of the apartment project to illustrate the process of mortgage underwriting. For this example, the borrower applied to a lender for a loan amount equal to 75% of the property's $48 million asking price, or $36 million.

The amortization schedule for a $36 million loan was presented in Chapter 8, and will serve as input to the lender's determination of whether to provide the loan, and for how much.

9.2.1 Ratios and Rules of Thumb

Several ratios are used to determine loan approval: the loan-to-value ratio, the debt coverage ratio, and the debt yield. Typically, the requested loan must satisfy all three of these very important ratios. Other ratios and calculations are also utilized as supplemental information for the lender in determining whether to offer a loan on the property, and if so, how much of a loan should be offered.

Loan-to-Value Ratio

The loan-to-value ratio (LTV) is straightforward, and is simply the ratio of the loan balance at origination relative to the value of the property. In the case of the apartment investment opportunity, with an asking price of $48 million, the loan request is for $36,000,000. These numbers indicate a LTV of 75%:

$$LTV = Loan\ amount\ /\ Property\ value = \$36{,}000{,}000\ /\ \$48{,}000{,}000 = 75\%$$

The lender will require the borrower to pay for a full and detailed appraisal of the building, to ensure that the $48 million accurately reflects the true market value of the property. As discussed in Chapter 8, the building serves as collateral for the loan, and the lender has a security interest in the building. If the borrower should default on the loan, the lender has a right to take over ownership of the building and sell it to attempt to recover the loan amount. Given the importance of the value of the property in mitigating risk for the lender, it is critical to get an independent appraisal or valuation of the property.

It is also clear that the lower is the LTV ratio, the lower is the risk to the lender. A low LTV ratio indicates that the equity investor has invested more of their own funds in the project. This higher equity stake reduces the likelihood that the investor will "walk away," or default on the loan.

In the case of an amortizing mortgage, the balance outstanding will decline over the life of the mortgage as each payment is made. Therefore, over time, the loan-to-value ratio decreases as long as the property value increases or remains stable, making the mortgage more secure. If, however, property values should decline over time, the borrower's equity account is eroded and in some cases eliminated, increasing the likelihood of borrower default. Although underwriting standards change over time as conditions in the real estate markets change, an LTV ratio of 75% or less is generally considered acceptable.

Debt Coverage Ratio

Table 9.1 shows the first-year income statement from our discussion of expected cash flows for the apartment project in Chapter 7 (Table 7.4).

TABLE 9.1 Expected cash flows, end of Year 1

Gross rental revenue	$5,145,240
– Vacancy	$257,262
Gross effective income	$4,887,978
+ Other income	$276,600
Total income	$5,164,578
– Operating expenses	$2,049,991
NOI	$3,114,587

TABLE 9.2 Before-tax property income, end of Year 1

NOI	$3,114,587
– DS	$2,652,858
BTCF	$461,729

Debt service payments are subtracted from the net operating income (NOI) to determine the before-tax cash flow earned by the investor on this property. Since all cash flows are assumed to be annual flows, the $221,071.50 monthly debt service calculated in Chapter 8 for the $36,000,000 loan is multiplied by 12 to get an annual debt service payment of $2,652,858.09. This adds another couple of lines to the property income statement, as shown in Table 9.2.

This cash flow statement will serve as the basis for calculation of underwriting ratios used by the lender in the loan underwriting process.

The debt service coverage ratio (DCR) is the ratio of income to debt service payments. Just as a low LTV ratio implies lower risk for the lender, so does a high ratio of NOI to debt service payments. Higher DCRs indicate a larger cushion of property income that is earned over and above the level of debt service required to repay the mortgage loan. Historically, the higher is the NOI relative to the amount of debt service payment each year, or the debt coverage ratio, the lower is the likelihood that an investor will be in financial difficulty arising from ownership of the property. In other words, the higher is this cushion of income over debt payment, the higher the credit quality of the loan.

In the $36-million-dollar loan example, annual debt service payments are fixed each year at $2,652,858. Net operating income in the first year is $3,114,587, so the first year DCR is 1.174:

$$DCR = NOI \,/\, Debt\ service\ payment = \$3{,}114{,}587 \,/\, \$2{,}652{,}858 = 1.174$$

This indicates that there is $1.17 of income for every dollar of debt service that is required to be paid under the terms of the mortgage. NOI would have to deteriorate by more than 14.5% ($0.17/$1.17) before cash flow is insufficient to pay debt service. DCRs required by lenders change over time, depending on the availability of the funds that they have to offer to the market, competitiveness in the lending market, and the lending market's perception of the risk involved in the commercial real estate market.

Historically, lenders require this ratio to be between 1.3 and 1.5, which means that the loan request by the investment group does not meet the DCR constraint that is required by the lender. For now, let's assume that the lender requires a DCR of 1.3 times, or $1.30 of NOI for every dollar of debt service.

With a DCR calculated for the requested loan equal to 1.17, and the lender's required DCR of 1.3, the lender would not be willing to offer the loan of $36 million. In this case, the lender would refuse to fund the loan based on its underwriting criteria, and ask the borrower to submit another request for a lower loan amount.

Debt Yield

Debt yield has become an important ratio for lenders, especially after the global financial crisis, and is simply NOI divided by loan amount, or:

$$\textit{Debt yield} = \textit{NOI} \,/\, \textit{Loan amount} = \$3{,}114{,}587 \,/\, \$36{,}000{,}000 = 8.65\%$$

Generally, lenders desire a debt yield that is greater than 9%, although when there is competition among lenders to originate a new loan, this requirement may be relaxed. Lenders use the debt yield because it is easy to measure, and does not require information on market conditions.

When capital is highly available, cap rates can decrease as competition to own assets increases, and valuations increase. These valuations may not be sustainable through the cycle, and future refinancing would be risky if valuations decline. The debt yield calculation does not require debt service payments, which can be affected by cyclical relaxation of debt coverage and loan-to-value ratios. Current interest rates or amortization periods have no impact on the debt yield calculation. The loan amount is solely determined by the lender, and NOI is the lender's informed estimate of first-year income.

If the borrower defaults on the $36,000,000 loan, the lender can foreclose and have access to the $3,114,587 NOI earned by the property. Lower debt yields indicate higher leverage relative to the NOI, and are more risky.

9.2.2 Determining the Maximum Loan Amount

The maximum loan amount measures the capacity of the property to carry debt at current mortgage rates and terms. In order to determine the maximum loan amount (MLA), the analyst needs to divide NOI ($3,114,587) by the debt coverage ratio (1.3). The resulting amount, $2,395,836.15, is the maximum annual debt service allowed by the lender based on the property's income. Dividing by 12, the maximum monthly payment is $199,653. Using this as the payment in the @PV function in Excel, along with the monthly rate of 0.458333% and a term of 300 months, the present value is the MLA of $32,512,142.

The lender can also calculate the maximum loan amount allowable for this project with the mortgage loan constant introduced in Chapter 8. The calculation is as follows:

$$\textit{Maximum loan amount} = \textit{NOI} \,/\left(\textit{DCR} * \textit{Mortgage loan constant}\right)$$

Based on the contract interest rate of 5.5% and the amortization period of 300 months, the mortgage loan constant, or installment to amortize one dollar of mortgage debt, was calculated to be 0.061408749 per month, and when multiplied by 12 to annualize, the result is 0.073690499. Using first-year NOI, the mortgage loan constant and the lender's required DCR, the MLA for the apartment project, which represents the maximum debt capacity of the project, is:[1]

$$MLA = NOI / (DCR * Mortgage\ loan\ constant)$$
$$= \$3,114,858 / (1.3 * 0.073690499) = \$32,512,144$$

The maximum that this lender should be willing to commit to a borrower for purchase of this property is $32,512,142. Assuming a purchase price of $48 million, the loan-to-value ratio is 67.73%. The investment group has to invest the difference between purchase price and loan amount, or $15,487,858.

An important point to be made here is that either the debt coverage ratio or the loan-to-value ratio will be the constraining factor when underwriting a loan. The $36 million loan request met the lender's required loan-to-value ratio of 75%, but at the 5.5% contract rate using the 300-month amortization period, the loan did not achieve the lender's DCR hurdle of 1.3 times. Typically, one or the other of these two underwriting criteria will be more stringent, and will limit the amount that the lender will be willing to lend.

Using a loan amount of $32,512,142, the loan rate of 5.5%, and an amortization period of 25 years or 300 months, we can calculate a monthly debt service payment of $199,653.00. The new amortization schedule is shown in Table 9.3. Over a full year, the payments are $2,395,836 ($199,653.00*12).

With the new mortgage amount, the first-year before-tax cash flow statement is modified as shown in Table 9.4.

As a check, the DCR using this set of cash flows is 1.3 times, or:

$$DCR = NOI / DS = \$3,114,587 / \$2,395,836 = 1.3\ times$$

TABLE 9.3 Amortization schedule for maximum loan amount

Month	Beg. loan balance	Payment	Interest	Principal	End loan balance
1	$32,512,142.41	$199,653.00	$149,013.99	$50,639.01	$32,461,503.39
2	$32,461,503.39	$199,653.00	$148,781.89	$50,871.11	$32,410,632.28
3	$32,410,632.28	$199,653.00	$148,548.73	$51,104.27	$32,359,528.02
4	$32,359,528.02	$199,653.00	$148,314.50	$51,338.50	$32,308,189.52
5	$32,308,189.52	$199,653.00	$148,079.20	$51,573.80	$32,256,615.72

(continued)

[1] The difference between the two calculations of MLA is due to rounding. The correct amount is $32,512,142.

TABLE 9.3 (Continued)

Month	Beg. loan balance	Payment	Interest	Principal	End loan balance
6	$32,256,615.72	$199,653.00	$147,842.82	$51,810.18	$32,204,805.54
7	$32,204,805.54	$199,653.00	$147,605.36	$52,047.64	$32,152,757.90
8	$32,152,757.90	$199,653.00	$147,366.81	$52,286.19	$32,100,471.71
9	$32,100,471.71	$199,653.00	$147,127.16	$52,525.84	$32,047,945.87
10	$32,047,945.87	$199,653.00	$146,886.42	$52,766.58	$31,995,179.29
11	$31,995,179.29	$199,653.00	$146,644.57	$53,008.43	$31,942,170.86
12	$31,942,170.86	$199,653.00	$146,401.62	$53,251.38	$31,888,919.48
13	$31,888,919.48	$199,653.00	$146,157.55	$53,495.45	$31,835,424.03
14	$31,835,424.03	$199,653.00	$145,912.36	$53,740.64	$31,781,683.39
15	$31,781,683.39	$199,653.00	$145,666.05	$53,986.95	$31,727,696.43
16	$31,727,696.43	$199,653.00	$145,418.61	$54,234.39	$31,673,462.04
17	$31,673,462.04	$199,653.00	$145,170.03	$54,482.97	$31,618,979.08
18	$31,618,979.08	$199,653.00	$144,920.32	$54,732.68	$31,564,246.40
19	$31,564,246.40	$199,653.00	$144,669.46	$54,983.54	$31,509,262.86
20	$31,509,262.86	$199,653.00	$144,417.45	$55,235.55	$31,454,027.32
21	$31,454,027.32	$199,653.00	$144,164.29	$55,488.71	$31,398,538.61
22	$31,398,538.61	$199,653.00	$143,909.97	$55,743.03	$31,342,795.58
23	$31,342,795.58	$199,653.00	$143,654.48	$55,998.52	$31,286,797.06
24	$31,286,797.06	$199,653.00	$143,397.82	$56,255.18	$31,230,541.88
36	$30,594,455.02	$199,653.00	$140,224.59	$59,428.41	$30,535,026.60
48	$29,863,059.44	$199,653.00	$136,872.36	$62,780.64	$29,800,278.80
60	$29,090,407.41	$199,653.00	$133,331.03	$66,321.97	$29,024,085.45
72	$28,274,171.73	$199,653.00	$129,589.95	$70,063.05	$28,204,108.68
84	$27,411,893.94	$199,653.00	$125,637.85	$74,015.15	$27,337,878.79
96	$26,500,976.91	$199,653.00	$121,462.81	$78,190.19	$26,422,786.72
108	$25,538,677.00	$199,653.00	$117,052.27	$82,600.73	$25,456,076.26
120	$24,522,095.80	$199,653.00	$112,392.94	$87,260.06	$24,434,835.74
132	$23,448,171.44	$199,653.00	$107,470.79	$92,182.21	$23,355,989.22
144	$22,313,669.30	$199,653.00	$102,270.98	$97,382.02	$22,216,287.28
156	$21,115,172.32	$199,653.00	$96,777.87	$102,875.13	$21,012,297.19
168	$19,849,070.69	$199,653.00	$90,974.91	$108,678.09	$19,740,392.60
180	$18,511,550.98	$199,653.00	$84,844.61	$114,808.39	$18,396,742.59
192	$17,098,584.65	$199,653.00	$78,368.51	$121,284.49	$16,977,300.16
204	$15,605,915.90	$199,653.00	$71,527.11	$128,125.89	$15,477,790.02
216	$14,029,048.91	$199,653.00	$64,299.81	$135,353.19	$13,893,695.71
228	$12,363,234.22	$199,653.00	$56,664.82	$142,988.18	$12,220,246.04
240	$10,603,454.49	$199,653.00	$48,599.17	$151,053.83	$10,452,400.66
252	$8,744,409.35	$199,653.00	$40,078.54	$159,574.46	$8,584,834.89
264	$6,780,499.45	$199,653.00	$31,077.29	$168,575.71	$6,611,923.74
276	$4,705,809.60	$199,653.00	$21,568.29	$178,084.71	$4,527,724.89
288	$2,514,090.93	$199,653.00	$11,522.92	$188,130.08	$2,325,960.85
300	$198,742.10	$199,653.00	$910.90	$198,742.10	0.00

TABLE 9.4 First-year before-tax cash flow statement

	Year 1
NOI	$3,114,587
– DS	$2,395,836
BTCF	$718,751

This must be the case because 1.3 was used as the DCR in the calculation of maximum loan amount.[2]

Before-tax cash flows from operations over the holding period are shown in Table 9.5. The debt coverage ratio should be calculated for each year and this is as shown in Table 9.6. In some years, extraordinary expenses may be incurred as tenant lease terms end and the owner has to pay leasing commissions and/or costs to refit existing space for new tenants. Upon rollover of a significant tenant, there may also be a period of vacancy during which no income will be earned between when the old tenant vacated and the new tenant's lease term begins. It is important that, even in these periods of lower income, NOI exceeds debt service and the DCR remains above the lender's requirement.

TABLE 9.5 Operational before-tax cash flows

	Year 1	Year 2	Year 3	Year 4	Year 5
Gross rental revenue	$5,145,240	$5,299,597	$5,458,585	$5,622,343	$5,791,013
– Vacancy	$257,262	$264,980	$272,929	$281,117	$289,551
Gross effective income	$4,887,978	$5,034,617	$5,185,656	$5,341,226	$5,501,462
+ Other income	$276,600	$284,898	$293,445	$302,248	$ 311,316
Total income	$5,164,578	$5,319,515	$5,479,101	$5,643,474	$5,812,778
– Operating expenses	$2,049,991	$2,101,241	$2,153,772	$2,207,616	$2,262,807
NOI	$3,114,587	$3,218,274	$3,325,329	$3,435,858	$3,549,971
– DS	$2,395,836	$2,395,836	$2,395,836	$2,395,836	$2,395,836
BTER	$718,751	$822,438	$929,493	$1,040,022	$1,154,135

TABLE 9.6 Debt service coverage ratio

	Year 1	Year 2	Year 3	Year 4	Year 5
DCR	1.300	1.343	1.388	1.434	1.482

[2]The debt yield using the new loan is $3,114,587/$32,512,142 = 9.58%.

Because of the assumption that rents charged to tenants will increase at a faster rate than operating expenses during the holding period, and that annual debt service payments stay constant, the DCR increases each year.

Operating Expense Ratio

When underwriting a mortgage loan, the lender will want to ensure that operating expenses do not differ greatly from market norms for that property type. For the apartment project, the operating expense ratio (OER) in the first year of operations is simply:

$$OER = Operating\ expenses\ /\ Gross\ effective\ income = \$2,049,991\ /\ \$4,887,978 = 41.94\%$$

This percentage is typical of multi-family rental OERs, which are likely to fall within the 35–50% range. The OER represents the efficiency with which the project is being managed. If the OER is high relative to comparable properties, management may be spending too much on certain expenses incurred to deliver the units to the market, or perhaps not be delivering the space to the market in the most efficient manner. An OER that is low relative to competing properties may indicate that the owner is skimping on operating expenses, and not providing full service to the tenants.

The lender should project the OER for every year of the holding period, and attempt to anticipate recurring and non-recurring expenses. For example, operating expenses such as repaving the parking lot or re-shingling the roof should be forecast and incorporated into the OER. The annual OERs for the apartment example are as shown in Table 9.7.

Well within the acceptable range, and improving each year, the OER will be seen as a positive for this loan in the underwriting process.

Breakeven Ratio

The breakeven ratio (BER) measures the ability of the income generated from the property to pay all expenses related to the operation of the property and all costs of repaying the mortgage. By dividing the sum of operating expenses and debt service payments by the gross rental revenue that is generated by the property, the lender can determine the vacancy rate that would be required for the owner of the property to break even. In the case of the apartment project, the BER is calculated as follows:

$$BER = \left(Operating\ expenses + Debt\ service\right) /\ Gross\ possible\ income$$
$$= \left(\$2{,}049{,}991 + \$2{,}395{,}836\right) / \$5{,}145{,}240 = 86.41\%$$

TABLE 9.7 Operating expense ratio

	Year 1	Year 2	Year 3	Year 4	Year 5
OER	41.94%	41.74%	41.53%	41.33%	41.13%

In effect, this ratio tells the lender that an 86.41% occupancy level is required for the property to break even, in the sense that all property-related and debt-related expenses are covered. If vacancy rises above 13.59% (100% – 86.41%), the project will be unable to pay off its expenses. Typically, depending on the property type being considered, BERs of 75–90% are acceptable to lenders. Above this, the borrower is more likely to default. Below these levels, the likelihood of default due to cash flow shortages is lower. To exhibit a 13.59% vacancy rate, 50 units would have to be vacant for an entire year. Since the project has rarely experienced a vacancy rate above 5% (equivalent to 13 units), the underwriter would see the BER as a favorable characteristic.

As with the other ratios, it is important to calculate this ratio from the pro forma cash flow analysis for each year of the prospective holding period. The BER for each of the 5 years in the apartment project case is as shown in Table 9.8.

In this case, the BER declines each year as NOI increases. Although operating expenses increase as well, the fixed debt service payments generate a declining BER throughout the holding period.

Debt Yield

Table 9.9 shows the annual debt yield calculations for the apartment project.

The debt yield ratio exceeds the 9% hurdle in each year, and grows due to the annual increase in NOI.

Once the lender feels comfortable that the property and the borrower fall within reasonable ranges for these underwriting criteria, the loan will be approved and the investor will be able to obtain the property with a combination of debt and equity capital. Conservatism in underwriting criteria leads to lower subsequent default rates. In some cases, however, when lenders are competing to commit funds, these criteria could be relaxed (e.g. lower DCRs and higher LTVs) so that lenders will be more willing to originate a larger loan for the same value or amount of cash flow. In retrospect, this relaxing of loan underwriting criteria was a strong contributing factor to the real estate collapse in the late 1980s and early 1990s, and certainly to the credit crisis of 2008–9.

TABLE 9.8 Breakeven ratio

	Year 1	Year 2	Year 3	Year 4	Year 5
OER	86.41%	84.86%	83.35%	81.88%	80.45%

TABLE 9.9 Debt yield

	Year 1	Year 2	Year 3	Year 4	Year 5
Debt yield	9.58%	9.90%	10.23%	10.57%	10.92%

9.3 INVESTMENT FEASIBILITY WITH LEVERAGE: BEFORE-TAX ANALYSIS

In this section, we add the effects of leverage to the unleveraged apartment case presented in Chapter 7. We use the maximum loan amount of $32,512,142 and debt service calculated earlier in this chapter as our starting point for analysis.

9.3.1 The Two-Part Nature of Cash Flows: Operating Income and Disposition Income

As with an investment in a financial asset, and as was shown for the unleveraged example in Chapter 7, there are two components of expected cash flows for a real estate investment. The first source of income is generated by leasing and operating the real estate asset. In most cases, we use annual cash flows earned in each year of the holding period as our focus for analysis. The second major part of the cash flow from a real estate investment comes from the disposition of the asset, which is earned at the end of the expected holding period.

Both the operating and disposition income can each further be broken down into sub-components. The first step in generating cash flow income statements requires calculating income from the property itself, or NOI, which was the focus of Chapter 7. Operating income flows come from the rents that the property earns, net of all the costs which the owner of the property bears to produce the product the tenant is paying for: space, over time, with certain services.

In the case of the disposition income, the net cash flow generated from sale of the asset is equal to the sales price less all of the expenses incurred by the seller that are required to transfer the property to the new buyer. This net cash flow is the net selling proceeds.

The second step is to determine the effect of financing on the cash flows earned by the equity investor. As shown earlier, debt service is subtracted from NOI to get before-tax cash flow. Similarly, at the end of the holding period any balance outstanding on any loan that was taken out on the project must be fully repaid upon sale of the property. Debt-related cash flows are the focus of this section.

9.3.2 Financing Impact on Investor Income Statements: Adding Debt Service Cash Flows

The annual amount that is paid to the mortgage lender must be subtracted from NOI to determine the residual, or free, cash flow earned by the investment group on a before-tax basis. The monthly payment required to pay down the maximum loan amount over the 300-month maturity is $199,653.00. The annual payment amount, used in the annual income statement, is 12 times this amount, or $2,395,836.

Subtracting debt service payments from NOI gives a before-tax cash flow in the first year of operating the asset of $718,751. This represents the amount that the equity investor gets to keep after all other claims have been paid. In this sense, it is the residual cash flow earned by the equity investor.

TABLE 9.10 Before-tax cash flows over the holding period

	Year 1	Year 2	Year 3	Year 4	Year 5
NOI	$3,114,587	$3,218,274	$3,325,329	$3,435,858	$3,549,971
– DS	$2,395,836	$2,395,836	$2,395,836	$2,395,836	$2,395,836
BTCF	$718,751	$822,438	$929,493	$1,040,022	$1,154,135

In subsequent years, as NOI increases, the debt service remains constant so the BTCF increases. Because of the fixed payment of debt service, BTCF growth will exceed rental growth over the holding period. Before-tax cash flow for the 5-year holding period is as shown in Table 9.10.

Income from Disposition

When a project is sold, the remaining balance outstanding on the loan, or unpaid mortgage (UM), must be paid back to the lender. For the apartment example, the maturity or term of the mortgage is 5 years, whereas the amortization schedule used to calculate payments is 25 years. If prepaid prior to maturity, there will be a balloon payment due that is equal to the unpaid balance of $29,024,085 (from Table 9.3, the loan balance for month 60), which must be repaid from the sale proceeds.[3]

The difference of net selling proceeds (NSP) less the UM equals the BTER, as shown in Table 9.11.

The residual cash flows earned from operating the asset and selling it at the end of a 5-year holding period are summarized for the apartment investment in Table 9.12. These cash flows represent the investment group's best guess at future income that will be earned from owning the property, after taking into account the characteristics of the financing that is available from the lender. These cash flows are used by the investor and the lender to ensure that the investment meets the investor's investment criteria.

TABLE 9.11 Before-tax equity reversion

	Year 5
NSP	$50,907,026
– UM	$29,024,085
BTER	$21,882,940

[3] For an interest-only loan, this amount would be the full principal amount originally borrowed. By contrast, for a fully amortizing loan that is not prepaid prior to maturity, there is no unpaid mortgage at time of sale.

TABLE 9.12 Equity investor cash flows

	Year 0	Year 1	Year 2	Year 3	Year 4	Year 5
Equity investment	($15,487,858)					
BTCF operations		$718,751	$822,438	$929,493	$1,040,022	$1,154,135
BTER disposition		$0	$0	$0	$0	$21,882,940
Total cash flows	($15,487,858)	$718,751	$822,438	$929,493	$1,040,022	$23,037,075

9.3.3 Determining Investment Feasibility: The Leveraged Before-Tax Case

Investors use two types of measures to evaluate the expected investment performance of prospective investments. The first set of measures comprises static measures, meaning ratios calculated using single-year or single-point cash flows. The second set of measures utilizes expected cash flow estimates over the full 5-year holding period to calculate NPV and IRR.

Static or Single-Year Measures of Investment Performance

Ratios that relate income earned to investment outflows help provide better understanding of the investment performance of a real estate investment. Measures such as return on investment (ROI) and return on equity (ROE) are useful for showing the income return that is earned, and allow for comparisons with other investments that may also be under consideration.

Return on Investment

The ROI is calculated by dividing NOI expected to be earned by the property by the initial cost of the building, and can be calculated for each year of the holding period:

$$ROI = NOI\ /\ Initial\ building\ cost$$

ROI does not reflect debt or income taxes, and demonstrates the income earning potential from renting the apartment units. As mentioned above, NOI is a measure of the property's productivity, so this measure gives an indication of the return earned from that productivity.

Using first-year cash flows, the ROI for the apartment opportunity is:

$$ROI = NOI\ /\ Initial\ building\ cost = \$3{,}114{,}587\ /\ \$48{,}000{,}000 = 6.49\%$$

The ROI calculations for each of the 5 years of the holding period are as shown in Table 9.13.

These ROI calculations show that this project throws off strong cash flows relative to the initial cost of the building. ROI grows over the holding period because we have assumed that rental growth is faster than the rate of growth of expenses.

TABLE 9.13 Return on investment

	Year 1	Year 2	Year 3	Year 4	Year 5
ROI	6.49%	6.70%	6.93%	7.16%	7.40%

The reader should notice that the ROI in the first year is equal to the going-in capitalization rate that was presented in Chapter 7.

Return on Equity

Our investor is using debt to help pay for the initial cost of the building, and will be interested in how much cash is earned relative to the equity investment that he has made. ROE provides such a measure. The before-tax return on equity (BTROE) is calculated as the before-tax cash flow (BTCF) divided by the initial equity contribution used to purchase the property. In this case, a $15,487,858 equity investment is required.

The BTROE is used to see how much of the return expected to be earned is coming from operating the building, and is useful as a comparison with other asset classes such as stocks or bonds. These returns are called "cash-on-cash" returns because they are given by the ratio of the actual cash that is earned (on a before-tax basis) divided by the actual cash that is invested by the equity investor.

For the first year of operations, the BTROE is:

$$\begin{aligned} BTROE &= BTCF \,/\, Initial\ equity \\ &= \$718{,}751 / \$15{,}487{,}858 = 4.64\% \end{aligned}$$

The BTROE for each of the 5 years of the holding period is as shown in Table 9.14.

Different investors will have different opinions on how high the ROE should be. The first-year BTROE may be considered to be a bit low for this investment, but with increasing NOI, the ratio improves in each year of the holding period. In all 5 years, the ROE indicates that cash earned is not only sufficient to pay all operating expenses incurred by the owner of the property, but also debt service, leaving substantial cash flow to distribute to the equity investor.

A useful comparison of the ROE measure is given by the dividend yield on common stock investments. The dividend yield is calculated as the dividend expected to be paid in the next year on a share of stock divided by the current price of the stock. Since 2000, the average 12-month dividend yield on the 500 stocks that are included in the

TABLE 9.14 Return on equity

	Year 1	Year 2	Year 3	Year 4	Year 5
ROE	4.64%	5.31%	6.00%	6.72%	7.45%

Standard and Poor's (S&P) 500 Stock Index is 1.94%, and in September 2019 the dividend yield on the S&P 500 was 1.92%. Against this comparator, the relatively high ROE earned by the apartment investment opportunity in particular, and for real estate more generally, illustrates one of the major benefits of real estate investment.

Determining Investment Feasibility Using Multiple Year Cash Flows

The bottom line before-tax cash flows earned by the investment group are shown in Table 9.15 and extracted from Table 9.12 above.

Discounted at a 10% before-tax required rate of return for the investment group, this set of cash flows produces a NPV of $1,558,155. Given the standard rule of investment analysis, this project, with a positive NPV, should be accepted as it increases the investor's wealth. The reader should verify that the IRR for this project is 12.32%, which is above the 10% hurdle rate. Given that positive signals are given by both investment criteria, the investment group should continue to analyze the apartment project as a potential investment opportunity.

Equity Multiple

The equity multiple (EM), also known as the return on invested capital (ROIC), is calculated as the ratio of the sum of all cash inflows over the outflow. For the leveraged case, using the cash flows from Table 9.15, the sum of all inflows is $26,547,779. Note that this sum is not discounted to a present value. It is simply the sum of all cash flows earned from operating the asset and from disposition. The outflow is $15,487,858, so the leveraged equity multiple is:

$$EM = \$26,547,779 / \$15,487,858 = 1.714 \textit{ times}$$

For each dollar of equity invested, $1.71 is earned from the investment. Another way of saying this is that 171% of cash flows invested is returned over the lifetime of the investment. Many investors hope to earn an equity multiple of greater than 2.0 times, so this may fall short for them.

Partitioning the IRR and NPV

From the above analysis, this investment should be accepted because the NPV is positive at the 10% required rate of return, and the IRR of 12.32% exceeds the 10% hurdle rate. Beyond these calculations, it is also useful to partition the two investment criteria to determine the source for the cash flows. As discussed above, the two sources of

TABLE 9.15 Equity investor cash flows

Year 0	Year 1	Year 2	Year 3	Year 4	Year 5
($15,487,858)	$718,751	$822,438	$929,493	$1,040,022	$23,037,075

TABLE 9.16 Partitioning the IRR

	Dollars	Percentage	IRR
PV operational cash flows	$3,246,835	21.0%	2.6%
PV dispositional cash flows	$12,241,023	79.0%	9.7%
PV total cash flows	$15,487,858	100.0%	12.32%

income are from operations and from disposition. In most cases, a project whose primary source of return arises from lease contracts that generate cash flows from operations exhibits a lower level of risk than a project that earns most of its return from the more speculative increases in property value that generate cash flow from disposition. Since the sale of the project occurs at the end of the holding period, the price received at disposition is dependent on conditions that exist in the market well into the future, and forecasting market conditions that far in advance is extremely speculative.

To determine the relative contribution of operational and dispositional cash flows, we partition the IRR (see Table 9.16). The first step uses the before-tax cash flows from Table 9.12, and discounts each by the IRR to calculate the present value of each cash flow. The sum of the present values of each of the five before-tax cash flows is $3,246,835. The present value of the $21,882,940 BTER earned in year 5 is $12,241,023. The sum or present value of all cash flows is $15,487,858.

Dividing the present value of operating cash flows by the total present value of cash flows, we see that 21.00% of all cash flows come from operations. Similarly, the ratio of disposition to total cash flows is 79.00%. When these proportions are multiplied by the 12.32% IRR, the proceeds from disposition provide a 9.7% return, while the operating cash flows generate a 2.6% return.

The total present value of cash flows should be equal to the equity investment being made. These sums will be equivalent because the stream of cash flows is discounted by the IRR, which by definition is the rate that is calculated to equate the inflows to the outflows.

In this case, the proceeds from disposition dominate the cash flows from operations as a source of return. A project that is more heavily dominated by the disposition cash flows should be viewed as more speculative or risky than a project that provides a higher share from operating cash flows. In these cases, the investor would be wise to increase their required return to compensate for the higher risk. Typically, a project will exhibit proportional cash flows that are 30% or 40% weighted toward the operational cash flows. Since this project exhibits a lower proportion than typically experienced, the risk is a bit higher, although the partition is affected by the short (5-year) holding period assumed.

Determining the Maximum Price to Pay with Leverage

As we did with the unleveraged example from Chapter 7, we can also calculate the maximum price that the investor can pay and still earn their 10% required return. For the leveraged case, it is a bit more complex due to the constraints on maximum loan available from the lender due to the loan-to-value and debt coverage ratio constraints.

That is, the maximum loan amount will remain at $32,512,142 given the lender's required DCR and the NOI of the property. Therefore, if a higher price than $48 million is paid for the property, the increase must be funded with additional equity. In the analysis that follows, we'll assume that the investment group can raise this additional capital as equity.

The maximum amount of equity that the investors would be willing to pay for the asset is simply the present value of the residual before-tax cash flows discounted at the required rate of return of 10%. Taking the present value of the operational and dispositional cash flows, the maximum equity for the group to break even (from a required rate of return perspective) is $17,046,013. Adding this to the maximum debt obtainable from the lender of $32,512,142, the maximum that the group would be willing to pay is $49,558,155. With a first-year NOI of $3,114,587, the implied cap rate at this price is 6.2847%.

9.4 SENSITIVITY ANALYSIS

We tested for the sensitivity of investment results in Chapter 7 (Table 7.11) by seeing how the IRR changed when certain important variables were changed. We can also perform this analysis for the leveraged case. Table 9.17 shows the IRR of 12.32% for the base-case assumptions discussed throughout this chapter (3% rent growth, 2.5% expense growth, vacancy of 5%, and cap rates increasing by 50 points between acquisition and disposition). Results are also shown for variations of the base case.

When annual rent growth is increased from 3% to 4% and all other assumptions are the same as the base case, IRR increases to 16.24% from 12.32%. When the rent growth assumption is lowered to 2% from 3%, the IRR drops to 7.96%. When vacancy is increased from 5% to 7%, IRR drops 104 basis points to 11.28%. A lowering of the vacancy rate assumption to 3% leads to an increase in IRR of 117 basis points to 13.49%.

When capitalization rates are expected to increase by 100 basis points rather than the 50 basis points of the base case, the IRR drops significantly to 9.13%. If capitalization rates are assumed to remain the same as at acquisition, the IRR increases to 15.59%. As with the unleveraged example in Chapter 7, investment results are most impacted by estimates of future cap rates. This is not surprising given that disposition represent 79% of the total present value of expected cash flows.

When the most optimistic assumptions are made for all of the variables (e.g. 4% rent growth, 1.5% expense growth, 3% vacancy, and no change in capitalization rate), the IRR is 21.95%. When the most pessimistic assumptions are made, the IRR is 1.53%.

It is clear that the assumptions that you make can have a significant impact on investment results. Assumptions should be made based on a thorough understanding of the local market in which a prospective asset is located, as well as of the capital markets. We have assumed that growth rates and vacancy are constant through the holding period, which is unlikely. Growth rate forecasts for these variables should be carefully determined based on local supply and demand conditions during the holding period.

It is also clear that leveraged returns are more sensitive to changes in outcomes than are unleveraged returns. Comparing Table 9.17 to Table 7.11 shows much higher IRR differences across assumptions for the leveraged case.

TABLE 9.17: Results of sensitivity analysis

	Assumption	IRR impact
	4%	16.24%
Rent growth	3%	12.32%
	2%	7.96%
	3.50%	10.64%
Expense growth	2.50%	12.32%
	1.50%	13.86%
	7%	11.28%
Vacancy	5%	12.32%
	3%	13.49%
	100 bps	9.13%
Cap rate increase	50 bps	12.32%
	0 bps	15.59%
Best case		21.95%
Base case		12.32%
Worst case		1.53%

9.5 CONCLUSION

This chapter has been a thorough analysis of many features that are important when adding leverage or debt to investment feasibility analysis. The first section showed how a lender looks at a loan request from an investor interested in purchasing a property. In many cases, the borrower will ask for a loan that is higher than the lender is willing to give. The lender will apply their underwriting criteria to the property cash flows and determine the maximum amount that they would be willing to lend. In the apartment case, the lender's maximum loan amount was lower than the amount requested by the borrower. In order to be able to pay the asking price for the property, the investor will have to commit more funds as equity to the property.

Using the lower loan amount, we showed how an investor would determine investment feasibility using before-tax cash flows. Consistent with our unleveraged analysis in Chapter 7, this investment (even with the higher equity investment) still achieves the desired investment performance of the investment group. The IRR is higher than the group's 10% required rate of return, and the NPV is positive. Taking the present value of the before-tax cash flows to the equity investor, we see that the group would be willing to pay up to $49,558,155 for the property, which is above the asking price, and still earn a 10% return. Either the $48 million asking price or the $49,558,155 maximum value compares favorably to the estimated market value of $50.235 calculated using the first-year NOI and a cap rate estimated in Chapter 7 (Section 7.4).

A large proportion of the investment benefits from this opportunity comes from disposition of the property at the end of the holding period, as shown by the IRR partitioning. Since sales proceeds that far into the future are subject to large estimation error, a project with such characteristics would be considered more risky than a project that has more balance between the return that is provided by the operations and the disposition of the asset.

Developing a pro-forma income statement requires making numerous assumptions about property cash flows in the future. Since the cash flows occur in the future, they are subject to mis-estimation. Analysts can determine how sensitive the feasibility results are to changing assumptions by re-running the numbers for different scenarios. In general, assumptions about the going-out cap rate and vacancy rates are expected to have the most impact on IRR and NPV.

CHAPTER 10

Real Estate Development

10.1 INTRODUCTION

The supply of buildings is fixed in the short term. At any point in time, a certain number of square feet is available in the existing building stock, and the demand for that space determines the price, or rents, that will be paid by tenants. Excess demand for space relative to the fixed supply will drive rents higher. Conversely, if demand is insufficient for the space available, rents will decrease.

If capitalization rates are assumed to be constant or falling, values will increase. As discussed in Chapter 2, increasing investor demand to own a fixed supply of assets will lead to declining capitalization rates, and investors will be willing to pay higher amounts for each dollar of rent. With increasing rents and constant or decreasing cap rates, values may increase to levels significantly above the cost to replace or build new buildings. If market values are sufficiently higher than costs, developers have an incentive to introduce new space to the market and sell it upon completion. The difference between sales price and cost represents developer profit.

When a developer recognizes that a profit can be earned, several hurdles must be cleared prior to the time that the building is opened and earning rents. Among these hurdles are gaining approvals from the local jurisdiction to build, and raising equity and debt capital to pay for all costs incurred during the construction process.

Obtaining entitlements requires proving to the jurisdiction that the new project will not create negative externalities. The duration of the approval (or entitlement) process is uncertain, and dependent on the local jurisdiction's appetite for new construction. This appetite is typically independent of the potential profitability for the developer. In markets where supply is constrained by geographic limitations, administrative processes, or other reasons, it may take years to obtain approval to build. The developer's ability to raise debt and equity capital is dependent on obtaining entitlements, and on the size and likelihood of earning a profit from development and sale.

If entitlements are granted and debt and equity capital is available, the developer can begin to construct the building. The construction period length will depend on the size and complexity of the project. During construction, the developer will make every effort to identify tenants who will rent space in the building after it is completed, and pay rents sufficient to cover expenses. A developer who starts construction prior to obtaining tenants is a "speculative" developer. Developers who contract with tenants prior to the start of construction are "build-to-suit" developers, and incur less risk than speculative developers.

Unless he has access to long-term equity finance, the developer will also attempt to identify potential investors to acquire the building upon completion, and earn the difference between the value that is paid relative to the total cost of bringing the space and building to market. Selling on completion introduces more risk, because the developer gives away or loses the option to wait (to sell when values are higher).

The length of time between the developer recognizing that a development will be profitable and project completion, lease-up, and sale may be several years. During this time, market demand conditions could change.

Other developers may have also recognized that development could be profitable and brought competing buildings to the market. If the new supply of space grows faster than demand, realized rents on a completed building may fall short of the rents expected to be earned at the beginning of the development process. If the demand to own assets falls, cap rates will increase and values per dollar of rental income will decrease. Either of these circumstances would decrease the profitability for the developer.

In contrast, the developer may be a first mover and attract tenants paying above-market rents, property investors who will pay higher prices, and earn higher profits than expected.

The uncertainty of outcomes or risk is high for developers given the approval process and the potential for a significant change in market conditions during the development period. Because of this, developers and their equity investors require higher rates of return than investors in well-occupied existing buildings.

In this chapter, we provide an overview of the approval process, then present an office development example.

10.2 THE DEVELOPMENT PROCESS

The development process[1] is similar whether entire projects (office, industrial, retail, and multi-family) are built and sold, or if projects are built and sold in small parts (residential and office condominiums, single-family houses). The developer is the conductor – pulling all of the pieces and people together so that construction can be achieved on schedule and on budget.

Developers identify new opportunities in two ways. The first is to identify an underserved sector of the local real estate market (e.g. moderate income multi-family, convenience retail, co-working office space). This determination is based on the developer's perception of the market demand and available supply for that kind of use. Once the use is identified, the developer searches for a suitable site. Not surprisingly, this is called a use in search of a site.

[1] Miles *et al.* (2015) and Peiser and Hamilton (2012) serve as useful background for the material in this chapter.

The second is to identify a site that is in search of a use. The site could be well located and available for sale. If the property is not currently on the market, the developer could make an unsolicited offer to buy the building, hopefully at a price that creates an opportunity to earn a profit. If control of the site can be obtained, the developer will identify the highest and best use for that site.

The following is a brief summary of the activities that a developer must perform to take a project from the idea stage through completion.

- Identify a use in search of a site or a site in search of a use.
- Find land and gain control of the land through a letter of intent (LOI) or option.
- Perform initial due diligence.
  - Preliminary analysis of lot size, zoning requirements, allowable building size, setbacks, height, maximum buildable area, etc.
  - Preliminary market analysis to determine market rents, vacancy, operating expenses, down to net operating income (NOI) (perhaps for different uses). Also, determination of cap rates so that market value can be calculated.
  - Preliminary determination of all construction costs.
  - Compare market value to construction costs to determine if development would be profitable.
- If there is a high probability of profitability, begin process to obtain approval (also known as entitlements to build) from the local jurisdiction for the intended project. Bearing in mind that the developer's main priority is to minimize costs, he/she will:
  - Hire architects, engineers.
  - With architectural plans in place, contract with general contractor to create detailed budget.
  - Begin discussions with potential equity and debt sources.
  - Do thorough market analysis to generate best expectation of cash flows after completion of the project; come up with multi-year cash flow estimates.
  - Identify all potential competing projects in local area.
  - Identify and begin discussions with potential tenants about pre-leasing if relevant (office, retail, industrial, senior housing), or advertise completion date (multi-family, self-storage).
  - Contract with property management team.
  - Make presentations at public hearings, get feedback from city, town. and/or county planning department.
  - Have legal team create documents/contracts for leases, form of ownership, equity, and debt.
  - If approved, move forward.
  - If not, move on to next project (costs are sunk costs).
- Begin construction: the developer's primary objectives are now to minimize the time to completion, and to stay on schedule and on budget.
  - General contractor provides detailed schedule of all activities on site during construction period.
  - Equity paid in first, paid out last.
  - After equity is consumed by project, developer can start to draw from construction loan.

  - Operating deficits while building is in lease-up are usually funded by loan until stabilization.
- Complete construction and operate.
  - Lease rest of building if necessary.
  - Finish tenant improvement work.
  - Manage property.
- Continue to own, or sell project.

10.3 PRELIMINARY ANALYSIS OF "THE STATION" DEVELOPMENT

A local developer has identified a 4.35-acre site where an office development would be profitable. The site consists of flat land and fully connected infrastructure (water, sewer, and electric utilities). The site is currently owned by the city, and is used to house a fire station that will be demolished and relocated on another site.

The site is located 200 feet from a major thoroughfare in the rapidly growing suburbs of a major metropolitan area. The developer has 30 years of local experience building mixed-use single- and multi-family residential, office, hotel, and retail projects. The local market is supply constrained and the local government is notorious for the length of time that is required to make decisions regarding land use, and for denying approvals or requiring modifications which are often too costly to provide sufficient developer profit.

The first step taken by a developer is to demonstrate that the project is feasible on a "back-of-the-envelope" (BOE) analysis prior to introducing it to the local authorities and going through the entitlement process. Information that is used in the BOE analysis is based on the developer's local market knowledge regarding construction costs and market conditions. The determination of whether market value at completion exceeds the total of construction and land costs can be done using the income statements and valuation techniques that were introduced in Chapters 7 and 9.

10.3.1 "Back-of-the-Envelope" Analysis

Based on experience, zoning, and land use requirements, and using cost information, the developer can estimate the size of building that would currently be allowed under land use regulations, and the total costs that are expected to be incurred in building the project.

Most jurisdictions limit the size of building on each site within its boundaries using several measures. One of these measures is the floor area ratio (FAR). The FAR is determined by the local planning jurisdiction, and is the ratio of the building's total floor area square footage to the overall square footage of the land. In highly dense urban areas, FARs will be very high (e.g. 5.0). In less dense areas, FARs will be lower. In this case, the city's maximum FAR for office buildings is 0.264.

The site that has been identified for the office building development comprises 4.35 acres, and 1 acre contains 43,560 sq. ft. Therefore, the total land area is 189,486 sq. ft. Given the city's FAR requirement of 0.264, 50,024 (0.264 * 189,486) sq. ft of development can occur on the site. The developer will propose a 50,000 sq. ft office building.[2]

[2] Note that for a FAR of 5.0, the total area allowed is 947,430 sq. ft.

The maximum building height that is allowed on the site is four stories, so if a 50,000 sq. ft office building is to be built, the average area for each of the four floors is 12,500 sq. ft. This is referred to as the floorplate, and can also be used as an approximation of the building's site footprint.

Impervious surface is another aspect of development regulated by local jurisdiction, and is defined as the area through which water does not seep. When it rains on impervious surface, storm water runs off to adjacent properties and could cause flooding. Limits on a site's impervious surface allow the jurisdiction to attempt to ensure that non-impervious surface is sufficient to absorb any runoff of storm water. The local regulation is that a maximum of 24% of the site can be impervious surface. For a site of 189,486 sq. ft total, the maximum impervious surface is 45,477 sq. ft.

Asphalt and concrete used for parking, driveways, and sidewalks are impervious surface, as is the building's footprint. The jurisdiction requires 2.75 parking spaces per 1,000 sq. ft of space and the developer has agreed to build 132 parking spaces using a surface parking lot. The average parking space is 180 sq. ft, and with driving and turning lanes the total area per parking space is approximately 300 sq. ft. If each of the 132 spaces requires 300 sq. ft, the total area of parking is 39,600 sq. ft.

Adding the impervious surface used by the surface parking lot (39,600 sq. ft) to the building footprint (12,500 sq. ft), the total impervious surface coverage of the site is 52,100 sq. ft, which exceeds the jurisdiction's maximum. The developer's solution is to build a two-story parking deck, which effectively halves the parking footprint to 19,800 sq. ft. Adding the 12,500 sq. ft of building to the 19,800 sq. ft of parking, the total impervious surface ratio is 17.05%, which is well below the jurisdiction's requirement and allows flexibility in providing ingress and egress to the site, and also for sidewalks and other ways to access the building and parking.

Estimating Construction Costs

Using information from other projects in the local market, the developer estimates that the total cost to build a Class A office building, exclusive of land costs, is $300/sq. ft. This includes all materials and labor to complete the building and parking, as well as all infrastructure costs. The owner of the land parcel is asking $2,000,000 for the site, or $40/sq. ft for a 50,000 sq. ft building. Total costs of land and building are $340/sq. ft.

Estimating Market Value

To estimate market value, the developer needs to estimate local rents, vacancy rates, operating expenses, and also make a guess at what capitalization rates will be when the project is completed. The new office building is adjacent to a mixed-use development that was built by the same developer. The adjacent property comprises 75,000 sq. ft of retail space, 200 high-end condominiums, 200 apartment units, and 113,000 sq. ft of office space that is 98% occupied. Due to this experience, the developer is extremely familiar with the market and confident that a new Class A office building will quickly be occupied after completion at rents that are above current market rents.

The developer has performed initial due diligence on the site, and is comfortable that the office space will lease up quickly at the gross market rent of $35.00/sq. ft. Local vacancy rates are 5%, so gross effective income is $33.75/sq. ft ($35.00 – (5% * $35.00)). The developer estimates that operating expenses in the market are $9.50/sq. ft. Using these numbers, NOI for the new building is expected to be $23.75 ($33.75 – $9.50)/sq. ft. The developer expects that cap rates will be 6.5% in the local market when the project is completed. Dividing NOI of $23.75/sq. ft by a 6.5% cap rate gives an estimate of market value of $365.38/sq. ft.

Table 10.1 shows the market value and construction cost estimates using these assumptions. The developer's objective is to build projects where the market value (gross development value in UK terminology) exceeds construction costs. The difference is profit that is earned by the developer. The larger is the project market value at completion relative to costs, the more wealth that the developer can create, and the higher the return that the equity investors can earn.

Subtracting the total cost estimate of $340.00/sq. ft from the market value of $365.38 leaves a difference of $25.38/sq. ft, which is the profit per square foot. Dividing the profit per square foot of $25.38 by the total construction costs of $340 gives an estimate of the unleveraged gross profit margin of 7.47%, below normal required levels.

The yield to cost (YTC) is the ratio of NOI to the total cost of development, or $23.75 / $340.00, equaling 6.99% for this project. Most developers will compare this ratio to the stabilized expected cap rate, which in this case we assume is 6.5%. The spread between YTC and the cap rate is 49 basis points in this example (6.99% – 6.5%), which will likely be seen as too narrow by the developer. Desired spreads are more typically in the 100–200 basis point range, which equates to higher project gross profit and gross profit margin.

TABLE 10.1 Back-of-the-envelope feasibility analysis (per sq. ft)

Revenues and market value		**Construction costs**	
Gross rent PSF	$35.00		
– Vacancy	$1.75		
Gross effective income	$33.25		
– Operating expenses	$9.50		
Net operating income	$23.75		
		Building cost PSF	$300.00
Cap rate	6.50%	+ Land cost	$40.00
Market value	$365.38	Total cost	$340.00
		Yield to cost	6.99%
Profit/sq. ft	$25.38		
Gross profit margin	7.47%		

Note: PSF = per square foot.

The same result expressed in total dollars expected to be earned and expended is as shown in Table 10.2.

The developer's best estimate of market value is $18,269,231, and his best estimate of the total cost of development is $17,000,000. The dollar profit expected to be earned by the developer and equity investors is the difference, or $1,269,231. When this amount is divided by the cost of $17 million, the same gross profit margin of 7.47% obtains. The YTC and cap rates are the same as shown in Table 10.1, and the spread is 49 basis points.

10.3.2 Adding Construction Financing

Most developers will finance their development projects with debt and equity. For this office development, the developer assumes that a loan will be available at a loan-to-cost ratio of 70% based on recent transactions in the local market. With a total cost of $17 million, a loan of $11.9 million is attainable. The rest of the cost of the project will be funded by equity totaling $5.1 million. The equity will be provided by the developer and outside equity investors (Table 10.3).

If the property is sold for $18,269,231 million at the end of the construction period, the loan of $11.9 million will be paid back and the remainder of $6,369,231 is earned by the developer and equity investors. The equity profit margin is calculated as the ratio of equity profit to equity investment, less 1, or:

$$\textit{Equity profit margin} = \textit{Equity profit} \,/\, \textit{Equity invested}$$
$$= \left(\$6,369,231 \,/\, \$5,100,000\right) - 1 = 24.89\%$$

TABLE 10.2 Back-of-the-envelope feasibility analysis

Revenues and market value		Construction costs	
Gross rent PSF	$1,750,000		
– Vacancy	$87,500		
Gross effective income	$1,662,500		
- Operating expenses	$475,000		
Net operating income	$1,187,500		
		Cost estimate PSF	$15,000,000
Cap rate	6.50%	+ Land	$2,000,000
Market value	$18,269,231	Total cost	$17,000,000
		Yield to cost	6.99%
Dollar profit	$1,269,231		
Gross profit margin	7.47%		

Note: PSF = per square foot.

TABLE 10.3 Analysis of equity return

Loan to cost	70%		$11,900,000.00
Equity	30%	=	$5,100,000.00
Total	100%		$17,000,000
Market value			$18,269,231
– Loan amount			$11,900,000
Profit to equity			$6,369,231
Equity profit margin			24.89%

Note that financing improves the equity profit margin from the unleveraged case. This occurs for two reasons. First and most importantly, the spread between cap rates and the yield to cost is positive. If the spread were negative, the equity profit margin in the leveraged case would be negative and lower than the unleveraged profit margin. Second, the lender provides financing and is paid back interest and construction loan principal at the end of the construction period. The lender does not share in the upside, which is wholly earned by the developer and equity investors. With a positive spread between cap rate and yield to cost, the more that is borrowed, the higher will be the profit margin.

Most developers would continue to the entitlement process given a 24.89% profit margin and return, despite the relatively narrow spread of cap rates over the yield to cost.

10.3.3 Sensitivity Analysis

It is probably wise to think about risk at this point. As defined earlier, a way to think about risk is to consider uncertainty of outcomes, and there are many aspects of the development process that could lead to future uncertainty. Since developer profit is earned when the property is sold for a market value that exceeds construction costs (or replacement value), market conditions that affect either market value or construction costs have a significant impact on feasibility.

Construction costs increase when labor, materials, land, financing, and other costs used in the development process increase. Market values decrease when rents fall between the time that the BOE analysis is completed and when property is built and earning rental income. Higher vacancies and operating expenses lead to lower NOI, which also decreases market value. Finally, higher cap rates at the end of the construction period decrease the market value for a given NOI. Holding construction costs constant, any of these negative events will provide lower sales proceeds for the developer and equity providers, and lower profits.

Sensitivity analysis, as discussed in Chapters 7 and 9, is a "What if?" analysis. For example, what happens to financial feasibility if rents are not $35.00, but instead drop to $33.00 between the BOE analysis and completion of the project? What if a large number of competitive projects come to market at the same time that the Station is completed, leading to a vacancy rate of 10% instead of the 5% that is assumed in the base case? What if construction costs increase over the construction period? Changes in any of these variables could impact the critical requirement that market value exceed construction costs.

Table 10.4 shows the sensitivity of profits to gross rents and land price. The first column in Table 10.4 provides the base-case analysis, and is the same result as was shown in Table 10.3. Market value exceeds construction costs by $1,269,231 and with an equity profit margin of 24.89%, the developer would likely continue to pursue this project. This analysis assumes that the land transacts at the land seller's asking price of $2,000,000. The yield to cost is 6.99% and the cap rate is 6.5%, providing a spread of 49 basis points.

The second column of Table 10.4 shows what would happen if gross rents are $33.00/sq. ft, which is lower than the $35.00 rent assumed in the base case. This leads to a decrease in market value. All other assumptions are the same as in the base case. If rents are $33.00/sq. ft, the yield to cost is 6.43%, which is below the cap rate of 6.5%. The market value of $16,806,692 is less than the total of $17 million of construction and land costs. The difference is a loss to the developer of $192,308, which means that the project profit margin and the equity profit margin are negative. The feasibility of this project turns from positive to negative for a small $2.00/sq. ft change in rents.

TABLE 10.4 Sensitivity analysis results for 5% vacancy

Assumptions	(1) Land cost	(2) $2m	(3) Land cost	(4) $1.75m
	$35 rents	**$33 rents**	**$35 rents**	**$33 rents**
Rent (per sq. ft)	$35.00	$33.00	$35.00	$33.00
Vacancy	5%	5%	5%	5%
Loan to cost	70%	70%	70%	70%
Land cost	$2,000,000	$2,000,000	$1,750,000	$1,750,000
Replacement value	$17,000,000	$17,000,000	$16,750,000	$16,750,000
Loan amount	$11,900,000	$11,900,000	$11,725,000	$11,725,000
Equity amount	$5,100,000	$5,100,000	$5,025,000	$5,025,000
Feasibility results				
Market value	$18,269,231	$16,807,692	$18,269,231	$16,807,692
Yield to cost	6.99%	6.43%	7.09%	6.52%
Profit (per sq. ft)	$25.38	−$3.85	$30.38	$1.15
Profit	$1,269,231	−$192,308	$1,519,231	$57,692
Profit margin	7.47%	−0.01%	9.07%	0.34%
Equity profit margin	24.89%	−0.04%	30.23%	1.15%

Columns 3 and 4 in Table 10.4 show feasibility results assuming that the land seller is willing to sell the property for $1.75 million instead of $2 million, and for rents of $35 and $33/sq. ft. Replacement value drops, leading to better feasibility results. The yield to cost in this case increases to 7.09% from the base case 6.99%, and the spread between yield to cost and cap rate is now 59 basis points. The unleveraged profit margin increases to 9.07% and equity profit margin rises to 30.23%.

If rents are $33.00/sq. ft, the project is not feasible despite the lower land price. The profit per square foot is only $1.15 for a total project profit of $57,692. This represents an overall profit margin of 0.34% and an equity profit margin of 1.15%.

Table 10.5 shows feasibility results for a 10% vacancy rate, as compared to the 5% vacancy rate assumption used in Table 10.4. Market value is lower with the assumption of a higher vacancy rate, and the spread between market value and replacement value shrinks, making the project less profitable for the developer and investors. In the first two columns, where the assumed land price is $2,000,000, the 10% vacancy assumption leads to negative overall profit margin and equity profit margin. The results are slightly better when land is assumed to cost $1,750,000, but are insufficient to persuade the developer to continue with the project.

Analysts perform sensitivity analyses to determine the impact of assumptions on profit margins and returns. Many things can go wrong, or right, between the time at which capital is expended and the time at which the project is sold and capital is returned to the developer and investors. Tables 10.4 and 10.5 show the impact of several variables, but there are numerous other variables that could also be tested for their

TABLE 10.5 Sensitivity analysis results for 10% vacancy

Assumptions	Land cost	$2m	Land cost	$1.75m
	$35 rents	**$33 rents**	**$35 rents**	**$33 rents**
Rent (per sq. ft)	$35.00	$33.00	$35.00	$33.00
Vacancy	10%	10%	10%	10%
Loan to cost	70%	70%	70%	70%
Land cost	$2,000,000	$2,000,000	$1,750,000	$1,750,000
Replacement value	$17,000,000	$17,000,000	$16,750,000	$16,750,000
Loan amount	$11,900,000	$11,900,000	$11,725,000	$11,725,000
Equity amount	$5,100,000	$5,100,000	$5,025,000	$5,025,000
Feasibility results				
Market value	$16,923,077	$15,538,462	$16,923,077	$15,538,462
Yield to cost	6.47%	5.94%	6.57%	6.03%
Profit (per sq. ft)	−$1.54	−$29.23	$3.46	−$24.23
Profit	−$76,923	−$1,461,538	$173,077	−$1,211,538
Profit margin	−0.45%	−8.60%	1.03%	−7.23%
Equity profit	−1.51%	−28.66%	3.44%	−24.11%

impact on feasibility results. The overall result stems from the notion that market value must be sufficiently higher than replacement value for the developer to profit from building the project. Anything that negatively impacts the sale price after the project is completed (e.g. lower rents, higher vacancy, higher operating expenses, or a higher cap rate) will reduce the spread between market value and replacement cost. By contrast, anything that positively impacts the sale price after completion will increase the spread and developer profitability.

Similarly, anything that adversely impacts replacement value (increase in land price, hard costs, or soft costs) will reduce the spread between market value and replacement value. Conversely, if construction costs or land costs decrease for some reason between the time that the preliminary feasibility study is completed, the spread will increase.

10.4 FORMAL ANALYSIS OF DEVELOPMENT OF "THE STATION"

Despite the potential risks, the developer has elected to continue with the project and begin the process of obtaining entitlements from the local jurisdiction to build the office building. During the entitlement period, the developer engaged an architect to draw up preliminary plans for the building, a transportation engineer to do a traffic study to determine the impact of the office building on local roadway congestion, a landscape architect to do a preliminary design, and also a soils and environmental engineer to test for whether the soil will support the building and if it is contaminated and requires remediation. The developer also contracted with a general contractor (GC) who developed a budget for the project based on local knowledge of the costs of labor and materials. Total expenditures paid by the developer for pre-development costs prior to receiving entitlements were $184,055.

Twelve months elapsed during the entitlement period, and after consideration of floor to area ratios, impervious surfaces, and setbacks from the street and adjacent property boundaries, the local jurisdiction approved a four-story office building consisting of 48,301 leasable square feet, with each floorplate comprising 12,075 square feet. The core factor is 12%, so the usable square footage totals 43,126 (48,301/1.12). The jurisdiction requires 2.75 parking spaces per 1,000 square feet of space and the developer has agreed to build 132 parking spaces. Total costs for developing the office buildings have been provided by the GC and are as shown in Table 10.6 below.

The developer successfully negotiated land price down by $250,000 from the $2,000,000 estimate in the preliminary feasibility study, so replacement value is lower than in the BOE analysis. The developer and general contractor agreed to a guaranteed maximum price (GMP) for all building hard costs, tenant improvement costs, and for the cost of the parking deck. The GMP contract limits the developer's risk related to increasing construction costs over the construction period, and will typically include a premium to actual costs to insulate the general contractor against unexpected cost increases.

Construction is conservatively estimated to take 11 months. During that period, the developer will attempt to attract tenants and be fully leased up to a market rate of vacancy by the end of the 14th month in the development period, which is 3 months after completion.

Given the demand to own assets in this rapidly growing metropolitan area, the developer hopes to sell the office project after only 3 months of operations. Capitalization rates in the local market are 6.5%, and are expected to remain at that level throughout the construction period.

10.5 BUDGET FOR "THE STATION" OFFICE PROJECT

All financial and non-financial costs incurred during site improvement and building completion are shown in Table 10.6.

The land was put under contract by the developer just prior to the start of the entitlement process. The purchase price, to be paid when construction begins, is $1.75 million. An earnest money deposit of 5%, or $87,500, was paid to the seller when it was put under contract, but the developer was able to negotiate a refundable deposit. If entitlements to build a 50,000 square foot building were not awarded by the local jurisdiction, the full deposit would have been returned to the developer.[3] With the approval of the

TABLE 10.6 Development budget for The Station

Construction costs	Dollars	Dollars PSF	Percentage of total costs
Land acquisition	$1,750,000	$36.23	11.29%
Demolition and site costs	$669,541	$13.86	4.32%
Parking deck	$2,643,623	$54.73	17.05%
Architecture & engineering	$567,500	$11.75	3.66%
Hard costs	$5,577,908	$115.48	35.98%
Tenant upfit	$2,415,050	$50.00	15.58%
Pre-construction costs	$244,055	$5.05	1.57%
Development fee	$429,063	$8.81	2.74%
Commissions	$583,235	$12.08	3.76%
Closing costs and fees	$139,500	$2.89	0.90%
Loan fees	$54,280	$1.12	0.35%
Loan interest	$256,854	$5.32	1.66%
Total construction costs	$15,330,609	$317.32	98.85%
Contingency	$177,821	$3.68	1.15%
Total budget	**$15,508,430**	**$321.00**	**100.00%**

Note: PSF = per square foot.

[3] In many cases, a seller may require a non-refundable deposit, meaning that if the developer did not follow through on the acquisition for any reason, the seller would keep the $87,500.

project, the seller keeps the deposit and the rest of the $1.75 million land cost is paid at the beginning of the construction period.

When acquired, there was an old two-story building on the site that has to be demolished. All costs to demolish the existing building and prepare the site for development total $669,541, or $13.86/sq. ft of building. The total costs for site preparation and land acquisition are $50.09/sq. ft, or 15.66% of total costs.

A two-story above-ground parking structure will be built on the site next to the building. The GC has estimated that each of the required 132 spaces will cost $20,027 to build, so the total cost of the parking structure is $2.644 million, or $54.73/sq. ft of building.

The GC estimate of hard costs is $5,777,908, or $115.48/sq. ft, and includes all materials and labor to build the building on the site. To attract tenants the developer must contribute a market rate for tenant upfit (or tenant improvements). Owners of newly built competitive Class A office projects offer tenants $50 per leasable square foot for new space. Recall that the building contains 48,301 usable square feet. The cost of tenant upfit is typically included in the development budget, since it is a cost that must be incurred by the developer to attract tenants to the building. Total tenant upfit costs are $2,415,050, comprising 15.43% of the total construction budget.

Pre-construction costs are discussed above, and include all costs that are expended to successfully gain entitlements. These are referred to as deal pursuit costs. The developer paid for these items, even though the outcome of the process was uncertain. If entitlements were not obtained, these would be sunk costs. Because the project was able to gain entitlements to build, development costs are added into the budget.

The development fee compensates the developer for the work that is done to gain entitlements to build, as well as for assembling the team and the capital to successfully build the office building. During the pre-construction period, the developer was actively engaged in the planning, design, and entitlements process. In addition, the developer raised debt and equity capital prior to construction. During construction, the developer will seek out qualified tenants to fill the building, and also oversee all construction activities of the GC. The total developer fee for The Station is 4% of the sum of the hard costs, the costs of building the parking deck, and tenant upfit costs.

Additional fees for acquisition of the land and to pay back the developer for overheads and other costs during the entitlement process total 0.9% of all costs less the construction loan interest, or $139,500. Engineering and architectural work performed during the construction period totals $567,500.

Commissions are fees that are paid to leasing brokers after leases are signed, and are based on the expected rents to be paid at the time of the building's completion (see Chapter 6). Closing costs and other fees include other costs of buying the land, building the building, obtaining a loan to help pay for construction, and raising equity capital.

Loan fees are 0.5% of the total construction loan, and construction loan interest is determined by the construction loan amount and the interest rate charged by the lender. Calculation of these two items is described in Section 10.6.

10.6 FINANCING DEVELOPMENT

Funding of the budget is required in four different stages of development.

10.6.1 Stage One: Pre-construction

Pre-construction costs relate to gaining control of the land, doing preliminary feasibility studies, and pursuit costs (site plans and engineering work paid for by the developer). Until entitlements are received, this capital is completely at risk. If entitlements are ultimately not received, or if they are received for a substantially lower amount of square footage or with substantial additional public requirements (such as improved roads and traffic signals), this money is lost.

10.6.2 Stage Two: Construction

The second stage of development is the construction stage. When the entitlements are obtained, the developer will immediately pay the remainder of the land cost ($1,750,000 less the $87,500 deposit, or $1,662,500) and start the construction process.

As mentioned above, the construction of the building will take 11 months to complete. The lender stands ready to loan $10,855,901 to the developer over this 11-month period. The lender will forward payments to the developer only after all equity has been contributed. For providing this loan, the lender will charge a fee of $54,280 (approximately 0.5% of the total loan amount).

After entitlements have been obtained, horizontal development begins to prepare the site for the building, parking, and landscaping. This step includes levelling the land, installing water, sewerage, and utility infrastructure underneath the property, remediating contaminated soils, and demolishing the existing building, among other tasks.

After preparation of the land, vertical development of the parking structure and office building begins. The first expenditures made are paid out of the equity that was raised by the developer until the equity balance is depleted. After all the equity has been paid in, a construction loan is used to pay the remainder of the anticipated development costs in each month. The construction lender agrees to provide a certain maximum dollar amount to the developer, and the developer accesses the loan during each month of construction by drawing pre-specified monthly amounts from the construction loan amount as specified in a draw schedule.

As construction proceeds, and after the initial equity balance is depleted, the developer draws enough capital from the construction loan in each month to fund that month's expenditures. The lender requires invoices from the general contractor and all sub-contractors who have performed work at the site before any payments are made to the developer. By the end of construction, all equity will be invested and the construction loan will be at its maximum balance.

After each draw from the construction loan, the amount drawn will accrue interest for the remainder of the construction loan term. The balance outstanding in each month increases by the amount of draw taken, as well as the interest that accrues on the total amount of draws that have been taken.

Construction Loan Calculations

The developer sent information about the project to several lenders, and the highest loan amount offered is $10,855,901, which is 70% of the total construction budget of

$15,508,901. The remaining 30%, or $4,652,529, has been raised from equity investors. The construction loan interest rate is 4.4366%.

The loan has a 14-month maturity, after which the lender agrees to extend the loan for up to three 1-year intervals. After 14 months, the rate remains 4.4366%, and the developer will be contracted to pay interest-only payments for 3 months before the property is sold. During these 3 months, the payments will be paid out of NOI earned by the property.

In addition to the fee, the developer of the project will pay all legal fees that were incurred by the lender during the process of making the loan. In addition, the developer will pay an appraiser to determine the value of new construction on a month-by-month basis as a requirement of the lender, assuring the lender that the loan disbursements to the developer are being used for the construction of the building, and that the loan balance does not exceed the total cost of construction. Other costs funded by the loan at the beginning of the construction period include title insurance, builder's risk insurance, and general liability insurance while the project is being completed. These costs are all assumed to occur in the first month of the construction period, and the sum of these costs accrues interest throughout the remainder of the construction loan period.

The developer and general contractor have prepared a monthly budget and schedule to indicate when contractors will be on site throughout construction, and what their contracted labor, material costs, and fees will be in each month. The schedule shows the dollar amount of the total development budget, as well as the percentage of the total budget that is to be completed in each month, and is shown in Table 10.7.

Monthly costs are paid using equity until it runs out, and then using debt. Unlike a permanent loan that provides funding at the beginning of the term, the construction lender agrees to provide a maximum amount to the developer. As monthly costs are paid, the lender draws from this maximum loan amount.

The draw schedule is as shown in Table 10.7. The second column shows the schedule of monthly development expenditures, expressed as a percentage of the total project budget. The developer and equity partners pay the first expenditure of $1,750,000 to the land seller. The actual disbursement is the land price less the option payment that was paid at the beginning of the entitlement process, or $1,662,500 ($1,750,000 less $87,500). This happens at the very beginning of the development process, which we assume is at time 0.

At the end of the first month, the developer's schedule shows that 5% (Column 2) of the total budget less the construction lender's estimate of loan interest ($15,508,439 – $256,854 = $15,251,576), or $762,579 (Column 3) has been expended. This amount is used to pay back some of the developer's expenses incurred to that point, begin the demolition of the existing building, and start site work.

In the second month, the developer's timeline shows that 6% of the total construction costs (less construction interest) will be paid for by the developer and equity partner, for a total of $915,095 (Column 3). The monthly expenditure for month 3 is 8% of the total budget, and by the end of month 3, 30.47% of the project (or $4,647,800) has been completed and paid for entirely by the equity investors. The reader should recall that the total equity committed is $4,652,529. This leaves only $4,730 of additional equity to be funded from the developer and equity investors.

TABLE 10.7 Draw schedule and interest calculation

Month	Percentage drawn	Total draw	Equity draws	Debt draws	Accrued interest	Cumulative debt	NOI	Interest paid	BTCF
0	11.47422%	$1,750,000	$1.750,000	0		0			
1	5.00%	$762,579	$762,578.81	0		0			
2	6.00%	$915,095	$915,095	0		0			
3	8.00%	$1,220,126	$1,220,126	0		0			
4	8.00%	$1,220,126	$4,730	$1,215,396		$1,215,396			
5	8.00%	$1,220,126		$1,220,126	$4,494	$2,440,016			
6	9.00%	$1,372,642		$1,372,642	$9,021	$3,821,679			
7	10.00%	$1,525,158		$1,525,158	$14,129	$5,360,966			
8	10.00%	$1,525,158		$1,215,396	$19,820	$6,905,944			
9	8.00%	$1,220,126		$1,220,126	$25,532	$8,151,602			
10	7.00%	$1,067,610		$1,067,610	$30,138	$9,249,351			
11	9.00%	$1,452,831		$1,452,831	$34,196	$10,736,378			
12	0.00%				$39,694	$10,776,072			
13	0.00%				$39,841	$10,815,913			
14	0.00%				$39,988	$10,855,901			
15	0.00%					$10,855,901	$97,508	$40,136	$57,372
16	0.00%					$10,855,901	$97,508	$40,136	$57,372
17	0.00%					$10,855,901	$97,508	$40,136	$57,372
Total	**100.00%**	**$15,251,576**	**$4,652,529.08**	**$10,599,047**	**$256,854**	**$10,855,901**			

In month 4, 8% of the budget, or $1,220,126 of costs, is incurred by the developer. With only $4,730 (Column 4) left to be funded by the developer and equity partner, the remainder ($1,220,126 – $4,730 =) $1,215,397 (Column 5) becomes the first draw from the construction lender. In successive months of the development period, this amount will accrue interest.

Total expenses incurred in the fifth month are 8% of the total, or $1,220,126. Since the equity has been depleted, the entire amount will be paid with a construction loan draw. Two draws have been taken (in months 4 and 5), so the total draws on the construction loan are $2,435,523 ($1,215,397 + $1,220,126).

In addition to this amount, the construction loan outstanding increases by interest that accrues on the draw taken in month 4. Interest on the $1,215,397 draw in month 4 is equal to the interest rate of 4.4366% divided by 12 to make it monthly, multiplied by $1,215,397, or $4,494 (Column 6). This interest accrual is added to the sum of the first two draws to give a construction loan balance at the end of month 5 of $2,440,016 (Column 7).

The same process continues in the remaining months of the construction period. In month 6, 9% of the total budget is drawn down from the construction loan, for a total of $1,372,642. The construction loan balance at the beginning of month 6 of $2,440,016 accrues interest at the 4.4366% monthly rate to generate accrued interest at the end of month 6 of $9,021. The sum of the previous balance ($2,440,016), plus the month 6 draw of $1,372,642, plus the accrued interest of $9,021, is the construction loan balance at the end of the sixth month, or $3,821,679.

The construction loan balance continues to grow by the remaining draws over the next 5 months and the increasing amount of interest as the loan balance grows. After the last draw is taken, the total balance of the loan is $10,736,378.

10.6.3 Stage Three: Lease-Up

The third stage of development is the lease-up stage, which in the case of The Station is expected to comprise 3 months. For well-conceived projects, substantial lease-up will occur during the construction period, but there may still be some space that needs to be leased after construction is completed. A construction loan term will typically extend beyond the construction period to provide time for the project to be leased up to a stabilized market rate prior to the maturity of the loan. For The Station, stabilized occupancy is 95%, which is expected to be achieved by the end of Month 14.

During the lease-up period, no further draws will be taken from the construction loan, but the cumulative balance of the draws plus all accrued interest earned over the construction loan period continues to increase until the construction loan is paid off with sale proceeds.

At the end of Month 11, the balance is $10,736,378, and this amount earns 4.4366% (divided by 12) in interest over the following month to increase the loan balance by $39,694. This interest accrual amount is added to the loan balance at the end of Month 13 so that the balance grows to $10,776,072. During the subsequent 2 months, accrued interest totals $79,829, which is also added to give a total balance of $10,855,901 at the end of the 14th month of the construction loan term, which is also the maturity of the loan. This is the amount that had been calculated by the lender at the beginning of construction, when the budget was drawn up and the loan fee and loan interest balances were determined.

We are assuming that no income is earned in months 11 through 14. If income had been earned, it would have offset all or part of the monthly interest accrual.

10.6.4 Stage Four: Operations

Let us assume that two tenants have signed leases to occupy 95% of the 48,301 square feet of space, and that their leases start paying rent after the end of Month 14. The two tenants have agreed to pay $36.84/sq. ft, which is $1.84 higher than estimated using the BOE analysis. With 5% vacancy and $9.50 operating expenses, the NOI per square foot earned in the first year of operations is $25.50 ($36.84 – (–0.05) * $26.84 – $9.50), and the property will earn $1,170,092 in NOI (48,301 square feet * $25.50/sq. ft). Monthly NOI is $97,508.

Also in Month 14, the construction loan rolls into its first extension and monthly interest accruals are paid from property income. The loan balance at the end of Month 14 is $10,855,901. Using a 4.4366% rate, the monthly interest payment is $40,136. Monthly NOI will be used to pay the interest payment, leaving $57,372 to be distributed to the equity investor.[4] Assuming that rents do not grow over the 3-month operation period, this amount ($57,372) is earned in Months 15, 16, and 17.

More detail on the Month 17 cash flow is shown in Table 10.8. The property is assumed to be sold at the end of month 17 at a 6.5% cap rate. Annual NOI is $1,170,091.73, so the value at which the property will be sold is $18,001,411. After accounting for 2% selling expenses ($360,028), the net selling price is $17,641,383. The before-tax equity reversion is this amount less the mortgage balance of $10,855,901, or $6,785,482. Adding in the before-tax cash flow earned in Month 17 of $57,732 gives a total of $6,843,214 earned by the developer and equity investor in Month 17.

Lender Yield Calculation for the Construction Loan

The stream of cash flows disbursed and received by the lender is shown on the timeline in Table 10.9. Note that the lender's first disbursement to the developer is in the

TABLE 10.8 Cash flow earned in Month 17

Sale price	$18,001,411
– Selling expenses	$360,028
Net sale price	$17,641,383
– Loan balance	$10,855,901
Equity reversion	$6,785,482
+ NOI Month 18	$57,732
Cash flow Month 17	$6,843,214

[4] If this income were to be earned over a full year, the total annual before-tax cash flow would be $681,576. The total equity investment was $4,652,529, which produces a 14.34% return on equity.

TABLE 10.9 Lender yield calculation

Month	Lender cash flow
4	−$1,215,397
5	−$1,220,126
6	−$1,372,642
7	−$1,525,159
8	−$1,525,159
9	−$1,220,126
10	−$1,069,610
11	−$1,452,831
12	0
13	0
14	0
15	$40,136
16	$40,136
17	$10,896,037
Yield/month	0.3677%
Yield/year	4.5032%

fourth month. Additional draws on the loan amount are made in months 5 through 11 when construction is completed. For months 12 through 14, the loan balance continues to accrue interest monthly, as we have assumed that no income is being earned. During months 15 and 16, income earned by the property is sufficient to pay interest that is accrued on the loan in those months, and in Month 17, the final interest payment of $40,136 is paid out of property income, and the total loan balance of $10,855,901 is paid when the property is sold. The total of these two payments is $10,896,037.

The monthly yield (or IRR) on this stream of cash outflows and inflows is 0.3677%, and when annualized the lender's yield (or IRR) is 4.5032%. Note that this is higher than the interest rate of 4.4366% due to the 0.5% loan fee that is paid out of equity when the lender agrees to provide the loan to the developer.

10.7 DEVELOPER PROFIT AND RETURN

Using the above information, we can also determine the investment performance for the developer and the equity investors. The first capital spent was the developer and/or the equity investors, and represented the outflows in the first 4 months of the construction period. While the construction loan is being drawn, there is no more requirement for equity to be expended. At stabilization, the property earns NOI of $57,732 for 2 months. In the final month, the property is assumed to be sold at a 6.5% cap rate. With an assumed NOI of $1,170,092, the gross selling price is $18,001,415.

TABLE 10.10 Equity return calculation

Month	Equity cash flow
0	–$1,750,000
1	–$762,579
2	–$915,095
3	–$1,220,126
4	–$4,730
5	0
6	0
7	0
8	0
9	0
10	0
11	0
12	0
13	0
14	0
15	$57,732
16	$57,732
17	$6,843,214
Yield/month	2.61%
Yield/year	36.17%

The total stream of cash inflows and outflows is as shown in Table 10.10. The outflows for the first 5 months total $4,652,529, and the inflows total $6,958,678. Total profit is the difference, or $2,306,149, for a profit margin of 49.57%. If we ignore the net operating earned and divide sale proceeds ($6,785,482) by the equity invested ($4,659,529), the profit earned on development is $2,132,953, for a profit margin of 45.85%. The equity multiple for the equity investors is 1.50. The monthly IRR is 2.61%, and the annualized return is 36.17%.

10.8 COMPARISON TO "BACK-OF-THE-ENVELOPE" ANALYSIS

The main differences between the back-of-the-envelope analysis and actual results are that land price is $1,750,000 instead of $2,000,000, gross rents earned by the property at completion are $36.84 as opposed to $35.00, and the building size is 48,301 square feet and not 50,000 square feet. In addition, total actual construction costs are $15,508,430, compared to the estimated total construction costs of $16,750,000 in the back-of-the-envelope analysis (when using $1.75 million as land cost). The results of the comparison are shown in Table 10.11.

The first column of Table 10.11 is the same as shown in the third column of Table 10.4. Key calculations are the 7.09% yield to cost, the profit and profit margin of

TABLE 10.11 Comparison of actual results and back-of-the-envelope analysis

Assumptions:	BOE $35 rents	Results $35 rents
Rent (per sq. ft)	$35.00	$35.00
Vacancy	5%	5%
Loan to cost	70%	70%
Land cost	$1,750,000	$1,750,000
Replacement value	$16,750,000	$15,508,430
Loan amount	$11,725,000	$10,855,901
Equity amount	$5,025,000	$4,652,529
Feasibility results		
Market value	$18,269,231	$17,641,383
Yield to cost	7.09%	7.54%
Profit (per sq. ft)	$30.38	$44.16
Profit	$1,519,231	$2,132,953
Profit margin	9.07%	13.75%
Equity profit margin	30.23%	45.85%

$1,519,231 and 9.07%, respectively, and the equity profit margin of 30.23% in our back-of-the-envelope analysis.

The actual results are better than we had expected because the achieved results are better than expected (land cost is lower, rents are higher, construction costs are lower). The building size was smaller than expected due to the regulatory requirements of the local jurisdiction, but the difference was relatively small.

The second column of Table 10.11 shows the returns earned by the developer, the numbers being taken from our discussion in Sections 10.6 and 10.7. Total development costs are $15,508,430, and the net sales price ($18,001,411 – $360,028) as shown in Table 10.8 is $17,641,383, for a profit of $2,132,953. Net operating income is $1,170,092, so the yield to cost is 7.54% ($1,170,092 / $15,508,430).

The unleveraged profit margin is profit divided by total cost, or $2,132,953 / $15,508,430, or 13.75%. This is higher than the 9.07% expected in Table 10.4. The lender financed 70% of the construction costs, or $10,588,901, so total equity investment is $4,652,529. Since the upside in the development is paid to the equity investors, the equity profit margin is the profit divided by the equity invested, which is 45.85%. This compares favorably to the 30.23% profit margin that was shown in Table 10.4.

10.9 A LONDON OFFICE DEVELOPMENT THROUGH THE CYCLE

This is the ongoing story of developing London's largest office building – the Bishopsgate Tower, or the Pinnacle (Figure 10.1), or the Helter Skelter, or Twentytwo Bishopsgate.

FIGURE 10.1 The Pinnacle in the London skyline
Source: Pinnacle project brochure.

In 2003, DIFA (a German open-ended fund) instructed architects KPF to design a tower on the site of Crosby Court, Bishopsgate, in the City of London. As at 2005, the existing building, a 1986 construction of 250,000 square feet, had a rental value of around £35/sq. ft, and was valued at a cap rate of 6.25%. The total value was around £140 million.

The design brief called for an iconic design (given a sudden interest in tall buildings by the City planners at the time, which led to the Gherkin, Heron Tower, Shard, Cheesegrater, and Walkie Talkie).

The KPF design featured a variety of floorplates, a tapering top, and a design reminiscent of a fairground helter skelter. Between 2005 and 2007, the planning consultation process led to several revisions: the Civil Aviation Authority imposed a 2,000 ft (305 m) height restriction, which led to a loss of area equivalent to five office floors, and there were revisions to the massing plan. The result was a plan for 850,000 square feet on 60 floors.

The rental value of the new building as at 2005 added a healthy £10/sq. ft to the existing £35, and the cap rate for the brand new completed asset was pushed down to 5%. The gross development value was £765 million. Given estimated building costs of around £480 million, DIFA and their advisors reckoned that a developer could pay up to £200 million for the opportunity to buy Crosby Court and develop the Helter Skelter, or (its formal name) the Pinnacle. This would leave them with a profit of nearly £90 million, around 13% of total costs. The rent would deliver a yield of 5.6%, which, relative to an investment cap rate of 5%, offered a developer's reward for risk. These margins all look slightly thin to experienced developers, who might look for a profit of at least 25% of costs, but 2005 was a hot market, and a small increase in rents or reductions in cap rate would deliver much bigger margins, so it was not unreasonable to expect someone to be interested at this sort of price. For DIFA, the boom in interest in tall buildings delivered a profit of £60 million on the current valuation of £140 million (Table 10.12).

In 2007, a consortium of 60-odd Middle East investors, including SEDCO and WAFRA, and fronted by a developer, Arab Investments, which was appointed by the investor consortium – despite it being rumoured that Arab Investments had no previous experience in large-scale projects, completed the acquisition of the site for £200 million.

At this point the site was "ready to go," with planning permission granted for the 850,000 square foot office development. Multiplex was appointed as construction partner on a £500 million fixed-price construction contract, and completion was planned for 2013.

The building was beautiful to many eyes, but the floorplans were inefficient, irregular, and different on every floor; the elevator design did not permit rapid vertical travel, as three separate trips were required to get to the top of the building; and the amount of steel involved in the highly complex construction project was much greater than would be normal for a building of this size.

TABLE 10.12 The Pinnacle, 2005 appraisal

Size	850,000 sq. ft
Rent	£45/sq. ft
Cap rate	5.0%
Gross development value (GDV)	£765,000,000
Cost	£450/sq. ft
Cost inc. fees	£478,125,000
Site cost	£200,000,000
Yield to cost	5.6%
Profit	£86,875,000
Profit	**12.8%**

Note: yield on cost = (850,000 * 45)/(£478,125,000 + £200,000,000).

TABLE 10.13 The Pinnacle, 2007 appraisal

Size	850,000 sq. ft
Rent	£58/sq. ft
Cap rate	4.5%
GDV	£1,086,111,111
Cost	£475/sq. ft
Cost inc. fees	£504,687,500
Site cost	£200,000,000
Yield to cost	7.0%
Profit	£381,423,611
Profit	**54.1%**

Nevertheless, by 2007 the purchase looked inspired. Rental values had risen and the estimated cap rate was down to 4.5% as London benefitted from a huge property boom. The completed development value was now well over £1 billion. Costs were up, but the developer's yield was now a very healthy 2.5% over the yield on a competed development and the estimated (projected) profit was close to £400 million, 54% of total costs (Table 10.13).

Work started immediately, and the usual problems arose. There were inevitably some developer variations which pushed up costs. The archaeological excavation did not turn up any particular problems, but neighboring tenants took out an injunction for interference with their rights of light, causing 3 months' delay, so that demolition work did not start on site until 2008. And then unusual problems arose. September 2008 saw the Lehman crisis, with the capital markets in distress, potential tenants such as banks suddenly contracting or bust. The first and only pre-let – the penthouse restaurant – was announced in October 2008, but by the time that piling works began in March 2009, no office tenants were showing any interest.

By 2009, costs had risen to £575 million, due to developer variations, despite the fixed-price Multiplex contract. The scheme was now severely loss-making (Table 10.14).

Due to the very difficult letting conditions and a need for more capital, construction of the core was halted in 2010 after getting up to the seventh floor (at which point the market nickname for the building became "the Stump").

At this point the developers and investors took a deep breath and reflected. £480 million had been sunk into the site, design costs, and foundations. Another £300 million was needed to finish the building, not all of which had been committed by the investors, who had expected £700 million to cover everything. SEDCO invested more equity in 2011, but this was not enough and CBRE was instructed to look for new funding in March 2011. At this point, HSBC and HSH Nordbank agreed to provide a £500 million debt facility with the scheme's owners to allow above-ground construction to recommence; not enough equity funding had been secured, but Arab Investments announced that development was set to recommence in June 2011; nevertheless, it was obvious to anyone that the site remained on go slow.

At last, in January 2012, fatally injured by the second Greek leg of the global financial crisis, the scheme was halted. In October 2012, Brookfield Multiplex sued the owners of the Pinnacle for breach of contract and claimed £16 million in unpaid fees. Arab

TABLE 10.14 The Pinnacle, 2009 appraisal

Size	850,000 sq. ft
Rent	£45/sq. ft
Cap rate	6.5%
GDV	£588,461,538
Cost	£542/sq. ft
Cost inc. fees	£575,875,000
Site cost	£200,000,000
Yield to cost	4.9%
Profit	–£187,413,462
Profit	**–24.2%**

Investments decided to try to offload the problem to someone else and instructed CBRE to find a buyer for their interest. In February 2013 it was revealed that Lipton Rogers Developments (LRD) was circling the scheme and contemplating a completely new design using the existing piling, but CBRE rejected LRD's approach in July, insisting that the original building had to be constructed by any buyer.

Meanwhile, LRD worked for 2 years with its professional team to attack what they saw as a great opportunity, and to address what they saw as fundamental issues with the design of the Pinnacle, including the floorplates (size, uniformity, and occupational density), the lifting strategy, and the excessive construction costs. They engaged the original architects, PLP, to design a scheme built on the design principles of the consented scheme, but one which was much more efficient. By now, the City authorities' high-rise plans had firmed up and the Pinnacle was the centrepiece of the City's emerging group of towers. Indeed, it was now unthinkable to planners that the scheme would not go ahead, and the Stump was a horrible embarrassment in the London 2012 Olympic year.

The new PLP brief was to design a skyscraper of similar height, building on the existing foundation and podium, thereby avoiding the inevitable cost, risk, and time in the ground which would be necessitated by ripping up and then repeating any archaeology, piling, and basement work. The result was a much simpler design, and one which was to cost considerably less to build per square foot than the other new London landmarks such as the Shard.

In November 2014, at last, Lipton Rogers were in exclusive talks to buy the site. As merchant developers, or development consultants, they had no direct access to the capital needed to buy the site and complete the development. Their financial model is to charge investors a fee and a profit share for their work in conceiving and managing the project.

The capital was not especially hard to find. In 2013–14, London was bouncing back from the 2008 shock, with finance-sector occupiers back in the market and increasing activity in the technology, media, and telecoms sectors. Office vacancy rates in the City were low, and new developments available to buy were few and far between. However, a single capital source ready and willing to take on a risky development project costing in the region of £800–900 million was not going to be easy to find.

As it turned out, another intermediary was needed to pull the finance together. This was a real estate fund and asset manager, albeit one backed and owned by a large insurance company with its own capital to invest. AXA-REIM stepped forward as asset or investment manager for the Pinnacle, having secured capital totalling 25% of the capital required from three AXA insurance funds, and then – with LRD help – finding three further investors to take 25% each.

In February 2015, a deal was agreed. A price of £300 million was paid to Arab Investments, some of it unconditional, but £18 million was used to pay off a bank loan, £20 million was paid to Multiplex to settle their breach of contract claim, and £100 million was paid to Arab Investments conditional on certain milestones being achieved. Arab Investments also retained the top two floors (worth maybe £25–50 million) on a long lease at a peppercorn rent. Having spent around £500 million by this point, the Arab Investors consortium crystallized a loss of around £150 million.

The three investors who joined the AXA consortium were Temasek (a Singaporean sovereign wealth fund), PSP (a Canadian pension fund manager acting for public pension plans including the army and police), and British Columbia Investment Management Corporation (a Canadian pension fund manager acting on behalf of local pension funds, now known as Quadreal). 25% of the required equity was to be provided by each; no debt was to be employed; and decision-making was to be unanimous, with both AXA-REIM and LRD providing advice as necessary, but each with their own fee-based financial motivations.

While securing the finance, LRD and AXA-REIM proceeded to develop detailed plans for the scheme. This was to be the tallest building in the City cluster. Issues with other City schemes led to a series of planning concerns having to be dealt with; these included wind, solar glare, the provision of a viewing gallery, rights of light, and delivery traffic. The latter, driven by online retailing amongst other issues, required the developers to reduce the expected number of 400 deliveries a day to 200 by establishing an offsite logistics facility and consolidating package deliveries to the site during the night and at non-peak hours during the day.

The consultation process started in 2012 and bi-weekly meetings were held throughout 2014, with both sides motivated and keen to secure a quick agreement. Planning approval was granted in November 2015. The new Pinnacle, now to be known as 22 Bishopsgate, was 278 m high – the tallest office development in the City – with 1.4 million square feet of offices (later reduced to 1.25 million), including 100,000 square feet of amenity space, capacity for 12,500 people, and 2 million square feet of gross external area. The result was a highly profitable project, about to be restarted at a time of considerable optimism (Table 10.15).

And then ...

The June 2016 Brexit vote in the UK caused the investors to delay signing the building contract and to generally consider their options. There were many arguments against continuing; and a few for. The arguments against are clear – major uncertainty regarding possible lettings, rising commodity and construction costs as the pound weakens, possible labor shortages as EU workers are unsure of their rights, a general reluctance to sink more capital into a damaged and more risky market. The arguments for are more subtle. Brexit also cast further doubt on the development of rival schemes, 150 Bishopsgate and 40 Leadenhall; a cheaper pound means fewer euros, Canadian

TABLE 10.15 The Pinnacle, 2015 appraisal

Size	1,400,000 sq. ft
Rent	£70/sq. ft
Cap rate	5.0%
GDV	£1,960,000,000
Cost	£575/sq. ft
Cost inc. fees	£1,006,250,000
Site cost	£300,000,000
Yield to cost	7.5%
Profit	£653,750,000
Profit	**50.0%**

and Singaporean dollars to commit; and it is always hard to write off £370 million of sunk capital (a further £70 million having been spent since the purchase). In addition, it was estimated that a further £70 million might have to be spent in the winding-down process.

LRD and AXA-REIM and their professional advisory teams worked very hard over the June to October 2017 period to persuade investors to proceed, and succeeded (Figure 10.2). Confidence in London had been boosted by recent tech property deals (by Google, Amazon, and others), and it was agreed that the developers make as much noise about the decision as possible in order to deter other developments and reduce the competing supply of space.

The developers also took the opportunity to make a virtue out of the huge lettable area and changes in occupier preferences towards lifestyle facilities and co-working. Convene – a hospitality provider – signed up for 100,000 square feet. Space was set aside for food markets, gyms, innovation and fitness hubs, a club, a cycling park, and reflective areas.

By 2018, the anticipated profit was down from the heady days of 2016, and (assuming a successful letting programme) settling around a "normal" level of 25% of costs, and a development yield premium of 1.3% (Table 10.16).

By 2019, construction was almost complete and letting activity was well underway. Completion was planned for the end of 2020. The eventual success of 22 Bishopsgate was about to be settled once and for all.

NEWS

Why AXA's backing of 22 Bishopsgate is backing for Brexit Britain

FIGURE 10.2 22 Bishopsgate goes ahead
Source: Architects' Journal.

TABLE 10.16 The Pinnacle, 2018 appraisal

Size	1,250,000 sq. ft
Rent	£65/sq. ft
Cap rate	5.3%
GDV	£1,547,619,048
Cost	£600/sq. ft
Cost inc. fees	£937,500,000
Site cost	£300,000,000
Yield to cost	6.6%
Profit	£310,119,048
Profit	**25.1%**

10.10 CONCLUSION

This chapter has provided an in-depth analysis of the techniques utilized by a developer to determine the profitability of building an office project. For the developer of "The Station," the actual results exceeded the expected results. Market conditions improved during the entitlement and construction periods, leading to higher rents and lower costs than were expected. This led to higher profits. However, rents could have dropped over the time period, vacancy rates could have been higher, and the cap rate at which the asset was sold could have been higher.

For the developers of 22 Bishopsgate, it has been a very bumpy ride. As Figure 10.3 shows, this is a highly cyclical industry. It is worth repeating that development is very risky, but with the risk often comes high returns.

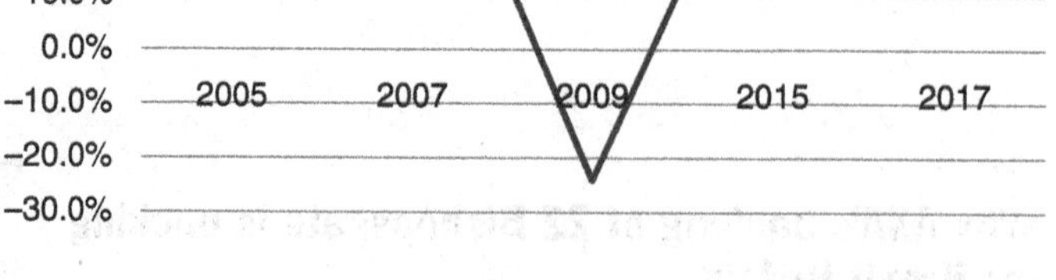

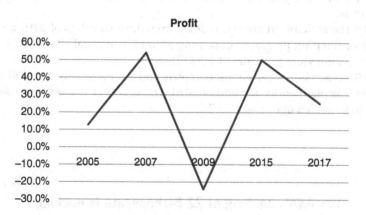

FIGURE 10.3 Development can be risky – 22 Bishopsgate's profit, 2005-18

PART Three

Real Estate Investment Structures

CHAPTER 11

Unlisted Real Estate Funds

11.1 INTRODUCTION TO UNLISTED REAL ESTATE FUNDS

One of the primary drawbacks of investing in real estate directly is the lumpy, illiquid nature of the asset class (see Chapter 1). Indirect investment via a property fund is an appealing alternative. The major appeal of a fund is that it can pool investor capital, so that each investor can own a share of a more diversified portfolio of assets than would be achievable using only its own capital.

A second drawback of real estate is its illiquidity. As this chapter will illustrate, real estate funds are not designed to solve the problem of illiquidity. While this opens the door for REITs and other listed forms of real estate (see Chapter 12), some unlisted fund formats can be more liquid than direct real estate holdings. Liquidity can be improved by the manager arranging matched bargains between buyers and sellers, or by the manager dealing directly with the market through an open-ended structure. In addition, there is often a healthy secondary market for units in both open- and closed-ended funds. Much current activity is addressed at the digital tokenisation of assets, and unlisted funds are a natural target for this. Ony time will tell whether this will permit more liqudity in the unlisted fund market.

The universe of unlisted real estate funds includes two different types of vehicle. Open-ended 'core' (low risk, or Type A) funds such as PRISA (Prudential Property Investment Separate Account) have existed in the USA since the 1970s, but are also popular in Europe, especially in the UK and Germany. There are also some lower-risk closed-ended funds that are traded actively in secondary markets, but higher-risk closed-ended private equity (Type B) real estate funds have been popular in the USA since the 1990s.

Open-ended core funds are very different in many ways from the very private, higher-risk, illiquid opportunity or private equity real estate fund. The structures including co-investment, carried interest structures, or preferred returns which we discuss in Chapter 12 are more relevant to private equity real estate funds; core funds are unlikely to have these features.

11.1.1 The US Market

In the USA, the meaning of the term 'private equity real estate' has changed considerably over the past 30 years. Prior to 1990, private equity referred to small groups of investors pooling their capital into general or limited partnerships with the intent to purchase a single property or a portfolio of properties. These investors (sometimes called syndicators) are still active in real estate markets, usually operating locally, but do not make up a large portion of transactions.

In the late 1980s, the USA saw the launch of a new generation of co-mingled funds looking to buy cheap, distressed property assets popularly known as 'vulture funds'. These were the first generation of closed-ended real estate funds, usually set up in a corporate or partnership format. For many reasons the format became discredited, but the access provided to difficult markets for foreign investors, tax efficiency, and a lack of alternatives all helped to overcome resistance to the vehicle. A more acceptable name ('opportunity funds') was found for these funds in the 1990s; later, 'private equity real estate funds' became a popular broader descriptor for higher-risk, higher-return, illiquid closed-ended real estate funds modelled on private equity structures.

As discussed in Chapter 2, the Resolution Trust Corporation (RTC) was formed to sell off assets in the early 1990s, and private equity firms were formed to bid at the auctions and buy at a discount, hold until markets improved, and then sell for higher amounts. Funds created by firms like J.E. Robert, Goldman Sachs, Morgan Stanley, and others were able to earn high returns over short periods of time. The experience that was gained in the 1990s, and the success of the participating firms, spawned the private equity real estate industry as it is now known in the USA. A list of the top 20 US private equity real estate firms, ranked by the amount of capital raised over the 5 years ending in 2017, is provided in Table 11.1.

Private equity real estate funds are always closed-ended, and it follows that they usually have a limited life in order that investors can force a sale to receive a return of equity. As we will see in Chapter 12, fee structures in such vehicles, modelled initially on US private equity and venture capital funds, typically attempt to 'align' the interests of investor and manager by rewarding the manager on a performance basis. The fund manager often has an investment alongside clients. The manager may charge a base fee calculated as a percentage of the value of the assets managed, and additionally take a proportion (say 20%) of the total return over a minimum hurdle (say 8%).

11.1.2 The Global Market

The higher-risk, return-seeking nature of these funds sent them in search of attractive markets, and this opened up the way for the first real wave of global property investment. It is not an accident that the growth of unlisted funds has since tracked the geographical expansion of real estate investment strategies.

The pace of change in investor attitudes in the 2000s was rapid. Taking UK pension funds as an example, balanced, unlisted real estate funds began to dominate institutional investment strategies early in the new millennium, and domestic multi-manager mandates which focused on these funds rather than direct real

TABLE 11.1 US private equity real estate firms ranked by capital raised (2013–17)

Rank	Name of firm	Capital raised
1	Blackstone	$83.1bn
2	Lone Star Funds	$56.6bn
3	Brookfield Property Group	$25.9bn
4	Carlyle Group	$18.7bn
5	Morgan Stanley Real Estate Investing	$17.6bn
6	CBRE Global Investors	$16.6bn
7	Goldman Sachs Merchant Banking Division	$16.0bn
8	Starwood Capital Group	$15.7bn
9	AXA Investment Managers – Real Assets	$15.4bn
10	Colony NorthStar	$13.1bn
11	PGIM Real Estate	$14.6bn
12	Global Logistic Properties	$12.7bn
13	Angelo, Gordon & Co.	$12.3bn
14	LaSalle Investment Management	$12.2bn
15	Rockpoint Group	$10.4bn
16	PIMCO	$10.2bn
17	Oaktree Capital Management	$9.2bn
18	AEW Capital Management	$8.7bn
19	Westbrook Partners	$8.4bn
20	Blackrock	$8.3bn

Sources: Preqin, PFR.

estate became common. Later, pan-European pension fund mandates became typical and global multi-manager mandates and global listed/unlisted mandates started to appear. Global Type A funds such as CBRE Global Investors' Global Alpha, a long-life fund of funds and assets, became established with over $5 billion of gross asset value, while global Type B funds managed by firms like Blackstone typically raised $10 billion in equity.

Thanks to the development of these unlisted structures, the standard pension fund mandate has become increasingly global, and investors continue to require the development of more global listed and unlisted funds accessing more and more markets. Emerging markets in particular will offer both diversification and the highest rewards, and unlisted real estate funds play a significant part in this process whereby these markets enter the institutional investment universe.

As a result, these structures often involve complicated cross-border structures which are purpose made and tax effective for certain investor domiciles and types (see Chapter 16). Gearing is common in Type B funds, at levels of up to 60%, both for performance and tax purposes. This type of vehicle carried much of the US-originated 1990s investment in markets such as Eastern Europe and China.

The leading managers shown in Table 11.2 are now truly global, managing nearly $1,150 billion between them, up from $400 billion in 2010.

TABLE 11.2 Managers ranked by value of unlisted vehicles managed (as at July 2019)

	# Unlisted funds	GAV unlisted funds	# Listed funds	GAV listed funds	Total # funds	Total GAV of funds
Blackstone	8	$201,197m	1	$16,973m	9	$218,170m
Nuveen/THRealEstate	58	$64,776m	0	$36,736m	58	$101,512m
Brookfield	18	$82,114m	0	–	18	$82,114m
UBS Global Asset Management	36	$49,803m	11	$31,688m	47	$81,491m
GLP	21	$56,300m	1	$6,400m	22	$62,700m
PGIM	18	$55,469m	8	$4,658m	26	$60,127m
JP Morgan Asset Management – Global Real Assets	10	$58,254m	0	–	10	$58,254m
Starwood Capital Group	2	$33,996m	2	$16,718m	4	$50,714m
Deka Immobilien Investment/ WestInvest	21	$48,462m	0	–	21	$48,462m
Tishman Speyer Properties	16	$46,258m	0	–	16	$46,258m
AXA Investment Managers – Real Assets	102	$40,681m	1	$3,600m	103	$44,281m
Credit Suisse Asset Management	17	$24,441m	30	$18,728m	47	$43,169m
Union Investment	14	$43,123m	0	–	14	$43,123m
CBRE Global Investors*	35	$35,600m	28	$6,000m	63	$41,600m
DWS	5	$38,584m	150	$2,919m	155	$41,503m
AEW Global	72	$36,400m	10	$3,254m	82	$39,654m
Invesco Real Estate	0	$27,465m	18	$9,324m	18	$36,789m
Prologis	2	$24,789m	2	$8,518m	4	$33,307m
Morgan Stanley Real Estate Investing	15	$33,204m	0	–	15	$33,204m
Aberdeen Standard Investments	28	$28,511m	4	$2,957m	32	$31,468m
Clarion Partners	10	$30,316m	0	–	10	$30,316m

* Data from 31 March 2019.
Source: PFR 2019.

11.2 THE GROWTH OF THE UNLISTED REAL ESTATE FUND MARKET

Pension funds and insurance companies typically invest in property to achieve diversification and liability matching (see Chapter 4). Because some of the diversification advantages of real estate will be lost by using liquid securities, unquoted vehicles offer advantages.

Over the period 1998–2007, a change in the investment strategy of pension funds and other professional investors generated an increased investor appetite for global real estate investment. The world's top investors went global, and real estate investment managers facilitated this through the creation of innovative indirect real estate investment solutions.

While the REIT market saw steady growth in the USA and in European and Asian markets as the necessary legislation was passed, it is the universe of unlisted real estate vehicles that grew more dramatically over this period.

11.2.1 The Global Unlisted Property Market Universe

Property Funds Research (PFR)'s estimate of the size of the global unlisted market is around \$2.7 trillion. This accounts for around 8% of all global investable property (see Chapter 1). The largest markets in PFR's vehicle universe are those of continental Europe, the UK, and North America.

In Europe, the number of funds in the PFR universe grew on average by over 20% p.a. over the 10-year period to 2008. Over the same period, gross asset values (GAV) grew by 14% annually in the European market while explosive, albeit more recent, growth was evident in Asia and the emerging markets. This became a truly global phenomenon, which greatly facilitated executable global real estate investment strategies and expanded the investable opportunity set for the benefit of many. Following a slowdown in 2007–10, the unlisted fund universe resumed its impressive growth thereafter: see Figure 11.1.

From 2009 onwards, Asia in particular experienced a boom, as shown in Figure 11.2.

Table 11.3 shows the number of funds launched in each market over the period 1995–2018.

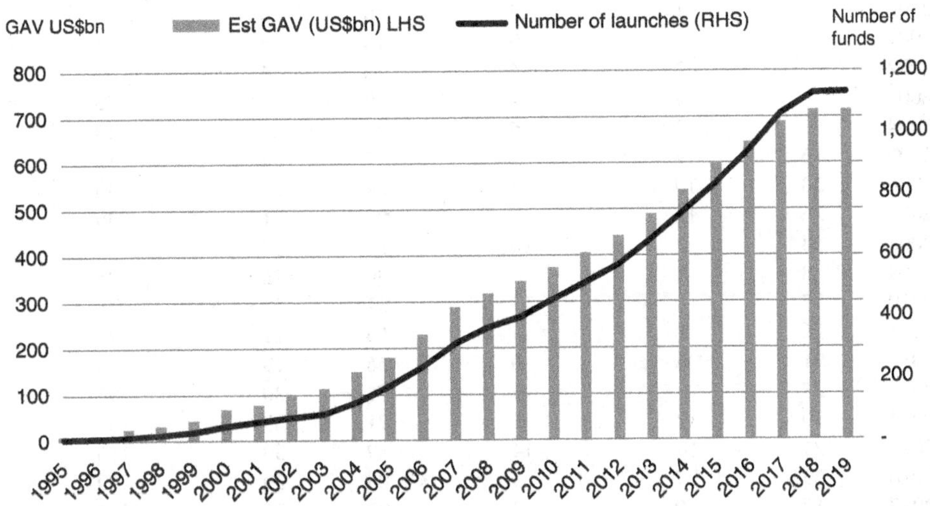

FIGURE 11.1 Europe unlisted market growth (GAV, \$bn)
Source: PFR 2019.

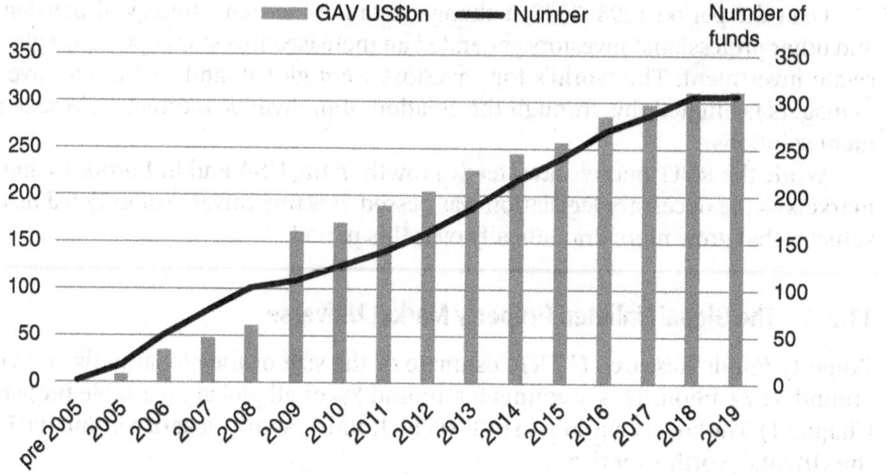

FIGURE 11.2 Asia unlisted market growth (GAV, $bn)
Source: PFR 2019.

TABLE 11.3 Funds launched, 1995–2018

Year	Asia	Australasia	Emerging	Europe	Global	North America
1995		5	1	5	1	1
1996		4	1	3		
1997	1		0	3	1	1
1998		2	0	6	1	4
1999			0	7		1
2000		1	2	18	3	1
2001			0	10	3	1
2002		2	4	16	4	1
2003		4	1	9	1	3
2004	1	3	5	33	7	13
2005	16	9	1	45	14	11
2006	33	10	5	64	24	40
2007	26	12	10	80	41	49
2008	24	2	10	57	39	48
2009	8	3	6	36	25	25
2010	15	7	15	61	23	48
2011	16	1	5	55	21	76
2012	21	6	6	56	19	83
2013	25	3	9	75	30	93
2014	30	12	8	71	39	103
2015	24	10	14	89	30	116
2016	29	7	3	88	29	109
2017	17	9	3	97	26	103
2018	20	1	1	49	10	60
Total	306	113	110	1,033	391	990

Source: PFR 2019.

11.2.2 How Much Global Real Estate is in Unlisted Funds?

The value of global commercial real estate owned by institutional investors was estimated to be around $35 trillion by PFR in 2019 (see Chapter 1). This is the investable stock, meaning stock that is of sufficient quality to be acquired by an institutional investor. The $35 trillion investable stock of real estate can be broken down to the regional level and further disaggregated by ownership structure (see Table 11.4).

Publicly available REIT and property company market capitalisation data has been used and grossed up as shown to reflect the use of debt in the capital structure of the typical listed company. This represents around $4.5 trillion, or 13% of the global market gross asset value.

PFR estimates that of the much less mature unlisted real estate fund market of $2.7 trillion, around 8% of the investable stock, Europe (including the UK) represents the biggest component, holding around 32% of the global unlisted fund market by value (see Table 11.5).

TABLE 11.4 The global real estate investment universe

Region	Asia	Australasia	Europe	UK	Latin America	Middle East/ Africa	North America	Total
Investible stock	$11,490bn	$730bn	$8,453bn	$1,591bn	$1,627bn	$1,537bn	$9,992bn	$35,420bn
Listed universe	$2,354bn	$146bn	$736bn	$175bn	$102bn	$193bn	$850bn	$4,556bn
Unlisted universe	$346bn	$186bn	$710bn	$176bn	$55bn	$14bn	$1,261bn	$2,748bn
Direct market	$8,790bn	$397bn	$7,007bn	$1,240bn	$1,470bn	$1,329bn	$7,882bn	$28,116bn

Sources: PFR, PGIM, IMF and EPRA 2019.

TABLE 11.5 PFR's unlisted fund vehicle universe

Region	Estimated GAV	# Funds
Asia	$312,588m	308
Australasia	$129,038m	121
Europe (ex UK)	$680,704m	984
Global (pan-region)	$807,172m	396
Latin America	$29,389m	77
Middle East/Africa	$10,465m	36
North America	$883,518m	1016
UK	$143,232m	228
Total	**$2,996,108m**	**3,166**

Source: PFR 2019.

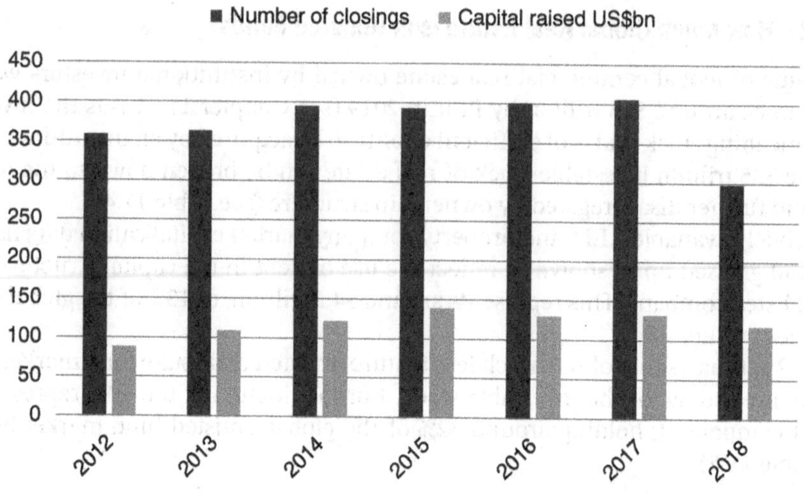

FIGURE 11.3 Private equity real estate capital raised, global, 2012–18
Source: Preqin 2018.

The majority (47% by number) of the unlisted funds in the PFR database are diversified. Debt (11%), residential (10%), and retail (6%) are the most popular sectors. The fund market is over-represented relative to direct property indexes in residential and 'other' real estate, including healthcare, student housing, and infrastructure.

Sponsors of private equity funds raise capital from an increasingly wide range of investors and in substantial quantities. Figure 11.3 shows the total amount of capital raised globally by private equity real estate funds between 2012 and 2018. In 2017, for example, $132 billion was raised by 406 funds.

11.3 UNLISTED FUND STRUCTURES

Being unlisted means there is no requirement to be public, so unlisted fund data can be hard to find. INREV (the European Association for Investors in Non-listed Real Estate Vehicles) and sister organisation ANREV (the Asian Association for Investors in Non-listed Real Estate Vehicles) track the market and promote best practice, while there are a few private information sources including Preqin and PERE, aimed primarily at the higher-risk opportunity fund (Type B) sector.

There are three popular legal structures in use globally. These are: (i) companies; (ii) partnerships; and (iii) trusts. These fund types are all supported by the general body of law relevant to each. In addition, contractual agreements, backed by a special law (in Germany, the KAGG and, later, the KAGB), are especially common in Germany, France, and Luxembourg.

Type A real estate funds are often open-ended, while higher-risk Type B funds are typically closed-ended limited-life structures. Liquidity is the key issue which defines the relevant structure. A REIT or listed fund can usually be traded quickly on a major stock exchange, but an unlisted fund cannot. Investors in unlisted funds need to know how they can get their money back, and how much they will receive.

In the absence of an active secondary market for units in unlisted funds, which appears from time to time but cannot generally be relied upon, the open-ended fund appears to guarantee 'redemption' of capital by the manager at something close to net asset value. In the absence of this, closed-ended funds need to have a termination date at which point all assets can be sold and capital returned.

Roughly twice as many funds by value are closed-ended rather than open-ended (over 70% by number). Around one-third of live funds by value are closed to new investment (this is the proportion of the closed-ended universe comprised of funds which have completed capital raising).

11.3.1 Open-Ended Funds

Some funds operate as open-ended funds, allowing investments and dispositions (redemptions) at any time. They also have an indefinite life. Unlike other private equity investments, there is a modicum of liquidity in open-ended private equity funds. This liquidity is provided through redemptions, often after an initial lockup period.

The redemption price is determined based on the value of all properties owned by the fund, typically appraised on a quarterly basis. Investors in open-ended funds will often seek to redeem when returns are expected to deteriorate, and in a declining market investors will seek redemption at the last quarterly price, which has not yet fully reflected the downturn in the industry. Hence the open-ended structure can be fatally flawed in 'one-way' markets, where there is a large preponderance of sellers. Also problematic is a market where there is a fashion for investors to try to get invested in these funds, such as happened in the UK in 2006–7. A rush of buyers can flood the manager with cash, thereby diluting the real estate return delivered by the fund or encouraging panic buying, damaging the manager's performance.

While no such restrictions typically apply in Europe, a US open-ended fund will usually be required to fund redemption requests out of income earned on the underlying property, and not through sales of property. To the extent that earned income is insufficient to fund redemption requests, prospective sellers of units or shares in US funds must queue up behind others who have asked to redeem shares and only when income is sufficient will they get their capital back. In a hot real estate market, queues will similarly form to get in to these funds.

This US Type A universe is usually defined as the NCREIF ODCE (Open-Ended Diversified Core Equity) universe. These open-ended funds are generally defined as infinite-life vehicles consisting of multiple investors who have the ability to enter or exit the fund on a periodic basis, subject to contribution and/or redemption requests. The 'Diversified Core Equity' style typically reflects lower-risk investment strategies utilising low leverage, and the constituent funds are usually invested in equity positions in stabilised US operating properties diversified across regions and property types.

The property unit trust or PAIF (property authorised investment fund) is the main open-ended vehicle used by pension funds to gain access to diversified portfolios of UK real estate, in a form that allows replication of direct market performance characteristics. It is unlisted, unit prices are determined by valuation, and liquidity is limited to a small amount of secondary market trading activity and the guarantee that managers will buy and sell units, albeit at spreads which replicate the cost of buying and selling property direct.

Property unit trusts are tax free for qualifying pension funds. While they have to invest in domestic property to protect this status, they can be established offshore to appeal to international investors.

The UK open-ended fund came under fire in late 2007: see Box 11.3 later.

11.3.2 Closed-Ended Funds

Closed-ended funds are more prevalent in the private equity industry, and they inhabit the higher-risk end of the real estate fund spectrum (Type B). A closed-ended fund raises capital from investors before investments are made, and generally prescribes a specific investment period and fund termination period. The investment period could be 3 years, for example, during which time the sponsor (manager) would attempt to place all committed capital into real estate investments. Once the investment period is over, the fund usually has another 3–5 years before the termination period expires, at which time the fund must distribute all cash flows (including sales receipts) back to investors. Specific investment periods and termination periods can be extended by a vote of the limited partners.

After the initial fundraising process, additional funds are not raised from new or existing investors, and liquidity is not available to investors in the form of redemptions or an active secondary market for shares or units, although stakes will usually be tradable on a matched bargain basis.

Most private equity funds in the USA are formed as limited partnerships or limited liability corporations (LLCs), and the most common form of closed-ended fund globally is the limited partnership. In partnerships and LLCs, the fund sponsor serves as the general partner (GP) or manager, and the investors are limited partners. The fund sponsor or GP usually has total control over all management activities of the fund, and the limited partners are passive investors. While a GP would typically incur unlimited liability for the activities of the fund, in most cases the fund sponsor will set up a shell corporation with the sole purpose of being the GP for a specific private equity fund which helps to limit liability. Limited partners have limited liability by definition and theoretically cannot lose more than their original investment.

Limited partnerships are tax-neutral or tax-transparent vehicles, meaning that the vehicle itself does not attract tax, and partners are treated exactly as if they owned the assets of the limited partnership directly. This creates an enormous advantage for the vehicle, which has become increasingly popular as the standard vehicle for co-mingled property ownership.

It is common practice that limited partnerships have a predetermined lifespan, usually between 6 and 10 years. There is a statement of intent, when the partnerships are established, that at the end of the period the partnership will be wound up and the assets disposed of, although this need not be the case if the partners vote to extend the vehicle life.

In establishing the pool of capital required, the GP may appoint a promoter to raise capital from limited partners; in some cases, the promoter may be the originator of the concept and seek a GP to act as lead investor. Limited partners will contribute capital and may form an advisory board, but cannot be seen to be making decisions without losing their limited liability status.

In recent years, limited partners have been faced with an interesting test of limited liability. Many of the 2005–8 vintage real estate private equity funds invested in property with high loan-to-value ratios with relatively short maturities at the peak of the cycle. As properties lost value during the credit crisis, the loans matured and sponsors were forced to refinance or sell properties. With lower property values, the amount that could be refinanced fell short of the remaining balance of the maturing loan. Further, since property values had fallen, sales proceeds would have fallen short of the balance on the maturing loans. Therefore, to retain ownership and not default, sponsors would have to inject capital into each of the properties. In many cases, the sponsors would offer investors the 'opportunity' to invest more capital to cover the equity requirements on the refinanced loan through a fund recapitalisation. To the extent that this increased the equity stake above the initial capital contribution, and that the total capital was at risk, the total loss could be greater than the amount initially invested at the start of the fund.

The first private equity funds were extremely successful in generating large returns for investors, and they are still active in the market. While firms that got into trouble have had a hard time, those with a track record of performance have an easier time returning to the market to raise subsequent funds. They can point to their success in sourcing and analysing deals, managing transactions to maximise income and value, and a record of providing strong returns to investors.

11.3.3 Funds of Funds

There are several ways in which investors choose to invest in unlisted funds. Investors may select a single diversified fund; they can use advisors or an in-house team to select specialist funds; they may appoint a discretionary manager to select a group of specialist funds (this is called a multi-manager mandate); or they may invest in a fund of funds.

The multi-manager and fund of funds models are highly appropriate for pension funds without expert in-house teams. A fund of funds is a wrapper placed around other wrappers (the underlying real estate funds). As in a multi-manager mandate, two sets of fees are charged: one by the fund of funds manager, and a second by the managers of the underlying funds. The fund of funds manager needs to justify the additional layer of fees, either by the additional diversification and risk reduction produced by the strategy, or by its skill in identifying and sourcing excellent underlying funds, by negotiating lower fees with the underlying fund managers, or any combination of these.

The first large real estate fund of funds was launched in the early 2000s, and this market grew rapidly before falling back when investors responded to poor performance in 2006–9. After the global financial crisis (GFC) it became fashionable to take back control by forming investor clubs or employing in-house staff. At the end of 2019, PFR held data on over 65 real estate fund of funds products, down from 120 in 2009.

11.4 CHARACTERISTICS OF UNLISTED REAL ESTATE FUNDS

Funds are differentiated by many factors. Competing to attract capital from investors, private equity funds offer different strategies and investment terms, as well as different management fees and profit-sharing arrangements. This section outlines the key differences that can exist across funds.

11.4.1 Style

As with any other asset class, there is a broad range of opportunities within which to invest. Some opportunities exhibit low levels of risk, or uncertainty of outcome, while others exhibit higher levels of risk. A general hierarchy of risk and return in real estate and for private equity real estate funds in particular is shown in Figure 11.4.

Some industry participants have distinguished funds using four styles: core, core-plus, value-add, and opportunity. The European trade body, INREV, recommends three styles: core, value-add, and opportunistic. This classification system has become the industry standard, although there is an increasingly strong case for simplifying this again and distinguishing Type A – lower risk, core/core-plus – from Type B – higher risk, value-added/opportunity.

Core funds are low-risk funds with no or low gearing, often open-ended, and should aim to closely replicate returns on the relevant index of direct real estate. Core funds invest in well-located buildings that are highly occupied, often in 'gateway' cities with large populations and employment levels. A core fund will often be restricted to investing with no or low leverage.

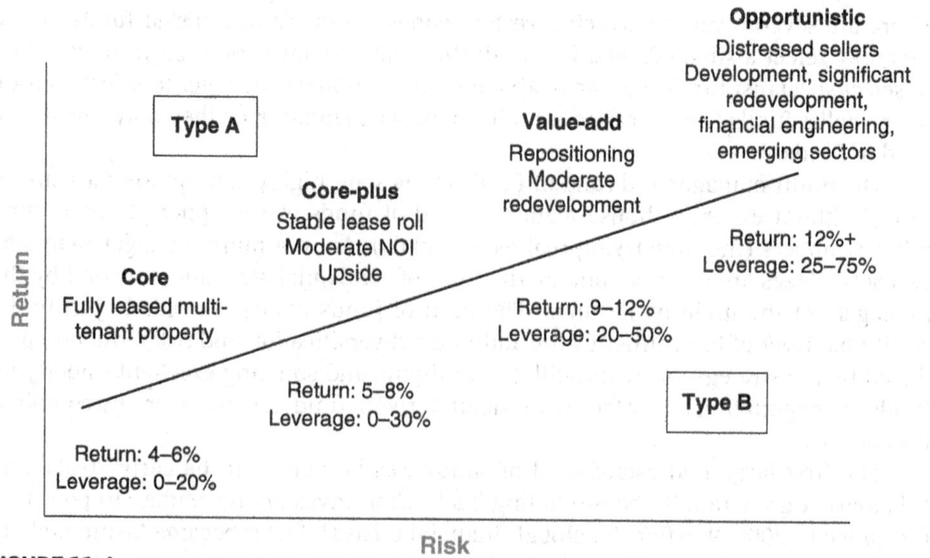

FIGURE 11.4 Unlisted real estate fund styles

Core-plus funds take a little more risk than core funds, usually by incurring a little more lease-up risk, buying properties that are at 90% occupancy or lower, for example, and hoping to increase occupancy rates, or by minor refurbishment.

Value-add funds invest in properties that exhibit risk but have the potential to earn high returns. An example of a value-add investment is a property that has been under-managed or has a relatively high current vacancy rate due to mismanagement and/or obsolescence. The value-add fund that buys the property may plan capital expenditure to improve the property to the current market standard, and/or bring in a more efficient management team to improve cash flows with more professional leasing and a reduction in operating expenses. The typical value-add strategy is often known as 'buy–fix–sell'. In addition, these funds usually allow a higher degree of leverage than core or core-plus funds.

Opportunistic funds make investments in properties, companies, or other structures that exhibit the highest degree of complexity or risk in the spectrum, but also offer the highest potential for return. These funds typically employ high degrees of leverage, which increases financial risk and the volatility of cash flows. They might also focus on development or redevelopment, taking on the risk of bringing speculative space to the market.

Opportunity funds experienced rapid growth between 2000 and 2003, but value-add funds then emerged as the style of choice. The majority of funds launched between 2005 and 2008 were value-added. As competition to place capital into real estate investments increased during the 2000–7 period, required rates of return on funds decreased without a corresponding decrease in the risk taken. In the early part of the period, core funds were targeting between 8% and 10%, value-add funds were targeting 18–20%, and opportunistic funds were targeting returns that exceeded 20%. In the latter part of the period, as prices increased across all sectors, targeted returns dropped to 6–8%, 12–15%, and 15% plus for the core, value-add, and opportunistic funds, respectively.

By 2019 the continuing low interest rate environment had suppressed target returns in the major markets even further, to (say) 4–8% for Type A funds, and 9–12% and above for Type B value-add and opportunistic funds.

11.4.2 Investment Restrictions

The vehicles in PFR's universe have a variety of investment restrictions aimed at limiting the risk of a particular portfolio of investments. Diversified funds may be permitted to invest between 30% and 50% of GAV in a particular sector. Pan-European funds may have prescribed limits on the countries in which they can invest, which may be anywhere between 30% and 50% of GAV in each country. Development is limited to anywhere between 10% and 30% of GAV, depending on fund style. There is likely to be some kind of investment restriction based on the amount invested in any single asset, typically in the region of 15% of GAV. Similarly, income restrictions are likely to be placed on a fund. Income derived from a single tenant/company is typically limited to around 15% of GAV.

11.4.3 Property Sector and Geographic Focus

To attract investors, some funds elect to target a specific property type or geographical focus where they can demonstrate expertise. A sponsor with a successful track record in the multi-family sector, for example, would raise funds from investors with the intent to develop and/or own multi-family assets. The investors gain the expertise of the sponsor, and earn returns as earned by the assets in the fund. Similar strategies are undertaken in the office, retail, industrial, and hotel sectors. Other funds take a broader approach and invest across all property types, providing a diversified portfolio within the real estate asset class.

In a similar way, some funds focus their investment and development activity on a specific region where they have gained some expertise. By focusing on a fast-growing region, an investor could hope to outperform the overall real estate market. By investing in the fund of an experienced sponsor, the investor could gain access to investments outside of the local markets, and by investing in several geographically focused funds an investor could create a diversified portfolio.

Figure 11.5 shows that Type A funds tend to be the style of choice for the more developed markets of the UK, continental Europe, and Australasia, while Type B funds are a more significant proportion of all funds in the USA and developing markets.

PFR also records permitted gearing based on the level of debt in a vehicle as a percentage of GAV. Funds have permitted gearing levels ranging up to 85%, although typical gearing levels are far more conservative than this. Gearing levels average 20% for core funds, 35% for value-add funds, and around 40% for opportunity funds.

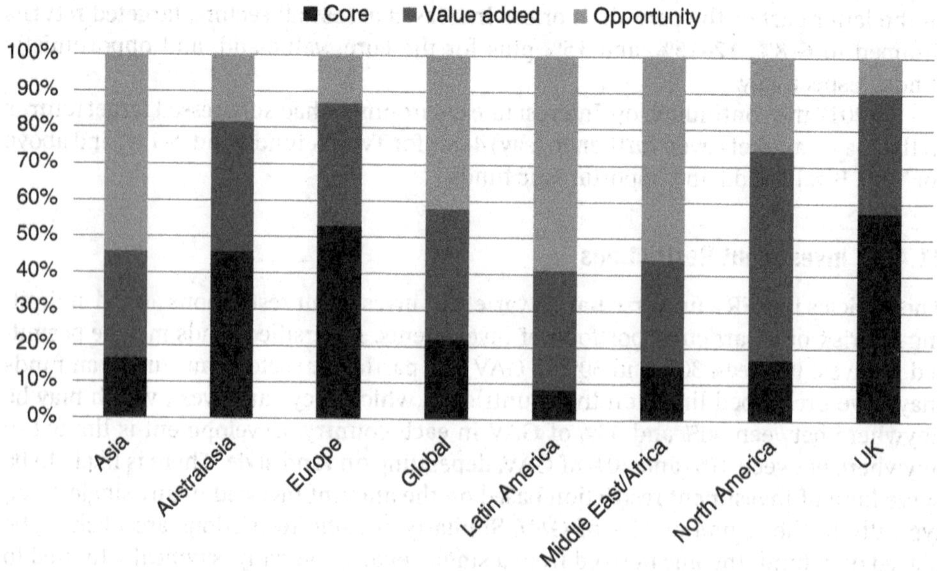

FIGURE 11.5 Vehicle style by regional focus
Source: PFR 2019.

11.5 LIQUIDITY AND VALUATION ISSUES

11.5.1 Liquidity

The lumpy, illiquid nature of real estate as an asset class means that indirect investment may be an appealing alternative. However, liquidity in unlisted funds is generally limited. Open-ended funds offer monthly, quarterly, or annual redemptions, although sometimes with an initial lock-up period of 3 or 4 years, in which case the term 'semi open-ended' may be appropriate. Following the example provided by the relatively mature UK market, there is an increasingly active secondary market in European closed-ended funds and this may develop in international markets. Nonetheless, closed-ended funds generally offer little liquidity.

Given that unlisted funds are not stock market traded, an alternative mechanism is needed to provide this liquidity. The key issue is whether the fund is open-ended, semi-open-ended, or closed-ended.

Open-ended fund units can (in principle, at least) be redeemed on demand, and new investors will normally be allowed and encouraged to buy new units. In some markets, though not typically in the USA, the manager will issue units at net asset value (NAV) plus an allowance for the costs of buying new properties with the new cash (the offer price), and will undertake to return capital to the investor at the latest NAV estimate less a deduction for trading costs (the bid price). (Technically, the NAV is adjusted to offer price by adding real estate acquisition costs and offer is reduced to bid by deducting the round-trip costs of buying and selling real estate.) In the USA, the typical mechanism involves no bid–offer spread.

Semi-open-ended funds will have a 'lock-up' period, typically up to 5 years, during which investors are not allowed to redeem units and after which limited redemptions will be permitted.

Open-ended and semi-open-ended funds can have infinite lives, and this is an obvious attraction for managers. Closed-ended funds, in contrast, have a limited number of units in issue at any time (hence the term) and do not have a redemption facility, so that investors are reliant upon secondary market trading, which – with some notable exceptions – may be thin or non-existent. The manager of a closed-ended fund is therefore forced to offer a termination date at which investors can force assets to be sold and capital returned. This is typically 6–10 years from launch.

The open-ended structure can benefit from twin liquidity mechanisms. Investors can redeem units in return for cash from the manager at a given bid price relative to NAV, but may also be able to sell units in the secondary market for a higher price. Equally, new investors will not subscribe for new units if they can buy units for less than the offer price in the secondary market.

Where there is a balance of buyers and sellers, buyers and sellers will deal directly with each other at something close to mid-price (halfway between bid and offer), and the bid–offer spread imposed by the manager is not justified because there is no need to undertake any direct real estate trading to grow or reduce the real estate portfolio. The manager may then wish to orchestrate a secondary market, either in search of broking fees or to offer a service to investors and to maximise the market appeal of the fund.

However, the open-ended structure can be fatally flawed in 'one-way' markets. If a majority of investors feels that the time is right to sell real estate units, this may be for either or both of two reasons. First, investors may feel that the units are fairly priced but that the future market return will be relatively unattractive. Second, investors may feel that the units are over-priced and will wish to exploit a pricing anomaly by selling. On several occasions, with the UK in late 2007 and June 2016 being the latest examples, these two factors combined to create a crisis.

In 1990, Rodamco, then an open-ended Netherlands fund, was forced to close its doors to prevent investors from exiting. In 2005, German open-ended funds suffered a large exodus of investors, forcing an immediate revaluation and audit of one large fund and the risk of its closure through mass withdrawals. Following this, the pricing of German open-ended funds was publicly debated, new regulations were introduced, fraud was discovered in two cases, and questions about investor protection were raised openly. In 2007, in the UK, a weakening real estate market was coupled with the predictable conservatism of valuers reluctant to mark prices down without clear evidence, with strong external evidence in the derivatives and REIT markets of much lower real estate prices. The September quarter-end valuation of most open-ended funds was too high. Professional investors, primarily fund of funds managers, wished to exploit this anomaly by selling over-valued units in open-ended funds. The reaction of several open-ended fund managers was to defer redemptions and reduce the valuation retrospectively, thereby preventing investors from exiting at valuation (see Box 11.3 later). In June 2016, the UK Brexit vote created an immediate market lock-up. Within days of the vote, several funds had suspended redemptions, opening again within a month. As the Brexit crisis dragged on in 2019, another fund suspended redemptions. See Box 11.1.

Box 11.1: Innovations in Fund Structures

The launch of the International Property Securities Exchange (IPSX) in London in 2019 promised a primary and secondary market for units or shares in single properties. At the same time, a fashion for the tokenisation (digital fractionalisation or unitisation) of single assets – and potentially funds – was also gathering strength, although no serious business was yet being done. London had a reasonably successful set of listed and unlisted property fund structures to work with, but a limited range of onshore structures authorised for sale to the non-professional investor. There was a growing risk that inappropriate offshore structures with light investor protection might begin to damage the credibility of the industry.

It was strongly believed that as a leading global centre for real estate investment, London and the UK should be able to provide investors and managers with a full range of appropriately regulated fund vehicles. This range includes listed REITs and unlisted funds, with the latter either open-ended or closed-ended.

Investor protection requires that managers are regulated, but also that the vehicles they promote are fit for purpose. This requires that the funds will be capable of returning capital to investors in an orderly way. The dominant form of lower-risk UK property fund had hitherto been open-ended, as the return of capital is ensured via the manager making a market (issuing new units and redeeming existing units). This mechanism has been found wanting in periods of market stress (2007–8 in the USA and UK and June 2016 in the UK provide good examples). Nevertheless, this format has its place, and a secondary market for units has become well established, providing a second way for investors to redeem capital.

Closed-ended funds – ones for which a manager will not make a market, and where the number of units in issue at any time is a fixed amount determined by the initial capital raised – are also commonly traded on the same secondary market. But – in the UK – they are not authorised for sale to the public. This is presumably because of concerns about liquidity, as the depth of the secondary market is limited. For some closed-ended products, there may be no liquidity – indeed, the fund documentation (usually a limited partnership agreement or LPA) may inhibit sales or impose limitations such as pre-emption rights. This is not a matter of great concern where the investors are focused on a value-add strategy with a specific maturity and the fund has a limited life, necessitating the sale of all fund assets after say 5 or 7 years. However, investors and managers will prefer the option of a longer-life closed-ended product.

For several reasons, by 2019 it was felt by industry groups – including AREF (the Association of Real Estate Funds) – that the time had come to modernise, standardise, and regulate a form of tax-transparent closed-ended fund. The reasons are as follows:

1. Identical, but in the UK unregulated, products are commonplace and established in offshore jurisdictions. It would be better to bring these onshore.
2. Technical innovations, in particular the development of websites and phone apps, has made possible the development of highly efficient secondary markets for all things, and it is to be expected that a standardised closed-ended property fund format freed from the trading limitations that are currently typical will quickly develop its own secondary market liquidity.
3. The world is awash with talk of tokenisation, in effect, informal, unregulated secondary markets for single assets and closed-ended funds. It would be preferable by far to create a regulated framework for a superior and standardised form of such offerings.
4. Investor protection in the event of disappointing liquidity is possible via limited life or, for an evergreen product, a standardised mechanism to ensure the sale of the fund's assets in the event of a majority vote with minority protection.

The AREF submission on a new UK closed-ended real estate fund was being prepared at the time of writing.

11.5.2 Valuation

As the secondary market trading of funds has begun to grow, pricing of these units has begun to take place at discounts and premiums to net asset value. This challenges market convention, as – unlike REITs which trade in the stock market at market-determined prices in real time – unlisted funds are priced by reference to market valuations. For higher-risk Type B funds, valuations may be irregular and unimportant, as investors expect to see a return of capital within 3–7 years and interim valuations may not be helpful where development or other value-adding activity is the key focus of the fund. For low-risk Type A funds with longer or indefinite lives, regular valuation is a more accurate and necessary indicator of the manager's progress, and monthly valuations are not uncommon, so secondary market premiums and discounts can appear to challenge the published valuation.

11.6 THE CASE FOR AND AGAINST UNLISTED REAL ESTATE FUNDS

11.6.1 The Case for Unlisted Real Estate Funds

Unlisted Real Estate Funds can Diversify Real Estate-Specific Risk

A lot of money is needed to build a diversified real estate portfolio. The capital investment required to mimic the performance of a real estate index depends on both the efficiency of diversification within the segment and the average lot size within each segment. Investors with higher levels of risk aversion require more capital investment in real estate segments in order to reduce the specific risk component of the portfolio to the desired level.

For example, Baum and Struempell (2006) found that over £1 billion is needed to build a diversified portfolio of London offices with a 2% tracking error. This presents a very strong case for using an unlisted fund focused on London offices. Assuming that such a fund is financed by 50% debt and 50% equity, 20 investors committing £25 million each will produce enough capital to achieve the diversified fund. Yet the investor's £25 million is enough to buy only one or two London offices of average lot size. For more on this issue, see also Baum and Colley (2017).

Unlisted Funds are Priced by Reference to NAV

The above argument could also be used to justify investments in listed property securities. However, the pricing of listed REITs and property companies will differ from real estate prices, and in the short to medium term (0–5 years) this will distort the performance of securities relative to the underlying real estate market. Since 1990, US REITs have traded at discounts and premiums varying from −35% (in 1991) to +30% (in 1997), and hit these levels again in 2009 (discount) and 2010 (premium). At the end of 2018, US REITs were trading at an 18% discount.

In contrast, open-ended Type A funds appear to track real estate NAVs. This could be highly misleading. Appraisal-based returns on core funds will track appraisal-based returns on the index, but this does not show how secondary market trading prices track the index. This became a problematic issue in 2007–8, as described later in Box 11.3.

Unlisted Funds Provide Access to Specialist Managers

It is likely to be the case that specialist managers, meaning experts in a market sector or a specific geography, will produce better performance than a manager or investor located in a single market but attempting to buy and manage assets globally. PFR global data shows that the majority of closed-ended unlisted funds are typically focused on a geography (India, London) and sector (shopping centres, London offices). Good fund and manager selection can lead to the holy grail of lower risk and higher returns.

11.6.2 The Case Against Unlisted Real Estate Funds

Investing in unlisted funds suffers from four key challenges. First, cash may not be taken immediately by the discretionary manager, fund of funds, or selected fund(s). This produces a slow expected cash drawdown profile and an 'agency problem' (a conflict of interest arising between investors and managers because of differing goals). Second, the initial performance will be coloured by the costs involved in the manager buying the initial portfolio, producing what is known as the J-curve effect. Third, manager fees can challenge thoughtful investors. Finally, trading prices may not track NAV, even for open-ended funds.

The Drawdown Profile

Managers will not wish to draw cash immediately for a variety of reasons, the key issue being their desire to deliver real estate returns not coloured by cash, and the potential for the manager to maximise IRR-based performance fees (see Chapter 12). Hence cash is drawn from investors as and when it is needed to complete the purchase of assets. The result is a delay in the investor being able to attain full exposure. See Box 11.2 for a potential solution to this.

Box 11.2: Evergreen Property Funds

Tristan Capital Partners (€7.5bn AUM) has its roots in Curzon Global Partners, a joint venture between real estate advisors DTZ (now Cushman and Wakefield) and American fund manager AEW, who were looking to establish a European platform in 1998 and felt they needed a London partner to do so.

Curzon's original business focused on Type A real estate, and the Curzon fund series is now regarded by the firm as a core-plus franchise. Having launched four closed-ended European core-plus funds (Curzon Capital Partners I, II, III in 2011 and IV in 2014), Tristan and its investors decided in 2016–7 that Fund V should adopt a different format. Investors were impressed by the speed of investment and

(continued)

(*continued*)

asset disposal achieved by the firm, driven by an orientation towards IRR-based performance rewards, yet frustrated by the rhythm of capital deployment (delayed drawdowns and the early return of capital), which meant that they were not fully invested in real estate for as long as they wished. Tristan, meanwhile, was reluctant to engage in a continual series of fundraising exercises for core-plus business when they were also raising for a value-add series. Both sides felt that this was not the most efficient way to achieve long-term exposure to core-plus real estate in Europe. So an exercise was launched to fund the best alternative.

Open-ended funds in European real estate were interesting, but Tristan felt that the legal and tax structure of these vehicles was usually set up to favour domestic investors (UK pension funds in European funds set up by UK managers, German pension funds in European funds set up by German managers, and so on). In addition, open-ended real estate funds with a UK origin used bid–offer spreads to manage entry and exit while US managers used NAV pricing and the ODCE queuing system. Tristan was aware that Blackstone had launched its first core-plus fund real estate in the USA using the ODCE type of structure, and was planning to repeat this model in Europe, with its fund due to launch in 2018.

Meanwhile, semi-open-ended funds had been used by J.P. Morgan and others in European real estate, and the perpetual or evergreen nature of hedge funds was seen as an efficient structure for managers.

Tristan decided to set up a perpetual or evergreen fund, using the ODCE type of entry and exit queuing method, but on a semi-open-ended basis initially so that the founding investors – who would have priority rights thereafter – were locked up (could not redeem) for an initial period. After 10 years, investors could vote to wind up the fund by forcing its conversion to a closed-ended limited life structure, but if they failed to do this the fund would continue indefinitely.

Investors subscribe to a UK LP, a familiar and tax-transparent structure, but the fund has a sub-structure in the form of a Luxembourg Reserved Alternative Investment Fund, or RAIF. This gives Tristan the flexibility to move the structure to Luxembourg if the UK becomes unatttactive to European pension plans from a regulatory stance.

Tristan succesfully raised an initial €1bn for this fund in 2017–8.

Gearing and the J-curve Effect

The performance of an allocation to unlisted funds will also be damaged in the short term by the costs involved in buying the initial portfolio. The result can be poor short-term performance. In the early years, newly launched funds' performance can be negative relative to the direct real estate index, because $100 million invested in a fund will, depending on the level of transaction costs, be immediately converted into (say) $95 million. (This is no different when buying in the direct market, of course.) After fund costs are amortised, it is hoped that unlisted funds can outperform the direct market to recover the lost ground, and gearing is one mechanism used to achieve the desired result.

Hence the typical closed-ended fund, whether core or value-add is likely to be geared and adjustments will need to be applied to the direct real estate risk, return, and correlation data which encouraged the original decision to invest in real estate. A financial structure of 50% equity and 50% debt means that half of the required investment only is needed to attain the same exposure. This increases the appeal and efficiency of unlisted vehicles even more, but unfortunately this factor carries with it financial risk, which to some extent will offset the reduction in specific risk.

It is known that gearing increases risk and volatility. It also makes performance more responsive to interest rates and the bond market, depending on whether the interest rate is fixed or floating. Debt will alter the cash flow, and will typically affect the investor's cash on cash return or net income return on equity (see Chapter 9).

In summary, the risk of a geared fund is likely to be higher than the risk of an ungeared fund. Hence, the price of specific risk reduction achieved by unlisted vehicles may be higher volatility introduced by gearing – albeit sometimes balanced by higher prospective returns (see Alcock *et al.*, 2013).

Fees and Performance Persistence

Fees charged by the manager of a real estate fund (or a fund of funds) will usually be charged on an annual *ad valorem* basis, typically between 50 and 150 bps every year in the UK (and 100 to 300 bps in the USA) on a hopefully growing gross asset value, despite the fact that much of the manager's activity is front-loaded. In addition, performance fees may be charged and related to absolute returns or returns relative to an index. Often, the use of high gearing will mean that the manager has increased the risk profile of real estate investing but, to the extent that this delivers extra returns, will be paid for the risks taken with client's capital. These issues are challenging for managers to justify: see Chapter 17.

In addition, double fees charged in funds of funds may be hard for clients to swallow. Managers need to be able to justify the additional fee layer by proven added diversification and risk reduction, or alternatively by the provision of expert access to outperforming managers at a reduced cost. Evidence of this is elusive, as is any evidence that good performance is persistent. Aarts and Baum (2016) found strong evidence for performance persistence across directly consecutive funds, but little support for a relationship between the performance of other prior funds and the current fund, suggesting that performance persistence is a short-term phenomenon.

Do Trading Prices Track NAV?

A large component of the case for unlisted real estate funds, as argued above, is that unlisted funds are priced by reference to NAV and can therefore be expected to deliver property-style performance, whereas REITs and listed property companies exhibit volatility and correlation with equities. But the events of 2007–8, described in Box 11.3, call this into question.

Box 11.3: Pricing an Open-Ended Fund in Late 2007

It is mid-2007, the peak of a bull market for property, and we are working for a UK open-ended fund. The fund is valued monthly by a well-known chartered surveying practice/property services provider. The valuation instruction is to estimate the asset value of the properties in the fund; any adjustments needed to estimate the fund NAV are usually undertaken simply as an accounting function, dealing with the addition of cash holdings and the deduction of debt.

From January 2007 to June 2007, the IPD monthly index had been showing positive capital growth of between 0.27% and 0.46% for each of the 6 months of the first half of the year (see Figure 11.6). The fund also showed positive NAV growth.

In the summer of 2007, there was a change in market sentiment. This was evidenced by some circulars from fund managers to their clients warning of poor returns to come. It was reflected to some extent in the IPD monthly index, which produced its last positive total return of the cycle in July, disguising a tiny fall in capital value of 0.22%, followed by a negative capital return in August of 0.4%, marking a turning point in retrospect – yet hardly indicative of a crash.

The fund's values were flat over this period, as they were through the end of September. However, the IPD monthly index for September had taken a more significant downward turn of over 1.5%, a figure which was not available to the valuer of the fund's properties at the time the September valuation was produced. The effect of this was that the fund's values stayed flat over the summer quarter, while the IPD monthly index fell by over 2% for the quarter.

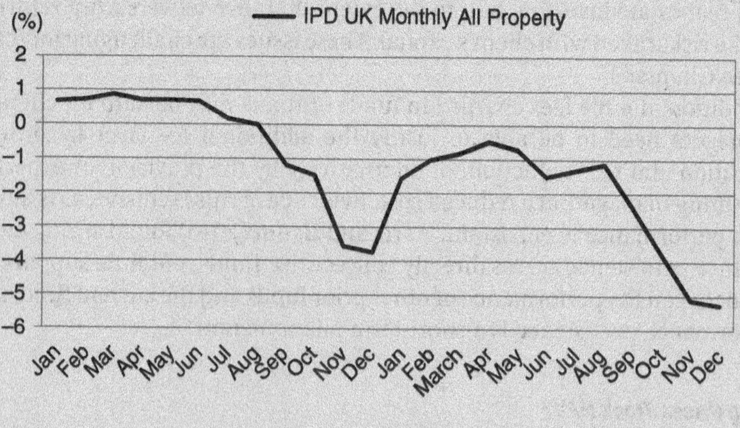

FIGURE 11.6 IPD UK monthly index, monthly total returns, 2007–8
Source: IPD.

Open-ended fund units can be redeemed on demand, and in the UK typically have quarterly redemptions. The quarter-end NAV is important, as it sets the bid and offer price. For example, the relevant data for the fund might be as follows:

- The fund's NAV is £995.05 million. The number of units in issue is 19,082,778. The NAV per share is £995.05 million/19,082,778 = £52.15.
- The offer price – the price paid by an investor on entry – is set at NAV plus 4.75% = £52.15 * 1.0475 = £54.63.
- The bid price – the price received by an investor on exit – is set at offer price less 6.25% = £54.63 * 0.9375 = £51.21.
- The bid–offer spread = (offer – bid)/offer = (£54.63 – £51.21)/£54.63 = 6.25%.
- Mid price = (bid + offer)/2 = (£54.63 + £51.21)/2 = £52.92.

In mid-October 2007, the fund's manager found itself in a 'challenging' position. Market sentiment had clearly changed. The UK REIT market had moved to huge discounts to NAV, moving downwards from a small premium in March 2007 to a discount touching 20% in September 2007. Meanwhile, the fund's NAV had stayed flat over the summer. Unlisted funds in general were in a strange position – secondary trading had dried up as the market sought a new price level. Only by November had the re-pricing become evident.

Professional investors could see a clear arbitrage opportunity, and were prompted to exploit it. They served redemption notices effective at the end of September, expecting to be paid out at the NAV-based bid price. This was broadly the same as it had been in June, at the peak of the market, but by October values were clearly falling. The manager was faced with the prospect of selling properties in a very weak market for prices which would clearly not be as high as the September NAV.

This might be a fair game as far as the exiting professional investor would view it, but it might not be fair from the perspective of an existing unit holder who wishes to stay in the fund. If a large number of properties are sold considerably below NAV but existing unit holders are paid out at NAV, the remaining unit holders suffer the loss. If this is the case, then all unit holders will be tempted to exit at the same time, challenging the continued existence of the open-ended fund, which had been a perfectly acceptable and stable investment for many small pension funds.

The trust deed allowed the manager to defer redemptions, and also to make adjustments to the NAV in exceptional market circumstances. It was judged that these circumstances were indeed exceptional, and a large (12%) discount was applied to the NAV in October, and a further discount (8%) was applied in January.

Given the downward price revision, exiting investors were able to withdraw their redemption notices under the trust deed. Some investors withdrew their redemption notices, as their arbitrage strategy had been thwarted by the small print in the trust deed. Some redemptions were made at the lower bid price, and some property sales took place. Exiting investors were paid out on time, albeit at around 80% of the September NAV.

11.7 CONCLUSIONS

Direct real estate is lumpy and illiquid in nature. Indirect investment is an appealing alternative. Unlisted real estate funds are not designed to solve the problem of illiquidity, although there is often a healthy secondary market for units in both open- and closed-ended funds; the major appeal of a fund is that it can pool investor capital and investors can own a share of a more diversified portfolio of assets. This also opens up the possibility of global investment, and the growth of unlisted funds has accompanied the geographical expansion of real estate investment strategies.

Thanks to these funds, the standard pension fund mandate has become increasingly global, and investors are likely to continue to require the development of more cross-border funds. However, the consequences of leverage and the market crisis of 2007–9 were disturbing for real estate funds. While unlisted fund NAVs may continue to track the direct property index in stable markets, there is less reason to suppose that NAVs will be reflected either in trading prices of funds on the increasingly active secondary market, or in the prices received by investors exiting open-ended funds at the wrong time. We can expect to see innovations in this field.

CHAPTER 12

Real Estate Private Equity: Fund Structure and Cash Flow Distribution

12.1 INTRODUCTION: THE FOUR QUADRANTS AND PRIVATE EQUITY

Figure 12.1 shows the so-called four quadrants of real estate investing. First introduced in the 1990s, the concept of four quadrants has become standard for classifying the investment opportunities available to investors in real estate. Some have argued (erroneously in our opinion) that the four quadrants can be used to drive a portfolio strategy, but we see it as merely a way to categorize products and market real estate services. The four-quadrant diagram segments the overall investment market into public investments in debt and equity, and private investments in debt and equity.

In general, an equity investment in real estate allows an investor to participate in the residual cash flows earned by a property or portfolio of properties. As discussed in Chapters 7 and 9, these cash flows are earned from leasing and operating property, and from disposition of the asset at the end of the holding period. The residual cash flows from both sources represent free cash flows that remain after all other claims have been paid.

Debt investment, introduced in Chapter 8 and described in more detail in Chapter 14, earns the lender a series of cash flows that arise from a borrower's contractual obligation to repay principal and interest with regular payments over a fixed period of time. If the borrower ceases to make payments as obligated, the lender has the right to force a sale of the property in the hope that the proceeds from the sale are sufficient to repay the outstanding balance of the mortgage.

Within the real estate investment universe, it is possible to invest in public (listed) equity and debt securities, or in private (unlisted) equity and debt investment opportunities. The difference between private and public markets lies in the liquidity of, or the ability to trade, the investment. Private market entities can hold debt or equity investments, and are formed as partnerships or companies to own a pool of assets. Investors own a share of the partnership or company that owns the underlying real estate equity or debt investments. Once a private market entity has been created and investors

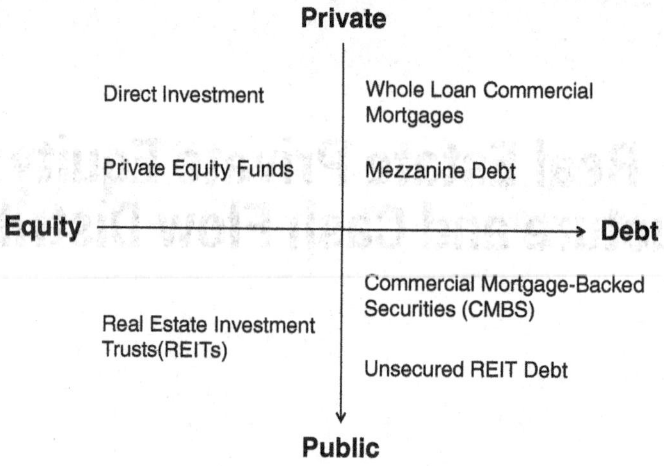

FIGURE 12.1 The four quadrants of real estate investing
Source: Baum (2009).

have provided capital to purchase debt or properties, subsequent trading of ownership shares does not occur.

Privately held entities are typically owned by investors until the underlying assets are sold. While many such larger entities have some secondary market liquidity, active central markets for trading private investments do not exist, so share value can only be estimated based on an estimate of the value of the underlying assets. When the underlying assets are sold, the private investment vehicle generally ceases to exist.

By contrast, investors in public market entities own shares of companies that trade on open exchanges. Like private entities, public entities can hold equity or debt assets. Examples of public entities are Real Estate Investment Trusts (REITs), which own portfolios of properties or mortgages and pass income and capital gains on to shareholders. Real Estate Operating Companies (REOCs) or Property Companies (PropCos) are also publicly traded real estate securities. As with any public company, shares can be bought or sold on public exchanges providing liquidity to shareholders, and prices are public information.

Investors in both public and private equity invest to obtain the benefits argued to be provided by real estate, including competitive returns, low levels of volatility, diversification of portfolios that hold other financial assets, an inflation hedge, and a return that includes a large income component. The pooling of capital into private and public equity investment vehicles is intended to deliver these benefits while attempting to minimize the problems that are involved (as described in Chapter 1).

It is helpful as a start to cover the responsibilities of the sponsor (or manager) of an unlisted private equity fund, and the economics of the relationship between the sponsor and the investors. Most private equity funds are created as limited partnerships, which create two sets of claims. The general partner (GP) has expertise in real estate investment and controls all real estate and fund-level decisions. The limited partners (LPs) are by definition passive investors and provide most, if not all, of the equity capital that is used by the GP to acquire properties. In return, they hope to achieve the investment benefits of investing in real estate.

12.2 PRIVATE EQUITY FUNDS: THE BACKGROUND

The advent of the private equity fund in the USA occurred just after the savings and loan crisis in the late 1980s. As described in Chapter 2, the Resolution Trust Corporation (RTC) received properties from failed saving and loan institutions, and was charged with liquidating the assets. The RTC's strategy was to auction portfolios of properties off to potential investors. The first auctions generated few bids, and those who won the bid would often end up owning a pool of properties at significant discounts to the amount of debt outstanding, and to the market value of the properties. These assets were repackaged and sold quickly at higher than their purchase price, or held for longer periods in the hope of selling when real estate markets and property values recovered.

The auction bidders often formed limited partnerships, with themselves as general partners or sponsors, and with capital providers as passive limited partner investors. These general partnerships were among the first private equity funds in the USA, and included companies like Goldman Sachs, Salomon Bros. Inc., Morgan Stanley, Hines, Trammell Crow, and other familiar investment banking and real estate companies. Many of these firms are still active in the real estate private equity industry, and many others have entered the market. Many of the newer firms are spin-offs of the early entrants.

The typical structure for early private equity funds was for the GP to invest no, or a small amount (say 5%) of, capital, and the LPs to provide a much larger stake (say 95% or 100%). The GP would acquire properties with a combination of LP equity and debt financing. As the properties earned income and were subsequently sold, hopefully for much higher values than at acquisition, the LPs might earn 80% of the income earned, and the GP 20%. If values decreased after acquisition, LPs had a lot more to lose than GPs and hence, incurred higher risk. It is not hard to imagine that a GP might only invest in extremely high-risk assets in hopes of a large payout when the asset was sold. Both LPs and GPs win if that occurs. However, we have defined risk as uncertainty of outcomes, and if the property should drop substantially in value, the LP stands to lose much more (if not all) of their investment. The incentives of the GP were not aligned with those of the LP, and asymmetric outcomes could occur. GPs, in contrast, were not at risk in the downside scenario.

Incentives between GPs and LPs are most aligned when the sponsor of the fund has a financial stake in the fund. In some cases, the general partner invests a small percentage, maybe 1–5% of the total equity raised, as their stake in the fund. Although small, this allows the GP to stand "side-by-side" with the limited partner investors, winning when they win and losing if they should lose. Some fund sponsors will also require their employees who are directly related to the fund's management to invest a material amount (relative to their own personal net worth) in the fund. Both of these types of investments serve to align the interests of the fund sponsor, those investing for the fund, and the limited partner investors.

As the private equity industry has evolved, so have incentive structures. Modern structures typically reward GPs with increasing proportions of investment upside after the LPs have earned a target level of return. Different methods of distributing equity cash flows between GPs and LPs will be discussed, after an explanatory section on the lifecycle of a private equity fund.

12.3 THE LIFECYCLE OF A PRIVATE EQUITY FUND

The general partner controls all fund decisions, and all property investment, management, and cash distribution decisions. There are several steps in the lifecycle of a private equity fund, as outlined below.

12.3.1 Initial Fundraising

In this stage, the sponsors of the fund raise capital from qualified investors that will subsequently be invested as equity in real estate properties. A partnership agreement and an offering (or private placement) memorandum provide the general framework and terms of the fund, giving information on the fund's investment proposition, the target rate of return sought to be provided to investors by the fund sponsor, the expected term of the fund, the spectrum of allowable investments, maximum leverage allowed, legal rights and obligations of the sponsor and the investors, how profits from owning property will be shared between the sponsors and the investors in the fund, and many other items.

Most real estate private equity funds are closed-ended funds. Capital is committed by equity investors at the beginning of the fund life, and no new investors are allowed after that point. In addition, the fund has a prescribed and finite life, at which time all assets will be liquidated, and the fund terminated.

Private equity funds are also "blind pool" investments, meaning that there are no assets in the fund when capital is committed, and the sponsor has full discretion to invest in assets that are deemed to fulfill the fund's mandate. Typically, the mandate is purposefully broad, and the investor relies on the sponsor to source deals that will generate a return equal to or greater than the fund's target. Sponsors with a good reputation and track record are more likely to be able to attract investors based on past performance.

The investment proposition may indicate that the fund will invest in a specific property type (e.g. office, hotel, retail, multi-family, industrial), in a specific region (e.g. southwest, Midwest, California, North and South Carolina), or even in a specific market (e.g. office buildings in the Dallas, TX market). Alternatively, the fund could have a broader mandate to invest in a diversified portfolio of assets across regions, countries, and property types.

As discussed in Chapter 11, private equity funds can have many different mandates. Some hold low-risk core properties that are held for long periods of time. Others may have a value-add mandate, and acquire properties that are flawed in some way. These properties could be mis- or under-managed, have significant vacancy, need to be updated with renovations, or repositioned in the market to create value. A third type of fund is more opportunistic, investing in more risky development deals.

After careful due diligence regarding the terms and investment goals and objectives of the fund, and their confidence in the ability of the sponsor to execute the strategy, investors commit to provide a specific amount of capital by signing a subscription agreement. The subscription agreement indicates the amount of capital committed by each limited partner. The fund will "close" when commitments from investors meet or exceed the sponsor's targeted amount of capital. The closing date is the date after which no further investors will be allowed to invest in the fund, although second and third closings are not uncommon.

The general partner will usually require that some proportion of the committed capital be remitted when the fund is closed. The subscription agreement obligates investors to provide the remainder of their capital when it is requested, or called, by the sponsor, as specified within the Limited Partnership Agreement and Offering Memorandum. Typically, an investor is given 10 days to wire money to the sponsor after it is called.

Considerable expense is incurred by the sponsor in drawing up fund documents, marketing to prospective investors, and developing the infrastructure to manage the fund once capital is committed by investors. When a fund is closed, the sponsor will typically charge a management fee to investors to cover fund operating expenses. These fees typically range from 0.5% to 2% of either committed or invested capital, depending on fund strategy. For example, core funds are at the lower end of the fee spectrum, while more management-intensive opportunistic funds are at the higher end.

12.3.2 Acquisition Stage

The limited partner agreement will define an investment period during which the fund can call capital from investors and make investments. The length of the investment period can vary, but 3 years is common. When the sponsor finds investment opportunities that fit with the fund's strategy and are expected to earn returns that meet or exceed the fund's targeted return, capital will be called from LPs. Capital calls can occur until the end of the 3-year investment period, or earlier if all capital is called prior to that time.

Stocks and bond investments are usually made with an up-front investment followed by a series of cash inflows based on dividend or coupon payments, and ultimate sale of the investment. Unlike these asset classes, private equity investors commit a certain amount of capital when partnership documents are signed, and provide some proportion of their commitment (say 10%). When the sponsor is successful at sourcing investments, additional capital is called from the investors to fund the transaction. Sponsors can call capital at any time during the 3-year investment period, and often do so at differing intervals, which creates uncertainty for investors as to the timing of their investment (unlike the typical stock or bond investment). The total amount of the commitment could take the entire 3-year investment period, or with success at acquiring assets, the commitment could be called far sooner. Hence, actual investment of the committed amount could come at any time during the investment period, and investors must hold relatively liquid assets to be able to fund their commitments.

Let us assume that a fund obtains commitments from investors of $360 million to be paid in when called throughout a 3-year investment period. If investments come sequentially, the fund invests $10 million in each of the 36 months, which is unlikely. Hypothetically, the fund could call the entire $360 million in the first year, or, in a period where it is difficult to find investments that meet the target return, the entire amount could be called during the last few months of the 36-month investment period.

Potential transactions are sourced from as many market participants as possible, and analyzed to determine if the investment will meet the fund's return hurdle. Careful due diligence is performed by fund employees to determine the expected risks and returns of each transaction. Once it is determined that an investment meets the fund's criteria, the deal is presented to the fund's investment committee, who vote to decide if the investment should be made. If the transaction is approved, the acquisitions and transaction team is given approval to acquire the property or portfolio. Each acquisition will usually require extensive legal documentation, and the use of internal or external legal counsel.

Additional capital cannot be called from limited partners for further investments after the investment period ends, unless an amendment to the initial limited partnership agreement is approved by the fund's governing Board of Directors.

12.3.3 Asset Management

Acquired properties are turned over to the asset management team, which is charged with the responsibility of efficiently managing the properties owned by the fund and ensuring that cash flows and market values are maximized to provide the targeted return to investors. Asset managers may propose capital expenditure strategies for individual properties, hire leasing brokers and property managers, and determine overall property strategy regarding rental rates, operating expenses, and the marketing, among other responsibilities. For a value-add or opportunistic fund, the asset management team will oversee renovation and development projects to ensure that they are delivered on time and on budget.

12.3.4 Portfolio Management

The portfolio manager is responsible for overall strategy for the properties owned by the fund. Responsibilities include, but are not limited to, monitoring properties and markets so as to dispose of an asset when its market value is highest, proposing capital expenditure strategies for individual properties so that value can be added in the form of higher rents for an improved property, and generally managing the portfolio to achieve investment results as targeted in the fund's offering documents. For a small fund, the portfolio managers could be responsible for all owned properties, whereas a larger fund may employ many portfolio managers with responsibility over sub-portfolios of properties.

Income is paid to investors from operating and disposition of fund investments. Opportunistic and value-add investments typically have shorter-term lives, and the return is mostly based on cash flows from disposition. Other investments have longer-term holding periods, and may provide a stream of income from operations, followed by a sale, perhaps toward the end of the fund life, or in an extension of the fund. The end result is that the timing of receipt of cash flows by investors is extremely uncertain.

If a fund invests in 10 assets, any of them could be sold at any time, and some may even be sold before the end of the investment period. In this case, the fund could either return the capital to investors, or if allowed by the partnership documents, reinvest in new acquisitions. Since any of the 10 assets could be sold at any time during the fund's life, cash returned to investors and duration of the fund life is uncertain. This uncertainty of asset duration makes it difficult for an investor to match liability duration.

12.3.5 End of Fund Life

The limited partnership agreement will specify the fund's life, before the end of which all assets must be sold and all income from the assets net of fund expenses distributed to LPs. Traditional funds have a life of 7 years, but fund life can often be extended, usually by up to 3 years.

12.4 FUND ECONOMICS

Investments made by the fund management team are expected to earn cash flows from operation and from disposition. These cash flows are shared by the sponsor and limited partners, as predetermined in the fund's formation documents. It is important to note that all cash flows, net of fund expenses, will be distributed to either the sponsor or the limited partners.

12.4.1 Management Fees

The general partner earns a management fee that is used to offset the expenses of the partnership. These expenses include start-up costs of forming and registering the partnership, as well as any legal and other fees incurred, and all other costs that would be incurred in the acquisition and management of properties and the operations of the partnership. Management fees are initially paid out of capital contributions made by the investors, or subsequently out of investment cash flows.

Management fees are typically paid quarterly in advance, based on an annual percentage. For example, let us assume that investors commit $100 million in capital to a sponsor, and that the sponsor charges a 2% p.a. management fee, payable quarterly in advance. Annually, the sponsor earns management fees of $2 million, with $500,000 payable immediately at the closing of the fund, and an additional $500,000 paid at the beginning of each quarter for the remainder of the year.

12.4.2 Limited Partner Distributions

The underlying benefits from investing in real estate pass through to investors in a private equity fund, and these benefits flow from residual operational and dispositional income earned by the properties in which the fund invests. In most cases, there are four different ways that investors receive a return of capital, and a return on their capital. The components of cash flow to investors and the fund sponsor are as follows:

- A return of initial capital investment to investors.
- A preferred return.
- A carried interest (or share) in the profits earned.
- A promoted interest that is earned when certain return hurdles are achieved.

The priority of cash flows differs by fund, and can significantly impact the actual return earned by investors.

The system by which cash flows are distributed is known as a waterfall. The idea is that cash gets poured into the entity from the underlying properties, and then is directed into "buckets" based on a strict priority system or distribution framework that is specified in the limited partnership agreement that all parties sign when capital is committed to the fund by the investors. As a higher-priority bucket is filled, subsequent cash flows earned fill buckets lower in the priority structure. The "buckets" that are filled up usually fall into the following categories.

Return of Initial Capital

Funds will often return capital prior to the distribution of any profits earned from the underlying property investments. Let us assume that a private equity fund has raised $300 million of equity from a single pension fund investor who is the limited partner. The fund has a 75% targeted leverage ratio, so the $300 million of equity has $1.2 billion of leveraged purchasing power. With the $1.2 billion, properties are purchased, and cash flows are earned. Every dollar of before-tax cash flow that is earned from the underlying properties is first paid to the investor until their $300 million initial investment is completely returned.

Preferred Return

Typically, preferred returns to the LP investors are the second form of cash flow distribution, payable after the initial capital investment has been returned. A preferred return resembles a dividend payment on a preferred stock, and is paid prior to other claims on the underlying property cash flows.

The preferred return offered by most private equity funds ranges between 8% and 12%. The preferred return (or PREF) is paid based on the initial capital that was provided by the investor. For example, an 8% preferred rate on $300 million of equity would earn $24 million annually in preferred return cash flow before additional cash flows are distributed. After the preferred is paid, a total of $324 million has been earned by investments, and all of it has been distributed to the limited partners. To this point, the general partner has not received any cash flows other than management fees.

Carried Interest

After all capital has been returned, and the preferred return payment made, any additional cash flows earned by the properties owned by the fund will be distributed to LP investors and the GP sponsor according to the terms that were specified in the offering memorandum and limited partnership agreement. A sponsor might, for example, agree to distribute 80% of the remainder of the cash flows to the LPs, and retain 20%. The 80% is referred to as the LPs' carried interest, and the 20% is the fund sponsor's carried interest.

Promoted Interest

In many funds, the sponsor's carried interest will increase, or be promoted, as certain return hurdles are achieved. For example, the 80/20 splits may hold until the investors have earned a 15% internal rate of return (IRR). Once that hurdle has been achieved, the cash flow split to the sponsor may be promoted to 40%, and the investors' share declines to 60%. Another hurdle may exist above which the carried interest amounts change again. For example, the splits might be 60/40 until an IRR of 18% is earned, after which any additional cash flows are split 50/50.

To summarize the waterfall system using the cash flow priority outlined above, any cash flows earned by the underlying properties in the fund are distributed:

- First, to return capital to the investors of the fund.
- Second, to pay an 8% preferred return to the investors of the fund.
- Third, by distributing 80% of any additional cash flows to the investors of the fund, and 20% to the sponsor of the fund, up until the investors of the fund have earned an IRR of 15%.
- Fourth, after the 15% IRR hurdle is achieved, by distributing 60% of any additional cash flows to investors, and 40% to the sponsor of the fund, up until the investors of the fund have earned an IRR of 18%.
- Fifth, after the 18% IRR hurdle is reached, by distributing any additional cash flows 50% to the investors and 50% to the sponsor.

In this structure, the sponsors earn a higher percentage of the overall fund's cash flows as the investors in the deal earn higher returns. This is thought to align the interests of the GP and LPs, as it incentivizes the sponsor to earn the highest possible returns for investors. A contrary argument might be that a promote structure incentivizes the sponsor to take greater risks in the underlying properties, as they will only earn higher proportions of cash flows when higher returns are earned.

One important thing to note is the dilution of return that exists for the LPs relative to the underlying property return. If a fund targets a 15% return for its investors, returns of higher than 15% must be earned on the underlying properties given the 20% carried interest and any promote that exists. More on this will be presented in the numerical examples provided below.

Most offering memoranda and other documents prepared by fund sponsors target an absolute rate of return. Investors provide capital in the hope that they will receive this stated return. Another metric used by investors is the equity multiple (EM) or return on invested capital (ROIC), which is calculated as the sum of all cash flows to the investor divided by the amount invested. An example of the use of this metric was shown in Chapter 9.

Unlike other investment vehicles, there is typically no mention of the other benefits that are purported to be provided by investment in real estate, such as its inflation hedging ability or its ability to diversify a mixed-asset portfolio.

Further, since many of the closed-ended funds report a distinct ending period, few of them are long-term real estate investors. Instead, the strategy of most funds in the 2000–7 period was to buy an asset cheaply, turn it around by adding value through management, leasing, or development, and sell within a few years for a much higher value than the price at which the asset was purchased.

12.5 WATERFALL STRUCTURES

12.5.1 Introduction

The sequence of cash distributions differs across funds, and has a significant impact on cash flows earned by the LP investors and the GP sponsor. It is essential that both parties earn a sufficient return, both to keep the GP operating in the best interests of the LPs and to ensure that the LPs earn the return that was targeted in the initial fund documents.

Let us start with a fund that raises equity from a single investor, and that invests in a single property. The fund consists of $1,000 of equity, which was combined with a $3,000 loan to purchase a $4,000 property. The fund targets a 15% net return to investors, after payment of all fees to the sponsor, and after accounting for the sponsor's carried and promoted interests. This is a simple example, but clearly shows the differences that can arise across fund structures in terms of the return that is earned by the limited partner.

Leveraged funds will distribute before-tax cash flows earned by the underlying property. After paying debt service, the property cash flows are as shown in Table 12.1.

Typically, two calculations are made to determine the performance of private equity funds. They are the IRR, introduced in an earlier chapter, and the equity multiple (EM, sometimes also referred to as the return on invested capital [ROIC] or multiple on invested capital [MOIC]), which is simply the sum of the inflows divided by the outflows. In this case, the only outflow is the initial investment, and the sum of all cash flows earned over the 5-year holding period is $2,125. Therefore, the multiple is ($2,125 / $1,000), or 2.125 times. This means that the sum of all cash flows earned is 2.125 times the amount invested.

TABLE 12.1 Property cash flows

Year:	**0**	**1**	**2**	**3**	**4**	**5**
Outflow	–$1,000					
Before-tax cash flows		$125	$125	$125	$125	$125
Before-tax equity reversion						$1,500
Total cash flows	–$1,000	$125	$125	$125	$125	$1,625

The IRR for this investment is 19.31%. Clearly, there is a relationship between the IRR and the multiple. The initial investment is more than doubled over the course of the investment. Generally, a doubling of cash flows implies a 20% IRR per year in each of the 5 years of the holding period for the investment. Assuming compounding (as the IRR does), the annual IRR will be lower than the 20% simple compounding case. For the investment described above, a 2.125 equity multiple earned over a 5-year period coincides with a 19.31% IRR.

12.5.2 Pro-rata Investment and Distribution

The first scenario that we will analyze assumes that the sponsor and the investor both invest in the deal and their cash flow distributions are made based on how much they invest relative to the total equity investment made. The GP sponsor invests $200, and the LP invests $800. The GP earns 20% of the before-tax cash flows, and the LP 80%. The distributions of cash flows to each party are as shown in Tables 12.2 and 12.3.

The sponsor earns an IRR of 19.31% and an equity multiple of 2.125, which mirrors the performance of the overall deal.

The limited partner's equity multiple is 2.125 and his IRR is 19.31%. Since all cash flow distributions are made pro rata with the initial investment, the multiple and IRR earned by each party are exactly the same as provided by the investment.

12.5.3 All Equity Provided by Limited Partner, 80%/20% Carried Interest

A second case provides the GP sponsor with cash flows as a reward for sourcing and acquiring the underlying property, but the sponsor does not provide any of the initial equity capital required to buy the property. The LP puts up the entire equity stake of $1,000, and receives 80% of the cash flows earned. The sponsor earns 20% of the cash

TABLE 12.2 Cash flows to the sponsor (20% equity invested)

Year:	0	1	2	3	4	5
Outflow	−$200					
Before-tax cash flows		$25	$25	$25	$25	$25
Before-tax equity reversion		$0	$0	$0	$0	$300
Total cash flows	−$200	$25	$25	$25	$25	$325

TABLE 12.3 Cash flows to the limited partner (80% equity invested)

Year:	0	1	2	3	4	5
Outflow	−$800					
Before-tax cash flows		$100	$100	$100	$100	$100
Disposition cash flows		$0	$0	$0	$0	$1200
Total cash flows	−$800	$100	$100	$100	$100	$1,300

TABLE 12.4 Cash flows to the sponsor (20% carried interest, no equity)

Year:	0	1	2	3	4	5
Outflow	$0					
Before-tax cash flows		$25	$25	$25	$25	$25
Before-tax equity reversion		$0	$0	$0	$0	$300
Total cash flows	$0	$25	$25	$25	$25	$325

TABLE 12.5 Cash flows to the limited partner (80% interest, 100% equity invested)

Year:	0	1	2	3	4	5
Outflow	–$1,000					
Before-tax cash flows		$100	$100	$100	$100	$100
Disposition cash flows		$0	$0	$0	$0	$1,200
Total cash flows	–$1,000	$100	$100	$100	$100	$1,300

flows. The cash flows earned over the 5-year holding period by each party are as shown in Tables 12.4 and 12.5.

The sponsor's equity multiple and IRR are infinite, but the wealth of the sponsor is increased by the net present value (NPV) of $232.96.[1]

Several things are important to notice. First, when determining the sponsor's investment performance, the multiple and IRR are undefined, since there was no initial investment made. Instead, we calculated the present value of the stream of sponsor cash flows at an arbitrary discount rate of 15%, which we assume is the investor's required rate of return. This present value is what would need to be invested to earn the stream of cash flows representing 20% of the total deal cash flows, and earn a 15% return. This is a useful way of summarizing the investment benefits of the fund for the sponsor. In effect, the sponsor receives a grant equivalent to $232.96, payable with cash flows to be earned over 5 years, in exchange for providing the investor the opportunity to invest in this transaction.

The limited partner's returns are diluted because of the cash flow payments made to the sponsor, who has made no investment. The multiple for the investor drops to 1.7 from 2.125 in the previous example. The investor's IRR has fallen to 13.08% from 19.31%, a drop of 623 basis points. Under these cash flow splits, the net return to the investor does not meet the 15% required rate of return.

12.5.4 Adding a Preferred Return

More typical of private equity funds is a scenario where the LPs provide the entire equity amount, and earn a preferred return. In this example, the sponsor does not invest in the partnership, but, as a reward for providing access to real estate exposure, retains a 20% carried interest in the upside of the investments that are made. The preferred return is

[1]The NPV calculation uses a discount rate of 15%.

TABLE 12.6 Cash flows with preferred return

Year:	0	1	2	3	4	5
Outflow	–$1,000					
Before-tax cash flows		$125	$125	$125	$125	$125
Preferred return		$80	$80	$80	$80	$80
Remainder		$45	$45	$45	$45	$45
LP share (80%)		$36	$36	$36	$36	$36
GP share (20%)		$9	$9	$9	$9	$9
Before-tax equity reversion						$1,500
LP share (80%)						$1,200
GP share (20%)						$300

TABLE 12.7 Cash flows to the sponsor (20% after preferred return)

Year:	0	1	2	3	4	5
Outflow	$0					
Before-tax cash flows		$9	$9	$9	$9	$9
Disposition cash flows						$300
Total cash flows	$0	$9	$9	$9	$9	$309

paid out of operating cash flows in each year, and any residual cash flows are split 80% to the LPs and 20% to the sponsor. Net sales proceeds are also split on an 80:20 basis.

The cash flows earned by the entire project and the calculation of preferred return and residual cash flows from operations are as shown in Table 12.6.

As the name "preferred" implies, the investor is entitled to receive 8% of his original investment, or $80, each year prior to any other distributions. Splits between the sponsor and the investor are based on the residual cash flow left after the preferred return has been paid.

When the project is sold at the end of the period, the $1,500 in disposition proceeds is split in the prescribed 80:20 fashion, with $1,200 distributed to the limited partners and $300 distributed to the sponsor. The total cash flows earned by each party in this scenario are as shown in Tables 12.7 and 12.8.

The sponsor's EM and IRR are infinite, but he increases his wealth by the NPV of $179.32.[2]

Despite the priority of payment of the preferred return before any cash flow splits are made, the IRR of the fund for the limited partner still falls short of the 15% return target. The multiple and IRR are slightly higher than in the case where no preferred payment was made, and the present value of the cash flows earned by the sponsor is slightly lower than in the previous case. Again, the dilution of cash flows generated by

[2]The NPV calculation uses a discount rate of 15%.

TABLE 12.8 Cash flows to the limited partner (80% after preferred return)

Year:	0	1	2	3	4	5
Outflow	–$1,000					
Preferred return		$80	$80	$80	$80	$80
Residual before-tax cash flows		$36	$36	$36	$36	$36
Before-tax equity reversion						$1,200
Total cash flows	–$1,000	$116	$116	$116	$116	$1,316

paying the sponsor 20% of the upside dilutes the overall IRR to 14.59% from the total deal IRR of 19.31%. The equity multiple is 1.78.

12.5.5 Return of Capital, Simple Interest Preferred Return, Carried Interest

In this case, as would be typical of private equity funds in the market, the investor's initial capital is returned prior to any other claims. After return of capital, a preferred return of 8% is paid to the equity holders based on their original equity investment. Since cash flows are insufficient in any year, or over the full 5-year period, to pay back all of the invested capital, the preferred return accrues over the 5-year holding period and is paid out of sale proceeds. Once all capital has been returned and the accrued preferred return payments are paid, any additional cash flows are split according to the 80/20 carried interests. The cash flows earned and distributed under this scenario are as shown in Table 12.9.

As shown in Table 12.10, the LP receives the entire before-tax cash flows earned by the property over the 5-year holding period. This is paid as a return of capital. The sum of the 5 years' cash flows is (5 * $125), or $625. Since they invested $1,000 at the

TABLE 12.9 Project cash flows with simple interest preferred return and carried interest

Year:	0	1	2	3	4	5
Outflow	–$1,000					
Before-tax cash flows		$125	$125	$125	$125	$125
Return of capital		$125	$125	$125	$125	$125
Capital account balance	$1,000	$875	$750	$625	$500	$375
Preferred return		$80	$70	$60	$50	$40
Accrued preferred			$150	$210	$260	$300
Disposition cash flows						$1,500
– Capital to be returned						–$375
Residual						$1,125
– Accrued preferred						$300
Residual						$825
LP share (80%)						$660
GP share (20%)						$165

TABLE 12.10 LP cash flows with preferred return and carried interest

Year:	0	1	2	3	4	5
Outflow	–$1,000					
Return of capital		$125	$125	$125	$125	$125
Return of capital (disposition)						$375
Accrued preferred						$300
80% of residual						$660
Total cash flows (LP)	–$1,000	$125	$125	$125	$125	$1,460

TABLE 12.11 Sponsor cash flows with preferred return and carried interest

Year:	0	1	2	3	4	5
Outflow	$0					
Before-tax cash flows		$0	$0	$0	$0	$0
20% of residual						$165
Total cash flows	$0	$0	$0	$0	$0	$165

beginning of the fund, they are still owed $375 ($1,000 less $625) in order to have their full capital investment returned. This is paid out of the $1,500 before-tax equity reversion, leaving $1,125 for further distributions.

During each of the 5 years in the holding period, an 8% preferred return is accrued, but not paid, since all cash flows are returned to the investor to partially return the initial investment. The accrued amount in the first year is (8% * $1,000), or $80. At the beginning of the second year, the capital balance for the LPs is reduced by $125 in capital returned in Year 1. Because of this, the preferred return earned by the LP is (8% * ($1,000 – $125)), equal to $70. The accrued preferred return decreases each year, declining as the capital balance is paid down. Over 5 years, the sum of the shortfall in preferred return payments is a total of $300. This must be paid out from the remainder of the before-tax equity reversion that is left after returning the LPs' capital. After the $300 is paid to provide the accrued preferred return to the LP, the remainder to be distributed out of the before-tax equity reversion is ($1,125 – $300), or $825.

Now that capital has been returned and the accrued preferred return has been paid, the remainder can be distributed according to the carried interest proportion. The LP gets 80%, or $660, and the GP gets 20%, or $165.

Since the limited partners get paid their return of capital and preferred returns first, the IRR is higher than in the previous cases, which were more favorable to the sponsor, and the multiple is higher. The IRR is 17.26%, which exceeds the investor required rate of return of 15% targeted in the fund's offering materials. The equity multiple is 1.96.

The sponsor's cash flows are shown in Table 12.11. Equity multiple and IRR are infinite, but the sponsor increases his wealth by the NPV of $82.03.[3]

[3]The NPV calculation uses a discount rate of 15%.

This figure represents the amount that the sponsor would have had to invest to earn sufficient cash flows to generate a 15% return. Another thing to note is that of the total $2,125 before-tax cash flows that are earned by the property, $1,960 (92.2%) goes to the limited partner, and $165 (7.8%) goes to the sponsor.

A distribution structure like this can lead to sponsor incentives to invest in properties that have shorter holding periods. Since capital is fully returned and accrued preferred returns must be paid prior to any distribution to the sponsor, it is likely that sponsor cash flows will only be earned upon sale of the property.

Adding Management Fees

Another permutation includes management fees. Let us assume that the sponsor charges 2% management fees based on the capital balance of the equity investor. Going back to the simple interest case and a $1,000 investment at time zero, the management fee owed to the sponsor is $20 (2% * $1,000) in Year 1. This management fee is paid out of the $125 before-tax cash flow earned in the first year, as shown in Table 12.12. The remaining cash flow of $105 is used to pay down the LP's capital balance to $895 at the end of Year 1.

Cash flow of $125 is also earned in the second year of the holding period, and the management fee owed to the sponsor is 2% of the reduced capital balance of $895, or $17.90. This management fee payment is paid to the sponsor, which leaves $106.10 to be returned to the investor as return of capital. After paying the investor, the capital balance declines to $788.

Using the same logic, the cash flow to the equity investor is $15.76 in Year 3 and the equity capital balance is reduced to $679. Moving forward to the fifth year, the

TABLE 12.12 Project cash flows with simple interest preferred return and carried interest

Year:	0	1	2	3	4	5
Outflow	–$1,000					
Before-tax cash flows		$125	$125	$125	$125	$125
Management fees		$20	$17.90	$15.76	$13.57	$11.34
Return of capital		$105	$107	$109	$111	$114
Capital account balance	$1,000	$895	$788	$679	$567	$454
Preferred return		$80	$72	$63	$54	$45
Accrued preferred			$152	$215	$269	$314
Disposition cash flows						$1,500
– Capital to be returned						–$454
Residual						$1,046
– Accrued preferred						$314
Residual						$732
LP share (80%)						$585.70
GP share (20%)						$146.42

TABLE 12.13 LP cash flows with preferred return and carried interest

Year:	0	1	2	3	4	5
Outflow	–$1,000					
Return of capital		$105	$107	$109	$111	$114
Return of capital (disposition)						$454
Accrued preferred						$314
80% of residual						$586
Total cash flows (LP)	–$1,000	$105	$107	$109	$111	$1,467

TABLE 12.14 Sponsor cash flows with preferred return and carried interest

Year:	0	1	2	3	4	5
Outflow	$0					
Management fees		$20	$18	$16	$14	$11
Before-tax cash flows		$0	$0	$0	$0	$0
20% of residual		$0	$0	$0	$0	$146
Total cash flows	$0	$20	$18	$16	$14	$158

management fees paid to the sponsor are $11.34 (2% of $567), the return of capital to the equity investor is $114, and the ending capital account balance is $454.

When the asset is sold, the first priority is paying the remainder of the capital balance ($454) and the accrued preferred return of $314. After these have been paid, the remainder is split 80/20 between the investor and the sponsor, respectively.

A summary of the investor's cash flows is shown in Table 12.13. The total return of capital over the first 5 years is $546, and the remainder of capital ($454) is paid in Year 5. After that is paid, the investor earns the preferred return of $314, and their share of the remaining cash flow in Year 5 is $586. The operating and disposition cash flows due to the LP investors provide an IRR of 16.01% and an equity multiple of 1.9.

The sponsor's cash flows include the management fee earned in each of the 5 years, plus their 20% share of the Year 5 residual (Table 12.14). Discounting at a rate of 15%, the present value of the sponsor's cash flows is $127.41.

Of the $2,125 in total cash flows earned by the property, the investors earn a total of $1,900, or 89.41%. The sponsor earns the remainder, which is $225, or 10.59% of the total.

12.5.6 Return of Capital, Compounded Interest Preferred Return, Carried Interest

The examples in the previous section assumed that the preferred return is calculated using simple interest. Many unlisted funds will provide for compounded interest, which means that if preferred return is not paid in any year, it will earn interest at the preferred return rate (in this case 8%) until it can be paid. The project cash flows are exactly the same as before.

TABLE 12.15 Project cash flows with compounded preferred return and carried interest

Year:	0	1	2	3	4	5
Outflow	–$1,000					
Before-tax cash flows		$125	$125	$125	$125	$125
Return of capital		$125	$125	$125	$125	$125
Capital account balance	$1,000	$875	$750	$625	$500	$375
Preferred return earned		$80	$70	$60	$50	$40
Yr 1 pref. compounded						$109
Yr 2 pref. compounded						$88
Yr 3 pref. compounded						$70
Yr 4 pref. compounded						$54
Accrued preferred						$361
Disposition cash flows						$1,500
– Capital to be returned						–$375
Residual						$1,125
Accrued preferred						$361
= Residual						$764
LP share (80%)						$611
GP share (20%)						$153

The impact of compounding on the cash flows is as shown in Table 12.15. In Year 1, the investor earns an 8% preferred return, or $80, but the property's cash flow is insufficient to provide this payment. For the remaining 4 years, the $80 earns 8% interest, and grows to $108.84 ($80 * (1.08)^4) at the time that the property is sold in Year 5.

In Year 2, a preferred return of $70 is unpaid to the limited partner, and as such will earn 8% in each of the remaining 3 years to grow to a total of $88.18. The unpaid $60 preferred in Year 3 grows over two more years to $69.98, and the Year 4 unpaid return of $50 grows over one more year at 8% to total $54. Adding the last payment of $40 to these amounts gives an accrued compounded preferred payment of $361 that must be paid in Year 5 when the property is sold.

As before, the property is sold for $1,500 in Year 5, the remaining capital balance of $375 is deducted to get a residual of $1,125, and then the accrued compounded return of $361 is deducted to get the net residual of $764 (Table 12.16). This amount is then split 80/20 between the limited partner and the sponsor, respectively.

The LP return in this case is 17.41%, which is higher than in the simple interest case (which was 17.26%), as would be expected. The equity multiple is also higher at 1.972.

With simple interest, the residual cash flow owed to the sponsor was $165, while in the compounded case, the sponsor's claim on the residual is lower, at $153 (Table 12.17). The present value of this amount at 15% is $76.07. This represents a difference of only $5.96, or 0.6% of the initial fund investment of $1,000. For a $1 billion fund, this difference would be $5.96 million.

TABLE 12.16 LP cash flows with compounded preferred return and carried interest

Year:	0	1	2	3	4	5
Outflow	–$1,000					
Return of capital		$125	$125	$125	$125	$125
Return of capital (disposition)						$375
Accrued preferred						$361
80% of residual						$611
Total cash flows (LP)	–$1,000	$125	$125	$125	$125	$1,472

TABLE 12.17 Sponsor cash flows with compounded preferred return and carried interest

Year:	0	1	2	3	4	5
Outflow	$0					
Before-tax cash flows		$0	$0	$0	$0	$0
20% of residual						$153
Total cash flows	$0	$0	$0	$0	$0	$153

12.6 PRIVATE EQUITY STRUCTURES IN THE CREDIT CRISIS

The bulk of capital raised outside Europe by private equity funds in the 2005–7 period was for value-add or opportunistic strategies. These strategies relied on a turnaround in the prospects of invested assets over a relatively short period of time, followed by a sale at a much higher price to another real estate investor, after value had been added. This strategy works as long as asset values increase over the holding period.

Instead, as we saw during the credit crisis, as investors repriced the risk of real estate debt and equity, and required higher rates of return on both, prices actually fell. In some instances, the declines in value were estimated to be between 35% and 45% from peak prices in 2007.

Let us assume that an investor placed capital with a fund sponsor with the same distribution policy as in the last example in Section 12.5, and that instead of the asset increasing in value by 50% over the 5-year holding period, it declined in value by 40%. Therefore, the final before-tax cash flow earned was not $1,500 as presented in that example. Instead, the final before-tax cash flow from sale of the asset was $600. The cash flows earned under this scenario are as shown in Table 12.18.

Under the distribution waterfall, the cash flows and return earned by the limited partners are as shown in Table 12.19.

Notice that after returning the final $375 of capital to investors, there is only $225 left to distribute. The investors are owed an accrued preferred return of $300 but only $225 can be paid from available cash flows. After that, there is nothing available to pay back the remainder of the preferred return owed, and no cash flow left to distribute as carried interest. The IRR of 5.30% falls well short of the 15% target, and the multiple is 1.23.

TABLE 12.18 Project cash flows with simple interest preferred return and carried interest – credit crisis example

Year:	0	1	2	3	4	5
Outflow	–$1,000					
Before-tax cash flows		$125	$125	$125	$125	$125
Return of capital		$125	$125	$125	$125	$125
Capital account balance	$1,000	$875	$750	$625	$500	$375
Preferred return		$80	$70	$60	$50	$40
Accrued preferred			$150	$210	$260	$300
Disposition cash flows						$600
– Capital to be returned						–$375
Residual						$225
– Accrued preferred payment						$225
– Residual						$0
LP share (80%)						$0
GP share (20%)						$0

TABLE 12.19 LP cash flows with preferred return and carried interest – credit crisis example

Year:	0	1	2	3	4	5
Outflow	–$1,000					
Return of capital		$125	$125	$125	$125	$125
Return of capital (disposition)						$375
Accrued preferred						$225
80% of residual						$0
Total cash flows (LP)	–$1,000	$125	$125	$125	$125	$725

Since the investor's capital is returned out of before-tax cash flow, and the preferred is paid prior to any distributions to the sponsor, there is no cash flow left to be distributed as a residual, and hence no cash flow from the investment earned by the sponsor. The sponsor's cash flows are as shown in Table 12.20, and as expected, all are zero.

In this case, the only income from sponsoring this fund is from management fees charged to investors.

This example is fairly typical of events during the credit crisis, if not a bit optimistic. Many opportunistic funds invested in real estate development projects with the hope of selling a building upon completion. The developer borrowed the cost of construction from a short-term lender, who was to be paid either from sale of the project at the end of the development period, or from a permanent loan takeout. No cash flows are earned over the development period, so the return of capital, preferred return payments, and any carried interest would be paid out of proceeds from the sale or refinancing.

TABLE 12.20 Sponsor cash flows with preferred return and carried interest – credit crisis example

Year:	0	1	2	3	4	5
Outflow	$0					
Before-tax cash flows		$0	$0	$0	$0	$0
20% of residual						$0
Total cash flows	$0	$0	$0	$0	$0	$0

As values declined, any sale that would occur would be at a value well below that which was expected at the time the capital was raised. Additionally, any attempt to refinance would be at much tighter underwriting criteria, which meant that the amount that could be borrowed would fall far short of that needed to repay the construction loan. This negative equity situation led many fund sponsors to default on loans, meaning that not only did investors not get the cash flows that they had expected, they did not even get their initial investment back.

12.7 CONCLUSION

Within the real estate investment universe, it is possible to invest in public (listed) securities, or in private (unlisted) investment opportunities. Private market structures can hold debt or equity investments, and partnerships or companies are often created to own a single asset or a pool of assets. Investors can then own a share of the partnership or company that owns the underlying real estate equity or debt investments.

Incentives are most aligned when the sponsor of the fund has a share of the fund equity return through a co-investment with the limited partners. Often, equity participation is achieved through a carried interest or performance fee structure which enables the general partner to participate in the upside but not have to risk equity capital.

Subsequent trading of shares in such private investments does not normally occur. However, the type of structure we have discussed in this chapter is used in large-scale private equity real estate investment funds, sometimes called unlisted funds, many of which have some secondary market liquidity, as we discussed in Chapter 11.

CHAPTER 13

Listed Equity Real Estate

13.1 INTRODUCTION

The benefits of real estate investment were described in Chapter 1 as follows:

- Property appears to be a diversifying asset. The returns earned by property tend to exhibit low correlations with other assets that are typically held in investor portfolios, such as stocks, bonds, and Treasury bills.
- Property appears to be an inflation hedge. Leases are often indexed to inflation or another measure, so that income return rises and falls along with general price levels. This is important for investors with indexed liabilities.
- Property appears to be a medium-risk asset. While measurement of property returns is problematic given the lack of frequent transactions of individual properties, several indices that measure the performance of privately held real estate indicate that the overall risk is low. Income produces a substantial proportion of total return, and since rent is a contractual obligation of the tenant, it will typically be paid prior to dividends.

Investors have long sought to achieve these benefits without the more harmful effects of real estate. Among the difficulties involved with real estate that were mentioned in Chapter 1 are two key issues:

- Property is illiquid. It may take months or even longer to sell a real estate asset, during which period market fundamentals can significantly change. Converting property investments into cash takes much longer relative to more liquid investments in common stocks or bonds.
- Property assets are generally large in terms of price and value, meaning that it is difficult to diversify both within the real estate asset class, and when adding real estate to a portfolio of stocks and bonds.

As we saw in Chapter 11, unlisted real estate investments provide some of the benefits of real estate investment, but also the less attractive characteristics. In addition, unlisted funds are typically available only to institutions and individuals that meet minimum net worth and income criteria. Through the years, investment managers have attempted to find ways to offer investment vehicles that provide diversification, an inflation hedge, and a low-risk profile, while also allowing for liquidity and the ability to invest in small amounts. One possible alternative is to invest in publicly traded forms of real estate investment.

By public real estate we mean listed real estate securities – securities that can be traded on public markets. In this chapter, we focus on listed securities that provide exposure to equity real estate. These can be split further into equity instruments – Real Estate Investment Trusts (REITs) and Real Estate Operating Companies or Property Companies (REOCs or PropCos). The definition can be expanded to include mutual funds and exchange-traded funds (ETFs).

13.2 REITs AND REOCS

REITs are generally distinguished from property companies or REOCs by two factors: tax treatment and regulation.

A property company is a taxable entity, like any company. Profits are taxed within the firm, and management has unlimited discretion to distribute dividends to shareholders from post-tax income. Tax-paying shareholders are then taxed on the dividend income that they receive, so double taxation arises.

REITs generally do not pay taxes at the company level provided that they conform to a number of restrictions which typically include the following:

- They discharge a majority of taxable income as dividends.
- Real estate assets comprise a significant proportion of their asset holdings.
- The portion of income derived from merchant development is limited.

Tax is one reason why investment in non-REIT property companies has, generally, not been popular. Taxes on capital gains are paid when shares of the REIT are sold, and not as individual assets are sold by the REIT.

In some markets, the UK being a prime example, long-term property company returns have been no better than returns from direct property, while risk has been much higher. Performance has been strongly linked to equities in the short term – so property companies have not diversified equity portfolios. Finally, tax leakage has put all investors in property company shares at a disadvantage to direct property. REITs, however, have been more popular and both the tax advantage and improved performance characteristics appear to have been significant.

13.3 LISTED FUNDS AND MUTUAL FUNDS

The distinction between a company and what is commonly thought of as a fund is not based on the legal structure but on the way the two are managed. The typical listed property company is internally managed, meaning that there is no legal separation of assets and the management team, while a fund has external management and a contract is put in place between the fund manager and the assets, which are held in a separate corporate structure.

A mutual fund is a listed fund that invests in other listed companies, also known in the UK as an investment trust. This is similar in effect to a fund of funds (see Chapter 11), but a mutual fund invests in publicly traded companies rather than in private funds. Hence, there are listed (mutual) funds in the USA that invest in UK, European, and global REITs, providing a diversified exposure to the sector. Outside of the USA, these are more commonly known as property securities funds.

13.4 EXCHANGE-TRADED FUNDS

Traded like normal shares, but more like mutual funds in their investment performance characteristics, ETFs allow investors to spread investments even more by tracking the performance of an entire index through buying a share in a single asset that represents that index.

The range of ETFs includes the EPRA (European Public Real Estate Association) universe of European REITs and real estate stocks, and the global listed real estate sector can be accessed through the EPRA/NAREIT[1] Global Property Yield Fund. ETFs provide exposure to global property companies and REITs without the manager selection risk – or possible benefit – of a mutual fund. Also available are short and ultra-short ETFs, which provide returns that are perfectly negatively correlated with the underlying index returns. This is a useful tool for a hedge fund.

13.5 THE US REIT EXPERIENCE

13.5.1 Introduction

REITs were created in the USA in 1960 to allow smaller investors to participate in property markets and invest in institutional quality real estate.[2] They are tax-neutral, or tax-transparent, vehicles provided they meet the qualification rules. In the USA, these rules include the following:

- There must be a minimum of 100 shareholders, with limited insider dominance.
- At least 75% of total assets must be held in real estate assets, cash, or government securities.
- At least 75% of gross income must be generated from rents of real property, interest on mortgages, gains on sales of property, and dividends from other REITs.
- At least 90% of the REIT's taxable income must be distributed to shareholders.

[1] NAREIT is the National Association of Real Estate Investment Trusts, based in the USA.

[2] The history of real estate investment trusts was described in some detail in Chapter 2, as they played a key role in past real estate cycles, particularly in the 1970s and 1990s.

US REITs can be public or private vehicles; in this chapter we focus on the listed (public) variety.[3] The market consists of equity REITs, mortgage REITs, and hybrid REITs. Equity REITs own property directly, and may be focused on a particular property sector (e.g. office, retail, hotel, multi-family) or a specific region of the USA (e.g. southeast, Midwest, California). Mortgage REITs provide loans to residential or commercial real estate borrowers, or invest in mortgage-backed securities. Hybrid REITs are a combination of both equity and mortgage REITs, and comprise a relatively small portion of the overall REIT market. In this chapter we focus on equity REITs.

The major growth period for US REITs began in 1991, as the vehicle proved ideal for re-capitalizing a distressed real estate market. The creation of the Umbrella Partnership REIT (UPREIT) in 1992 allowed a boom in securitization through the REIT vehicle. Property investors who owned real estate could contribute assets to a REIT in return for units in an operating partnership (OP). The OP units were transferable into shares of the REIT at the owner's option. By trading assets for the partnership units, owners who sold their assets to REITs would not have to pay capital gains taxes that otherwise would have to be paid at the time of sale. Instead, payment of capital gains taxes was deferred until the OP units were converted into shares, and then sold.

US REITs are now one of the longest-standing and most researched tax-transparent property vehicles in existence. The key question is whether they perform more like the underlying property market, or like the equity markets upon which they trade.

13.5.2 Distributions

A possible reason why REITs may be expected to perform like direct real estate is the regulation regarding dividend payments, which should mean that income returns closely resemble the income earned on privately held property.

When REITs were introduced in the USA in 1960, a high compulsory income distribution level of 90% was set. This was designed to ensure that the risk to investors was reduced (after all, "a bird in the hand is worth two in the bush").

The distribution level was later increased to 95% of net income. These required distributions were calculated by deducting expenses, interest, and (as is common in accounting for any company) a depreciation allowance from income, recognizing the following:

- Real estate vehicles need the ability to retain some earnings through which reinvestment and renewal of the buildings that they own can be made.
- In a particular year, a real estate owner can be faced with significant costs to repair and maintain buildings for existing or prospective occupiers.

More recently, in the 1999 REIT Modernization Act, the compulsory distribution level was reduced back to 90% of net income. The change did not appear to have a

[3]Private REITs must satisfy all of the requirements of a REIT, and if they do so, are exempt from taxes at the corporate level. Since they are private, they do not trade on an open exchange and are not liquid.

big impact on US REIT values, largely because REIT dividends are only partially constrained by the minimum distribution requirement.

The reason that these high payout proportions are not particularly restraining for REITs is that there is a big difference between reported net income and the net cash flow that an equity (property-owning) REIT has available to distribute. This difference is created by provisions for depreciation and amortization, associated with the cost-based treatment of commercial real estate assets in financial statements.

13.5.3 Measuring REIT Net Income

To satisfy the requirements to be a REIT, 90% of net income must be passed through to shareholders as dividends. However, when analyzing a REIT, net income is not considered the "true" earnings of the company, but is thought of as an accounting convention. Other alternatives to net income have become widely accepted by REIT analysts as being more effective measures of "true" earnings, and will be discussed in this section.

Defining Net Income

For any company, net income is defined using Generally Accepted Accounting Principles (GAAP) as:

Revenues
– Operating expenses
– Depreciation and amortization
– Interest expense
– General and administrative expenses
+/– Other items
Net income

All financial statements of companies in the USA that are under the jurisdiction of the Securities and Exchange Commission (SEC) must report net income that complies with GAAP requirements. As discussed, REITs must pass 90% of their net income in any year through to shareholders as dividends.

As an example, Highwoods Properties, Inc. (Highwoods) began as a private company owning an office park in Raleigh, NC in the late 1970s. Highwoods (ticker symbol HIW) was converted into an umbrella partnership REIT, or UPREIT, in 1994, and now develops and owns office properties in eight US markets: Raleigh, NC; Charlotte, NC; Richmond, VA; Pittsburgh, PA; Atlanta, GA; Nashville, TN; Orlando, FL; and Tampa, FL. The REIT is known for the high quality of its management team, and the quality of its portfolio. Highwoods shareholders earned $1.76 and $1.85 in dividends per share in 2017 and 2018, respectively. At the end of 2018, Highwoods shares were trading for $38.49 per share. The dividend yield was 4.8%.

Table 13.1 shows excerpts of the income statement for Highwoods in 2017 and 2018.

The income statement shows that rental and other revenue totaled $720,035 million in 2018, the most recent full year of operations. Expenses include operating expenses

TABLE 13.1 Income statement for Highwoods Properties, Inc., 2018 and 2017 ($'000)

Revenues	2018	2017
Rental and other revenues	$720,035	$702,737
Other income	$1,940	$2,283
Total revenue	$721,975	$705,020
Expenses		
Rental property and other expenses	$242,415	$236,888
Depreciation and amortization[1]	$229,955	$227,832
Interest expense	$71,422	$69,105
General and administrative expenses	$40,006	$39,648
Impairments of real estate assets	$423	$1,445
Total expenses	$584,221	$574,918
Net income before gain on sale	$137,754	$130,102
Equity in earnings of unconsolidated affiliates	$2,238	$7,404
+ Gain on sale of real estate	$37,638	$54,157
Net income (GAAP)	$177,630	$191,663
Distributions on preferred shares	−$2,492	−$2,492
Other items[2]	−$5,795	−$6,298
Net income available for shareholders	$169,343	$182,873
Common shares outstanding	103,439,000	102,682,000
Net income per share	$1.64	$1.78
Dividend paid to common shareholders	$1.85	$1.76
Dividend as a percentage of net income	113.00%	98.82%

Source: Highwoods Properties, Inc.

Notes:

1. Includes real estate depreciation of $227,045 in 2018 and $225,052 in 2017. The remainder is non-real estate depreciation.
2. Other items include income and losses from JV and other partnerships.

related to the ownership of properties, interest payments on debt, depreciation and amortization of real estate and non-real estate assets, general and administrative expenses arising from operating the REIT, and other non-recurring expenses. Expenses total $584,221 million and the difference between revenues and expenses is $137,754 million. Highwoods owns a small number of properties in unconsolidated affiliates, and the earnings of $2,238 million are added back before calculating net income. Gains on sale of properties of $37,638 million are also added. The total net income according to GAAP measures is $177,630 million in 2018.

To get to net income that is available to common stockholders, dividends on preferred stock must be subtracted, as must be other items that represent earnings on properties that are partially held by other entities. Net income available to common shareholders is $169,343 million. At the end of 2018, there were 103,439 million shares held by common shareholders, so net income per share was $1.64. Applying the 90% pass-through requirement, HIW would be required to pay $1.48 in dividends.

Instead, HIW paid a $1.85 dividend in 2018, which was 125% of what was required, and 113% of net income, so net income would appear to be insufficient income to pay the shareholder dividend. However, net income is not a good representation of total income for a REIT, and adjustments must be made to generate a more informative and accurate measure of recurring real estate income that is earned by Highwoods.

Rental revenue increases from 2017 to 2018, as do many of the expense items. However, 2018 GAAP net income is less than 2017 net income, which some may read to imply that overall results were weaker. The largest contributor to the difference is gain on sale of real estate. In 2017, gains of this type were $54,157 million, as Highwoods sold non-core properties that weren't in its top eight markets from the portfolio. Non-core properties were also sold in 2018, reducing net income, but at a lower level than in 2018. Sale of properties occurs for strategic purposes as market conditions are favorable, and not on a recurring or annual basis.

Funds from Operations

Funds from operations (FFO) is a measure that has become widely accepted, and more closely represents recurring income from property ownership for REITs. It should be noted here that there are many interpretations of how to convert net income to FFO, and that different REITs apply different conventions, making it difficult at times to compare performance across REITs.

There are two primary reasons that net income is not a good reflection of true REIT income. First, since depreciation is deducted from revenues to determine net income, and depreciation is a non-cash expense, GAAP net income underestimates true income for a REIT. Real property, if well located and maintained, is expected to appreciate in value. Further, if property values fall, decreases in value are unlikely to be correlated with depreciation entries determined using cost accounting conventions.

Second, gains or losses on sale of properties are one-time events, and not a component of recurring cash flow. To calculate FFO, depreciation is added, and one-time gains from sale of property are deducted. Additional items related to joint venture properties have a minor impact. The result is an approximation of core cash flow earned by the REIT.

The calculation of FFO for Highwoods Properties, Inc. (HIW) provides some insights into the difference between net income and FFO. FFO calculations for 2017 and 2018 are shown in Table 13.2.

FFO in 2018 was $3.45 per share, which is much higher than both the $1.85 dividend and the $1.64 in GAAP net income. In fact, the 2018 dividend is only 53.69% of the FFO earned by the REIT.

FFO growth between 2017 and 2018 is 2.4% ((($366,164 / $357,689) - 1) * 100), while net income was down by 7.4% ((($169,343 / $182,873) - 1) * 100). Net income is also more variable than FFO, mostly because of the unpredictable nature of asset sales. For these and other reasons, FFO is a more accurate measure of the income earned by HIW.

Some analysts go a step further to calculate cash available for distribution (CAD). FFO from Table 13.2 is modified by several items that require cash expenditures, and that are considered the cost of doing business for an office REIT (see Table 13.3). The first is dividends paid to preferred shareholders. Highwoods issued 125,000 preferred shares that pay 8 5/8%, or $86.25 per year in 1997, and approximately 29,000 of these shares are still outstanding, so the total preferred dividend paid in

TABLE 13.2 Calculation of Highwoods funds from operations (FFO, $'000)

	2018	2017
Net income	$177,630	$191,663
+ Depreciation of real estate assets	$227,045	$225,052
– Gain on sale of real estate	–$37,096	–$53,170
– Other items[1]	$1,077	–$3,558
Fund from operations	$368,656	$359,987
Less dividends on preferred stock	–$2,492	–$2,298
FFO for common shareholders	$366,164	$357,689
Common shares outstanding (diluted)[2]	106,268	105,594
FFO per share	$3.45	$3.39
Dividends paid to common shareholders	$1.85	$1.76
Dividends as percentage of FFO	53.69%	51.96%

Source: Highwoods Properties, Inc. and authors.
Notes:
1. Other items include real estate depreciation, and gains on sale of assets, held in JVs and other affiliates.
2. Diluted shares include those held by insiders that were granted as options or restricted shares.

TABLE 13.3 Calculation of Highwoods cash available for distribution (CAD, $'000)

	2018	2017
Funds from operations available to common shareholders	$368,656	$359,987
– Dividend paid to preferred shareholders	–$2,492	–$2,492
– Building improvements	–$37,960	–$38,676
– Tenant improvements	–$75,296	–$60,562
– Leasing commissions	–$25,329	–$19,849
– Straight-line rental income	–$22,604	–$30,838
+/– Other items	$6,959	$8,335
Total adjustments	–$156,722	–$144,082
–	–	–
CAD	$211,934	$215,905
/ Number of shares outstanding	106,268	105,594
CAD per share	$1.99	$2.04

2018 was $2.492 million. Additional cash was expended for building improvements, which include the cost to maintain, improve, and modernize building features and functions. In addition, leasing commissions and tenant improvements must be paid prior to new tenants taking occupancy. Combined, these two items cost $100,625 million in 2018, an increase from the previous year due to a larger number of tenants rolling over, and also to large developments that were brought to market by Highwoods in 2018.

The logic behind the straight-line rent item is a little more subtle, and a result of using GAAP accounting to define net income. In most leases (except for apartments), tenants sign long-term leases to occupy space. As was discussed in Chapter 6, office leases often have escalation clauses whereby the lease amount increases annually at a pre-specified rate. For example, an office lease might include a clause that states that rents will increase at 3% per year over a 5-year lease term. Rents of $26.00 in the base year grow as shown in Table 13.4.

GAAP for rents mandate that the average rent over the five periods be booked as income in each year of a tenant's lease term, or $27.61/sq. ft. This is the number that must be used to calculate GAAP rental income for a newly signed tenant during each year of their lease, despite it having no basis in reality.

For longer-term leases, the differences are more striking, as shown in Table 13.5. In this example, the tenant signed a 20-year lease for a Highwoods building with a starting rent of $26.00 in Year 1, and 3% escalations over the lease term. Rent paid in the final year is $5.48, and the average straight-line rent over the period is $33.60. GAAP

TABLE 13.4 Straight-line rent calculation (5-year term)

	Year 1	Year 2	Year 3	Year 4	Year 5
Rent	$26.00	$26.78	$27.58	$28.41	$29.26
Straight-line rent	$27.61				

TABLE 13.5 Straight-line rent calculation (20-year term)

Year	Rent	Straight-line rent
1	$26.00	$33.60
2	$26.78	
3	$27.58	
4	$28.41	
5	$29.26	
6	$30.14	
7	$31.04	
8	$31.97	
9	$32.93	
10	$33.92	
11	$34.94	
12	$35.99	
13	$37.07	
14	$38.18	
15	$39.33	
16	$40.41	
17	$41.62	
18	$42.87	
19	$44.16	
20	$45.48	

accounting requires that the $33.60 straight-line rent be reflected in net income calculations in each year of the 20-year term.

In both cases, the straight-line rent is higher in the early part of the lease term, and in the last part, the straight-line rent is lower than the amount paid by the tenant. Understatements and overstatements are larger for leases with longer terms. Highwoods booked a $22.644 million deduction for straight-line rents in 2018, indicating that actual rents received were lower than reported using the GAAP calculation.

As shown in Table 13.3, the sum of the adjustment to get from FFO to CAD in 2018 is –$156.722 million, and CAD is $211.934 million. Highwoods shows a negative number for the straight-line adjustment in both years, indicating that the average rent is higher than rents being paid by Highwoods tenants (or customers).

The CAD per share in 2018 is $1.99. The $1.85 per share dividend in 2018 is paid from $1.99 of cash available for distribution, for a CAD payout ratio of 92.97%.

While these different metrics offer alternative ways of assessing REIT earnings, there is a lack of consistency in how they are calculated between firms.

13.5.4 Performance

Table 13.6 shows the annual returns earned in the USA by a number of different asset classes over several different time periods, ending in June 2019. The returns are annualized from quarterly data, and include returns for:

- equities (as measured by the S&P 500);
- bonds (as measured by the Merrill Lynch Bond Index);
- direct property (as measured by the NCREIF Property Index, or NPI);
- REITs (as measured by the Wilshire Real Estate Securities Index (WRESI));
- global REITs (as measured by EPRA);
- small stocks (as measured by the Russell 2000);
- the Consumer Price Index (CPI).

Over all time periods except for the most recent 3 years, the US REIT market outperformed all other asset classes. The 12.49% 30-year REIT average return since the second quarter of 1989 exceeds returns earned by all other asset classes. In all periods,

TABLE 13.6 Annualized returns for US asset classes, periods ending Q2 2019

Period	S&P 500	Bonds	NCREIF	REITs	EPRA	R2000	CPI
3 year	15.03%	2.37%	6.89%	6.67%	6.01%	13.85%	2.05%
5 year	11.34%	3.00%	8.83%	9.70%	6.33%	8.37%	1.46%
10 year	15.66%	3.95%	9.29%	17.41%	12.54%	15.17%	1.73%
15 year	9.92%	4.32%	8.84%	12.29%	10.28%	10.09%	2.03%
20 year	7.27%	4.99%	8.98%	13.07%	10.83%	10.02%	2.20%
25 year	11.33%	5.57%	9.45%	12.56%	10.26%	11.44%	2.23%
30 year	11.29%	6.07%	7.85%	12.49%	9.52%	11.47%	2.45%

Sources: Clarion Partners Investment Research, NCREIF, NAREIT, EPRA, S&P, Bloomberg.

TABLE 13.7 Variability of asset returns, periods ending Q2 2019

Period	S&P 500	Bonds	NCREIF	REITs	EPRA	R2000	CPI
3 year	12.75%	3.39%	0.27%	12.82%	11.06%	16.88%	1.11%
5 year	11.02%	3.22%	1.33%	12.93%	10.53%	15.70%	1.42%
10 year	13.29%	3.22%	2.82%	16.42%	14.54%	17.60%	1.43%
15 year	14.76%	3.28%	5.20%	22.43%	20.70%	18.86%	2.00%
20 year	16.07%	3.42%	4.55%	20.48%	19.33%	20.42%	1.89%
25 year	15.90%	3.63%	4.17%	19.17%	18.60%	19.98%	1.71%
30 year	15.29%	3.88%	4.39%	18.74%	19.23%	19.99%	1.62%

Sources: Clarion Partners Investment Research, NCREIF, NAREIT, EPRA, S&P, Bloomberg.

REITs earned a return that was greater than inflation, but the same is true for all other asset classes.

Table 13.7 shows the annualized standard deviations of the quarterly returns, and demonstrates wide variation across assets. As previously stated in this and other chapters, the standard deviation of the NCREIF returns is artificially low due to the method of calculation used. The increase in variability of the NCREIF Property Index, however – even when using appraisal-based returns – is observably higher in periods that contain the global financial crisis and its aftermath.

US REITs, shown to have the highest 30-year average annualized return in Table 13.6, also exhibit the third highest standard deviation among all of the assets exhibited. The Russell 2000 index demonstrated the highest volatility at 19.99%, with global REITs (as measured by the FTSE EPRA NAREIT Global Index) a close second. US REITs are next in line, and their variability is 345 basis points higher than the S&P 500 index. Not surprisingly given the relatively stable interest rate environment throughout the period, bonds demonstrated the lowest standard deviations over the 30-year horizon. Interestingly, NCREIF variability is only 51 basis points higher than the bond index: valuation smoothing is discussed elsewhere in this book.

Table 13.8 shows the returns earned by the US REIT sector and the privately held real estate sector as measured by the NCREIF Property Index in the period surrounding the global financial crisis. Several observations can be made about the relative performance of the two indices during this period. First, recall that Lehman Brothers declared bankruptcy in September 2008, and that mortgage-backed securities defaults were one of the main reasons it happened. Variability in REIT returns is quite high starting in the fourth quarter of 2008, with REIT returns falling 38.8%, on a quarterly basis, and losing 31.9% in Q1 2009. The overall decline in return for REITs was 70%, as investors exited the REIT market, unloading the most liquid real estate investment in their portfolio and driving prices down. In the second quarter of 2009, investors came back into the market, recognizing that prices had fallen below the value of the underlying properties. For this reason, REITs rebounded in Q2 and Q3 2009.

Another interesting observation is the lag in the measurement of the real estate downturn in the NCREIF index relative to the REIT index. REIT investors sold from the market in Q4 2007 and in Q2 2008, perhaps recognizing that risk had increased and utilizing the liquidity provided by the REIT market. NCREIF returns dropped in Q4

TABLE 13.8 Quarterly returns, US real estate, Q1 2007–Q1 2010

Quarter	REITs	NCREIF
Q1 2007	3.5%	3.6%
Q2 2007	−9.0%	4.6%
Q3 2007	2.6%	3.6%
Q4 2007	−12.7%	3.2%
Q1 2008	1.4%	1.6%
Q2 2008	−4.9%	0.6%
Q3 2008	5.6%	−0.2%
Q4 2008	−38.8%	−8.3%
Q1 2009	−31.9%	−7.3%
Q2 2009	28.8%	−5.2%
Q3 2009	33.3%	−3.3%
Q4 2009	9.4%	−2.1%
Q1 2010	10.0%	0.8%
Average	−0.21%	−0.66%
Annualized	−0.85%	−2.60%
SD	20.35%	4.28%

Sources: Clarion Partners Investment Research, NCREIF, NAREIT, EPRA, S&P, Bloomberg.

2009, but the decrease was less on an absolute basis, and it took from Q4 2008 to Q4 2009 for the private real estate index to decrease 26.2%.

From this, it appears that the REIT market reacted to negative news from the economy more quickly and recovered more quickly. Private real estate reacted more slowly given the "rear view" nature of appraisal-based index return calculations, and was also slower to recover. Note that these analyses are based on annual data, and it is clear that REITs and private real estate are not correlated using annual returns.

Hoesli and Oikarinen (2012) published a prize-winning paper on the long-run relationship between REITs and private real estate. They found that, while the short-term co-movement between REITs and stocks is substantially stronger than that between REITs and direct real estate, REITs are likely to bring the same exposure to various risk factors into a long-horizon investment portfolio as will direct real estate. REITs are expected to have the same diversification properties as direct real estate investments in the long horizon, defined as around 4 years, after which holding period REITs and real estate exhibit similar performance characteristics. So in the short term, REITs do not perform like real estate, probably due to valuation smoothing and the noise introduced by stock market volatility, while they are driven by the same factors in the long run.

Table 13.9 presents correlations of REITs with other asset classes. Do REITs provide diversification and inflation hedging benefits? Over the latest 20-year period (ending in June 2019), REITs are shown to be fairly highly correlated with the three public equity indexes (S&P 500, EPRA, and the R2000), and hence are not likely to provide strong diversification benefits. In addition, the correlation with the CPI is 0.17, and a finding of inflation hedging would require a correlation that is much higher.

TABLE 13.9 Correlations of real estate with other assets

Asset	20-Year horizon		3-Year horizon	
	REITs	NCREIF	REITS	NCREIF
S&P 500	0.65	0.18	0.72	0.66
Bonds	0.07	−0.12	0.50	−0.31
NCREIF	0.25	1.00	0.47	1.00
REITs	1.00	0.25	1.00	0.47
EPRA	0.92	0.22	0.96	0.52
R2000	0.69	0.15	0.62	0.81
CPI	0.17	0.23	0.48	0.28

Sources: Clarion Partners Investment Research, NCREIF, NAREIT, EPRA, S&P, Bloomberg.

The correlation of REIT returns with bonds is much lower, indicating diversification potential from holding these two asset classes in a portfolio. Both public and private real estate exhibit positive correlations with the CPI, indicating that real estate assets demonstrate at least a partial hedge against inflation.

Summary

REITs provide some diversification benefits with bonds, but not with traded equities (e.g. S&P 500, Russell 2000). REIT returns are also shown to provide a positive correlation with inflation, indicating the provision of a partial hedge. They exhibit higher volatility than all other asset classes over a 15-year and 20-year horizon, largely due to the fact that they can be bought and sold like stocks. Apparently, the benefit of liquidity is offset by the cost of higher volatility. In the short term, REITs do not perform like real estate, probably due to valuation smoothing and the noise introduced by stock market volatility, while they are driven by the same factors in the long run.

13.6 THE GLOBAL MARKET

13.6.1 The Global Property Company Universe

The global listed property company universe, including REITs, includes all companies that invest in real estate or real estate-related assets. Figure 13.1 shows that the combined market capitalization of developed and emerging Asian property companies exceeds the market capitalization of developed North American (mostly US) property companies. Asian and North American countries comprise over half of the total global property company universe.

13.6.2 The Global REIT Universe

As at 2020, 39 countries had adopted some form of REIT legislation, including all of the G7 countries. Many countries have long-standing REIT industries, including the

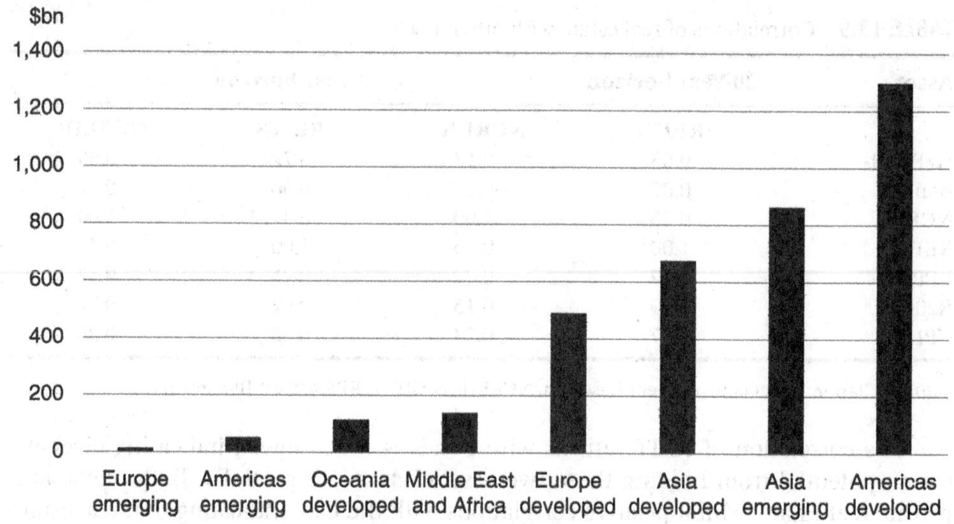

FIGURE 13.1 The global universe of all property companies
Source: EPRA, June 2019.

G7 countries, Australia, Hong Kong, the Netherlands, Singapore, and South Africa. Portugal has the most recent REIT market, passing REIT legislation in early 2019, and according to the National Association of Real Estate Investment Trusts (NAREIT), many other countries are considering REIT legislation (Argentina, Cambodia, Ghana, Indonesia, Malta, Nigeria, Sweden, and Tanzania). The REIT has become an integral part of the investable universe for individual and institutional investors around the globe.

We show REIT market capitalizations in each country with more than $1 billion. The USA is nearly 10 times larger than Japan, which is the next largest REIT market. North American REITs (USA and Canada) comprise over 65% of the $1.9 trillion global REIT market, while Asian REITs are the next largest proportion at just over 15%, followed by the European market which is 11%.

Market capitalizations from 2010 are shown in parentheses in Table 13.10, and show the rapid growth of most REIT markets. The US REIT market grew at an annual rate of 13.16% to $1.184 trillion in 2019 from $389 billion in 2010, more than tripling market capitalization. The Japanese REIT market grew at a rate of 18.64% per year to $135.32 billion from $29.43 billion during the same period. Of the markets with greater than $20 billion of assets in 2019, Singapore, Canada, Hong Kong, and South Africa all grew by more than 300%.

The level of specialization of the publicly traded real estate vehicles is shown in Table 13.11. Diversified REITs dominate the industry in terms of the number of companies and also market capitalization, followed by retail, office, residential, and industrial REITs. The level and type of diversification varies significantly by country. In the USA,

TABLE 13.10 Global REIT market capitalizations

Country	Market cap ($bn)
USA	$1,184.42 (389.0)
Japan	$135.32 (29.43)
Australia	$99.82 (80.00)
UK	$72.87 (37.18)
Singapore	$67.08 (23.13)
Canada	$60.55 (20.61)
France	$58.09 (64.53)
Hong Kong	$38.58 (9.52)
Spain	$26.14 (NA)
Netherlands	$24.50 (11.23)
South Africa	$23.50 (3.40)
Belgium	$18.59 (6.76)
Thailand	$14.88 (NA)
Mexico	$14.65 (NA)
China	$13.18 (NA)
Malaysia	$7.27 (1.54)
New Zealand	$5.14 (2.54)
Germany	$4.83 (0.71)
India	$4.11 (NA)
Ireland	$3.57 (NA)
Brazil	$3.55 (NA)
Taiwan	$3.53 (NA)
Saudi Arabia	$3.35 (NA)
Turkey	$2.94 (1.89)
Greece	$1.74 (NA)
South Korea	$1.61 (0.13)
Israel	$1.56 (NA)
Indonesia	$1.12 (NA)
Italy	$1.10 (NA)
Poland	$0.82 (NA)
UAE	$0.81 (NA)
Russia	$0.21 (NA)
Pakistan	$0.14 (NA)

Source: EPRA, June 2019.

REITs tend to be specialized by property type. Australia, Canada, and the UK also offer property type specialization, albeit to a lesser degree than the USA. Small public real estate companies in China are specialized, but the large public REITs in Asia tend to be more diversified. This is true even in countries with highly developed public real estate markets, such as Japan, Singapore, and Hong Kong, where large, publicly traded real estate operating companies are active in developing and holding a wide array of real estate and infrastructure, often across multiple countries.

TABLE 13.11 Global REIT market sector breakdown

Property sector	# Companies	Market cap ($'000)	Avg. market cap ($'000)
Data Centers	4	$38,819	$9,705
Diversified	167	$498,516	$2,985
Health Care	22	$140,140	$6,370
Industrial	38	$169,112	$4,450
Industrial/Office	12	$26,182	$2,182
Lodging/Resorts	18	$54,321	$3,018
Office	55	$210,226	$3,822
Residential	65	$326,014	$5,016
Retail	85	$317,218	$3,732
Self-Storage	7	$63,993	$9,142
Specialty	3	$24,946	$8,315
	476	$1,869,487	$3,927

Sources: FTSE, NAREIT, EPRA.

13.6.3 The UK REIT

In contrast to the US REIT, the UK REIT market began trading much more recently, on January 2, 2007. A small number – but all of the largest by value – of traditional property companies became (at the price of a one-off tax charge) early converters. The converting companies included Land Securities, Hammerson, and British Land.

The rules under which they must operate include requirements to:

(a) Be a "property rental business," with 75% of income arising from that business and 75% of assets dedicated to it (2006 Finance Act, s.108). However, as long as these tests are satisfied, a UK REIT may carry out taxable ancillary activities, which can include property (re-)development.
(b) Distribute at least 90% of the profits of the property rental business (2006 Finance Act, s.107). This does not include capital gains from selling property, though, which can either be distributed or reinvested in the portfolio (2006 Finance Act, s.118).

The qualifications to each requirement are important, as they appear to give UK REITs flexibility to renew their portfolios. It is important that distributions will be from profits rather than gross income. These steps have, on the face of it, reduced the level of dividends to investors. However, because UK and European property companies adopt accounting standards that do not permit the deduction of depreciation (as happens with GAAP accounting in the USA), those profits (and therefore the distributions) are higher than would be the case in the USA.

Because UK REITs are required to carry properties at market value in their accounts and no allowance for depreciation is made to offset taxable income, values change with market conditions rather than being written down each year. This key difference from the US treatment means that the distributable profits of a UK REIT will be much closer to its cash flow, and FFO or AFFO adjustments are of much less importance and use.

Other differences exist between accounting practices and various REIT regimes that may influence distribution and retention decisions. In particular, the terms and conditions of leases granted will determine whether the REIT or the tenant is responsible for repairs and maintenance. This, in turn, not only influences the pattern of income and expenditure, but potentially also the extent and amount of depreciation in the portfolio (Baum and Turner, 2004).

Although UK leases have become shorter and opportunities to break have increased, traditional repairing and rent review provisions still predominate (Crosby *et al.*, 2005). In the USA, leases are shorter on average and more of the repairing obligations are borne by the landlord. This means that there are more opportunities for the US owner to actively manage their buildings and more incentive to do so, owing to the need to achieve re-lettings more often. In contrast, UK leases have encouraged more passive management of the stock. Responsibility for regular maintenance to combat physical deterioration is passed to the tenant, especially in single-let (single-tenant) buildings, but there is no guarantee that the tenant will perform these obligations in the same way and, often, they are discharged through payment of a dilapidations charge at the end of the lease. While, in theory, this compensates the landlord for lost value, the impact of not performing work when it is necessary may mean greater depreciation in value overall.

Because of these differences, which exist when comparing other countries as well, the experience and performance of the US and other markets are of limited value when attempting to determine performance for UK, and even other European, REITs. These differences may lead to differences in performance though, which could lead to greater diversification benefits.

13.7 REIT PRICING

13.7.1 Using Earnings to Value REITs

The valuation of a REIT involves different approaches in different regimes. In the USA, REIT valuations are typically made by reference to earnings (defined in different ways, see above) and a price-to-FFO ratio, or a variant of this model. In the UK, valuations of assets are available and pricing by reference to net asset value (NAV) is common.

It has also become common to analyze UK REIT prices by reference to implied yields. For example, a City office building yielding 5.5% may appear unattractive if the "correct yield" (see Chapter 4) is assessed as 6.5%. A listed property company owning City offices and trading at a 30% discount to NAV would have a higher implied yield, say 7%, which may be attractive.

Although the pricing of listed securities is linked to that of the real estate portfolio, there is also a significant degree of variability around the underlying NAV. This is because both REITs and property company shares are influenced by price movements in the equities markets in general (as was shown in the correlations statistics presented above). Consequently, there can be price anomalies compared with the underlying real estate market which can be exploited tactically. (It is commonly suggested by REIT analysts that property equities, unconstrained by valuations and comparable evidence, forecast the direct market up to 18 months ahead.) However, this issue can also increase the risk of REITs underperforming the underlying property market, and REITs are unlikely to provide access to the same level of pure real estate performance in the short term as the unlisted market.

REIT analysts in the USA use FFO multiples (REIT share price divided by FFO) as an indicator of the relative value of REIT shares. Within the office sector, for example, REITs with holdings in central business districts (CBDs) might be expected to trade at higher FFO multiples than REITs that hold suburban office buildings. This is due to the fact that, generally, it is more difficult to bring new space to CBD markets as they are thought to be more supply constrained due to high land prices and more rigorous planning processes. Used like a price-to-earnings ratio in the general equity market, low FFO multiples may suggest that REITs are cheap.

13.7.2 Market Capitalization and Net Asset Value

EPRA and NAREIT maintain REIT and listed property vehicle data of the type one would expect to find in listed securities markets. The market capitalizations of the global REIT markets are therefore readily available. One method of determining the relative value of a REIT is to compare the value of its market capitalization to the value of the underlying real estate that it owns less its debt. This value is called the net asset value, and is similar to the valuation techniques used by appraisers (valuers).

Calculating NAV is inexact, especially for REITs that hold diversified assets in numerous markets. The first step is to estimate the net operating income (NOI) from each property owned by the REIT. The analysis should then divide the NOI by the relevant capitalization rate for the property's location, property type, and building quality. Often, properties within a market (for example Dallas office buildings) will be aggregated and the NOI earned by these properties divided by the market's capitalization rate to determine an estimate of property value in that sector. The analyst will then add the total asset values of all the REIT's properties to get the total value of the portfolio. From this, the REIT's liabilities are subtracted, leaving the NAV, which is then compared to the equity market capitalization of the REIT.

13.7.3 Premium or Discount to NAV?

Data produced by Green Street Advisers suggests that over the period 1990–2019, US REITs traded at an average premium to NAV (this is estimated NAV – REITs are not required to value their assets) of approximately 5%. In the 1998–9 period, the REIT price to NAV premium was 35%, but by the middle of 2008, the estimated discount to NAV exceeded 40%, rivalling the record discount seen in 1991. Since 2012, the REIT prices have generally ranged between a 10% premium and a 10% discount to NAV.

When REIT shares trade at premiums, the sector can be expected to grow, as REITs can buy comparable property in private markets for a lower price per dollar of income than the share price. Once owned by the REIT, the value should adjust to the REIT's pricing. When REIT share price is above NAV, the issuance of shares becomes attractive to investors as prospective shareholders expect the REIT to buy bargain properties in the private market.

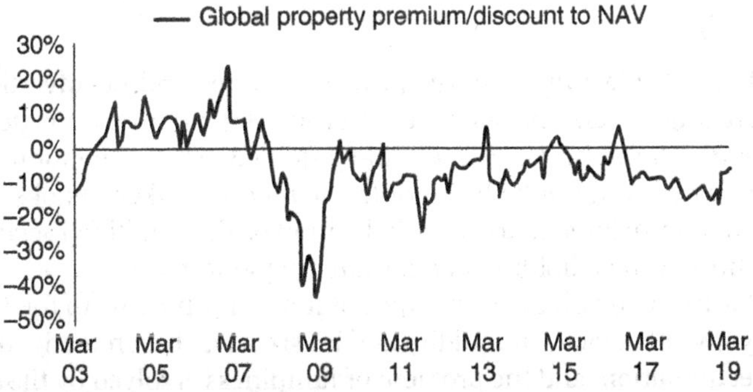

FIGURE 13.2 Global property markets trade at discounts to NAV
Sources: UBS, data from March 2003 to March 2019; FTSE EPRA/NAREIT Global Index.

What explains the premium, or discount? Figure 13.2 shows UBS estimates of discounts and premiums in the global REIT sector from 2003 to 2019. The charts show that global property companies have traded at fairly consistent discounts to NAV since 2007.

Arguments about the source of this variation can become heated. This is because the well-known valuation smoothing issue which affects direct real estate prices is seen by some – REIT proponents included – as wholly destructive of the value of appraisal-based estimate of value and, by extension, NAV estimates. Compared to "real" pricing in the stock markets, this is mere opinion, and systematically flawed at that. To proponents of direct property, valuations can and should be professional estimates of the most likely selling price of a property in the absence of a distressed market, while stock market prices are volatile, unreliable reflections of short-term sentiment in the absence of a more objective logic. The debate is philosophical and unresolvable.

Assuming that both NAV estimates and REIT trading prices contain useful information, why might the price of a REIT share be higher (or lower) than its NAV per share? In our opinion, the following arguments are the most convincing.

Instant Exposure

In Chapter 11, we examined the so-called J-curve effect. This describes the phenomenon which affects any investor in direct real estate or in a blind (unpopulated by assets) real estate fund. $100 million invested in either of these formats is converted, all things held equal, into around $95 million of assets, because management fees, legal fees, other due diligence costs, and property taxes (stamp duty, for example) will likely add up to around 5% of the acquired property's value.

Investors in REITs and REOCs do not suffer this problem. The investor usually gains instant exposure to a fully invested real estate portfolio in the assembly of which these costs have already been incurred. All things held equal, this should drive REIT prices to a natural premium to the observed average premium in the USA of, say, 5%.

Liquidity/Divisibility

What creates liquidity? Listing a security provides a shop window, advertising the product and encouraging buyers and sellers to transact. But a quotation is not sufficient to attract the attention of a market maker. Many quoted assets – including many small property companies – will not be taken onto the market maker's books. To encourage trades, they will require large market capitalization of the combined sector of standard vehicles plus short average holding periods and frequent trading.

The case for REITs revolves around the solution they provide to the twin problems direct property investors face – illiquidity and lot size. The best remedy for illiquidity is a public market quotation, and the problem of lumpiness is solved by the securitization of real estate and the consequent divisibility of the REIT instrument.

Given a REIT's potential liquidity, these advantages should drive REIT prices to a premium to NAV.

Asset Values are Higher than the Reported NAV

If asset values are perceived to be higher than the reported NAV, then efficient REIT pricing will drive share prices above NAV. Because valuation smoothing is expected to depress valuations below trading prices in a rising market, this is a likely phenomenon in a strong market for property investing. (Observed or estimated US REIT premiums have generally been positive in strong markets and negative in weak markets: see Figure 13.2.)

If asset values are perceived to be lower than the reported NAV, then REIT prices can be expected to be below NAV. This is a likely phenomenon in a falling or weak market for property investing.

Projected Asset Values are Expected to Exceed the Reported NAV

If asset values are expected to rise, REIT prices might act as a coincident indicator of these expectations and a leading indicator of property prices. Because property prices are somewhat auto-correlated, this is a likely phenomenon in a strong market for property investing, and will work in the same direction as the perceived difference between current and reported NAVs. Note, however, that these are different, albeit related, factors.

If asset values are expected to fall, then REIT prices will be expected to be below NAV.

Management Skills

If management skills and efficiency are perceived to be of high quality relative to the overheads of running the business, it is argued that this would drive REIT share prices to a premium against NAV. The opposite would occur if management is perceived to be value destroying.

Tax

If there is an embedded tax liability (usually a capital gains tax liability which is contingent on the sale of assets), this is likely to drive prices to a discount to the gross of tax NAV. As with many factors, it is difficult to estimate how large this effect will be. If a property company is sold with such an embedded contingent liability, there is usually a negotiation about how much of that tax risk is deducted from the price, as it is not possible to be certain how large the tax will be or, indeed, if any tax will arise, without knowledge of when the assets will be sold, or for how much.

Debt

REITs will fund asset acquisitions through secured and unsecured financing. REIT analysts and markets generally favor management that maintains lower levels of debt to assets, and lower debt payments to income levels. Secured financing (as discussed in Chapters 8 and 9) encumbers the asset, and limits flexibility, so price may drop relative to NAV for companies with higher secured financing as a percentage of asset value.

13.8 CONCLUSION

REITs are here to stay as a way for individual and institutional investors to gain exposure to real estate in their portfolios. Providing a modicum of liquidity relative to other equity sectors, but a great deal of liquidity compared to private real estate ownership, this sector of the market has grown since its first introduction in the USA in 1960. Indeed, market capitalizations around the globe have grown significantly over the past 10 years as existing REITs have grown and accessed the public markets with follow-on offerings, as new REITs were formed, and as legislation was adopted in a large number of countries to allow the REIT form of ownership.

Some investors utilize the REIT market as their sole entry into real estate investment. In contrast to the private markets, where information is held very closely, public reporting by REITs allows large amounts of information to be available to the investing public. In addition, lot size is sufficiently small to allow investors access to the market without requiring large net worth and income.

REITs may also be held as part of a real estate portfolio that holds illiquid unlisted or directly owned property. REITs can provide some portfolio liquidity as well as the opportunity to tactically allocate a portfolio around benchmark sector holdings to rapidly increase or decrease holdings in the real estate portfolio. Given lags involved in measuring private real estate performance, there may be opportunities to arbitrage price differences between public and private markets.

Institutional investors may also allocate a portion of their real estate holdings to a dedicated REIT portfolio that can be held either in an indexed fund that mirrors the overall REIT market, or in a managed fund where a professional investment manager is hired to choose REITs that are expected to outperform the index.

In the short term, REITs do not perform like real estate, probably due to valuation smoothing and the noise introduced by stock market volatility, while they are driven by the same factors in the long run. The excessive volatility and value loss experienced in both the direct and unlisted markets during the credit crisis of 2008 provided a strong case for REITs and other forms of public real estate investing. We can expect markets to continue to grow, and for investors to become even more willing to own and trade REIT shares.

CHAPTER 14

Real Estate Debt Markets

14.1 INTRODUCTION

Until the 1990s, the way in which finance was used by real estate investors was relatively simple. A first (or senior) mortgage loan was used as debt financing, and the remainder of the capital needed to buy an asset was raised from equity investors.

Until the 1990s, underwriting criteria (see Chapter 9) were fairly standard across the lending industry, with long-term loan-to-value (LTV) ratios in the 65–75% range, and debt coverage ratios (DCRs) in the 1.25–1.5 times range. With the advent of the Commercial Mortgage-Backed Securities (CMBS) market, which really took hold with the expansion of Nomura's activities in the 1990s, the world of commercial real estate finance changed, as did the methods that lenders used to compete against each other.

Traditionally, commercial banks, life insurance companies, and savings institutions provided the bulk of debt financing to the commercial real estate market. There were periods during which other institutions competed (for example, mortgage REITs in the 1970s as discussed in Chapter 2), but from 1980 through roughly the year 2000 the lion's share of debt financing came from these three sources.

The CMBS market grew rapidly through the early years of the 21st century until in 2007 CMBS providers originated $230 billion of commercial mortgages, which was roughly 55% of all mortgages originated that year. The CMBS market was thought to be a permanent part of the lending environment for many reasons, largely because it provided a relatively transparent vehicle that allowed investors to gain access to the commercial mortgage corner of the fixed-income market where they had previously not been able to invest, and offered higher yields in an increasingly yield-compressed bond market. Being "gradable and tradable," CMBSs were rated by independent and well-known rating agencies and provided liquidity, as they could be traded after issuance. In the four-quadrant diagram that we showed in Chapter 12, these became the major component of the public debt market sector.

These securities proved to be in extremely high demand by investors, who bought the $230 billion of securities backed by commercial mortgages in 2007. During the 2003–7 period, investors such as pension funds, high net worth individuals or families, global investors, and anyone in search of a few basis points of yield above similarly rated corporate bonds flocked to buy rated CMBS issues. The CMBS market matched willing investors, investment bankers who were very willing to create CMBS for investors (given their profitability), and rating agencies who provided a method for investors to compare and contrast risk. In combination, all of these events helped lead to the enormous and unprecedented growth in this new sector of the commercial mortgage and fixed-income markets.

In addition to the public debt markets, borrowers could access mezzanine debt from private lenders. Similar to a junior mortgage, mezzanine debt – when added to the senior loan – allowed investors to buy properties at very high LTV ratios. With first mortgage and mezzanine debt widely and cheaply available, investors were required to provide only small equity stakes to take ownership of properties in the commercial real estate market. Almost all first and mezzanine debt was non-recourse (see Chapter 8), which meant that owners had an option on the upside of the property with very little money invested, and the ability to default on their loans if things took a turn for the worse.

The combination of cheap and easy debt led to over-investment in real estate assets, which in turn led to an unprecedented increase in the prices of individual commercial properties that was not based on the underlying fundamentals of the markets. Instead, a low cost of debt capital allowed buyers to increase bid prices. In addition, numerous investors had large amounts of funds to invest, which allowed a great deal of liquidity to wash over all investable markets.

As the excess liquidity attempted to find a home, competition to buy and own assets became destructive. This led to large numbers of bidders for each property that was placed on the market, and an auction-like environment further pushed up asset prices. In this seller's market, investors had to reduce their required rates of return on equity below prudent levels to be able to bid enough to own assets. The combination of a low cost of debt capital, a low cost of equity capital, and enormous flows of funds into real estate led to unprecedented increases in asset values and decreases in real estate capitalization rates.

As is the case with most real estate cycles, the growth in values was unsustainable and markets began to adjust from mid-2007 and 2008 levels. As values dropped, lenders reduced their allocations to the commercial mortgage market, CMBS originators were priced out of the market, and equity investors tried to figure out how to protect their capital.

Defaults and foreclosures were common in the latter parts of the first decade of the 21st century, although the outcome for many owners was unlike previous downturns in the real estate industry. Instead of foreclosing on properties, many lenders delayed taking over properties and instead extended the maturity and modified the terms of loans. By delaying foreclosure, the lenders hoped for improvements in market conditions, and gambled on borrowers being able to make full payment on their loans at some time in the future. A low interest rate environment and job growth in the economy helped with this strategy, and lenders modified loan terms by reducing the contract rate to a current rate which allowed lower payments than had been contractually agreed upon in the original mortgage documents.

The economy strengthened in the second decade of the 2000s, creating new jobs and demand for space. At the same time, interest rates dropped and lenders slowly returned to the debt market. After a period of declining prices and uncertainty regarding the risk of real estate investment, equity investors took advantage of low values and the demand for asset ownership increased after several years of sitting on the sidelines. Values increased, and by 2017 real estate pricing exceeded the peak levels experienced in 2007.

The long recovery continued into early 2020 with no sign of abatement. As we write this, the US economy and real estate markets have been on a general upswing since 2008, representing an unprecedented 12-year recovery in real estate markets. A turnaround is inevitable at some point in the future, but the usual boom-to-downturn predictors of oversupply, undisciplined lending, and a recession are not yet apparent.

This chapter provides a history of lending in the USA, which clearly led the global market, as well as the story of how the secondary market for commercial mortgages was created. The factors that led to the downfall of the CMBS market are also discussed. We also discuss the subsequent post-crisis recovery of mortgage and real estate markets, with new securities that more closely align the risk exposure or originators of mortgage loans, issuers of securities, and investors. As we discussed in Chapter 2, though, history often repeats itself and cycles drive real estate markets.

14.2 A BRIEF HISTORY LESSON

14.2.1 Banking in the 1960s and 1970s

In the 1960s and 1970s, community bankers, including commercial banks, savings and loan institutions, and mutual savings banks, attracted deposits from the local community and lent that money out to local borrowers as mortgages to be used to purchase homes. Figure 14.1 highlights the relationship between a community banker and his borrowers: banks were intermediaries between those who needed capital (borrowers on home loans) and those who had capital (depositors).

Bank regulators limited the amount of interest that could be paid on these deposits, based on fears that destructive competition among banks would lead to increases in rates paid (Reubling, 1970). Deposits held at banks were either demand deposits (checking accounts available for withdrawal on demand) or time deposits (savings accounts available for withdrawal with notice). These short-term deposits served as the bulk of a bank's liabilities, and the banks were totally dependent on the supply of deposits. Without them, banks could not sustain a lending program.

The rates that banks charged on home mortgages were stable in the 1960s and early 1970s, and lending out money at those rates while paying out constrained rates on deposits allowed bankers to earn a nice spread on the money that flowed through the bank. As "spread bankers," they could earn 7% on their assets (mortgages) while paying 4% on deposits. This 300 basis point spread was the profit earned by the bank, and provided a good living for bankers.

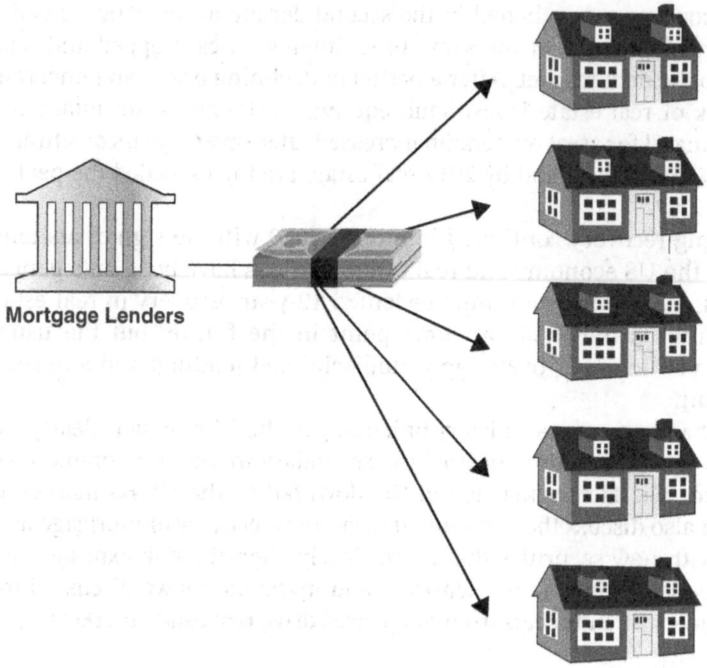

FIGURE 14.1 The traditional property lending process

The typical mortgage at the time was a constant payment, fully amortizing loan with a maturity of 30 years.[1] There was, however, a mismatch between the short-term nature of the liabilities (time and demand deposits) and the long-term nature of the assets (30 years).

The bank would carefully underwrite each mortgage, which was used by a local borrower to buy a local house. Typically, for many small community banks, the lender personally knew the borrower, the house, and the neighborhood, and provided a thorough analysis of the borrower's potential to pay back the promised mortgage principal and interest. Community bankers felt a fiduciary responsibility to their depositors, who were entrusting their money to the bank.

Banks held the mortgages as assets on their balance sheets until loan maturity or loan prepayment (typically due to household mobility). The bank incurred the risk of mortgage default for the entire length of time that the mortgage was outstanding.

[1] Like now, most borrowers did not pay principal and interest for the full 30 years, although there were lower levels of household mobility. Borrowers might prepay the mortgage if they were moving to a larger house, moving out of a particular neighborhood, community, or city, divorcing (less common), or defaulting because they were unable to make their promised payments.

14.2.2 The Volcker Era of High and Volatile Interest Rates

Paul Volcker became the Chairman of the Federal Reserve Board in the fall of 1979, inheriting an economy with historically high and volatile inflation and interest rates. Volcker altered the Fed's long-standing policy of pegging interest rates, and instead focused on tightening the money supply. The thinking was that short-term pain in the form of rapidly rising rates would ultimately lead to gain in the sense that economic activity would slow and inflation and interest rates would decline.

Rising interest rates created at least two major problems for community bankers. First, rational depositors withdrew their money out of interest rate-constrained deposits at banks and placed them in short-term money market funds where they could earn higher, market-based returns. This process was called disintermediation, in effect taking funds away from traditional financial intermediaries. Disintermediation greatly reduced the amount of funds that could be lent out to local mortgage markets. Without deposits (the source of funds for lenders), banks could not make new loans (the use of funds).

Second, the asset side of the balance sheet was also greatly impacted. Banks had made loans for 30-year terms at the low rates of the 1960s and early 1970s. As the general level of inflation, interest, and mortgage rates increased, these fixed-income bank assets declined significantly in value. The mismatch between long-term assets (declining in value) and short-term liabilities (declining with withdrawals) created a difficult environment for community bankers all across the USA, and banks of all types were looking for ways to stay in business and earn profits.

14.3 WALL STREET ACT I: THE EARLY RESIDENTIAL MORTGAGE-BACKED SECURITIES MARKET

In September 1980, a law was passed that allowed banks with underwater mortgage portfolios to sell them off to willing investors. Since they would incur losses from the sale, treasury allowed the banks to use the losses to offset income from the past 10 years, hence reducing their tax liabilities.

This created a huge incentive for bankers to sell mortgages, but there was little opportunity for them to do so. In fact, there was only one possible window available to them. A team of investment bankers at Salomon Brothers, Inc., led by Lewie Ranieri, hit on the notion that investors would be willing to hold securities that offered to pay them principal and interest payments made by residential mortgage borrowers.[2]

While most of Wall Street thought he was crazy to invest the firm's money in the mortgage group, Ranieri began to assemble a team of mortgage and math experts in an attempt to figure out how to create, price, and trade these securities. When the tax legislation was passed in 1980 allowing banks to offset past income from portfolio sale

[2] For a great review of the advent of the mortgage securities market, see *Liar's Poker* (Lewis, 1989). In it, he provides a detailed review of life at Salomon Brothers in the late 1980s, and the mortgage-backed securities department at Salomon.

losses, the banks ran to Ranieri's mortgage group to try to get liquidity for their previously illiquid portfolios.

Although the early securitizations of underwater mortgage loans were sold at huge discounts, banks were able to liquidate their mortgage holdings for cash and re-lend the money to new borrowers at higher interest rates. Willing investors were found to buy the securities, and Salomon Brothers (and later other investment banks) collected principal and interest payments from the individual borrowers and passed them through to the investors. Buying at low prices, the investors earned large returns, and a market was created.

14.3.1 The Securitization Process Explained

As the market matured, investors and lenders gained familiarity with mortgage payment mechanics, mortgage-backed security pricing, and risk. Investment bankers sold the idea of securitization to banks by highlighting the profitability of originating mortgage loans and selling them directly into the secondary mortgage market. By doing so, banks would no longer hold long-term mortgage assets in their portfolios, but could originate and sell loans to the investment bankers over much shorter periods of time. Doing so increased return on equity for the banks, and opened up a new and potentially large sector of the credit markets. They would move from "loan-to-hold" strategies to "loan-to-sell" strategies.

Figure 14.2 illustrates the process, which begins with an investment banker promising to buy a pool of mortgage loans that exhibit a standard set of characteristics. For example, an investment banker might tell a loan originator that they will promise to buy $100 million of loans made in an originator's local market if the mortgages are

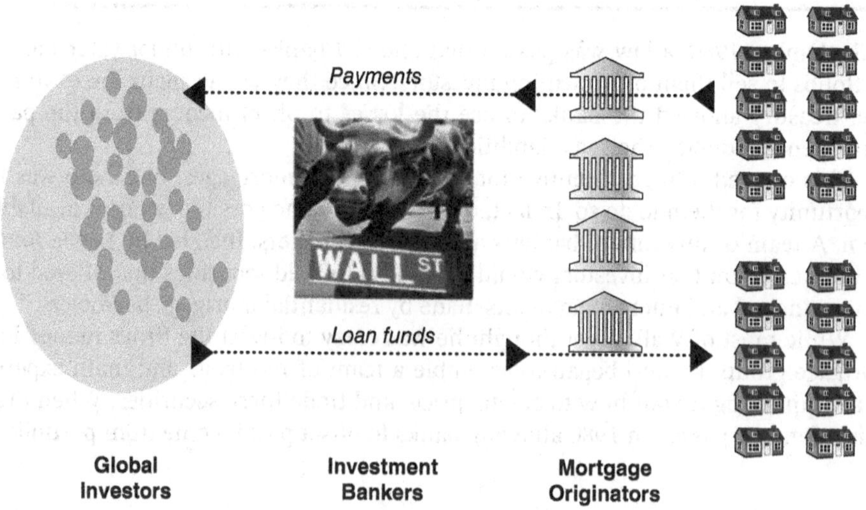

FIGURE 14.2 Wall Street enters the mortgage market

made at a specific interest rate, for a specific term (say 30 years), and with specific underwriting criteria (for example, the monthly housing expense is less than 28% of gross monthly income, and the LTV ratio is less than 80%). In addition, the loans would have to be delivered to the investment bank within 90 days. With this promise in hand, the originator draws off a line of credit as loans are made in the local market.

The originator generates one form of revenue by charging points or fees when the mortgage loan is made. For example, a loan origination fee of 1% may be charged, in essence providing up-front cash to the lender. There may be other up-front fees earned by the bank as well.

Once the originator has accumulated $100 million of loans, the pool of mortgages is sold to the investment bank and taken off the originator's balance sheet. The investment bank now owns the loans, and the originator is typically engaged to collect payments from the individual borrowers and pass them through to the investment banker. The process of passing through payments is known as servicing, and for this the originator receives a portion of the pass-through payments each time a payment is made by borrowers and passed through to the security holders, generating a second stream of revenue for the originator.

The role of the originator is similar in some ways to the function performed by the community banker in the traditional lending role, but is different in some very important aspects. The local borrower still borrows from the local lender, but the lender no longer holds the mortgage in the portfolio until the ultimate repayment of the loan. Instead, the lender sells a pool of mortgages to the investment banker within 90 days, and incurs no further risk after that transaction is consummated. In other words, the bank bears no risk on the loans that it originates in its local market, as it has passed on all default and interest rate risk to the investment banker by this point.

The originator has a strong incentive to increase the volume of loans originated and sold off to investment bankers. The more loans that are originated and serviced, the higher is the profit and revenue for the originator.

Once the investment banker takes ownership of the loans, they are aggregated with other pools of loans that have been accumulated from other originators. In keeping with the above example, let us assume that they arrange to buy $100 million pools of mortgage from 10 lenders, hence accumulating $1 billion of mortgages at the end of the 90-day contract period. They will then sell the rights to the underlying mortgage cash flows to investors who purchase securities.

The simplest form of mortgage-backed security is a pass-through security. As the name implies, the cash flows that are paid by individual borrowers are passed through from originator to investment bank, and then again from investment bank to investors. There may be a large number of diverse investors who buy the securities offered by the investment banker.

The investment bankers earn fees in several ways. They earn a fee for issuing the securities, and also may profit to the extent that they can offer the securities to investors at lower rates than the rate at which they bought the mortgage from the originators (because the pool is better diversified, it appears to be of lower risk and can deliver a lower yield). Rarely do investment bankers retain securities, passing all default and interest rate risk onto the investors.

Through this process, investors buy securities from investment bankers, who then buy mortgages from originators, who have made loans in their local markets to home buyers. In this way, the security investors ultimately provide mortgage funds to local home buyers. This has (at least) three distinct advantages over the traditional "loan-to-hold" system.

First, it encourages a flow of funds into the mortgage market from investors that had never before invested in mortgages. Prior to the advent of securitization, the majority of mortgage loans were made by local commercial banks, savings and loan institutions, and mutual savings banks. Securitization allows institutions such as pension funds, life insurance companies, foreign banks, mutual funds, and other investors to buy mortgage-backed securities. This expands both the sources and availability of mortgage funds.

Second, before the advent of securitization banks were constrained to lend only on mortgages to local borrowers in the local market. If the local economy experienced distress, the loan portfolio was not at all diversified. By buying mortgage-backed securities that were originated in California, Texas, or any other region of the USA, a bank could geographically diversify its mortgage portfolio. To the extent that the underlying mortgages in mortgage-backed securities were in cities whose economic activities were not correlated with those in the bank's local market, diversification benefits could be obtained. Further, by buying mortgage-backed securities backed by mortgages outside of the bank's local market, banks are indirectly providing mortgage financing in those markets. A savings and loan based in California could diversify its mortgage holdings by buying mortgage-backed securities backed by mortgages in Delaware and in other locations around the country.

Third, to the extent that the investors in mortgage-backed securities are based outside of the local markets where the mortgages are originated, capital now flows from across the globe to fund local mortgages. When APG (the Dutch Public Employees' Pension Fund) buys mortgage-backed securities, funds flow from the Netherlands to provide cash to mortgage borrowers in small towns and large cities all across the USA. Similarly, when Japanese banks, German mutual funds, California savings and loans, and a host of other types of investors buy mortgage-backed securities, funds flow from their locations into local US markets to fund mortgage loans.

An additional enticement to investors is provided by government-sponsored enterprises like the Federal National Mortgage Association (FNMA, or Fannie Mae) and the Federal Home Loan Mortgage Corporation (FHLMC, or Freddie Mac). For mortgages that meet certain criteria, Fannie Mae and Freddie Mac stand ready to make payments to investors if they are not made by the individual borrower. For instance, if a borrower does not pay his scheduled payments of principal and interest in a given month so that the servicer cannot pass the payment through to the investor, Fannie Mae or Freddie Mac will make the payment to the investor and then attempt to get repayment from the borrower. In this way, the credit of Fannie Mae or Freddie Mac replaces the credit of the individual borrowers, giving investors greater confidence when they buy mortgage-backed securities.

The end result is that mortgage markets have a much more efficient inter-institutional and inter-regional funds flow. While the extent is open to debate, this arguably leads to lower overall mortgage rates for borrowers in US housing markets.

14.3.2 Lender Profitability from Securitization

While greater overall efficiency and the ability to diversify portfolios are good outcomes from securitization, lending institutions will not sell mortgages into the secondary market unless it is profitable to do so. A simple example will help to compare the profitability of the traditional lending operation versus the securitization alternative.

In the "loan-to-hold" strategy, a bank lends and holds loans as assets for the long term. Using an example from earlier, let us assume that a lender pays 4% on deposits and lends the money out to mortgage borrowers at 7%, creating a spread of 3% (or 300 bps profit). In addition, assume that the lender has $100 of assets with debt equal to 80% of assets, or a 4:1 debt-to-equity ratio. The equity in the bank is the difference between asset value and debt, or $20. The 300 basis points of profits represent $3 per year in revenues, and assuming overhead costs of 1.5% of assets (or $1.50 per year), net profit to the bank is $1.5 per year ($3 revenue less $1.50 in overhead costs). Dividing the net profit of $1.50 by the equity of $20 gives a return on equity to the "loan-to-hold" banker of 7.5% per year. The credit risk of the underlying mortgages arising due to delinquency, default, or foreclosure is completely borne by the bank throughout the loan maturity.

Now assume that the same bank follows an originate-to-sell strategy using the same $100, financed 80% with debt and 20% with equity. The bank lends the $100 over the first quarter of the year, receiving 1% origination fees on each dollar loaned, and a 0.375% servicing fee throughout the rest of the year. In the first quarter, the bank receives $1 of origination fees. Annual servicing fees (assuming no amortization of principal) equal (0.375% * $100) = $0.375 per year, or ($0.375 / 4) = 0.09375 per quarter.

Servicing for the loans originated in the first quarter does not begin until the second quarter, and fees are earned for the last three quarters of the year. These fees equal ($0.09375 * 3) = $0.28125 for the mortgages originated in the first quarter of the year.

At the end of the first quarter, the bank sells the mortgages to an investment banker, and receives another $100 in capital, which can be used to make further loans. If the $100 of mortgages are originated in the second quarter, another $1 of origination fees is earned in the second quarter, and the loans originated in the second quarter earn ($0.09375 * 2) = $0.1875 in servicing fees for the last half of the year.

At the end of the second quarter, the loans made in the second quarter are sold to an investment banker, and the $100 received is lent back out to the local mortgage market. Another $1 of origination fees is earned in the third quarter, and those mortgages originated in the third quarter are serviced in the fourth quarter of the year, earning the bank $0.09375. As before, mortgages originated in the third quarter are sold to an investment banker, the bank receives $100 from the sale, and the $100 is lent back out into the mortgage market in the fourth quarter of the year, earning the bank another $1 in origination fees.

In the originate-to-sell strategy, the $100 is lent out to the local mortgage four times. In the originate-to-hold strategy, it is lent out to the mortgage market only once. Therefore, the velocity of money churning through the bank increases fourfold.

Total profits earned by the bank include the origination fees and the servicing fees. The $1 origination fee is earned four times throughout the year, and the servicing fees total ($0.28125 + $0.1875 + $0.09375), or $0.5625 in this simple example. Revenue for the year totals $4.56, and after subtracting the $1.50 of overhead, leaves profit of $3.06. Dividing the profit by the $20 of equity, the ROE is 15.3%, more than double the 7.5% ROE that was earned in the loan-to-hold strategy. In addition, the bank with the loan-to-sell strategy incurs no further credit risk due to delinquency, default, or foreclosure because that is passed through to the investors in the mortgage-backed securities after the loans are sold to the investment banker. The loan-to-hold banker would still be subject to this risk.

The incentive structure of the originate-to-sell strategy is to generate as much loan volume as possible. For each dollar loaned, another dollar of origination fees is earned. For each dollar of loan serviced, another 0.375% of servicing fees are earned. The quicker the bank can roll the money through the bank by originating and selling, the more can be earned. Further, the marginal cost of adding additional borrowers to information systems is relatively small.

14.4 WALL STREET ACT II: SENIOR-SUBORDINATED SECURITIES, THE ADVENT OF STRUCTURED FINANCE

14.4.1 The Coast Federal Savings and Loan Deal

At Salomon Brothers in April 1987 one of the mortgage traders and a member of the mortgage finance group called everyone into a conference room to discuss an innovation that they had dreamed up in conjunction with the firm's lawyers. Calling it a "senior-subordinated" security, they described a way of taking the cash flows earned from mortgage borrowers and (instead of passing them through to investors like a simple pass-through security), creating pools of investors who would receive cash flows in a strict priority system.

The precise details are forgotten (at least by the authors), but here is the general gist of the first senior-subordinated security deal. A southern California savings and loan association (S&L) came to Salomon looking to sell a pool of mortgages it had originated in the southern California apartment market. The loans had been originated to weak borrowers who had bought weak properties that were leased by weak tenants in weak markets. If sold as a pool, the price that Salomon would have received for them would be at a huge discount to the par value of the loans, which is the balance outstanding at the time. This was not a good outcome for the S&L, so they asked Salomon to come up with something a bit more creative.

We are going to make up some numbers here, but the general idea works as follows. Assume that the S&L had made 15 loans of $20 million each to the apartment borrowers, for a total loan portfolio of $300 million. Further assume that the rate on the loans was 9%, and that they were non-amortizing, or interest only. Therefore, in each year, each of the borrowers was obligated to pay $1.8 million to the S&L. For all 15 loans, the total amount to be received by the S&L was $27 million.

When the loans were made, the net operating income (NOI) earned by the properties totaled $35 million. Unfortunately, conditions in the southern California property markets had worsened, so that the NOI earned by the properties totaled only $27 million, equal to the total amount of debt service owed on the individual mortgages.

Therefore, at the time that the S&L came to Salomon, the DCR (the ratio of income to debt service) was equal to 1.0 times. The income earned was just enough to cover the debt service, so that if there was any further reduction in income, borrowers could not pay their total mortgage payments out of property cash flow. This is a distressed pool of loans.

It is commonly suggested that performing commercial mortgage loans historically default in a similar way to a BBB bond, so the interest rate on a commercial mortgage should be roughly equal to a BBB bond. At the time, BBB bonds yielded about 9%. Typically, a performing commercial loan has a DCR of 1.3 or higher, indicating that there is a sizeable cushion of income above debt service. Clearly, the loans in the S&L's pool were of less credit quality than BBB, given their 1.0 times DCR. Rational investors would require a higher return than the 9% BBB rate.

Given the weakened credit quality of these mortgages, investors priced them at a 15% rate, for a total value of $180 million ($27 million of interest divided by 0.15).[3] This was an unacceptable "haircut" of $120 million to the S&L, which is why they asked Salomon to come up with something creative.

The breakthrough event was the Salomon team charged with selling the mortgage portfolio coming to the realization that each dollar of the $27 million of debt service paid had a different level of risk. For example, if the mortgages were pooled, the total income earned by the 15 properties was $27 million. The first dollar must be almost risk free, because to lose that dollar would require that the properties with a rental value of $27 million produced a zero income. But the last dollar is risky, because a tiny (one dollar, or 0.0000037%) fall in NOI will wipe it away.

For discussion purposes, suppose we create two classes of securities. The first is sold to an investor (Class A) who gets the right to receive the first dollar of debt service that is paid, and another security is sold to a second investor (Class B) who gets the rest of the debt service payments, but only after Class A has been paid his dollar. If the full $27 million in debt service is paid by the 15 borrowers, Class A gets a dollar, and Class B gets whatever else is paid of the $27 million promised by the borrowers.

Since they are promised the first dollar of debt service payments, and the total expected NOI is $27 million, the DCR (equal to NOI divided by debt service) for the Class A investors is $27 million to one. Clearly this is far higher than the overall pool, so the risk incurred by the Class A investor is quite low. The only way that the Class A investor will not get paid is if, for the entire pool of 15 mortgages, no debt service payments are made at all, which is an extremely low probability event. If the Class A security were to be sold to investors, their required rate of return would be far less than the 9% contract rate on the original mortgages.

Extending the example, the second dollar of mortgage payments in the pool has a debt coverage ratio of $13.5 million to one (the first dollar has $27 million of NOI to one

[3]The calculation is a bit simplified, but for any interest-only loan (bond), loan payments are equal to the interest rate times the balance outstanding, or LPMT = Rate * Balance. In our case, the rate is 15% and the loan payment is $27 million. Solving for Balance, by dividing LPMT by Rate, or $27 million / 0.15, provides the value, or price offered, of $180 million.

dollar of debt service; the second dollar has $27 million of NOI to two dollars of debt service). Each successive dollar of payment has a slightly lower DCR, and a higher level of risk, than the previous dollar.

For a more realistic example, assume that we designate a class of investors (again Class A) who will receive the first $10.5 million of debt service payments from the pool of 15 $20 million mortgages. The S&L will collect all payments, and the first $10.5 million will be distributed to these investors. With $27 million expected to be earned as NOI, the DCR for Class A is $27 million over $10.5 million, or 2.57 times. That is, the income earned by the properties is 2.57 times the debt service to be distributed to the Class A investors.

Again, this is a higher DCR, and represents lower risk, than a standard commercial mortgage that has a 1.3 times DCR and a rate of 9% (or a BBB-rated bond). Assume that Salomon is able to convince a rating agency that the risk to the Class A investors is similar to a AA corporate bond, and that AA corporate bonds yield 7%. If investors require 7% for the AA-equivalent mortgage-backed security, they will be willing to pay $150 million ($10.5 million / 0.07) for the right to receive the first $10.5 million of debt service payments from the pool of multi-family mortgages in Southern California.

So far, the investment banker has promised $10.5 million of the $27 million debt service payments, so there is $16.5 million more that can be sold to other investors. Assume that Salomon promised the next $8.5 million to another group of investors (Class B), but they are only paid after Class A has received their full payment of $10.5 million. The Class A investors have a senior claim to the cash flows, and the Class B investors have a subordinated claim. The DCR for the Class B investors is $27 / ($10.5 + $8.5), or 1.42 times. Since this ratio is above the traditional 1.3 times DCR for commercial mortgages, assume that a rating agency gives the Class B securities a BBB+ rating, and that BBB+ bond investors require an 8.5% yield in the bond market.

The BBB+ Class B security promising $8.5 million of debt service payments, but only after the Class A investors have received their total $10.5 million, can be sold to the public at a par value of $100 million ($8.5 million / 0.085 = $100 million). The securitization process so far is summarized in Table 14.1.

So far, remembering that the whole distressed loan portfolio had a market value of $180 million, Salomon has sold $250 million of bonds and promised $19 million of annual payments to the Class A and Class B investors, and there is still $8 million of debt service payments made by the borrowers left to be distributed.

Assume that Salomon designates a third class of investors, and agrees to pay them the next $4 million of debt service payments from the underlying pool of mortgages. These cash flows are subordinated to the Class A and Class B investors, so the Class C

TABLE 14.1 The securitization process (1)

Class of bond	Rating	Cash flow promised	Rate	Proceeds
A	AA	$10.5m	7%	$150m
B	BBB+	$8.5m	8.5%	$100m
Total		$19m		$250m

TABLE 14.2 The securitization process (2)

Class of bond	Rating	Cash flow promised	Rate	Proceeds
A	AA	$10.5m	7.0%	$150m
B	BBB+	$8.5m	8.5%	$100m
C	NR	$4m	18%	$22.22m
Total		$23m		$272.22m

investors will not get paid unless the Class A and Class B investors get their full payments, totaling $19 million.

Class C exhibits a DCR of 1.18 times, small relative to typical commercial mortgage underwriting. Given the relatively higher risk, this class will be unrated. Assume that investors in Class C require 18% on their investment, and will pay $22.22 million (Table 14.2).

With the addition of Class C, $23 million of debt service payments have been promised to the three classes of investors ($10.5 million to Class A, $8.5 million to Class B, and $4 million to Class C), and $272.22 million has been raised from the sale of securities. Since there is $27 million of total debt service, $4 million more is expected to be paid by the 15 multi-family borrowers.

In the first senior-subordinated security transaction, the S&L that originated the mortgage agreed to hold the "equity" in the deal. That is, they retained the highest-risk, first-loss position in the security structure. If less than $27 million was paid by the borrowers, the first cash flow stream to be impacted is the S&L's cash flow stream. The resulting "capital stack" is shown in Figure 14.3.

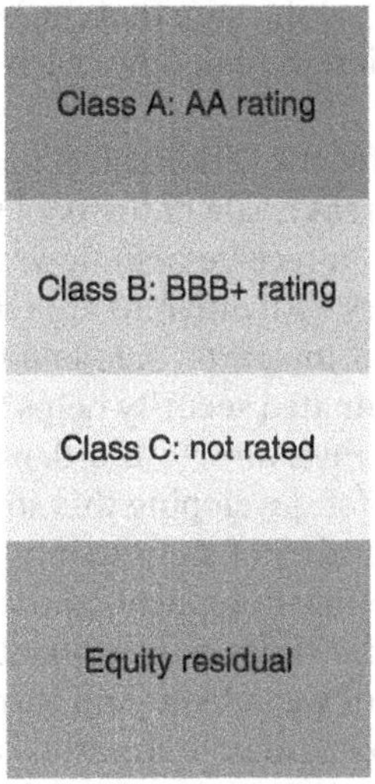

FIGURE 14.3 A simple senior-subordinated security – the Coast Federal Savings and Loan deal

14.4.2 Risk and Return Characteristics of the Senior-Subordinated Structures

What is the resulting position of the S&L and the various investors? For example, assume that only $26 million of debt service payments are made. Salomon pays the Class A investors their $10.5 million, the Class B investors their $8.5 million, and the Class C investors their $4 million. The S&L gets whatever is left, and in this case would receive $3 million. Similarly, if only $23 million is received from the borrowers, each of the three investment classes gets full payment as expected, but the S&L receives nothing.

If $21 million is received from the borrowers, then the Class A and Class B investors get full payment as expected, the S&L gets nothing, and the Class C investors get a payment of only $2 million. Notice that the Class B investors receive less than expected if debt service payments are less than $19 million, meaning that $8 million of debt service payments must default before this will happen.

Clearly, the real estate risk impacts the security holders from the bottom of the security structure, which is why each successive class requires a higher rate of return. With the credibility of an AA rating from an independent rating agency, the Class A security might be purchased by an insurance company, pension fund, or other investor in high-grade securities. Similarly, although lower in credit quality, the Class B investor might also include investors looking for higher yield, but still investment-grade credit quality.

The Class C investors would more carefully underwrite the risk of each of the properties and loans, given that they hold the first loss position within the issued securities. These investors would assess the quality of the individual properties, the surrounding real estate markets, the mortgage terms, and the payment history of the borrowers.

The S&L is happy to offload its portfolio of loans, but still receives cash flow from the borrowers if they stay current with their payments. In a sense, the S&L is in the first-loss position, in that if there is any cash flow degradation it will receive a smaller payment stream. Requiring the original lender to hold the first-loss piece ensures that it will retain a strong interest in making sure that the borrowers continue to make their payments. It will receive $4 million in cash flows each year if all contractual payments from the borrower are made.

The securitization solution for the S&L in question allowed it to raise $272.22 million (less a fee to Salomon), whereas a sale of the pool would have brought it only $180 million. By prioritizing the right to receive cash flows from the underlying mortgages, Salomon was able to find investors with different appetites for risk, and satisfy their risk preferences. In effect, the "sum of the parts" was sold for more than the whole.

In a sense, the senior-subordinated security helps to complete the investment market, creating new securities for investors with a demand for different levels of risk. Salomon earned a very large fee for developing this structure, and as a first mover was able to earn large fees from a number of transactions until the rest of the investment banking community figured out how to replicate the security structure.

To summarize, everyone in the chain of securitization profits from the transaction. The S&L monetized its portfolio of weak loans and earned a premium in the securitization process relative to a portfolio sale. Salomon earned a large fee, and the rating agency also earned a nice fee from Salomon. Investors were able to match their risk preferences with different classes of security and ratings, and a new form of security was created.

By prioritizing cash flows, Salomon was able to create something different from the traditional pass-through security described in Section 14.3.1. Managing the cash flows within a security is called "structured finance,". Following its introduction, this has been used in different ways in a large number of transactions. We will come back to structured finance in Section 14.6, when we discuss collateralized debt obligations (CDOs).

14.5 WALL STREET ACT III: THE EVOLUTION OF STRUCTURED FINANCE

The senior-subordinated securities market had evolved through the 1990s to become a major profit center for investment banks. From the humble beginnings of the savings and loan issuance in California, the structured finance market has grown and changed in some important ways. An updated example of a senior-subordinated issuance will provide some intuition before the CDO is introduced.

14.5.1 An Updated Look at the Senior-Subordinated Security

By 2007, the senior-subordinated security and structured real estate finance had reached a highly evolved form. Figure 14.4 illustrates a senior-subordinated security with classes rated AAA, AA, A, BBB, BB, and B, and a small residual equity class.

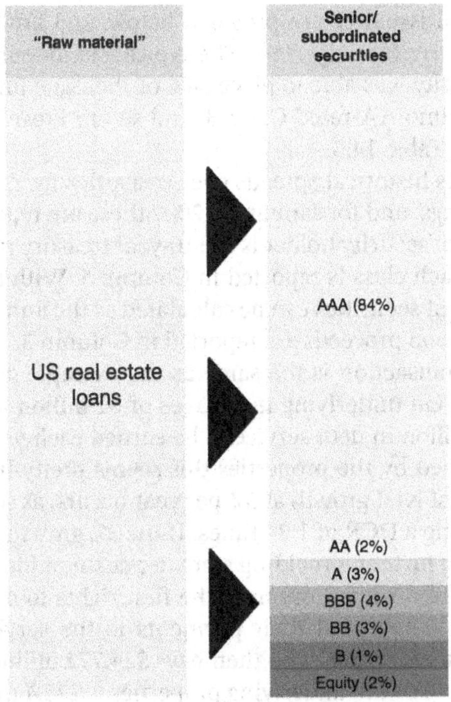

FIGURE 14.4 The structure of a senior-subordinated security, 2007
Source: Commercial Mortgage Alert, Goldman Sachs.

TABLE 14.3 Typical senior-subordinated issuance

Rating	Percentage	Proceeds	Spread	Rate	Interest	DCR
AAA	84%	$840m	0.68%	5.33%	$44.772m	1.68
AA	3%	$30m	0.79%	5.44%	$1.632m	1.62
A	3%	$30m	0.90%	5.55%	$1.665m	1.57
BBB	4%	$40m	1.2%	5.85%	$2.340m	1.59
BB	3%	$30m	2.95%	7.60%	$2.280m	1.43
B	1%	$10m	6.75%	11.40%	$1.140m	1.40
Equity	2%	$25.28m	11.85%	16.5%	$4.171m	1.30
Total		$1,005.28m			$58.00m	

Assume that, in early January 2007, an investment banker creates a $1 billion commercial mortgage portfolio by purchasing separate pools of loans originated by several lenders. The 10-year Treasury rate is 4.65%, and the current mortgage credit spread is 1.15% above Treasuries for a mortgage rate of 5.8%. On the $1 billion of mortgages, this means that $58 million of debt service payments will be earned on the pool each year. Assume that the NOI for the thousands of underlying properties is 1.3 times the debt service, so total income in the first year is $75.4 million. The NOI is expected to increase by 3% each year for the 10 years that the loans will be outstanding. For simplicity, assume the loans pay only interest, and do not amortize principal over their 10-year terms.

Details of a typical issuance are provided below, and are based on terms available in the market in early January 2007. The typical senior-subordinated commercial mortgage-backed security was able to place 84% of the issue into the AAA-rated Class A, 3% of the issuance into AA-rated Class B, and so on. Proceeds from each class are shown in Column 3 of Table 14.3.

J.P. Morgan reports historical spreads over treasuries for mortgage-backed securities with different ratings, and for January 4, 2007 these are reported in Column 4. The rate paid to each class of security holder is the 10-year treasury rate plus the spread, and the total rate paid to each class is reported in Column 5. With interest-only loans, the proceeds from the sale of securities can be calculated as the annual payment divided by the rate paid, and the total proceeds are reported in Column 3.

The logic of the transaction is the same as the example described previously for the S&L in California. On underlying mortgages of $1 billion at 5.8%, the investment banker expects $58 million in debt service to be earned each year, and with $75.4 million of NOI being earned by the properties this seems pretty likely. This is especially true if the expectation of NOI growth at 3% per year occurs, as second-year NOI will be $77.66 million, providing a DCR of 1.34 times. If the 3% growth rate continues into the future, NOI grows even further, providing a greater cushion for the security holders.

The AAA-rated Class A investors have the first rights to debt service paid by the borrowers in the pool. They send their payments to the servicer, who passes them through to the investment banker, who then pays $44.772 million to the AAA security holders. Because the NOI of the underlying properties is $75.4 million, this class enjoys a 1.68 times DCR ($75.4 million in NOI divided by $44.772 million in debt service to the AAA-rated class). The high DCR is the rationale behind the AAA rating.

Once the AAA-rated investors get their full $44.772 million in payments, the AA-rated Class B investors are eligible to receive their payments. The next $1.632 million of debt service payments made by borrowers flows to the AA-rated investors. Likewise, after the AAA-rated and AA-rated investors receive their payments, the A-rated Class C investors are eligible to start receiving their $1.67 million of payments. After the AAA-rated, AA-rated, and A-rated securities are paid what they are promised, only then will the BBB-rated investors get their $2.34 million of payments. The rest of the holders get what is left over only after all higher-rated investors get their payments. This process is called a "waterfall," because cash flows are directed to each class until their "bucket" is filled. Once the AAA-rated bucket is filled, for example, the water then flows over to begin to fill the AA-rated bucket, and so on.

In this case, we assume that the investment bank sells the equity class to another investor, whose required yield of 16.5% will be based on the overall quality of the underlying mortgages. Since the equity class will receive the residual cash flows resulting from earning $58 million and paying out $53.829 million to the rated classes, they expect to receive $4.171 million of payments each year that the mortgages are outstanding. This, of course, only occurs if all $58 million of debt service payments are made by the individual borrowers in the transaction. Since the equity investor receives $4.171 million and requires 16.5%, the equity class is sold for a total of $25.28 million (($4.17 / 0.165) = $25.28).

If, for some reason, the full $58 million in debt service payments is not made by the underlying borrowers, the equity is the first to see a diminution of cash flows.

Assume that only $54 million of debt service payments are made by the borrowers. The AAA-rated investors get their $44.772 million, the AA-rated security holders get their $1.632 million, and the A-rated security holders get their $1.667 million of payments. At this point, $48.071 million of debt service has been paid to the three highest classes within the security structure. Since $54 million comes in, the BBB-rated security holders get full payment of their $2.34 million, the BB-rated securities will receive $2.28 million, and the B-rated security holders will receive $1.14 million. The total paid to the rated classes is $53.829 million. Since the servicer received only $54 million, the remaining cash flow to be paid to the equity investor is $0.17 million.

A large number of the borrowers in the pool would have to default on their payments for such an extreme event to occur. Each investor in each class will attempt to determine the expected cash flows under various default scenarios and pay a price based on their perception of the risk that some portion of the cash flows will be discontinued.

The investment banker has promised a total of $58 million in cash flows to the six classes of security owner, and the equity owner, in the security. The investment banker earns a profit from the securitization of $5.28 million because he can sell the "sum of the parts" (the six security classes and the equity) for $1.00528 billion, which is more than the whole (the $1 billion in mortgages). This occurs because the mortgage market values the mortgages at the average rate of 5.8%, while the security market values each marginal piece of the deal at different rates for different risk classes. The weighted average of these marginal rates is lower than the 5.8% rate on the underlying mortgages. In this case, the total amount of interest paid on all classes is $58 million, and for the $1.00528 billion of securities issued this represents a weighted cost of capital of 5.77% ($58 million divided by $1.00528 billion). This 5.77% is therefore the investment bank's cost of capital in raising funds to buy the $1 billion of mortgages that pay 5.8%. Since the assets earn more than the liabilities, a profit is earned.

An obvious strategy for the investment banker is to try to push as much of the security as possible into the higher-rated classes. Since the cost of capital for the AAA class is only 5.33%, the investment banker can earn a larger profit by placing as much of the 5.8% mortgages as she can in this class. Fortunately, the rating agency in this case allowed her to put 84% of the issuance into the AAA-rated class, in effect allowing the investment bank to earn 47 basis points (5.8%–5.33%) from this part of the transaction. Similarly, each security paying a rate less than 5.8% contributes something to the investment banker's profit. Those classes paying a higher rate than 5.8% are a smaller proportion of the overall deal, and the loss implied by paying more than 5.8% on these classes is more than offset by gains on the classes that pay less than 5.8%.

14.5.2 Who Profits from these Transactions?

As long as the cost of capital (the weighted-average of the size of each security class times the yield paid to investors) is less than the rate earned on the underlying mortgages, the investment bankers' incentive is to create as many of these securities as they possibly can. They earn a nice fee for selling the securities, and the more securities they sell, the more profit they earn. Unless they hold the equity, which was rare prior to the global financial crisis, they have completely passed on the risk of delinquency, default, and foreclosure to the security owners.

Similarly, the lenders of the underlying mortgages earn an origination fee based on $1 billion of mortgages. Their incentive is to originate as many mortgages as they possibly can, and will continue to lend as long as investment bankers stand willing to buy their mortgages. The mortgage lenders, like the investment bankers, incur no further risk once the mortgages have been sold. Lenders often compete aggressively to make the loans, and historically have loosened their underwriting standards to increase their origination volume. That is, if a borrower is looking at several options for a mortgage loan, he or she will rationally borrow from the lender that is willing to lend a larger amount of money relative to the value of the property or the level of income earned by the property.

Rating agencies earn fees based on the total number of securities that they rate. During the period of heightened security issuance before the global financial crisis, there were three rating agencies: Standard and Poor's, Moody's, and Fitch. These rating agencies model the cash flows of the underlying mortgage pool, "stressing" the cash flows under assumptions of weak economic activity to determine how each class will perform. For each class, the rating agency determines the amount of cash flow and principal value that might be affected under "worst-case" scenarios. Using the outcome of these models, they provide ratings that are intended to give investors the same level of confidence that they might have in a similarly rated corporate bond.

One interesting outcome of the securitization wave was that investment bankers would "shop around" for rating agencies that would give them the largest amount in the higher-rated securities. If a rating agency wanted to earn a fee, it would have to compete against the other rating agencies in terms of placing more of the security in the more highly rated classes. The rating agencies, serving only as independent assessors of the risk of each class not getting their assigned cash flows, incur no further risk (other than loss of reputation) once the security is issued.

The borrowers on the underlying mortgages are able to access a larger loan pool, as the total amount of funds available increases with the level of securitization. To the extent that lenders are competing for their business, borrowers may also be able to borrow a larger amount relative to the income earned by the property. This, in turn, also allows them to bid more for a property, which increases the overall price level in real estate markets.

The final participants are the investors in the various classes of the senior-subordinated security. The investors in the more highly rated securities have the comfort of an independent rating of AAA, AA, A, or BBB from one or more of the three rating agencies. As long as the rating agencies were properly assessing the risk, investors could sleep well at night knowing they had an investment-grade security.[4]

14.6 COLLATERALIZED DEBT OBLIGATIONS

A CDO is a security that bundles together parts of other securities. To start at the beginning, we will use the same senior-subordinated security discussed in the previous section. It was backed by $1 billion of loans, and carved into seven classes (including the equity).

From the large pool of mortgages, 84% of the security issued backed by those mortgages receives a rating of AAA. Lower credit classes of the senior-subordinated security are much smaller components of the security (totaling $140 billion). If there are defaults or other discontinuations of cash flows, the equity will be the first to incur losses, and then losses will flow up the security structure, through the lowest-rated classes first.

The capital stack of a 2007 CDO can be seen in Figure 14.5. Assume an investment banker collects the pieces of the original security that were not rated AAA and do not comprise the equity in the deal. In this case, the AA, A, BBB, BB, and B classes of securities are placed into a separate portfolio called "Mortgage-Backed Security (MBS) collateral." In addition, similarly rated classes from a host of other MBS deals are also collected and placed into the collateral pool.

Assume that the investment banker has accumulated $1 billion of these classes of previously issued securities. Once these have been accumulated, the investment banker creates a new senior-subordinated security. Of all the cash flows that are earned by the classes held as MBS collateral, the first are directed to a group of investors who buy "super-senior" CDO securities representing 70% of the security issue. If there are sufficient cash flows beyond those promised to the super-senior investors, the next group of investors gets their payments. In Figure 14.5, these investors buy

[4] Investment grade refers to securities rated BBB or higher. Many institutional investors, like pension funds, may only invest in investment grade securities.

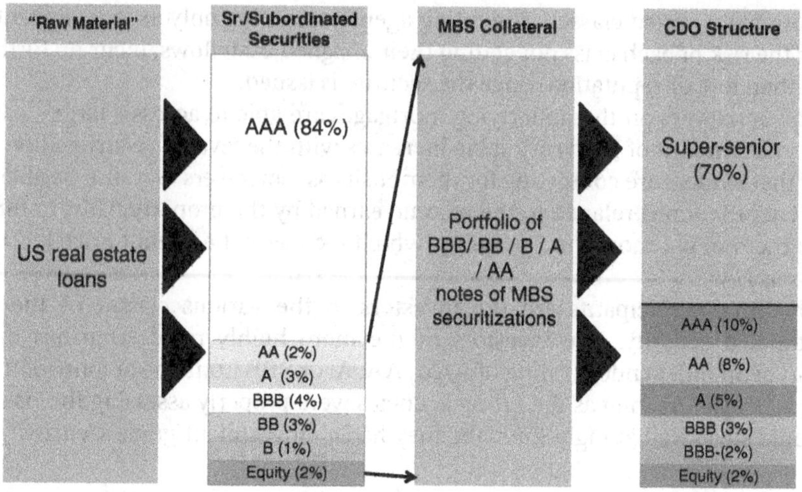

FIGURE 14.5 2007 CDO structure
Source: Commercial Mortgage Alert, Goldman Sachs.

10% of the pool, and they hold a security with AAA rating. If there is sufficient cash flow from the MBS collateral after paying the super-senior class and the AAA-rated class, the AA class investors (representing 8% of the transaction) begin receiving the cash flows on which they hold a claim. Each class that follows is subordinate to the string of senior classes above them in the capital stack. The first-loss position is, as always, the equity piece.

By now, the reader should be getting a feel for how complex these securities can be. To value them, an analyst must estimate the cash flows that are earned by each class of the CDO. Each class of the CDO is backed by "MBS collateral," which consists of a large number of investment classes from a large number of previously issued MBS deals. Each class of MBS collateral is backed by separate pools of mortgages originated all over the USA. Therefore, to accurately model the CDO class an analyst first has to estimate the debt service payments for each of the mortgages in the pool and as a whole. From there, the analyst must attempt to estimate the cash flows earned by the classes of securities in the first senior-subordinated security, as well as all the other senior-subordinated securities from which the MBS collateral was accumulated. After that is done, the analyst must then estimate the expected cash flows on the classes that make up the CDO structure.

This highlights the difficulty that investors have in accurately pricing the classes of a CDO structure. This is especially true for the rating agencies that rate these classes. Events in 2008 indicate that the rating agencies did not effectively model these cash flows, and their assessments of risk of loss for almost all CDO classes were not accurate. Since most investors believed in the independence of the rating process and the accuracy of the ratings provided, they purchased securities backed by these classes of CDOs based solely on their ratings. To the extent that these ratings implied lower risk than that which would actually be incurred, investors paid too much for CDO securities.

Here are the major conclusions to be drawn so far in this chapter.

- Asset-backed securitization began in the early 1980s, and grew substantially until the beginning of the global financial crisis.
- Lenders can make higher profits by originating and selling their loans than they can by originating and holding.
- Securitization provides benefits to mortgage markets, allowing funds to flow across regional boundaries and from institutions that were previously not able to fund mortgages.
- Senior-subordinated securities were issued by investment bankers so that investors with different risk tolerances could satisfy their risk and return appetites.
- The CDO market was spawned from the senior-subordinated security, and aggregated classes of previously issued senior-subordinated securities. Using these pools of classes from a large number of previously issued securities as collateral, new securities were issued.
- The derivative nature of these CDOs made them very difficult to model, to determine their riskiness, and to price.
- Many investors purchased CDO classes based on the rating that was placed on them by independent rating agencies.
- To this point, all of the participants in the mortgage markets made enormous amounts of money. Originators increased their lending, earning fees for doing so. Investment bankers increased their issuance of mortgage-backed securities and CDOs backed by the mortgage-backed securities. Rating agencies rated more and more mortgage-backed security classes, and more and more CDO classes, earning more and more fees as they did so. In addition, there was an increase in the percentage of securities that were rated at the highest levels, indicating that the risk of the MBS and CDO classes had decreased over time.
- Borrowers were able to borrow more and more, as lenders competed to give them loans by lowering underwriting standards, effectively allowing them to pay more for properties using bigger loans than they probably should have been able to borrow. CMBS and CDO investors, who believed that the risk of the securities was accurately rated by the rating agencies, bought enormous amounts of securities at relatively low yields, given the relatively low risk assessments as provided by the rating agencies.
- Everyone was operating rationally within the rules that were handed to them by the market.

14.7 MEZZANINE DEBT[5]

14.7.1 Mezzanine: The Background

As the CMBS market grew, it crowded out traditional mortgage lenders such as commercial banks, life insurance companies, and savings institutions from the market. Competing to make loans but maintaining traditional, relatively conservative, underwriting

[5] Greater detail on mezzanine debt structures can be found in Watkins *et al.* (2003). Some of the material in this section is taken from that article.

standards proved very difficult. The CMBS market was willing to provide mortgages at (say) 90% or higher LTV ratios, but life insurance companies were only willing to provide LTVs of (say) 70%.

The mezzanine debt market expanded to satisfy investor needs and allow lenders to make higher-risk loans. Equity investors with life insurance company relationships were often dissatisfied with these lower debt levels requiring (say) 30% equity investment. They more typically liked to invest a maximum of 15–25% of the costs of the property as equity.

As a result, mezzanine loans were often used to close the gap between the desired equity investment and the amount that a first mortgage loan provider was willing to lend. As a theater mezzanine may sit between the orchestra and the balcony, the mezzanine lender sits between the first mortgage debt provider and the equity investor.

For example, let us assume a property with a value of $100. The equity investor would like to invest $15, and the mortgage lender would be willing to lend $65. The gap between the two amounts, or $20, would be provided by a mezzanine lender.

As we discussed in Chapter 8, a lender receives contractual payments from a borrower over the term of a mortgage based on the prevailing interest rate in the debt markets. The payment stream to a mortgage resembles that of a fixed-income security, and if this is paid to maturity, the yield earned by the lender is the coupon rate on the mortgage. The risk is that the borrower might default, and the lender is forced to take over the property through foreclosure proceedings. Let us also assume that the first mortgage lender requires a 6% yield.

Equity investors receive residual cash flows, but only after all other claims (operating expenses, debt service, and so on) are paid. Their upside is based on market conditions. If rents and values increase, the upside can be substantial. The downside is that cash flows decline below debt service payments, and/or the property value falls below the loan amount, which in a non-recourse situation may lead the investor to default. In the worst case, the lender forecloses and the investor loses their equity.

Since equity investors face a greater degree of uncertainty than debt investors, the risk premium used to determine a required rate of return will be higher. For this example, let us assume that the equity investor requires a 15% rate of return.

Mezzanine debt, different because it is private or unlisted, otherwise resembles the tranches of a CMBS issuance that are subordinated to the AAA tranche. Let us assume that the mezzanine portion of the capital stack is $20 in our example. The first mortgage lender has first claim on cash flow, mezzanine providers are next in line, and equity investors receive the residual.

Similar to a CMBS, the equity investor/owner makes payments to the first mortgage lender, and if there are additional cash flows available, the mezzanine lender gets paid according to the terms of the mezzanine loan. If there are funds available after debt service payments to both debt providers, the equity receives the residual. Figure 14.6 illustrates.

14.7.2 Mezzanine Structures

Since the mezzanine lender has a subordinated position, the risk of getting paid is higher than that of the first mortgage lender, and the mezzanine lender will require a rate of

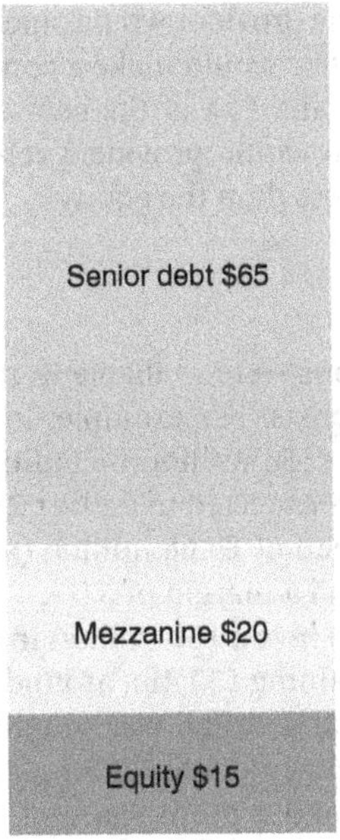

FIGURE 14.6 Mezzanine, debt, and equity

return that is higher than the first mortgage lender, but not as high as the equity provider. The return earned will depend on how far up the capital stack they go. In our example, the mezzanine lender provides debt from 65% to 85% of the value of the property.

In other cases, mezzanine debt might be junior to an 85% loan, and provide additional funding up to 95% of the value of the property. The latter is more risky since the combined LTV ratio is higher.

Mezzanine structures can vary greatly, but broadly fall into two categories. The mezzanine piece can be structured as straight debt, where the borrower makes regular debt service payments based on a higher interest rate than that of the first mortgage debt. In other cases mezzanine lenders provide a loan with a combination of the features of debt and equity, where the lender earns a regular debt service payment, and also participates in the cash flows earned by the property.

In the most straightforward approach, the mezzanine provider offers a debt instrument to the property investor or owner. Lenders typically receive a fixed-income yield, and in our example the yield might be in the 8–10% range. In this example, the mezzanine provider is purely a lender to the borrower, providing junior debt. The DCR required by the mezzanine lender would assure that the income available from the property is sufficient to pay debt service payments on both the senior or first mortgage loan and on the junior or mezzanine loan.

Owners who seek higher LTV ratios are willing to allow the mezzanine provider to share in the cash flows of the property. A typical example would incorporate a fixed payment to the mezzanine provider, usually at a rate that is lower than that which would have been required of a junior mortgage as described above (say 5–6%). Above this base payment, the mezzanine provider would share or participate in the cash flows of the property. The equity investor would make a contractual payment, but also allow the lender to earn between 10% and 15% of the before-tax cash flows from operations and from sale. The combination would provide a return, in our example, of 10–13% (more than the junior loan but less than the equity).

14.7.3 A UK Example

Attractive mezzanine propositions were available in most globally developed markets in the aftermath of the credit crisis. For example, in 2009 a UK industrial portfolio could be acquired for a total of £156 million including acquisition costs, delivering a 10.1% yield at acquisition. It was expected to deliver 2% p.a. rental growth. A prospective buyer had raised a senior loan of £93.6 million (at a 60% LTV ratio) with interest charged at a fixed rate of 3.5% and a margin of 3.0%.

The buyers were prepared to invest £30 million in equity, but did not have enough equity capital to supply the remaining £32.4m, around 21% of the total purchase costs. A mezzanine loan for this capital shortfall was sought. The terms agreed were a 14% coupon (interest rate), a 4% arrangement fee, 2.5% p.a. amortization (2.5% of the loan amount paid back every year), and a profit share of 30% of the cash flows once the internal rate of return (IRR) exceeded 14%.

On the basis of an assumed 10% exit yield, the IRRs available were 17.7% for the mezzanine lender and 18.8% for the equity investor, a very high relative return for the mezzanine lender. On the basis of the 8% exit yield which was achieved on sale, the delivered IRRs were 20.7% for the mezzanine lender and 27.9% for the equity investor, demonstrating the lower risk for the lender but the higher upside for the borrower, and the appeal of high leverage in a recovering market, even at what appear to be punitively expensive finance costs.

14.8 WHOLE LOANS AND SYNTHETIC MEZZANINE

Following the global financial crisis, bank debt became scarce and the prospective returns available to lenders looked appealing. As a result, real estate debt funds became popular. By 2020, Property Funds Research (PFR) held data on 277 real estate debt funds, almost 10% of the PFR universe.

Real estate debt funds are typically private equity funds (see Chapter 11) which raise capital to lend to property investors and developers. Some offer moderate returns for low risk, as would be expected from senior debt. Some, however, offer value-add level returns. A typical strategy for a high-return debt fund is to lend using what is known as a whole loan or stretch senior. The LTV ratio in a whole loan is higher (say 80%) than in senior debt (limited to say 60%). A whole loan will earn a higher rate of interest than senior debt – say 8% rather than 6%. This creates an opportunity for the debt fund to manufacture a higher return.

By lending $80 million at an 80% LTV, earning 8%, the fund earns interest of $6.4 million. If the fund then borrows $60 million of senior debt from a bank, giving the senior lender a first charge over the asset, it will pay 6% interest or $36 million on the

TABLE 14.4 Synthetic mezzanine

Year	Capital out	Capital in	Interest in	Interest out	Net cash
0	$80m	$60m			−$20m
1	0	0	$6.4m	$3.6m	$2.8m
2	0	0	$6.4m	$3.6m	$2.8m
3	0	0	$6.4m	$3.6m	$2.8m
4	0	0	$6.4m	$3.6m	$2.8m
5	£60m	$80m	$6.4m	$3.6m	$22.8m
				IRR	14.0%

senior loan. It earns a margin of $24 million. If it issues the debt (and borrows) for a 5-year period, its cash flow is as shown in Table 14.4. $80 million goes out and comes back (hopefully) at the end of the whole loan term; $60 million is received on day 1 and has to be repaid at the end of the term. The cash flow delivers an IRR of 14%, higher than the 8% that would have been earned on the whole loan without leverage. This is known as synthetic mezzanine, as the debt fund now has a second charge over the asset and is exposed to the capital stack between 60% and 80% LTV. Lender risk arises if the asset falls in value by more than 20% and the borrower defaults. This higher-risk, higher-return debt exposure is made possible by the financial engineering or structured finance techniques first observed in Wall Street Act II (see Section 14.4 above).

14.9 INCOME STRIPS

Income stripping is another example of financial engineering applied to real estate assets, or of arbitrage, meaning the nearly simultaneous purchase and sale of an asset in different markets in order to profit from price discrepancies. In the case of income strips, the different markets are (i) the real estate market, in which assets are typically priced using the rent divided by cap rate approach, and (ii) the bond markets, which price assets using discounted cash flow.

The freehold ownership of an office building leased to a bank for 20 years for £1 million annually can be thought of as having at least two, and if the lease has upward-only rent reviews, three valuable components (see Figure 14.8). The first is the lease rent, or an annuity; the second is the residual interest in the building and land when the lease ends; and the third is the right to call a higher rent at every 5-year rent review.

All or part of the lease rent – the annuity in Figure 14.8 – could be split off from the asset and sold to a fixed-income investor such as a pension fund. Let us assume that the entire asset is available for sale at a cap rate of 8% (it may be old, poorly located, and less attractive than a prime asset). Its market price is £12.5 million.

Government bonds sell on a 2% yield. The annuity is a fixed-interest asset, albeit less liquid than a bond, and the required return for such an "income strip" would be higher – say 3.5%. A 20-year annuity of £1 million discounted at 3.5% is £14.2 million. This is more than the price of the whole property asset. There is a clear arbitrage: a profit

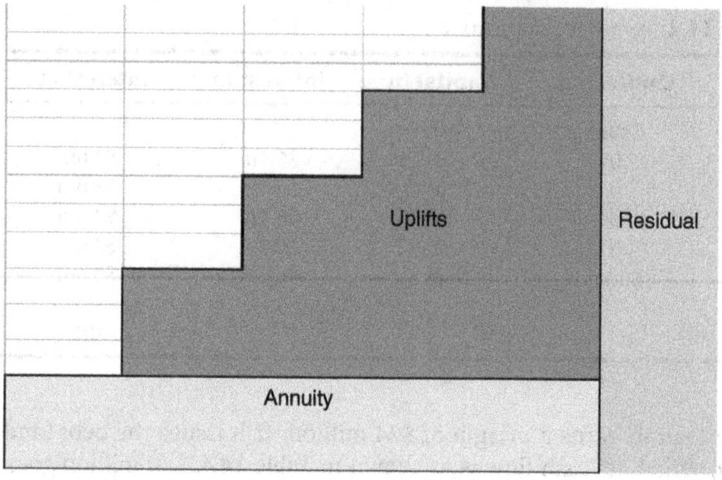

FIGURE 14.8 A UK long lease asset

can be made by buying the asset, simultaneously selling the income strip, and retaining both the residual and the right to call a higher rent.

Income strips are popular when (as in 2020) interest rates are low and cap rates for property assets are typically higher. To execute the arbitrage, the income is assigned to a special purpose company, which is then sold to an investor (see Figure 14.9).

The annuity could be further split vertically into a low-risk income of £250,000 (it would be easy to re-lease the space at this rent if the bank went bust) and a higher risk £750,000. These two income streams are known as tranches (from the French word for slice or portion). Slicing real estate income into tranches can be achieved via the property owner designing and agreeing appropriate contracts, rather than through splitting the legal ownership of the asset. We are more likely to encounter tranching in the context of securitization, when income streams are bundled into different classes of bond with different interest rates and priorities (for example, the CMBS and CDO structures discussed above).

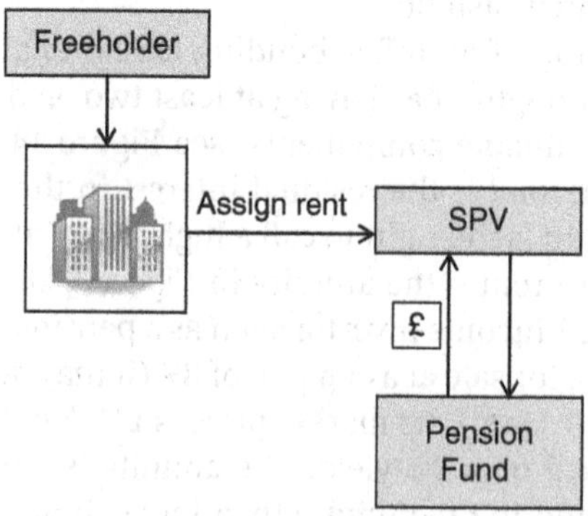

FIGURE 14.9 Income strip rent assignment

14.10 CASH-OUT REFINANCING

With different types of lenders willing to compete to originate loans to investors prior to the global financial crisis, risk premiums required by lenders dropped and underwriting criteria became less stringent. Meanwhile, during the period from 2000 to 2007, income earned by real estate properties increased, as did real estate values. The combination of these factors allowed investors a new way to take equity out of a property, in the form of a cash-out refinancing. An example of a cash-out refinancing is shown in Table 14.5.

For the sake of the example, let us assume that an investor purchases a property for $8 million at the end of 2000. The cap rate at the time of purchase is 8%, so the first-year NOI is $640,000. The investor obtains an interest-only loan with a 70% LTV ratio at an interest rate of 8%. The loan amount is $5.6 million, so the equity investor provides $2.4 million of equity when the property is purchased. The debt service payment on this loan is $448,000 per year.

During 2001, the before-tax cash earned by the investor is $192,000. The ratio of NOI to debt service, or DCR, is 1.43 times.

Three years later, real estate market conditions improved, driving up market values and driving down capitalization rates. In 2004, the capitalization rate had fallen to 7% and the value of the asset had risen to $10,000,000. The NOI was therefore $700,000. Underwriting criteria had loosened a bit, and now lenders were willing to provide 80% of the value of the property, or $8 million, as debt. Commercial mortgage interest rates had fallen to 7%, so the annual payment on the loan was $560,000.

In 2004, the property earns a before-tax cash flow of $140,000. The DCR has dropped a bit given the higher LTV ratio, to 1.25 times, but this still demonstrates a sizeable cushion of income over debt service.

Notice in this case that the owner borrowed $8 million, and had to pay back the original loan taken out in 2000 of $5.6 million. Therefore, the owner is able to take $2.4

TABLE 14.5 Cash-out refinancing example

	2001	2004	2006
Value	$8,000,000	$10,000,000	$12,000,000
Cap rate	8%	7%	6%
NOI	$640,000	$700,000	$720,000
LTV	70%	80%	90%
Loan	$5,600,000	$8,000,000	$10,800,000
Rate	8%	7%	6%
DS	$448,000	$560,000	$648,000
DCR	1.43	1.25	1.11
NOI	$640,000	$700,000	$720,000
− DS	$448,000	$560,000	$648,000
BTCF	$192,000	$140,000	$72,000

TABLE 14.6 Owner cash flows 2001–6

Year	2001	2002	2003	2004	2005	2006
Property cash flow	−$2,400,000	$192,000	$192,000	$192,000	$140,000	$140,000
Refi proceeds				$2,400,000		$2,800,000
Total	−$2,400,000	$192,000	$192,000	$2,592,000	$140,000	$2,940,000

million of cash out of the property without having to sell.[6] Since the initial equity investment was $2.4 million, the owner would have felt that his capital had been returned, and that any cash flow earned in the future was pure profit. A further benefit is that, in the USA, debt proceeds do not represent taxable income.

Two years later, rental and property markets had improved again, with cap rates dropping to 6% and the value of the property increasing to $12 million. NOI in 2006 – as shown in the far right column of Table 14.5 – was $720,000. Interest rates on commercial mortgage loans had dropped to 6%, partly due to competition among lenders, but also because the general level of rates in the USA had declined. Further, lenders were willing to provide up to 90% LTV loans because this risk could be pooled and passed on to CMBS investors, so the owner could borrow $10.8 million. Debt service payments on this loan were $648,000.

After the second refinancing in 2006, the before-tax cash flow had fallen to $72,000 and the DCR was only 1.11. But, by borrowing $10.8 million and paying back the old loan of $8 million, the owner was able to take another $2.8 million out of the property without selling the asset.

To summarize, the owner invested $2.4 million, earned $192,000 in before-tax cash flow for 3 years, took out $2.4 million on the first refinancing, earned $140,000 for 2 years, and then took out another $2.8 million on the second refinancing. By the end of 2006, a total of $6.056 million had been earned by the owner in exchange for the initial $2.4 million investment. These cash flows are as shown in Table 14.6. The reader should verify that the owner has earned a 28.2% internal rate of return and an equity multiple of 2.52 at this point.

Needless to say, this is extremely strong performance, and the property is expected to earn $72,000 per year from that point forward. In addition, the owner likely expected values to continue to increase, rates to drop further, and another cash-out refinancing opportunity to present itself in the next few years.

One clear outcome of the abundance of capital willing to provide loans at high LTV ratios for both purchase loans and cash-out refinancing is that overall levels of leverage in the commercial real estate industry increased. As we saw in earlier

[6] In this example, we assume that there were no prepayment penalties due at the time of refinancing. However, even with prepayment penalties, many owners executed the strategy demonstrated in the example because the cash they could take out with a refinancing was usually much larger than the penalty that would have been incurred. A useful exercise for the reader would be to replicate the results presented here with the addition of prepayment penalties and amortization. The results will still be positive, but not as strong as presented.

chapters, leverage induces risk, and risk implies that there is a downside for every upside. The downside for commercial real estate came during the credit crisis that began in 2008.

14.11 ALL GOOD THINGS MUST COME TO AN END

The beginning of the end for the real estate bubble was created by activities in the residential mortgage and housing market. Egregious lending practices allowed home-buyers to purchase homes that were worth far more than they could afford. Creative "sub-prime" mortgage instruments were developed and marketed by originators and sold into the secondary mortgage market, just as was demonstrated by our discussion of the commercial mortgage market above. Many of these mortgages had floating rates with upward-only resets, or negative amortization features. When rates reset, or when borrowers were faced with increasing principal balances, they found themselves unable to continue to make payments.

However, the originators had already taken their fees out at origination, the investment bankers (for the most part) had already sold the mortgages as mortgage-backed securities and taken their fees, while the investors who bought tranches of securities or CDOs were faced with the risk of default and foreclosure. In many cases they had bought highly rated tranches expecting very little risk.

As more and more borrowers realized that they could not continue to make the debt service payments, defaults and foreclosures became endemic in the housing market. Security owners of even the highest-rated securities began to suffer losses, and it was quickly realized that the entire housing market capital structure was in danger of collapse. It was also clear that the rating agencies had erred in granting strong credit ratings to securities that were backed by sub-prime mortgages.

As investors lost confidence in the credit quality of highly rated residential mortgage-backed securities and the CDOs that were backed by them, they exited credit markets in general. The thinking among those who had invested so much money in these securities was no doubt driven by the fact that it was impossible to understand the credit risk of mortgage-backed securities that are highly rated, so that maybe the ratings across the entire debt markets were equally flawed. In some sense, the "toxic" nature of residential mortgage-backed securities was felt to be contagious, affecting other securities backed by similar assets in the same way. Commercial mortgage-backed securities and a host of other asset-backed securities suffered from this contagion.

This distrust of the quality of ratings led to a massive exodus of capital from every fixed-income security except for those of the highest quality. As investors sold securities due to their uncertain prospects, they bought securities that were less complex, including treasury securities and bonds of the highest ratings. This "flight to quality" by investors depressed prices for commercial mortgage and other asset-backed securities, representing an increase in the required yield to compensate for the perceived higher risk. Prices of CMBS tranches fell precipitously, and yields rose to unprecedented levels.

Investment bankers could no longer make a profit issuing CMBS, so none were issued. The $230 billion of loans originated in commercial markets in 2007 shrank to nearly zero in 2008. While $12 billion of CMBS were issued in 2008, they were mostly deals that had already been pooled prior to the crisis, and were sold at a loss. Net new issuance was actually negative, as more loans were paid off to reduce CMBS principal balances than were included in new CMBS issuances. When the conduits stopped pumping loans, the largest source of mortgage capital dried up.

Lenders who were used to selling their loans into the CMBS market were also having difficulties, as they owned warehouses of mortgage assets that they had been holding in anticipation of pooling them and selling to investment bankers, who would subsequently sell securities. As investors shunned the CMBS market, and as spreads on the securities increased, the investment banks were unable to sell them. The value of these assets on their books fell, and they began to have to write off the losses of value. As they tried to figure out how to operate in the new credit environment, this source of capital also dried up for commercial real estate debt.

Together, the CMBS market and commercial banks issued 90% of new debt for commercial real estate purchases between 2005 and 2007. By 2008, they had largely ceased lending. Investors were forced to look for new sources of loans, most notably insurance companies and smaller regional commercial banks. Together, these sources fell far short of the void left by the collapse of lending from the CMBS market and from commercial banks.

Real estate is traditionally a debt-intensive industry. Banks have historically felt comfortable providing 60–80% of the value of purchased property, as loans and investor equity has historically been in the 20–40% range. As capital to lend dried up, property investors had fewer dollars available from debt to buy property. Those lenders who were still making loans required higher levels of equity, and applied stricter underwriting criteria. Investors could not earn their required returns unless prices were significantly discounted. Lower prices equate with much higher capitalization rates, especially compared to cap rates that investors accepted between 2001 and 2007.

Mortgage originations reached their peak in 2007, with $508 billion of new loan volume, and $229 billion were originated through CMBS conduits. Originations continued through the early part of 2008, but total 2008 originations decreased to $181 billion for the whole year, with CMBS originations virtually non-existent. By 2009, originations of commercial mortgages totaled only $82 billion.

14.11.1 The Cash-out Refinancing Example Extended

The cash-out refinancing example above is extended to 2011 in Table 14.7 to show what would have happened to the owner of that property. Let us assume that the loan taken out in 2006 had a 5-year term, so it matured at the end of 2011. By that time, market conditions had considerably weakened through the credit crisis, and the value of the property had declined by 30% to $8.4 million. This was about the same as the value at which the property had been purchased 10 years earlier in 2001.

Cap rates had risen to 8%, so the property's NOI had dropped to $672,000 and underwriting conditions had become more stringent. At maturity, the loan balance remained at $10.8 million, and the property was worth only $8.4 million, which represents an LTV ratio of 128.57%, and a negative equity situation for the owner. The only positive outcome is that the BTCF is higher than the debt service payment, but the DCR is only 1.04.

TABLE 14.7 Loan terms and consequences in 2011

	At maturity 2011	New loan 2011
NOI	$672,000	$672,000
/ Cap rate	8.00%	8%
Value	$8,400,000	$8,400,000
× LTV	128.57%	70%
= Loan	$10,800,000	$5,880,000
× Rate	6.00%	6.00%
= Interest	$648,000	$352,800
BTCF	$24,000	$319,200
DCR	1.04	1.9

One option available to the owner is to obtain a new loan. If a new loan could be found, lenders would require a 70% LTV, so the investor could only qualify for a maximum loan of $5.88 million – as shown in the far-right column of Table 14.7. Of course, at maturity the last loan taken as a cash-out refinancing has to be paid back. With a balance outstanding at maturity of $10,800,000, and a maximum new loan of $5.88 million, the owner must come out of pocket for the difference of $4.92 million. Many borrowers were unwilling to make this payment because they had insufficient cash flows, and defaulted.

Let us think through other options that are available to the owner. A second option would be to attempt to sell the property, but the owner would be lucky to get a price of $8.4 million in a distressed market. Even if the property was sold for $8.4 million, the owner would still have to pay back the $10.8 million loan, for a net loss of $2.4 million. At the 6% interest rate prevailing in the market, a $5.88 million loan would require a debt service payment of $352,800. With this NOI and this debt service payment, the before-tax cash flow earned by a new owner is $319,200.

As was discussed in Chapter 8, a third option would be for the owner to exercise their put option and simply "sell" the property back to the lender for the balance outstanding of the loan. By not making the payment at maturity, the owner will be in default, and the lender would likely foreclose on the owner's equity on the property. It could be argued that the owner has already earned a good return, and default for many owners during the credit crisis was a rational option.

The cost of default, however, is that the owner would likely not be able to borrow again for a long time. If the owner is in the business of real estate investment, having access to debt capital market is critical. A default and foreclosure would have to be disclosed to future lenders, which would effectively disqualify the owner from future borrowing. This is a cost that professional investors will not wish to incur.

The fourth option is to attempt to negotiate with the lender to either extend the loan and continue making the same payments, or reduce payments by extending the amortization period or reducing the interest rate.

In this case, the owner realized that this loan was likely the least of the lender's worries. Cash flow as shown in Table 14.7 was positive even with the outstanding $10.8

million loan, with a wafer-thin debt coverage ratio of 1.04. NOI is $672,000, the debt service payment is $648,000, so before-tax cash flow is $24,000. While a small drop in NOI would eliminate the margin of income-to-loan payment, at least for now the loan can be paid out of property cash flows and the loan is current with respect to payments. A large number of loans were in both a negative equity position (e.g. LTV > 1), and a negative cash flow position (BTCF < debt service payment), and would have merited far more concern by lenders and special servicers than this loan.

In reality, the owner took the fourth option and negotiated a 1-year extension of the loan. To get the extension, the lender required that the owner pay down the loan by $2 million in 2011, decreasing the outstanding loan balance to $8.8 million. At the end of 2012, the lender agreed to extend the loan for another 2 years to 2014, and the owner agreed to pay another $1 million of principal. At this point the loan was paid down to $7.8 million.

For less fortunate investors who could not provide an equity infusion, the outcome was far worse with a loss of property and the equity that was initially invested. For others, the collapse in the real estate market provided opportunities to take advantage of the fall in values.

The collapse in the real estate market did create opportunities for some investors to take advantage of the fall in values. Box 14.1 provides an example of investment opportunities in the marketplace in the UK that were available to investors in 2009.

Box 14.1: Equity, Debt, and Mezzanine Compared

INTRODUCTION

This case study is a hypothetical exercise based on market conditions in the UK in the early part of 2009. It reflects the opportunity that was available for real estate investors who had the flexibility to invest across the capital structure in debt, mezzanine, and equity.

The reference assets are three identical office blocks, all part of the 3Towers development. Investors had several available investment conduits to access these assets. These were an equity purchase, supported by a senior loan; a mezzanine investment; and CMBS interests which could be purchased on the secondary market at a discount to par value (100). The aim of the case study is to assess the relative merits of each alternative investment in terms of the expected returns and risk, over a 5-year investment horizon from June 2009.

The three office blocks were each valued at £500 million in June 2007 (the market peak) on the basis of a 5% cap rate. By June 2009, all three saw their values slip to £277 million, using a 7.5% cap rate and a 15% decline in income, from £26 million to £22 million. Table 14.8 summarizes.

Grey Tower

You can buy Grey Tower outright for £277 million. 5.75% acquisition costs and other sundry expenses will boost the total outlay to £293.33 million. You will use debt

TABLE 14.8 Loan terms and consequences after the credit crisis

Year	Rent	Cap rate	Price	Costs	Net value
2007	£26m	5.00%	£520m	£20m	£500m
2009	£22m	7.50%	£293.33m	£16.33m	£277m

finance to produce a leveraged equity position, and can achieve a 60% LTV ratio by way of an interest-only loan with a 1% arrangement fee. Interest charges will be 1.75% over LIBOR.

Blue Tower

Another buyer has been found for Blue Tower at £277 million. As in the case of Grey Tower, the buyer is using debt finance at a 60% LTV (£160 million), with an interest-only loan and interest charges of 1.75% over LIBOR. But the borrower only has £85 million of equity available and is £40 million short. You have the opportunity to provide mezzanine finance, a 15% "plug" between 60% (the debt proportion) and 75% (25% being the equity portion) of the capital structure. The borrower will pay a 2% arrangement fee, a 12% coupon, and a simple 20% profit share.

Green Tower

The loan on Green Tower was securitized and you have the opportunity to acquire an existing CMBS interest. The loan was made in June 2007 at a 70% LTV ratio. All securities were issued with 7-year maturities (5 years from expected deal completion).

You can buy discounted secondary market AAA1, AAA2, and BBB CMBS tranches secured on the rental income from Green Tower and, on default, the capital value. The available price discounts to par value are 30% for AAA1, 35% for AAA2, and 75% for BBB.

The offered deals are summarized in Table 14.9.

TABLE 14.9 CMBS tranches

Security	Tranche size	Coupon	Acquisition discount
AAA1	£200m	5.5%	30%
AAA2	£55m	5.7%	35%
AA	£35m	5.9%	Not available
A	£35m	6.1%	Not available
BBB	£25m	6.2%	75%

(continued)

(continued)

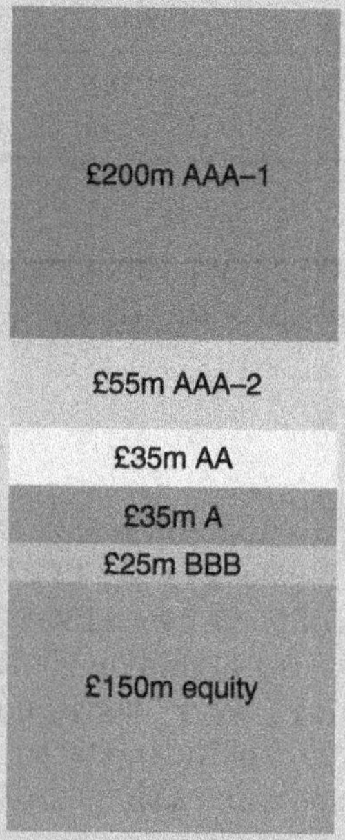

FIGURE 14.7 Subordination levels for CMBS issues
Source: authors.

Figure 14.7 shows the subordination levels of the different issues. The BBB tranche will fail to produce 100% of its coupon and capital repayment when the rental income and capital value, respectively, fall by more than 30%; for AAA1, representing the lowest-risk 40% slice, the fall would have to be more than 60%.

MARKET CONDITIONS

You envisage three alternative market scenarios: optimistic, base, and pessimistic. These are shown in Table 14.10.

TABLE 14.10 Market scenarios

Scenario		Year 1	Year 2	Year 3	Year 4	Year 5
Base	Income growth	−10%	0%	0%	5%	10%
	Cap rate	7.50%				7.00%
Optimistic	Income growth	−10%	0%	0%	10%	15%
	Cap rate	7.50%				6.50%
Pessimistic	Income growth	−15%	0%	0%	0%	5%
	Cap rate	7.50%				8.00%

Assumed LIBOR (bank interest) rates for each of the following 5 years are 1.5%, 2%, 2.5%, 3%, and 4%.

EXPECTED RETURNS

Grey Tower

Table 14.11 shows the modeled returns for a 100% equity purchase and a 60% leveraged purchase of Grey Tower, and (for comparison) the average return achieved by the senior loan provider (LIBOR plus the margin and an arrangement fee).

The senior lender has a non-variant (apparently zero risk, although we know this not to be true), low-return investment. Your own return is likely to be boosted by leverage but, as is always the case, the riskiness of the acquisition increases.

Blue Tower

Table 14.12 shows the modeled returns for the mezzanine provider and the borrower (the leveraged buyer).

The borrower faces a more risky and less remunerative set of returns than the buyer would in the case of the leveraged Grey Tower acquisition, both because of the amount of leverage (75% vs. 60%), but also the increased cost of borrowing. The returns to the mezzanine provider, in contrast, look reasonably invariant and quite high.

TABLE 14.11 Grey Tower returns

	Pure equity	Leveraged equity	Senior loan
Pessimistic	3.10%	0.60%	4.60%
Base	8.60%	14.60%	4.60%
Optimistic	12.00%	20.40%	4.60%

TABLE 14.12 Blue Tower returns

	Mezzanine	Borrower return
Pessimistic	14.60%	−7.90%
Base	14.00%	14.50%
Optimistic	16.70%	21.80%

(continued)

(continued)

Green Tower

Table 14.13 shows the modeled returns for discounted secondary market purchases of AAA1, AAA2, and BBB CMBS tranches secured on the rental income from Green Tower.

The AAA1 issue is very unlikely to default. Having collapsed by around 45% in the last 2 years, the value of Green Tower would have to fall by another 28% to £200 million, 40% of its peak price, before default is threatened. This means the return of around 15% is almost invariant with respect to market out-turns.

The AAA2 issue is more likely to default. For this to happen, the value of Green Tower would have to fall by another 8% to around £255 million, 51% of its peak price. There is therefore some uncertainty of return, and some damage in the pessimistic scenario, but returns are higher to compensate for this, thanks to the bigger discount and higher coupon. The (simplified) cash flow expected is shown in Table 14.14.

For the heavily discounted BBB note to pay back 100% of its issue value, the value of Green Tower would have to *rise* by 26% to £350 million. This is a risky investment. However, if prices were to recover in line with the optimistic scenario (a value increase of 33% over 5 years), this is an investment which will "shoot the lights out." The annualized (and therefore simplified) expected cash flow in this scenario is shown in Table 14.15.

Table 14.16 shows the IRRs available, taking account of the quarterly cash flows for the three tranches under the three market scenarios. (The difference between the estimated IRR returns of 48% and 53.9% for BBB in the optimistic scenario is explained by the different impact of annual and quarterly discounting.)

TABLE 14.13 Green Tower AAA1 cash flow and IRR

	Price	Year 1	Year 2	Year 3	Year 4	Year 5
Coupon		£5.5	£5.5	£5.5	£5.5	£5.5
Capital	−£70					£100
Total	−£70	£5.5	£5.5	£5.5	£5.5	£105.5
IRR						14%

TABLE 14.14 Green Tower AAA2 cash flow and IRR

	Price	Year 1	Year 2	Year 3	Year 4	Year 5
Coupon		£5.7	£5.7	£5.7	£5.7	£5.7
Capital	−£65					£100
Total	−£65	£5.7	£5.7	£5.7	£5.7	£105.7
IRR						17%

TABLE 14.15 Green Tower AAA2 cash flow and IRR

	Price	Year 1	Year 2	Year 3	Year 4	Year 5
Coupon		£6.1	£6.1	£6.1	£6.1	£6.1
Capital	−£25					£100
Total	−£25	£6.1	£6.1	£6.1	£6.1	£106.1
IRR						48%

TABLE 14.16 Green Tower IRRs

	AAA1	AAA2	BBB
Pessimistic	14.90%	14.20%	1.50%
Base	14.90%	17.20%	9.90%
Optimistic	14.90%	17.20%	53.90%

CONCLUSIONS

The mezzanine, AAA1, and AAA2 investment all looked exceedingly attractive in June 2009. As it turned out, these would have been great investments, but the BBB tranche would have been the best buy, as values recovered rapidly (see Chapter 2). The rewards available to senior debt providers appear to be miserable by comparison, although this return is (supposedly) bullet-proof.

14.12 POST-CRISIS RECOVERY

It took many years for investors to return to real estate markets. As is the case in the trough of most real estate cycles, the increased perceived risk premium of investors and lenders increased required rates of return, and bid prices dropped well below ask prices. Buyers and sellers could not agree on asset prices, and few properties were transacted. Prices continued to drop until they were low enough to attract buyers back into the market. Other investable markets also suffered as investors sought low-risk options in government bond markets and high-grade corporate bonds.

As this "flight-to-quality" occurred, and with low overall property values, the first investors back into the market sought "trophy" assets, or core investments in gateway markets that were thought to provide stability even in time of great risk. Cyclical low values provided an opportunity for investors to earn unleveraged yields of 6–8%, far exceeding treasury and corporate bond yields. Cash-rich investors that had been on the sidelines of the market during the global financial crisis could enhance their yields by utilizing debt, although low LTV ratios reflected the restrictiveness of lender underwriting.

The drop in real estate values provided a significant investment opportunity for first movers into risky real estate assets as well. As prices of core property in gateway markets increased and cap rates dropped, investors began looking for distressed opportunities at the historically low prices existent due to the crisis. High levels of defaults and foreclosures led commercial banks and CMBS special servicers to offer properties to markets at distressed prices, and investors were able to enter the market at large discounts.

The mortgage market slowly began to recover as transactions increased, but lenders continued to require more equity and higher debt coverage ratios from investors.

Mortgage originations grew slowly in subsequent years, but CMBS markets never returned to their pre-crisis levels. Key reasons for slower CMBS originations are related to more stringent regulations that were put in place after the crisis. For example, issuers are now required to hold 5% of the most risky securities, which provides them with an incentive to more closely monitor the risk of the mortgage that they originate. A large portion of recent CMBS issuances have either had smaller numbers of loans as collateral, and many are specific to individual properties.

By 2014, total mortgage originations had grown to be at similar levels to 2006. 2018 was the first year that total mortgage origination volume had grown to be higher than at the peak of the market in 2007. Whereas CMBS lending was nearly 50% of 2007 originations, conduit lenders represented only 20% of the total mortgage originations in 2018. Government agencies and bank loans now have a much higher share of the origination market than they did at the previous cyclical peak, and life insurance company lending has remained at similar levels throughout the market recovery.

14.12.1 A Final Update to the Cash-out Refinancing Example

As mentioned above, the owner had paid back $3 million to the lender in 2014 to extend the loan's maturity, leaving a balance on the original 2006 loan of $7.8 million. Market conditions (rents and vacancy levels) had improved by 2014, which led to an increase of NOI earned by the property of $749,000. Cap rates at the time were 7%, and the market value was $10.7 million. Lenders were willing to provide up to 75% LTV, and the owner borrowed $8.025 million interest only for a 5-year term. Interest rates had dropped to 5%, so the owner's new debt service payment was $401,250 per year, which provided the lender a very comfortable DCR of 1.87. The before-tax cash flow in 2014 was the difference between NOI and debt service, or $347,750. The income statement for 2014 after refinancing is shown in Table 14.17. The owner was able to take $225,000 in cash out of the property (new loan balance of $8.025 million less the old loan balance of $7.8 million) at the time of refinancing, and earn $347,750 in before-tax cash flow per year.

The 5-year loan matured in 2019, when market conditions had further improved. NOI grew to $812,000, and cap rates decreased slightly to 6.5%, so market value increased to $12,493,408 over the 5-year period. Lender LTV requirements stayed at 75%, so the borrower obtained a 5-year loan for $9,369,231 at a 5% interest rate. Assuming an interest-only loan, the debt service or interest payment totaled $468,462, providing a DCR of 1.73. The BTCF earned by the owner is $343,538. When the loan was refinanced in 2019, the owner was able to take $1,344,231 in cash out of the property by borrowing $9,369,231 and paying back the old loan of $8.025 million.

TABLE 14.17 Update on owner's cash flows and value

	2014	2019
NOI	$749,000	$812,000
/ Cap rate	7.00%	6.5%
Value	$10,700,000	$12,492,308
× LTV	75.00%	75.00%
= Loan	$8,025,000	$9,369,231
× Rate	5.00%	5.00%
= Interest	$401,250	$468,462
BTCF	$347,750	$343,538
DCR	1.87	1.73

This example shows the impact of real estate cycles on leveraged investors over a full cycle. Our investor was able to enjoy the upside of the cycle as rents increased, and as cap rates and interest rates decreased. NOI increased, and by refinancing twice, he was able to earn far more capital than he had originally invested, yet still own the property and its upside. Distress caused by the global financial crisis led to a decrease in NOI and an increase in cap rates, leading to a drop in property value. Our investor was fortunate in that he was able to maintain a positive BTCF, but he was also required to inject $3 million in additional equity when the 2006 loan was extended.

By 2014, markets had recovered, and the investor was able to earn a large amount of BTCF from the property after refinancing. Market conditions and liquidity continued to improve so that in 2019, our investor was able to pull out another significant amount of equity by refinancing. Naturally, as a long-term investor, he also knows that at some point another cyclical downturn will occur.

14.13 CONCLUSION

Ironically, securitization is touted as increasing the transparency and level of information in markets, and as a dampener of the amplitude of the real estate cycle. During the second decade of the 21st century, we saw that securitization of commercial mortgages neither increased transparency nor dampened the real estate cycle. Instead of relying on their own due diligence, investors depended solely on the ratings provided by rating agencies and CDOs were far too complex to be transparent. As the years following the crisis unfolded, untold losses for investors in CMBS and CDO issues revealed themselves.

At the time of writing, lenders have returned to the market and annual originations of commercial mortgages exceed pre-crisis levels, but the CMBS market is only about half of its former size. Investors see the income and appreciation opportunities of real estate as far exceeding those that can be obtained from other asset classes, and equity capital is abundant from a large number of domestic and international sources. Lending at this stage of the cycle is relatively disciplined, but, as we stated in Chapter 2, participants in real estate markets often forget the past and are doomed to repeat it. As we write this in early 2020, commercial real estate prices in all sectors are far above prices at the peak of the crisis. Debt and equity are readily available from many sources, and market fundamentals are strong. Debt providers are much more conservative than they were before the global financial crisis, so excessive leverage does not appear to be a problem.

As is always the case at this stage of the cycle, investors should be asking themselves what will cause the next downturn in the cycle, and how will the debt market contribute or react when the market turns?

PART Four

Creating a Property Investment Portfolio

CHAPTER 15

Building the Portfolio

15.1 THE TOP-DOWN PORTFOLIO CONSTRUCTION PROCESS

15.1.1 Introduction

The development of indexes and benchmarks which measure the performance of real estate has been an extremely helpful contribution to our understanding of the risk and return characteristics of this asset class. The NCREIF Property Index in the USA and the work of IPD/MSCI in several countries allows asset allocators to form risk and return expectations founded on data, albeit flawed data. While 'valuation smoothing', which reduces apparent price volatility and distorts the reported returns, produces a limitation on the value of this information – see, for example, Barkham and Geltner (1994) – investors continue to use this data as the basis of asset allocation modelling. We can credibly use the same data and models to build what appear to be efficient property portfolios.

However, apart from smoothing, there are other limits to the usefulness of this data. First, an issue which is directly connected with valuation smoothing is the illiquidity of real estate, which creates difficulties for investors/asset allocators struggling with the challenges involved in mixing traded securities with privately traded assets. Listed equity real estate – shares in Real Estate Investment Trusts (REITs) and non-REIT property companies – becomes attractive in this context. However, the performance of listed real estate stocks is believed to have characteristics that differ from those of direct, illiquid real estate (see Section 15.3.2). Research and analysis suggests that real estate stocks are much more volatile than (smoothed) private real estate, that real estate stock prices might lead the price of private real estate with a lag of 6–12 months, and that there is little or no correlation between the returns on public and private equity real estate over rolling periods of up to (say) 5 years. Thereafter, over periods of more than 5 years, public and private real estate might behave more similarly. These issues have been well documented by Clayton and MacKinnon (2003), Pagliari *et al.* (2003), Hoesli and Oikarinen (2012), and others. We can expect that the tracking error of listed real estate portfolios against a direct benchmark will be very large (see Section 15.3.3).

Second, it is widely accepted that portfolios comprising private real estate will likely contain significant specific risk. Real estate is said to be a 'lumpy' asset, with large and non-standard lot sizes. The sampling that takes place in the assembly of a private real estate portfolio is largely without replacement, because one asset cannot generally be shared between two owners (which is not true of divisible listed securities). These characteristics, when taken together, mean that a typical real estate portfolio will not be large enough to be well diversified and will exhibit a significant tracking error against an index or universe of private real estate. This issue has been explored most in the UK context by, among others, Morrell (1993), Byrne and Lee (2001), Baum and Struempell (2006), and Callendar *et al.* (2007). Hence, we can expect that the tracking error of direct real estate portfolios against a direct benchmark will be significant and will vary inversely with portfolio size.

These limitations on the usefulness of private real estate universe data provide significant challenges to investors. The universe data describes performance characteristics for the asset class that, according to the literature referred to above, cannot be captured by investors in direct real estate (because of the specific risk they take on) or by investors in real estate equity securities (because of the short- to medium-term divergence in returns between public and private real estate markets).

Recently, more efficient access to real estate has become possible through the growth of the unlisted real estate fund (see Chapter 11). Baum and Struempell (2006) found that over £1 billion is needed to build a diversified portfolio of London offices with a 2% tracking error. This presents a very strong case for using an unlisted fund focused on London offices. Assuming that such a fund is financed by equity alone, 20 investors committing £50 million each will produce enough capital to achieve the diversified fund. Yet the investor's £50 million is enough to buy only two or three London offices of average lot size.

Kennedy and Baum (2012) suggested that highly leveraged value-add or opportunity funds and funds focused on debt are likely to be sufficiently non-correlated with direct property indexes as to cause significant difficulties for asset allocators. However, we can suggest that core unlisted funds will be correlated with direct property indices and will diversify away much of the specific risk held by direct portfolios.

The development of the unlisted fund has expanded the apparently investable real estate universe, and with it has come the multi-manager proposition (a separate account portfolio by means of which an investor's capital is spread across a number of unlisted real estate funds) and funds of funds (a similar proposition, but in a fund format and thereby pooled between a number of investors), with the result that professional investors now select from a variety of routes to exposure (see e.g. Andonov *et al.*, 2013 and Baum, 2015). These routes are: investing directly in real estate assets; investing in REITs and listed property companies; investing directly in core unlisted funds; and investing indirectly in core unlisted funds using a multi-manager approach.

In this section we use data from Baum and Colley (2017), who employ a random stochastic simulation of historic UK performance data from 2003 to 2012 in order to test a series of hypotheses about the risk and return characteristics of multi-manager and fund of fund solutions. Using these results, we compare the risk and return characteristics of real estate investment approaches (direct exposure, balanced and specialist unlisted funds, a multi-manager approach and listed securities) relative to a domestic market index.

As we will see in Chapter 16, international property investment is not straightforward and adds a further layer of complexity to real estate portfolio construction. Tax and currency issues are considerable, and there are many other barriers. The data required to fully support a case in the face of these obstacles is not yet available, and the solutions available appear to offer limited efficiency. Nevertheless, many investors are committed to building a global exposure to real estate, seeking either higher returns than are available domestically and/or diversification of real estate exposure. Later in this chapter we describe a recommended approach for a large institutional investor with, say, $1,000 million to invest.

In this approach, we assume a focus on public and private *equity* investments. We believe that it is likely that new forms of real estate return and risk objectives will be used by global investors to take account of the more attractive characteristics of real estate debt in combination with equity investments and, in time, derivatives. However, for this exercise we assume an investment objective based on the replication of the real estate return and risk characteristics discussed in Chapter 1, which are thought to be represented (to some extent at least) by unleveraged, direct property indexes such as those maintained by NCREIF and MSCI. This means we omit allocations to debt, including mezzanine, senior, and distressed debt, as well as an exposure to new or secondary CMBS issues.

While direct investment is popular with individuals, family offices, and wealth managers, as well as some return-seeking institutional investors, unlisted funds and/or club investments are another natural route to gaining global property exposure for most institutional investors of this scale. This is because the performance characteristics of these funds should be most in line with the direct market over the short to medium term, meaning that efficient diversification is possible against financial market assets. In Chapter 11 we saw (and in Chapter 17 we will see again) that these funds can fail to deliver what is required, but unlisted funds with the appropriate risk and return characteristics continue to be used as the standard real estate channel to gain access to most markets, with some exceptions where listed REITs are the dominant routes to market.

So, for the vast majority of investors without large in-house teams and with inadequate capital to build a direct global portfolio, investing in a portfolio of unlisted funds is an attractive way to gain exposure to diversified global property markets, as these funds should provide a means of accessing property-style returns and diversification at the property level.

REITs may be a useful addition to this type of portfolio, providing useful liquidity, a different and sometimes more attractive tax treatment, and on occasion very attractive pricing. The limits to direct property and unlisted fund investment in certain geographies, coupled with the occasional pricing advantages of the listed sector, means that the addition of a selection of REITs brings several benefits at the property portfolio level.

Given this starting point, we use Figure 15.1 to illustrate a view of the relative strengths of direct property, the unlisted fund, and public equity routes to international investment.

Direct property is the purest form of real estate exposure, offering maximum control and good diversification qualities against stocks and bonds. Management quality should be good or bad, depending on who is appointed, but there are many direct portfolios which are unprofessionally managed. Diversification is difficult because the required investment size tends to be large, and direct private real estate is not liquid.

	Direct	Unlisted funds	Listed REITs
Pure property exposure	* * *	* * *	*
Diversification against other assets	* * *	* * *	* *
Management quality	* *	* * *	* * *
Investment size	*	* *	* * *
Diversification of specific risk	*	* *	* * *
Liquidity	*	*	* * *
Control	* * *	*	*

FIGURE 15.1 Direct property, unlisted fund, and REIT characteristics

REITs offer very different qualities. They perform as equities in the short run, providing limited diversification against other public assets, and control is handed over to the board of the REIT manager. But those managers can be expected to be very professional, the minimum investment size is very small, diversification of specific risk is easy, and the shares should normally be liquid.

Unlisted funds can offer investors a little more control if: there is a small number of investors and some sit on an investment committee or advisory board; liquidity is not usually on offer; there is more diversification, but there are many small unlisted funds with 5–10 assets; minimum investment sizes are generally larger than for REITs but less than for direct real estate. A good-quality manager can be expected, and the nature of the performance of unlisted funds is such as to provide property-style performance and good diversification against publicly traded assets.

There will, of course, be good and bad unlisted funds and good and bad REITs, and it will be someone's task to identify the better managers and platforms in each of these sectors. As we discussed in Chapter 11, investors may select a single diversified fund plus a REIT fund, use advisors or an in-house team to select specialist funds, appoint a discretionary manager to select a group of specialist funds and REITs (this is called a multi-manager mandate), or invest in an unlisted fund of funds and a REIT fund.

15.1.2 Risk and Return Objectives

There are three possible performance objectives for an investment portfolio. First, it may have an absolute target return: this should, but may not, be subject to an understanding of the risk that might be accepted in the pursuit of that target.

Second, it may have a set of liabilities to meet. These may include interest payments for a property company portfolio, annuities and bonuses for a life fund, or pension payments for a pension fund. These are appropriate objectives for managers to pursue for the benefit of the client investor. Typically, however, the property portfolio will be only one part of a larger fund. It is therefore unlikely that there will be any consideration of liabilities at the property level: if liabilities are considered explicitly, this issue will be dealt with at the multi-asset level.

Third, it may have relative performance objectives. These are commonly in place primarily for the benefit of the manager, but may also be relevant for trustees and anyone on the investor side responsible or accountable for execution solutions.

Several criteria should determine the precise framing of the performance objective. These will have an impact on the return target and risk tolerance, the benchmark adopted, and the timescale over which performance is measured.

Objectives should be achievable, yet testing. They should also be marketable, in other words capable of attracting or satisfying investors. It is unrealistic to expect investors to be happy with below-average returns, but equally unrealistic to expect fund managers or investment portfolios to deliver returns of (say) 2% above average every year. This target level is testing, and return consistency or persistence is nearly impossible to find (Aarts and Baum, 2016). 1% above the median return has typically been sufficient to produce upper-quartile performance. In addition, property-specific risk means that it is more realistic to set a target in terms of 3- or 5-year averages; the effects of valuation timing, illiquidity, and specific risk are then reduced.

Objectives must be quantifiable, so that performance measurement (see Chapter 17) is capable of determining success or failure. This should then be capable of leading to a reward of some sort (a performance fee or bonus). Finally, the objective must be specific in terms of risk control.

No asset can guarantee the delivery of a return fixed in nominal or real terms, apart from conventional bonds or indexed bonds held to redemption and assets for which an efficient hedge can be put in place. Yet many property funds have been launched with *absolute* target returns (say 10% nominal, or 6% real) rather than *relative* returns (say 1% above the MSCI or NCREIF benchmark).

In the Property Funds Research global fund universe at the end of 2018 (Figure 11.5), core/core-plus or Type A funds had a composite value of around 40% of the universe. Opportunity/value-add or Type B funds were worth around 60% of the universe. Simplifying, this suggests that the absolute return fund universe is around one-and-a-half times bigger than the relative return universe. This is probably a function of three drivers: first, the desire by managers to replicate the leveraged IRR-based performance fee structures of hedge funds; second, the acquiescence of investors attracted to the somewhat unrealistic ideal of absolute return promises; and third, the absence of appropriate or acceptable benchmarks for Type B international property funds. The relative return model is more obviously appropriate for Type A funds. Opportunity funds will no doubt wish to protect absolute return targets, but even for these funds, dual absolute and relative objectives should emerge.

Investors may therefore express their return objectives in absolute terms, meaning a quantified nominal or real total return over a given time period. An Australian superannuation fund, for example, might express its real return objective for a real estate portfolio as follows: *to achieve a 5% return in real terms, after fees and taxes, for the lowest possible risk*. A nominal return objective might be 6–8% at a time when inflation is expected to run at 1–3%. This is designed to allow the pension fund to pay out future pensions at a rate which covers wage inflation and to reduce the contribution rate made by employers and employees in the longer run. If the real estate portfolio can deliver these returns as well as diversifying the risk of the multi-asset portfolio and operating as a hedge against unexpected inflation, this is an attractive proposition.

Investors may, however, provide fund managers with different, relative, return targets. This is because investor trustees or pension plan sponsors may need to prove that their selected manager has done a good job in order that they will be retained for a further investment period.

The Relative Return Target

Return objectives are best expressed relative to a benchmark. This could be to achieve average performance, to achieve above median performance, to achieve 2% (or any other number) above average, to achieve upper-quartile performance, or a combination of these. The return objective should be realistic when considered against the current structure of the portfolio, possible restructuring and transaction costs, staff levels and other constraints, as well as the quality of appropriate benchmarks.

Fund managers are generally content with relative return targets. Financial services organisations, like other businesses, concentrate on market share as one of the ways to grow profits. Like any business, they are also concerned with the performance of their competitors and business risk. To prove that they are delivering value as fund managers, there is a requirement to measure return relative to a competitor benchmark. The property fund manager is therefore concerned not only with absolute return, but also with return relative to a performance benchmark such as that provided in many property markets by MSCI.

Table 15.1 shows how the fund manager views relative risk. Absolute volatility, as measured by standard deviations, shows Manager B (28.06%) to be much worse than Manager A (0%). However, this is of less concern than the riskiness of excess returns (the standard deviation of delivered returns relative to an index or benchmark), called tracking error.

In the table, Manager A has no volatility, but the index does. Hence, the returns achieved by A relative to the index (A excess) are volatile (the tracking error, or standard deviation of relative return, is 21.97%). They are in addition more volatile than the excess returns, or the tracking error, on B (6.14%). Manager B produced more volatile returns, but they were more in line with the market and probably introduced less business risk for Manager B than Manager A, who would have been uncomfortable in all years except Year 3.

Any investment carries risk and there is a trade-off between return and risk. Thus, the higher is the required return, the higher is the risk to be taken. If the manager

TABLE 15.1 Excess returns and tracking error (%)

Year	Index	A	B	A excess	B excess
1	18	10	20	−8	2
2	17	10	20	−7	3
3	−30	10	−40	40	−10
4	20	10	25	−10	5
5	21	10	25	−11	4
Average	9.2	10	10	0.8	0.8
SD	21.97	0.00	28.06	21.97	6.14

seeks to achieve top-quartile performance, he must take a higher risk of achieving lower-quartile performance than if the objective is median performance. Risk tolerance should be made explicit.

Because information is relatively scarce, properties are heterogeneous and there is no central marketplace, property is traded in a relatively inefficient market. As a result, and because specific risk is such a significant problem (see Chapter 1), it is arguably easier to outperform (or underperform) the index by sector structure and by stock selection (see Chapter 17) than it is in the securities markets. Considerable data exists to enable this potential to be measured.

Good or widely accepted benchmarks are not, however, available in all property markets. Hence, a reversion to an absolute return objective is understandable, but can be dangerous for investor and manager alike. Investors are unlikely to be satisfied with 5% real returns when the market booms and is believed to deliver very strong returns of 20%, and managers will be unhappy to be charged with failure to deliver if the market turns down badly. A global benchmark remains a key requirement for a professional sector, and work continues to bring this closer.

The Absolute Return Target

The absolute return objective is common in the absence of acceptable benchmarks.

Where an absolute return target is unqualified by a benchmark, the investment manager may be tempted to employ a form of modern portfolio theory (MPT)-based optimisation process. This approach is challenged by the limitations listed in Chapter 1, and applications in practice tend to be heavily qualified and adjusted.

Alternative approaches include the equilibrium model (Litterman, 2003). When applied within a property portfolio, we would begin with a neutral position, determined by the value of the market, with positions taken against that neutral weight determined by the attractiveness of market pricing. This more closely reflects the practice of professional and institutional market participants.

Given an absolute return target, risk should be measured and expressed as a standard deviation of return, or using value-at-risk (VaR) approaches (Figure 15.2).[1]

Return objective	Return type	Risk measure
10% nominal return	Absolute	Standard deviation/VaR
5% real return	Absolute	Standard deviation/VaR
1% above benchmark	Relative	Tracking error
Top quartile of peer group	Relative	Avoid bottom quartile

FIGURE 15.2 Typical return objectives and risk measures

[1]VaR is a measure of how much value a set of investments might lose (with a given probability), given normal market conditions, in a set time period such as a day, a year, or (for property) say a 5-year period. It is typically used by firms and regulators in the financial industry to gauge the amount of assets needed to cover possible losses.

TABLE 15.2 The MSCI UK universe, end 2018

Sector	# Properties	Value	Proportion
Retail	3,472	£78,399	36%
Offices	2,016	£53,868	24%
Industrial	2,637	£47,424	21%
Other	5,005	£41,132	19%
All Property	13,130	£220,823	100%

Source: MSCI.

15.1.3 Benchmarks

The universe used to compile the MSCI UK annual index at the end of 2018 comprised over 13,000 properties worth around £220 billion. Table 15.2 shows the breakdown of this universe by sector.

The neutral or equilibrium portfolio comprised 36% retail property, 24% offices, 21% industrial, and 19% other. This is suggested as a reasonable portfolio shape to begin with. As noted in Chapter 1, the tracking error between a real estate portfolio and a benchmark can be very high, but a portfolio constructed with this shape is likely to perform more closely in line with the return delivered by the universe in that year than a portfolio with different constituent weights.

15.2 STRENGTHS, WEAKNESSES, CONSTRAINTS: PORTFOLIO ANALYSIS

The portfolio analysis examines the current portfolio structure and assesses the strengths, weaknesses, and constraints affecting the organisation in the context of the stated performance objective.

Fund manager appointments in property are most commonly made subject to a 3- or 5-year review. The performance objective may be framed in these terms. Whether or not this is the case, the manager's strategy will be influenced by his recent performance. There will be times when greater risks are encouraged to recover lost ground; there will other times when the appropriate strategy will be designed to lock in the fruits of good past performance by eliminating tracking error from the portfolio.

15.2.1 Current Portfolio Structure

If the portfolio structure is identical to the benchmark, the only risk remaining relative to the benchmark is specific to individual buildings – or funds – rather than systematic. This could be diversified away by having a large number of buildings or funds, although in practice this is rarely possible because of costs and lot size (see Chapter 1).

The analysis of structure identifies those sector/countries/regions or cities in which the fund has an above- or below-average representation relative to the benchmark. This analysis is combined with forecasts of the sector/countries/regions. If the fund has less than the benchmark in a sector/country/city that does well, the fund will perform at a below-average level. If the fund has more than the benchmark in a sector/country/city which does poorly, the fund will also perform below average.

When taken together with market forecasts and the fund objectives, an analysis of the structure of the fund relative to the benchmark will suggest sector/country combinations to buy or sell.

15.2.2 Strengths, Weaknesses, Constraints

Implementation of a strategy may be helped or hindered by a number of factors. A number have already been covered. Others include the following:

- The scope for changing the shape of a portfolio or fund will depend on whether new money is coming in or money is being withdrawn. Cash inflows can create opportunities to change the fund shape, or apply capital to active management. Cash outflows can create enormous pressures on performance, especially in an illiquid market.
- It is also necessary to consider practicalities: for example, whether it will be possible to undertake the proposed level of sales and purchases in a sensible time. This is a particular concern in inactive or small markets and for large funds. Can a position in a closed-ended fund be liquidated at net asset value before it terminates?
- Particularly for small funds, there may be stock-specific factors (such as lease renewals) which mean that the required sales cannot or should not be made at a particular time.
- The cost of sales and purchases should be included in the analysis.
- The impact of taxation needs to be considered for some vehicles.
- For small funds, it may not be possible to gain exposure to large-value markets with large lot sizes, such as shopping centres. Using unlisted funds may be an option, but this brings other challenges (see Chapter 17).
- The fund may not have the necessary expertise in-house and may require external advice.
- The timing of any change in strategy and changes in tactics is important: it is necessary to anticipate market movements and to buy and sell at the most advantageous moments. In property, as is the case with many investments, it is rarely a good time to buy or sell when the consensus agrees with you.

15.2.3 Structure and Stock Selection

The most commonly accepted way of summarising the skills available to a property fund manager is to separate the performance impact of portfolio structure from the performance produced by stock selection. This is covered in more detail in Chapter 17.

In considering a plan for altering the structure of a portfolio, relevant issues include: the appropriateness or otherwise of sector/region (or city) classifications; the accuracy and value of forecasts; and portfolio size as it impinges upon the manager's freedom to balance the portfolio across 3, 5, 10, or 50 sector/country/regions. This will also be affected by research staff size and expertise and by the culture of the organisation, which may or may not apply similar processes to those used for other asset classes.

Managers and investors may believe in their ability to spot underpricing in property types – for example, secondary or high-yield property. In equity fund management, this is called style management. An investor could hold the benchmark proportion for the asset class but select particular styles – opportunity or Type B funds, for example – within the class. Forecasts (see Chapter 4) can help to identify the sector/country/region to buy. This provides a basis for stock selection (investing in a particular fund, or buying and selling individual properties) and focuses the work of those who have to identify investments. An investment that appears 'good' in its own right need not be good in a portfolio context.

A large property investment fund or organisation with a belief in its central research and forecasting capabilities might reasonably expect to add to its returns by taking active positions against a benchmark. This is the expected behaviour of a large balanced fund such as an insurance fund.

An organisation with a highly skilled and motivated acquisitions team which enjoys the benefit of asset-specific performance fees or carried interests (see Chapter 12) might reasonably be expected to focus on a small number of deals which it expects to add to performance rather than to buy a large number of properties whose performance will tend towards the mean return for the sector or market. This is the expected behaviour of a private equity real estate fund or opportunity (Type B) fund.

True excellence might imply that the investment manager can both take sector positions and focus on good deals (Figure 15.3). Realism, modesty, very thin resources, or compensation packages that do not provide a performance fee or bonus might suggest holding benchmark sector weights and diversifying at the asset level in order to limit the tracking error of the fund relative to the benchmark.

Investors who employ fund managers should focus on their investment objectives and on the fee structures of their managers in order that behaviour appropriate to the investor's requirements is encouraged. Performance fees and carried interest have a particularly powerful effect: see Chapter 17.

	Market forecasting ability	
Stock selection skills	**Good**	**Poor**
Good	Concentrate on underpriced properties	Concentrate on underpriced properties
	Shift sector weights based on forecasts	Hold market weights
Poor	Diversify: hold many properties	Diversify: hold many properties
	Shift sector weights based on forecasts	Hold market weights

FIGURE 15.3 Passive and active strategies

15.3 PORTFOLIO CONSTRUCTION

15.3.1 Top-Down or Bottom-Up?

Given our understanding of stock selection and portfolio structure as the twin drivers of portfolio return and risk, how can we think about the portfolio construction process?

Where good benchmarks are available, as in the UK and USA, a top-down strategic approach has become popular in property portfolio management, particularly for Type A funds, portfolios, and managers. This involves an analysis of the structure of the portfolio relative to a benchmark; forecasts of return and risk for the portfolio, often top down by property type or location; and a strategy which involves buying and selling. The top-down investment process, which applies equally well to a portfolio whose investor or manager has absolute or relative return objectives, is shown in Figure 15.4.

Commonly, forecasts of rental growth and yield movement are applied at the market, sector, region, city, and property level. These, fed through a discounted cash flow valuation model, will suggest market buys and sells – those sectors, towns, and buildings where the returns on offer, as estimated by the investment manager, exceed the risk-adjusted required return.

A valuation model is simply a way of comparing the expected or forecast return with the required return (the risk-adjusted cost of capital) or, equivalently, the correct initial yield with the current market yield. The inputs into a valuation model are the investor's views on rental growth, depreciation, and risk. These are used to establish the correct yield or the expected return. This is compared with the current market yield or the required return to establish whether the asset is correctly priced, underpriced, or overpriced. This produces market buy and sell decisions. This process is described in detail in Chapter 4.

Deciding whether assets or markets look cheap is not sufficient to determine a portfolio strategy. The current portfolio structure is also significant, and a portfolio analysis will be undertaken to identify where the manager is underweight or overweight relative to a given benchmark. In addition, the manager's or trustees' objectives must be

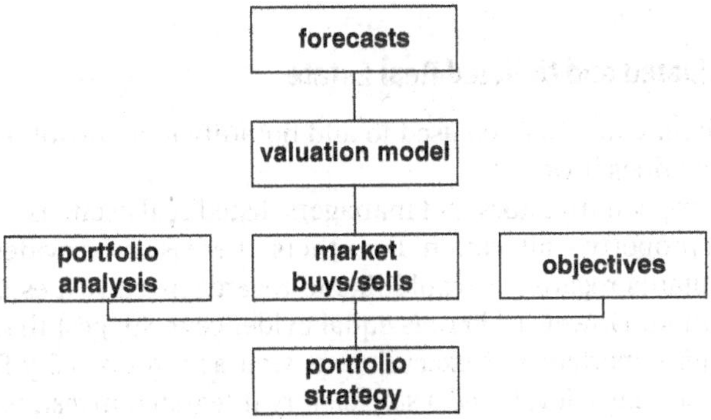

FIGURE 15.4 The top-down investment process

taken into account in determining what action needs to be taken. That action will be prescribed in the form of a business plan or portfolio strategy.

As Figure 15.3 illustrates, not all organisations will choose to adopt a top-down process. Confidence in rent forecasting has been damaged by shocks such as on-line retailing and its largely unanticipated impact on retail rents, and cap rate forecasting has always been challenging. As we discussed in Chapters 3 and 4, real estate data quality is generally poor, and the more focused is the location under consideration, the greater this difficulty becomes. At the same time, increasing attention is being paid to cities and sub-locations within cities as important drivers of value and return. Type B (poorly diversified) funds focus on asset-specific risk, and a top-down forecast of a country/sector/region may have little or no value to such an investor, who will focus on themes and assets.

The bottom-up process focuses on assets, and each asset under consideration will be 'underwritten' (analysed) by reference to asset-specific issues – the tenant, the lease, the opportunity to add value through refurbishment, and so on. A (typically) 5- to 10-year cash flow model will be built, requiring a forecast of rental value change but one which is driven more by the asset and its micro-location than by national or regional GDP growth and such macro variables. Such portfolios are modelled bottom-up, building by building or even lease by lease, rather than top-down.

So, we expect long-term returns from real estate as an asset class which are superior to bonds but inferior to equities. Volatility (by reference to appraised valuations) is low, but smoothed. Real estate is a good diversifier against bonds and equities, with a high Sharpe ratio. An optimiser can be used to model the ideal property weight, and the ideal geographical portfolio distribution.

Direct portfolios carry high property-specific risk, because property is not homogeneous and individual lot sizes may be large. We can employ top-down or bottom-up portfolio construction techniques, with top-down preferred for larger Type A portfolios and bottom-up preferred for smaller Type B portfolios.

Listed and unlisted funds can help to diversify specific risk; unlisted property is illiquid, but listed property companies and REITs provide limited diversification against stocks and bonds.

What evidence do we have that real estate investors can use this knowledge to build efficient portfolios in practice?

15.3.2 Mixing Listed and Unlisted Real Estate

First, to what extent can REITs be used to add liquidity to a portfolio? This is a highly attractive idea, but does it work?

For some European investors and managers, listed real estate is clearly part of the equity – and not property – allocation. For others, there is some evidence that pension funds and consultants regard (or would like to regard) listed real estate as part of the real estate allocation. However, there is equal evidence to suggest that asset managers (with their greater experience of execution as well as a propensity for business unit separation) may not have developed a satisfactory integrated investment process.

In a survey undertaken for EPRA (the European Public Real Estate Association), Baum and Moss (2012) found that only 20% of interviewee organisations believed that

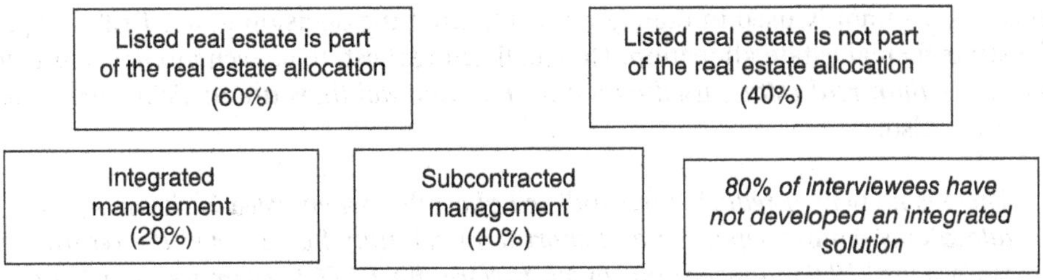

FIGURE 15.5 Integrating listed real estate
Source: Baum and Moss (2012).

they had developed an integrated process for the management of a portfolio of listed and unlisted real estate (see Figure 15.5). For 40%, listed real estate was not part of their real estate allocation at all. For two-thirds of the remaining interviewees for whom listed real estate was a part of their real estate allocation, they made no attempt to integrate the public and private portfolios and subcontracted the management of the listed stocks.

There was a strong view amongst many investors that property companies and REITs are securities and do not come within the real estate team's remit, sitting very firmly within the equity team. Listed property analysts may be close to the direct real estate team, exchanging notes on markets, but the investments are fundamentally different. Real estate securities and private real estate should be separate because (a) they are essentially different animals, with different correlations and different volatilities and (b) the skills sets for investing are different.

> *(Listed) is currently not within the mandate or IMA (investment management agreement). The client deals with real estate equities within the equity allocation. Real estate equities are not part of the real estate allocation. The client's view is that they are more 'equities' than 'real estate'.*

For some Dutch pension funds and others, listed real estate securities are a large part – as much as 50% – of the real estate allocation. But most of those investors and managers who do invest in REITs as part of their real estate allocation use a dedicated REIT team sitting outside the real estate group, sharing research only to a limited extent.

Some managers use listed securities where product development requires daily pricing and liquidity, defined contribution and retail (for sale to the public) property funds being the prime examples. Others invest in listed in a quest for further diversification within the sector, as well as for liquidity.

When portfolio returns and their consequent impact on returns, solvency, and funding models are driven by year-end valuations of private real estate, the volatility of the listed sector and the high correlation with general equities causes investors a significant problem.

Investors are interested in exploiting the arbitrage opportunities that should exist between public and private real estate, but struggle with the operational difficulties involved in trying to do this. There is a clear failure to separate the active tactical decisions commonly used in managing REITs from the decision to use REITs as part of a strategic real estate allocation. Hence, listed real estate is '*seen by clients as equities rather than real estate, used as a cash pot, and holdings are tactical rather than strategic*'. Also:

> *There is no way of reducing our unlisted allocation when listed is cheap, so the allocations remain separate; and short term volatility has affected the returns badly. Our REIT manager aims to out-perform his REIT benchmark on a 6–12 month basis but this has little to do with our overall objective.*

15.3.3 Can Real Estate Investors Build Efficient Portfolios?

Using MPT, the traditional asset allocation process employs measurements of risk and return delivered by asset classes – for example, stocks, bonds, and real estate – to build efficient portfolios. To build efficient portfolios in practice using this type of analysis requires that the risk and return characteristics of the asset class can be replicated in real portfolios. This may be true of stocks and bonds, but is it true of real estate?

Using an analysis based on the uniquely rich MSCI dataset for UK direct real estate, Baum and Colley (2017) compared the risk and return characteristics of real estate investment approaches (direct exposure, balanced and specialist unlisted funds, a multi-manager approach and listed securities) relative to a UK market index. Having applied a random stochastic simulation of historic performance data from 2003 to 2012 to hypothetical portfolios of £25, £50, and £100 million, deducting typical purchase, sale, and asset management fees, they drew several conclusions from their results (which are summarised in Table 15.3).

TABLE 15.3 Real estate investment strategy risk/return comparison, 2003–12

Universe	Strategy	TWRR	Excess return	Tracking error
Benchmarks	IPD All Property Index	6.31	n/a	n/a
	AREF Balanced Fund Index	4.25	−2.06	1.41
	AREF All-Pooled Fund Index	4.04	−2.27	3.71
Direct mandate	£25m	5.31	−1.00	7.59
	£50m	5.31	−1.00	5.35
	£100m	5.31	−1.00	4.06
Unlisted balanced fund universe	Single fund	4.27	−2.04	3.77
	Dual fund	4.31	−2.00	3.07
	£25m multi-manager	4.09	−2.22	2.12
	£50m multi-manager	4.11	−2.20	2.01
	£100m multi-manager	4.10	−2.21	1.95
Listed mandate	UK REITS	4.69	−1.62	22.43

Source: Baum and Colley (2017).

Firstly, the difficulty of diversifying away specific risk in such a lumpy asset class means that it is extremely difficult and/or costly to access or replicate direct property market returns. This suggests that an investor/manager setting out to deliver returns in line with a market index would have to demonstrate significant levels of skill. Secondly, listed real estate, which is more readily diversifiable, fails to deliver returns that are correlated with direct real estate in the short term (1–5 years). In contrast, it is clear that multi-manager strategies were able to deliver returns that more effectively replicated a direct benchmark.

However, multi-manager fees negatively impacted on returns and largely accounted for average underperformance of 0.15% against the direct benchmark. While it is estimated that over a 10-year analysis period both direct and listed investment strategies outperformed multi-manager strategies (by 121 bps and 59 bps p.a., respectively), this outperformance would have been delivered at the cost of significant tracking error against direct property benchmarks. Specific risk can be avoided by real estate investors, but at a cost.

Despite the direct benchmark outperforming all other strategies, for a given amount invested (£25, £50, or £100 million) a direct market strategy would have delivered the widest range of returns (apart from REITs) for investors. For example, the tracking error of a £100 million direct mandate would have averaged 4.06%, which compares to 1.95% for a £100 million multi-manager strategy and 3.77% for a single fund randomly selected from the all-balanced universe and 3.07% for a two-fund strategy. These are Type A funds; adding Type B funds over this period would not have been helpful.

Table 15.4 and Figure 15.6 show how various strategies deliver return and risk results which (roughly speaking) are efficient (more return means more tracking error), although REITs look inefficient given the massive short-term tracking error produced.

These results show risk–return combinations in line with expectations, with the coefficient of variation rising above the direct solution as more funds are added, with the exception of the listed approach, which offers more risk for less return than the direct solution, and the two-fund approach, which offers marginally more return than the single-fund approach for less risk. Otherwise, funds offer less return for less risk and the multi-manager solution appears especially efficient as measured by the coefficient of variation.

TABLE 15.4 Risk and return (£25m invested, all balanced universe)

	Return	Risk	CV
Direct	5.31	7.59	0.70
One fund	4.27	3.77	1.13
Two funds	4.31	3.07	1.40
Multi-manager	4.09	2.12	1.93
Listed	4.69	22.43	0.21

Source: Baum and Colley (2017).
Note: CV = coefficient of variation (defined as risk/return).

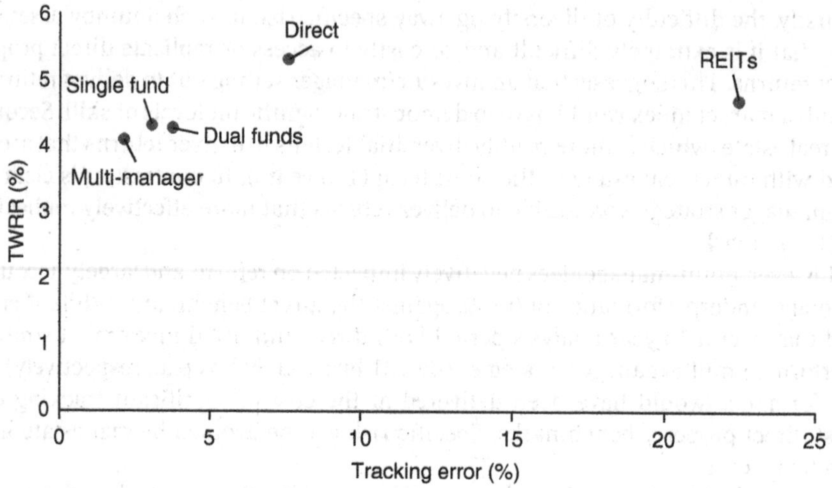

FIGURE 15.6 Risk and return (£25m invested, all balanced universe)
Source: Baum and Colley (2017).

Table 15.5 shows the risk–return results and the coefficient of variation (and Figure 15.7 shows the capital market line) for £50 million invested, plotting the risk and return for the direct solution against a single fund randomly selected, two funds randomly selected, and a multi-manager solution, all confined to the all balanced universe, plus the listed portfolio.

These results again produce risk–return combinations in line with expectations, similar to the £25 million result.

Table 15.6 shows the risk–return results and the coefficient of variation, and Figure 15.8 shows the capital market line, for £100 million invested, plotting the risk and return for the direct solution against a single fund randomly selected, two funds randomly selected, and a multi-manager solution, all confined to the all balanced universe, plus the listed portfolio.

TABLE 15.5 Risk and return (£50m invested, all balanced universe)

	Return	Risk	CV
Direct	5.31	5.35	0.99
One fund	4.27	3.77	1.13
Two funds	4.31	3.07	1.40
Multi-manager	4.09	2.01	2.04
Listed	4.69	22.43	0.21

Source: Baum and Colley (2017).
Note: CV = coefficient of variation (defined as risk/return).

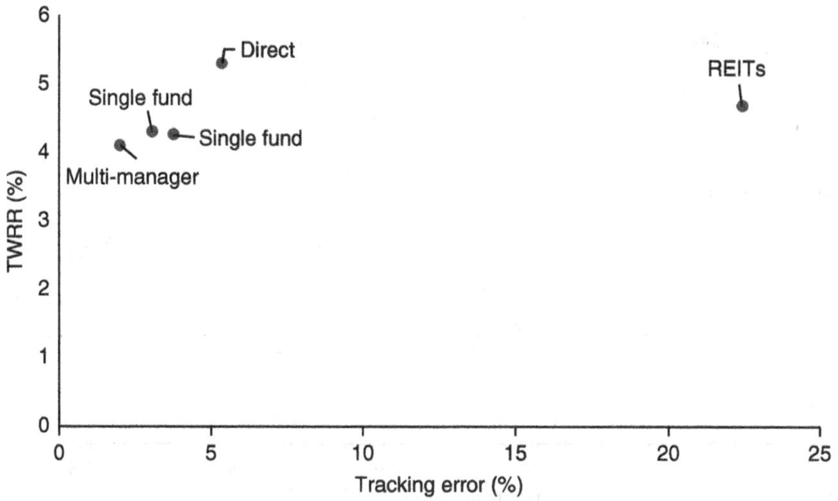

FIGURE 15.7 Risk and return (£50m invested, all balanced universe)
Source: Baum and Colley (2017).

TABLE 15.6 Risk and return (£100m invested, all balanced universe)

	Return	Risk	CV
Direct	5.31	4.06	1.31
One fund	4.27	3.77	1.13
Two funds	4.31	3.07	1.40
Multi-manager	4.10	1.95	2.10
Listed	4.69	22.43	0.21

Source: Baum and Colley (2017).
Note: CV = coefficient of variation (defined as risk/return).

These results are less clear. £100 million invested allows a direct approach to diversify some risk away. It appears that larger sums – say £100 million – are needed to justify a direct exposure for reasonable risk. For smaller investors, funds provide a more efficient investment strategy.

15.3.4 Possible Approaches

Case 1: Large US Endowment Fund

To illustrate a possible approach to building a portfolio for a large investor, we assume that optimisation tools are available, and focus on the appropriate variables as specified above.

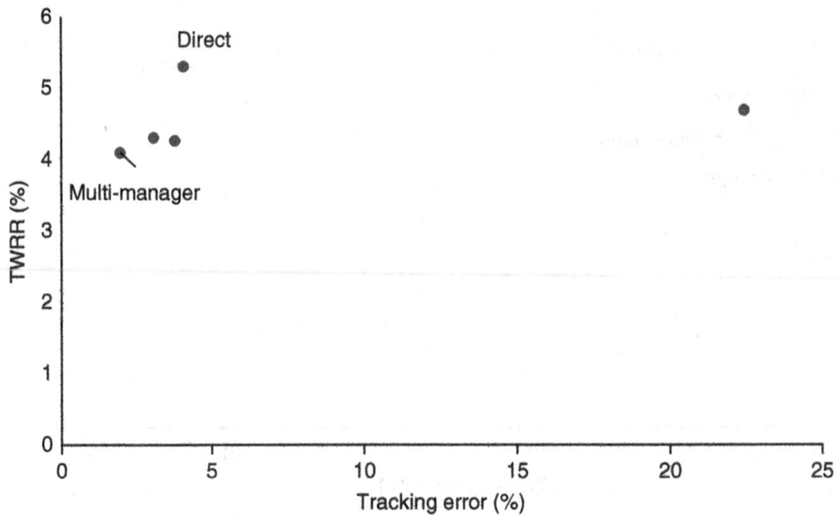

FIGURE 15.8 Risk and return (£100m invested, all balanced universe)
Source: Baum and Colley (2017).

We are a US investor with dollar-denominated liabilities. We manage an endowment fund with a new $1,000 million real estate investment allocation. We are seeking exposure to domestic real estate. The fund has no current exposure to real estate, has a long-term horizon, a moderate risk appetite, and a skeleton in-house team. The issues to be confronted are as follows:

- What allocations should be made to direct and indirect forms of property?
- How much of an indirect allocation should be to listed and how much to unlisted? How much should be allocated to funds with core, value-add, or opportunity styles?
- What regional and geographic split of the allocation is advisable? What sector split is to be recommended? Should we use optimisation, or an equilibrium (market value-weighted) approach?
- What execution model is appropriate? Should the fund hire in-house personnel and choose funds? If so, where should they be located? If not, what mandate can be designed and how many advisors or managers are required? Should funds of funds or a multi-manager approach be used?

The board has determined the following. The key decision made was that there will be no direct property – this is regarded as too lumpy for a global $1,000 million allocation, and the lack of any internal property expertise suggested outsourcing acquisitions, disposal and asset management to a fund manager. A segregated or separate account could be employed, in which case the mandate could include direct assets, but focusing all risk on one manager was not appealing when several managers were used for the endowment's public securities and private equity investments.

Several managers of Type B funds in which the endowment were interested had indicated that they would offer so-called sidecar or co-investment opportunities to the endowment fund. Under this arrangement, attractive assets that are too large or in some other way unsuitable for the relevant fund are offered to individual fund investors, who may invest in the asset alongside the fund or manager, or with other fund investors. So some semi-direct exposure might be available via the Type B fund allocation.

As a US investor, the fund focuses on US assets because liabilities are dollar-denominated and the tax treatment of domestic assets is favourable. The long-term investment horizon and limited requirement for liquidity encourages an exposure to unlisted funds at the expense of listed securities, but there is a preference for the risk profile of REITs over REOCs and other listed property securities.

The fund's risk appetite allows an exposure to some Type B (value-added/opportunity) funds. The minimum/maximum investment to each fund is $25/50 million (say 30 unlisted funds maximum). A single advisory manager is to be used to guide fund selection and ongoing review, with the fund board retaining discretion over investment decisions.

After a working session between fund and advisor, using a neutral or equilibrium approach adjusted by an optimisation of excess net returns, the recommended regional and sector allocations and fund style choices have been made. The regional and sector allocations are shown in Tables 15.7 and 15.8. The recommended weights by risk style are summarised in Table 15.9.

Our advisor has reminded the fund that gearing – typically 20% for Type A, 30% for listed, and 50% for Type B funds – will alter the equity required to attain the desired geographical and sector exposure. Given that gross asset value exposure is the key determinant of tracking error risk, we show the required equity positions in Table 15.10.

TABLE 15.7 Regional allocations

	Neutral	Position	Bet
East	32%	40%	+8%
MidWest	8%	5%	−3%
South	20%	25%	+5%
West	39%	30%	−9%
	100%	100%	0%

TABLE 15.8 Sector allocations

	Neutral	Position	Bet
Office	40%	25%	−15%
Retail	25%	15%	−10%
Industrial	10%	20%	10%
Residential	15%	25%	+10%
Other	10%	15%	+5%
	100%	100%	0%

TABLE 15.9 Property style allocations

	Neutral	Position	Bet
Direct	0%	0%	0%
Listed	44%	30%	−14%
Type A funds	49%	55%	6%
Type B funds/sidecars	7%	15%	8%
	100%	100%	0%

TABLE 15.10 Equity allocations

	Position	Gearing	Equity
Direct	0%	0%	$0m
Listed	30%	30%	$290m
Type A funds	55%	20%	$607m
Type B funds/sidecars	15%	50%	$103m
	100%		$1,000m

Case 2: UK Family Office

The ABC Trust has an allocation to real estate of around £40 million. To date, this has been invested in smaller single assets, but recent experience has been troublesome, with vacancies and complex refurbishment works taking up too much management time. Following a strategic asset allocation review, the ABC Trustees wish to consider a slightly lower long-term investment in indirect UK commercial property using pooled property funds and REITS. As direct assets are sold, the indirect portfolio will be built up to around £30 million over time, with 60% of the portfolio held in more liquid investments (open-ended funds and REITs). The benchmark employed will be the MSCI UK All Balanced Property Funds Index.

An investment manager has been appointed to select and monitor funds on an advisory basis from the pool of funds/listed securities available to the trust. The appointed manager has proposed a three-part portfolio shape. This is based on a core/liquid/specialist breakdown of the market opportunity set (balanced open-ended unlisted or Type A funds, REITs, and specialist open or closed-ended funds, some of which would be Type B).

Sector weightings have been defined by reference to the following sectors:

- Office
- Retail
- Industrial/logistics
- Residential
- Social infrastructure

Model portfolio weightings are based on the advisor's house views of the expected return on the UK real estate market, disaggregated as above, leading to a preferred overweight position to industrial/logistics and social infrastructure and underweight positions to retail and offices. There will be agreed ranges of exposure to Type A funds, Type B funds, and REITs, with a focus on open-ended funds and REITs (in combination, at least 60% of the portfolio).

The advisor also maintains a view on regional and city exposure, preferred investment themes – including preferred gearing levels, stock quality expressed through yield levels, value or growth orientation, and exposure to development – and will monitor and limit the portfolio exposure to these variables.

The advisor's fund selection process involves a series of distillations from the total fund universe with the objective of identifying target funds in each category of the fund universe. Funds are targeted following a meeting with the manager and a review of the fund materials, by reference to a standard set of selection criteria in four dimensions, as follows:

- Manager
- Property portfolio
- Fund structure
- Pricing

Investments are sourced both through the primary and secondary market. Primary issues include new fund launches, re-openings of closed-ended funds to raise additional equity, and issues by open-ended funds. A pro-forma financial model is applied for all prospective investments to project total returns and to assess relative value across competing opportunities. Key inputs into these models are the economic/property market views that drive the market outlook.

Secondary dealing platforms will be utilised to deal in secondary trades which can on occasion offer better value. The selection of listed security exposures may be subcontracted to a qualified specialist advisory firm.

Reports will typically be received from managers on a quarterly basis and the advisor will deliver standardised aggregated data to ABC on a quarterly basis. The advisor will expect to be proactive in seeking more information from managers as required, and will hold annual meetings with managers of core holdings.

Disposals of holdings may be prompted by considerations of portfolio shape, by expected fund underperformance, or by opportunities to crystallise a profit in the secondary market and reinvest the proceeds on a more accretive basis in other opportunities.

Target return objectives and risk constraints will be agreed to cover the following:

- Leverage (on a look-through basis)
- Development exposure
- Exposure to a single manager
- Exposure to a single fund
- Minimum income requirement

The advisor will also identify any client-specific factors constraining fund selection, including making sure legal and tax structures are compatible with third-party client advice, and environmental, social, and governance issues, or other ethical restrictions.

Iterating between the client's objectives and constraints, the model portfolio, and the preferred funds in each category, a target portfolio structure has been recommended, comprising a set of target allocations to a portfolio of funds. The target portfolio is as shown in Table 15.11, with 63% of the gross asset value allocated to more liquid funds.

As the investment programme developed, market conditions suggested a cautious approach and after 1 year, three funds had been committed to, but none in the liquid category. Equity of £3.5 million had been drawn, with £4.8 million committed. Various analytics are shown in Table 15.12, while Figure 15.9 shows the exposure of committed capital relative to the benchmark. It was agreed between the trust and the manager that liquid funds would be the next target investments, but only when pricing was attractive.

TABLE 15.11 Equity allocations and exposure

	Target equity commitment	Leverage	Equity	Exposure
Fund 1: Type A	£7,500,000	0%	25%	21%
Fund 2: Type A	£6,000,000	10%	20%	19%
Fund 3: specialist, core, Type A	£5,100,000	20%	17%	17%
Fund 4: Type B	£1,500,000	22%	5%	5%
Fund 5: Type B	£2,100,000	30%	7%	8%
Fund 6: Type B	£1,800,000	30%	6%	7%
Fund 7: Type B	£4,500,000	30%	15%	17%
Fund 8: REIT	£1,500,000	35%	5%	6%
Total	**£30,000,000**	**15%**	**100%**	**100%**

TABLE 15.12 Equity commitments, 1 year on

	Portfolio
Equity committed	**£4.8m**
Equity drawn	**£3.5m**
Number of funds	**3**
Liquid exposure (% GAV)	**0**
GAV	**£112.5m**
Number of assets	**21**
LTV current/expected (% GAV)	**15/27**
Standing investments (% GAV)	**21**
Planning risk (income producing, % GAV)	**44**
Development risk (% GAV)	**36**
Non-income producing planning/development	***23%***
Pre-let/ forward funding	***13%***

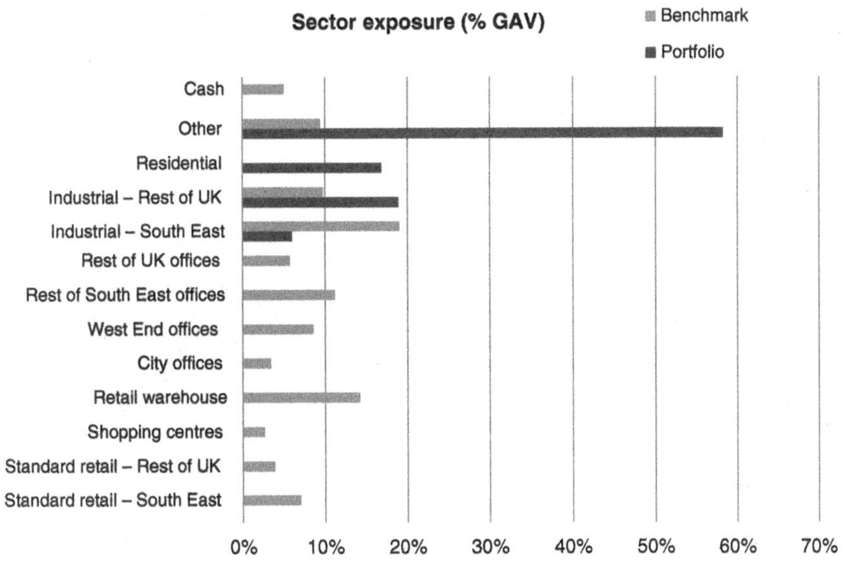

FIGURE 15.9 Sector exposures relative to benchmark

15.4 CONCLUSION

The objective of a property fund or investment portfolio might be to achieve good 'absolute' returns, meaning good returns relative to other assets, or good 'relative' returns, meaning good returns relative to the market benchmark for domestic or global real estate investments or investors.

In this chapter we described a recommended approach for a large institutional investor. We suggest that direct property investing will suit the very largest investors, but that funds and/or club investments are the natural route to gaining global property exposure for most institutional investors of scale. This is because their performance characteristics are most in line with the direct market over the short to medium term. These funds can fail to deliver what is required, but unlisted funds with the appropriate risk and return characteristics continue to be created in most markets, although listed REITs are the dominant routes to some markets.

In constructing a large Type A property portfolio for a professional investor, we suggest using a top-down approach feeding from capital market, economic, and property pricing data, and assume we will allocate between direct property, unlisted funds, and REITs. We assume that tax and structuring issues are generally soluble without prohibitive cost. We consider, in particular, market pricing leading to regional allocations and property type allocations; we also consider fund risk style allocations, and the impact of leverage, tax, and fees.

In Chapter 16 we move on to consider the particular issues which arise when investing internationally.

CHAPTER 16

International Real Estate Investment: Issues

16.1 INTRODUCTION: THE GROWTH OF CROSS-BORDER REAL ESTATE CAPITAL

In 1972, over 94% of the floor space in a large database of City of London office properties (see Lizieri *et al.*, 2000) was owned by UK firms; just less than 3% of space was owned by Middle Eastern interests; and around 2% was European owned. Research found no properties owned by German, Japanese, or US firms at that time.

By 1997, 21.9% of the buildings covered in the survey were in overseas ownership. 7% of the properties were in Japanese hands, 5% were German owned, 4% were owned by US firms, and just under 3% were, as in 1972, in Middle Eastern ownership.

By 2006, 45% of the office space in the City was owned by non-UK firms. Japanese ownership had been in decline, while the US and German presence had been on the increase, but the most interesting change had been the emergence of international vehicles with indeterminate ultimate ownership – Luxembourg, the Cayman and Channel Islands funds, for example.

The globalisation of business activity was, prior to 2007–8, a continuing process, driven both by the conversion of ownership of successful companies from domestic to multinational concerns and by the increasing opportunities offered to corporations and institutional investors and banks to own overseas assets through globally traded stock markets. The result has been a surge in foreign direct investment, with Asia-Pacific a particular beneficiary. In this region, real estate investment (the construction of manufacturing facilities, for example) accounted for more than 40% of all foreign direct investment in the decade to 2001. Both occupier demand and the ownership of corporate real estate facilities have become increasingly driven by the needs of the multinational enterprise.

An increased investor appetite for global investment in equities and bonds, and later property, has generated a structural market shift observable since the mid-1990s.

Diversification by institutional investors is a powerful driver of this activity, while other investor groups look for higher returns by seeking markets about to boom. If returns going forward in a domestic property market are perceived to be disappointing, that capital will look abroad. The rise of international benchmarks and improvements in data provision, coupled with globalisation in general and the growth of the international investment house in particular, have added to the appeal of international investment. Sheer weight of money drives some funds – such as the Abu Dhabi Investment Authority (with estimated assets of around $1 trillion) – to place their investments abroad. Others, such as the Government Investment Corporation (GIC) of Singapore, are forced by government regulation to invest outside their domestic markets.

Home bias remains an observable phenomenon. Imazeki and Gallimore (2010), for example, find clear evidence of this even in funds of liquid real estate stocks. Nonetheless, the world's largest real estate investors have become global investors. To a significant extent, currency risk has disappeared for Euroland investors and international investing has been much simplified for non-Europeans entering Europe. Regulation and taxation rules have very slowly begun to converge. Investment benchmarks are slowly becoming global. This will create a significant change in investor behaviour: from a position where any exposure to overseas assets is a risk against a domestic benchmark, growing recognition of wider non-domestic benchmarks would lead to a need to invest overseas to *reduce* risk relative to these benchmarks.

The credit crunch of 2007–8 and the political events of 2016 onwards threatened a return to protectionism and trade barriers, and clearly slowed down the globalisation process. The strategic trend to international real estate investing nonetheless appears irreversible. Where currency risk remains, hedging is, however, expensive and difficult to achieve efficiently (Lizieri *et al.*, 1998) and vehicles are rarely fully hedged. This problem leaves investors at the mercy of currency movements. Other perceived difficulties, including the dangers of operating from a distance with no local representation, increase the attraction of investing internationally through liquid securitised vehicles and unlisted funds, but barriers to international exposure by asset managers remain.

Financial globalisation has helped to create new investment vehicles to solve many of the problems that are characteristic of this asset class (Baum, 2008). International real estate investment through unlisted funds has included Type A strategies, through which capital has been allocated largely to developed markets, and Type B funds, which have also allocated capital to developing and emerging markets (Baum, 2009).

As a result, cross-border property investment grew more quickly than domestic investment over the period leading up to the global financial crisis, as evidenced by various publications by INREV (the Association of Investors in Non-Listed Real Estate Vehicles) and most firms of leading real estate brokers (for example, CBRE and Jones Lang LaSalle). Running in parallel with this development has been a boom in the number and value of unlisted property funds (see Chapter 11). Investing in unlisted real estate vehicles has become an increasingly standard route to attaining international real estate exposure.

16.2 THE GLOBAL REAL ESTATE MARKET

16.2.1 The Global Universe

The global investable stock of real estate has been estimated (as at 2017) at around $35 trillion (see Chapter 1).

Asia (the developed part, including Japan, Korea, Singapore, Hong Kong, Taiwan, Australia, New Zealand, and increasingly China), Europe, and North America dominate this universe. The developing and emerging markets in Asia, Africa, and Latin America are under-represented. More stark are the statistics shown in Table 16.1, which relate the value of investable real estate to each head of population, with a global average of $4.68 of real estate for each person – but $17.26 per person in North America, $19.21 in Oceania (Australasia), $13.59 in Europe, and only $2.51 in Asia and $1.26 in Africa/Middle East, a figure massively boosted by the Middle East markets. There is a long way to go before economic development is evenly spread and the typical real estate portfolio is properly geographically diversified.

16.2.2 Core, Developing, Emerging

Many US investors and most UK investors looked for their first overseas investments in continental Europe. This is explained wholly by familiarity and perceptions of risk. However, US opportunity funds opened up the new emerging markets of Central and Eastern Europe in the early 1990s and entered Latin American and Asian markets in force in the following decade.

Type A investors focus on what have been called core markets; Type B investors will also consider developing and emerging property investment markets; all will typically avoid opaque markets. This distinction is somewhat arbitrary and changes over time. Nevertheless, broadly speaking, core markets have a benchmark (for the relevance of this, see Chapter 15), are politically stable, have a stable currency, offer professional services necessary for institutional investment, and are liquid and transparent. Developing markets generally have no benchmark, are smaller, have less liquid markets (but liquidity is either growing or is expected to grow), and are politically stable with a stable currency. Emerging markets have low liquidity, less political or currency stability, fewer professional services, and no benchmark.

Continuing attention to these distinctions places an increasing focus on the powerhouse economies of China and India. The global geography of real estate market

TABLE 16.1 The investable real estate universe per capita

	Africa/ME	Asia	Oceania	Europe	South America	North America	Total
Market size	$1,537bn	$11,490bn	$730bn	$10,044bn	$1,627bn	$9,992bn	$35,420bn
Population	1,216bn	4,581bn	38bn	739bn	422bn	579bn	7,575bn
Coefficient	$1.26	$2.51	$19.21	$13.59	$3.86	$17.26	$4.68

attractiveness is constantly changing, and forms the first key challenge in developing an investment strategy.

16.2.3 Transparency

In addition to the core, developing, and emerging markets there are also perceived 'red-lined' or non-investable markets. These are also defined as 'opaque' by Jones Lang LaSalle (JLL) in its Real Estate Transparency Index, first published in 1999 (latest version 2018). This survey-based measure uses judgements about the following:

a. the availability of investment performance indexes;
b. market fundamentals data;
c. listed vehicle financial disclosure and governance;
d. regulatory and legal factors; and
e. professional and ethical standards.

This information is used to arrive at a single index measure, with the highest transparency scores in the 2018 report awarded to the UK (see Table 16.2).

China and India are ranked 33 and 35, respectively, and defined as semi-transparent. The biggest improvers were Bulgaria and Serbia.

16.2.4 The Limits to Globalisation

Baum (2008) focuses on the development of unlisted funds as intermediary structures carrying institutional capital from developed to developing markets. The research relates the number of funds targeting particular countries to population and GDP per capita. It finds that there is a very strong relationship between the popularity of a country for investment through this vehicle format and these independent variables.

TABLE 16.2 Jones Lang LaSalle Transparency Index rankings 2018

Rank	Country	Score
1	UK	1.2
2	Australia	1.3
3	USA	1.4
4	France	1.4
5	Canada	1.5
6	Netherlands	1.5
7	New Zealand	1.6
8	Germany	1.9
9	Ireland	1.9
10	Sweden	1.9
11	Finland	2.0
12	Singapore	2.0

Source: Jones Lang LaSalle.

More interesting, perhaps, is the identification of outlier countries where the amount of investment is significantly less – or greater – than that predicted by population and GDP per capita.

The predicted number of funds targeting the country can be compared with the observed number. The countries receiving significantly more investment than that predicted by the equation are Brazil, Malaysia, Mexico, Argentina, and Vietnam. Three of these are located close to the USA, the main supplier of capital in the survey. The countries receiving significantly less investment than that predicted by the equation are Taiwan, Saudi Arabia, Venezuela, Indonesia, Iran, Pakistan, Columbia, Nigeria, Bangladesh, Algeria, Thailand, and Peru.

The research found that the JLL Transparency Index results and political issues fit well with countries receiving significantly less investment than that predicted, while the countries receiving significantly more investment than that predicted by the equation are generally semi-transparent or improving.

16.3 THE CASE FOR INTERNATIONAL REAL ESTATE INVESTMENT

Two dominant styles of international real estate investment vehicle have emerged since the 1990s, driving much of the recent international activity. These are distinguished by the objective being pursued. The key drivers for investing outside the domestic property market and buying global property are the increased opportunities for either or both of (i) diversification and (ii) enhanced return.

These potential benefits come at a cost of increased complexity of execution. The diversification drive has been characterised by Type A property funds for diversifiers, and the search for return by Type B funds. This latter property fund type has commonly explored emerging markets. Western Europe, North America, and the Pacific Rim still represent the majority in terms of volume of activity (Lizieri, 2009), but it is clear that property investment in emerging markets, especially by unlisted opportunity funds, had become common prior to the credit crunch of 2007–8.

Investors and fund managers typically allocate capital to regions and countries before selecting buildings or funds (Baum, 2009). The main arguments for country relevance are to do with the way data (for example, national government economic growth and inflation statistics) is collected and made available, the influence of national regulations, currencies, and taxes, and the interaction facilitated by spatial proximity helping to build the trust and rapport which is vital as investors gather market information (Leyshon and Thrift, 1997; Agnes, 2000). For these reasons, geography still matters for portfolio choice, savings, and investment, and can have a great influence on investors' decisions and returns (Stulz, 2005). Of course, this is even more relevant in international real estate investing, as spatial characteristics are a key feature of the asset class.

16.3.1 The Case for International Real Estate Investment: Diversification

It is common to find simplistic assertions that international real estate investment will provide effective diversification for pension plans. This model, which assumes an investor objective defined in terms of expected return and the standard deviation of

TABLE 16.3 Real estate returns, selected markets, 2001–18

	2001	2002	2003	2004	2005	2006	2007	2008	2009
Australia	10.7	9.81	12.2	14	15.7	19.2	18.3	−0.26	−2.15
Canada	9.25	8.81	8.33	12.9	18.7	18.3	15.8	3.69	−0.32
Ireland	8.08	2.35	12.4	11.4	24.4	27.2	9.85	−34.5	−23.3
UK	6.79	9.64	10.9	18.3	19.1	18.1	−3.42	−22.1	3.51
USA	7.28	6.74	8.99	14.5	20.1	16.6	15.8	−6.46	−16.9

	2010	2011	2012	2013	2014	2015	2016	2017	2018
Australia	9.3	10.4	9.4	9.2	10.4	14.0	11.8	12.0	10.2
Canada	11.2	15.5	14.1	11.0	7.1	8.0	5.7	6.7	7.4
Ireland	−2.4	−2.4	3.1	12.3	36.2	25.2	12.6	8.0	9.6
UK	15.1	7.8	3.4	10.8	17.8	13.1	3.9	9.6	5.1
USA	14.5	14.5	10.7	11.1	11.7	12.1	7.8	7.0	7.3

Source: IPD.

TABLE 16.4 Real estate return correlations, selected markets, 2001–18

	Australia	Canada	Ireland	UK	US
Australia	1	0.77	0.80	0.54	0.87
Canada	0.77	1	0.47	0.41	0.82
Ireland	0.80	0.47	1	0.75	0.75
UK	0.54	0.41	0.75	1	0.61
USA	0.87	0.82	0.75	0.61	1

Sources: IPD, authors.

expected return, is highly flawed, both because it fails to recognise the diversity of real investor objectives and because there are many costs of international diversification which are unrecognised in the measure.

Table 16.3 shows local currency returns in selected markets for which good data is available.

Table 16.4 shows the correlations between these markets. Two conclusions should be drawn, one from the data and one from intuition. First, the data does not provide a strong case for the benefits of diversification, with the possible exception of the UK against Australia and Canada. Second, the data is almost useless. Tables 16.3 and 16.4 do not represent the net of tax and fees, domestic currency, leveraged, and specific risk-laden returns available to investors. Data such as this should only be presented with reservations and should only be received with healthy scepticism. It covers too short a period; it is restricted to too few countries; it describes something that is uninvestable, specifically the fully diversified unleveraged direct property index in each country. These correlations describe the past, probably a very unusual period, and should be adjusted for future expectations when used to model a potential portfolio. In addition, they describe returns in local currencies, which any single-country investor cannot achieve. This issue requires much more attention – see Section 16.5.

Nonetheless, the nature of the economics driving local rental markets, coupled with the clear difference between the developed markets of North America, Northern and Western Europe, and developed Asia, plus the developing and emerging markets of Latin America, Africa, and elsewhere, suggests that, theoretically at least, diversification benefits should be available. The extension of the euro and the expansion of mature Europe suggests less diversification benefit for a commitment to emerging Central and Eastern Europe (but see Lizieri *et al.*, 2003 and McAllister and Lizieri, 2006). However, it is very likely that the risk and return characteristics of a domestic portfolio, combined with a diversified global exposure to both the core and emerging markets, will be significantly better than the global portfolio alone.

16.3.2 The Case for International Real Estate Investment: Enhanced Return

Europe, Asia, and the Americas all combine large and relatively mature, liquid and lower-risk markets with risky emerging markets, with the result that investments are available across the risk spectrum in what are known as core, core-plus, value-add, and opportunity categories (see Chapter 11, which summarises the risk/return characteristics of typical property funds in these categories, simplified as Type A and Type B funds). Enhanced returns are likely to be available in the riskier markets and funds.

International investment can clearly provide access to higher potential returns than are available domestically. As an example, Figure 16.1 demonstrates the returns that would have been achieved in different markets in one year, 2005. UK returns were strong at 19%, but well behind those achieved in South Africa (31%). Meanwhile, Germany suffered capital value falls and struggled to deliver a positive

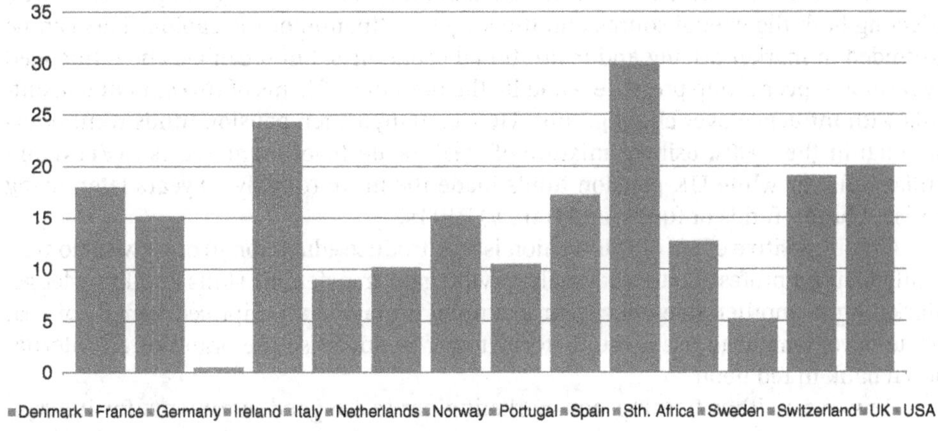

FIGURE 16.1 Direct property total returns, 2005
Source: IPD composite indices, 2006.

return (0.5%). The range of these (local currency) returns means that a global unconstrained mandate is usually likely to offer the potential for higher returns than a domestic-only strategy.

16.3.3 Other Drivers of International Property Investment

Insurance companies build books of liabilities to pay out insurance claims and savings income in international markets. As an example, the UK insurance conglomerate Norwich Union changed its trading brand to Aviva in 2009, probably as a sign that its business was no longer local, nor national, but international. The insurance fund has to match liabilities with assets in order to remain in business, so it is natural to build investment portfolios in different markets and currencies, including real estate assets.

In addition, there are stark examples of very wealthy investors or savings generators based in one domicile which contains a very small real estate market in global terms. These investors are forced to invest internationally. Examples include sovereign funds in the Middle East (Qatar, Abu Dhabi) and others. The argument has also been used by pension funds in larger markets, such as the Netherlands and Australia.

In addition, the Government Investment Corporation (GIC) of Singapore and other sovereign wealth funds are prevented by their mandates from investing in their domestic (real estate) market. This is related to the size of the domestic market and is designed to prevent (i) overheating of the market through weight of capital, (ii) poor return prospects, and (iii) poor diversification.

Part of the wave of international real estate investing has been encouraged by investment managers making a stronger case for diversification than the data permits, while higher fees can be earned from an international property fund. Because higher fees can be earned does not mean there is more profit to be made, but there is little doubt that fund management businesses with a mission to build a global franchise have been very keen to sell international products and take capital across national boundaries.

It has also been evident that international real estate investing happens in waves, affecting both the capital source and the target destination of the capital. This can be grounded in market pricing and institutional economics, but it can also be influenced by fashion – peer group pressure – and by the opinions of firms of investment consultants with influence over client groups. Hence, many Dutch pension funds went international in the 1990s, using a mixture of Real Estate Investment Trusts (REITs) and unlisted funds, while UK pension funds made the move roughly 10 years later, using unlisted funds, funds of funds, and (rarely) REITs.

A more positive effect of this fashion is to introduce education to otherwise domestically focused professionals and analysts who gain transferable skills and knowledge. Marketing is another side-effect. For example, it may be an unpriced benefit of real estate development to use a multi-storey tower to advertise the brand of an international bank in red neon.

However, neither training nor marketing *per se* are good arguments for international real estate investing which, to return to the beginning of this section, should be driven either by diversification or by the search for high returns. But what are the costs?

16.4 THE PROBLEMS

16.4.1 Introduction

Baum and Murray (2010) undertook research designed to add to previous studies of barriers to global investment and to focus this work in the context of real estate investment. Through interviews and a literature review they explore the following issues: why some countries receive real estate capital and others do not; how investors make their decisions; how much they know about barriers; and which barriers they consider more important.

'Push and pull factors' are terms used in economics to explain international capital flows. Push factors can be related to the lack of debt availability in the investor's country, while pull factors are related to the risk–return relationship in the host country (Montiel and Reinhart, 1999). While push factors provide reasons why investors choose to go abroad or not, pull factors can help to explain geographical asymmetries in capital flows.

Some countries try to eliminate or lessen the impact of the barriers that are most likely to isolate the local market from the global capital market. These barriers have been classified by academic work as *formal and informal* or *direct and indirect* barriers. The formal or direct barriers are those that primarily affect the *ability* of foreign investors to invest efficiently in emerging markets, for example in the form of taxes and laws; the informal or indirect barriers are those that affect an investor's *willingness* to invest, mainly due to reservations regarding cultural or political issues (Nishiotis, 2004). In an investment context, Baum and Murray offer the view that formal barriers are known variables which will affect either the ability to invest or the net return delivered; informal barriers represent risks which may affect the ability to invest or the net return delivered.[1]

16.4.2 Index Replication and Tracking Error

The problem of specific risk, introduced in Chapter 1, means that investors find it very difficult to replicate the return delivered by a national index without suffering a significant tracking error. This sampling error, amplified by the non-substitutability of real estate assets across portfolios, adds a layer of risk which is not represented in index data as shown in Table 16.3. The more global an investment strategy, the greater this problem becomes.

[1]Previous studies focused on general foreign direct investment, defined as *'a long-term investment by a non-resident, but with control (a 10% or greater share)'* (Lahiri, 2009). This is usually contrasted with portfolio investment, which is normally associated with investing in liquid securities and has a typical holding period of less than a year. Baum and Murray note that global real estate investment falls neatly into neither category, but because real estate is an illiquid asset this is closer to foreign direct investment.

16.4.3 Leverage

Leverage will often be used when investing internationally. There are several reasons for this. First, pension funds will often choose to invest internationally through a special purpose vehicle or unlisted fund. If the investment is through a fund, the fund manager will normally have a preference for using leverage. This is because debt can be easier to raise than equity, and boosts assets under management, and hence fees, as well as a mutually beneficial aspiration to increase return on equity and carried interest or performance fees (and, less mutually beneficial, risk). If a special purpose vehicle is used by the investor, he may choose to use leverage to boost return, but is more likely to be driven to do so for the following reasons: (i) it is tax efficient to do so; (ii) it permits greater diversification of specific risk; and (iii) it is believed it can partially hedge currency risk (but see Section 16.6.2 below).

The tax efficiency of a non-domestic property acquisition by an investor which is tax-exempt in its own market can be boosted by using leverage. This is because the tax penalty most likely to be suffered is a withholding tax, applied to income. If net taxable income can be reduced by offsetting loan interest payments against the rent, then income returns are effectively transformed into capital gains on equity, which are less likely to be taxed.

Borrowing money locally to buy real estate is usually possible in developed markets, offering what is known as a 'natural hedge'. A natural hedge is achieved where the adverse (or positive) impact of foreign exchange rate variations on cash inflows from the investment is offset by a positive (or adverse) impact on cash outflows to the lender.

Because leverage has so many advantages both for the fund manager and for the investor, it went hand in hand with international investing in the 1998–2007 period, and the withdrawal of debt facilities in 2008–9 slowed down international real estate investing. The market recovered gradually over the period 2012–20.

However, these good reasons produce an unfortunate side-effect, which is a significant increase in risk. Is a 60% leveraged, tax-efficient, currency hedged, diversified international real estate portfolio more or less attractive than an unleveraged, taxed, currency exposed, lumpy international real estate portfolio? This question is challenging and complex.

16.4.4 Global Cycles, Converging Markets

It has been argued, and there is some evidence to support this, that the diversification benefits of international investment have fallen as a result of the globalisation that cross-border investment illustrates. The more we are involved in other markets, the more our perspective will affect prices in those markets. As prices rise in developed markets, cheap property in foreign markets will become more attractive, and prices will rise.

As a particular example, the extension of the euro suggested that the diversification benefits offered within the mature Eurozone markets were weaker, and the expansion of mature Europe suggests less diversification benefits for a commitment to emerging Central and Eastern Europe. The implications of the already not-too-helpful correlations presented Table 16.4 are especially sobering in this context.

16.4.5 Execution Challenges

It may be the case that an investor or fund manager believes that the case for international diversification is strong, but how does he/she achieve this in practice?

At one extreme, we may seek a highly efficient, liquid exposure such as is available in stocks and bonds. Can we invest through liquid securities such as REITs? While this will be achievable, either directly or by employing a manager through a REIT fund or a separate account, it may not deliver the real estate performance characteristics we seek.

Using derivatives would be very appealing, but insufficient opportunities exist to deliver a truly global property derivative portfolio.

At the opposite extreme, we might buy buildings. The problems are clear: large sums of money will be needed so that diversification will be difficult to achieve and liquidity is limited. But how exactly do we buy the buildings? Do we travel a lot? Do we hire local employees? Can we trust an advisor appointed on an advisory mandate to do the best possible job? Alternatively, can we find a joint venture partner to work with in local markets?

To take a middle route, should we use unlisted property funds? If so, how do we choose them? Should we delegate this and use a manager (of managers) appointed under a discretionary separate account mandate, or invest in a fund of funds, each with double fees?

All of these approaches have costs, both direct and indirect, and benefits. To some extent, the choice of approach will depend on the motivation of the investor, whether it be to diversify through core investment or seek return; and to some extent it will depend on the nature and ambitions of the organisation, which will influence staffing levels. The choice of execution model is almost always more difficult in real estate than it would be for stocks, bonds, or other alternative assets, and seeking international exposure doubly complicates this choice.

16.4.6 Loss of Focus and Specialisation

For a REIT or investment manager which has a strong track record and long experience of a particular market, especially when specialised in a single sector, there is much to be said against diversification. It is commonly held that diversification is better achieved by the investor, and that REITs and funds should 'stick to the knitting'.

There are significant challenges involved in executing a global property investment strategy. We now deal with these issues.

16.5 FORMAL BARRIERS

Given our definition of formal barriers, it is clear that they must include restrictions on the removal of capital and legal barriers which relate to the foreign ownership of local assets. They also include differential, sometimes punitive, taxation of foreign owners.

16.5.1 Legal Barriers

Legal barriers arise from the different legal status of foreign and domestic investors. This could be in the form of ownership restrictions, which will clearly affect real estate investors (Bekaert, 1995). For example, governments in both developed and developing countries often impose ownership restrictions as a means of ensuring domestic control of local firms, especially those firms that are regarded as strategically important to national interests (Eun and Janakiramanan, 1986).

The degree to which this restriction applies to real estate ownership varies greatly, and research in this area is usually done case by case, given that there are often differences in practice within countries, as some land is more sensitive to nationalist protectionism. For example, there have been restrictions on ownership around coastal areas in Brazil which usually force foreign investors to find a local partner.

This is not a problem that is restricted to emerging economies. A fund manager interviewee reported by Baum and Murray (2010) recalled having to find a local partner in order to acquire a property asset that was close to a military base in Switzerland, where the government had imposed restrictions on foreign owners. These types of restriction can often be solved by finding a local partner. For large global investment firms that have regional offices and are sometimes considered 'local' in more than one market, this may not be a serious issue.

16.5.2 Capital Controls

Capital controls affect the ability of investors to repatriate their investment. If domestic savings are scarce in the host country, it is likely that capital account transactions will be restricted. A common direct restriction could be the imposition of a minimum period of investment (Bekaert, 1995); less common are absolute bans on the removal of capital from domestic banks.

It follows from this that restrictions on international financial flows are less prevalent in high-income countries with large domestic savings (Eichengreen, 2001) and more common in developing economies. Baum and Murray (2010) show that real estate investors consider restrictions to capital accounts to be a very high barrier to investment.

16.5.3 Tax

The residence principle means that incomes from the foreign and domestic income sources of residents of one country are taxed at equal rates, while incomes of non-residents are tax exempt (Razin *et al.*, 1998). Pension funds are usually tax exempt in their own domicile, but may suffer withholding taxes – and other taxes specific to the foreign environment – when investing abroad. Withholding tax is a tax on income, so called because the income is withheld from the foreign investor at source. Using leverage to reduce net income, if permitted, is a natural way to mitigate this. So institutional investors generally face a relative income tax disadvantage when investing in foreign real estate, while private individuals may not.

In addition, there may be differential tax treatment. Examples have included a French capital gains tax on non-EU owners of property, which is charged at 33.33%, but at 19% for EU residents, and higher stamp duty, a tax on transactions in the UK, paid by non-residents.

Sometimes, properties will be held within single asset companies to allow shares rather than the building to be sold at lower transfer tax rates, or to permit other taxes to be minimised. This may be tax advantageous, but introduces another taxable layer: as a result we will now have potentially taxable properties, companies, fund entities, and investors.

Taxes may be applied to investors in the domicile of the fund (for example, withholding tax and taxes on capital gains). Taxes may be applied to the investor in its home domicile (income tax, taxes on capital gains). Taxes may be applied to the investor in the domicile of the property (property taxes, stamp duty). Taxes may be applied to the holding entity in the domicile of the property (local corporate taxes), or the domicile of the fund (corporate taxes, withholding tax). Taxes may be applied to the entity in the domicile of the entity (corporate taxes). Taxes can be applied to the property in the domicile of the property (VAT, stamp duty, and other transfer taxes).

There are many other tax risks facing the global investor, and the complexity of the problem is perhaps best illustrated by case studies and examples – see, for example, Box 16.1. Suffice it to say, expert tax advice is unhesitatingly used by professional investors and fund managers when contemplating non-domestic investment and new international property funds, and the resulting structures can be mesmerising.

Black (1974) and Stulz (1981) show that taxes and other issues mean that the global market portfolio will not be efficient for any investor. The academic evidence suggests that high entry costs and taxation are both deterrents to investing in a foreign country.

To limit the impact of taxes may involve complex structuring of the investment and the payment of legal and consulting fees, and investment management fees for international mandates and products will often be higher than domestic fees. The structures set up to invest internationally can be very expensive to create and manage. Consulting fees, legal costs, directors' fees, accounting and audit fees, fees charged on the provision of debt, and the costs of annual reporting combine to produce a hefty initial and annual expense.

Box 16.1: A French Property Fund, Late 1990s

A UK investment manager with a captive (in-house) insurance fund has determined that performance prospects for French property, especially Paris offices, are attractive. There is also known to be demand from a Dutch pension fund as a likely co-investor. Attractive fees can be earned from an unlisted fund set up to access this market, and the in-house insurance fund will benefit from higher return prospects than are available in the UK.

However, there is a tax penalty for overseas investors in France. There was also (at the time) a transfer tax of 18.5% on the purchase of buildings.

There is a 1.75% tax on the transfer of companies. In addition, a company with limited liability is helpful in making sure there is a layer of protection between the fund's operations and the fund itself.

There is a tax treaty between France and the Netherlands, and a tax treaty between the UK and the Netherlands, but no tax treaty between France and the UK.

(continued)

(continued)

Tax treaties are set up to avoid double taxation of legal persons who are resident or domiciled, or otherwise have interests in two locations. The tax treaty also means that pension funds which do not pay tax at home may be shielded from tax when investing internationally.

There is income tax relief on loan interest in France, and lower taxation of loan interest than equity dividends in the Netherlands.

The structure used is shown in Figure 16.2. The way the fund works (in simplified terms) is as follows. The fund is a Dutch limited liability company, which must be controlled by a majority of Dutch nationals based in the Netherlands, where board meetings will be held. The Netherlands–UK tax treaty means that no tax is paid in the Netherlands by a tax-exempt UK life fund.

The fund owns a single limited liability holding company (BV) to allow a sale of the entire portfolio without collapsing the fund, and to insert a layer of limited liability. This in turn owns a series of special purpose Dutch BVs which in turn each own a single French property company. This structure widens the net of possible tax-efficient buyers.

The tax treaty between the Netherlands and France means that no tax is paid by Dutch tax-free entities on French income. The French companies own the French buildings in order to avoid the transfer tax of 18.5% on acquisitions and to put in its place a 1.75% company transfer tax. The French property companies use debt to reduce taxable income and to reduce French income tax on dividends paid.

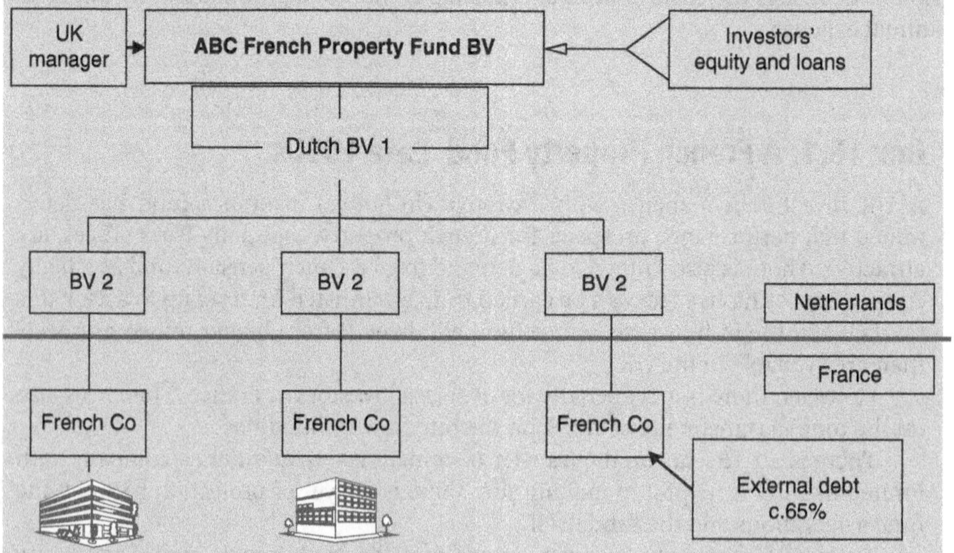

FIGURE 16.2 French property fund structure
Source: Manager.

At the fund level, the investors provide loans to reduce the tax on income received, but 'thin capitalisation' rules limit the extent to which loans can be used in place of equity. The loans pass down through the structure subject to the tax efficiency of the structure at each stage.

Each company will have its own cash and its own revenue statement. If the structure works well, the loans and equity pass down through the various companies and are used to provide the equity for the property acquisitions. The companies will receive rents, and pay operating expenses and two sets of loan interest (one to the local bank and one back up to investors), and make a small profit which is available for distributions up through the structure, with enough cash to fund them, but not so much cash that it becomes trapped (exceeding distributable profits) in the subsidiaries.

16.6 INFORMAL BARRIERS

16.6.1 Introduction

Informal barriers to international investment arise because of differences in available information, accounting standards, and investor protection. They also arise through ignorance ('information asymmetry') and prejudice (presumptions about corruption levels, for example). There are risks that are especially important in emerging markets, such as currency risk, political risk, and liquidity risk (Bekaert and Harvey, 2002; Nishiotis, 2004). Title risk (referred to in Baum, 2009) is a specific real estate issue that we can add to this group. Currency risk and currency management is particularly challenging.

16.6.2 Currency Risk

In order that an international investor can achieve local currency returns, there must either be no movements in exchange rates, or the investor must be able to perfectly and fully hedge his currency risk. This is not possible.

The MSCI (formerly IPD) Global Index was published for the first time in June 2008. It reports the market weighted returns for the 22 most mature markets measured by MSCI (Austria, Australia, Belgium, Canada, Denmark, France, Germany, Ireland, Italy, Japan, Netherlands, New Zealand, Norway, Portugal, South Africa, South Korea, Spain, Sweden, Switzerland, and the UK) plus KTI Finland and NCREIF in the USA, together worth an estimated €3.25 trillion as at the end of 2007. The returns shown in Table 16.5 are in local currency.

In 2007 the all-property total returns across global real estate markets in local currencies were lower than those in 2006, falling from 14.9% to 11.5%. But a dollar investor made 22.0% and 16.6%, while a euro investor made 9.3% and 5.2% – and for a sterling investor returns doubled, from 7.3% to 14.7%, as both the domestic market and the pound weakened.

Movements in currency exchange rates can have a large impact on delivered returns to investors, and greatly complicate a global strategy. Currency fluctuations can

TABLE 16.5 IPD global index returns, 2002–7

Currency	2002	2003	2004	2005	2006	2007
Euro	−1.4	−0.9	8.0	23.6	9.3	5.2
GBP	16.1	19.1	16.4	7.5	7.3	14.7
USD	5.0	7.1	8.6	20.1	22.0	16.6
JPY	5.2	7.5	11.3	23.4	23.3	9.3
Local	7.1	7.8	11.4	15.5	14.9	11.5

Source: IPD.

be significant and, if left unhedged, currency exposure would significantly increase the overall riskiness of the investment. Currency movements can have a dramatic impact on equity returns for foreign investors. (Surprisingly, many developing economies manage to keep exchange rate volatility lower than that which is typical in industrial economies. This is not surprising, as many developing economies try to peg their exchange rates to the US dollar or to a basket of currencies; Bekaert, 1995.)

Given that, as we have seen, as much as two-thirds of the returns from an international property portfolio can be explained by currency movements and one-third by property returns, it can be more important to develop a currency strategy than a property investment strategy. At the same time, given that property investors and property fund managers are not currency experts, and that forecasting currencies is notoriously difficult, our focus needs to be on the risk component of currency and not its return potential.

There are other side-effects of currency movements which can be damaging to investors and fund managers. The quick and steep devaluation of sterling in 2008, for example, had an unforeseen impact on investors who had committed to non-sterling investments. We saw in Chapter 11 how the drawdown period for an unlisted fund might extend to 3 years. Investors make forward commitments, say in euros, while their domestic currency may be sterling. There may be an initial drawing (say 10% of the commitment) but if 90% remains undrawn and sterling depreciates by 20%, the capital required is now 118% of the original sterling commitment.

Generally, investors and managers will focus on neutralising currency risk as much as they can. Three common approaches are: to use a currency overlay, common amongst larger multi-asset investors and managers who have the luxury of an in-house team of currency experts who maximise the risk–return profile of the house's net global currency exposure; to use local leverage, which partly hedges the investment; and to hedge the remaining equity through the use of currency swaps. These currency management approaches are developed below in Section 16.8.

16.6.3 Legal and Title Risk

The lack of a recognisable and reliable legal framework is considered seriously problematic among investors. Confidence in the legal system and the courts is vital for investors if faced with the contract and title disputes common in property. Protection in the case of tenant default and the risk of defective title are other examples of the legal risks seen as important by investors. In cases where tenants default, the different political systems of countries become relevant especially when landlords seek enforcement and/or compensation.

A particularly critical real estate issue is the risk of defective or unenforceable title. This has been a problem in newly democratised markets such as Eastern and South-Eastern Europe, where prior claims preceding communist state ownership have complicated acquisitions, and in other jurisdictions which have witnessed political interference or turmoil. This risk can be insured in many cases, but not in all. In Buenos Aires, for example, methods of piecemeal or tiered development can lead to multiple ownership and a scarcity of institutionally acceptable single-title assets. This problem is not particular to Buenos Aires; many Latin American cities present the problem of 'informal markets', the gradual populating of land around the peripheries of major urban centres that not only lacks infrastructure but also clear legal title (Abramo, 2010). The issue of state title 'resumption' has been problematic in Zimbabwe, and adds to the conception of title and legal risk associated with political risk.

16.6.4 Liquidity Risk

Liquidity risk captures the time it takes to execute trades, other factors such as the direct and indirect costs of trading, and risk and uncertainty concerning the timing of selling and the achievement of the expected sale price. The risk that arises from the difficulty of selling an asset is important in portfolio investment, with relatively liquid instruments, but liquidity risk is a much more serious issue for real estate investors.

The prospective 'take-out' is crucial in the issue of liquidity for emerging property markets, especially for Type B funds which try to buy and sell in a short space of time to maximise their (internal rate of) return and performance fees or carried interest payments. Who will buy the property when the investor wants or needs to sell it?

Baum *et al.* (2015) found that real estate market liquidity has the most significant impact on domestic and foreign inflows of real estate capital, suggesting that investors are particularly interested in market entry and exit options. Emerging markets are likely to have less well-developed local institutions and investment funds, and international owners are less likely to be represented in developing or emerging markets. In addition to potential shortages of equity players ready to buy, there may also be a shortage of bank debt. Local investors may find it hard to raise the cash to buy a property if local debt is not available, and international buyers will often use local debt to hedge some currency risk, so if debt is unavailable, liquidity can disappear.

16.6.5 Geographical Barriers

Some theories contest the inevitability of financial globalisation, claiming that geographical barriers remain significant. Even when operations are run from a central office in the home country of the investor, investors or fund managers still need to visit the target market, as real estate is a 'global market, local asset'. Geographical proximity is therefore an important factor.

If the host country is large enough to be worth opening a local hub, geographical or cultural problems (such as language and time zones) are reduced and can be accommodated within the local company. Real estate fund management businesses therefore tend to be clustered in financial centres (for example, New York, London, Paris, Frankfurt, and, in Asia, Tokyo, Singapore, and Hong Kong), especially given that a large part of the global real estate market is operated from these hubs. The difficulty of studying 30 countries, and another 30 legal and tax systems, may simply not be justified by a net improvement in return or reduction in risk.

16.6.6 Political Risk

In capitalist economies, public and private institutions can change or establish new economic rules. In other words, they can shape the characteristics of a country (laws, culture, history, politics, economics, and so on), and affect the country's economic performance, risk, and investment (North, 1990). Poor or stressed government action will often express itself in the form of excessive inflation, currency devaluation, high taxation, low economic growth, and other impacts which are not conducive to successful property investment.

A purer form of political risk can encompass a range of hazards, from the imposition of formal barriers such as the punitive taxation of foreign investors, exchange controls, new limits on non-domestic ownership of real estate assets, and even land and property nationalisation or expropriation.

Academic research also highlights the importance of pressure from powerful groups within countries. The most important difference between emerging and developed markets is the much more prominent role of politics in emerging markets and their larger public sectors, which can act as pressure groups (Bekaert and Harvey, 2002). Pressure groups are at the heart of political instability and can add substantial risk premiums to returns and therefore deter foreign investment.

Political risk can be exaggerated by international investors who are ignorant of a country's history and institutions. At its most extreme, however, grounded or ungrounded perceptions of political risk can make a country uninvestable.

16.6.7 Cultural Barriers

Real estate is a local business, and negotiations are human activities and not electronic, so knowledge of the culture is crucial to build good relationships and achieve transactions.[2]

Cultural barriers are exemplified when investors deal with assets based in Shariah-law countries with different religious beliefs, expressed through the structures used to achieve cross-border investment.

A local partner is often the solution to these problems. A failure to find the right local partner could jeopardise investment, although large funds with offices across the world typically hire locals in the host country. If that is not possible, then the usual

[2]The policy of Westfield, the largest listed property company in the world in 2010, is indicative. Originally Australian, Westfield invested as at 2010 in the USA, Canada, the UK, Australia, and New Zealand. It was acquired in 2018 by Unibail Rodamco, a similarly regionally (continental Europe) focused player, to create a global powerhouse, but the subsequent behaviour of the stock price of the merged entity suggested market doubts about the wisdom of this move.

way is to develop relationships with local joint venture partners or agents over a long time period.

16.6.8 Information Asymmetry

A large amount of capital is needed to purchase a portfolio of directly owned real estate assets. If this is concentrated in the domestic market, and the benchmark is domestic, then specific risk will be a challenge for all investors except the very largest. If the benchmark is global and the same amount of investment capital has to be spread around the world, then the specific risk – and tracking error – will be much greater, and a problem for everyone.

There is a perception that foreign assets are, dollar for dollar or pound for pound, more risky than domestic assets through 'information asymmetry', or the belief that local players know more about the asset, the legal and tax environment, and the market than a foreigner. If this is the case, perceived specific risk is a big issue in international investing, and this explains why international investors will often choose to invest through a joint venture with a local partner.

To some extent, and on occasion, this may be balanced by the perspective advantage an external buyer might have when looking into a market where local players have lost confidence (Baum and Crosby, 2008 describe a case where German buyers did very well in these circumstances in London in 1993).

Related to information asymmetry is perceived or actual corruption. This can have a large impact on the attractiveness of real estate investment. Corruption, while damaging, may be unavoidable in emerging markets, and some investors are willing to accept a certain degree of corruption in order to complete a transaction. The difficulty lies in quantifying what degree of corruption they are willing to accept and how they use middlemen to avoid a direct connection with it.

Corruption is particularly difficult for institutional fund managers who will not become involved in an economy perceived to be corrupt. Regulations such as money-laundering controls are important but are not globally standardised. This could be a barrier to entry for countries with weak institutions and high levels of corruption.

16.7 A PRICING APPROACH FOR INTERNATIONAL PROPERTY

We discuss pricing for domestic markets in Chapter 4, but the process of international portfolio investment is complicated greatly by currency effects. To develop a pricing approach for international investment, we begin with an example.

16.7.1 Example

A euro-domiciled fund is interested in buying a shopping centre in Istanbul. The cap rate is 12% and the expected internal rate of return (IRR) is 20%. The Turkish bond yield/interest rate is 14%.

It could alternatively buy a shopping centre in Brussels. The cap rate is 8% and the expected IRR is 10%. The euro bond yield/interest rate is 5%. Which is most attractive?

TABLE 16.6 Example cash flows (1)

Year:	0	1	2	3	4	5
NOI	−$1,000.00	$120.00	$129.60	$139.97	$151.17	$163.26
Exit						$1,469.33
Cash flow	−$1,000.00	$120.00	$129.60	$139.97	$151.17	$1,632.59
IRR						20.0%

The answer to this problem may seem obvious – high IRRs are better than low IRRs. But this ignores three issues. First, there may be a difference in the risk attached to the Istanbul and Brussels shopping centres. Second, there is a different currency risk involved in one asset – currencies can be volatile, subject to shocks, and difficult to manage. Third, and less obvious, financial markets may expect exchange rates to move in a particular direction. Where this is true, the apparently available IRR may be questionable. (This is the subject of much economic theory, which we need to understand and will explore below.)

If the pension fund is interested in buying a Turkish Istanbul shopping centre with a cap rate of 12% and an expected IRR of 20%, which implies rental and capital growth of 8% p.a., a 5-year cash flow may look like that shown in Table 16.6. We assume a notional price of $1,000.

For the purposes of this calculation, it is assumed that the rent is agreed 1 year in advance of payment at the end of each year. Rent then rises at 8% p.a. In Year 5, the asset is sold at the same 12% cap rate but on the basis of the rental value agreed at the end of year 5 and to be paid at the end of Year 6 ($176.32).

If the Turkish bond yield/interest rate is 14%, what is the leveraged return in Turkish lira? From Chapter 9, an approximation of this value is given by:

$$ke = \left[ka - \left(kd * LTV\right)\right] / \left(1 - LTV\right)$$

where:

ke = return on levered equity

ka = return on unlevered asset

kd = cost of debt

LTV = loan to value ratio

$$ke = \left[0.2 - \left(0.14 * 0.6\right)\right] / \left(1 - 0.6\right) = 0.116 / 0.4 = 29\% \left(approx.\right)$$

Running the cash flows produces a more accurate IRR estimate of 26.77%. This is shown in Table 16.7. Note that the cash flow in Year 6 is reduced by the repayment of the 60% loan.

The pension fund can easily borrow euros. The euro bond yield/interest rate is only 5%; so why not borrow euros to buy the shopping centre?

TABLE 16.7 Example cash flows (2)

Year:	0	1	2	3	4	5
Cash flow	–$400.00	$120.00	$129.60	$139.97	$151.17	$1,032.59
Interest		$84.00	$84.00	$84.00	$84.00	$84.00
Cash flow	–$400.00	$36.00	$45.60	$55.97	$67.17	$948.59
IRR						26.77%

If it does this, the new leveraged return in Turkish lira is given by the following:

$$ke = \left[ka - \left(kd * LTV\right)\right] / \left(1 - LTV\right)$$

$$ke = \left[0.2 - \left(0.05 * 0.6\right)\right] / \left(1 - 0.6\right) = 0.17 / 0.4 = 42.5\% \left(approx.\right)$$

Running the cash flows produces a more accurate IRR estimate of 37.34% (Table 16.8).

TABLE 16.8 Example cash flows (3)

Year:	0	1	2	3	4	5
Cash flow	–$400.00	$120.00	$129.60	$139.97	$151.17	$1,032.59
Interest		$30.00	$30.00	$30.00	$30.00	$30.00
Cash flow	–$400.00	$90.00	$99.60	$109.97	$121.17	$1,002.59
IRR						37.34%

Should investors borrow in low interest rate markets and invest in high interest rate markets (this is known as 'the carry trade')? If not, why not? What is the catch? To address this we need to consider some theories of interest rates and exchange rates.

16.7.2 Theories of Interest Rates and Exchange Rates

The Law of One Price

In an efficient market all identical goods must have only one price. If the price of a security, commodity, or asset is different in two different markets, then an arbitrageur will purchase the asset in the cheaper market and sell it where prices are higher.

Absolute Purchasing Power Parity

Under this theory, the purchasing power of different currencies is equalised for a given basket of goods. The Economist Big Mac index, for example, judges under- and over-valued currencies by reference to the local price of a Big Mac. Where this is higher than average, the currency could be considered overvalued.

Relative Purchasing Power Parity

Under relative purchasing power parity, the difference in the rate of change in prices at home and abroad – the difference in the inflation rates – is equal to the percentage depreciation or appreciation of the exchange rate. If this were not the case, consumers would travel to buy goods in low-inflation economies.

The Monetary Model of Exchange Rates

This theory suggests that the exchange rate is a function of prices, interest rates, and GDP. These forces act on the demand for, and the supply of, money – and the price of money (the exchange rate) moves to keep supply and demand in balance. Strong GDP growth, for example, would increase demand for the subject currency to buy the goods produced there, and in the absence of an increase in supply the exchange rate will rise. Germany provides a good example – it is often said that if the euro were to be abandoned, the new German currency would appreciate because Germany is a strong net exporter.

The Fisher Equation

In Chapter 4 we saw the Fisher equation, which explains the level of interest rates (R) in an economy as follows:

$$R = l + i + RP$$

where:

R = interest rate
l = a reward for liquidity preference (deferred consumption)
i = expected inflation
RP = risk premium

So the interest rate and the expected inflation rate are directly and positively related.

Interest Rate Parity

Interest rate parity is a theory which relates interest rates and exchange rates. The spot price and the forward or futures price of a currency incorporate any interest rate differentials between the two currencies.

To be more accurate, interest rate parity suggests that interest rate differentials and expected currency exchange rate movements are directly related.

Putting Relative Purchasing Power Parity and Interest Rate Parity Together with the Fisher Equation

These are generally just theories, and empirical evidence is sometimes supportive, sometimes not. Interest rate parity is somewhat different to the other theories summarised above, because the banking system prices currency futures on this basis, so the empirical evidence is generally undeniable.

Very roughly speaking, this is similar to saying that exactly the same amount of money will be made by investing cash in a bank in a low interest rate economy as investing it in a bank in a high interest rate economy, because the financial markets expect the currency in the low interest rate economy to appreciate by exactly the amount required to equalise the resultant gain.

As an example, assume that we are a euro investor and place cash on deposit in Turkey to earn 14% interest. If, as expected or indicated by the theories we have summarised, the Turkish currency devalues by 9%, then we will earn (14% – 9%) = 5% in euros. This is exactly what we can earn by placing cash on deposit in the Eurozone.

Using the Fisher equation, $R = l + i + Rp$, it is clear that the interest rate and the expected inflation rate are directly and positively related. Under relative purchasing power parity, the difference in inflation rates between two economies is equal to the percentage depreciation or appreciation of the exchange rate. So the expected inflation rate is directly related to currency depreciation.

Because we already know that the interest rate and the expected inflation rate are directly and positively related, the interest rate must be indirectly related to currency depreciation. Happily, interest rate parity confirms this: interest rate differentials and expected currency exchange rate movements are *directly* related. So, in theory, a high interest rate suggests high expected inflation, and currency depreciation.

Summarising:

Positive difference in interest rates = positive difference in expected inflation
= expected currency depreciation

After this brief excursion into monetary theories, we now return to our shopping centre in Turkey.

16.7.3 Putting Theory into Practice

If the Turkish interest rate is 14%, and the euro rate is 5%, the expected currency movement must be +9% in favour of the euro. Hence (if the theory holds in practice and currencies move as predicted), the euro investor in Turkish cash or bonds will earn 14% – 9% = 5%, or 5% by investing directly in the euro. A Turkish investor will earn 5% + 9% = 14% in euro bonds, or 14% by investing directly in Turkey.

In the case of our shopping centre, the Turkish investor will earn an IRR of 20%, while the euro investor will earn 20% – 9% = 11%.

Running the cash flows produces a more accurate IRR estimate of 10.09% (see Table 16.9).

How does the expected currency movement impact the investor using euro leverage to buy the Turkey shopping centre? The expected currency depreciation of 9% p.a. will damage returns in euros. Clearly, leverage will increase the damage. In fact, the 41.60% leveraged return falls to 18.03%. Table 16.10 shows the expected cash flow in euros.

TABLE 16.9 Example cash flows (4)

Year:	0	1	2	3	4	5
NOI	–$1,000.00	$110.09	$109.08	$108.08	$107.09	$106.11
Exit						$954.96
Cash flow	–$1,000.00	$110.09	$109.08	$108.08	$107.09	$1,061.07
IRR						10.09%

TABLE 16.10 Example cash flows (5)

Year:	0	1	2	3	4	5
Cash flow	–$400.00	$110.09	$109.08	$108.08	$107.09	$461.07
Interest		$30.00	$30.00	$30.00	$30.00	$30.00
Cash flow	–$400.00	$80.09	$79.08	$78.08	$77.09	$431.07
IRR						18.03%

The value of the cash flow is now falling, as it is subject to 8% local growth but also to 9% devaluation. So, is the Turkish shopping centre an attractive acquisition? The key issue for us to consider now is risk.

For a Turkish buyer, the prospective unleveraged return is 20%, and the prospective leveraged return is 26.77%. This seems a high number – but a Turkish investor can buy a government bond to earn a risk-free 14%. Expected returns on all assets are high, because inflation is expected to be high. This reveals an *available risk premium* of 6% (20% – 14%) unleveraged, and 12.77% (26.77% – 14%) leveraged. Is this enough to compensate for the risk of the investment? To begin to answer this question, we can go back to Chapter 4, where we dealt with the concept of the required return and suggested ways of building a *required risk premium* from an analysis of sector, location, and building-specific issues.

For a euro buyer, the prospective unleveraged return in dollars is 10.09%, and the prospective leveraged return in dollars is 18.03%. A euro investor can buy a government bond to earn a risk-free 5%. This reveals an *available risk premium* of 5.09% unleveraged, and 13.03% using dollar leverage, to be compared to the required risk premium. Note that this seemingly high available premium, which takes account of expected currency depreciation, is still subject to currency risk, as we cannot forecast currency movements with confidence no matter what the theories say, and in addition the investor now has an asset/liability mismatch (a leveraged asset denominated in Turkish lira and a liability denominated in euros).

If the Turkish lira were not to depreciate against the euro, then the available risk premium to the euro investor now appears to be (37.34% – 5%) = 32.34% (from Table 16.8). Surely this is enough to make anyone invest! Well, yes and no. This is the basis of the 'carry trade', using which large returns can be made by borrowing in low interest rate markets and investing in high interest rate markets. When using leverage, carry trade returns can be enormous. In the short term, interest rate parity can break down, as flows of capital into high interest rate markets can push up what should be the weak currency and exaggerate returns even more.

TABLE 16.11 Risk and return outcomes, Istanbul and Brussels

	1	2	3	4	5	6	7
Average return	20.34	11.94	27.18	4.02	1.05	10.18	15.07
SD	3.02	13.75	5.70	48.58	56.08	4.96	8.53
CV	6.74	0.87	4.77	0.08	0.02	2.05	1.77
Max	25.24	37.62	36.17	60.04	64.47	18.81	29.25
Min	16.29	−8.43	19.25	−100	−100	4.73	5.45
Premium over local bonds	6.34	6.94	13.18	−0.98	−3.95	5.18	10.07

Notes:
SD is standard deviation.
CV is coefficient of variation (return divided by risk).
(1) A Turkish buyer of the Istanbul asset, using no leverage.
(2) A euro-based buyer of the Istanbul asset, using no leverage.
(3) A Turkish buyer of the Istanbul asset, using 60% leverage.
(4) A euro-based buyer of the Istanbul asset, using 60% leverage in Turkish lira.
(5) A euro-based buyer of the Istanbul asset, using 60% leverage in euros.
(6) A euro-based buyer of the Brussels asset, using no leverage.
(7) A euro-based buyer of the Brussels asset, using 60% leverage in euros.

But this is hugely risky, as history shows that currencies can become overvalued and then collapse. And in our property case, borrowing euros to buy a Turkish asset is now a mixture of real estate investment and leveraged currency speculation. The risk premium for currency speculation must be much higher than any property risk premium – and we are leveraged!

The risks involved are illustrated in Table 16.11. In this table, we explore 35 scenarios for these two potential investments by our euro investor in Brussels and Istanbul, and compare the results with what happens to a Turkish investor buying in Istanbul.

Under the base case, the IRR in Brussels is 10% (8% income yield and 2% appreciation) and in Istanbul it is 20% (12% income yield and 8% appreciation). The exit cap rate for a 5-year hold is the going-in cap rate (8% and 12%, respectively). The expected currency movement is 9% against lira, or 9% in favour of the euro.

The other (equally weighted) scenarios we examine are as follows. First, the exit yield moves relative to the current cap rate by up to −3% and up to +3% in 1% steps (so the Brussels asset, for example, sells for 8%; or 7%, 6%, or 5%; or 9%, 10%, or 11%; and the Istanbul asset sells for 12%; or 11%, 10%, or 9%; or 13%, 14%, or 15%). This produces seven scenarios.

Second, currency depreciation, which is expected to be 9% against the lira, could be zero, or 18% against the lira, or 27% against the lira; or 9% in favour of the lira (all equally weighted and fairly distributed around −9%). This provides a further five scenarios, multiplying the seven exit cap rate scenarios to a total of 35 possible outcomes.

These 35 scenarios provide the alternative market conditions for seven different strategies: a Turkish buyer of the Istanbul asset, using no leverage; a euro-based buyer of the Istanbul asset, using no leverage; a Turkish buyer of the Istanbul asset, using 60% leverage; a euro-based buyer of the Istanbul asset, using 60% leverage in Turkish lira; a euro-based buyer of the Istanbul asset, using 60% leverage in euros; a euro-based buyer of the Brussels asset, using no leverage; and finally a euro-based buyer of the Brussels asset, using 60% leverage in euros.

A Turkish buyer of the Istanbul asset, using no leverage, had a base case return of 20%. The average return over 35 scenarios is 20.34%, suggesting a minor positive skew (although note that currency variations have no effect in this case). The standard deviation of seven exit yield scenarios is only 3%, producing a coefficient of variation of 6.74. The best return in the seven scenarios is 25.24%; the worst is 16.29%. Given a local bond yield of 14%, the mean return offers a 6.34% risk premium.

Contrast these results with the euro buyer of the same asset, using no leverage (Case 2). The base case return was 10.09%. The average return over 35 scenarios is 11.94%, suggesting a minor positive skew (with currency variations having a full effect). The standard deviation of 35 scenarios is 13.75%, producing a coefficient of variation of only 0.87. The best return in the 35 scenarios is 37.62%; the worst is –8.43%. Given a local euro bond yield of 5%, the mean return offers a risk premium of 6.94% – similar to Case 1, but for a deal which is much riskier.

In Case 4, where the euro buyer of the same asset uses 60% leverage, the base case return was 18.03%. The average return over 35 scenarios is 4.02%, suggesting a strong negative skew. Currency risk is now leveraged and the standard deviation of 35 scenarios is 48.58%, producing a coefficient of variation of only 0.08. The best return in the 35 scenarios is 60.04%; the worst is –100% (all equity is lost, and this happens in 13 out of 35 cases). Given a local euro bond yield of 5%, the mean return offers a negative risk premium. Case 5, where the currency of the debt is not matched by the currency of the asset, is even worse.

All domestic buyer cases (1, 3, 6, and 7) appear superior to the cross-border cases (2, 4, and 5).

We could adopt different decision rules to decide whether to buy this shopping centre, leveraged or not. What makes most sense?

Approach 1: Maximise IRR in the local (foreign) currency

We will buy where the IRR in the foreign currency is at a maximum or where it exceeds a target absolute return, say 20%. This may work out well, but ignores (i) the risk of the asset and (ii) currency risk. This rule will attract us to risky assets in high-inflation economies. It may be the appropriate goal for a risk-seeking Type B fund. Cases 4 and 5 offer the highest maximum returns; Case 7 offers the best mean return.

Approach 2: Maximise excess returns in the local currency

It is appealing to buy where the IRR in our home currency exceeds the required risk-adjusted return. Where:

R_d is the domestic interest rate

R_l is the local interest rate

The expected return in the domestic currency is given by $(K + G - D) - (R_l - R_d)$, so we will buy where:

$$\left[\left(K+G_N-D\right)-\left(R_l-R_d\right)\right]>\left(RF_N+R_p\right)$$

This means we will buy when ($K + G_N - D$) in the domestic currency > ($RF_N + R_p$) using the local risk-free rate. The expected return in the domestic currency is ($K + G_N - D$) adjusted for expected currency movement acting through the difference in interest rates, and the risk premium is also adjusted for currency risk. We have to take both property risk and currency risk into account in estimating R_p.

This approach was discussed in Chapter 4 (Box 4.1). In that box, we asked: What is the required return for a UK investor buying Japanese bonds? As a UK investor, the yen income converted to sterling is uncertain and may be volatile. A higher risk premium is necessary, and the result is that Japanese bonds are not attractive to UK buyers. This does not mean that the market is not priced in equilibrium: simply that the likely buyer, whose natural habitat this investment represents, is not based in the UK.

This creates a couple of interesting issues, or three, or more. First, how do we estimate this additional risk premium? Second, would not this approach penalise all investments in non-domestic currency and make them look less attractive, so that domestic buyers will always dominate markets? Third, and related to this, how does this square with the benefits of global diversification? Are we not making the mistake of discounting for specific risk when it can be diversified away? For these reasons, this approach may appeal to a private investor but is not highly recommended for large, professional, diversifying investors.

Instead, a Type A investor should seek to maximise *excess returns* in the *local currency*.

This rule is less obvious, but deals elegantly with both currency and property risk. It also avoids the estimation of a currency risk premium and the resulting lack of competitiveness.

The excess return in local currency is given by:

$$\left(K + G_N - D\right) - RFR - RP$$

$K + G_N - D = IRR$, so we are maximising $IRR - RFR - RP$. To use Case 2 in our example, the Istanbul property acquired by a euro buyer, assume we estimate a required risk premium of 8% over local bonds. If $RP = 8\%$ and $RFR = 14\%$, then:

$$IRR\left(K + G_N - D\right): 12\%\, cap\, rate\left(K\right) + 8\%\, net\, growth\left(G\right) = 20\%\ IRR$$

$$IRR - RFR - RP = 20\% - 14\% - 8\% = -2\% : \textit{this is unattractive}$$

(Note: this is unattractive because the available risk premium of 6.34% falls below the required risk premium of 8%.)

If we were to buy a Brussels property with an 8% cap rate and 2% expected growth, assuming $RP = 4\%$, $RFR = 5\%$, then:

$$IRR\left(K + G_N - D\right): 8\%\, cap\, rate\left(K\right) + 2\%\, net\, growth\left(G\right) = 10\%\ IRR$$

$$IRR - RFR - RP = 10\% - 5\% - 4\% = 1\% : \textit{this is attractive}$$

Our conclusion is therefore that the Brussels property is more attractive for a risk-averse investor such as a pension fund. Does this approach deal with expected currency depreciation?

Yes: in $(K + G - RFR) - RP$, inflation, which is assumed to be perfectly correlated with currency movements, drives both G and RFR, and therefore cancels out. If we assume that property is an inflation hedge, we can expand this to:

$$K+(Gr+I)-(L+I)-RP = K+Gr-L-RP$$

where:

Gr = real growth

I = inflation

L = liquidity preference or real risk-free rate

In words, this means that the real expected IRR is given by the cap rate plus real growth, and the excess return is given by the real IRR less the real required return (the real risk-free rate plus a risk premium).

The impact of inflation, and with it the impact of the associated currency depreciation, on return is removed. If inflation is high, growth is higher and IRR is increased; but RFR is also higher by the same amount, so the excess return is not affected by inflation nor, consequently, damaged by currency movement.

In practice, we have to estimate the required risk premium (RP), and we can then go in search of excess returns, defined as $IRR - RFR - RP$. Currency risk above and beyond the expected impact of interest rates and inflation is diversified away, and property risk is dealt with through the required return. This, we suggest, is the appropriate decision rule for a risk-averse (Type A) global real estate investor.

16.7.4 Using Local Excess Returns

For Type A, risk-averse investors, we recommend looking for high nominal excess returns in the local currency. High nominal excess returns are delivered where the expected return is higher than the required return. Because expected inflation is part of both the required and the expected return, this rule holds in theory in high- and low-inflation markets. A high nominal return is not attractive *per se*, other than to risk-seeking investors. Investors should therefore aim for high excess returns on property relative to returns on local bonds plus a risk premium (high excess returns).

We now illustrate this approach across markets. To do so, we revisit the example used in Chapter 4. To begin, we take four government bond markets: UK, Japan, France, and South Africa, with 10-year issues yielding 4%, 2%, 3%, and 10%, respectively. UK indexed bonds yield 1.5%.

A pricing analysis is shown in Table 16.12. The analysis is from the perspective of the local investor. All fixed-interest bond issues carry a small inflation risk premium of 0.5%: there is no currency risk. The real risk-free rate is given by the UK indexed bond yield of 1.5%. All markets, being efficient for local investors, are in equilibrium, as the required return ('req') is equal to the expected return ('exp') in all cases.

TABLE 16.12 Bond pricing analysis

	RFR_r	$+i$	$+RP$	Req	=	K	$+G_N$	$-D$	Exp
UK indexed bonds	1.5	2.0	0.0	3.5	=	1.5	2.0	0.0	3.5
UK bonds	1.5	2.0	0.5	4.0	=	4.0	0.0	0.0	4.0
Japan bonds	1.5	0.0	0.5	2.0	=	2.0	0.0	0.0	2.0
France bonds	1.5	1.0	0.5	3.0	=	3.0	0.0	0.0	3.0
South Africa bonds	1.5	8.0	0.5	10.0	=	10.0	0.0	0.0	10.0

The differences in expected inflation rates signify expected movements in currency exchange rates against the pound. The yen is expected to appreciate by (4% – 2% =) 2%; the euro is expected to appreciate by (4% – 3% =) 1%; and the rand is expected to depreciate by (10% – 4% =) 6%.

From the perspective of a UK investor, all fixed-interest bonds are expected to deliver the same return in sterling, as shown in Table 16.13, which adds *Gc*, growth from currency movements, to the analysis.

We can now extend the analysis to property. Let us assume that property yields in the UK, Japan, France, and South Africa are 6.5%, 4.5%, 5.5%, and 12.5%, respectively.

Table 16.14 is an equilibrium pricing analysis from a local perspective. Returns on offer to local players in the UK, Japan, France, and South Africa are 7.5%, 5.5%, 6.5%, and 13.5%, respectively. These are all excess returns over bonds of 3.5%, the additional risk premium for property over fixed-interest bonds.

From a UK perspective, growth in income from the expected currency movement must be added. The UK analysis is shown in Table 16.15.

All four property markets are offering the UK investor a return of 7.5% in sterling. However, this assumes that the investor estimates the same risk premium, the same rental growth potential, and the same depreciation for each market.

TABLE 16.13 Bond returns – UK perspective

	Return	=	K	$+G_N$	$+Gc$	$-D$
UK indexed bonds	3.5	=	1.5	2.0	0.0	0.0
UK bonds	4.0	=	4.0	0.0	0.0	0.0
Japan bonds	4.0	=	2.0	0.0	2.0	0.0
France bonds	4.0	=	3.0	0.0	1.0	0.0
South Africa bonds	4.0	=	10.0	0.0	–6.0	0.0

TABLE 16.14 Property returns – local perspective

	RFR_r	$+i$	$+RP$	Req	=	K	$+G_N$	$-D$	Exp
UK property	1.5	2.0	4.0	7.5	=	6.5	2.0	1.0	7.5
Japan property	1.5	0.0	4.0	5.5	=	4.5	2.0	1.0	5.5
France property	1.5	1.0	4.0	6.5	=	5.5	2.0	1.0	6.5
South Africa property	1.5	8.0	4.0	13.5	=	12.5	2.0	1.0	13.5

TABLE 16.15 Property returns – UK perspective

	RFR_r	$+i$	$+RP$	Req	=	K	$+G_N$	$+Gc$	$-D$	Exp
UK property	1.50	2.00	4.00	7.5	=	6.5	2.00	0.00	1.00	7.5
Japan property	1.50	0.00	4.00	5.5	=	4.5	2.00	2.00	1.00	7.5
France property	1.50	1.00	4.00	6.5	=	5.5	2.00	1.00	1.00	7.5
South Africa property	1.50	8.00	4.00	13.5	=	12.5	2.00	−6.00	1.00	7.5

In practice, these estimates will differ greatly. Given that rental growth is partly inflation driven, we can expect more rental growth in South Africa and less in Japan. The economies may be offering different real growth prospects. Market leasing practice and construction standards may drive differing depreciation. The risk premium in non-domestic markets is likely to be higher, largely to deal with the risk of currency movements but also to cover the costs and risks systematically incurred by international buyers.

Table 16.16 is a possible (hypothetical) analysis from a UK perspective. (On the required return side of the equation, remember that the UK investor needs to beat UK inflation.)

On the basis of this analysis, the UK market is a hold, Japan a sell, France a buy, and South Africa a sell: see Table 16.17.

Note that UK property is expected to deliver the UK bond yield plus the additional UK property risk premium over bonds. Japan property delivers the UK bond yield (4%) plus the additional Japan property risk premium (4.5%), less the excess (−1.5%) = 7%. France property delivers the UK bond yield (4%) plus the additional France property risk premium (4%), plus the excess (1%) = 9%. South Africa property delivers the UK bond yield (4%) plus the additional South Africa property risk premium (7.5%), less the excess (−2%) = 9.5%.

TABLE 16.16 Property returns – UK perspective, non-equilibrium

	RFR_r	$+i$	$+RP$	Req	K	$+G_N$	$+Gc$	$-D$	Exp
UK property	1.50	2.00	4.00	7.50	6.5	2.00	0.00	1.00	7.50
Japan property	1.50	2.00	5.00	8.50	4.5	1.00	2.00	0.50	7.00
France property	1.50	2.00	4.50	8.00	5.5	3.00	1.00	0.50	9.00
South Africa property	1.50	2.00	8.00	11.50	12.5	5.00	−6.00	2.00	9.50

TABLE 16.17 Property excess returns – UK perspective

	Expected	Required	Excess	Decision
UK property	7.50	7.50	0.00	Hold
Japan property	7.00	8.50	−1.50	Sell
France property	9.00	8.00	1.00	Buy
South Africa property	9.50	11.50	−2.00	Sell

TABLE 16.18 Property excess returns – recommended approach

	Bond	+ *RP*	Req	K	+ G_N	− *D*	Exp	Excess	Dec
UK property	4.00	3.50	7.50	6.5	2.00	1.00	7.50	0.00	Hold
Japan property	2.00	4.50	6.50	4.5	1.00	0.50	5.00	−1.50	Sell
France property	3.00	4.00	7.00	5.5	3.00	0.50	8.00	1.00	Buy
South Africa property	10.00	7.50	17.50	12.5	5.00	2.00	15.50	−2.00	Sell

Note: Dec = decision.

Our recommended simple rule is to look for high nominal excess returns in the local currency. This takes account of market risk, takes out the inflation – and currency – effect and requires no currency forecasting skill. Currency movements, represented in Table 16.16 by *Gc*, will disappear.

How would this rule work in the example? See Table 16.18 for an illustration.

The expected sterling returns remain as shown in Table 16.17. South Africa is not attractive, despite having the highest initial yield and the highest expected return in local currency; France is attractive, despite having a lower initial yield than the UK. (Note again that the risk premium in this table is the additional risk premium above the bond risk premium of 0.5%. This ensures that the local required return is correctly estimated.)

Seeking high nominal excess returns (expected returns less required returns) in the local currency will therefore put in place a process which is designed to deliver a minimum of the *domestic* risk-free rate plus the *local* risk premium, and to select markets on the basis of their excess returns without the complications of currency forecasts.

16.8 MANAGING CURRENCY EXPOSURE AND CURRENCY RISK

The analysis above assumes that investors have no way to avoid the currency risk which arises when investing internationally. Given the international context, so far we have been thinking about *analysing or measuring* risk; we now move on to *managing* risk, specifically currency risk and currency exposure. In addition to doing nothing, we discuss four alternative approaches: diversifying, using a currency overlay, using local debt, and hedging the equity exposure.

Before we embark on this, we should state a strong belief. Forecasting the future direction of currency exchange rates within a real estate investment organisation is absolutely not recommended, for two reasons. First, currencies are generally both more volatile and more efficiently priced and traded than real estate, and forecasting their short-term direction is notoriously difficult. (Some believe that the short-term direction of exchange rates is simply a 'random walk'.) Second, a real estate professional is taking an unjustified risk, and over-extending his/her professional and technical capability, by incorporating a currency forecast within the underwriting of a real estate investment, and should concentrate on what they should be good at – real estate investing.

In contrast, we have seen already that doing nothing about currency can lead to very high returns through the 'carry trade'; it can also lead to very low returns. Clearly, having a non-domestic currency exposure increases risk in terms of domestic returns.

When investing in funds, two different types of currency risk present themselves. If the currencies of a non-domestic currency-denominated fund *appreciate* against the domestic currency during the investment period, the non-domestic commitments will increase in cost in domestic currency terms. This could result in the investor having insufficient capital available to meet its commitments.

After the capital has been called and invested into funds, there is a risk that non-domestic currencies *depreciate* against the domestic currency, resulting in a fall in value of the investments in domestic currency terms.

16.8.1 Diversifying

A large real estate investment organisation engaged internationally has an advantage over a small competitor. If the organisation has enough capital and diversity of investments, it can diversify its currency exposure to the point where the rising currencies compensate for the falling currencies. It will have no market risk if it (indirectly) holds the global currency portfolio.

However, this strategy does not remove the single remaining risk, that of a movement between the domestic currency and the diversified basket of all other currencies. Where an investor has liabilities denominated in a single domestic currency, an increase in the exchange rate of that currency against all other currencies will damage the diversified investor relative to a domestic-only investor.

16.8.2 Using a 'Currency Overlay'

A large multi-asset investment organisation engaged internationally will already be exposed to currency risk (and diversification) through its equity, bond, cash/currency, and other alternative assets, including private equity, hedge funds, and cash, held either for liquidity or specifically to access an attractive currency. Such investors and managers may have the luxury of an in-house team of currency experts whose job it is to maximise the risk–return profile of the house's net global currency exposure. It will therefore have currency management expertise, and will be able to hold preferred currency exposures. In these organisations, the appropriate real estate decision may be to maximise risk-adjusted IRRs in local currency, and to leave the currency desk to manage the currency exposure.

The currency team's optimal currency exposure policy, perhaps influenced by liabilities, will measure the undesired currency exposure and manage it. It can use a variety of instruments to manage currency exposure, but the most common instrument used will be the currency swap, which hedges (neutralises) an undesired exposure. If a currency team operates in this way for the house, then a 'currency overlay' avoids any need for the property investment team to manage currency exposure. The price of this may be a directive to avoid or limit investment in certain property markets because the undesired currency exposure is too expensive to manage.

16.8.3 Using Local Debt

A natural hedge is achieved where the adverse impact of foreign exchange rate variations on cash inflows is offset by a positive impact on cash outflows, or vice versa. Given the popularity of leverage in real estate, both for the lender and for the borrower, this appears to be very helpful in international real estate investing, as leverage clearly provides a natural hedge.

Real estate investors find leverage helpful for a variety of reasons: it can be helpful in offsetting income tax, it can help increase diversification as it means more property can be bought with the same amount of equity, and it enhances return when the project IRR exceeds the costs of debt.

When and where debt finance is available, property funds investing in non-domestic property typically employ local currency leverage, in the 50–70% range. The leverage has more than one benefit. It enhances the income return (the cash-on-cash yield, or the income return on equity) if property yields exceed debt rates, so that dividend yields for continental European property funds were generally higher in nominal terms than for UK property funds when (as in 2000–7 and again in 2012–20) the UK interest rate exceeded the euro interest rate. For example, if we buy an asset for $100 million, with a $10 million income, we achieve a 10% income yield. If we use 50% leverage and an interest-only loan at a rate of 5%, we lose $2.5 million in interest but now receive a cash-on-cash return of $7.5 million, which as a percentage of equity is $7.5 million/$50 million = 15%.

Leverage also provides a partial hedge against the effect of currency movements on capital values. For example, if the leverage ratio is 50%, 50% of the property capital value will be hedged by equal and opposite changes in value of the local currency debt.

Acting as a currency hedge, leverage acts both on the net income earned and the capital received on exit. To use our US/Turkey example, if a US dollar investor invests $300 of equity and borrows $700 in Turkish lira to buy a Turkish shopping centre, then both the income and the interest/capital repayments are denominated in lira, such that the adverse impact of foreign exchange rate variations on cash inflows is offset by a positive impact on cash outflows – the income may fall in dollars, but so will the repayments. More obviously, the debt outstanding and to be repaid when the building is sold will decrease in dollars if the lira devalues against the dollar, as will the sale price; whereas appreciation of the lira will increase the sale price in dollars, but the loan outstanding will also increase in dollars.

Assume as before that we have an interest-only loan providing 60% leverage on a $1,000 asset in Turkey. At the outset, we owe $600 to a Turkish bank, but this debt is denominated in lira. The asset is expected to appreciate to $1,469.33 by the time it is to be sold in 5 years' time, but this is subject to foreign exchange movement. If, as expected, the lira depreciates against the dollar by 9% p.a., the asset will then be worth $955; but the outstanding loan will now be worth not $600, but $390. If the asset were purchased with 100% equity, the damage to the capital gain through currency movement is $514.33 ($1,469.33 – $955); using 60% leverage, the damage to the capital gain through currency movement is $204.33 [($1,469.33 – $700) – ($955 – $390)].

The effect on IRR has already been explored. Using 100% equity, a return of 20% is made if the exchange rate does not change, but this just about halves to 10.09% with 9%

devaluation. Using 60% leverage, 26.77% falls to 18.03% with 9% devaluation. Using 80% leverage, an all-equity return of 34.92% falls only to 31.91%.

But we must not forget that leverage introduces a risk all of its own! If the Turkish currency were to fall by 15% against the dollar for 5 years, then an all-equity return of 20% would fall to 4.35%; but using 80% leverage would drag the leveraged 34.92% down to a *negative* 1.92%. This was a key issue in the 'noughties' decade: the risk reduction introduced by leverage in terms of currency hedging and increased diversification was in many cases overwhelmed by the huge increase in financial risk it carried with it.

16.8.4 Hedging Equity

Finally, the investor could use the financial markets to formally hedge the equity exposure. To explore how this works, we will use a different example.

Assume that the expected return on a property in Paris is 8% (6% from income, 2% from capital growth). Assume that a similar property in London has an identical 8% expected return (6% income, 2% capital). Are these identical return propositions for a UK investor? What about the risk of each investment?

The base rate in the euro area is 3.25%, while the UK base rate is 4.25%. A UK investor can borrow at an interest rate of 1% over base in either market, and expects to hold the property for 5 years. The current exchange rate is €1.25 : £1, and the property values in London and Paris are £8 million and €10 million, respectively.

What is the expected value of the Paris property in 5 years' time? Annual growth expected is 2%, so €10m * $(1.02)^5$ = €11.04m. What is the value of €11.04 million in pounds? €11.04m/1.25 = £8.83m – but the exchange rate is expected to change.

Given a unity relationship between interest rates and expected inflation, and between inflation and currency exchange rates, the interest rate differential is a predictor of currency exchange movements. The banking system holds and uses this information on a real-time basis as it makes a market for currency swaps.

The euro is expected to appreciate by 1% each year, because it has an interest rate that is lower by 1%. The expected value of €11.04 million in sterling is [€11.04m * $(1.01)^5$]/1.25 = £9.28m. So, a UK investor in Paris could take the currency exposure and get a capital return of £9.28/£8 = 1.16 = 1.03^5 = 3% p.a. In this case, of the 3% capital return, 2% comes from property and 1% comes from currency.

But this return is subject to exchange rate risk, so the UK investor can earn 8% in London or 9% in Paris, but needs to take a currency risk to get the extra 1% return. This is where hedging comes in.

In derivative parlance, the UK investor is 'long euros', meaning he has a positive exposure to the euro. In 5 years' time he expects to have a property worth €11.04 million, but he has sterling liabilities and wishes to lock in a sterling return (he wishes to be 'long sterling'). He can do this by selling €1.25, 1 year forward for today's rate of £1.00. This is an attractive proposition for another party, which is being asked to take euros – a strengthening currency – in return for the weakening pound at today's exchange rate. Because banks will compete for this business, and using interest rate parity, the bank will expect to pay an annual margin of 1%, so the property investor will get £1.01 in return for €1.25. For a 5-year swap, he will get £1.01^5 = £1.051.

In 5 years' time, he will sell the property for €11.04 million, and swap euros for pounds at £1.051. This will produce 11.04m * £1.051 * 0.8 = £9.28m. The capital return is again

3% – £9.28m/£8.00m = 1.16 = 1.03^5. But this time, there is no currency risk. The Paris property is now more attractive to the UK investor – he earns 1% more return, less a small fee for the hedge, for the same risk, and this looks like a free – or almost free – lunch.

In practice, there are several inefficiencies in this process. First, hedging capital may be possible, but would we hedge income? Second, hedging will cost money – there will always be fees, and there will be a positive margin when going into a higher interest rate currency.

Third, the illiquidity of real estate causes difficulties. In the example, we might fix a 5-year swap. But how can we be certain that the property will be sold in 5 years' time? If we sell before this, we may have to break the swap, which will cost money. It is possible to enter into a consecutive series of shorter swaps – say a year, or even quarterly. The price – and risk – effect of this will be different.

As an example, Table 16.19 shows that a long-date swap will add more return and reduce risk when hedging US dollars for Japanese yen, but a long-date swap designed to reduce risk will cost more when hedging US dollars for Australian dollars. A short-date swap allows flexibility in timing the sale – but it will fail to lock in the 5-year hedge price that is available in the market, and it also introduces the problem of resetting the swap at a cost.

Assume we swap pounds for euros at Day 1, and switch £10 million for €12.5 million (at €1.25 : £1). We hedge currency movements by using 1-year forwards (a commitment to sell euros for pounds at a fixed exchange rate). The forward exchange rate will be determined by the spot rate (€1.25) plus the interest rate differential (1%), so it will be €1.26.

In 1-year's time, assuming no capital appreciation, we have a building worth £10.1 million, if the euro has appreciated as expected by 1%. Then, £10.1 million is the new amount to be hedged. The bank already has £10 million, but we are now short £100,000. This cash needs to be paid to the bank to reset the hedge. Cash may be available from net rental income, but it may not, in which case we have a liquidity mismatch (a short cash position, and a long illiquid real estate position).

In the real world of funds, hedging can be mightily complex. We have illustrated a simple case – an investor and a building. A less simple case would involve an investor, a fund, and a building. The investor might be US-domiciled. The fund might be euro-denominated. The building might be in Poland. Here there are two currency risk positions and two hedging decisions to be made.

In a complex case we might have an investor, a fund of funds, a fund, and a building. Assume, for example, a sterling investor in a dollar-denominated fund of funds investing in a Brazil/South America fund whose currency is the real, with an asset in Buenos Aires. Here there are three currency risk positions and three hedging decisions to be made.

Finally, what is the correct amount of the equity to hedge? Is this always 100%? Practice in other asset classes is instructive here. When investing in bonds, investors are

TABLE 16.19 The cost/benefit of hedging

Currency	Spot rate vs. $	3-Month rate	$ return	12-Month rate	$ return
JPY	91.17	91.05	0.13%	90.44	0.81%
AUD	0.842	0.833	−1.07%	0.810	−3.80%

Source: J.C. Rathbone Associates 2010.

likely to place a high value on certainty of income and capital receipts. When investing in international bonds, therefore, hedging currency makes sense to protect that low-risk characteristic. When investing in equities, investors are likely to accept high return volatility. When investing in international equities, therefore, hedging currency at a cost may make much less sense, as diversification effects may mean that the marginal impact on volatility may not even be negative.

Real estate may be characterised as a bond/equity hybrid. Core real estate may have bond characteristics; opportunistic real estate investing may be more equity-like. Partial hedging of the equity used to build a global property portfolio makes some sense, and a full modelling exercise is recommended in order to arrive at an appropriate policy.

16.8.5 Leverage, Tax, and Fees

How would the possibility of hedging affect the decision between investment in different countries?

As we saw above, investors can use local debt to reduce the capital at risk. The equity can be hedged, and the cost of hedging will be determined by interest rate and inflation differentials. This will add to return if the target market has low interest rates.

If a UK investor hedges an international investment, this will damage return if the target market has high interest rates. It will enhance return if the target market has lower interest rates. In addition, leverage will have a more positive effect on returns if there is a positive carry (property yields are higher than borrowing costs).

Using funds means that returns will be geared or leveraged. Returns will be net of tax, and also net of fees. In a pricing analysis, we need to use excess returns which are leveraged, and net of fees and taxes. If using a hedge is attractive because the target market has low interest rates, then this is easily taken into account, as shown in Table 16.20. (The analysis would be the same, albeit with more risk, if no hedge were used but we instead relied upon currency appreciation.)

Low interest rate markets are attractive because the currency risk can be managed more easily, and (if hedged) can even deliver return while reducing risk. They have other advantages, as less equity is needed and greater diversification is possible. In addition, positive leverage is more likely to be achieved in a low interest rate environment, and (as we saw in Chapter 1 and Chapter 9) this can add to return (and risk).

Table 16.20 is an illustration of the positive effect of leverage. Assume that a UK investor has a choice of buying a UK shopping centre for £100 million or one based in France, a euro currency area, for €100 million. He plans to use 50% gearing. The UK shopping centre has a yield of 5%, and throws off a rental income of £5 million. The French shopping centre has a yield of 5.5%, and throws off a rental income of €5.5 million.

Management fees of 6% (£300,000) in the UK are higher *pro rata* in France where there is less competition to provide such services, and where the structure used to shelter tax involves some administrative expenses, totalling in this case €500,000 or 9%. Interest is charged at 6.2% in the UK and 5.2% in the lower interest rate euro area, a cost of £3.1 million (6.2% of a £50 million loan) in the UK and €2.6 million (5.2% of a €50 million loan) in France. The net income on equity is £1.6 million and the cash-on-cash yield is 3.2% in the UK, and the net income on equity is €2.4 million and the cash-on-cash yield is 4.8% in France.

TABLE 16.20 Shopping centre comparison, Eurobloc and UK

£100m shopping centre with 50% leverage			€100m shopping centre with 50% leverage		
	£m	ROE		€m	ROE
Net rental income	5.0		Net rental income	5.5	
Management fees	−0.3		Management fees	−0.5	
Interest	−3.1		Interest	−2.6	
Net income	1.6	3.2%	Net income	2.4	4.8%
Capital growth	2.0		Capital growth	2.5	
Tax leakage	0.0		Tax leakage	−0.3	
Total return	**3.6**	**7.2%**	Total return	4.6	9.2%
			Hedging return		1.0%
			Total return incl. hedge		**10.2%**

It is reckoned that rental and capital growth in the UK will slightly underperform rental and capital growth in France, running at 2% and 2.5%, respectively, and adding £2 million and €2.5 million, respectively, to the investor's equity and total return each year.

The French centre will be held in a tax-efficient structure, but there will still be some leakage, estimated at €300,000 each year. The UK property shows a net annual total return of £3.6 million, 7.2% on equity, while the French centre shows a net annual total return of €4.6 million, 9.2% on equity.

Finally, the interest rate differential of 1% will add 1% to the sterling return each year, either through currency appreciation or through the hedge. The result is a return in sterling of 7.2% in the UK and 10.2% in France, the outperformance coming from a combination of property, leverage, and currency factors.

16.9 BUILDING A PORTFOLIO

For the international investor, how exactly can we use capital market, currency, economic, and property pricing data to assemble a global portfolio?

We suggest a top-down approach, and assume we will allocate between direct property, unlisted funds, and REITs. We assume that tax and structuring issues are generally soluble without prohibitive cost. We will need to consider, in particular, market pricing leading to country and regional allocations and property type allocations; we will need to consider the fund risk style allocation, currency management, and impact of leverage, tax, and fees (see Box 16.2). As a start, we need to identify investable and attractive markets. We have already considered which markets may be investable. Tax advice will be needed to further refine this checklist; otherwise, market attractiveness is a function of pricing.

Given the rule we have developed in this chapter, we would optimise excess returns in local currency. This puts in place a process which is designed to select attractive markets without the complications of having to make currency forecasts, and leaves us with the issue of whether to hedge currency.

Box 16.2: The Government Pension Investment Fund, Japan

In 2016, it was reported that Japan, the world's third-largest pension market, was poised to undergo a dramatic rebalancing of its investment portfolios, as Japanese pension funds were set to change their policy of investing only in bonds and equities. Collectively, they owned $2.63 trillion in assets in 2015, according to Willis Towers Watson. Some proceeds from maturing bonds were to be reallocated to alternatives – real estate, private equity, and infrastructure.

Japan's Government Pension Investment Fund (GPIF), the world's largest pension fund, was reported as being likely to make the first move into alternative assets. As of 30 September 2015, the $1.14 trillion GPIF had about 53% of its assets in bonds but was set to invest in riskier assets due to low bond yields. At $1.2 trillion in assets, the GPIF is 34% larger than the second-place fund on the list, the Government Pension Fund of Norway.

In 2017, GPIF was reported as starting to actively invest in domestic real estate funds in a bid to boost its returns. The GPIF, which has no internal real estate expertise, was set to invest up to 5% of its 156 trillion yen ($1.37 trillion) holdings in alternative assets such as infrastructure projects, private equity, and real estate. The fund was looking for outside asset managers specialising in those areas.

Late in 2017, GPIF announced that it had appointed Mitsubishi UFJ Trust and Banking, part of the Mitsubishi UFJ Financial Group (MTU), to oversee its domestic real estate investment strategy. This strategy was said to be focused on core properties including prime office buildings in Tokyo.

In 2018, it was clear that GPIF was looking to invest around $25 million in global (non-domestic) real estate over a 5-year timetable, 2019–23. Mitsubishi has already been appointed to manage half of that in domestic real estate. You are keen to pitch for the global (ex-Japan) mandate.

You need to prepare a proposal which will assist GPIF in developing its business plan for entry into ex-Japan real estate/real assets as an asset class. The project objectives are to determine: (i) a portfolio strategy and (ii) an appropriate execution method.

You are not qualified to provide specialist tax and accounting advice, and detailed advice will eventually have to be sought from a specialist. You are not qualified to advise the client on the liability implications of any recommended investment strategy. You do not need to have all of the details worked out – but what can you say in a 1-hour discussion (summarised in five or six slides) that will maximise your chances of being asked back for a second meeting?

Here is your pitch:

Strategy guidelines

Benchmark: an equilibrium portfolio approach, using market weights and 'bets'.

Country allocation: zero domestic, all international; regional allocation, then countries, then cities; currency hedged where possible. Around 42.5% USA and Canada; 32.5% Europe; 25% Asia ex-Japan.

Sector allocation: underweight traditional sectors (retail, office); overweight alternatives, residential, logistics. Some debt exposure via core unlisted funds.

Risk: risk appetite allows some opportunity fund bet and currency risk. Type A predominates – 80–90%; some Type B exposure – 10–20%. Some appetite for single property investment via fund sidecars.

Leverage: 30% look-through limit.

Income yield requirement: 3–5% net.

Liquidity: illiquidity premium and long-term horizon encourages unlisted over listed.

Risk controls: minimum/maximum investment to each fund/investment: €100/200m (say 50 investments maximum); gearing alters equity required for exposure. Limited development exposure, very limited build to sell.

Execution

Subcontract to an advisory firm who can: (a) source managers and funds and (b) source joint ventures and single property deals. It is too early to build an in-house real estate team, and GPIF will wish to learn from a global brand leader.

Advisory or discretionary? Discretionary: one subcontractor is required initially to simplify processes. More mandates may follow, and others might be appointed.

Employ research, strategy, allocation, accounting, reporting, monitoring (2/3 staff) in-house. Agree policy positions (fees, etc.). Employ or subcontract legal and tax advisors.

Recommendations

Private unlisted core/core-plus (Type A) vehicles: 40–70%

US 25–30%

Asia 5–10%

Europe 25–30%

US REITs and listed equities: 10–20%

Non-US REITs up to 10%

Europe 5%

Asia 5%

Type B private equity funds: 15% including operating platforms

JVs and co-investments: 30–40% (within the allocations to unlisted fund or REIT managers)

Debt up to 15% (via unlisted funds)

Who will be appointed?

GPIF will seek a global leader, appointed as a fiduciary, with limited conflicts of interest. A global scale and reach is vital, with execution capabilities across all real estate types including REITs. The appointee will have a real estate focus with a good track record of managing separate accounts and a focus on region/country Type A funds, with some Type B capability.

The appointee was a top-10 manager (see Chapter 1, Table 1.5). Which one, do you think?

16.10 CONCLUSION

International property investment can be complex, primarily because of the impact of tax and currency issues and other barriers which place non-domestic buyers at a disadvantage. Nevertheless, many investors are committed to building a global exposure to real estate, seeking either higher returns than are available domestically and/or diversification of real estate exposure.

Formal and informal barriers to international investment are important in determining cross-border real estate capital flows. Formal barriers are prevalent in real estate markets because real estate ownership is easily regulated, real property is easily taxed, and capital controls can be applied to real estate assets as easily as they can to any asset type. This may act to leave domestic investors in a better relative position and exclude foreign buyers.

Informal barriers are equally challenging. The large lot sizes involved in real estate means that diversification is less easily achieved (Baum, 2007) and this leaves systematic country risks with investors. Currency and title risks in particular are likely to loom large in investors' thinking. In an equity portfolio, emerging market currency risk can be diversified; for a real estate investor, this may be impossible, meaning that hedging is required, but this can be very costly or even impossible to achieve.

In constructing a property portfolio for an international investor, we suggest using a top-down approach feeding from capital market, currency, economic, and property pricing data, and assume we will allocate between direct property, unlisted funds, and REITs. Except for the largest investors with a commitment to big in-house teams, direct property is unlikely to be appropriate, other than through joint ventures with managers and/or fund sidecars.

We assume that tax and structuring issues are generally soluble without prohibitive cost. We consider, in particular, market pricing leading to country and regional allocations and property type allocations; we also consider fund risk style allocation, currency management, and the impact of leverage, tax, and fees.

We note that seeking high nominal excess returns (expected returns less required returns) in the local currency will put in place a process which is designed to select attractive markets without the complications of having to make currency forecasts. That leaves us with the issue of whether to hedge currency or not, and (especially if an investor uses unlisted funds) hedging can be complex. Partial hedging of the equity used to build a global property portfolio makes some sense.

In Chapter 17 we move on to examine how we can retrospectively measure the success of our plans.

CHAPTER 17

Performance Measurement and Attribution

17.1 PERFORMANCE MEASUREMENT: AN INTRODUCTION

This chapter is concerned with the science of performance measurement (How well did we do?) as it can be applied to real estate investments, and with an associated analytical tool – 'attribution analysis' (How did we do it?). After the 1990s and 2007 market corrections, and in an era during which false news is an increasingly ubiquitous plague, property investors and managers need to understand how to use performance measurement and attribution systems, to understand Who has added real value, and Why.

Performance measures exist, first and foremost, to show whether a portfolio has achieved a rate of return better or worse than the 'market' average, or has met specified investment objectives. Benchmarking has answered the question: *by how much* did we outperform (underperform) the target return or benchmark? There follows an inevitable demand for portfolio attribution analysis which addresses the question: *why* did we outperform (underperform) the target or benchmark?

An ideal system of portfolio analysis would identify the contribution of all aspects of portfolio strategy and management to relative returns. It would separate, for example, profits earned on the development of investments from the returns on held properties. Those profits arise from two distinctly separate activities with different return and risk characteristics, and reflect different features of management 'skill'. Among held properties, return may be influenced by anything and everything from the broadest allocation of investment between sectors to skill in selecting tenants, negotiating rent reviews, and controlling operating expenses. In practice, the heterogeneity of individual properties and the complexity of property management mean that the contributions of different functions and skills to portfolio performance are hard to disentangle.

In the long run, as we argued in Chapters 1 and 2, property in developed markets should deliver a return in line with its net income yield plus something close to the rate of inflation. If the net income yield is 5%, a net real return of around 6% should be achievable if inflation runs at 2% and depreciation takes away 1%. It is understandable, therefore, that many property funds have been launched with absolute target returns (say 6% nominal, or 4% real), as this reflects the objectives of the investor in allocating capital to the asset class.

In the shorter run, however, property is highly cyclical, as Chapter 2 illustrated. This means that over the 7- to 10-year life of a typical closed-ended property fund (see Chapter 11), returns may easily exceed, or fall well below, this long-term expectation. Over the typical 3-year term of a separate account mandate awarded by a pension fund to a fund manager, this is even more likely. In such cases the fund manager could find itself in trouble if the absolute returns are disappointing and it appears that the manager has done a poor job relative to the competitors who could have been appointed instead. For this reason, and because trustees need to be able to show that their decision to appoint and retain a manager has been justified, relative return targets (for example, 1% above the NCREIF or MSCI benchmark) are common.

In this chapter we present and discuss ways of *measuring* performance in order to judge whether investors or managers have been successful. Success may be measured against an absolute return target, which is not as simple as it sounds – how should return be calculated? – or against a relative return objective. We also present ways of *attributing* the performance of single properties, of portfolios and of funds, which is a means of understanding how the return was achieved in order to judge where the manager succeeded, or failed.

17.2 RETURN MEASURES

17.2.1 Introduction

There are many confusions concerning return measurement in property. This is largely due to the unique terminology which has been developed in the property world; it is also due to the unique nature of property, caused especially by lease contracts and the resulting reversionary or over-rented nature of interests.

There is also some misunderstanding of the difference between return measures which are used to cover different points or periods in time. Return measures may describe the future; they may describe the present; or they may describe the past. Measures describing the future are always expectations. They will cover certain periods of time and may, if that period begins immediately, be called *ex ante* measures. An example is the expected internal rate of return (IRR) from a property development project beginning shortly; another example is the required return on that project. Measures describing the present do not cover a period, but describe relationships existing at a single point in time (now). An example is the initial yield on a property investment; while this may imply something about the income return likely to be produced by an investment in future, it is simply the current relationship between the rental income and the capital value or price.

Measures of return describing the past, or *ex post* measures, are measures of (historic) performance. An example is the delivered return on a project. Performance measurement is a science which deals only with the past. It must therefore be distinguished from portfolio analysis, which is relevant to the present, and to portfolio strategy, which is relevant to the future. It deals wholly with delivered returns, and not expected or required returns (see Chapter 4).

The following definitions are the most commonly used performance measures.

Income Return

This is the net rent or net operating income (NOI) received over the measurement period divided by the value at the beginning of the period.

$$IR = Y_{0-1} / CV_0$$

where:

IR = income return
Y_{0-1} = net income received from time 0 to time 1
CV_0 = capital value at time 0.

Capital Return

This is the change in value over the measurement period divided by the value at the beginning of the period:

$$CR = \left[CV_1 - CV_0\right] / CV_0$$

where:

CR = capital return
CV_1 = capital value at time 1
CV_0 = capital value at time 0.

Total Return

This is the sum of income return and capital return:

$$TR = \left[Y_{0-1} + CV_1 - CV_0\right] / CV_0$$

where:

TR = total return
Y_{0-1} = net income received from time 0 to time 1
CV_1 = capital value at time 1
CV_0 = capital value at time 0.

Mixing income and capital together in one measure of return is challenging for investors in certain domiciles, as they quite reasonably question the direct comparability of the cash-based NOI and the non-cash capital return component, which (unless there has been both a purchase and a sale in the period examined) is based on at least one valuation, and probably the difference between two valuation estimates. This explains why, in continental Europe, it is common to talk about direct, indirect, and total return, with 'direct' reflecting income return or NOI, and 'indirect' the value increase.

Time-Weighted Return

This is the single rate of compound interest which will produce the same accumulated value over more than one period as would be produced by a series of single-period returns or interest rates. Some commentators refer to this as the geometric mean rate of return, although this is not strictly accurate.

Being an average, the time-weighted return (TWRR) is unaffected by the timing of cash injections and redemptions. It is therefore appropriate for open-ended funds and other co-mingled funds where the manager cannot control flows of capital into and out of the fund. It is an inappropriate measure where the manager has discretion over asset allocation and cash flows into and out of the portfolio or fund.

Internal Rate of Return

This is the most complete description of historic return. It takes account of the amount invested in each period, which is why it is sometimes known as a money-weighted return. It is appropriate where managers have discretion over the cash flow. It is not a mean of annual returns.

17.2.2 Example: IRR, TWRR, or Total Return?

By way of illustration, let us assume that the return on two funds, life fund A and pension fund B, was measured over the period 2018–20. The performance information shown in Tables 17.1 and 17.2 is available for these funds.

At year-end, the fund managers decide whether or not to buy new buildings and all expenditure takes place at that time. Expenditure is not taken into account in the year-end valuation completed immediately before each expenditure. It is assumed instead that expenditure adds to the portfolio value at the beginning of the following year. It is also assumed that rent is paid and received quarterly in advance.

TABLE 17.1 Life fund A

	Initial value	Value at year-end	Net income	New expenditure
2018	\$123.45m	\$94.51m	\$9.34m	\$17.86m
2019		\$165.50m	\$10.12m	\$1.45m
2020		\$177.09m	\$10.32m	

TABLE 17.2 Pension fund B

	Initial value	Value at year-end	Net income	New expenditure
2018	\$12.35m	\$9.53m	\$0.93m	\$0.00m
2019		\$14.00m	\$1.01m	\$1.45m
2020		\$16.50m	\$1.03m	

So, the total return for the life fund in 2019 is given by:

$$TR = \left[Y_{0-1} + CV_1 - CV_0\right] / CV_0$$
$$= \left[\$10.12 + \$165.50 - (\$94.51 + \$17.86)\right] / (\$94.51 + \$17.86)$$
$$= \left[\$175.62 - \$112.37\right] / \$112.65 = \$63.25 / \$112.37$$

$$TR = 56.29\%$$

The IRR for the pension fund in 2020 is derived from the following quarterly cash flow:

$$-\$14.00 - \$1.45 + (\$1.03/4); + (\$1.03/4); + (\$1.03/4); + (\$16.50)$$
$$= -\$15.19 + \$0.26 + \$0.26 + \$16.50$$

$$IRR = 14.04\%$$

The full results are as shown in Table 17.3.

The life fund achieved a higher IRR over 3 years than the pension fund. However, the pension fund achieved a higher TWRR. In 2018, the IRRs achieved by both funds were less than the total returns achieved. In 2019 and 2020, they were both higher. Which of these measures is appropriate?

TABLE 17.3 Life and pension fund performance

Year	Life fund	Pension fund
2018 total return	−15.88%	−15.30%
2018 IRR	−16.68%	−16.08%
2019 total return	56.29%	57.50%
2019 IRR	59.44%	61.32%
2020 total return	12.25%	13.46%
2020 IRR	12.74%	14.04%
2018–20 TWRR	13.85%	14.82%
2018–20 IRR	14.67%	13.87%

IRR or TWRR?

The pension fund achieved a higher TWRR (which is not money-weighted), in other words a higher average annual return. The life fund appears to have outperformed on an IRR basis because the IRR (which is money-weighted) reflects the additional investment made by the fund at the start of the strong year of 2019.

The responsibility for investing the cash determines the correct measure. Who decided to put more money in at the start of 2019? If the decision was the responsibility of the fund managers in each case, then the IRR is correct and the life fund outperformed. If the decision was the responsibility of a higher authority, then the TWRR is correct and the pension fund outperformed.

In addition, it should be noted that the IRR exceeds the TWRR for the life fund because more money was invested in the better years and the initial poor years of performance badly damaged the investment base for the TWRR calculation. The TWRR exceeds the IRR for the pension fund, largely because there was no new expenditure at the end of 2018/beginning of 2019.

IRR or *Total Return?*

In 2018, the IRRs achieved by both funds were less than the total returns achieved. In 2020, they were both higher. The differences in each case are simply the result of the timing of rental income, assumed to be quarterly in advance.

Normally, that is when returns are positive – the quarterly payment of rent is an advantage and produces a higher IRR than total return. The total return effectively assumes a single end-of-year rent payment. In this case the IRR assumes that the (quarterly) intermediate cash flows are reinvested at the IRR. Hence the 2020 returns are higher on an IRR basis than on a total return basis. In contrast, negative returns in 2018 mean that the reinvestment of quarterly income led to negative interest, a damaged IRR, and a relatively higher total return.[1]

17.2.3 Required and Delivered Returns

If investors have perfect foresight, the return delivered on an asset in an efficient market will always be the return they require to make them invest. Delivered returns (see Section 17.3) are not always the same as required returns.

The Required Return

Any investment should deliver a return – an opportunity cost, or required return – which exceeds the risk-free rate by a premium, which in turn compensates for

[1] The IRR is certainly a superior measure of return. It is more practical to measure total returns, but comparisons of IRRs with total returns can be misleading. Professional performance measurement agencies, such as IPD, adjust for the timing effect in their total return calculations, 'chain-linking' monthly returns to produce annual TWRRs [by taking the 12th root of $(1 + TR_1) * (1 + TR_2) * ... * (1 + TR_{12}) - 1$]. Nevertheless, great care needs to be taken when comparing reported fund returns with benchmark return measures, as they may be specified differently.

the disadvantages of the asset class. These are best summarised as risk, illiquidity, and other factors (see Chapters 1 and 4).

In the following section we show how to estimate both the required return and the delivered return. The easiest starting point for considering the required return or opportunity cost is to look at a risk-free asset. In nominal terms, this is represented very well by a government bond. In real terms, it is represented by an inflation-indexed bond. Whichever is used, the required return is given by:

$$\left(1+RF_N\right)\times\left(1+RP\right)$$

or, as an approximation:

$$RF_N + RP$$

where RF_N is the redemption yield offered by the appropriate bond and RP is the extra return – the risk premium – required to compensate for the disadvantages of the asset. While RF_N can be measured by examining the redemption yield offered by bonds, the required risk premium on any asset is expectations-based and is therefore harder to estimate (see Chapter 4).

The link between real and nominal risk-free rates is given by Fisher (1930) (see Chapter 4). The return available on index-linked bonds selling at par is the coupon plus realised inflation. The real return therefore equates closely with the coupon, and modern-day averages are around 2%.

This rate is defined by Fisher as the reward for time preference. According to Fisher, investors also require a reward for expected inflation, otherwise investment in real assets would be preferable and paper-based investments such as conventional bonds would sell at lower prices. Hence, if 4.5% was available on 15-year bonds, this might include 2% for inflation and 2.5% for time preference. In Fisher's terms:

$$R = l + i$$

where:

R = required return

l = time preference

i = expected inflation.

However, for an investor interested in real returns (say an immature pension fund), conventional bonds are less attractive than index-linked bonds. There is a risk of inflation expectations not being realised, so that higher than expected inflation will lead to lower than expected returns; and there is a general discounting of investments where investments are risky. In a market dominated by investors with real liabilities, risky (in real terms) conventional bonds would be discounted, meaning the required return would be higher. If required returns are equal to the available return in an efficient market, then the 4.5% available on the conventional bond must include a risk premium. Following Fisher again, the full explanation of a required return is:

$$R = l + i + RP$$

where:

$$RP = risk\ premium$$

$$(l + i) = RF_N = the\,(nominal)\,risk\text{-}free\ rate$$

so that, as before:

$$R = RF_N + RP$$

For conventional bonds, it is possible that:

$$4.5\% = 2\% + 2\% + 0.5\% = 4\% + 0.5\%$$

when inflation is expected to run at 2% and the extra return required to compensate investors for the risk that it does not is 0.5%.

The Delivered Return

Returns are delivered in two ways: through income (income return) and through capital (capital return). These combine to create total return.

Income return over any period is the relationship of income delivered over the period and the capital value of the asset at the start of the period. Capital values can be explained in terms of the relationship of the initial income on an asset and its multiplier:

$$Y \times \frac{1}{K}$$

where:

Y = current income

K = initial yield on the asset.

Hence, capital values can change when incomes change or when initial yields change. Following Gordon (1962):

$$K = R - G_N$$

where:

$$G_N = expected\ income\ growth\,(net\ of\ depreciation)$$

Example: The UK market in 2018

To develop this, let us use an example, based in the depressed UK market of 2008. Assume that at the beginning of 2008 a property is valued at a cap rate of 5%. The required return is 7%, incorporating a 3% risk premium over conventional bonds yielding 4%. It is priced at £20 with an expected initial dividend of £l. The expected growth in income is given as follows:

$$K = R - G_N$$

$$5\% = 7\% - G_N$$

$$G_N = 2\%$$

If expectations are correct, what total return will be delivered? Remember the required return is 7%:

$$TR = IR + CR$$

$$IR = \frac{Y_{0-1}}{CV_0} = \frac{£1}{£20} = 5\%$$

$$CR = \frac{CV_1 - CV_0}{CV_0}$$

What will CV_1 be? In 1 year, if expectations are correct, the income will have grown to £1.02. If initial yields do not change, the value is given by:

$$CV_1 = \frac{Y}{K} = \frac{£1.02}{5\%} = £20.40$$

$$CR = \frac{£20.40 - £20}{£20} = 2\%$$

$$TR = IR + CR = 5\% + 2\% = 7\%$$

The delivered return is equal to the required return, because expectations turned out to be correct.

17.2.4 Capital Expenditure

Capital expenditure will be necessary from time to time to repair, refurbish, extend, and improve property. How should this be dealt with in a measure of performance? There are two alternatives. Expenditure can either be dealt with as if it causes a reduction in income, or as if it requires an increase in capital invested.

Reduction in income

Strict comparability with equities would suggest that minor capital improvements (*CI*) should be financed out of cash flow, just as a company would use cash flow to maintain its capital assets. The appropriate treatment is then quite simple. The income return is reduced by the expenditure, while the capital return may be increased if the expenditure adds value to *CV*1:

$$TR = \left[\left(Y_{0-1} - CI\right) + \left(CV_1 - CV_0\right)\right] / CV_0$$

Increase in capital invested

However, capital improvements are not always minor, and major improvements – say, extending a building – are similar to purchasing new assets. The appropriate treatment would then be to say that the amount of capital expended adds to *CV*0 (and to *CV*1 as long as the expenditure adds value) but does not affect the income return:

$$TR = \left[\left(Y_{0-1}\right) + \left(CV_1 - CV_0 + CI\right)\right] / \left[CV_0 + CI\right]$$

Both MSCI and NCREIF have chosen to use variations of this formula. However, there is an argument in favour of the first measure (reduction in income). The effect can be significant: while the total return is unlikely to be much affected, the income return can go down (and the capital return can go up) by as much as 2% over typical periods. This raises an interesting question about the income return delivered by depreciating property assets, as conventional approaches may disguise depreciation by overstating income returns: see Chapter 1.

Timing of Expenditure

These formulae effectively assume that the expenditure takes place at the beginning of the year. This may not be true; for example, it may take place in stages during the year. The formulae can then be adjusted to take account of timing.

For example, using the capital invested approach, expenditure at the half-year stage can be dealt with by suggesting that half of the expenditure is invested for the year:

$$TR = \left[\left(Y_{0-1}\right) + \left(CV_1 - CV_0 + 0.5 * CI\right)\right] / \left[CV_0 + 0.5 * CI\right]$$

17.2.5 Risk-Adjusted Measures of Performance

At the beginning of this chapter we noted the possibility of managers setting absolute return targets (say 8% nominal, or 5% real), as this reflects the objectives of the investor in allocating capital to the asset class. We noted that managers are also interested in relative return targets (for example, 1% above the NCREIF or MSCI benchmark) to protect their competitive position.

TABLE 17.4 Fund A or fund B? (1)

Year	MSCI	Fund A	Fund B
1	8	9	14
2	15	16	11
3	25	26	28
4	28	29	26
5	4	5	6
Average	16	17	17
SD	9.32	9.32	8.58

In the following example, two fund performances over 5 years will be compared with that of the UK property market, represented by the MSCI annual index. Fund A outperforms by 1% every year. Fund B has the same average outperformance, but behaves more erratically relative to the index (see Table 17.4).

The most commonly used measure of volatility is the standard deviation. One simple route to risk adjustment, then, would be to divide the average return by the standard deviation of that return. This is the reciprocal of what is commonly called the coefficient of variation (CV) and ranks fund B as superior to fund A, which in turn is superior to the MSCI benchmark (see Table 17.5).

However, the fund manager may not be concerned about absolute volatility of performance. If he is measured relative to MSCI, he may be concerned about relative performance. Dividing outperformance by the tracking error gives a more useful measure, sometimes called the information ratio (see Table 17.6).

We now have the most appropriate ranking of performance for two managers each trying to beat an index. Fund A has achieved consistent outperformance with no tracking error – infinitely good risk-adjusted performance. Fund B is less successful.

TABLE 17.5 Fund A or fund B? (2)

	IPD	Fund A	Fund B
Average return	16	17	17
Standard deviation	9.32	9.32	8.58
1/CV	1.72	1.82	1.98

TABLE 17.6 Fund A or fund B? (3)

	IPD	Fund A	Fund B
Average excess return	0	1	1
Tracking error	0	0	3.58
Information ratio	0	Infinite	0.28

This is not the end of the story. Had fund B achieved very slightly higher returns, which would have been best? How much tracking error compensates for an extra unit of outperformance? This is a subjective judgement, and we can offer no scientific solution.

17.3 ATTRIBUTION ANALYSIS: SOURCES OF RETURN

It should be clear from Section 17.2.3 that there are two reasons why delivered returns can differ from required returns. First, expectations of income *return* can turn out to have been incorrect. Second, expectations of capital return can turn out to have been incorrect, either because initial yields change or because expectations of income *growth* turn out to have been incorrect.

In our UK 2008 example, we assumed that a property has a current yield of 5%. The required return is 7%, incorporating a 3% risk premium over conventional bonds yielding 4%. It is priced at £20 with an expected initial dividend of £1. The expected growth in income is given as follows:

$$K = R - G_N$$

$$5\% = 7\% - G_N$$

$$G_N = 2\%$$

Changes in Initial Yields

Let us assume now that the income grows as expected at 2% but that initial yields rise from 5% to 6%. Capital value in year 1 will be given by:

$$\frac{£1.02}{6\%} = £17.00$$

$$TR = 5\% + \frac{£17.00 - £20}{£20} = 5\% - 15\% = -10\%$$

Why do changes in initial yields happen? Given (following Gordon, 1962) that:

$$K = R - G_N$$

and (following Fisher, 1930) that:

$$R = l + i + RP$$

which simplifies to:

$$R = RF_N + RP$$

then

$$K = RF_N + RP - G_N$$

Delivered returns will differ from required returns where:

a. expectations of income return are incorrect at time *t*;
b. the risk-free rate changes at time $t + 1$;
c. expectations of income growth change at time $t + 1$; or
d. the risk premium changes at time $t + 1$.

Let us assume that the required return on UK property is currently driven by a risk premium of 3% and that this has been a constant over the past two decades. The required return on UK property in 2008 would have been around 7% (conventional bonds were yielding around 4%). Why, then, were UK property returns in 2008 as low as −22%?

a. *Were expectations of the income return incorrect?*
In 2008, the income return was around 5%, as expected.
b. *Did the risk-free rate change?*
Despite changes to short-term rates, the long-term government bond remained reasonably flat.
c. *Were expectations of income growth revised?*
In 2008, expectations for property rents were almost certainly revised down in the wake of the global financial crisis, given the expected negative impact on the real economy. A downward revision in expected growth from 2% to (say) 1.5% would push the capitalisation rate up by 0.5%. The capital return impact would be as follows:

$$K = 4\% + 3\% - 1.5\% = 5.50\%$$

$$CV_1 = \frac{£1.00}{5.50\%} = £18.18$$

$$CR = \frac{£20.00 - £18.18}{£20.00} = -9.00\%$$

Did the risk premium change?
There is no doubt that the risk premium shot upwards in 2008 during the global financial crisis. An upward revision in the risk premium growth from 3% to (say)

4.35% would push the capitalisation rate up by a further 1.35%. The capital return impact in isolation would be as follows:

$$K = 4\% + 4.35\% - 2\% = 6.35\%$$

$$CV_1 = \frac{£1.00}{6.35\%} = £15.75$$

$$CR = \frac{£20.00 - £15.75}{£20.00} = -21.30\%$$

17.3.2 *The Combined Impact*

An increase in the risk premium of (say) 1.35% and a downward revision to growth expectations to (say) 0.5% would add 1.85% to the cap rate (Table 17.7). For a building previously earning £1 in rent and valued at £20, the new value would be given as follows:

$$\begin{aligned} K &= 4\% + 4.35\% - 1.5\% \\ &= 6.85\% \end{aligned}$$

$$\begin{aligned} CV_1 &= \frac{£1.00}{6.85\%} \\ &= £14.60 \end{aligned}$$

The combined (non-additive) capital return impact would be as follows:

$$\begin{aligned} CR &= \frac{£20.00 - £14.60}{£20.00} \\ &= -27.00\% \end{aligned}$$

The combined total return impact would be as follows:

$$\begin{aligned} TR &= 5\% - 27.00\% \\ &= -22.00\% \left(\text{the delivered return in 2008}\right) \end{aligned}$$

TABLE 17.7 UK property market sources of return, 2008

	Total	Income	Capital	RFR	Growth	RP
Expected	7.00%	5.00%	2.00%	4.00%	2.00%	3.00%
Delivered	−22.00%	5.00%	−27.00%	4.00%	1.50%	4.35%
Impact	−29.00%	0.00%	−29.00%	0.00%	−9.00%	−21.30%

17.4 ATTRIBUTION ANALYSIS: THE PROPERTY LEVEL

We have already seen that total return is a simple additive function of income return and capital return. Capital return is driven by changes in capital value. Given the following simple function:

$$CV = \frac{Y}{K}$$

changes in capital value must be driven by changes in Y (income) and K (cap rate). This is almost, but not quite, a comprehensive explanation of capital return in practice.

Because of what we prefer to call the lease effect, or the reversion effect, rental growth and cap rate changes may not pass directly through to capital value. The lease effect describes the amount of capital growth that cannot be accounted for by changes in either rental value or cap rates. Within a single property, typical causes of this error (there are many) are changes in vacancy (a property becomes vacant), leasing empty space, the expected cash flow changes as the lease end approaches, or indexation changes the passing rent.

To illustrate, let us use an example from the Netherlands. In 2020, the contract rent to be paid is €10,000; the market rental value at the end of 2019 is €15,000, and rises to €16,500 at the end of 2020; there are 4 years to the lease end at the end of 2019, and 3 years to the lease end at the end of 2020; the cap rate is 6% at the end of 2019, and falls to 5.75% at the end of 2020; and the rent is indexed in line with inflation, which is 1% in 2020.

Using a layer or 'top-slice' valuation, we now explore the change in capital value from the end of 2019 to the end of 2020.

At end 2019:

Core income	€10,000
PV p.a. perp @ 6.00%	16.6667
Capital value	€166,667
Top slice income	€5,000
PV p.a. perp @ 6.00%	16.6667
PV 4 yrs @ 6.00%	0.7921
Capital value	€66,008
Total	€232,675

At end 2020:

Core income (indexed)	€10,100
PV p.a. perp @ 5.75%	17.3913
Capital value	€175,652
Top slice income	€6,400 (€16,500 – €10,100)
PV p.a. perp @ 5.75%	17.3913
PV 4 yrs @ 5.75%	0.8456
Capital value	€94,118
Total	€269,770

To calculate total return, we use the following formula:

$$TR = \left[Y_{0-1} + CV_1 - CV_0\right] / CV_0$$

The relevant data is as follows:

$$CV_0 = €232{,}675$$

$$CV_1 = €246{,}11$$

$$Y_{0-1} = €10{,}000$$

$$TR = \left[Y_{0-1} + CV_1 - CV_0\right] / CV_0$$

$$TR = \left[€10{,}000 + \left(€269{,}770 - €232{,}675\right)\right] / €232{,}675$$

$$TR = \left[€10{,}000 + €37{,}095\right] / €232{,}675$$

$$TR = €47{,}095 / €232{,}675$$

$$TR = 20.24\%$$

$$IR = 4.30\%; CR = 15.94\%$$

We can now ask: What are the drivers of the capital return? How much of the 15.94% comes from rental growth? How much from cap rate movement? How much from indexation? And how much from the approaching lease end?

To answer this, we repeat the 2019 and 2020 valuations, but this time holding all variables constant except the variable under consideration. This produces the 2020 valuations shown in Table 17.8, and the return impacts shown in Table 17.9. Note that the effects are not additive.

TABLE 17.8 Netherlands property – end 2020 values

Rental growth	Cap rate effect	Index effect	Reversion effect	Combined
€252,478	€243,444	€234,341	€236,635	€269,770

TABLE 17.9 Netherlands property – 2020 capital returns

Rental growth	Cap rate effect	Index effect	Reversion effect	Combined
8.51%	4.63%	0.72%	1.70%	15.94%

17.5 ATTRIBUTION ANALYSIS: THE PORTFOLIO LEVEL

17.5.1 Introduction

The standard approach to the analysis of equity portfolios (see, for example, Hamilton and Heinkel, 1995) starts from three primary contributors to portfolio return: policy, structure, and stock. (Unfortunately, the terminology for the last two contributors varies between sources. 'Structure' may alternatively be described as 'timing' or 'asset allocation'; 'stock' as 'selection' or 'property score'.)

We concentrate on structure and stock selection. By structure is meant the allocation of portfolio weights to 'segments' of the market, typically but not necessarily defined by a mixture of property types and geographical locations. By stock is meant the selection of individual investments within each segment which deliver returns above or below the average for that segment.

Hence, attribution analysis at the real estate portfolio level seeks to separate (at least) two components of a portfolio's relative return. The first is the relative return which is due to 'structure', or the allocation of investment to 'segments' of the market with different average rates of return. The second is 'stock selection', or the choice of individual assets within each market segment that have returns above or below the averages for that market segment.

Table 17.10 shows the performance of an unnamed UK fund benchmarked against the (then) IPD index in the late 1980s.

In 1989, for example, the fund delivered a return of 8.3%, which was nearly 6% below the average return for the universe of properties measured by IPD. It was in the 94th percentile in that year. (Over the 1980s, the fund achieved an annualised total return of 11% against the IPD average of 15%, and the management was replaced in 1990.)

The poor sector mix (sector component) explained roughly half of the underperformance. The fund was overweight in retail, the underperforming sector over the period; it was particularly overweight in Scottish retail, again a poor relative performer. The remaining underperformance is explained by poor stock selection (the property component). The reason for this is that one very large asset performed very poorly. However, it is misleading to suggest that these are separable factors, because the large asset was a Scottish shopping centre.[2]

TABLE 17.10 Components of performance

	IPD return	Fund return	Sector component	Property component
1987	24.3%	13.3%	−5.1%	−6.0%
1988	29.2%	23.8%	−2.4%	−2.9%
1989	14.1%	8.3%	−2.2%	−3.6%

[2]The contribution of structure to variation in returns depends on the scale of differences in returns across market segments. The variation reached a maximum in the boom and slump of the late 1980s and early 1990s, which contains the above example.

Attribution analysis is of some importance in property fund management, relevant to the specification of investment objectives, the selection of managers, and the payment of performance-related rewards. Yet the above example shows that property is likely to present a series of challenges.

17.5.2 The Choice of Segmentation

An initial choice in any attribution system is critical to all that follows: what segments of the investible universe should be used to define 'structure'? Burnie *et al.* (1998) state that:

> *To be useful as a tool for evaluating portfolio management, performance attribution analysis should be carried out within a framework that mirrors the investment policy and the decision-making process particular to the fund under examination. A comprehensive attribution methodology will account explicitly for each key component of the portfolio management process.*

In that view, the segment structure should reflect the way in which the managers of each individual portfolio choose to regard the 'structure' of their investible universe, specifically how that universe is broken down for the purposes of analysis, forecasting, and the setting of target portfolio weights. But in practice this would make it extremely difficult for performance measurement services to operate, as it would not be possible to compare allocation and selection skills across portfolios. For practical purposes, there has to be a standardised segmentation applied to the attribution analysis of all investors, at least as a first step. One standard system is shown in Table 17.11.

Several considerations bear upon the choice of segmentation: statistical, practical, and convention.

- Statistically, each segment should contain a sufficient number of properties for the average return to be reasonably robust: that is, each segment should ideally only reflect systematic risk. The optimum segmentation of the market is that which statistically explains the most variance in individual property returns.
- Practically, segments most usefully cover property categories or areas for which property market information, with supporting information on (say) demographic and economic factors, is readily available to support analysis and forecasting.
- And, by convention, segments will be most acceptable to investors where they follow the generally accepted ways of dividing and analysing the market and managing properties: it would be difficult to offer a detailed analysis service in France, for example, which did not show Paris offices as a 'segment'.

In real-world performance analysis services, the search for an appropriate segmentation will tend to resolve quite rapidly to a mixture of the dominant property types (shops, shopping centres, offices, industrials) and geographical areas (either towns or regions) linked to either well-recognised property 'markets' or the city/regional boundaries used in the production of official statistics.

TABLE 17.11 MSCI UK returns, 2009

Percentile/ segment	1	5	10	25	50	75	90	99	Mean	SD	Obs.
Standard shops	−15.5	−5.0	−1.2	4.1	8.3	13.5	21.1	46.7	9.5	11.5	4,221
Shopping centres	−5.0	0.1	2.9	6.9	11.1	16.3	20.8	27.6	11.4	7.3	259
Retail warehouses	−10.3	−2.9	1.4	5.5	9.9	15.0	21.5	42.4	10.8	9.9	738
Stores/supermarkets	−7.4	0.2	3.7	7.6	11.5	17.7	25.2	50.7	26.5	27.3	420
Other retail	−27.7	−4.4	−0.2	5.3	9.3	13.8	24.7	105.8	11.7	18.9	271
Standard offices	−17.6	−3.1	1.3	6.9	11.2	18.2	26.9	64.6	13.3	14.3	2,693
Office parks	−11.2	−1.7	2.8	6.8	10.8	15.8	25.4	46.5	12.4	10.4	242
Standard industrials	−4.5	4.0	7.3	10.2	13.3	18.2	22.0	62.1	14.3	8.8	62
Industrial parks	−6.8	0.0	4.2	8.2	12.4	15.8	21.2	39.9	12.6	8.3	294
Distribution warehouses	−8.7	−1.5	1.7	5.5	9.7	13.5	19.9	34.2	10.0	7.7	223
Other property	−39.2	−10.5	−6.3	1.0	10.5	16.3	31.2	212.5	15.6	35.5	394
All property	−14.9	−3.7	0.3	5.7	10.2	16.1	24.2	55.0	12.3	54.7	11,142

Source: MSCI.
Note: Obs. refers to the number of properties in each segment.

17.5.3 Style

Property fund managers may adopt asset allocation positions which are different from the segment weighting of the benchmark for a variety of reasons. This may be the result of forecasts driving tactical asset allocation, so that views of likely market returns influence a manager to adopt an underweight or overweight position relative to the benchmark in an attempt to produce outperformance. It may be the result of strategic asset allocation or policy, where issues other than pricing – for example, liability matching – influence the asset allocation mix. It may also be the conscious or unconscious result of the style of the fund manager, and what the team is thought to be good at.

The term is used here in an attempt to reflect more commonly used judgements of investment style in fund management. Is the manager style top-down (driven by a view of sectors) or bottom-up (driven by his choice of properties)? Is the manager a value manager or a growth manager? This definition of style implies a persistent bias in the property portfolio structure which is the result of preference or habit. It may lead to long-term outperformance, or it may not.

Style may be associated with investment houses, with individuals, or with funds. Arguably, there has been too little explicit differentiation between house styles in property fund management. This has begun to change, with a split between 'core' and 'value-add' styles emerging over the last decade.

17.5.4 Themes

As noted above, segment structure will typically be defined by reference to property use type and broad geographical region. Property fund managers invest in forecasting systems which enable managers to take a tactical view on prospective returns in the market 'segments' which are determined by this classification. It can be seen, then, that definitions of fund structure are of necessity rather stable. However, sector (type)/region segments are not necessarily optimal in permitting outperformance by asset allocation.

Table 17.12 shows the mean average deviation between the mean return on the (then) IPD index and the returns across different segment classifications for the Irish market over the period 1986–95. The table suggests that the mean difference between the return on the individual sectors and the market as a whole in each individual year ('the window of opportunity') is less than the mean difference between the return on different age groups within the industrial market. There is more dispersion of returns across age bands *within* the industrial and retail sectors alone than there is across the three market sectors; and it would seem that concentrating on age bands across the market would have introduced the potential for greater returns than concentrating on sector choice would have done.

While sector allocations may not, in Ireland over the period 1986–95, present the maximum potential for outperformance, there is no reason why this might not be the case over some future period. An excellent manager may be expected to anticipate when this might be. Equally, he would be expected to anticipate at what point size becomes important – or age. This is what we mean by themes.

The asset allocation process ideally takes account of themes as well as standard segmentation. These may be new themes – sensitivity to changes in internet shopping, for example – or they may be standard, such as high yield/low yield. Themes differ from styles, because themes imply no necessary persistence in the manager's preference for

TABLE 17.12 Mean average deviations, IPD Irish Funds, 1986–95

Segment	Mean average deviation
Sector	2.70
Locations within retail	4.40
Locations within offices	1.80
Subsectors within retail	4.60
Age within retail	4.30
Age within offices	1.30
Age within industrials	5.70
Size within retail	2.40
Size within offices	1.20
Size within industrials	2.40

Source: IPD.

segments; and themes differ from structure, because themes imply no persistence in the segment classification or reliance on external performance measurement standards.

17.5.5 City or Metropolitan Statistical Area Selection

An attribution system will preferably be stable and holistic. One major attraction of a regional classification in Germany, for example, is its completeness of coverage of Germany property. However, this does not mean that fund managers will more effectively control risk and seek outperformance by categorising their holdings in this way.

A regional forecasting system may or may not be effective in identifying regional markets that will outperform a national benchmark. Even if it is, this may not be of much use to the fund manager, because he/she may not recognise the region as a useful way to think about the market. A more technical challenge to the usefulness of the region is the possibility that there may be greater windows of opportunity within a region than between regions.

For US and UK cities, the windows of opportunity (mean average deviations from the mean) have been considerably greater at the city level than at the regional level. In addition, it appears that greater forecasting success has been associated with city-level work than with regional forecasts. City selection has been a vital input into fund management strategy. In China, for example, there has been a switch in focus from first-tier to second-tier cities, irrespective of region.

However, portfolio structure is difficult to categorise by city. This is not a holistic system, because even if every city and town in China was covered by the benchmark database, there would still be outliers that fall outside defined city boundaries. This presents an attribution problem.

17.5.6 Two or Three Terms?

The relative importance of structure and stock is as much a matter of philosophy as of statistical evidence. When calculating the attribution scores, there is also disagreement over the appropriate number of attribution components, and how they should be interpreted.

Brinson *et al.* (1986) identify three attribution components: timing (which is analogous to structure in our terminology), stock selection, and an 'other' or 'cross-product' term. The cross-product term is effectively a residual component that, mathematically, reflects an additional combined contribution of timing and selection. Their interpretation of what are termed timing and selection components broadly coincides with structure and stock selection components as defined in this chapter, but they do not offer an explanation of how the 'other' term relates to the objectives or management of the portfolio.

Subsequent authors, and suppliers of performance measurement services, divide into two camps. Experts either follow a decomposition method which calculates structure and selection scores separately from the cross-product component, or prefer to incorporate the cross-product term in either the structure or selection component, arguing that it has no useful meaning or is mathematically troubling.

According to Burnie *et al.* (1998), the cross-product term:

> *...represents the interaction of two other attribution effects but ... is not itself directly attributable to any one source of active management. It is therefore usually reallocated to another attribution effect or, if it remains isolated, is an ambiguous term whose value may exceed the measured effects of active management, thus rendering analysis results inconclusive.*

Hamilton and Heinkel (1995) and the Property Council of Australia, however, follow the three-component route, and go beyond Brinson *et al.* in suggesting how the cross-product term may be related to management decisions. As put by Hamilton and Heinkel:

> *...the cross-product credits a manager for overweighting an asset class in which he or she out-performs the properties in that asset class in the RCPI (Russell Canadian Property Index).*

The argument we adopt is to support the three-component approach: this is because, in practice, the cross-product rewards an observable management approach in real estate, where persistently overweighting a segment is justified by skilled staff demonstrating consistently good stock selection in that segment. The cross-product is also an increasingly important measure of manager/fund selection in a fund of funds or multi-manager context (see Chapter 11).

17.5.7 The Formulae

The dominant method of performance measurement expresses the performance of the portfolio against a benchmark as a relative return, based on the ratio of the two rates rather than the simple difference:

$$\textit{Relative return} = \left(\left(1 + \textit{portfolio return}\right) / \left(1 + \textit{benchmark return}\right) - 1\right)$$

So, a portfolio return of 10% against a benchmark return of 5% gives a relative return of 4.8%:

$$\textit{Relative return} = 1.10 / 1.05 - 1 = 4.8\%$$

This formula ensures that components of return and returns annualised over a run of years maintain consistent relative results, which is not possible if simple differences are used to compare returns.

Attribution scores are built up from comparisons of weights and returns in each segment of the market. Separate structure and selection scores in each segment are summed across the portfolio, to produce the portfolio-level structure and selection scores which account for relative return.

The two- and three-component methods of attribution calculate structure scores in exactly the same way. In each segment:

$$Segment\ structure\ score = (portfolio\ weight - benchmark\ weight) * benchmark\ return$$

The alternative ways of calculating stock selection scores are as follows:

Two-component attribution method segment selection score:

$$= Portfolio\ weight * ((1 + portfolio\ segment\ return) / (1 + benchmark\ segment\ return) - 1)$$

Three-component attribution method segment selection score:

$$= Benchmark\ weight * ((1 + portfolio\ segment\ return) / (1 + benchmark\ segment\ return) - 1)$$

The difference lies in a single term. The three-component method multiplies segment relative returns by the benchmark weight, while the two-component method multiplies by the portfolio weight. When calculated using the two-component method, the structure score and selection score in each segment add up to the weighted contribution to relative return. Summed across segments, the structure score and selection score add up to the portfolio's relative return.

In the three-term method, the structure and selection scores do not add up in this way, leaving a 'residual' term, the cross-product, which is the product of the segment relative returns multiplied by the difference between benchmark weight and the portfolio weight (sometimes known as the 'bet'). This is calculated as:

$$Cross\text{-}product = relative\ return - ((1 + structure\ score) * (1 + selection\ score) - 1) * 100$$

This cross-product or interaction term, as it is also known, has been a source of much disagreement amongst practitioners. Most studies and performance measurement suppliers use the two-component method outlined above or incorporate it in the structure score. However, we prefer to relate the cross-product term to management decisions. We suggest that a positive cross-product term reflects a manager's decision to focus on a segment where they have 'stock' skills or specialisation. Keeris (2005) highlights the potential importance of the cross-product term and shows that when portfolios are structured in increasingly different ways to the benchmark, the relative importance of this third, cross-product, term grows.

The cross-product is also of clear relevance to multi-manager or fund of funds portfolios, as it can be used to indicate the portfolio manager's success in allocating money to the best fund managers, particularly at the higher-risk (value-added or opportunity fund) end of the market.

17.5.8 Results from Different Attribution Methods

Case 1 stands as an example of the differences in the message delivered to a fund manager by different choice of attribution methods.

Case 1

A fund achieved the following result in 2020. Using simplified arithmetic for demonstration purposes and using the three-component attribution method:

$$Outperformance(1.0) = structure(0.1) + stock(-0.4) + cross\text{-}product(1.3)$$

What do these results signify concerning the relative importance of structure and stock? If the cross-product is treated as part of stock selection, as in the most common two-component system:

$$Outperformance(1.0) = structure(0.1) + stock(0.9)$$

Stock selection contributes 90% of outperformance.

If the cross-product is allocated to structure, as proposed by Burnie *et al.* for a portfolio constructed by bottom-up selection of individual assets with passive structure:

$$Outperformance(1.0) = structure(1.4) + stock(-0.4)$$

Stock selection damages performance.

The choice of method is clearly non-trivial in this example. Different methods show results which differ in direction as well as scale.

Case 2

The performance of a European property share vehicle which was managed by a UK fund manager was as follows, net of the effect of cash:

$$Outperformance(-2.9) = structure(-0.1) + stock(-2.0) + cross\text{-}product(-0.8)$$

The fund was overweight in countries where stock selection was poor and underweight in countries where stock selection was good, especially the UK. It would not be a surprise to the UK manager to learn that the stock selection score was better in the UK, but it may be distressing for him to realise that the stock selection underperformance was exaggerated by nearly a full point because of fund structure. Did he take account of expected superior UK stock selection in his asset allocation?

In the ideal world, an attribution analysis should be 'carried out within a framework that mirrors the investment policy and decision making process particular to the fund under examination' (Burnie *et al.*, 1998).

17.6 ATTRIBUTION AND PORTFOLIO MANAGEMENT: ALPHA AND BETA

17.6.1 Alpha and Beta Attribution: An Introduction

The best real estate performance analysis systems will begin to utilise performance concepts widely used in other asset classes which have also seen the development of fund formats. The asset classes that are most relevant are private equity funds and hedge funds, and the most interesting attribution development in these markets is the concept of alpha and beta separation.

What creates beta, and what drives alpha in real estate investment? How can these concepts be measured and isolated? How do they relate to traditional attribution systems? Can performance records and performance fees adequately distinguish between these drivers?

There are many references to alpha and beta as sources of risk-adjusted performance in alternative asset classes, with most work focused on hedge funds (see, for example, Litterman, 2003). The concept of alpha and beta is drawn directly from Sharpe's capital asset pricing model (CAPM): see Sharpe (1964). Anson (2002) describes the CAPM as a regression model which can be used to determine the amount of variation in the dependent variable (the fund return) that is determined or explained by variation in the independent variable (the appropriate market return):

$$\textit{Investment return} = \alpha + \beta * \textit{benchmark return} + \varepsilon$$

The important measure of manager performance is the intercept term α, which represents the excess return earned by the fund over and above that of the benchmark. However, it is important that this is measured as a risk-adjusted return, in other words that the effect of pure risk is taken out of the intercept.

The security market line (SML) posits that higher-risk assets and portfolios should earn higher returns. A higher-risk portfolio should outperform a lower-risk portfolio on a risk-unadjusted basis. This does not mean that the manager has shown any skill. However, outperformance of the SML implies that skill has been demonstrated and this is measured by the intercept term, or alpha, as illustrated in Figure 17.1.

It is possible to measure alpha and beta for a property fund, provided that we have a series of fund returns and a series of appropriate benchmark returns over the same period. This is achieved by regressing the fund returns on the benchmark returns and

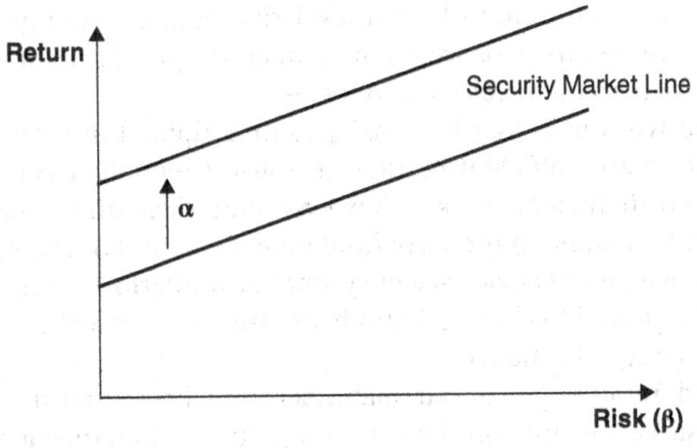

FIGURE 17.1 Alpha and beta

Source: Baum and Farrelly (2009), after Sharpe (1964).

observing the measured values of alpha (α) and beta (β). A value for β in excess of unity implies that fund returns are highly sensitive (or geared) to the market return, suggesting high-risk assets, a high-risk portfolio, or a high-risk strategy. A high value for α suggests that an excess return has been earned by the fund over the risk-adjusted benchmark return.

17.6.2 Sources of Alpha and Beta

Positive alpha represents outperformance of the SML and implies that the manager has demonstrated skill. In property fund management, managers can exercise skill when structuring their portfolios from a top-down perspective (allocating to markets and sectors) and at the stock level (sourcing and managing their assets). Outperformance at the portfolio structure is delivered by managers who, *ceteris paribus*, allocate relatively more to outperforming sectors or geographies. This implies that the manager has a forecasting capability, which is a source of outperformance.

As noted by Geltner (2003), alpha in property management can arise from operational cost control, tenant relationship management, asset maintenance, leasing strategy, marketing and capital expenditure applied to asset enhancement/refurbishment. Alpha can also be generated when assets are bought and sold. For example, managers who are able to purchase assets at discounts, recognise latent value that is not reflected in valuations, or negotiate attractive prices, and who have the ability to execute more complex deals and thus face less competitive pricing will, *ceteris paribus*, outperform their benchmarks.

Property investment risk (beta), like alpha, can be broadly separated into both structure and stock beta. Within the constraints of a domestic benchmark 'structure', beta arises from allocations to more volatile sectors such as central business district office markets. When mandates allow for global investment, exposures to more risky geographies – such as emerging markets – are then a source of additional risk.

Stock-level beta is an area of potential confusion. For example, development can often be referred to as a source of alpha in a given portfolio. This is incorrect *per se*, as development in itself is simply a more risky property strategy and should be reflected in a higher beta. Development alpha is obtained by being an outperforming development manager. There is a continuum of asset-level risk ranging from ground rent investments, to assets with leasing risk and high vacancy, to speculative developments, all of which should have a hierarchical range of betas.

The received wisdom is that it is easier to find alpha, those returns that are due to manager skill, in an inefficient market. It is also generally accepted that commercial property is an inefficient market; however, empirical studies do not find strong evidence of delivered alpha in property fund management. For example, Mitchell and Bond (2008) discovered little evidence of systematic outperformance for most property fund managers but found that a small number of funds in the top decile showed persistent risk-adjusted outperformance.

Mitchell and Bond suggest that manufacturing beta exposure (mimicking the returns of the market) is difficult, because property is a heterogeneous asset class. A large number of properties are required in order to get down to systematic risk levels, as suggested by Baum and Struempell (2006), who showed that specific risk is a function of lot size and diversification efficiency, meaning that it is difficult to diversify away risk if the portfolio is exposed to sectors in which the performance of individual assets is similar and where lot sizes are high.

When we consider these factors in the context of unlisted funds, alpha and beta separation is somewhat easier. This is dealt with in Section 17.7.

17.7 PERFORMANCE MEASUREMENT AND RETURN ATTRIBUTION FOR PROPERTY FUNDS

17.7.1 Introduction

Table 17.13 shows that over the 29-year period to 2018, UK property (as measured by the IPD annual index) delivered an average total return of 7.6% (4.8% in real terms). This covers a challenging period including two severe real estate corrections, but given that pension funds are believed to seek real returns of 4–5%, UK property appears to have delivered this. Over the same period, all UK property funds (core to opportunity) delivered an average return of 5.5% (2.6% in real terms), and balanced (diversified, generally lower-risk) funds delivered a return of 6.6% (3.7% real). Both had higher volatility than the IPD annual index. The average tracking error against the annual index over 1990–2018 was 3.82%, and 86% of funds in the IPD balanced universe delivered over 200 bps of tracking error.

These are worrying statistics, as (if the UK is representative) they question whether investors can capture the risk and return characteristics of the asset class through investments in funds. To this must be added qualifying questions derived from Chapter 11. Is it unfair or unwise to aggregate all funds? Are core and opportunity funds different?

From Chapter 11, we know that Type A funds typically have lower absolute risk and return objectives, but they may also be required to deliver against a relative return objective. If investors are seeking to capture the risk and return characteristics of the asset class, this implies that some degree of index tracking is available. This cannot easily be delivered through building a direct property portfolio, as specific risk is very great (see Chapters 1 and 15), derivatives are not widely available (see below), and REITs are more equity-like (Chapter 13). If a degree of index tracking is available from any executable property strategy, then (index derivatives apart) core/core-plus funds

TABLE 17.13 UK market and property fund return and risk, 1990–2018

	Return	Risk	CV
Equities	7.72%	15.46%	2.00
Government bonds	7.67%	8.60%	1.12
Property	7.64%	9.09%	1.19
IPD all funds	5.52%	13.07%	0.42
IPD balanced funds	6.58%	9.43%	1.43

Source: MSCI.

should be the best available route to this. Have core funds delivered? Have they tracked the direct property index?

How has the performance of core and opportunity funds compared over periods of market strength and market weakness? How risky are Type B relative to core funds? Can the relative performance be explained by leverage? What has been the alpha delivered, and what beta describes the performance of each fund category? In addition, we may want to know whether the vintage (launch date) of a fund is important, and whether managers can boost returns through good timing of money invested and withdrawn.

Type B funds will be expected to have higher absolute risk and return characteristics and (assuming that the index or benchmark is dominated by core property and unleveraged), should not be index tracking. Have these funds delivered higher returns? How risky have they been? Have performance fees been fairly earned?

17.7.2 The Asymmetry of Performance Fees

Performance fees may be charged by managers of unlisted funds, especially those at the riskier end of the spectrum, and will be related to absolute or relative returns. It can be expected that more focus is placed on defining and distinguishing alpha and beta investing in real estate funds, if only because performance fees charged purely for beta are commonplace, yet arguably unfair. This issue, among others, will add to the debate about transparency which is necessary to bring self-regulation to a growing and globalising market for real estate funds. Aided by the participation of world-class global managers and investors, real estate funds are likely to be the engine which drives best practice in a truly international real estate market.

Since the mid-1990s, fund managers have been able to raise significant capital for unlisted funds which reward them with performance fees, without the manager necessarily being able to provide clear evidence of historic outperformance against market benchmarks or targets. Higher fees should be earned only for demonstrable alpha, as pure risk-taking with client capital is not a skilful activity, and delivering leveraged market return is a pure beta activity. We also know that the impact of performance fees/carried interest is to create an asymmetric incentive for the manager: see Figure 17.2. If returns are low, investors participate fully in any loss of their capital; if returns are high, their participation in the upside is limited by carried interest.

Note: the manager's carried interest or performance fee is 20% on all returns over 10%, with no catch-up.

Table 17.14 shows the delivered and expected returns on a series of high-return funds with typical performance fees or carried interests. The average difference between the gross of fees IRRs earned by the fund and the net IRRs delivered to investors is just over 5%, or just over 20%, or one-fifth of the gross IRR. This is a substantial additional fee load for the investor and should therefore be justified in a relative context.

The fee impacts shown in Table 17.14, explained by 'carried interest' or performance fees (see Chapter 10), seem high. High fees may be justified if the manager has earned the fee through the exercise of skill. But, as we have seen, a higher-risk portfolio should outperform a lower-risk portfolio on a risk-unadjusted basis. This means that

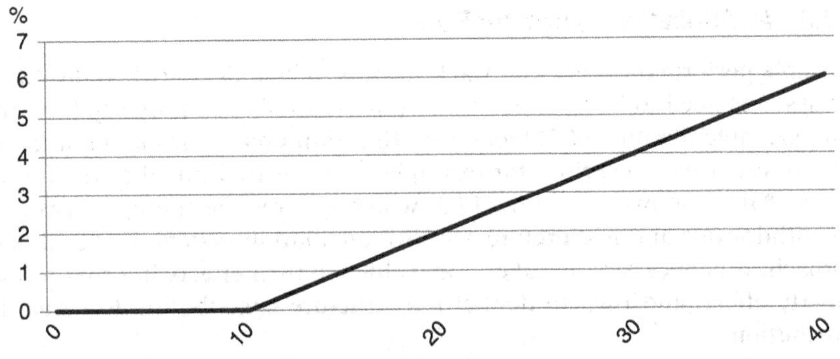

FIGURE 17.2 The impact of carried interest on investor returns (IRR, %)
Sources: PFR, ULI 2010.

TABLE 17.14 Total returns, fund series – fee impacts (rounded)

Fund	Gross IRR	Net IRR	Fee impact	Fee impact
1	29.0%	25.0%	4.0%	13.8%
2	17.0%	13.0%	4.0%	23.5%
3	33.0%	25.0%	8.0%	24.2%
4	35.0%	30.0%	5.0%	14.3%
5	27.0%	21.0%	6.0%	22.2%
6	46.0%	37.0%	9.0%	19.6%
7	21.0%	16.0%	5.0%	23.8%
8	34.0%	27.0%	7.0%	20.6%
9	16.0%	13.0%	3.0%	18.8%
10	20.0%	15.0%	5.0%	25.0%
11	18.0%	14.0%	4.0%	22.2%
12	20.0%	16.0%	4.0%	20.0%
13	14.0%	12.0%	2.0%	14.3%
14	20.0%	15.0%	5.0%	25.0%
Mean	25.0%	19.9%	5.1%	20.5%

Source: Baum and Farrelly (2009).

the manager could earn a high fee by taking risk with the client's capital. Performance fees should reward alpha, but they may reward pure beta.

In addition, performance fees may represent a form of free option (asymmetrical, as options tend to be) for the manager. High returns may lead to high fees (there is an 85% correlation between the gross IRR and the fee impact in Table 17.14) and limit the investor's upside without limiting the manager's upside; while the opposite situation may describe the downside, as the investor will suffer directly, but the manager will not. Hence there is a large incentive for managers to create high returns, which is good; but whether alpha or beta delivers those returns may be immaterial, and that is not good.

17.7.3 An Attribution System for Funds

To enable performance fees and track records to be judged, risk and return attribution systems need to be developed for property funds and property fund managers. As an example, Baum (2007) focuses on the additional return and risk contribution of fund structure – gearing, for example – to the traditional structure and stock factors. This is shown in Figure 17.3, which ignores the timing of cash injections and withdrawals and is therefore a TWRR attribution system. Under this proposed approach, it is necessary to take away vehicle return effects in order to expose the property effect, and then to deduct the structure contribution to reveal the stock contribution.

Fund structure is a factor specific to property held in a vehicle or wrapper. This factor will have an impact on the returns from listed REITs and property companies and from unlisted funds alike. There are two main drivers of the fund structure impact: fund expenses and management fees, and leverage.

If all portfolio segments are of similar risk, then positive excess returns generated by the portfolio structure relative to a benchmark will produce alpha. If they result from taking overweight positions in high-risk markets, then they generate beta. In the context of unlisted funds, which are largely owned by diversified investors or by fund of fund managers, much of this risk is diversified away. Hence, unless we can observe a strong bias to emerging markets in the portfolio structure, we can suggest that structure contributes alpha.

The same argument can be broadly applied to stock. Property selection can deliver higher initial returns through skill or through taking risk, but unless we can observe a strong bias to risky property types through, for example, pure development exposure or high vacancy rates, the stock impact can be assumed to deliver pure alpha. This taxonomy is illustrated in Figure 17.4.

Finally, the unlisted fund draws capital from investors over a period of time, which could be as much as 4 years (see Chapter 11). The timing of the drawdown is within the manager's control, meaning that an IRR approach is appropriate for return measurement. The benchmark, however, will report a time-weighted return, so that the difference can be attributed to investment timing and fund drawdowns.

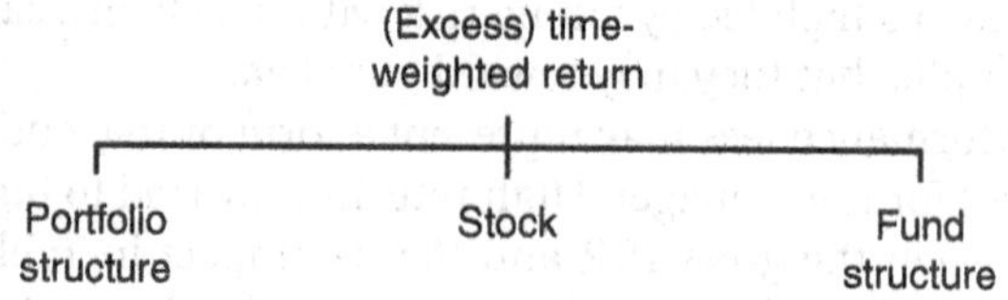

FIGURE 17.3 TWRR attribution for a property fund

Source: Baum and Farrelly (2009).

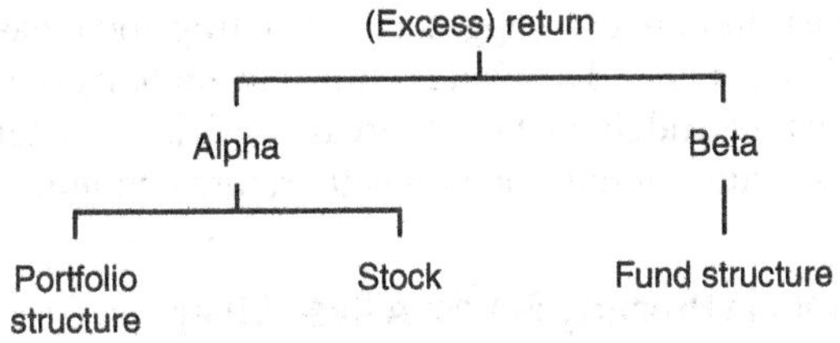

FIGURE 17.4 Time-weighted alpha and beta attribution for a property fund
Source: Baum and Farrelly (2009).

We arrive at a four-stage first tier of alpha/beta IRR attribution, illustrated by Figure 17.5. This is as follows:

- Fund structure, which is largely the leverage impact, will contribute primarily to beta. Fees will limit the return, however created, and performance fees create a non-symmetric return delivery which is problematic for investors and can, for ease, be assigned to beta.
- Portfolio structure needs to be judged as either an overweight position to more risky markets, or less risky markets, which will produce a beta impact, or as a set of positions with no greater or lesser market risk, in which case any extra return created through portfolio structure is wholly alpha. For most core and core-plus funds this is most likely to be an alpha-generating activity.
- Stock selection also needs to be judged as favouring more or less risky assets, which will produce a beta impact, or as a set of investments with no greater or lesser market risk, in which case any extra return created through stock selection is wholly alpha. For most core and core-plus funds, this is most likely to be an alpha-generating activity.
- The return impact of timing is attributed to the movement of capital into and out of the fund. The manager's skill in investment timing, which is an alpha activity, would be reflected in this effect. This will be of greater importance in value-added and opportunistic funds, which have shorter investment horizons and look to distribute capital back to investors more quickly.

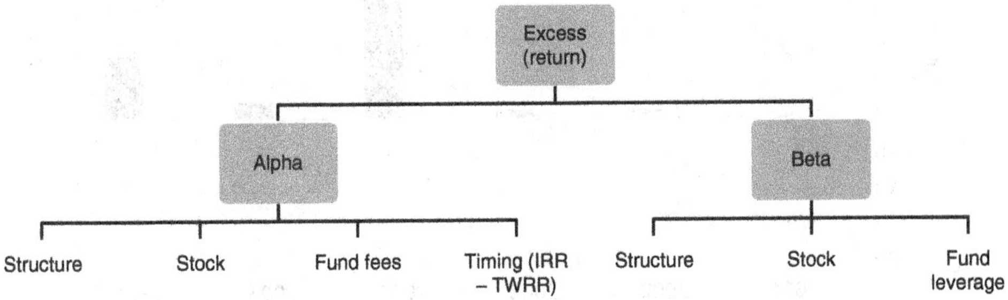

FIGURE 17.5 Money-weighted (IRR) return attribution for a property fund
Source: Baum and Farrelly (2009).

None of the above is intended to suggest that isolating and measuring alpha or beta will be easy or non-controversial. The choice and/or availability of benchmarks, in particular, are limiting factors. Judging whether greater risk is being taken at the structure or stock level will be a matter of opinion and is therefore a pragmatic question.

17.7.4 Alpha and Beta in Property Funds: A Case Study

We use a case study to illustrate the property fund attribution framework set out above.

The case study examines a closed-ended value-added UK-focused unlisted fund, which commenced its acquisition programme in the fourth quarter of 2001 and was effectively liquidated by the fourth quarter of 2006. Quarterly performance data was made available for this entire period, although we only had sufficient data to conduct full attribution analysis from the first quarter of 2002. The fund purchased 22 assets with an average book cost of £4.5 million and a total portfolio book cost of £99 million. Equity contributions totalled £26 million and leverage ranged from 65% to 70% throughout the fund's life.

The average holding period of the assets was 2.5 years. The manager was looking to exploit deal-making and transaction skills. This level of turnover is not unusual for value-added and opportunistic funds, but it is relatively high. As a result, capital was distributed back to investors soon after the investment period had been completed, as illustrated by the overall cash flows of the fund shown in Figure 17.6. Thus, the timing effect was expected to be significant.

For property fund attribution analysis, both the fund and property-level time-weighted returns were available, but only cash flow data at the fund level was available. The property-level time-weighted returns were calculated by IPD and the time-weighted fund returns and cash flow data for the fund were provided by the

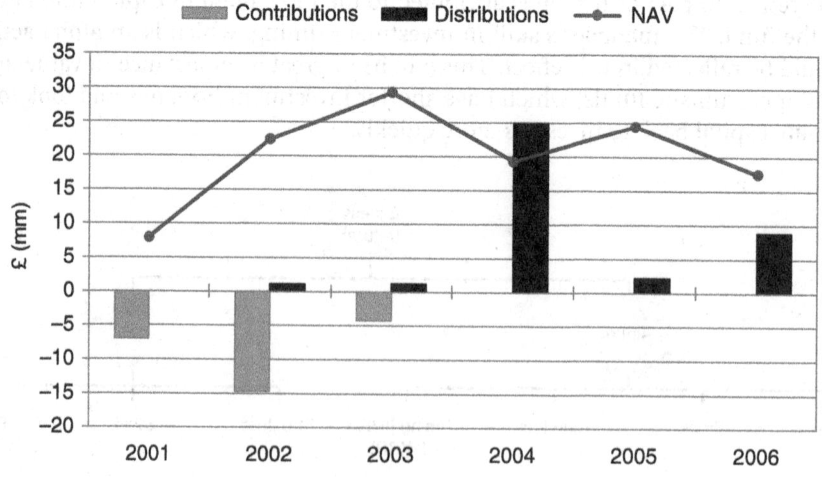

FIGURE 17.6 Cash flow profile, case study fund

Source: Baum and Farrelly (2009).

manager. (We excluded the first quarter's performance for detailed attribution analysis as time-weighted property level returns were not available.)

The fund had a mandate to invest across the UK, so we chose to perform the property fund attribution analysis against the UK IPD universe. The fund was very concentrated from a portfolio structure perspective, with holdings in only 4 of the 12 UK PAS segments and 55% in one of these. Under Baum and Key's (2000) style definitions, we would label this fund manager as specialist, where the manager is holding high weights in segments where selection skills are believed to be strong.

The results of the attribution analysis are detailed in Table 17.15. Addressing property-level performance first, the fund has produced relative outperformance of 1% p.a. over the 5-year measurement period. The manager has underperformed, due to portfolio structure, by almost 2% p.a.

Performance attribution suggests that the manager has outperformed due to stock selection. With such a relatively high stock score and relatively concentrated segment exposures, we can say that the manager has outperformed by concentrating on preferred segments. However, at this stage we cannot be sure whether this outperformance has been driven by any alpha, or is simply the result of higher relative risk in the portfolio.

TABLE 17.15 Property fund return attribution

	2002	2003	2004	2005	2006	*5 year*
Property level						
Property TWRR	12.6%	10.5%	23.7%	25.5%	8.8%	*16.0%*
Benchmark TWRR	9.2%	10.5%	17.4%	19.1%	18.5%	*14.9%*
Relative	3.1%	0.0%	5.4%	5.4%	−8.2%	*1.0%*
Structure score	−2.8%	−3.4%	−2.3%	0.6%	−0.2%	*−1.6%*
Selection score (two component)	5.7%	3.4%	6.9%	4.7%	−8.0%	*2.4%*
Fund level						
Gross TWRR	15.7%	20.1%	73.1%	52.3%	5.1%	*31.0%*
Gross fund structure score	2.8%	8.7%	40.0%	21.4%	−3.4%	*12.9%*
Net TWRR	11.8%	16.7%	57.6%	40.1%	8.7%	*25.6%*
Fee reduction	−3.4%	−2.9%	−8.9%	−8.0%	3.4%	*−4.1%*
Fee reduction	25.0%	17.1%	21.1%	23.3%	−70.1%	*17.2%*
Net fund structure score	−0.7%	5.6%	27.5%	11.6%	−0.1%	*8.3%*
Net IRR						*29.9%*
Timing score						*4.3%*

Source: Baum and Farrelly (2009).

The fund structure effect is presented on a gross and net basis. The gross total returns encompass leverage and all expenses associated with the fund bar investment manager fees, inclusive of performance fees.

The gross structure added 12.9% to the property-level return. Fees to the fund manager reduced the gross structure effect by 4.1% (or 17.2% in relative terms). Outperformance peaked in years 3 and 4 of the fund, when investments were being realised and value-added initiatives completed.

Finally, over the measurement period the timing of property cash flows added 4.3% to the time-weighted total return, to give investors an IRR of 29.9%. We were unable to conclude how much of this was attributable to alpha, although we suspected that the manager had delivered outperformance given the relatively short holding period of assets in the portfolio. (Whether IRR maximisation over TWRR is in the investor's interest is a moot point.)

The fund's annualised total time-weighted return over the measurement period was 25.6% against its benchmark return of 14.9%. However, the fund's annualised standard deviation was 23.0% compared to the benchmark equivalent of 5.3%. Figure 17.7 shows the annual return series relative to a fund benchmark.

We then employed the CAPM to assess the risk-adjusted performance of the fund in terms of alpha and beta to complement the above attribution analysis. The result is an alpha of zero but a positive and significant beta (see Table 17.16).

Unfortunately, the CAPM regression is not particularly robust statistically, with the alpha coefficient being insignificant. However, the beta coefficient is significant and the equation provides some insight into performance, suggesting that much of the delivered outperformance was a result of a high beta. The high beta reflects the level

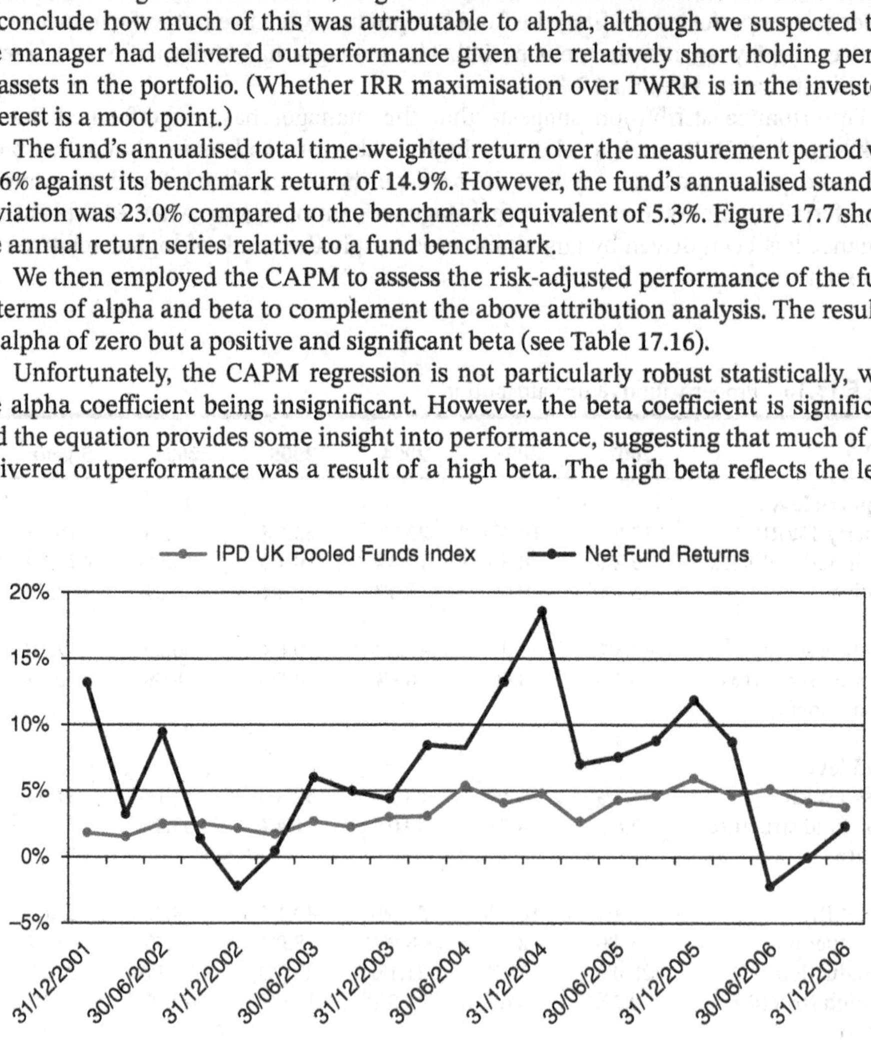

FIGURE 17.7 Quarterly time-weighted returns – fund vs. IPD index

Source: Baum and Farrelly (2009).

TABLE 17.16 Case study alpha and beta estimates for case study net total returns

	Alpha	Beta
Coefficient	0.00	1.73
***t*-statistic**	−0.04	1.98
R^2	0.18	
Observations	20	

Source: Baum and Farrelly (2009).

of gearing at the fund level, and the asset level and portfolio structure risk. The performance data suggests little evidence of alpha.

This is a small fund, and statistical significance may be elusive. Nonetheless, a regression-based CAPM approach confirms that there is no evidence of alpha in these performance results. Beta, in contrast, is significant. We now test whether this is a generalisable result by examining a large sample of core and opportunity funds.

17.7.5 Unlisted Fund Performance: Empirical Evidence

Property Funds Research (PFR) completed work for the Urban Land Institute (ULI) in 2010 which compared direct property returns with core/core-plus fund returns and opportunity fund returns. This work has enabled us to answer some challenging questions about fund performance.

The Data

The 2010 PFR work compared direct property returns, using the IPD global index and the indexes of the constituent countries/regions; core/core-plus fund returns using the IPD pooled fund indices and the NCREIF/Townsend US core fund index; and opportunity fund returns using investor reports, manager reports, and the NCREIF/Townsend US opportunity fund index. In addition, PFR collected primary data on fund performance with the result that the total sample included the accepted core fund universe and 273 opportunistic funds with a value of $428 billion, around 38% of the estimated opportunity fund universe.

It is important to state the limitations of this work. First, do we really know what investors want? If not, how can we challenge the delivered returns? Second, this was clearly a highly unusual period, and this is a relatively new industry, with insufficient consistent data to draw very strong conclusions. Third, we are not confident that measures of annual returns for opportunity funds are meaningful, as we are not sure that all the funds in our sample have revalued annually. Consequently, there is some potential confusion hidden within a multiplicity of different return measures, including annual total return, TWRR, and IRRs.

Relative Returns

Table 17.17 shows that opportunity funds outperformed in the strong market, and underperformed in weak markets, as should be expected. Over the whole period they outperformed core funds in all markets, as they should.

Alpha and Beta

With respect to alpha and beta, we would expect the following results. Core funds should deliver beta of around 1.0, index tracking, with low or no leverage. This should be statistically significant. Opportunity funds should earn higher returns, and show higher beta, although this should be less statistically significant. Opportunity funds will have a higher spread of returns than core, and much of the return will be explained by leverage.

Leverage has doubled in European core funds from 17% in 2003 to 30% in 2009: the average is 20–25%. However, the performance of European core funds, for example, appears to fit 35% leverage better, as shown in Figure 17.8, which compares the delivered returns on European core funds with the return that would have been delivered by the European property index had it been 35% leveraged. This is evidence of a high beta, which is only partly explained by leverage.

Table 17.18 shows that core funds have delivered statistically significant betas of between 1.4% and 1.6% p.a. in all markets, all higher than should be expected. Core funds have delivered tracking errors of around 5-6% in all markets, again higher than should be expected (strong doubts exist about the quality and replicability of the underlying benchmark in many markets around the world, but this is part of the problem for investors). This means that for 2 years in 3, returns will typically be the index return plus or minus 5–6%; 1 year in 3, returns will be more than 5–6% above

TABLE 17.17 Core and opportunity funds – relative returns

(Europe)	2003–6	2007–9	2003–9
Core	11.81	−8.71	2.5
Opportunity	24.5	−14.5	3.64
Relative	12.7	−5.79	1.13
(NA)			
Core	15.12	−9.87	3.66
Opportunity	32.89	−17.49	8.34
Relative	17.77	−7.62	4.68
(Global)			
Core	12.96	−8.62	3.15
Opportunity	37.73	−22.68	7.54
Relative	24.77	−14.06	4.39

Sources: PFR, ULI 2010.

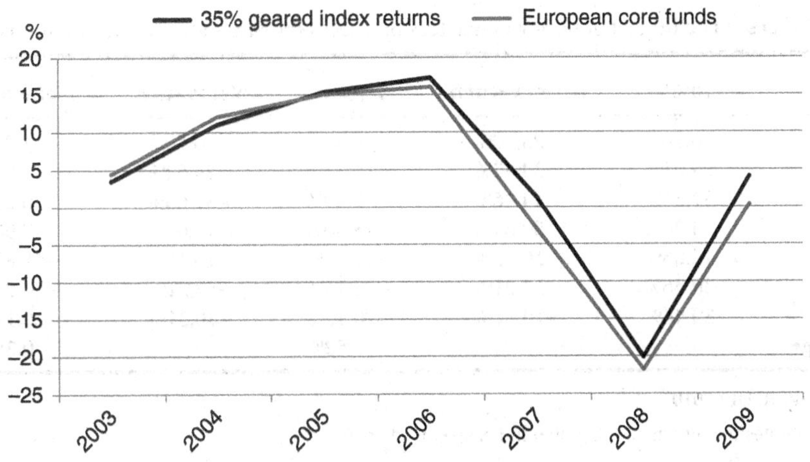

FIGURE 17.8 European core fund returns and the leveraged index
Sources: PFR, ULI 2010.

TABLE 17.18 Global core and opportunity funds – alpha, beta, and tracking error

	Alpha	Beta	*t*-Stat (α)	*t*-Stat (β)	R^2	Tracking error
Europe core	−3.88	1.61	−3.58	13.01	0.97*	5.45
NA core	−3.84	1.36	−4.11	20.63	0.99*	4.96
Global core	−6.30	1.63	−6.97	18.60	0.99*	5.81
Europe opportunity	−6.32	3.09	−1.40	5.96	0.88	19.37
NA opportunity	−2.41	2.34	−0.51	7.07	0.91	20.44
Global opportunity	−8.64	3.60	−0.91	3.89	0.75	29.01

Sources: PFR, ULI 2010.

or below the index return. Using the European core fund beta in a CAPM framework would imply a risk premium of 1.6 times the property risk premium, which is 4.8% if the market premium is 3%. This suggests that funds need to deliver returns 2% above the market, not more than 1% under the market as Table 17.16 suggests has been the case in the UK.

Table 17.18 also provides evidence of negative alpha everywhere, suggesting that it is difficult for managers to match the returns on a property index, even when the impact of fees is adjusted for.

Highly significant negative alphas of 4–6% are only partly explained by annual management fees, which are typically between 0.5% and 1%; in addition, the mean tracking error is over 5%, when the equivalent value for an equity market tracker would likely be below 20 basis points.

TABLE 17.19 The impact of performance fees on excess returns – all opportunity funds

	70%*	Gross return	Excess	Net return	Net excess
2003	16.70%	23.10%	6.40%	20.50%	3.80%
2004	24.61%	34.32%	9.71%	29.52%	4.91%
2005	37.37%	44.46%	7.09%	37.66%	0.29%
2006	34.74%	50.64%	15.90%	42.64%	7.90%
2007	22.05%	10.15%	−11.90%	10.15%	−11.89%
2008	−30.46%	−53.21%	−22.75%	−53.21%	−22.74%
2009	−30.46%	−10.31%	20.15%	−10.31%	20.15%
Average			3.52%		0.35%

Sources: PFR, ULI 2010.

Note: * denotes the return on the global index leveraged at 70%.

European opportunity funds have delivered a very significant beta of over 3. The (barely significant) alpha is negative, and more than 6% prior to performance fees. North American funds have been better performers. The highly significant negative alpha is about the same as in Europe, but core beta is lower, and opportunity alpha is less negative. Opportunity fund betas range from 2.3% in North America to 3.6% p.a. for the global fund sample, all statistically significant, around twice the core fund betas. Leverage explains the majority of the higher beta. There are some very big winners and losers (fat tails), and a negative skew, meaning that investors are more likely to do very badly than very well.

Table 17.19 shows the impact of performance fees in the global opportunity fund sample, which includes value-added and opportunity funds aimed at Europe, Asia, North America, and the global market. The excess return above a global benchmark adjusted for the average leverage level of 70% is around 3.5%. Unfortunately, when the impact of (notional) performance fees is taken away, the net excess just about disappears.

Timing: IRR and TWRR

Interestingly, it should be noted that opportunity funds typically change performance fees on IRRs, not TWRRs. Although the sample is very small, all funds for which we have data on IRR and TWRR over a complete fund life show a higher IRR and a positive timing effect.

IRRs and Vintage Year

Opportunity funds have delivered average IRRs of −7% with a standard deviation of over 30% in 2003–9 and a range of over 150% p.a. Average returns vary by vintage year, 2002 being best, and 2007 worst, and fund selection risk varies considerably by vintage year, peaking in 2006. Vintage year – and manager – diversification is clearly important for investors.

17.8 CONCLUSION

This chapter is concerned with performance measurement and attribution analysis. We presented and discussed ways of *measuring* performance in order to judge whether investors or managers have been successful. We also presented ways of *attributing* performance of single properties, of portfolios, and of funds, which is a means of understanding how the return was achieved in order to judge where the manager succeeded, or failed.

Performance measures exist, first and foremost, to show whether a portfolio has achieved a rate of return better or worse than the 'market' average, or has met specified investment objectives. Benchmarking has answered the question: *by how much* did we outperform (underperform) the target return or benchmark? There follows an inevitable demand for portfolio attribution analysis which addresses the question: *why* did we outperform (underperform) the benchmark?

We can separate total return into income return and capital return. We can examine the relative and separate impacts of cap rate change, rental growth, and lease effects. We can separate structure and stock contributions, and we can think about alpha and beta effects. All of these offer useful ways of thinking about success or failure *ex post*, and better strategies *ex ante*. Performance measurement can tell us whether a policy, or style, has delivered; whether it has been right to enter a particular market; and whether a manager or fund has been successful.

The growth seen in the unlisted market has helped facilitate growing cross-border property investment in Europe and across the world, and unlisted funds have become a preferred conduit. However, it appears that core funds have failed to track the property index, while opportunity funds have delivered higher returns only at the cost of taking large risks with investors' capital. It appears that many of the performance fees paid have not been fairly earned, and this lays down a clear challenge to the fund industry as it emerges from the credit crisis.

What will the future hold? We will examine the possibilities in Chapter 18.

CHAPTER 18

Conclusion

18.1 WHY PROPERTY?

Real estate is an interesting asset class. It appears to be capable of offering diversification against stocks and bonds, and good and steady real returns of around 4–5%. However, the experience of property investors in the early 1990s was enough to persuade many of them that it was time to abandon the asset class. The experience gained in the late 2000s will have had the same effect on some. Yet since 2000 many investors have discovered the appeal of private assets, or real assets, or alternatives, all of which categories include a high allocation to real estate. So the asset class remains of appeal to most professional investors, and the key question for these investors is not whether to invest, but how to invest.

Given the issues presented in Chapter 1, the fundamental problem confronting property investors and property investment managers is this: to achieve a diversified, reasonably liquid property portfolio which delivers pure property-style returns, replicating the return on a property index without specific risk, thereby offering steady real returns and diversification against stocks and bonds.

In Chapter 1, we showed how direct property indexes suggest that real estate offers moderate returns for low risk with reasonable diversification prospects, and that these three characteristics make a strong case for a significant real estate allocation. The result of using UK return, risk, and correlation data in a modern portfolio theory framework is a huge property allocation of between 55% and 80%; using more plausible US 1991–2018 data, shown again in Table 18.1, property comprises between 39% and 58% of the optimal or efficient portfolio at all target return levels.

Yet the actual allocation for UK institutional investors in 2019 was around 10%, a quarter to one-sixth of the optimised level. What explains the huge difference between unconstrained theory and practice? An explanation of the difference between theory and practice lies in the way in which property investment strategies can pragmatically be executed. These execution strategies have at various times overstated the attractions

TABLE 18.1 Illustrative asset class allocations (USA, 1979–2018)

Target return	Volatility	US property	US stocks	US bonds
8.00%	4.6%	39%	5%	56%
9.25%	6.2%	58%	24%	18%
10.50%	10.3%	41%	59%	0%

Sources: MSCI, PFR.

of direct real estate, of Real Estate Investment Trusts (REITs), and of unlisted funds, both core and opportunity. The reasons are as follows:

1. Standard deviations of returns from year to year understate true property risk, and correlations between property and other assets may be unreliable. In addition, year-on-year correlations between the asset classes may be said to be of limited interest to pension funds and insurance funds with longer-term liabilities, and in the longer term correlations between asset classes tend to increase.
2. The data used in optimisation exercises typically describes the returns available on the index universes of asset classes. For stocks and bonds, it is possible for investors to replicate these universes in an investment portfolio, as they are highly divisible assets and index-tracking products are available. For property, however, the universe is not investable. The investor therefore faces an additional layer of risk, specifically the sampling error created by the heterogeneity and specific risk of real estate.
3. The majority of property transactions involve the use of leverage. The use of the ungeared returns presented by MSCI and NCREIF in their performance analyses may not be fully representative of the risk and return profile of the (often geared) investment vehicles used by investors.
4. Real estate, unlike securities, is not a liquid asset class. This problem is not reflected in the unadjusted risk, return, and correlation data, which therefore overstates property's attractiveness. Yet, the introduction of liquidity into a property structure can significantly change the return characteristics of real estate to the point that it ceases to be attractive. Arguably, therefore, illiquidity is a necessary evil in justifying the role of real estate in a portfolio, but it is an evil that clearly reduces the attraction of the asset class.
5. Property investment may require the services of specialist fund managers who typically charge *ad valorem* annual management charges as well as performance fees.

These issues all challenge the value of a gross-of-tax-and-fees unleveraged universe of returns in deciding on an allocation to commercial property. Adding the operational challenges of investing in real estate alongside faster-moving securities, it is not surprising that allocations do not reflect the outputs of an MPT optimiser. Adding again the challenges of cross-border real estate investment (taxes, currency risk, and so on), it is hardly surprising that investors think twice before committing to an investment strategy which includes more than a notional real estate allocation.

However, the world is witnessing a fourth industrial revolution. What lessons have we learned to temper any excitement that tech-driven entrepreneurs might bring to the table? Given these lessons, to what extent can technology and innovation address real estate's fundamental challenges, and move real estate allocation closer to the optimised portfolio – or, alternatively, provide us with better data which finally puts to rest any idea that real estate should form more than (say) 15–20% of any portfolio?

18.2 LESSONS LEARNED

18.2.1 Liquid Structures

In the 1990s and in the run-up to the global financial crisis (GFC), it became acutely apparent that the liquidity of property was not the same as the liquidity of equities and bonds, and owners found it very hard to sell assets. The property investment market became fascinated by the potential for the securitisation or unitisation of real estate. REITs became popular, as did commercial mortgage-backed security (CMBS) structures.

But property is illiquid, which means that its required – and expected – return is higher than it would otherwise be. Theory suggests that introducing liquidity to property may damage returns, as the illiquidity premium may be eroded. Theory was borne out in practice. REITs have been volatile, and the securitisation of commercial mortgages neither increased transparency nor dampened the real estate cycle as expected. In the years following the crisis, untold losses for investors in CMBS and collateralised debt obligation (CDO) issues revealed themselves. More liquidity led to negative returns. It took a real estate crash and the consequent absence of liquidity to re-establish the conditions for good returns in the 2011–19 period.

More recently, wise investors have discovered that REITs can provide some portfolio liquidity as well as the opportunity to arbitrage public and private markets, without the volatility or stock market-dominated performance that a wholly public equity portfolio can deliver. Institutional investors can use REITs in this way as a tactical allocation device, shifting holdings within the real estate portfolio or to gain rapid exposure to real estate. However, for this to happen efficiently we will need to be able to sell direct or unlisted fund holdings when we want to upscale our REIT holdings. This is not possible at the time of writing, because there is not enough unpriced liquidity in the fund market to permit this arbitrage.

It would make sense for tech platforms to develop deep secondary markets both for assets and for unlisted funds. CBRE's Property Match has made some inroads, but there is no technical reason why a deeper and broader marketplace should not follow. Primary market capital raising is hugely inefficient, as is the exit process for closed-ended fund investors, and the technology is available to improve both processes. In 2019 we heard a lot about asset tokenisation (fractionalisation) and the liquidity improvements that might follow; if this idea gains traction, fund tokenisation could follow. But we remain unconvinced that real estate can become a truly liquid asset class while retaining the other investment characteristics which make it attractive in a multi-asset portfolio.

18.2.2 Unlisted Funds

Surveys have consistently shown that diversification is a powerful driver for pension funds and insurance companies to become involved with real estate as an investment. Diversification surely works only as long as the asset is truly different, so taking away the illiquidity and the physical, heterogeneous, commodity nature of real estate would take away a large part of its diversification potential, and a large part of its appeal. Hence, unlisted funds and joint ventures have become more popular than REITs for those seeking real estate exposure.

However, the consequences of leverage and the market crisis of 2007–9 are disturbing for real estate funds. While unlisted fund net asset values (NAVs) may continue to track the direct property index and demonstrate high correlation, there is less reason to suppose that trading prices of funds on the secondary market – or the prices received by investors exiting open-ended funds – will always stick closely to NAV. And as globalisation and the unlisted fund took off together in the real estate market, we discovered issues that made international investing challenging.

The credit crisis of 2008–9 made us think about the asset a little differently, and exposed dangerous practices related to leverage and the fund structures we developed. The combination of lumpiness, illiquidity, leverage, and cross-border investment, often inseparable, created a doubt as to whether it is possible to capture 'pure' real estate returns as they are often advertised.

The data we presented regarding fund performance in Chapter 17 has some sobering implications. Table 18.2 shows risk and return data and Table 18.3 shows correlation data for the UK, using the unleveraged real estate index, as before, but adding two more lines for somewhat leveraged but generally core-type funds.

Using property fund data suggests that property is a less attractive asset class than it appears to be using (largely uninvestable) property index data based on the valuations of directly held property assets. Although the correlations are largely unaffected, returns are lower and risk is higher. As we cannot yet buy an index exposure through a derivative in many markets (see below), the performance characteristics that produce the allocations in Table 18.1 are elusive. The best we can do may be even less attractive than what is expressed in Table 18.2, because we cannot buy all funds. Nonetheless, the data therein will undoubtedly be closer to something that is executable.

TABLE 18.2 Risk and return, major assets, and property funds (UK, 1990–2009)

	Return	Risk	CV
Equities	8.08%	17.54%	0.46
Gilts	8.61%	8.37%	1.03
Property	6.78%	10.77%	0.63
IPD all funds	5.52%	13.07%	0.42

Sources: MSCI, PFR.

TABLE 18.3 Correlations, major assets, and property funds (UK, 1990–2018)

	Equities	Gilts	Property
Equities	1		
Gilts	0.12	1	
Property	0.42	−0.14	1
IPD all funds	0.37	−0.18	0.98

Sources: MSCI, PFR.

While many core funds have failed to track the property index, opportunity funds have delivered generally higher but very variable returns, at the cost of taking large risks with investors' capital. It appears that many of the performance fees paid were not fairly earned, and this lays down a clear challenge to the property fund industry as it emerges from the credit crisis. Core funds need to focus on delivering consistent, index-type relative returns, while opportunity funds need to prove that extra returns can be delivered through skill, or alpha.

18.2.3 International Investing

In Chapter 16 we noted that international property investment can be complex, primarily because of the impact of tax and currency issues and other barriers which place non-domestic buyers at a disadvantage. However, the growth seen in the unlisted market has helped facilitate growing cross-border property investment in Europe and across the world, and unlisted funds have become a preferred conduit to international investing.

As a result, a professional investor may develop a global strategy using MSCI/NCREIF data and then collect together in one place the problems of currency and tax plus leveraged but imperfectly diversified funds. Will this give us diversification against stocks and bonds, and good and steady real returns? To answer this honestly requires a lot of thought on behalf of investors and managers. The best will make it worthwhile, but the others may be disappointed.

18.2.4 Best-Practice Real Estate Investing

To deliver good and steady real returns from real estate will require excellence in the investment process. To be an excellent global property investor will mean the following:

- understanding the nature of the asset class;
- being able to develop and execute a strategy that captures the asset's more attractive characteristics;
- using vehicles and structures that do not wreck the proposition;
- avoiding unmanageable and poorly understood international risks while making the most of the opportunities for diversification and return that are presented; and
- knowing at what price to buy.

If we had to rely on one skill alone, understanding prices and anticipating rises and falls in value would be the vital component of excellent investing. How can this skill be developed?

18.2.5 Pricing

In Chapter 2 we presented three lessons that might have told us we were heading for trouble in 2007. These were as follows.

First, too much lending to property is dangerous. The coincidence of geometric increases in lending and a following crash is not accidental.

Second, the risk premium in property cap rates should be mean-reverting relative to real bond yields, and the empirical evidence is highly supportive. It is easy to conclude that there is a natural or mean risk premium, and that when cap rates are driven to abnormally low levels, reducing the available premium as happened in 2006, a rise back towards the norm is inevitable.

Third, we should keep an eye on yields on index-linked bonds. UK property yields have moved in line with index-linked bond yields since the recovery from the 1990–2 crash, since when the average premium of property cap rates over index-linked yields was around 5%. By the end of 2006, the difference between property cap rates and index-linked yields had closed from a mean of 5% to a new level of around 2.5%. This suggested that property yields were already too low and the rise that followed was predictable. Since 2009, the gap has looked bigger than usual, creating the conditions for sustained good returns.

In Chapter 3 we suggested that both theory and empirical evidence suggest a strong long-run correlation between rents and inflation. If real rents rise strongly, a downward correction can be expected, and buying at low real rent levels is likely to be a good idea.

From this base, understanding the return delivered by real estate is not complicated. The delivered long-term return on real estate is produced by the cap rate, or initial yield, plus net nominal rental growth. There is a strong relationship between net nominal rental growth and inflation, and real rental growth has been close to zero.

We can therefore suggest that the delivered long-run return on real estate is produced by the cap rate, or initial yield, plus inflation. Cap rates have a rational or fair value relative to indexed bonds, and overpricing should be apparent by this measure. When cap rates are low by this measure, returns may be poor, as in the period following 2006; when cap rates are high, as in 2009, there will be an additional source of return to harvest.

18.3 THE FUTURE

18.3.1 The *PropTech* Explosion

As is happening with many other industries, technology is beginning to disrupt how the traditional real estate industry operates. The introduction of technology generally creates process efficiencies through automation, scale, and uniformity, which we believe is occurring in the real estate industry after years of underinvestment. These new technologies are creating better consumer experiences and more productive agents, all while the real estate industry is being tasked with becoming more compliant as the regulatory spotlight brightens.

In our opinion, these new technologies will either improve or replace most value propositions that have long been the status quo in the real estate market. Therefore, we view the next few years as an opportune time for entrepreneurs, venture capitalists, private equity, and corporations to re-evaluate how they perceive that technological advancements and changing consumer behaviors will drive the outcome for the next real estate cycle.

We expect that the single-family, multifamily, and commercial real estate sectors will be materially affected by technology, each at different speeds and in different ways.

William Blair, 2015

There is no denying the huge energy, creativity, and optimism behind the 2015–20 wave of activity that makes up the so-called PropTech explosion (Baum, 2017). Thousands of extremely clever people, backed by billions of dollars of often expert investment, were working extremely hard to change an old-fashioned and inefficient industry that can be improved by idealism and which earns huge fees for professional advisors. The heterogeneity and illiquidity of the industry goes some way to explaining those fees; advisory work is very often customised because there is no velocity of repeat business. Much of the activity was aimed at the way real estate is traded. Can it produce more velocity; more homogeneity; more commoditisation of processes; lower transaction fees; and a more tradeable, more liquid asset class?

Idealism also drove a smart building movement and the application of shared economy principles to real estate. According to CBRE (2017), technology will play an ever greater role in how occupiers use and manage their office space:

Growth in the use of sensors, 'big data techniques' and predictive analytics to create strategies and manage portfolios more efficiently will sustain this trend. Underlying all of this is a desire on the part of corporations for greater operational flexibility in their real estate arrangements.

There are bigger forces at work. Figure 18.1 (from Baum, 2017) suggests that big, or exogenous, tech will produce non-real estate innovations such as driverless cars, airborne cars, and drones which will change the configuration and locational qualities of logistics space, retail space, parking, and residential property. We can imagine a landscape of high-rise, high-density urban buildings surrounded by low-rise, low-density agriculture, warehousing, and parking sites.

Robotics and machine learning will lead to the automation of many office jobs. Some worry that this will seriously damage the demand for office space, and they might be right. But there will be some growth, if only for tech, robotics, drones, driverless

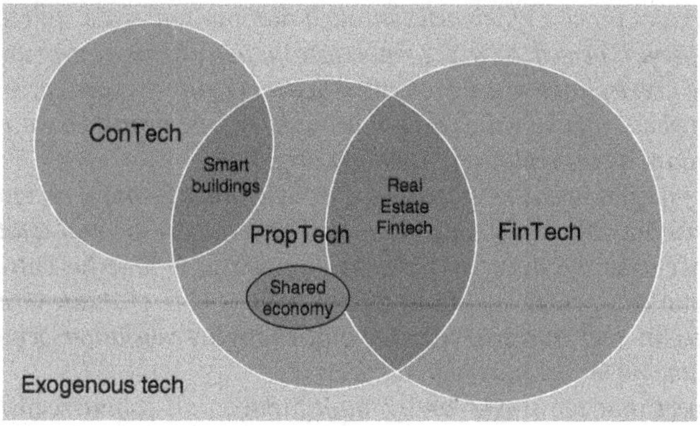

FIGURE 18.1 PropTech, ConTech, FinTech, and exogenous 'big tech'
Source: Baum (2017).

cars, and artificial intelligence (AI) lawyers, salesmen, and programmers. Co-working and automation are already here. Advances in voice recognition, AI, and mixed reality will change the way office workers interact with technology, and with each other. Software and hardware will continue to become cheaper and faster, with cheaper sensors and devices, significantly more data, and better transparency. According to IBM in 2017: '*90% of the data in the world today has been created in the last two years alone*'. We can expect to see more powerful analytics and predictive decision-making tools, decreased transactional friction, and increased resource optimisation – which may, of course, mean fewer office jobs and/or a radical change in the front-office/back-office relationship. The suburban office park could stage a comeback as a centre for more automated activities, with a blurring between the data centre and the decentralised, automated office building.

The growing confusion between retail and logistics space seems set to continue, as drones and driverless cars facilitate last-mile delivery. Again, the rebound of suburban development to hold warehousing and delivery functions alongside the automated office seems likely. Driverless and automated vehicles will change parking locations, which should move to the urban periphery.

Changing land use patterns will have a knock-on effect on residential locations. Continuing urbanisation and the vertical city – dependent on rail transport for lateral connections – will be encouraged by big tech, and it is those high-rise vertical constructs that will lend themselves to smart building technology and flexible use – co-living, co-working, and flexible rental/ownership.

Investable real estate will continue to migrate to new uses, mixed uses, and social infrastructure. As offices, retail, and logistics continue to evolve and mutate, the risk of these formats will rise, encouraging much greater investment in sectors that government is forced by budget rebalancing to retire from and which will require large private investment. This has already happened in student housing; other emerging private real estate sectors will include schools, universities, hospitals and medical centres, prisons, waste disposal and recycling facilities, parking for automated vehicles, fuel storage and generation facilities, and senior housing parks. Added to these will be the new investment sectors – data centres, co-working and co-living, rooftops, drone and driverless car parks, and a new generation of recycling plants creating energy and value from ever-increasing obsolescence and waste.

It seems highly likely that the sector definitions which we are currently familiar with – office, retail, industrial – will fade in importance as the multi-purpose high-rise building (already evident in cities such as Hong Kong and New York) will grow in dominance. More clustering of urban centres and vertical travel between co-living spaces, co-working spaces, corporate headquarters, hotels/gyms, shopping centres, schools, and medical centres is a natural development requiring only more flexible planning regulations and inventive design.

18.3.2 Smart Buildings and ESG

'Smart buildings' is a phrase used to describe technology-based platforms which facilitate the operation of real estate assets. The assets can be single property units or entire cities. The platforms may simply provide information about building or urban centre performance, or they may directly facilitate or control building services. This sector supports real estate asset, property, and facilities management.

Smart building tech is all about the efficient use of buildings and urban environments, about control and sustainable management. There is a huge appetite for power by tech firms, and energy costs will increasingly become internalised in property rents and pricing. New property sectors, including data centres, are emerging. Based on our expectations about the big tech impact on city form, there is a strong demand for growth in this sector. This is a natural growth area for PropTech, with the ConTech sector also playing a vital role, and requires much more focus by real estate professionals.

Given that the embedding of environmental, social, and governance factors into preferred investment criteria is likely to enhance performance and ensure that assets remain healthy, resilient and as obsolescence-proof as possible, we can expect smart buildings to drive ever-smarter real estate asset management.

18.3.3 Occupier Markets: Space as a Service

'The shared economy' describes technology-based platforms which facilitate the *use* of real estate assets. The assets can be land or buildings, including offices, shops, storage, housing, and other property types. The platforms may simply provide information for prospective users and sellers of space, or they may more directly facilitate or effect rent- or fee-based transactions. This sector supports the real estate occupier markets.

The shared economy could be a popular movement which is part way through a process of radically altering concepts of private property, health and safety regulation, and public liability. Airbnb and WeWork are immensely successful shared economy unicorns, but focused on the real estate industry.

However, an unlimited shared economy boom is very unlikely. While a continued increase in the use and supply of co-working spaces in more and more inventive locations (public facilities like schools and libraries, and shopping centres in particular) is to be desired and expected, and co-living propositions will cater for some slices of society, there are natural limits to this movement, which many see as a temporary fad. Co-living and co-working are economic necessities in the post-recession age, but have limited appeal for many of us. There are natural limits to sharing: collaborative consumption might be a long-term millennial preference, but it is much more likely to be age related. As families and responsibilities grow, a desire for more control is natural. The millennial generation for whom Uber, Airbnb, and the shared use of space are natural may be youthful idealists who will mutate into conservative property-owning and non-sharing parents. We have also seen that cultural differences reduce the appeal of sharing space in countries like China where there is weak copyright control.

Sharing will have limited appeal for users of real estate, and it will have even less appeal for operators. Co-working operators will naturally want to own and control buildings: successful operators of space often demonstrate conservatism and a desire to protect wealth by moving up the food chain and becoming property companies, and competition with traditional asset managers is inevitable.

Regulatory pushback may also inhibit the growth of this sector. We can imagine all sorts of disputes involving unprofessional lessors of not fit-for-purpose space and damaged renters. Because of concerns about its market impact and the potential misuse of residential property as quasi-hotels, Airbnb has already faced pushback in places like Barcelona and Berlin, and it has sued other cities, including its hometown of San Francisco, which recently passed a law requiring anyone who wants to rent out their home on Airbnb or similar platforms to register their property with the city of San Francisco. There is a limit to the idealism of collaborative consumption and the shared access economy.

18.3.4 Fractionalisation and Liquidity

Liquidity and Faster Transactions

Real estate FinTech describes technology-based platforms which facilitate the trading of real estate asset *ownership*. The assets can be buildings, shares or funds, debt or equity, freehold or leasehold, but must have a (negative or positive) capital value. The platforms may simply provide information for prospective buyers and sellers, or they may more directly facilitate or effect transactions. This sector supports the real estate capital markets.

The residential sector is clearly more compelling (bigger and more liquid) for investors than the commercial market. The greater the size of the capital stock, and the greater the velocity of turnover of assets in both sectors, the greater the volume of fee savings that will be made available for more investment in process improvements. The key question is therefore this: Can and will real estate FinTech improve liquidity and grow velocity?

We know that a significant financial benefit will flow to the innovators which can introduce more velocity and liquidity into real estate, and more efficient distribution. There is no doubt that information platforms are already helpful in lubricating the market. The main area of doubt is the potential for transactions to become faster and more efficient.

PropTech has the ability to bring increased market transparency, liquidity, and lower transaction costs. This should positively impact the value of investment assets. The digitalisation of both data and current processes is evident within the emerging technologies attempting to embed themselves into the transactions process. Digitalised data enables computer programs to automatically execute tasks without the need for human intervention. At its most ambitious and radical, the technology world imagines a single, distributed system of recording real estate ownership and transactions – the blockchain world – as the ultimate solution. This blockchain world is decades away, and may never happen unless it is mandated by regulation and/or supported by industry groups.

Within the commercial real estate sector, technology is digitising the current workflow, offering a more efficient transfer of information than a paper-based process. However, the lack of comprehensive digitalisation limits the automation of more arduous tasks. An openly accessible, single pool of up-to-date, standardised property information could reduce most of the causes for delay highlighted.

An example of standardised property information is the property passport, a digital file containing the legal and physical data relating to an individual property, held and transferred along with its title. The idea of a single property information database somehow attached to the plot of land to be transacted is currently also being explored through the use of geospatial technologies. Using mapping and satellite technology it is possible establish an irrefutable plot boundary identifier upon which to link its legal documentation. Clearly, despite many start-up businesses evangelising about their vision, only a centralised land registry can drive this degree of change, but a fully digitalised land registry is a long way off for the UK and other developed countries.

The impact of technology will (in the absence of top-down regulatory change) be restrained by old-fashioned risk aversion and conservatism. *Caveat emptor* adds a hugely powerful dose of realism when a pension fund is acquiring a very complex commercial property. To reverse this would require a change in contract law – a little unlikely for such a fundamental and deeply embedded principle – or an institutionally agreed innovation such as an economical and standardised insurance product. For less complex residential property, if we can imagine the veracity of the data held in a property passport being guaranteed and backed by insurance, then the due diligence phase may be significantly quicker.

The public – all of us – will need to develop a much clearer sense of responsibility for collecting and storing data describing our most valuable assets, and a much better sense of the value of this data. Human beings will protect themselves in a *caveat emptor* world by taking their time and being thorough in the research process before committing large capital sums. Until we arrive at the instantaneous transaction, buyers and sellers will wish to pay professional advisors for risk mitigation and, on occasion, risk transfer.

The capability of the technology will easily outpace the capacity of the system to employ it, and radical change will be slow.

Tokenization and Fractionalization

We have witnessed a steady push towards the unitisation, fractionalisation, or democratization of individual real estate assets. This push has consistently proved unsuccessful, either because market conditions have not been right, limiting either or both of the demand and supply sides, or because regulatory and tax issues have not been dealt with.

In 2019 IPSX, a regulated exchange, was set up in London to trade shares in single-asset property companies. At the same time there has been a lot of noise made about the digital tokenisation of assets. Can IPSX create a successful secondary market for units in commercial real estate? Scepticism would be very natural, given the various failed attempts to introduce such liquidity and unitisation in previous decades, particularly when it is not obvious that technology has changed the nature of the required solution (a heterogeneous offering, through an efficient platform, and a large pool of qualified buyers). Property is illiquid, and (we repeat) theory suggests that introducing liquidity to property may damage returns, as the illiquidity premium may be eroded. Is the perfect world – adding liquidity without damaging returns or diversification – really possible?

Fractionalisation of debt and the tokenisation of (already fractionalised) funds make more sense (see Baum, 2020).

18.3.5 Derivatives

Unfortunately, continuous improvement towards a more efficient real estate market cannot be guaranteed, and nothing demonstrates this better than the real estate derivatives market. In the first edition of this book, we included a chapter on real estate derivatives, which had gained some traction in the UK and US markets, and elsewhere, by 2007. One result of the global financial crisis, partly regulation-driven, was a decline in appetite amongst banks and investors to grow this marketplace, so that in this second edition we can no longer justify a full chapter. A healthy real estate derivatives market remains a possible innovation, but by 2020 it is not the established market we had hoped for.

A derivative is a financial instrument whose value is 'derived' from the value of another asset or index, so that real estate derivatives would derive their value from real estate indices representing the underlying real estate markets. In its simplest form, a derivative represents a contract between two parties where one party wishes to increase his exposure to a certain asset and the other party wants to reduce his exposure to the same asset without trading the asset itself. Real estate derivatives could allow investors to increase and decrease real estate exposure without buying or selling properties.

Derivative transactions take place with minimal legal fees and transaction costs, so that due diligence is focused on third-party credit risk rather than the complexities of properties. Hence, derivatives could offer less expensive access to real estate exposure than investing directly or in some other indirect vehicles. Thus, derivatives potentially overcome many of the negative factors involved in investing in direct real estate, for example specific risk, illiquidity, and high transaction costs, and deal directly with the traditional inability of investors to hedge market risk. Derivatives could offer a well-diversified market exposure, allowing smaller-scale investors to achieve the desired result.

In the last decade many innovative property vehicles have been offered as solutions to this challenge. We have seen (in Chapter 12) that listed real estate equity securities are imperfect property investment vehicles due to their return characteristics. We also suggest in Chapter 11 that unlisted vehicles have their own particular challenges. Derivatives, or synthetics, on the other hand, appear to have the potential to overcome many of those challenges. Commercial real estate was, until recently and once more, the only major asset class without a well-developed derivatives market.

The first real estate-linked swap was launched in 1991 in the USA, but property index certificates (PICs), launched by Barclays in the UK in the mid-1990s, were the first popular commercial property derivative investments. Through these instruments, buyers were provided with synthetic returns matching the annual return on the IPD annual index. As in the bond market, the buyer pays a capital sum which is either par value or a price representing a premium or discount to par depending on demand in the market. The issuer provided a quarterly-in-arrears income based on the IPD annual income return, and following expiry the par value was repaid together with a large proportion of the capital appreciation in the IPD index.

A subset of a broader derivative 'structured note' market had been developed in the UK and more widely in the period post-2004 when tax and regulatory clarification made a property derivative market more efficient for institutional investors. Between 2004 and 2007 the UK property derivative market experienced significant growth until market expansion became capped by the global crisis. The UK accounted for 95% of global property derivative trading volume in 2010.

In 2006, the S&P CME housing futures and options contracts were launched in Chicago, based on the Shiller–Weiss indices, and in 2007 derivatives based on the Residential Property Index (RPX) developed by Radar Logic were created, with some initial success. CMBS swaps had also existed for some time in the USA, but a commercial derivatives market aimed at creating long/short US real estate equity exposure was slower to emerge. A total return swap based on the NPI was announced and offered by Credit Suisse First Boston (CSFB) in the USA in 2005, and in 2006 Real Capital Analytics and MIT announced a set of indices tracking US commercial property prices which were designed to be the basis for derivative trading. Total notional traded values reached $0.6 billion at the end of the first quarter of 2008 and then stalled.

The emergence of financial intermediaries (derivatives brokers, in particular) and the leading banks prepared to take positions, warehouse deals, and carry inventory costs was critical in the development of a more liquid market and the emergence of price signals, as were partnerships between real estate service providers and derivatives brokers (CBRE and GFI, DTZ and Tullett Prebon, for example). Initially, almost all trades were over-the-counter bipartite deals, although investment banks were active in arranging these deals. The UK market grew rapidly from this beginning, with outstanding notional principal passing the £1 billion mark by the end of 2005, £6 billion by the end of 2006, and £9 billion by the end of 2007.

Although trading volume fell as underlying asset market conditions worsened, there were 802 recorded trades in the UK in 2008, and for the first time volumes in the underlying market – albeit weak – began to converge with derivative volumes. The UK property derivatives market traded around £7.1 billion of trades in 2008; by comparison, there was £24 billion trading of direct UK property investments in 2008, down nearly 25% on 2007.

Since then, it is sobering to have to report that the volume of trading in the UK property futures market has fallen to zero following the result of the Brexit referendum in 2016. In what appears to have been a watershed moment following hot on the heels of the GFC, the uncertainty following the EU referendum has proven to be the death of the market in its current state. Fund managers and investors have instead chosen to manage market risk by using traditional asset allocation and risk management techniques.

MSCI Property Futures contracts continue to be listed on the Eurex Exchange, but in 2020 there was not enough expressed demand to get the market started again. In time, hopefully, this market is likely to make a comeback.

Outside the UK and USA, Listed Property Trust futures contracts have been traded on the Australian Stock Exchange and there are exchange-traded products based on the European EPRA indices. Residential property derivatives have been traded in Switzerland, and commercial real estate total return swaps based on MDCI/IPD indices have been traded in Australia, Canada, France, Spain, Germany, and Japan. In Hong Kong, Sun Hung Kai Financial and ABN AMRO jointly executed the market's first ever Asian property derivative, which was based on Hong Kong residential property.

The implications of an active property derivatives market are substantial, as the availability of property derivatives may increase the aggregate demand for commercial property as efficient risk management becomes possible. A successful traded futures market would mean that counterparty risk will disappear and more efficient price discovery will reduce barriers to entry. As the global commercial real estate derivatives market re-examines its options in the aftermath of the GFC and more invasive and inhibiting bank regulation, it is to be hoped that at some appropriate point property derivatives will offer increasing benefits to real estate investors, including risk management, more efficient portfolio rebalancing, and the potential for immediate exposure to new markets.

18.4 CONCLUSION

Looking into the future, there are opposite forces at work. The excesses demonstrated during the lead-up to the GFC created a reaction that values conservatism, low leverage, more modest fee structures, and stricter – or better – governance. At the same time, we must continue to innovate.

The real estate sector is ripe for change, being famous for its lack of capacity for deep and continuing innovation. Its capacity to resist change should not be underestimated. However, PropTech businesses will survive if they solve problems without duplication. If they do not, they are unlikely to gain a market. Some exist because technology makes things possible, but they do not serve an obvious need. The majority, however, create building blocks towards a more efficient property market.

A truly transformative PropTech movement is under construction. These firms will eventually bring efficiency and alignment to the market, but they will encounter behavioural obstacles, establishment reaction, and often financial calamity. There is an oversupply of activity in real estate FinTech, an excess of optimism in shared economy real estate, and a real need for smart buildings.

A reaction from protective governments and big business is inevitable. We have already described Airbnb's problems; other successful FinTech will run into similar issues. Unauthorised deposit holding, unregulated investment advice, unprofessional governance, inaccurate advertising and misrepresentation are all charges made against real estate FinTech start-ups.

The notion that qualified, experienced professional advisors can be replaced by customer feedback is fanciful. The human factor will reassert itself in a variety of ways. Traditional business formats capturing tech for their own benefit will hit back and compete with purely digital offerings.

An improvement in the liquidity of unlisted holdings can be expected. While real liquidity is neither possible nor clearly desirable in the private equity real estate market, we can expect to see secondary trading platforms that help investors to manage mixed portfolios of listed and unlisted property, particularly at the core end of the market. But the world cannot be perfect.

In Chapter 1, we listed the perceived problems associated with real estate as an asset class.

1. Property is a real asset, and it wears out over time, suffering from physical deterioration and obsolescence, together creating depreciation.

   Can technology remove this problem? Will the limitations of physical space designed for a specific purpose clash with shared economy and multi-use repurposing? We will see winners and losers. It is clear that some buildings will be repurposed, but we will need more urban high rises and some property types will find themselves in the wrong locations, too far from the front office, the communications network and power.

   The increased pace of change will likely increase obsolescence, especially of energy-inefficient buildings that are incapable of becoming smart buildings.
2. The cash flow delivered by a property asset is controlled or distorted by the lease contract agreed between owner and occupier. US leases can be for 3 or 5 years, fixed or with pre-agreed annual uplifts. Leases in continental Europe may be 10 years long, with the rent indexed to an inflation measure. Leases in the UK for high-quality offices are commonly for 10 years, with rents fixed for 5-year periods after which they can only be revised upwards.

   The shared economy and the increasing pace of change both point to the need for shorter and more flexible leases, a development which is already in motion. We can expect to see more owner-operator landlords, characterised by the student housing and multi-family PRS sectors, as co-working and co-living operators merge with traditional property owners in their joint mission to create, own, and operate multi-purpose, energy-efficient, flexible space.

3. The supply side is controlled by planning or zoning regulations, and is highly price inelastic. This means that a boom in the demand for space may be followed by a supply response, but only if permission to build can be obtained and only after a significant lag, which will be governed by the time taken to obtain a permit, prepare a site, and construct or refit a property.

   Can tech really disrupt the real estate cycle? The much greater availability of information might just help to regulate and smooth away the boom and bust nature of the office market, as may the multi-purpose design of new space, but we would do well to remember that 'no developer ever turned down a bank loan'.
4. The returns delivered by property are likely to be heavily influenced by appraisals rather than by marginal trading prices. This leads to the concept of smoothing.

   Appraisals of commoditised property may become machine-generated in real time, but this is unlikely to affect large, complex assets. Shorter, more flexible leases may make real estate harder to value, as it will take on more equity-like qualities and look less like a bond. More liquid and unitised secondary markets might just begin to provide real-time transaction evidence and the much-needed velocity/liquidity, but this is not likely to happen quickly.
5. Property is highly illiquid. It is expensive to trade, there is a large risk of abortive expenditure, and the result can be a very wide bid–offer spread (a gap between what buyers will offer and sellers will accept).

   Crowdfunding platforms, on-line secondary market platforms, and blockchain make this the most intriguing of FinTech questions. Given the experience of the last 30 years, more liquidity will be very hard to effect, but it would change the nature of the asset class – not always for the best, as more volatility and equity market correlation is likely. However, greater unitisation and liquidity is something of a holy grail, and PropTech could just provide the key.
6. Property assets are generally large in terms of capital price. This means that property portfolios cannot easily be diversified, and suffer hugely from specific risk.

   Again, unitisation or fractionalisation is possible through the primary and secondary market platforms now being established. In 2011, we could see the potential for the development of a listed market for single assets; in 2019, this was introduced in the UK. Only time will tell whether this can lead to serious change.
7. Leverage is used in the vast majority of property transactions. This distorts the return and risk of a property investment.

   Nothing is likely to change, as peer-to-peer lending platforms and on-line mortgage apps will make sensible leverage easier to obtain.
8. The risk of property appears low. Rent is paid before dividends, and as a real asset property will be a store of value even when it is vacant and produces no income. Its volatility of annual return also appears to be lower than that of bonds. This is distorted somewhat by appraisals, but the reported performance history of real estate suggests a medium return for a low risk, and an apparently mispriced asset class.

   On-line marketplaces, if successful, will allow real-time pricing and introduce more volatility. As ever, the holy grail of greater liquidity without volatility will prove elusive.

Through wise reflection on what went wrong in 2006–9, coupled with sensible innovation, intelligent risk-averse professionals will strive to achieve reasonably diversified, not very liquid property portfolios which deliver something close to pure property-style returns, replicating the return on a property index without too much specific risk, thereby offering diversification against stocks and bonds and good and steady real returns in the long run. Others will continue to strive to 'shoot the lights out'. We wish them all success.

REFERENCES

CHAPTER 1

1. Barras, R. (1994). Property and the economic cycle: Building cycles revisited. *Journal of Property Research*, 11, 183–197.
2. Baum, A. (2007). Managing specific risk in property portfolios. *Property Research Quarterly (Netherlands)*, 6(2), 14–23.
3. Baum, A. and Crosby, N. (2008). *Property Investment Appraisal* (3rd edn). Blackwell: Oxford.
4. Baum, A. and Saull, A. (2019). *The Future of Real Estate Transactions*. University of Oxford Future of Real Estate Initiative: Oxford.
5. Baum, A. and Struempell, P. (2006). *Managing specific risk in property portfolios. Pacific Rim Real Estate Society Conference*, Auckland.
6. Brown, G.R. (1988). Reducing the dispersion of returns in UK real estate. *Journal of Valuation*, 6(2), 127–147.
7. Brown, G.R. and Matysiak, G.A. (2000). *Real Estate Investment: A Capital Market Approach*. Financial Times/Prentice Hall: London.
8. CBRE (2017). *How Much Real Estate? A Global City Analysis*.
9. DTZ (2015). *Money into Property*.
10. Elton, E. and Gruber, M. (1977). Risk reduction and portfolio size: An analytical solution. *Journal of Business*, 50(4), 415–437.
11. Evans, J. and Archer, S. (1968). Diversification and the reduction of dispersion. *Journal of Finance*, 23(4), 761–767.
12. Hodes Weill & Associates/Cornell University (2018). *2018 Allocations Monitor*. https://irei.com/news/target-allocations-real-estate-institutional-portfolios-continue-climb-2018
13. Litterman, R. (2003). *Modern Investment Management: An Equilibrium Approach*. Wiley: Chichester.
14. MacGregor, B. (1994). *Property and the economy. RICS Commercial Property Conference*, London.
15. Markowitz, H.M. (1952). Portfolio selection. *Journal of Finance*, 12(March), 77–91.
16. Morrell, G.D. (1993). Value-weighting and the variability of real estate returns: Implications for portfolio construction and performance evaluation. *Journal of Property Research*, 10, 167–183.
17. Pensions and Investments Online (2018).
18. Schuck, E.J. and Brown, G.R. (1997). Value weighting and real estate risk. *Journal of Property Research*, 14(3), 169–188.
19. Scott, P. (1998). *The Property Masters*. E&FN Spon: London.

CHAPTER 2

20. Galbraith, J.K. (1955). *The Great Crash*. Penguin: Harmondsworth.
21. MSCI (2019). *Real Estate Market Size* 2018.
22. World Bank (2020). *Doing Business*. https://www.doingbusiness.org/en/doingbusiness

CHAPTER 3

23. Lizieri, C. (2009). *Towers of Capital: Office Markets and International Financial Services.* Wiley-Blackwell: Oxford.
24. McCann, P. and Gordon, I. (2005). Innovation, agglomeration and regional development. *Journal of Economic Geography*, 5(5), 523–543.
25. Ricardo, D. (1817). *On the Principles of Political Economy and Taxation.* John Murray: London.
26. University of Aberdeen and IPD (1994). *Economic Cycles and Property Cycles.* RICS Books: London.
27. von Thünen, J.H. (1826). *The Isolated State.* Pergamon: Oxford [1966].

CHAPTER 4

28. Brown, G.R. and Matysiak, G.A. (2000). *Real Estate Investment: A Capital Market Approach.* Financial Times/Prentice Hall: London.
29. Fisher, I. (1930). *The Theory of Interest.* Porcupine Press: Chatham, MI [1977].
30. Gordon, M.J. (1962). *The Investment, Financing and Valuation of the Corporation. Irwin: New York. [Reported in Brigham, E. (1982). Financial Management: Theory and Practice (4th edn). Dryden Press: San Diego, CA.]*
31. Investment Property Forum (2011). *Depreciation in Commercial Property Markets.* IPF Educational Trust: London.
32. Van der Spek, M. and Hoorenman, C. (2007). *Duration Perspective of Real Estate Funds.* Europe Real Estate Yearbook.

CHAPTER 5

33. Baum, A. (1991). *Property Investment Depreciation and Obsolescence.* Routledge: London.
34. Damodaran, A. (2001). *The Dark Side of Valuation.* Pearson: London.
35. Investment Property Forum (2005). *Depreciation in Commercial Property Markets.* IPF Educational Trust: London.
36. Williams, J.B. (1938). *The Theory of Investment Value.* Harvard University Press: Cambridge, MA.

CHAPTER 6

37. Baum, A. and Crosby, N. (2008). *Property Investment Appraisal* (3rd edn). Blackwell: Oxford.
38. Grenadier, S. (1995). Valuing lease contracts: A real-options approach. *Journal of Financial Economics*, 38, 297–331.
39. Lizieri, C. and Herd, G. (1994). *Valuing and appraising new lease forms: The case of break clauses in office markets. RICS Cutting Edge Conference*, London.
40. Patel, K. and Sing, T.F. (1998). *Application of contingent claim valuation (real option) model for property investment analysis. RICS Cutting Edge Conference*, London.
41. Rowland, P. (1999). *Pricing lease covenants: Turning theory into practice. Pacific Rim Real Estate Society Conference*, Kuala Lumpur.

42. Ward, C. (1997). *Risk neutrality and the pricing of specific financial aspects of UK leases. RICS Cutting Edge Conference*, London.

CHAPTER 10

43. Miles, M., Netherton, N., and Schmitz, A. (2015). *Real Estate Development*, 5th edn. Urban Land Institute: London.
44. Peiser, R. and Hamilton, D. (2012). *Professional Real Estate Development*, 3rd edn. Urban Land Institute: London.

CHAPTER 11

45. Aarts, S. and Baum, A. (2016). Performance persistence in real estate private equity. *Journal of Property Research*, 33, 236–251.
46. Alcock, J., Baum, A., Colley, N., and Steiner, E. (2013). The role of financial leverage in the performance of core, value-add and opportunistic private equity real estate funds. *Journal of Portfolio Management*, 39(5), 99–110.
47. Baum, A. and Colley, N. (2017). Can real estate investors avoid specific risk? *ABACUS Journal of Accounting, Finance and Business Studies, Issue* 3.
48. Baum, A. and Struempell, P. (2006). *Managing specific risk in property portfolios. Pacific Rim Real Estate Society Conference*, Auckland.

CHAPTER 12

49. Baum, A. (2009). *Commercial Real Estate Investment: A Strategic Approach*. Elsevier: Amsterdam.

CHAPTER 13

50. Baum, A. and Turner, N. (2004). Retention rates, reinvestment and depreciation in European office markets. *Journal of Property Investment and Finance*, 22(3), 214–235.
51. Crosby, N., Hughes, C., and Murdoch, S. (2005). *Monitoring the 2002 Code of Practice for Commercial Leases*. Office of the Deputy Prime Minister: London.
52. Hoesli, M. and Oikarinen, E. (2012). *Are REITs real estate? Evidence from international sector level data. Swiss Finance Institute Research Paper No. 12–15.*

CHAPTER 14

53. Lewis, M. (1989). *Liar's Poker*. Hodder & Stoughton: London.
54. Reubling, C. (1970). *The administration of Regulation Q. Federal Reserve Bank of St. Louis Review*, Feb, 29–40.
55. Watkins, D., Egerter, D., and Hartzell, D. (2003). *Commercial real estate mezzanine finance: Market opportunities. Real Estate Issues*, Fall.

CHAPTER 15

56. Aarts, S. and Baum, A. (2016). Performance persistence in real estate private equity. *Journal of Property Research*, 33, 236–251.
57. Andonov, A., Kok, N., and Eichholtz, P. (2013). A global perspective on pension fund investments in real estate. *The Journal of Portfolio Management*, 39(5), 32–42.
58. Barkham, R. and Geltner, D. (1994). Unsmoothing British valuation-based returns without assuming an efficient market. *Journal of Property Research*, 11, 81–95.
59. Baum, A. (2015). *Real Estate Investment – A Strategic Approach* (3rd edn). Routledge: London.
60. Baum, A. and Colley, N. (2017). Can real estate investors avoid specific risk? *ABACUS Journal of Accounting, Finance and Business Studies, Issue* 3.
61. Baum, A. and Moss, A. (2012). *Are Listed Real Estate Stocks Managed as Part of the Real Estate Allocation?* EPRA: London.
62. Baum, A. and Struempell, P. (2006). *Managing specific risk in property portfolios. Pacific Rim Real Estate Society Conference*, Auckland.
63. Byrne, P. and Lee, S. (2001). Risk reduction and real estate portfolio size. *Managerial and Decision Economics*, 22, 369–379.
64. Callender, M., Devaney, S., Sheahan, A., and Key, T. (2007). Risk reduction and diversification in UK commercial property portfolios. *Journal of Property Research*, 24(4), 355–375.
65. Clayton, J. and MacKinnon, G. (2003). The relative importance of stock, bond, and real estate factors in explaining REIT returns. *Journal of Real Estate Finance and Economics*, 27, 39–60.
66. Hoesli, M. and Oikarinen, E. (2012). *Are REITs real estate? Evidence from international sector level data. Swiss Finance Institute Research Paper No. 12-15.*
67. Kennedy, P. and Baum, A. (2012). *Aligning asset allocation and real estate investment: Some lessons from the last cycle.* Henley Business School Working Paper.
68. Litterman, R. (2003). *Modern Investment Management: An Equilibrium Approach.* Wiley: Chichester.
69. Morrell, G.D. (1993). Value-weighting and the variability of real estate returns: Implications for portfolio construction and performance evaluation. *Journal of Property Research*, 10, 167–183.
70. Pagliari, J., Scherer, K., and Monopoli, R. (2003). Public versus private real estate equities. *The Journal of Portfolio Management*, 29(5), 101–111.

CHAPTER 16

71. Abramo, P. (2010). *Mercado informal y la producción de la segregación espacial en América. Latin American Real Estate Society Conference*, Chicago, IL.
72. Agnes, P. (2000). The "end of geography" in financial services? Local embeddedness and territorialization in the interest rate swaps industry. *Economic Geography*, 76, 347–366.
73. Baum, A. (2007). Managing specific risk in property portfolios. *Property Research Quarterly (Netherlands)*, 6(2), 14–23.
74. Baum, A. (2008). *Unlisted property funds: Supplying capital to developing property markets? International Real Estate Research Symposium*, Kuala Lumpur.
75. Baum, A. (2009). *Commercial Real Estate Investment: A Strategic Approach.* Elsevier: Amsterdam.
76. Baum, A. and Crosby, N. (2008). *Property Investment Appraisal* (3rd edn). Blackwell: Oxford.
77. Baum, A. and Murray, C.B. (2010). *Understanding the barriers to real estate investment in emerging economies.* University of Reading School of Real Estate and Planning Working Paper.

78. Baum, A., Fuerst, F., and Milcheva, S. (2015). Cross-border capital flows into real estate. *Real Estate Finance*, 31(3), 103–122.
79. Bekaert, G. (1995). Market integration and investment barriers in emerging equity markets. *World Bank Economic Review*, 9, 75–107.
80. Bekaert, G. and Harvey, C. (2002). Research in emerging markets finance: Looking to the future. *Emerging Markets Review*, 3, 429–448.
81. Black, F. (1974). International capital market equilibrium with investment barriers. *Journal of Financial Economics*, 1(4), 337–352.
82. Eichengreen, B. (2001). Capital account liberalization: What do cross-country studies tell us? *The World Bank Economic Review*, 15, 341–365.
83. Eun, C.S. and Janakiramanan, S. (1986). A model of international asset pricing with a constraint on the foreign equity ownership. *The Journal of Finance*, 41, 897–914.
84. Imazeki, T. and Gallimore, P. (2010). Domestic and foreign bias in real estate mutual funds. *Journal of Real Estate Research*, 26, 367–390.
85. Lahiri, S. (2009). Foreign direct investment: An overview of issues. *International Review of Economics and Finance*, 18(1), 1–2.
86. Leyshon, A. and Thrift, N. (1997). A phantom state? The de-traditionalisation of money, the international financial system and international financial centres. In Leyshon, A. and Thrift, N. (Eds.), *Money/Space: Geographies of Monetary Transformation*. Routledge: London.
87. Lizieri, C. (2009). *Towers of Capital: Office Markets and International Financial Services*. Wiley-Blackwell: Oxford.
88. Lizieri, C., Worzala, E., and Johnson, R. (1998). *To Hedge or Not to Hedge?* Royal Institute of Chartered Surveyors, June.
89. Lizieri, C., Baum, A., and Scott, P. (2000). Ownership, occupation and risk: A view of the City of London office market. *Urban Studies*, 37(7), 1109–1129.
90. Lizieri, C., McAllister, P., and Ward, C. (2003). Continental shift? An analysis of convergence trends in European real estate equities. *Journal of Real Estate Research*, 23(1), 1–23.
91. McAllister, P. and Lizieri, C. (2006). Monetary integration and real estate markets: The impact of the euro on European real estate equities. *Journal of Property Research*, 23(4), 289–303.
92. Montiel, P. and Reinhart, C. (1999). Do capital controls and macroeconomic policies influence the volume and composition of capital flows? Evidence from the 1990s. *Journal of International Money and Finance*, 18, 619–635.
93. Nishiotis, G.P. (2004). Do indirect investment barriers contribute to capital market segmentation? *The Journal of Financial and Quantitative Analysis*, 39, 613–630.
94. North, D. (1990). *Institutions, Institutional Change and Economic Performance*. Cambridge University Press: Cambridge.
95. Razin, A., Sadka, E., and Yuen, C.W. (1998). A pecking order of capital flows and international tax principles. *Journal of International Economics*, 44, 45–68.
96. Stulz, R.M. (1981). A model of international asset pricing. *The Journal of Financial Economics*, 9(4), 383–406.
97. Stulz, R.M. (2005). The limits of financial globalization. *The Journal of Finance*, 60, 1595–1638.

CHAPTER 17

98. Anson, M. (2002). *Handbook of Alternative Assets*. Wiley: Chichester.
99. Baum, A. (2007). Managing specific risk in property portfolios. *Property Research Quarterly (Netherlands)*, 6(2), 14–23.

100. Baum, A. and Farrelly, K. (2009). Sources of alpha and beta in property funds. *Journal of European Real Estate Research*, 2(3), 218–234.
101. Baum, A. and Key, T. (2000). *Attribution of real estate portfolio returns and manager style: Some empirical results. European Real Estate Society Conference*, Bordeaux.
102. Baum, A. and Struempell, P. (2006). *Managing specific risk in property portfolios. Pacific Rim Real Estate Society Conference*, Auckland.
103. Brinson, G., Hood, L., and Beebower, G. (1986). Determinants of portfolio performance. *Financial Analysts Journal*, 42(4), 39–44.
104. Burnie, S., Knowles, J., and Teder, T. (1998). *Arithmetic and geometric attribution. Journal of Performance Measurement*, Fall, 59–68.
105. Fisher, I. (1930). *The Theory of Interest*. Porcupine Press: Chatham, MI [1977].
106. Geltner, D. (2003). IRR-based property-level performance attribution. *Journal of Portfolio Management*, 29(5), 138–151.
107. Gordon, M.J. (1962). *The Investment, Financing and Valuation of the Corporation. Irwin: New York. [Reported in Brigham, E. (1982). Financial Management: Theory and Practice (4th edn). Dryden Press: San Diego, CA.]*
108. Hamilton, S. and Heinkel, R. (1995). *Sources of value-added in Canadian real estate investment management. Real Estate Finance*, Summer, 57–70.
109. Keeris, W. (2005). *An improved specification of performance; the interaction effect in attribution analysis. European Real Estate Society Conference*, Dublin.
110. Mitchell, P. and Bond, S. (2008). *Alpha and Persistence in UK Property Fund Management.* Investment Property Forum: London.
111. Sharpe, W.F. (1964). Capital asset prices: A theory of market equilibrium under conditions of risk. *Journal of Finance*, 19(3), 425–442.

CHAPTER 18

112. Baum, A. (2017). *Proptech 3.0: The Future of Real Estate. Said Business School, University of Oxford.*
113. Baum, A. (2020). *Tokenisation: The Future of Real Estate Investment?* Said Business School, University of Oxford.
114. CBRE (2017). *How Much Real Estate? A Global City Analysis.*
115. Baum, A. (2017). *Proptech 2020: The Future of Real Estate.* Said Business School, University of Oxford.

Glossary

Adjustable rate mortgage A mortgage loan whereby the interest rate changes on specific dates.

AFFO Adjusted funds from operations – recurring income delivered by properties owned by REITs adjusted for non-real estate depreciation and amortization and a straight-line rent adjustment.

Alpha The return delivered when the manager uses skill to outperform the market competition at the relevant risk level.

Amortization The process whereby the principal amount of a liability is reduced gradually by repayment over a period of time until it is paid off. The contrast to amortization is a bullet repayment, whereby the entire principal amount is repaid at closing. Scheduled amortization is not prepayment, which is the repayment of principal in advance of its scheduled date for payment.

Arbitrage The simultaneous purchase and sale of an asset in order to profit from a difference in its price, usually on different exchanges or marketplaces. An example of this is where a domestic stock also trades on a foreign exchange in another country, where its price has not adjusted in line with the exchange rate. A trader purchases the stock where it is undervalued and short sells the stock where it is overvalued, thus profiting from the difference.

Asset-Backed Securities (ABS) Bonds or notes backed by pools of financial assets. Such financial assets will generally have predictable income flows (for example, credit card receivables or vehicle loans) and are originated by banks and other credit providers.

ATER After tax equity reversion.

B loan The subordinate tranche in an AB structure.

B note The subordinate tranche in a CMBS structure.

B pieces Tranches of a CMBS issuance which are rated BB or lower and are therefore below investment grade.

Balloon loan A loan in which monthly payments of principal and interest during the period until maturity are not sufficient to fully amortize the loan. The balloon payment is the amount of remaining principal which is due upon maturity of the loan.

Basis Point (bp) One basis point is 1/100 of a percent, or 0.01%.

Basis ris The risk that payments received from an investment do not match the necessary payments out to bondholders. This arises from discrepancy between the indices to which the investment and liability are linked.

BER The breakeven ratio, which measures the ability of the income generated from the property to pay all expenses related to the operation of the property and all costs of repaying the mortgage.

Beta The return delivered when the manager exposes the client's capital to the market, taking a particular amount of market risk.

Blind pool or blind fund A real estate fund which has raised capital but not yet acquired any assets.

Bottom-up approach to investing A strategy adopted by an investor whereby the focus is aimed at individual asset deals, as opposed to top-down investing, whereby large-scale trends in the general economy are examined and assets selected which are likely to benefit from those trends.

BTCF The before-tax cash flow.

BTER The before-tax equity reversion.

Bullet loan A loan whereby principal is repaid in its entirety through a single payment at maturity.

Capital adequacy The obligation on a regulated entity (such as a bank or building society) to maintain a certain minimum level of capital in proportion to the risk profile of its assets. Such regulated entities may be able to meet the capital adequacy requirement by securitizing their assets and removing them from their balance sheet without recourse, thereby negating the obligation to maintain capital with respect to the securitized assets.

Capital return The change in value over the measurement period divided by the value at the beginning of the period.

Capitalization rate A measure of a property's value based on current rent and also a measure of investors' expectations. Calculated by dividing the net operating income for the year by the value of the property.

Carried interest The additional cash flow earned by a fund to be distributed to limited partner investors and the general partner sponsor according to the terms that were specified in the offering memorandum and limited partnership agreement. A fund might, for example, agree to distribute 80% of the remainder of the cash flows to the investors, and retain 20%. The 80% is referred to as the carried interest of the investor, and the 20% is the carried interest of the fund sponsor.

Cash flow waterfall The order in which the cash flow available, after covering all expenses, is allocated to investors or holders of the various classes of issued securities.

Cash-on-cash return A measure of the short-term return on property investment calculated by dividing the cash flow received from the property by the equity invested in the property.

Cash-out refinance mortgage loan A mortgage loan taken in order to refinance an existing mortgage loan in a situation where the amount of the new loan exceeds (by more than 1%) the amount required to cover repayment of the existing loan, closing costs and repayment of any outstanding subordinate mortgage loans. The borrower can put the additional cash to whatever use it pleases.

Catch-up A form of promoted interest designed to achieve a certain split of return between GP and LPs after a preferred interest has been provided.

Closed-ended fund A real estate fund from which investors cannot demand to have their capital redeemed or paid back, and which are not normally open to new investors to subscribe for new units for cash other than when formally capital raising. They are normally limited-life structures, but the term "closed-ended" means that a finite number of units will be in issue for long periods of time, unlike an open-ended fund.

Collateral Assets that have value to both a borrower and a lender and which the borrower pledges to the lender as security for the funds borrowed. Should the borrower default on its obligations under the loan agreement, the lender can apply these pledged assets to make good the default.

Collateralized Debt Obligation (CDO) A security backed by a pool of various types of debt, which may include corporate bonds sold in the capital markets, loans made to corporations by institutional lenders, and tranches of securitizations.

Commercial Mortgage-Backed Securities (CMBS) Securities that are backed by one or more pools of mortgages secured by commercial real estate, such as shopping centers, industrial parks, office buildings, and hotels. All principal and interest from the mortgages flow to the noteholders in a predetermined sequence.

Conduit The legal entity which provides the link between the lender(s) originating loans and the ultimate investor(s). The conduit purchases loans from third parties and once sufficient volume has been accumulated, pools these loans to sell in the CMBS market. In the European CMBS market the pool is generally of less than 20 loans with a wide or narrow range of properties. However, in the USA the pool may consist of anything between 50 and 100 loans secured on a wide range of properties.

Core-plus real estate investments Property investments that are relatively safe, but are riskier than core investments. Core-plus properties provide investors more opportunities to increase the rate of return but are slightly more risky.

Core real estate investments Property investments that have the following defining characteristics: they are substantially rented, they have an orderly lease expiration schedule, they are of high quality and are from the four basic property types – offices, industrial, retail, and multifamily. Core property must also be well maintained in a major city, carry no more than 50% debt, have low roll-over and an investment structure with significant control.

Credit default swap A contract whereby the protection seller agrees to pay to the protection buyer the settlement amount should certain credit events occur. This gives protection to the protection buyer, in return for which the protection buyer will pay the protection seller a premium.

Credit enhancement An instrument or mechanism which operates alongside the mortgage collateral to enhance the credit quality of mortgage-backed or other securities and thereby support the desired credit rating of the securities.

Cross-collateralization A provision by which collateral for one mortgage also serves as collateral for other mortgage(s) in the structure. This is a technique for enhancing the protection provided to a lender which adds value to the structure and therefore is a form of credit enhancement. Generally seen in connection with commercial mortgage loans.

Debt service The scheduled payments on a loan, including principal, interest, and other fees stipulated in the credit agreement.

Debt service coverage ratio (DCR, or DSCR) The net cash flow generated by an income-generating property on an annual basis divided by the annual debt service payments required under the terms of the mortgage loan or loans entered into for the purpose of financing the property. This is generally expressed as a multiple and gives a measure of a property's ability to cover debt service payments. Should this ratio drop below 1.0, there will be insufficient cash flow from the property to cover debt payments.

Defeasance The setting aside of cash or a portfolio of high-quality assets to cover the remaining interest and principal payments due with respect to a debt.

Delinquency Failure to comply with a debt obligation by the specified due date.

Depreciation The decline in value of an asset as it ages.

Drawdown profile The time period over which capital is taken for investors to put into deals.

Due diligence The investigation and fact-finding exercise carried out by a potential purchaser to allow him to make a more well-informed decision about whether to purchase or invest. In legal terms this is a measure of prudence, as can be expected from a reasonable and prudent person in the circumstances of the particular deal.

EBITDA Earnings before interest, taxes, depreciation, and amortization.

EPRA The European Public Real Estate Association.

ERISA (or Employee Retirement Income Security Act of 1974) U.S. legislation which stipulates the standard of risk suitable and acceptable for private pension plan investments.

Exchange-traded funds (ETFs) Traded like normal shares and allow investors to spread investments even more by tracking the performance of an entire index.

Expense stops Lease clauses which limit the amount of a landlord's obligation for expense on a property, with expenses in excess of this amount being met by the tenant.

Face rent Rental payments without adjustments for any lease concessions (for example, rent-free periods).

Fannie Mae (or Federal National Mortgage Association, FNMA) A quasi-private U.S. corporation which purchases and pools conventional mortgages then issues securities using these as collateral. Holders of Fannie Mae certificates are guaranteed full and timely payment of principal and interest.

FFO Funds from operations, recurring income delivered by properties owned by REITs.

First loss piece The most junior class of a CMBS which suffers losses from a mortgage pool before any other classes suffer.

Floating-rate notes A class of securities having a variable (or floating), rather than fixed, interest rate, but typically a margin above a market index.

Foreclosure A proceeding, in or out of court, brought by a lender holding a mortgage on real property seeking to enable the lender to sell the property and apply the sale proceeds to satisfy amounts owed by the owner under the related loan.

Freddie Mac (or Federal Home Loan Mortgage Corporation, FHCMC) A quasi-private U.S. corporation. This entity is charged with providing liquidity to the secondary market for single-family mortgages and issues securities using these mortgages as the underlying collateral. Holders of Freddie Mac certificates are assured of timely payment of interest and eventual payment of principal.

Funds of funds Funds (wrappers or vehicles) placed around other wrappers (the underlying real estate funds).

GAAP Generally accepted accounting principles. There are various sets worldwide, such as in the USA, UK, and Germany.

Gearing An accounting term used to define the debt-to-equity ratio of a company.

Granularity Achieved where an underlying pool of loans is made up of smaller loans. Pools which contain a small number of higher-value loans are said to be less granular, or more lumpy.

Gross asset value The appraised value of the properties in a REIT or real estate fund.

Ground lease A lease of either undeveloped land or land excluding any buildings and structures thereon.

Haircut The expression given to the reduction in the value attributed to an asset or the income or cash flow anticipated to be received from a property, usually by applying a percentage to this value.

Headline rent Rental payments without adjustments for any lease concessions (for example, rent-free periods).

Hedge funds Investment vehicles that can "go short" – in other words, sell the liability to pay out cash based on the future performance of a security or an index. Hedge funds may also be investment vehicles aiming to be market neutral – delivering a good return even if the market performs badly.

Hedging A general term used to refer to strategies adopted to offset investment risks. Examples of hedging include the use of derivative instruments to protect against fluctuations in interest rates or currency exchange rates.

Hurdle rate The required rate of return.

Income return The net rent or net operating income (NOI) received over the measurement period divided by the value at the beginning of the period.

INREV The European Association for Investors in Non-Listed Real Estate Vehicles.

Interest rate risk 1) The risk that a change in interest rates results in the interest earned on assets in a low interest rate environment being insufficient to service the payments required in respect of liabilities incurred in a higher interest rate environment, thereby leading to a shortfall. The risk of such shortfall (and the corresponding change in a security's value) is the interest rate risk. 2) The risk of value loss in a bond or fixed-income security when market interest rates change. Generally, fixed-income security values will increase when market interest rates decrease, and decrease when market interest rates increase.

Interest rate swap A binding agreement between two counterparties to exchange periodic interest payments on a predetermined principal amount, which is referred to as the notional amount. Typically, one counterparty will pay interest at a fixed rate and in return receive interest at a variable rate, with the opposite applying to the other counterparty.

Internal rate of return (IRR) The most complete description of historic return, including the contribution of capital, income, and timing. It takes account of the amount invested in each period, which is why it is sometimes known as a money-weighted return.

Investment grade AAA, AA, A, and BBB-rated investments, which are deemed suitable for regulated institutional investors.

IPD The Investment Property Databank, now part of MSCI.

IRS The U.S. Internal Revenue Service.

Issuer A party that has authorized the creation and sale of securities to investors.

J-curve The time-variant profile of the performance of an unlisted fund which expends fees and taxes as it acquires assets.

Junk bonds A colloquial term applied to below investment grade securities.

Leverage (or gearing) The addition of debt for the acquisition of a property.

Lien An encumbrance against a property which may be voluntary (as in the case of a mortgage) or involuntary (as in the case of a lien for unpaid property taxes), and acts as security for amounts owed to the holder of the lien.

Limited partnership (LP) A partnership structure which enables a pool of investors to invest together in one or more assets. The general partner (GP) must have unlimited liability, while the other partners (LPs) have limited liability. The investment vehicle is tax transparent.

Liquidity A measure of the ease and frequency with which assets can be traded. It is a function of both the time it takes to close a particular action and the ability to trade the asset at market prices.

Liquidity risk The risk that there will only be a limited number of buyers interested in buying an asset if and when the current owner of the asset wishes to sell it, and the resulting risk that an owner of an asset will not be able to dispose of that asset.

Listed real estate investments Property investments that are traded on exchanges and priced on the basis of supply and demand for shares in the companies.

Loan-to-value (LTV) ratio The balance of a mortgage loan over either the value of the property financed by the loan or the price paid by the borrower to acquire the property; provides a measure of the equity the borrower has in the asset that secures the loan. The greater the LTV ratio, the less equity the borrower has at stake and the less protection is available to the lender by virtue of the security arrangement.

Lock-out period The time period following origination during which the borrower cannot prepay the mortgage loan.

London Interbank Offered Rate (LIBOR) The rate of interest that major international banks in London charge each other for borrowings. There are LIBOR rates for deposits of various maturities.

Mark to market To restate the value of an asset based on its current market price.

Master servicer The party responsible for servicing mortgage loans.

MSCI A global provider of equity, fixed income, hedge fund and real estate indices.

Mezzanine debt Debt which is paid off after a first mortgage.

Mortgage A security interest in real property given as security for the repayment of a loan.

Mortgage-Backed Securities (MBS) Includes all securities whose security for repayment consists of a mortgage loan (or a pool of mortgage loans) secured on real property. Payments of interest and principal to investors are derived from payments received on the underlying mortgage loans.

Mortgagee The lender with respect to a mortgage loan.

Mortgagor The borrower with respect to a mortgage loan.

Multi-family property A building with at least five residential units, often classed as high-rise, low-rise, or garden apartments.

Mutual fund A listed security which invests in other listed securities.

NAREIT The National Association of Real Estate Investment Trusts.

Negative amortization Where the principal balance of a loan based on the amount paid periodically by the borrower is less than the amount required to cover the amount of interest due. The unpaid interest is generally added to the outstanding principal balance.

Net asset value The appraised value of the properties in a REIT or real estate fund less the REIT's or fund's liabilities (debt).

Net effective rent The gross rent less all operating expenses, rental concessions, tenant improvements, etc. This can be a negative figure.

Net net lease (or double net lease) A lease which requires the tenant to pay for property taxes and insurance in addition to the rent.

Net net net lease (or triple net lease) A lease which requires the tenant to pay for property taxes, insurance, and maintenance in addition to the rent.

Net operating cash flow (NOCF) Total income less operating expenses and adjustments but before mortgage payments, tenant improvements, replacement revenues, and leasing commissions. This is used as the basis for many financial calculations (for example, debt service coverage ratios).

Net operating income (NOI) Total income less operating expenses and adjustments and after mortgage payments, tenant improvements, replacement revenues, and leasing commissions.

Non-performing A loan or other receivable with respect to which the obligor has failed to make at least three scheduled payments.

Net present value The sum of the present values of all future incomes less the sum of the present values of all costs, including purchase price, discounted at the required return.

OER The operating expense ratio, given by (operating expenses/gross effective income).

Open-ended fund A real estate fund from which investors can demand to have their capital redeemed or paid back. These are usually also open to new investors who can subscribe for new units for cash.

Opportunistic real estate investments Investments that are the most risky are in non-traditional property types, including speculative development, seek high internal rates of return, and often have higher then average debt levels. They are characterized by property assets that have low economic occupancy, high tenant roll-over, are in secondary or tertiary markets, and have investment structures with minimal control. Foreclosed properties, debt on distressed properties, and construction projects are examples of opportunistic real estate investments.

Origination The process of making loans.

Over-collateralization A capital structure in which the value of assets exceeds the value of liabilities, and is a form of credit enhancement (used most regularly in certain asset-backed transactions). For example, an issuance of £100 million of senior securities might be secured by a pool of assets valued at £150 million, in which case the over-collateralization for the senior securities would be 33%.

Percentage lease Rent payments which include overage as a percentage of gross income which exceeds a certain amount, as well as minimum of base rent. Common in large rental stores. Also known as turnover rents (Europe).

Performing A loan or other receivable with respect to which the borrower has made all scheduled interest and principal payments under the terms of the loan.

Portfolio manager An individual or institution that manages a portfolio of investments.

Preferred equity Financing that is similar to a mezzanine loan but structured as a senior equity position rather than as a loan. A preferred equity interest will typically have a stated preferred return and control rights similar to or greater than those of a mezzanine lender.

Preferred returns The second form of cash flow distribution in a fund, payable after the initial capital investment has been returned. A preferred return resembles a dividend payment on a preferred stock, and is paid prior to other claims on the underlying property cash flows.

Premium An amount in excess of the regular price paid for an asset (or the par value of a security), usually as an inducement or incentive.

Prepayment A payment by the borrower which is greater than and/or earlier than the scheduled repayments.

Prepayment penalty or prepayment premium A levy imposed on prepayments made on a mortgaged loan to discourage prepayment.

Prepayment risk The risk that the return on an investment will be adversely affected if some or all of the principal amount invested is repaid ahead of schedule. Commercial mortgages often reduce this risk through lockout periods, prepayment premiums, and/or yield maintenance. Prepayment risk can also be taken to include extension risk, which is related to the repayment of principal more slowly than expected.

Private placement The sale of securities to investors who meet certain criteria and who are deemed to be sophisticated investors (for example, insurance companies, pension funds).

Private real estate investments Direct real estate investments and indirect real estate investments such as open-ended and closed-ended funds that invest directly in real estate and are not traded on the exchanges.

Promoter A placement agent or fundraising consultant hired by the originator of the concept or GP to attract investors.

Property Unit Trusts (PUTs) Collective investment schemes in a vehicle or wrapper format based on UK trust law, with a trustee and beneficiaries (investors).

Prospectus The document which contains all the material information about a security.

Protection buyer The party transferring the credit risk associated with certain assets to another party in return for payment, often seen in transactions such as credit default swaps. Payment is typically an up-front premium.

Protection seller The party that accepts the credit risk associated with certain assets (often seen in transactions, such as credit default swaps, as mentioned above). Should losses on the assets exceed a specified amount, the protection seller makes credit protection payments to the protection buyer.

Public real estate investments Indirect property investments in exchange-traded companies that invest in real estate, or exchange-traded bonds secured on real estate assets.

Rated securities Securities to which a rating agency has given an issuer credit rating.

Rating agency Agencies which examine investments and their underlying collateral, and attribute a rating to the notes based on compliance with their criteria. Ratings range from AAA (highest) to CCC (lowest).

Real estate fund A legal entity which acts as a wrapper or vehicle into which investors place capital and which then invests in property.

Real Estate Investment Trust (REIT) A tax-transparent, (usually) listed and regulated property investment vehicle similar to a property investment company.

Real Estate Mortgage Investment Conduit (REMIC) A pass-through entity which can hold loans secured by real property which receives favorable tax breaks. Such entities help facilitate the sale of interest in mortgage loans in the secondary market.

Real Estate Operating Company (REOC) A listed real estate development, investment, or management company that owns assets but does not have REIT status.

Receivables A general term referring to the principal and interest-related cash flows generated by an asset and payable to (or receivable by) the owner of the asset.

Refinancing risk The risk that a borrower will not be able to refinance the mortgage on maturity, thus extending the life of a security which uses this mortgage as collateral.

Reinvestment risk The risk of an adverse affect on the return on an investment if the interest rate at which interim cash flows can be reinvested is lower than expected.

Residential Mortgage-Backed Securities (RMBS) Debt securities backed by a homogenous pool of mortgage loans which have been lent against residential properties.

Residual The term applied to any cash flow remaining after the liquidation of all security classes in a CMBS.

Reversion The ultimate sale or releasing of a property after a holding period (this can be a theoretical sale).

Reversionary cap rate The capitalization rate applied to the expected sale price of a property after a holding period. This will be higher than the going-in cap rate.

Reversionary value The expected value of a property upon reversion.

ROI Return on investment, given by net operating income/initial building cost.

Secondary market A market in which existing securities are re-traded (as opposed to a primary market in which assets are originally sold by the entity that made those assets).

Secured debt Borrowing that is made, in part, on the basis of security pledged by the borrower to the lender.

Securities and Exchange Commission (SEC) The U.S. government agency which issues regulations and enforces provisions of federal securities laws and its own regulations, including regulations governing the disclosure of information provided in connection with offering securities for sale to the public. The SEC is also responsible for regulating the trading of these securities.

Securitization An issuance of securities representing an undivided interest in a segregated pool of specific assets such as commercial mortgages.

Self-amortizing loans A loan whereby the full amount of principal will be paid off at termination.

Senior/junior A common structure of securitizations that provides credit enhancement to one or more classes of securities by ranking them ahead of (or senior to) other classes of securities (junior classes). In a basic two-class senior/junior relationship, the senior classes are often called the class A notes and the junior (or subordinated) classes are called the class B notes.

Servicer The organization that is responsible for collecting loan payments from individual borrowers and for remitting the aggregate amounts received to the owner or owners of the loans.

Shariah Islamic law.

Special servicer Responsible for managing loans which have defaulted.

Structured finance A type of financing in which the credit quality of the debt is assumed to be based not on the financial strength of the debtor itself, but on a direct guarantee from a creditworthy entity or on the credit quality of the debtor's assets, with or without credit enhancement.

Subordinated debt Debt which ranks junior to other debt. Such debt is usually paid after amounts currently due (or previously due) to holders of senior debt, before paying amounts currently due (or previously due) to holders of the subordinated debt.

Subordination A form of credit enhancement whereby the risk of credit loss is disproportionately collected amongst classes.

Swap An agreement pursuant to which two counterparties agree to exchange one cash flow stream for another, for example fixed-to-floating interest-rate swaps, currency swaps, or swaps to change the maturities or yields of a bond portfolio.

Swap provider The party that writes a swap contract.

Synthetic CDO or synthetic CMBS A CDO or CMBS transaction in which the transfer of risk is effected through the use of a credit derivative as opposed to a true sale of the assets.

Target rate The required rate of return.

Tenant improvements The expense, generally met by the tenant, of physically improving the leased property or space.

Top-down approach to investing A strategy adopted by an investor whereby large-scale trends in the general economy are examined and assets, industries, and companies chosen for investment which are likely to benefit from those trends, in contrast to a bottom-up approach to investing.

Total return The sum of income return and capital return.

Time-weighted rate of return (TWRR) The single rate of compound interest which will produce the same accumulated value over more than one period as would be produced by a series of single-period returns or interest rates. Some commentators refer to this as the geometric mean rate of return, although this is not strictly accurate.

Tranche The collective description of the discreetly rated classes of CMBS securities. Each class is paid a predetermined coupon and principal based on a payment sequence. The lower-rated tranches generally have higher coupons (to compensate for increased risk) and longer life spans, as they do not receive principal payments until higher-rated tranches have been paid off. This term is also used to describe any partitioned cash flow.

Trigger event In a securitization structure, the occurrence of an event which indicates that the financial condition of the issuer or some other party associated with the transaction is deteriorating. Such events will often be defined in the transaction documents, as are the changes to the transaction structure and/or the priority of payments that are to be made following the occurrence of such an event.

Trophy asset A large commercial property that enjoys a high profile as a result of some combination of prestigious location, highly visible owners, prominent tenants, and often striking design.

Trustee A third party, often a specialist trust corporation or part of a bank, appointed to act on behalf of investors. In the case of a securitization, the trustee is given responsibility for making certain key decisions that may arise during the life of the transaction.

Turnover rent Rent payments which include overage as a percentage of gross expenses which exceed a certain amount, as well as the minimum of base rent. Common in large rental stores. Also known as percentage rents (US).

Underwriter Any party that takes on risk. In the context of the capital markets, a securities dealer will act as underwriter to an issuance and commit to purchasing all or part of the securities at a specified price, thereby giving the issuer certainty that the securities will be placed and at what price and eliminating the market risk. In return for assuming this risk, the underwriter will charge a fee.

Unlisted real estate investments Direct investments in real estate and securities collateralized by real estate that are issued by wholesale and retail companies and trusts that are not traded on an exchange.

UPREIT An umbrella partnership REIT.

Value The fair market value of a property determined in an appraisal.

Value-add real estate investments Property investments that are slightly more risky than core-plus and generally seek higher internal rates of return. Buyers of value-add properties usually acquire the major property types, plus other retail, hospitality, senior living, and storage properties. Value-add real estate investments often carry significant debt, and rely more on local knowledge than core or core-plus investment. They are also moderate to well-leased, have moderate roll-over, are in an institutional or emerging markets, and have investment structures with significant or moderate control.

Waterfall The term applied to the cash flow payout priority in a CMBS or other property fund. Generally, cash flow pays principal and interest to the highest-rated tranche, but interest only to lower-rated tranches. Once the notes from the highest-rated tranche are paid down, cash flow then pays principal and interest on the next highest-rated tranche, and so on. The sequence will be stipulated in the prospectus at the time of issue.

Weighted-average cost of capital The weighted-average rate of return that an issuer must offer to investors as a combination of required returns on borrowed funds and equity investments.

Yield to maturity The calculation of the return an investor will receive if a note is held to its maturity date. This takes into account purchase price, redemption value, time to maturity, coupon, and the time between interest payments.

Index

Page references followed by *fig* indicate a photograph or illustration; followed by *t* indicates a table; followed by *b* indicates a box.

Q

R

U